MAY 2007

ALSO BY HENRY KISSINGER

Does America Need a Foreign Policy?:
Toward a Diplomacy for the 21st Century

Years of Renewal

Diplomacy

Observations: Selected Speeches and Essays, 1982–1984

Years of Upheaval

For the Record: Selected Statements, 1977–1980

White House Years

American Foreign Policy: Three Essays

Problems of National Strategy: A Book of Readings (editor)

The Troubled Partnership: A Reappraisal of the Atlantic Alliance

The Necessity for Choice: Prospects of American Foreign Policy

Nuclear Weapons and Foreign Policy

A World Restored: Metternich, Castlereagh and the Problems of Peace:
1812–22

HENRY KISSINGER

★ ★ ★

ENDING *the* VIETNAM WAR

A History of America's Involvement in and
Extrication from the Vietnam War

★ ★ ★

SIMON & SCHUSTER
NEW YORK   LONDON   TORONTO   SYDNEY   SINGAPORE

SIMON & SCHUSTER
Rockefeller Center
1230 Avenue of the Americas
New York, NY 10020

SIMON & SCHUSTER and colophon are registered trademarks
of Simon & Schuster, Inc.

Portions of this text previously appeared in *White House Years* copyright © 1979
by Henry A. Kissinger, *Years of Upheaval* copyright © 1982 by Henry A. Kissinger,
Diplomacy copyright © 1994 by Henry A. Kissinger, and *Years of Renewal* © 1999
by Henry A. Kissinger.

For information about special discounts for bulk purchases,
please contact Simon & Schuster Special Sales:
1-800-456-6798 or business@simonandschuster.com

Designed by William P. Ruoto

Manufactured in the United States of America

10   9   8   7   6   5   4   3   2   1

Library of Congress Cataloging-in-Publication Data

Kissinger, Henry, date.
    Ending the Vietnam War : a history of America's involvement in and
extrication from the Vietnam War / Henry Kissinger.
        p.   cm.
    Includes bibliographical references and index.
    1. Vietnamese Conflict, 1961–1975—United States.   2. Vietnamese Conflict,
1961–1975—Diplomatic history.   I. Title.
DS558 .K59   2002
959.704'32—dc21   2002017996
ISBN 0-7432-1532-X

To the memory of Ambassador Ellsworth Bunker and General Creighton Abrams, who manned the ramparts of freedom at a difficult time

CONTENTS

FOREWORD

This book deals with the way the United States ended its involvement in the longest war in its history, the one fought at the greatest geographic distance from America, with the least obvious relationship to previous concepts of national security, and the only war in which well-known Americans traveled to the enemy's capital to express solidarity with the enemy's goals and, on occasion, to broadcast from there.

No war since the Civil War has seared the national consciousness like Vietnam. The controversies surrounding it tore the country apart while the war was raging, and its legacies shaped the national approach to foreign policy for a generation. Absolute distinctions between moral values and the national interest, between ideals and power, were invoked and, in time, supplanted the previous policy disputes of the Cold War period. This near civil war constrained American policy for long after the war itself was concluded.

But history presents unambiguous alternatives only in the rarest of circumstances. Most of the time, statesmen must strike a balance between their values and their necessities or, to put it another way, they are obliged to approach their goals not in one leap but in stages, each by definition imperfect by absolute standards. It is always possible to invoke that imperfection as an excuse to recoil before responsibilities or as a pretext to indict one's own society. That gap can be closed only by faith in America's purposes. And that was increasingly challenged during the Vietnam war and its aftermath.

The domestic divisions that grew out of Vietnam were generally treated in the public discourse as a clash between those who were "for" the war and those who were "against" it. That, however, was not the fundamental issue. Every administration in office during the Vietnam war sought to end it— nearly desperately. The daunting and heartrending question was how to define this goal.

For Richard Nixon, who inherited the task of extrication from Vietnam in 1969 in the fifth year of a massive overseas deployment, the overriding issue was how to keep faith with the tens of millions who, in reliance on American assurances, had tied their destiny to ours. Too, he sought to maintain American credibility toward allies and America's deterrent posture toward adversaries, attributes on which, in the judgment of four successive administrations of both major parties, the peace of the world depended. The critics thought the quest for credibility illusory and draining of America's substance. They saw the key issue as salvaging America's moral core by scuttling a doomed and allegedly immoral enterprise on almost any terms.

In this manner, the war in Vietnam became for the United States the defining experience of the second half of the twentieth century. Even for those who lived through it at the center of events, the mood of that period is nearly impossible to recapture: the brash confidence in the universal applicability of America's prescriptions with which it all began and the progressive disillusionment with which it ended; the initial unity of purpose and the ultimate divisive trauma.

It was the so-called greatest generation that entered Indochina in the heyday of American self-confidence. The Truman and Eisenhower administrations involved the United States in Indochina in the aftermath of the Berlin blockade and the Communist invasion of South Korea. The Kennedy and Johnson administrations sent combat troops to South Vietnam when North Vietnam occupied portions of Laos and Cambodia and engulfed Vietnam in a guerrilla war backed by regular North Vietnamese forces. The four Presidents from both major parties were applying—with wide public support—the strategy that had achieved the historic transformations of the decade following the Second World War: the Berlin blockade had been overcome, Europe had been rebuilt, Germany and Japan had been restored to the community of nations, the Soviet advance into Europe had been arrested, and Communist aggression in Korea had been checked. This strategy drew from the experiences of World War II a faith in the ability to deter aggression by building military positions of strength and from Roosevelt's New Deal a belief in economic and social progress to remove Communist opportunities for internal upheavals. At the time, there was virtually no opposition to this open-ended commitment to a global mission or to the conventional wisdom that Indochina was an essential outpost in the defense of liberty.

But, by the end of the Johnson administration in 1968, frustration had set in. The strategy that had worked in every previous American war—of wearing down the adversary by attrition—could not succeed against guerrillas defending no specific territory, in a position to choose when and where to fight, and possessing supply lines through Laos and Cambodia. These countries became sanctuaries because of a bizarre interpretation of their neutral status that proscribed retaliation against North Vietnamese military bases from which Americans and South Vietnamese were being killed daily. Nor did the non-Communist countries of Indochina practice anything like the democracy of our European allies, throwing into question the moral purpose of the war. For those who had made the decision to send American troops, mounting self-doubt about the American role in Indochina compounded the despair caused by Kennedy's assassination.

National comity and mutual respect gave way—at least in intellectual, media, and policy circles—to a rancorous and clamorous distrust. (General public support remained well above 50 percent throughout the war years.) The once near-universal faith in the uniqueness of America's values—and their global relevance—was replaced by growing self-doubt. Successive administrations became the target of critics who increasingly challenged the moral essence of American involvement abroad. Early doubts as to whether the war was winnable and concerns lest its cost exceed any possible benefits escalated into the proposition that the frustrations of Vietnam were caused by moral rot at the core of American life. Critics moved from questioning the worthiness of America's allies to challenging the worthiness of America itself, assailing its conduct not only in Vietnam but around the world.

Nixon, who inherited this cauldron, held values which, for all his railing against the Establishment, paralleled those of the "greatest generation." He would not consider the unconditional withdrawal and overthrow the Saigon structure on which the North Vietnamese insisted until the end of his first term in 1972 and toward which American critics of the war were moving gradually but relentlessly. He was eager to end the war but not at the price of imposing a Communist government on the millions who had cast their lot in reliance on the promises of his predecessors. Nixon's motives were a mixture of moral and geopolitical conviction as he sought to reconcile America's postwar policy based on alliances and deterrence with domestic passions which, in his view, threatened the long-term American ability to build a world order based on free societies. Nixon feared for our alliances if America abdicated in Indochina; he was concerned about the impact on Soviet restraint if the United States simply abandoned what four administrations had affirmed, and he believed that a demonstration of American weakness in Asia would destroy the opening to China based in part on America's role in thwarting Soviet moves toward hegemony in Asia.

But as he entered office, he found that by the end of the Johnson administration, the goal of victory had been abandoned and a commitment had been made to end the bombing of North Vietnam and to seek a negotiated compromise solution. These objectives had been affirmed by both candidates in the presidential campaign. No significant American political or intellectual leader opposed them.

When a negotiated solution proved unattainable, Nixon proceeded unilaterally to implement his concept of an honorable withdrawal. In the process, he cut U.S. casualties from 1,200 a month at the end of the Johnson administration to thirty a month at the end of Nixon's first term. He unilaterally reduced American troops from 550,000 in 1969 to 30,000 in 1972. And he concluded an agreement to end the war when it was possible to do so without abandoning the allies that America had sustained.

The stages in this process were often highly controversial partly because the liberal Establishment, which had launched America into the quagmire, had become demoralized and left the field to the radical protesters who, certain of their moral superiority, saw no need for restraint in the methods they used to pursue their ends. At the same time, the conservatives had abandoned the cause of Indochina in frustration while those who later emerged as passionate neoconservatives were as yet besieging the barricades from the side of the protest movement. Nor did Nixon possess the qualities to transcend the gulf in American society by an act of grace.

Unexpectedly, I was drawn into the vortex. Though I had been the principal foreign policy adviser of Governor Nelson A. Rockefeller, Nixon's political opponent for a decade, and though I had met the President-elect only once and then only for a few minutes, he did me the honor of appointing me as National Security Adviser. In that role, I was to become the principal adviser to the President on the policy for the extrication from Vietnam and eventually the chief negotiator.

Like almost everyone involved in decisions affecting the future of Vietnam, I was beset by ambivalence. I was intellectually convinced that Hanoi would settle only if deprived of all hope of victory by a determined military strategy. But I was emotionally close to many of the more moderate of the protesters who had been my contemporaries at university; therefore I was also the principal advocate in the administration for negotiations for a political solution to give the people of Indochina a genuine opportunity to choose this future. It turned out to be a rough ride, rougher by far than I imagined when I started on the task.

Since then, the categories of our national debate on Vietnam have remained largely unchanged, compounded with the passage of time by an amnesia that suppresses events but remembers encrusted hatreds. A balanced judgment on Vietnam continues to elude us—and therefore the ability to draw lessons from a national tragedy which America inflicted on itself. As a result, Vietnam has become the black hole of American historical memory.

The essence of the Vietnam tragedy was the tension between America's idealism and the perception we have of ourselves as a nation with a special mission—and our growing involvement in a world of power, hence of relative judgment. How to strike the balance between these competing realities is not a simple matter, and practitioners of foreign policy have struggled with that problem for much of American history. The task is likely never to be completed, but we will not manage it unless we have sufficient confidence in ourselves to risk a definition of the issues reflecting their complexity.

This has not yet happened.

Ending the Vietnam War is composed of fourteen chapters drawn from texts heretofore scattered through four long treatises: the three volumes of my memoirs and my study *Diplomacy.* I have rearranged and occasionally rewritten the material to provide a consecutive narrative, reshaped the narrative from the anecdotal tone of memoirs to a more general account of the period, provided a connecting text where necessary, and added new material.

My purpose in undertaking this task is not to settle the debate of a generation ago retroactively but to leave for a new generation, hopefully untouched by the passions of the past, an opportunity to obtain as accurate an account as possible of how one group of America's leaders viewed and tried to surmount a tragic national experience. Like all autobiographical writings, it cannot be free of the righteousness inherent in describing actions in which one was involved—actions one obviously would not have undertaken unless one thought them right or at least necessary. Where I have had second thoughts, I have tried to record them. In a number of chapters, I have referred to and footnoted books with a different perspective. These works contain their own bibliographies.

The Vietnam debate has so far produced no ultimate answers. The administration that ended the war was too abstractly analytical when, in the face of massive media and congressional opposition, it insisted on its geopolitical design dictated by its view of the long-range national interest. The critics were too abstractly passionate in their refusal to relate their moral proclamations to an operational strategy reflecting America's responsibility for peace and world order. The administration had concept without domestic consensus; the critics had passion without analysis. Watergate destroyed the last hopes for an honorable outcome. For the only time in the postwar period, America abandoned to eventual Communist rule a friendly people which had relied on us and were still fighting when we cut off aid. The pattern of domestic discord did not end quickly. We paid for a long time for the divisions into which we stumbled in that period, now seemingly so distant.

As these lines are being written, America finds itself once again at war—this time with no ambiguity about the nature of the threat. While history never repeats itself directly, there is at least one lesson to be learned from the tragedy described in these pages: that America must never again permit its promise to be overwhelmed by its divisions.

1

AMERICA'S ENTRY INTO
THE MORASS (1950–1969)

It all began with high aspirations. For two decades after the end of the Second World War, America had taken the lead in building a new international order out of the fragments of a shattered world. It had rehabilitated Europe and restored Japan, faced down Communist expansionism in Greece, Turkey, Berlin, and Korea, entered into its first peacetime alliances, and launched a program of technical assistance to the developing world. The countries under the American umbrella were enjoying peace, prosperity, and stability.

In Indochina, however, all the previous patterns of America's involvement abroad were confounded. For the first time in America's international experience, the direct, almost causal relationship the nation had always enjoyed between its values and its achievements began to fray as Americans turned to questioning those values and why they should have been applied to so distant a place as Vietnam. A chasm opened between the Americans' belief in the unique nature of their national experience and the compromises and ambiguities inherent in the geopolitics of containing Communism. In the crucible of Vietnam, American exceptionalism turned on itself. American society did not debate, as others might have, the practical shortcomings of its policies but America's worthiness to pursue *any* international role.

This universalist approach had a long pedigree. From the beginning of the twentieth century, one president after another had proclaimed that America had no "selfish" interests, that its principal, if not its only, international goal was universal peace and progress. Truman, in his inaugural ad-

dress of January 20, 1949, had committed his country to the objective of a
world in which "all nations and all peoples are free to govern themselves as
they see fit." No purely national interest would be pursued. "We have sought
no territory. We have imposed our will on no one. We have asked for no privileges we would not extend to others." The United States would "strengthen
freedom-loving nations against the dangers of aggression" by providing "military advice and equipment to free nations which will cooperate with us in
the maintenance of peace and security." [1] The freedom of every single independent nation had become the national objective, irrespective of those nations' strategic importance to the United States.

In his two inaugural addresses in 1953 and 1957, President Dwight D.
Eisenhower took up the same theme in even more exalted language. He described a world in which thrones had been toppled, vast empires had been
swept away, and new nations had emerged. Amidst all this turmoil, destiny
had entrusted America with the charge to defend freedom unconstrained by
geopolitical considerations or calculations of the national interest. Indeed,
Eisenhower implied that such calculations ran counter to the American value
system, in which all nations and peoples are treated equally: "Conceiving the
defense of freedom, like freedom itself, to be one and indivisible, we hold all
continents and peoples in equal regard and honor." [2]

John F. Kennedy, in his inaugural address in 1961, carried this theme of
missionary duty to the world yet another step forward. Proclaiming his generation to be the linear descendant of the world's first democratic revolution,
he pledged his administration, in soaring language, not to "permit the slow
undoing of those human rights to which this nation has always been committed, and to which we are committed today at home and around the
world. Let every nation know, whether it wishes us well or ill, that we shall
pay any price, bear any burden, meet any hardship, support any friend, oppose any foe to assure the survival and the success of liberty." [3] Kennedy's eloquent peroration was the precise reverse of the famous dictum of British
Prime Minister Lord Palmerston that Great Britain had no permanent
friends, only permanent interests.

By the time of Lyndon B. Johnson's inaugural on January 20, 1965, conventional wisdom had culminated in the proposition that America's foreign
commitments, springing organically from its democratic system of government, had erased altogether the distinction between domestic and international responsibilities. For America, Johnson asserted, no stranger was

beyond hope: "Terrific dangers and troubles that we once called 'foreign' now constantly live among us. If American lives must end, and American treasure be spilled, in countries that we barely know, then that is the price that change has demanded of conviction and of our enduring covenant."[4]

Much later, it became fashionable to cite such statements as examples of the arrogance of power, or as the hypocritical pretexts for America's quest for domination. Such facile cynicism misreads the essence of America's political faith, which is at once "naïve" and draws from that apparent naïveté the impetus for extraordinary practical endeavors. Most countries go to war to resist concrete, definable threats to their security. In the twentieth century, America went to war—from World War I to the Kosovo war of 1998—largely on behalf of what it perceived as moral obligations to resist aggression or injustice as the trustee of collective security.

This commitment was especially pronounced among the generation of American leaders who had in their youth witnessed the tragedy of Munich. Burned into their psyches was the lesson that failure to resist aggression— wherever and however it occurred—guarantees that it will have to be resisted under much worse circumstances later on. From Cordell Hull onward, every American secretary of state echoed this theme. It was the point on which Dean Acheson and John Foster Dulles agreed.[5] Geopolitical analysis of the specific dangers posed by the Communist conquest of a distant country was deemed subordinate to the twin slogans of resisting aggression in the abstract and preventing the further spread of Communism. The Communist victory in China had reinforced the conviction of American policymakers that no further Communist expansion could be tolerated.

Policy documents and official statements of the period show that this conviction went largely unchallenged. In February 1950, four months before the start of the Korean conflict, NSC document 64 had concluded that Indochina was "a key area of South East Asia and is under immediate threat."[6] The memorandum marked the debut of the so-called Domino Theory, which predicted that, if Indochina fell, Burma and Thailand would soon follow, and that "the balance of Southeast Asia would then be in grave hazard."[7]

In January 1951, Dean Rusk, then Assistant Secretary of State and later Secretary of State for eight years, declared that "to neglect to pursue our present course to the utmost of our ability would be disastrous to our interests in Indochina and, consequently, in the rest of Southeast Asia."[8] In April of the year before, NSC document 68 had concluded that the global equilibrium was at stake in Indochina: ". . . any substantial further extension of the area under the domination of the Kremlin would raise the possibility that no coalition adequate to confront the Kremlin with greater strength could be assembled."[9]

Much later such reflections were dismissed if not ridiculed as the expression of an overwrought Cold War mentality. But the context is important. The policymakers of the early 1950s had experienced the Iron Curtain descend on Europe, Communist coups in a series of East European countries, the Berlin blockade, and the Communist invasion of South Korea.

Even so, some fundamental questions were avoided. Was it really true, as the document implied, that every Communist gain extended the area controlled by the Kremlin—especially given the experience of Tito's Yugoslavia which, though Communist, broke with Moscow? There were in fact vast differences in the nature of the threat. In Europe, the principal threat emanated from the Soviet superpower. In Asia, the threat to American interests came from secondary powers which were at best surrogates of the Soviet Union and over which Soviet control was—or should have been understood to be—questionable. In reality, as the Vietnam war evolved, America came to fight the surrogate of a surrogate (China), each of which deeply distrusted the respective senior partner. In the American analysis, the global equilibrium was under assault by North Vietnam, assumed to be controlled from Beijing, which, in turn, was conceived to be controlled by Moscow. This turned out not to be the case. In Europe, America was defending historic states; in Indochina, America was dealing with societies that, in their present dimensions, were building states for the first time. The European nations had long-established traditions of how to cooperate in the defense of the balance of power. In Southeast Asia, statehood was just emerging, the concept of the balance of power was foreign, and there was no precedent of cooperation among the existing states.

These fundamental differences between the geopolitics of Europe and Asia, together with America's interests in each, were submerged in the universalist, ideological American approach to foreign policy. The Czech coup, the Berlin blockade, the testing of a Soviet atomic bomb, the Communist victory in China, and the Communist attack on South Korea were all lumped together by America's leaders into a single global threat—indeed, a centrally controlled global conspiracy. *Realpolitik* would have sought to limit the Korean war to the narrowest possible dimension; America's Manichean view of the conflict worked in the opposite direction. Truman coupled his dispatch of American troops with an announcement of a significant increase in military aid to France in its own war against the Communist guerrillas in Indochina (then called the Vietminh). American policymakers drew an analogy between Germany's and Japan's simultaneous assaults in Europe and Asia in the Second World War, and Moscow's and Beijing's maneuvers in the 1950s, the Soviet Union replacing Germany, and China standing in for Japan. By 1952, a third of the French expenditures in Indochina were being subsidized by the United States.

America's entry into Indochina introduced a whole new moral issue. NATO defended democracies; the American occupation of Japan had imported democratic institutions to that nation; the Korean war had been fought to turn back an assault on the independence of small nations. In Indochina, however, the case for containment was initially cast in almost exclusively geopolitical terms, making it all the more difficult to incorporate into the prevailing American ideology. For one thing, the defense of Indochina ran head-on into America's tradition of anticolonialism. Technically still French colonies, the states of Indochina were neither democracies nor even independent. Although, in 1950, France had transformed its three colonies of Vietnam, Laos, and Cambodia into the "Associated States of the French Union," this new designation stopped well short of independence because France feared that, if it granted full sovereignty, it could do no less for its three North African possessions—Tunisia, Algeria, and Morocco.

By the end of 1950, the Truman administration had decided that the security of the free world required Indochina, a French colony, to be kept out of Communist hands—which in practice meant bending America's anticolonial principles by supporting the French war against the Communist insurgents in Indochina. Truman and Secretary of State Dean Acheson saw no other choice because the Joint Chiefs of Staff had concluded that the American armed forces were stretched to the limit by simultaneous commitments to NATO and to the ongoing war in Korea, and that none could be spared for the defense of Indochina—even if it were invaded by China.[10]

As it turned out, America's initial commitment to Indochina in 1950 established the pattern for its future involvement: large enough to get America entangled, not significant enough to prove decisive. In the early stages of the quagmire, this was largely the result of ignorance about the actual conditions and the near impossibility of conducting operations through two layers of

French colonial administration, as well as whatever local authorities the so-called Associated States of Indochina (Vietnam, Laos, and Cambodia) had been permitted to establish.

Fearing to be tarred as a party to colonialism, both the Joint Chiefs of Staff and the State Department sought to protect their country's moral flank by pressing France to pledge eventual independence.[11] The State Department expressed its awareness of the complexities of this delicate balancing act by naming its Indochinese program Operation Eggshell. The label, unfortunately, conveyed an understanding of the predicament far greater than its contribution to the solution. The basic strategy was to prod France into granting independence to Indochina while urging it to continue waging the anti-Communist war.[12] Why France should risk lives in a war designed to end its presence in Southeast Asia was not explained.

By the time the Truman administration prepared to leave office, evasion of the hard choices had matured into official policy. In 1952, a National Security Council document formalized the Domino Theory and gave it a sweeping character. Describing a military attack on Indochina as a danger "inherent in the existence of a hostile and aggressive Communist China,"[13] it urged that the loss of even a single Southeast Asian country would lead "to relatively swift submission to or an alignment with Communism by the remainder. Furthermore, an alignment with Communism of the rest of Southeast Asia and India, and in the longer term, of the Middle East (with the possible exceptions of at least Pakistan and Turkey) would in all probability progressively follow."[14]

Obviously, if that estimate was correct, such wholesale collapse was bound to endanger the security and stability of Europe as well as to "make it extremely difficult to prevent Japan's eventual accommodation to Communism."[15] Nor was the perception of the long-range danger to Europe shared by America's European allies, which, in the years to come, consistently refused to participate in the defense of Indochina.

On the other hand, the arguments of the NSC memorandum were not as superficial as they later were represented to be. Even in the absence of a central conspiracy, and for all the West knew at the time, the Domino Theory might *nevertheless* have been valid. Singapore's savvy and thoughtful Prime Minister, Lee Kuan Yew, clearly thought so, and he has usually been proven right. In the immediate postwar era, Communism still possessed substantial ideological dynamism. A demonstration of the bankruptcy of its economic management was another generation away. Many in the democracies, and especially in the newly independent countries, considered the Communist world to be poised to surpass the capitalist world in industrial capacity. The governments of many of the newly independent countries were fragile and threatened by domestic insurrection. At the very moment the NSC memorandum was prepared, a Communist guerrilla war was being waged in Malaya.

Washington policymakers had good reason to be concerned about the conquest of Indochina by a movement which had already engulfed Eastern Europe and taken over China. Regardless of whether Communist expansion was centrally organized, it seemed to possess enough momentum to sweep the fragile new nations of Southeast Asia into the anti-Western camp. The real question was not whether some dominoes might fall in Southeast Asia, which was likely, but whether there might not be better places in the region to draw the line—for instance, around countries where the political and security elements were more in harmony, such as in Malaya and Thailand.

Truman's legacy to his successor, Dwight D. Eisenhower, was an annual military assistance program to Indochina of some $200 million and a strategic theory in search of a policy. The Truman administration had not been obliged to face the potential gap between its strategic doctrine and its moral convictions, or to confront the necessity of making a choice between the geopolitical rationale and American capabilities. Eisenhower was left with the responsibility of dealing with the first challenge; Kennedy, Johnson, and Richard Nixon with the second.

The Eisenhower administration did not question America's commitment to the security of Indochina, which it had inherited. It sought to reconcile its strategic doctrine and its moral convictions by stepping up pressures for reform in Indochina. In May 1953—four months after taking the oath of office—Eisenhower urged the American ambassador to France, Douglas Dillon, to press the French to appoint new leaders with authority to "win victory" in Indochina, and at the same time to make "clear and unequivocal public announcements, repeated as often as may be desirable," that independence would be granted "as soon as victory against the Communists had been won." [16]

For France, the issue by then had already gone far beyond political reform. Its forces in Indochina were enmeshed in a frustrating guerrilla war, with which they had no experience whatever. In a conventional war with established front lines, superior firepower usually carries the day. By contrast, a guerrilla war usually is not fought from fixed positions, and the guerrilla army hides among the population. A conventional war is about control of territory; a guerrilla war is about the security of the population. As the guerrilla army is not tied to the defense of any particular territory, it is in a position to determine the field of battle to a considerable extent and to regulate the casualties of *both* sides. Whereas in a conventional war, a success rate in battle of 75 percent would guarantee victory, in a guerrilla war, protecting the population only 75 percent of the time ensures defeat. While the conventional army is bound to lose unless it wins decisively, the guerrilla army wins as long as it can keep from losing.

Neither the French nor the American army, which followed in its footsteps a decade later, ever solved the riddle of guerrilla war. Both fought the only kind of war they understood and for which they had been trained and equipped—classical, conventional warfare based on clearly demarcated front lines. Both armies, relying on superior firepower, strove for a war of attrition. Both saw that strategy turned against them by an enemy who, fighting in his own country, could exhaust them with his patience and generate domestic pressures to end the conflict. Casualties kept mounting while criteria to define progress remained elusive.

France conceded defeat more rapidly than America, because its armed forces were spread more thinly in their effort to hold all of Vietnam with a third of the forces America would eventually commit to defending half of the country. France was being whipsawed as America would be a decade later: whenever it concentrated its forces around population centers, the Communists would dominate most of the countryside; when it attempted to move out to protect the countryside, the Communists would attack the towns and the forts, one by one.

Something about Vietnam consistently blighted the reasoning power of foreigners who ventured into it. Bizarrely, the French Vietnam war came to a climax at a road junction called Dien Bien Phu, which was located in the remote northwestern corner of Vietnam, near the Laotian border. France had placed an elite force there in the hope of luring the Communists into a pitched battle and, in the process, maneuvered itself into a no-win situation. If the Communists chose to ignore the French deployment, these forces would be wasted in a position far from areas of any strategic consequence. If the Communists took the bait, their sole motive had to be the belief that they were within sight of decisive victory. France had reduced its options to irrelevance or defeat.

The French vastly underestimated the toughness and the ingenuity of their opponents—as the Americans would do later. On March 13, 1954, the North Vietnamese launched an all-out attack on Dien Bien Phu which, already in its initial assault, overran two outlying forts that were supposed to dominate the high ground. They did so using artillery they were not thought to possess, and which had been supplied by China in the aftermath of the Korean war. From then on it was only a matter of time before the remainder of the French force would be ground down. Exhausted and seeing little purpose in fighting only to have to withdraw from Indochina under American pressure, the French government accepted a Soviet proposal to hold a conference on Indochina to begin that April in Geneva. Representatives of the United States, Britain, France, and the Soviet Union met with those of the Indochinese countries (Vietnam, Laos, and Cambodia), Communist China, and North and South Korea. Then, on May 7, even as the diplomats were discussing Indochina in Geneva, Dien Bien Phu fell.

The fall of Dien Bien Phu obliged the Eisenhower administration to choose between its theories and its possibilities. France would be forced to yield a substantial portion, if not all, of Vietnam to the Communists. Yet Dien Bien Phu could only be saved by a major military escalation for which France had neither the resources nor the will. The United States would have to decide whether to back the Domino Theory with direct military action.

The domestic debate over intervention at Dien Bien Phu demonstrated the growing difficulty of reconciling geopolitical analysis, strategic doctrine, and moral conviction. If it were true that a Communist victory in Indochina would cause the dominoes to fall from Japan to Indonesia, as Eisenhower predicted in a letter to British Prime Minister Winston Churchill and in a press conference on April 7, America would have to draw the line regardless of the reaction of other countries, especially since the military contribution of the potential participants would have been largely symbolic. (According to Secretary of State John Foster Dulles's plan, United Action, the United States envisaged the cooperation of Great Britain, France, Australia, New Zealand, and the Associated States of Indochina.) Although collective action was preferable, it was not a precondition to the defense of the global balance, if that was indeed what was at stake. This was especially true because at about the same time, the Eisenhower administration had changed its military doctrine to "massive retaliation," which depended, above all, on unleashing America's nuclear strength against the source of aggression. This, in practice, meant that a war over Indochina would be directed against China. Yet there was no political basis for air attacks against a country that was only indirectly participating in the Vietnam war and for a cause that Churchill had characterized as too peripheral and too dangerous to be sustainable for very long in Western public opinion.

Whatever their private reservations, Dulles and Eisenhower made a major effort to bring about United Action. On April 4, 1954, in a long letter, Eisenhower appealed to Churchill, who was then in his last year as Prime Minister:

> If they [France] do not see it through, and Indochina passes into the hands of the Communists, the ultimate effect on our and your global strategic position with the consequent shift in the power ratio throughout Asia and the Pacific could be disastrous and, I know, unacceptable to you and me. It is difficult to see how Thailand, Burma and Indonesia could be kept out of Communist hands. This we cannot afford. The threat to Malaya, Australia and New Zealand would be direct. The offshore island chain would be broken. The economic pressure on Japan which would be deprived of non-Communist markets and sources of food and raw material would be such, over a period of time, that it is difficult to see how Japan could be prevented from reaching an accommodation with the Communist world which would combine the manpower and natural resources of Asia with the industrial potential of Japan.[17]

Devoted as he was to the "special relationship" with America, Churchill was an Englishman first and perceived more dangers in Indochina than benefits to be gained. He did not accept the proposition that the dominoes would fall quite so inexorably, or that one colonial setback would automatically lead to global catastrophe.

Churchill and Foreign Minister Anthony Eden believed that the best place to defend Southeast Asia was at the borders of Malaya; Churchill therefore returned the noncommittal response that Eden would convey the Cabinet's decision to Dulles, who was about to leave for London. Churchill's avoidance of substance left little doubt that Great Britain was groping for ways to cushion its rejection of United Action. Had the news been favorable, Churchill would no doubt have conveyed it himself. Even prior to the Secretary of State's arrival, Eden "thought it unrealistic to expect that a victor's terms could be imposed upon an undefeated enemy." [18]

On April 26, Churchill expressed his reservations personally to Admiral Radford (Chairman of the Joint Chiefs of Staff), who was visiting London. According to the official record, Churchill warned of "war on the fringes, where the Russians were strong and could mobilize the enthusiasm of nationalist and oppressed peoples." [19] There was no political rationale for Great Britain to become involved in a cause which Churchill described this way:

> The British people would not be easily influenced by what happened
> in the distant jungles of SE Asia; but they did know that there was a
> powerful American base in East Anglia and that war with China,
> who would invoke the Sino-Russian pact, might mean an assault by
> hydrogen bombs on these islands. [20]

Stalin had died in 1953, and the post-Stalinist leaders in the Kremlin would have been extremely loath in their first year of power to confront America for China's sake. However, since America's military leaders were incapable of describing the likely outcome of massive retaliation against China (or within Indochina, for that matter), and since the independence of the countries of Indochina was still only a plan, Eisenhower deferred a showdown.

Both the Soviet Union and China feared American intervention, and therefore the Eisenhower-Dulles diplomacy of making implicit threats did help to bring about an outcome to the Geneva Conference that on the surface was far better than the military situation on the ground warranted. The Geneva Accords of July 1954 provided for the partitioning of Vietnam along the 17th parallel. To leave the way open for unification, the partition was described not as a "political boundary" but as an administrative arrangement for facilitating the regrouping of military forces prior to internationally supervised elections. These were to be held within two years. All outside forces were to be withdrawn from the three Indochinese states within 300 days; foreign bases and alliances with other countries were proscribed.

Cataloguing the various provisions, however, gives a misleading impression of the formality and stringency of the Geneva Accords. There were many signatories to different parts of the agreement but no contracting parties, therefore no "collective obligations."[21] Richard Nixon later summed up the hodgepodge as follows: "Nine countries gathered at the conference and produced six unilateral declarations, three bilateral cease-fire agreements, and one unsigned declaration."[22]

What it all amounted to was a way of ending the hostilities, partitioning Vietnam, and leaving the political outcome to the future. Amateur analysts often invoke the ambiguity of such agreements as a demonstration of the confusion or the duplicity of the negotiators. Yet, most of the time, ambiguous documents such as the Geneva Accords reflect reality; they settle what it is possible to settle, in the full knowledge that further refinement must await new developments.

The immediate difficulty was that the United States refused to participate officially at the Geneva Conference (or to sign the multilateral declaration). It tried to be both present and absent—sufficiently on the scene to uphold its principles, yet far enough to the side to avoid domestic obloquy for having to abandon some of them. America's ambiguity was best expressed in a concluding statement which declared that the United States "takes note" of the final declarations and would "refrain from the threat or the use of force to disturb them." At the same time, the statement warned that "it would view any renewal of the aggression in violation of the aforesaid arrangements with grave concern and as seriously threatening international peace and security."[23] I know of no other instance in diplomatic history of a nation guaranteeing a settlement it has refused to sign, and about which it has expressed such strong reservations.

Eisenhower's decision not to become involved in Vietnam in 1954 proved to be tactical, not strategic. After Geneva, he and Dulles remained convinced of Indochina's decisive strategic importance. While Indochina sorted itself out, Dulles put the finishing touches on a collective security framework, the Southeast Asian Treaty Organization (SEATO), which came into being in September 1954 and was composed, in addition to the United States, of Pakistan, the Philippines, Thailand, Australia, New Zealand, the United Kingdom, and France. What it lacked was a common political objective or a means for mutual support. Indeed, the countries refusing to participate in SEATO were more significant than its members. India, Indonesia, Malaya, and Burma preferred to seek safety in neutrality, and the Geneva Accords prohibited the three Indochinese states from joining. As for America's

European allies, France and Great Britain were not likely to run risks on behalf of an area from which they had so recently been ejected. Indeed, France—and to a lesser degree Great Britain—almost certainly joined SEATO primarily in order to gain a veto over what they considered the potential for rash American actions.

The formal obligations contained in SEATO were rather nebulous. Requiring the signatories to meet a "common danger" by their "constitutional processes," the Treaty neither established criteria for defining the common danger nor assembled the machinery for common action—as NATO did. Nevertheless, SEATO served Dulles's purpose by providing a legal framework for the defense of Indochina. This is why, strangely enough, SEATO was more specific about Communist aggression against the three nations of Indochina—barred from membership by the Geneva Accords—than with respect to a Communist attack on the signatories. A separate protocol designated threats to Laos, Cambodia, and South Vietnam as being inimical to the peace and security of the signatories, in effect providing a unilateral guarantee.[24]

Everything now depended on whether the new states of Indochina, especially South Vietnam, could be turned into fully functioning nations. None of them had ever been governed as a political entity within its existing borders. The French had divided Vietnam into three regions—Tonkin, Annam, and Cochinchina—governed by Hanoi, Hue, and Saigon respectively. The area around Saigon and in the Mekong Delta had only been colonized by the Vietnamese relatively recently, during the nineteenth century, at about the same time that the French arrived. The existing authorities consisted of a combination of French-trained civil servants and a maze of secret societies— the so-called sects—some of which had religious affiliations, but all of which supported themselves and maintained their autonomous status by shaking down the population.

Dulles all along had urged backing Ngo Dinh Diem, a former French administrator who had broken with the French administration over its refusal to implement some of his proposed reforms. A Catholic and a nationalist, Diem had spent two decades as a scholar recluse in his own country and in exile—mostly in America—refusing offers from the Japanese, the Communists, and the French-supported Vietnamese leaders to participate in their various governments. No democrat, Diem was chosen by Dulles as "the only horse available" and became president of Vietnam with American support.

In October 1954, Eisenhower made a virtue of necessity by writing to Diem with a promise of aid contingent on standards of "performance . . . in undertaking needed reforms." American assistance would be "combined with" an independent Vietnam that was "endowed with a strong Government . . . so responsive to the nationalist aspirations of its people" as to command both domestic and international respect.[25]

For a few years everything seemed to fall into place. By the end of the Eisenhower administration, the United States had given South Vietnam more than $1 billion in aid; 1,500 American personnel were in South Vietnam; the United States embassy in Saigon became one of our largest missions in the world. The United States Military Advisory Group, containing 692 members, had ignored the limits on foreign military personnel established by the Geneva Accords.[26]

Against all expectations and with massive American intelligence support, Diem suppressed the secret societies, stabilized the economy, and managed to establish central control—astonishing achievements which were well received in the United States. But events ultimately revealed that America had been celebrating a lull in Communist pressure, not a permanent condition. America's assumption that its own unique brand of democracy was readily exportable turned out to be flawed. In the West, political pluralism had thrived among cohesive societies where a strong social consensus had been in place long enough to permit tolerance for the opposition without threatening the survival of the state. But where a nation has yet to be created, opposition may appear as a threat to national existence, especially when there is no civil society to provide a safety net. In these conditions, the temptation is strong, often overwhelming, to equate opposition with treason and to thwart the emergence of a pluralistic system.

All of these tendencies become magnified in a guerrilla war. In Vietnam guerrilla activity had never ceased, and in 1959 it moved into high gear. The guerrillas' initial goal is to prevent the consolidation of stable, legitimate institutions. Their favorite targets are the worst and the best government officials. They attack the worst in order to win popular sympathies by "punishing" corrupt or oppressive officials; and they attack the best because it is the most effective way of preventing the government from achieving legitimacy and of discouraging an effective national service.

By 1960, some 2,500 South Vietnamese officials were being assassinated every year.[27] Only a small number of the most highly motivated, and a much larger percentage of the most corrupt, would run such risks.

As Eisenhower prepared to leave office, Laos was his main concern. In his memoirs, *Waging Peace*, he described that country as the linchpin of the Domino Theory. He considered the independence of Laos so crucial, in fact, that he was prepared to "fight . . . with our allies or without them." [28] Defending Laos was to be the most specific recommendation he made to President-elect Kennedy during the transition period prior to January 1961.

As the third consecutive President obliged to deal with Indochina, John F. Kennedy inherited a set of well-established policy premises. Involvement in Vietnam was not—as the critics were later to assert—a conspiracy of the best and brightest brought into government by Kennedy and inherited by Johnson but the application of principles pursued for a decade by two presidents of both parties. Like his predecessors, Kennedy considered Vietnam a crucial link in America's overall geopolitical position. He believed, as had Truman and Eisenhower, that preventing a Communist victory in Vietnam was a vital American interest. Like his predecessors, he viewed the Communist leadership in Hanoi and in Beijing as a surrogate of global Kremlin designs.

By choosing Vietnam as the place to draw the line against Communist expansionism, America ensured that grave dilemmas would lie ahead. If political reform was the way to defeat the guerrillas, did their growing power mean that American political recommendations were not being correctly applied or that these recommendations were simply not relevant, at least at that stage of the struggle? And if Vietnam was indeed as important to the global balance as nearly all of America's leaders were asserting, did it not mean that geopolitical necessities would, in the end, override all others and oblige America to take over a war 10,000 miles from home?

Although Kennedy's Vietnam policy was in many ways a continuation of Eisenhower's and Truman's, there were important differences. Eisenhower had viewed the conflict the way a soldier would—as a war between two distinct entities, North and South Vietnam. To the Kennedy team, the attacks on South Vietnam did not represent a traditional war so much as a quasi–civil conflict characterized by the relatively new phenomenon of guerrilla warfare. At the same time, the Kennedy team interpreted the geopolitical aspect of the conflict in even more apocalyptic terms than had its predecessors. Whereas Eisenhower had seen the military threat to Vietnam through the prism of conventional warfare, the Kennedy team believed— prematurely as it turned out—that a nuclear stalemate already existed between the United States and the Soviet Union which made general war, in the words of Secretary of Defense Robert McNamara, unthinkable. The Kennedy administration was convinced that its military buildup would remove the Communists' opportunity to wage Korean-type limited wars. By a process of exclusion, it came to consider guerrilla warfare as the wave of the future and resistance to it the ultimate test of America's ability to contain Communism.

On January 6, 1961, two weeks before Kennedy's inauguration, Soviet Premier Nikita Khrushchev described "wars of national liberation" as "sacred" and pledged Soviet support for them. Kennedy's young New Frontier treated this pledge as a declaration of war against its hope of giving new emphasis to America's relations with the developing world. Today Khrushchev's speech is widely perceived as having been aimed primarily at his ideological tormentors in Beijing, who were accusing him of lapsed Leninism because he had just extended an ultimatum to change the status of Berlin for the third time, and because of his oft-expressed reservations about nuclear war. At the time, however, Kennedy, in his first State of the Union address, on January 31, 1961, treated Khrushchev's speech as proof of the Soviet Union's and China's "ambitions for world domination—ambitions which they forcefully restated only a short time ago." [29]*

The Kennedy and Johnson administrations' interpretations of Communist pronouncements caused Indochina to be no longer perceived as one battle among many in the Cold War. To the New Frontier, Indochina represented the *decisive* battle that would determine whether guerrilla war could be stopped and the Cold War won. Kennedy's interpretation of the conflict as a coordinated global conspiracy caused him to conclude that Southeast Asia was the place to establish his credibility: "Now we have a problem," he told James Reston of the *New York Times*, "in trying to make our power credible, and Vietnam looks like the place." [31]

As in a classical tragedy in which the hero is led step by imperceptible

---

* In September 1965, the same misunderstanding would occur during the Johnson administration with respect to China, when Chinese Defense Minister Lin Piao's manifesto on "People's War" spoke grandly of "encircling" the world's industrial powers by revolutions throughout the Third World. [30] The Johnson administration interpreted this as a warning that China might intervene in Hanoi, ignoring Lin's subtext, which stressed the need for self-reliance on would-be revolutionaries. Reinforced by Mao's comment that Chinese armies did not go abroad, it was meant as well to provide a strong hint that China did not intend to become involved again in Communist wars of liberation. Apparently both sides in the Korean war had learned the same lesson; they were determined not to repeat it.

step to his destiny by seemingly random events, the Kennedy administration's entry into Vietnam was by way of a crisis from which its predecessors had been spared—the future of Laos. Few peoples have less deserved the suffering that befell them than the gentle, peace-loving Laotians. Wedged between forbidding mountain ranges that face Vietnam and the broad Mekong River, which marks the border with Thailand, the peoples of Laos asked nothing of their bellicose neighbor except to be left alone. That was one wish, however, that North Vietnam never granted them. Once Hanoi had launched its guerrilla war in South Vietnam in 1959, pressures on Laos inevitably increased. Had Hanoi tried to supply the guerrilla forces in the South through Vietnamese territory, it would have had to infiltrate across the so-called Demilitarized Zone, the demarcation line dividing Vietnam which extended for about forty miles along the 17th parallel. That distance could have been sealed off by the South Vietnamese army with American support. Or else the North Vietnamese would have had to launch an attack by organized military units across the 17th parallel, which would almost certainly have triggered American and perhaps SEATO intervention—something Hanoi appeared unwilling to risk until 1972, quite late in the Vietnam war.

By the cold-blooded logic that marked Communist strategy during the entire war, Hanoi concluded that infiltration into South Vietnam via neutral Laos and Cambodia would involve fewer international penalties than an overt thrust across the 17th parallel. Even though the neutrality of Laos and Cambodia had been guaranteed by the Geneva Accords of 1954 and reaffirmed by the SEATO Treaty, Hanoi made its judgment stick. In effect, it annexed the panhandle of sovereign Laos and established base areas both there and in Cambodia without significant opposition from the world community. Indeed what passed for world opinion fell in with Hanoi's bizarre reasoning: it was American and South Vietnamese efforts to interrupt the vast infiltration network on neutral soil and of bases used to sustain guerrilla war that became castigated as "expansions" of the war.

The panhandle of Laos provided the North Vietnamese with access routes under a jungle canopy of some 650 miles along the entire border of South Vietnam with Laos and Cambodia. Over 6,000 North Vietnamese troops moved into Laos in 1959 with the ostensible mission of supporting the Communist Pathet Lao, who, since the Geneva Accords of 1954, had been imposed by Hanoi in the northeastern provinces along the Vietnamese border.

As a military man, Eisenhower concluded that the defense of South Vietnam had to begin in Laos. He apparently told Kennedy during the transition that he was prepared to intervene in Laos, if necessary unilaterally. Kennedy's first statements on Laos were consistent with Eisenhower's recommendations. At a press conference on March 23, 1961, he warned: "The security of all Southeast Asia will be endangered if Laos loses its neutral independence. Its own safety runs with the safety of us all—in a real neutrality observed by all." [32]

Yet in April 1961, shaken by the Bay of Pigs fiasco, Kennedy decided against accepting Eisenhower's recommendation to intervene in Laos. Reluctant to risk war in Laos—on the border of China and in a country of which very few Americans had ever heard—Kennedy decided to draw the line in South Vietnam. In the meantime, Kennedy chose to rely on negotiations to buttress Laotian neutrality. As a matter of fact, it was the second time that Hanoi was peddling Laotian neutrality, having already undertaken to respect it at the Geneva Conference in 1954.

While developing the logistics network which was later dubbed the Ho Chi Minh Trail through Laos, Hanoi stalled the negotiations for a year, finally concluding them with an agreement providing for the removal of all foreign forces from Laos. Following its by now well established pattern, Hanoi failed to remove any of its military forces.

Eisenhower turned out to have been right. If Indochina were indeed the keystone of American security in the Pacific, as the leaders in Washington had claimed for over a decade, Laos was a better place to defend it than Vietnam; indeed, it was perhaps the only place to defend Indochina. Even though Laos was a remote and landlocked country, the North Vietnamese, as feared and hated foreigners, could not have waged a guerrilla war on its soil. America could have fought there the sort of conventional war for which its army had been trained, and Thai troops would almost certainly have supported American efforts. Faced with such prospects, Hanoi might well have pulled back to await a more propitious moment for full-scale war.

So geopolitical a strategic analysis, however, was deemed inappropriate for a conflict still perceived largely in ideological terms. For a decade, American leaders had been making a case for defending Vietnam because it represented a key element in an Asian defense concept. Eisenhower's emphasis on Laos in the closing days of his administration was a new concept.

For all these reasons, Kennedy and his advisers concluded that Indochina had to be defended in South Vietnam, where Communist aggression had some meaning for Americans, regardless of the fact that they had just made a decision which made that task nearly impossible militarily. Once the Ho Chi Minh Trail was opened, the crafty, mercurial ruler of Cambodia, Prince Norodom Sihanouk, concluded that the game was up and acquiesced in the establishment of Communist base areas all along Cambodia's border with South Vietnam. Thus was set up another catch-22 situation: if the Cambodian sanctuaries and the Ho Chi Minh Trail were left undisturbed, the North Vietnamese could attack the South and withdraw into safety for rest and re-fitting, making the defense of South Vietnam nearly unmanageable; if the base areas were attacked, South Vietnam and its allies would be pilloried for committing "aggression" against "neutral" countries.

Kennedy had a record of public comment on Indochina that extended over a decade. As early as 1951, he had struck the theme he would never abandon: force alone was not enough to stop Communism; America's allies in that struggle had to build a political foundation for it. In April 1954, during Dulles's United Action campaign to save Dien Bien Phu, Kennedy, in a Senate speech, opposed intervention so long as Indochina remained a French colony.[33] But in 1956, after France had withdrawn and South Vietnamese independence had been achieved, Kennedy was ready to join the prevailing orthodoxy: "This is our offspring—we cannot abandon it." At the same time, he reiterated that the conflict was not so much a military as a political and moral challenge "in a country where concepts of free enterprise and capitalism are meaningless, where poverty and hunger are not enemies across the 17th parallel but enemies within their midst. . . . What we must offer them is a revolution—a political, economic and social revolution far superior to anything the Communists can offer." Nothing less than America's credibility was at stake. "And if it falls victim to any of the perils that threaten its existence—Communism, political anarchy, poverty and the rest—then the United States, with some justification, will be held responsible, and our prestige in Asia will sink to a new low."[34] And in June 1961, as we have seen, Kennedy defined Vietnam as the place to vindicate American credibility.

Each new administration obliged to deal with Indochina felt compelled to take another step into the morass. Truman and Eisenhower had established the military-assistance program; Kennedy's emphasis on reform led to growing American involvement in the internal politics of South Vietnam. The problem was that reform and nation-building in South Vietnam would take decades to bear fruit. In Europe and in the 1940s and 1950s, America had bolstered established countries with strong political traditions by extending Marshall Plan aid and by means of the NATO military alliance. But Vietnam was a brand-new country and had no institutions to build upon. The central dilemma became that America's political goal of introducing a stable democracy in South Vietnam could not be attained in a time span relevant to the needs of a victory over the guerrillas, which was America's strategic goal. America would have to modify either its military or its political objectives.

When Kennedy entered office, the guerrilla war in South Vietnam had reached a level of violence sufficient to prevent the consolidation of the Ngo Dinh Diem government without as yet raising doubts about its survival. This seeming plateau of guerrilla activity tempted the Kennedy administration into the belief that a relatively small additional effort could achieve complete victory. The temporary lull, however, was due primarily to Hanoi's preoccupation with Laos; it turned out to be the calm before the storm. Once the new supply routes through Laos were opened, the guerrilla war in the South began to accelerate again, and America's dilemmas grew progressively insoluble. By the fall of 1961, the security situation had deteriorated to a point where it could only be alleviated by some kind of American military intervention. General Maxwell Taylor, the President's military adviser, and Walt Rostow, director of the State Department Policy Planning Staff, were sent to Vietnam to develop an appropriate policy. The real purpose of their mission was to determine the scale and the manner in which America should increase its commitment, not whether to undertake it.

In the event, Taylor and Rostow recommended a massive increase in the American advisory role at all levels of the Vietnamese administration. The result was a compromise between those who wanted to confine American participation to an advisory role and those who favored the immediate introduction of combat troops. The latter school was far from unanimous about what the mission of American combat troops ought to be; they were at one only in vastly underestimating the magnitude of the problem. Acting Assistant Secretary of Defense William Bundy estimated that the introduction of up to 40,000 combat troops, as recommended by the Joint Chiefs of Staff, had a 70 percent chance of "arresting things."[35] Because guerrilla war has rarely discovered a halfway point between victory and defeat, "arresting things" would, of course, likely postpone the moment of decision while staking America's global credibility.

Bureaucratic compromise often reflects the unconscious hope that something will happen in the interim to cause the problem to go away. But in the case of Vietnam, there was no conceivable basis for such a hope. With the official estimates ranging between 40,000 men for stalemate and 205,000 men for victory (the estimate of Secretary of Defense Robert McNamara and the Joint Chiefs of Staff), the Kennedy administration had to view the commitment of 8,000 troops (Taylor and Rostow's recommendation for increasing the American advisory role) as either woefully inadequate or as a first installment in an ever greater American role. And while odds of 70 percent for "arresting things" might seem attractive, they needed to be weighed against the global impact of a disaster such as France had suffered. Failure, of course, would be 100 percent.

The momentum was clearly all in the direction of further increases, as Kennedy had not changed his assessment of what was at stake. On November 14, 1961, he told his staff that the United States's reaction to Communist "aggression" would be "examined on both sides of the Iron Curtain . . . as a measure of the administration's intentions and determination." If America chose to negotiate rather than to send reinforcements, it might "in fact be judged weaker than in Laos." [36] He rejected a proposal from Averell Harriman, who was negotiating the Laos Accords on Vietnam, for a "negotiation" to implement the Geneva Accords of 1954, a euphemism for abandoning the effort to protect South Vietnam.

However, if negotiation was rejected and reinforcement treated as inevitable, an open-ended American commitment could only be avoided if Hanoi backed off—an outcome that would have required massive, not incremental, reinforcement, assuming it was achievable at all. The Kennedy administration was not prepared to grasp the nettle: the most dangerous course was gradual escalation.

The American objective, according to Roger Hilsman, then Director of the State Department's Bureau of Intelligence and Research, was to reduce the Vietcong to "hungry, marauding bands of outlaws devoting all their energies to staying alive." [37] But what guerrilla war in history offered a precedent for such an outcome? In Malaya, it had taken 80,000 British and twice that number of Malayan troops some thirteen years to defeat an opponent numbering no more than 10,000 and who had no significant outside support or secure lines of communication, and few opportunities of adding to its numbers. In Vietnam, the guerrilla army numbered in the tens of thousands, and the North had organized itself as the rear area for the struggle, had built

base areas along hundreds of miles of border, and retained the permanent option of intervening with an experienced North Vietnamese army whenever
the guerrilla army came under too much pressure.

America had maneuvered itself into what could at best be a stalemate, according to the Bundy estimate's requirement of 40,000 troops, of which it
was still well short. When Kennedy took office, the number of American
military personnel in Vietnam was close to 900. By the end of 1961, it had
risen to 3,164; by the time Kennedy was assassinated in 1963, the figure was
at 16,263, with more in the pipeline. The military situation, however, had
not significantly improved.

The more America's military role in South Vietnam expanded, the more
America emphasized political reform. And, the more insistent Washington
became on domestic change, the more it Americanized the war. In his first
defense review, on March 28, 1961, Kennedy restated his central theme:
that, no matter how powerful America's strategic weapons were, it could nevertheless be nibbled away slowly at the peripheries "by forces of subversion,
infiltration, intimidation, indirect or non-overt aggression, internal revolution, diplomatic blackmail, guerrilla warfare" [38]—dangers which could, in
the end, only be overcome by political and social reform enabling the potential victims to help themselves.

The Kennedy administration took for a truism what would turn out to be
one of Indochina's many insoluble dilemmas: the insistence on simultaneous
political reform and military victory. This set up a vicious circle. Within wide
limits, the guerrillas were in a position to determine the intensity of warfare,
and hence the level of security which was, in the short run, quite independent
of the pace of reform. The greater the insecurity, the more heavy-handed the
Saigon government was likely to become. And as long as Washington considered guerrilla successes the result, even in part, of lagging reform, Hanoi could
maneuver in a way that would magnify American pressures on the Saigon
government it was seeking to undermine. Trapped between fanatical ideo-
logues in Hanoi and inexperienced idealists in Washington, Diem's government froze into rigidity and was eventually ground down.

Every new American administration had sought to make increased aid to
Vietnam conditional on reform. Eisenhower had done so in 1954; Kennedy
was even more insistent in 1961, linking a massive increase of aid to obtaining for the United States an advisory role on all levels of government. Pre-
dictably, Diem refused; leaders of independent struggles rarely see merit in

exchanging colonialism for tutelage. Senator Mike Mansfield, visiting Vietnam at the end of 1962, reversed his own earlier judgment and agreed that the Diem government "appears more removed from, rather than closer to, the achievement of popularly responsible and responsive government."[39]

Relations between the administration and the Diem government deteriorated throughout 1963. Media reporting from Saigon, which until then had been supportive of America's involvement, turned hostile. The journalists did not on the whole question American objectives, as they would later, but the feasibility of bringing about a democratic, non-Communist South Vietnam in association with a ruler like Diem. Diem was even accused of considering compromise with Hanoi—the very course which, a few years later, a subsequent South Vietnamese President, Nguyen Van Thieu, would be condemned for rejecting.

The final break with Diem was provoked by a conflict between the South Vietnamese Buddhists and the Saigon government, which had issued an edict prohibiting the flying of flags by sects, religious groups, or political parties. Implementing the order, troops fired at protesting Buddhist demonstrators, killing several of them in Hue on May 8, 1963. The protesters had real grievances which were soon taken up by the international media—though the lack of democracy was not one of them. The Buddhists, who were as authoritarian as Diem, refused to state any terms to which Diem might have responded, had he been so inclined. Paralyzed by the guerrilla war and by its own inadequacies, the Diem government refused to make concessions. Washington multiplied its pressure on Diem to do so, and urged the removal of his brother, Ngo Dinh Nhu, who was in charge of the security forces, a démarche which Diem interpreted as designed to leave him at the mercy of his enemies. The final breach occurred on August 21, when Nhu's agents raided a number of pagodas and arrested 1,400 monks.

On August 24, newly arrived Ambassador Henry Cabot Lodge was instructed to demand Nhu's removal and to warn Diem that, if he refused, the United States must "face the possibility that Diem himself cannot be preserved."[40] Saigon's military leaders were to be put on formal notice that future American aid depended on the removal of Nhu, something Lodge's Vietnamese interlocutors understood to mean that Diem had to be overthrown. Kennedy and McNamara subsequently repeated essentially the same demands publicly. Lest the generals failed to appreciate the hint, they were told that the United States would provide them with "direct support in any interim period of breakdown of central government mechanism."[41] It took the South Vietnamese generals nearly two months to gather their courage and to act on proddings by their insistent ally. Finally, on November 1, they overthrew Diem, killing him and Nhu in the process.

By encouraging Diem's overthrow, America cast its involvement in Vietnam in concrete. Every revolutionary war is ultimately about undermining governmental legitimacy; Diem's overthrow achieved that objective for Hanoi. As a consequence of Diem's personal style of government, his removal affected every tier of civil administration down to the village level. Authority now had to be rebuilt from the ground up. And history teaches this iron law of revolutions: the more extensive the eradication of existing authority, the more its successors must rely on naked power to establish themselves. For, in the end, legitimacy implies the acceptance of authority without compulsion; its absence turns every contest into a test of strength. Prior to the coup, there had always existed, at least in theory, the possibility that America would refuse to become directly involved in military operations, much as Eisenhower had done when he pulled back from the brink over Dien Bien Phu. As the coup had been justified to facilitate a more effective prosecution of the war, withdrawal disappeared as a policy option.

Moreover, Diem's removal did not unify the people behind the generals, as Washington had hoped. In 1964 alone, seven more changes of government took place, none of which brought about a semblance of democracy. Diem's successors, lacking his prestige as a nationalist and as a mandarin-style father figure, had little choice but to turn the war over to the Americans—with the result that "the question was not going to be how to encourage a regime in South Vietnam that America could support, but of finding one that would support her in keeping up the struggle against the jubilant Communists."[42]

The power brokers in Hanoi grasped the opportunity immediately. A Communist Party Central Committee meeting in December 1963 laid down the new strategy: guerrilla units would be strengthened, and infiltration into the South accelerated. Most important, North Vietnamese regular units would be introduced: "It is time for the North to increase aid to the South, the North must bring into further play its role as the revolutionary base for the whole nation."[43] Soon thereafter, the 325th North Vietnamese regular division began moving into the South. Before the coup, infiltration from the North had consisted largely of Southerners who had been regrouped in 1954; afterward, the percentage of Northerners rose steadily until, after the Tet offensive of 1968, nearly all the infiltrators were North Vietnamese. With the introduction of regular North Vietnamese army units, both sides crossed their Rubicons.

Shortly after Diem's overthrow, Kennedy was assassinated. The new President, Lyndon Baines Johnson, interpreted intervention by regular North Vietnamese units as a classic case of overt aggression. The difference between the two sides by then was that Hanoi was implementing a strategy, while Washington was riven by competing theories, none of which was pressed to its conclusion.

Suspended between its yearning for a nonmilitary victory and its foreboding of a military disaster, the new administration faced a quandary. On December 21, 1963, McNamara reported to President Johnson that the security situation within South Vietnam had become very disturbing. America could no longer avoid facing the choice which had been implicit all along: dramatic escalation of its military involvement or the collapse of South Vietnam. The Kennedy administration had feared intervening on the side of an undemocratic ally; the Johnson administration feared abandoning the new, undemocratic Saigon government more than it did participation in the war.

In retrospect, the last moment at which America could have withdrawn from Vietnam at tolerable—although still heavy—cost would have been either just before or just after Diem was overthrown. In light of what followed, it would have been easier for America to disengage by letting Diem collapse of his own inadequacies or, at a minimum, by not standing in the way of the negotiations he was suspected of planning with Hanoi. Kennedy had been analytically correct to reject any such scheme on the ground that it would inevitably lead to a Communist takeover. The problem was that America was prepared neither to face the implications of the remedy nor to accept the probable outcome of letting matters run their course.

Kennedy's assassination made America's extrication from Vietnam even more difficult. If indeed Kennedy had realized that America had embarked on an unsustainable course—as has been argued by some of his entourage—he needed to reverse only his own decisions; Johnson, on the other hand, would have had to jettison what appeared to be the policy of a revered fallen predecessor, especially as none of the advisers inherited from Kennedy made the recommendation to disengage; indeed, they urged full-scale military commitment (with the notable exception of Undersecretary of State George

Ball, who, however, was not in the inner circle). It would have taken a leader of truly extraordinary self-confidence to undertake a retreat of such magnitude so soon after taking office. And when it came to foreign policy, Johnson was extremely unsure of himself.

The new President would have done well to undertake an analysis of whether the military and political objectives on behalf of which America had already invested so much were attainable, by what means, and over what period of time. Still, had such an analysis been undertaken, the outcome almost certainly would not have been significantly different. McNamara's Defense Department and National Security Adviser McGeorge Bundy's White House staffs were gluttons for analysis; the trouble was that they had no criteria to assess a challenge so at variance with the American experience.

In August 1964, a presumed North Vietnamese attack on the U.S. destroyer *Maddox* led to an American retaliatory strike against North Vietnam that was endorsed nearly unanimously by the Senate via the so-called Gulf of Tonkin Resolution. This resolution was used in turn to justify continuous air raids a few months later. In February 1965, an attack on an American advisers barracks in the Central Highlands city of Pleiku triggered an American retaliatory raid on North Vietnam, which quickly turned into a systematic bombing campaign code-named Rolling Thunder. By July 1965, American combat units were fully committed, and the American troop presence began to grow, reaching 543,000 by early 1969.

Subsequently, the issue of whether the Johnson administration had been entirely candid with the American people about the attack on the *Maddox* became part of the increasingly acrimonious Vietnam debate. It was used to discredit both the Gulf of Tonkin Resolution and America's participation in combat. To be sure, the Tonkin Resolution was not based on a full presentation of the facts, even allowing for the confusion of combat. But neither was it a major factor in America's commitment to ground combat in Vietnam. Rather, it was a small step along a road which would have brought America to the same destination, given the convictions of all the leading personalities. The cause of the frustration of Vietnam was not the way in which America entered the war, but that it did so without a more careful assessment of the likely costs and potential outcomes. A nation should not send half a million military personnel to a distant continent or stake its international standing and domestic cohesion unless its leaders are in a position to describe victory. This implies a definition of attainable political goals and a realistic strategy for achieving them.

One of the principal lessons of the Korean war ought to have been that protracted, inconclusive wars shatter America's domestic consensus. Yet Washington seemed to have gleaned exactly the opposite lesson: that the source of frustration in Korea had been MacArthur's advance to the Yalu and his quest for all-out victory. In this view, the Korean war was interpreted as a success because it prevented a Communist victory. America's involvement in Vietnam became consciously confined to a similar goal: without triggering Chinese intervention, to demonstrate to North Vietnam that it would not be permitted to take over South Vietnam and that, therefore, its only choice was negotiation. But negotiation for what end—especially in view of an enemy who equated compromise with defeat?

Theoretically, only two strategies have any chance of prevailing in a guerrilla war. One is essentially defensive and seeks to deprive the adversary of control of the population. General Taylor seemed to have had such a strategy in mind when he recommended establishing a series of enclaves protected by American forces while the South Vietnamese army would seek to prevent consolidation of a clearly defined Communist zone without trying to hold every last district day and night. The second possible strategy is to attack targets that the guerrillas have to defend, such as sanctuaries, supply depots, and home bases—for example, by interdicting the Ho Chi Minh Trail by ground forces and blockading both North Vietnam and the Cambodian ports servicing the sanctuaries. That strategy—at least conceptually—might have produced the relatively rapid war of attrition which the American military sought so desperately—and forced a negotiated outcome.

What could not work was the strategy that America in fact adopted: the mirage of establishing 100 percent security in 100 percent of the country, and seeking to wear down the guerrillas by search and destroy operations. No matter how large the expeditionary force, it could never prove sufficient against an enemy whose supply lines lay outside of Vietnam and who possessed extensive sanctuaries immune to attack and a ferocious will. At the end of 1966, North Vietnamese Premier Pham Van Dong told Harrison Salisbury of the *New York Times* that, although the United States was far stronger militarily, it would lose in the end because more Vietnamese than Americans were prepared to die for Vietnam.[44]

Johnson meanwhile resolutely rejected any territorial "expansion" of the war. Elite opinion in America had convinced itself that the four Indochinese states were separate entities, even though the Communists had been treating them as a single theater of operation for two decades. Moreover, Washington's assessment of the overall international context left it too preoccupied with Chinese intervention, ignoring Mao's statement that Chinese armies would not go abroad, which was reiterated by Mao to Edgar Snow, an American journalist sympathetic to the Chinese Communists. Thus it was that, in two separate wars a decade and a half apart, America paid a price for not taking Chinese statements seriously: in Korea, it had ignored Chinese warnings and marched to the Yalu, triggering Chinese intervention; in Vietnam, it had failed to understand strong hints by the Chinese that they would not intervene, causing America to reject the only strategy that might have brought victory.*

Though Washington was trying to prove that aggression does not pay and that guerrilla war was not going to be the wave of the future, it did not understand how its adversary calculated the costs and benefits. Johnson thought the way out was to demonstrate moderation, to reassure Hanoi, and to offer compromise. Yet all of these moves were much more likely to convince Hanoi to persist. Americans across the political spectrum kept appealing to Hanoi to participate in some democratic outcome, and racked their brains to devise workable election schemes. Yet none of the staples of American thought on international affairs held the slightest attraction for Hanoi except as tools by which to confuse its adversaries. Having established one of the world's most rigorous dictatorships, the Hanoi Politburo would never accept simply becoming one political party among many in the South—the core of the schemes presented by those most eager to end the war by negotiation. Hanoi had no conceivable incentive to stop using force; after all, it was bound to win as long as it did not lose, and it was certainly not losing.

Johnson wanted the Communist leaders in Hanoi to understand that

> . . . the minute you realize that a military victory is out of the question and you turn from the use of force, you will find us ready and willing to reciprocate. . . . We want an honorable peace in Vietnam. In your hands is the key to that peace. You only have to turn it.[45]

Johnson did not deserve the hatred and ridicule which such appeals evoked. He was, after all, restating traditional American verities. But neither he nor

---

* All this is clearer to me with hindsight. My own views evolved only gradually, paralleling the increasing ambivalence of our society, as I shall discuss in the next chapter.

his society had any concepts for an adversary who found such reassurances derisory; an adversary, moreover, to whom the American definition of compromise sounded like a call for surrender in the struggle of a lifetime.

To the tough, dedicated leaders in Hanoi, the concept of stability had no operational meaning. They had spent their adult lives fighting for victory, first against France, now against a superpower. In the name of Communism, they had brought incredible suffering to their people. "Leaving their neighbor alone" was the one thing Hanoi's leaders were inherently unable to do.

Once the tide of American public opinion turned against the war, Johnson's critics blamed him ever more stridently for the diplomatic stalemate. Insofar as these charges implied that Johnson was reluctant to negotiate, they missed the point. Johnson's eagerness to start negotiations was palpable to the point of being self-defeating. And it convinced Hanoi that procrastination was likely to elicit ever more generous offers. Johnson ordered one bombing pause after another, leaving no doubt that the United States would pay a significant unreciprocated entrance price just to get the negotiations started; Hanoi had every incentive to make that price as high as possible.

Almost by accident I had an opportunity to observe—and play a role in—the desperate efforts of President Johnson to find a way out of the war. In the summer of 1967, I attended one of the so-called Pugwash Conferences of scientists concerned with nuclear disarmament. Two participants who had heard of my visits to Indochina approached me with what seemed like an intriguing proposition. Raymond Aubrac, an official of the World Health Organization, had become acquainted with Ho Chi Minh in 1946, when the Vietnamese Communist leader had stayed at his home in Paris during negotiations with France. Aubrac offered to visit Hanoi, accompanied by a fellow scientist, Herbert Marcovich, to appeal personally to Ho Chi Minh on the subject of negotiations. I informed William Bundy, the Assistant Secretary of State, and Defense Secretary McNamara. They encouraged the visit, provided that the two scientists traveled in a private capacity and did not purport to represent official American views.

Aubrac and Marcovich journeyed to Hanoi, where they were received by Ho Chi Minh. After delivering a ritualized condemnation of American "aggression," Ho Chi Minh hinted that Hanoi would be willing to negotiate provided America stopped bombing North Vietnam. Mai Van Bo, Hanoi's diplomatic representative in Paris, was designated as the official contact.

Several exchanges followed by means of a complicated and decidedly undiplomatic procedure. Since Hanoi would not communicate directly with Washington prior to a bombing halt, I, a private citizen, served as intermediary. Even so, Hanoi, hoarding its every last negotiating chip, would not authorize its representative to deal with even an unofficial American. Thus, messages were passed to me from Washington, usually by Secretary McNamara, and then from me on to the two Frenchmen, who would deliver them to Mai Van Bo with whatever explanations I had been authorized to provide. McNamara was desperate to end the war, and repeatedly implored me to extract from my invisible interlocutors any hint, however oblique, that would enable him to promote the cause of a negotiated outcome.

In pursuit of that strange negotiation, I attended part of the meeting between President Johnson and his advisers in the Cabinet Room at which an American offer was prepared. The participants were Dean Rusk, the Secretary of State; Nicholas Katzenbach, Undersecretary of State; McNamara; Rostow; and Abe Fortas, then an unofficial adviser to Johnson. It was a melancholy experience. Clearly, Johnson's every instinct rebelled against a halt in bombing. Unsure as he was of his mastery of foreign policy, Johnson had had enough experience in politics to doubt the benefit of opening a negotiation with a unilateral concession. Yet he was desperate to end the war, battered as he was by domestic critics and unwilling to overrule advisers who were eager to attempt diplomacy. In the end, Johnson yielded. The upshot was the so-called San Antonio formula, devised after I had left the room, which Johnson presented in a speech in that city on September 29, 1967.

The San Antonio proposal turned into one of the turning points of the war. America offered to stop military action against North Vietnam—a precise obligation—in return for "productive" talks, so long as Hanoi did not take advantage of the bombing halt. No criteria were put forward to define either "productive" or "advantage." Yet, having demonstrated its capacity to manipulate the American domestic debate, Hanoi could have had few doubts that any American attempt to abrogate a bombing halt would be both controversial and time-consuming. Taking "no advantage" certainly did not seem to oblige Hanoi to stop guerrilla warfare, or, for that matter, to abandon anything it was already doing; at most, the provision meant that Hanoi was not to escalate a winning strategy. Hanoi turned the San Antonio formula down in 1967 but, aware of the floor under its risks, returned to it after the Tet offensive in 1968.

Criticism of America's Vietnam policy had started out fairly conventionally, with reasonable questions being raised about whether the war could be won and about the relationship of means to ends. On March 11, 1968, Walter Lippmann applied his already well-established critique of containment to Vietnam. America, he argued, had overextended itself, and the policy of containment was destroying any rational balance between national goals and the resources by which they might be achieved. Withdrawal, in that view, would strengthen America's overall geopolitical position.

The critics of the war traveled along the same road as the leaders who were conducting it, only in the opposite direction. They began by basing opposition on eminently practical grounds: the war was unwinnable; the costs exceeded the benefits; and America was overextending itself. But the critics, who were the products of the same American idealism, rapidly extended their critique to the moral plane as well in two stages: first, on the ground that, morally, there was really little difference between Hanoi and Saigon, which dispensed with the ideological reason for the war, and, second, that America's persistence in the war reflected not flawed practical judgment but a moral rot at the core of the American system. As a result, a policy which had enjoyed nearly universal support turned, in the course of two years, into an indictment of the morality of America's entire foreign policy and, a short while later, into a critique of American society itself.

In 1968, the noted *New York Times* columnist James Reston asked the question which had been tormenting so many Americans. "What is the end that justifies this slaughter? How will we save Vietnam if we destroy it in the battle?" [46]

Television was then just coming into its own. The regular evening newscasts were attracting audiences in the tens of millions, far more people than even the most popular print journalists could ever hope to reach in a lifetime. And they possessed the advantage of visual images to provide a running editorial commentary. The newscasts reflected a craving for drama and showmanship that, even with the best of intentions, could not always be balanced, if only because it was technically impossible to cover the atrocities the Vietcong were committing in the areas under their control. The news anchor turned into a political figure, in the sense that only a president could have reached as many people—and not with such regularity.

Throughout the postwar era, Americans had responded to their leaders' appeals for sacrifice in order to assist distant societies. In the crucible of Vietnam, America's exceptionalism—the belief in the universal application of American values—which had conferred such momentum on postwar reconstruction, began turning on itself and adopting a kind of moral scorched-earth policy. As casualties mounted, the critique of American foreign policy shifted from challenging the effectiveness of the policy to questioning the necessity for it—from an assault on the worthiness of America's Vietnamese ally to challenging the worthiness of America, not just in Vietnam but globally as well.

What lent a special poignancy to the attacks on America's fitness to conduct a global policy was that they originated to a large extent in the universities and the intellectual community, which up to that time had produced the dedicated defenders of America's international idealism.[47] Now, challenging the assumptions of twenty years of bipartisan foreign policy, the radical wing of the Vietnam protest movement ridiculed anti-Communism as being archaic. No less a figure than Hans Morgenthau, the doyen of American philosophers of the national interest, was moved to a proclamation of America's immorality: "When we talk about the violation of the rules of war, we must keep in mind that the fundamental violation, from which all other specific violations follow, is the very waging of this kind of war."[48]

In the post–World War II period, America had been fortunate to have never had to choose between its moral convictions and its strategic analysis. All of its key decisions had been readily justified as both promoting democracy and resisting aggression. South Vietnam, however, could by no stretch of the imagination be described as democratic. All of Diem's successor regimes felt beleaguered; South Vietnamese generals, who up to that time had been unknown to the public, were less than anxious to test their popularity at the polls. A convincing argument might have been made for the proposition that Saigon's new rulers were far less repressive than Hanoi's. That argument was, in fact, often made but never taken seriously. Moral relativism was unacceptable to a nation brought up on faith in the absolute distinction between good and evil.

Critics increasingly argued that, if Saigon failed to meet full democratic standards—which they knew in their hearts to be impossible—it deserved to be jettisoned altogether. As time went on, the Domino Theory, the central security premise on which the defense of Vietnam had been based for nearly two decades, was first abandoned and then ridiculed.

Johnson reacted to his critics by appealing to the orthodoxies of his predecessors, from Truman through Kennedy. But these had already begun to sound outdated, even irrelevant, to the critics. His offers for unconditional negotiations were rejected by Hanoi's leaders, who were far too subtle to provide a safety valve for America's domestic upheaval. To stem the tide, Johnson gradually modified his negotiating position, moving from demanding North Vietnamese withdrawal before America would stop hostilities to the San Antonio formula for suspending bombing prior to negotiations, and from refusing to talk to Hanoi's front in the South, the National Liberation Front (or NLF), to agreeing to talk to individual representatives of it, and, finally, to conceding NLF participation as a political entity in the negotiations. He also tried to tempt Hanoi with an economic aid program for all of Indochina. Each of these moves was dismissed by Hanoi as inadequate, and by the majority of U.S. domestic critics as insincere.

The administration's more moderate critics urged a negotiated compromise. The real obstacle to that, however, was not Washington but Hanoi. The North Vietnamese Communists had not spent a lifetime in mortal struggle to end it by sharing power or by de-escalating the guerrilla war, their most effective means of pressure. Johnson's frequent assurances that he would be flexible and open-minded seemed to Hanoi as either naïveté or political cynicism.

Ironically, America would have to pay the same price for compromise that it would for victory. Hanoi would accept compromise only if it felt too weak to win—that is, after it had been defeated. America would be able to show moderation only after the war, not during it. All the standard "solutions"—of both the administration and its moderate critics (myself included)—were rendered irrelevant by Hanoi's implacable determination. A cease-fire, which to Americans seemed a desirable way of ending the killing, would, in Hanoi's view, remove America's incentive to withdraw. A coalition government that was more than a mere fig leaf on the road to a Communist takeover seemed to Hanoi's leaders to guarantee Saigon's survival.

The real choice before America was not between victory and compromise, but between victory and defeat. The difference between North Vietnam and America was that Hanoi grasped that reality while neither Johnson nor his moderate critics would bring themselves to admit it. The practitioners of *Realpolitik* in Hanoi were convinced that the fate of Vietnam would be settled by the balance of forces on the ground—not at the conference table.

In retrospect, there can be little question that America did not need to pay any price for the opening of negotiations. Hanoi had decided to negotiate before America's 1968 presidential election, if only to deter both political parties—but especially the Republicans—from an intensified prosecution of the war by committing it to a negotiating process. But Hanoi's leaders would not enter negotiations without first making an effort to tilt the military balance in their own direction. Hence the Tet offensive, which occurred during the lunar new year, or Tet. In each year of the guerrilla war, including 1968, a truce had been agreed on for the holiday. Nevertheless, on January 30, Communist forces launched a broad offensive against thirty South Vietnamese provincial capitals. Achieving total surprise, they seized key targets in Saigon, reaching even the grounds of the United States embassy and General William Westmoreland's command headquarters. The ancient capital of Hue fell to the Communists and was held by them for twenty-five days.

Militarily, Tet is now generally recognized as a significant Communist defeat.[49] It was the first time that the guerrillas surfaced and engaged in open combat. The decision to launch a nationwide assault forced them to fight on battlefields they normally would not have chosen. Superior American firepower wiped out almost the entire guerrilla infrastructure, just as U.S. Army textbooks had predicted. Throughout the remainder of the war, the Vietcong guerrillas ceased being an effective force; almost all of the fighting was done by the North Vietnamese army's regular units.

Nevertheless, the Tet offensive turned into a major psychological victory for Hanoi. One can reflect with some melancholy on the course of events had, in its aftermath, American leaders stepped up pressure on the North Vietnamese regular combat units, which were now deprived of their guerrilla shield. Had Johnson done so, it is probable that he would have achieved the unconditional negotiations he was so desperately seeking, and maybe even an unconditional cease-fire. This is suggested by the rapidity—less than seventy-two hours—with which Hanoi accepted Johnson's renewed offer to negotiate, which was coupled with a unilateral partial bombing halt based on the San Antonio formula.

American leaders, however, had had enough and not because public opinion had deserted them. Polls showed that 61 percent of the American people considered themselves hawks, 23 percent doves, while 70 percent favored continuation of the bombing.[50] Those who abandoned the struggle were the very Establishment figures who had urged intervention in the first place. Johnson assembled a group of leaders from previous administrations, including such stalwarts as Dean Acheson, John McCloy, the "dean" of the Establishment who had served in many high positions, McGeorge Bundy, and Douglas Dillon, the former Secretary of the Treasury. By a large majority, they advised that escalation be ended and the liquidation of the war begun.

On February 27, 1968, television anchorman Walter Cronkite, then at the height of his influence, sent shock waves through the White House by predicting failure:

> It seems now more certain than ever that the bloody experience of Vietnam is to end in a stalemate. This summer's almost certain standoff will either end in real give-and-take negotiations or terrible escalation; and for every means we have to escalate, the enemy can match us.[51]

The *Wall Street Journal,* which up to that point had supported the administration, also jumped ship, asking rhetorically whether developments were "making hash of our original commendable objectives? . . . If practically nothing is to be left of government or nation, what is there to be saved for what?"[52] On March 10, NBC television concluded a special program on Vietnam with what was fast turning into a common refrain: "Laying aside all other arguments, the time is at hand when we must decide whether it is futile to destroy Vietnam in order to save it."[53] *Time* magazine joined the chorus on March 15: "Nineteen sixty-eight has brought home the awareness that victory in Viet Nam—or even a favorable settlement—may simply be beyond the grasp of the world's greatest power."[54]

Under the impact of such attacks, Johnson buckled. On March 31, 1968, he announced a unilateral partial bombing halt for the area north of the 20th parallel (that is, the heavily populated part of North Vietnam), to be followed by a total bombing halt as soon as substantive negotiations began. He indicated that no further significant reinforcements would be sent to Vietnam, and again repeated the oft-invoked reassurance that "our objective in South Vietnam has never been the annihilation of the enemy."[55] Finally, he also announced that he would not stand for reelection. The President who had sent 500,000 troops to Southeast Asia would leave their extrication to his successor.

By simultaneously de-escalating, renouncing his candidacy, and offering negotiations, Johnson embarked America on a treacherous passage. His aspirant successors vied with one another in making promises of peace, but without defining the term. Thus were created the conditions for public disillusionment once negotiations actually started. Hanoi had gained a bombing halt in exchange for essentially nothing but procedural talks, and was given the opportunity to restore its infrastructure in the South, albeit with North Vietnamese personnel. It had no incentive to settle with Johnson, and every temptation to repeat the same test of strength with his successor.

2

EVOLUTION OF A STRATEGY

What the Nixon Administration Found

On January 20, 1969, when Nixon took his oath of office, over a half million American troops were in Vietnam, and the number was still rising toward the ceiling of 549,500 that had been established by the previous administration in April 1968. (The actual peak of troop strength was 543,000 in April 1969.) The cost of the Vietnam effort had been $30 billion in fiscal year 1969.* American casualties had been averaging 200 men killed in action per week during the second half of 1968; a total of 14,592 Americans died in combat in 1968. On January 20, the cumulative total of Americans killed in action in Vietnam since 1961 stood at over 31,000; South Vietnamese casualties were close to 90,000.

The fighting was stalemated. The Tet offensive had been defeated in 1968, but it undermined public support for the war in America. The bombing halt multiplied pressures for withdrawal. The regular forces of South Vietnam numbered 826,000; they were also increasingly well equipped. But their task was daunting: to guard a jungle frontier of 600 miles and at the same time assure security for the population. And while the Vietcong cadres had been decimated in the Tet offensive, North Vietnamese regular army forces took up

---

* Of this, $24 billion was the "additional cost" of the war—that is, excluding the costs that would have been incurred anyway in maintaining American forces had the war not been taking place.

the slack. Almost all of the fighting was now done by *North* Vietnamese regular army units—contrary to the mythology of a "people's war."

The need to understand what America was facing produced the first study directive issued by the new administration. In National Security Study Memorandum (NSSM) 1, entitled "Situation in Vietnam," I requested the departments and agencies to respond to twenty-eight major and fifty subsidiary questions to pinpoint controversial issues and different points of view. Each agency was asked to respond separately and to describe any disagreements with other agencies.

Unfortunately, questions sometimes confirm the perplexities that have given rise to them rather than lead to their resolution. The responses to the NSSM 1 questionnaire arrived in February; the NSC staff summarized and analyzed them in a forty-four-page paper that was circulated to the members of the NSC Review Group on March 14.[1] Perhaps not surprisingly, the summary found that the bureaucracy was divided along lines very similar to those dividing the rest of the country. There was a relatively optimistic school of thought that included Ellsworth Bunker (the U.S. ambassador in Saigon), the Joint Chiefs of Staff, General Abrams (the commander in Vietnam), and Admiral John McCain (the commander of the Pacific theater). This group believed that the North Vietnamese had agreed to peace talks in Paris because of their military weakness, that pacification gains were real and "should hold up," and that "the tides are favorable." The opposite point of view reflected the civilian side of the Pentagon, the Central Intelligence Agency, and to a lesser extent the State Department. It acknowledged the improvements in South Vietnamese capabilities but held that "these have produced essentially a stalemate." It argued that pacification gains were "inflated and fragile," that "inadequate political progress" was being made, that the enemy was not dealing from weakness either in Paris or on the ground, and that "a compromise settlement is the only feasible outcome for Vietnam." There were, in addition, significant disagreements within the intelligence community over such elementary facts as the size and deployment of enemy forces, and the importance of Cambodia, particularly the port of Sihanoukville, as a supply route.

Politically South Vietnam seemed more stable than at any time in the previous four years. Nguyen Van Thieu, a northerner by birth, had been elected President in 1967 and broadened his government to include respected nationalists, such as Prime Minister Tran Van Huong. The American embassy in Saigon estimated that a Communist infrastructure still existed in 80 percent of the hamlets. Sixty-five percent of the total population and 81 percent of the rural population were estimated to be subject to some Communist influence, if only to Communist levies on their rice and agricultural production.

In the second half of 1968, General Creighton "Abe" Abrams had replaced General William Westmoreland as United States commander in Vietnam. Abrams had been a tank commander under George Patton in the Second World War and had led the battalion that broke the German siege of Bastogne in the Battle of the Bulge. Abrams had altered the American strategy in Vietnam by abandoning large-scale offensive operations against the Communist main forces and concentrating on protecting the population, which was the real prize of the war. American troops were deployed for defense in depth around major cities. In pursuit of that objective, he had redeployed two American divisions from the northern part of the country to the more populated southern part.

Another legacy inherited by the Nixon administration was the halt to U.S. bombing, which had come about for essentially two reasons. Opponents of the war had focused on the bombing partly because it was something the United States could halt unilaterally (unlike the rest of the fighting), partly because Hanoi had skillfully suggested that an end of the bombing would lead to rapid negotiation and negotiation would produce a quick settlement. On March 31, 1968, President Johnson announced his withdrawal from the presidential race and a bombing halt above the 20th parallel. A negotiation began in Paris between the United States and the Democratic Republic of Vietnam,* confined to the question of starting substantive talks in return for a complete bombing halt. On November 1, President Johnson agreed to a complete bombing halt, though bombing of the North Vietnamese supply corridor through Laos (the so-called Ho Chi Minh Trail) and reconnaissance flights continued. There was an "understanding" that there would be "no indiscriminate attacks on the major cities" (such as Saigon, Danang, and Hué); no firing of artillery, rockets, or mortars from, across, and within the DMZ; no movement of troops from, across, or within the DMZ; and no massing or movement of troops near the DMZ "in a manner threatening to the other side." Hanoi never explicitly agreed to these pro-

---

* The Democratic Republic of Vietnam (abbreviated DRV or DRVN) was the official name of North Vietnam.

visions but rather "assented by silence" to unilateral American statements to that effect. These were reinforced by an assurance from Soviet Premier Alexei Kosygin to President Johnson in a letter of October 28, 1968, that "doubts with regard to the position of the Vietnamese side are groundless." American chief negotiator Averell Harriman told the North Vietnamese in Paris on November 4 that indiscriminate attacks on the major cities "would create a situation which would not permit serious talks and thus the maintenance of a cessation [of the bombing]."

The bombing halt was an extraordinarily ambiguous arrangement. What did indiscriminate shelling mean? Was discriminate shelling allowed? What was the meaning of the arrangements regarding the DMZ, since the DMZ had been respected throughout the previous period—probably as an inhibition against a ground invasion from South Vietnam? There was the oddity that the bombing halt proscribed the bombing of belligerent North Vietnam but allowed the continued bombing of the supply corridors through "neutral" Laos.

Above all, the bombing halt did not lead rapidly to the productive talks Hanoi had led the Johnson administration to expect. The reason was that, no sooner was the bombing halt agreed to, than Hanoi insisted that the NLF, its front organization in South Vietnam, be included as an equal partner in the substantive talks—a first step toward delegitimizing the Saigon government as the government of South Vietnam. This was guaranteed to produce a deadlock. In every revolutionary conflict, the acceptance of the guerrillas as a negotiating partner has proved to be the single most important obstacle to negotiations, for it obliges the government to recognize the legal status of the enemy determined to overthrow it. This happened in the negotiations between France and the guerrillas in Algeria and between Israel and the PLO in the 1970s and 1980s before the Oslo agreement and again after the second intifada. A deadlock following the bombing halt was therefore nearly inevitable.

A generation later, a reckless journalist propagated the myth that Nixon produced this deadlock by conveying to Thieu that better terms were available if he waited for the Nixon administration. Therefore, according to this fairytale, Nixon and his associates bear a personal responsibility for all the casualties after 1968.[2] What appears to have happened on the basis of memoirs, the public record, and circumstantial evidence is that, after Johnson received the breakthrough message from Kosygin on October 28, he informed Nixon that a bombing halt was imminent. Nixon may thereupon have sent a message to Thieu through intermediaries though Nixon never admitted this. It would have been highly inappropriate if true. But neither did the Johnson administration cover itself with glory in that respect. For in his memoirs, former Soviet Ambassador Anatoly Dobyrin has reported that, at the same time, Secretary of State Dean Rusk was urging the Soviet Union to speed up the negotiations in order to elect Hubert Humphrey, who was likely to offer better terms than his opponent.[3]

As it turned out, neither appeal made any difference. The bombing halt went into effect on November 1, whatever Nixon did. As to the substantive talks, Thieu needed no incentive to stonewall; agreeing to the legitimacy of the NLF would be tantamount to a major political defeat. Thieu was bound to dig in, whatever Nixon urged.

As for Hanoi, it was following a timetable established, at the latest, when it launched the Tet offensive. It had agreed within seventy-two hours to negotiations about a bombing halt in April and, in a style we came to learn well, had stalled for five months to exact the best possible terms. From their point of view, the optimum time to settle that limited issue was just before the elections. Afterward a lame-duck president might be tempted to resume full-scale bombing without restraint, and whichever president emerged would be under less time pressure to settle the issue.

Thus the imperatives of Saigon and Hanoi tended to cancel each other out and would have produced an initial deadlock no matter what Nixon told Thieu or Dean Rusk told Soviet Ambassador Anatoly Dobrynin.

But the more vicious misrepresentation is that, but for the procedural deadlock—wrongly blamed on Nixon—peace would have been concluded in the last three months of the Johnson administration. An examination of the official positions of the two sides in the fall of 1968 shows that there was not the slightest possibility of this.

The official position of the Johnson administration, backed less than three months earlier by the Democratic Convention, called for the mutual withdrawal of all external forces, with the American withdrawal beginning only six months after the completion of the North Vietnamese retreat and only if the level of violence had subsided and internationally supervised free elections were in train. The Communist program announced by the NLF on November 3, 1968, two days after the bombing halt went into effect, demanded the unconditional unilateral withdrawal of United States forces and the overthrow of the Saigon government at the *beginning* of the process. There was no way to bridge this gap; this is why, in the public and private negotiations conducted by Harriman and Vance with Le Duc Tho, the principal North Vietnamese negotiator and a member of the Hanoi Politburo, no American comprehensive proposal was ever put forward.

Nor did Harriman or Vance during the transition make any suggestions to the incoming Nixon administration that could have led to a rapid breakthrough. They told us that a peace settlement should require the removal of all of North Vietnam's troops and cadres and even the North Vietnamese fillers in guerrilla units. To supervise this, "some [US] forces may have to remain in Vietnam for a considerable period until we are satisfied that all the North Vietnamese have withdrawn." Procedurally, Harriman (backed by Cyrus Vance, his deputy) favored a two-track approach, with the military issues to be discussed between the United States and North Vietnam and the political issues left to the Vietnamese parties.

The Nixon administration was later to adopt these procedural suggestions and put forward more flexible military terms only to see them rejected for four years. No agreement was imminent in 1968 because Hanoi was not prepared then or for the four years afterward to settle for anything other than total victory, including the unconditional withdrawal of all U.S. forces and the overthrow of the Saigon political structure.

As it turned out, Nixon helped break the procedural impasse in a way that enabled the departing Johnson administration to salvage a measure of success from the negotiating impasse. For three months, Saigon had resisted Hanoi's proposal for a four-sided table at which Hanoi, the NLF, Saigon, and the United States were each accorded equal status. By this proposal Hanoi sought to use the beginnings of the negotiations to establish the NLF as an alternative government.

In mid-January, less than a week before Nixon's inauguration, the Soviet Union suddenly offered a compromise on behalf of the North Vietnamese. The agreement that quickly emerged was a circular table without nameplates, flags, or markings—an arrangement ambiguous enough for the Communists to speak of four sides and for the United States and South Vietnam to speak of two sides (the allies versus the Communists). The Communists' motive was transparent. If the deadlock continued into the new administration, the new President, whose public pronouncements certainly sounded tougher than his predecessor's, might abrogate the bombing halt. If the deadlock were to be broken after the inauguration, the new administration would be able to use this sign of "progress" to strengthen its public support and therefore its endurance against the psychological warfare that Hanoi was about to unleash upon it. Settling with an outgoing administration in its last days in office solved both problems for the North Vietnamese.

It would have been easy to block the accord until after the inauguration on January 20. Saigon would surely have done so nearly automatically. But Nixon stood behind his Secretary of State-designate, William Rogers, in authorizing the outgoing Secretary of State, Dean Rusk, to urge Saigon to accept the compromise on behalf of the President-elect.

Nixon's gesture was all the more generous because of the intransigent rebuff he had received from Hanoi even before he took the oath of office.

On December 20, 1968, Nixon had sent a message to the North Vietnamese summarizing his readiness for serious negotiations:

1. The Nixon administration is prepared to undertake serious talks.
2. These talks are to be based on the self-respect and sense of honor of all parties.
3. The Nixon administration is prepared for an honorable settlement but for nothing less.
4. If Hanoi wants, the Nixon administration would be willing to discuss ultimate objectives first.
5. If Hanoi wishes to communicate some of their general ideas prior to January 20, they will be examined with a constructive attitude and in strictest confidence.

The North Vietnamese reply of December 31, 1968, was little concerned with honor or self-respect. It stated brutally two fundamental demands: the unilateral withdrawal of *all* American forces and the replacement of what Hanoi called the "Thieu-Ky-Huong clique," its standard pejorative phrase for the leadership in Saigon with which Hanoi was supposed to be negotiating in Paris.

The Nixon administration inherited this looming deadlock amidst an increasingly deep domestic schism. With every month, opposition to the war became more organized and insistent. It was composed of many strands: pacifists, who hated war; pragmatists, who could discern no plausible outcome; isolationists, who wished to end American overseas involvement; idealists, repelled by the horrors of a war brought home for the first time on television. These groups were given focus by a minority expressing the inchoate rage of the 1960s with shock tactics, expressing their hatred of America—which they derided as "Amerika"—its "system," and its "evil." I will discuss their impact later in this chapter.

Groping for a Strategy: The North Vietnamese Offensive and the Bombing of Cambodia

The Nixon administration entered office determined to end American military involvement in Vietnam. But it almost immediately came up against the same dilemmas that had bedeviled its predecessors. For nearly a generation, the security and progress of free peoples had depended on confidence in America. Nixon believed that he could not simply walk away from an enterprise involving four administrations, five allied countries, and 31,000 dead as if he were switching a television channel. Many urged him to "emulate de Gaulle"; but they overlooked that it had taken de Gaulle five years to extricate France from Algeria and as an act of policy, not as a collapse.

Such an ending of the war was even more important for the United States. No serious policymaker could allow himself to succumb to the fashionable debunking of "prestige" or "honor" or "credibility." For a great power to abandon a small ally to tyranny simply to obtain a respite from its own domestic travail seemed to Nixon—and still seems to me—profoundly immoral and destructive of efforts to build a new and ultimately more peaceful pattern of international relations. Clearly the American people wanted to end the war, but every poll, and indeed Nixon's election (not to mention the 13 percent vote for pro-war George Wallace), made it equally evident that they saw their country's aims as honorable and did not relish America's humiliation. The new administration had to respect the concerns of the opponents of the war but also the views of the majority and the anguish of the families whose sons had suffered and died for their country and who did not want it determined—after the fact—that their sacrifice had been pointless.

Before the administration could even address the issue of negotiations, it found its energies absorbed by the need to respond to a countrywide offensive launched by Hanoi on February 22—or four weeks after Nixon took office. The 1968 understanding with the North Vietnamese that led to the bombing halt included the "expectation" that there would be no indiscriminate attacks on major cities or across the DMZ. When Nixon took office, enemy infiltration was mounting, however, indicating that a new offensive was in the offing. It finally broke on February 22, the day before Nixon was leaving on his first visit to Europe as President. Its cost was 400 dead a week for a period of four months. Nearly half of all the casualties of the Nixon period were suffered in the first six months, 60 percent in the first year, as a result of a Communist offensive whose planning clearly antedated Nixon's inauguration.

After four weeks of casualties—and about 1,500 dead Americans—Nixon responded by ordering what has entered the demonology on the Vietnam war as the "secret bombing of Cambodia." In the presentations of its acolytes, this has produced a myth by which responsibility for the eventual abandonment of Cambodia has been justified. It runs like this:

Cambodia was a peaceful, happy land until *America* attacked it. There was no reason for this attack; it was the product of the psychosis of American leaders determined to act out their own insecurities on the prostrate body of an innocent people. American bombing turned a group of progressive revolutionaries, the Khmer Rouge, into demented murderers. By this self-hating hypothesis, American actions in 1969 and 1970 are held principally responsible for the genocide carried out by the Cambodian Communist rulers *after we left* in 1975—two years after all American military actions ceased—as well as for the suffering imposed by the North Vietnamese invasion of 1978.[4] This thesis can best be dealt with by describing the careful process by which the decision to attack the Cambodian sanctuaries was reached.

The only plan of the Johnson administration for dealing with an enemy offensive involved renewal of bombing of the North. On November 24, 1968, Secretary of Defense Clark Clifford had declared on ABC-TV's *Issues and Answers:* "If they, at some time, show us that they are not serious and that they are not proceeding with good faith, I have no doubt whatsoever that the President will have to return to our former concept and that is to keep the pressure on the enemy and that would include bombing if necessary." Averell Harriman made the same point in a White House briefing on December 4, 1968. General Earle Wheeler, Chairman of the Joint Chiefs, was only following inherited doctrine when he told Nixon at an NSC meeting of January 25, 1969, that everything possible was being done in Vietnam "except the bombing of the North."

No senior official in the new administration, however, was prepared to face resumption of the bombing in those early days. Nixon was savoring the honeymoon that follows the inauguration of a new President; he had never previously enjoyed the approval of the media, and he was reluctant to squander it. None of his colleagues had the stomach for the domestic outburst renewed bombing would provoke—even if it were the direct result of North Vietnamese violation of the understandings that had led to the bombing halt. Above all, Nixon and his associates had not yet given up hope, in the first month of the new presidency, of uniting the nation on a program for a negotiated settlement of the war.

Vietnam was briefly discussed at the first NSC meeting, on January 21, and more extensively at an NSC meeting on January 25. But the Nixon team was too new and the career officials too demoralized to offer imaginative ideas to a new President eager for them. Throughout the Johnson administration, the Pentagon had been complaining about being held on a leash by the civilian leadership. But when Nixon asked the Joint Chiefs of Staff for recommendations, their sole proposal was to resume the bombing of the North. The only new instruction issued by Nixon at this meeting was to stop bureaucratic harassment of the Saigon government; he had no intention of playing Hanoi's game of undermining the political structure of South Vietnam.

On January 30, I met at the Pentagon with Defense Secretary Melvin Laird and General Wheeler to explore how we might respond to the imminent North Vietnamese offensive. Wheeler reiterated that American forces within South Vietnam were already fully committed; the only effective riposte would be operations in the DMZ or renewed bombing of the North. Laird demurred at the latter suggestion; he stressed that the bombing halt had encouraged public expectations that the war was being wound down and that escalation would restart the public protests. Nor did I favor it, on what I now consider the fallacious reasoning of giving negotiations a chance.

This conceptual stalemate caused minds to turn to bombing the North Vietnamese sanctuary areas in Cambodia. The often heard argument that the Nixon administration assaulted the "neutral" status of a "peaceful" country flies in the face of indisputable realities. The territory under discussion was no longer Cambodian in any practical sense. For four years, as many as four North Vietnamese divisions had been operating on Cambodian soil from a string of base areas along the South Vietnamese border averaging about ten miles in depth. In 1978, the Communist victors in Cambodia put the uninvited North Vietnamese presence in northeastern Cambodia in 1969–1970 at 300,000, which far exceeded our estimates.[5] Cambodian officials had been excluded from the soil of their own country; most, if not all, of the population had been expelled. From these illegally occupied territories, North Vietnamese forces would launch attacks into South Vietnam, inflict casualties, disrupt government, and then withdraw to the protection of alleged Cambodian "neutrality." American critics seemed far more eager to vindicate this weird neutrality than was the government of Prince Sihanouk, who all but invited the American attack on the Communist bases and repeatedly justified these attacks, as I will show below.

The decision to bomb Cambodia was not taken lightly or by an isolated President egged on by his security adviser. It capped weeks of hesitation and even anguish on the part of all policymakers. The first suggestion came from General Wheeler. When Laird on January 30 had expressed doubt that a renewed bombing of the North was politically supportable, Wheeler proposed, as an alternative, attacks on the complex of bases that the North Vietnamese had established across the border in Cambodia. On February 9, General Abrams cabled General Wheeler from Saigon to say that recent intelligence from a deserter, as well as photo reconnaissance, showed that the Communist headquarters for all of South Vietnam was located just across the Cambodian border.* (As it turned out, the Communist leaders in Phnom Penh eight years later also confirmed that the deserter's information had been accurate on that score.) Abrams requested authority to attack the headquarters from the air with B-52s. Ambassador Bunker endorsed the proposal in a separate cable through State Department channels.

These recommendations fell on fertile ground with Nixon. In the transition period, on January 8, 1969, the President-elect had sent me a note: "In making your study of Vietnam I want a precise report on what the enemy has in Cambodia and what, if anything, we are doing to destroy the buildup there. I think a very definite change of policy toward Cambodia probably should be one of the first orders of business when we get in." General Andrew Goodpaster, former chief of staff to President Eisenhower and a Nixon consultant for the transition, had drafted a reply for my signature with detailed

---

* The Communist deserter who helped pinpoint the location of the North Vietnamese headquarters reported that no Cambodians were permitted in the headquarters area. General Abrams reported this to the President in February along with an assurance that the target was at least a kilometer distant from any known Cambodian hamlets.

information about the North Vietnamese base areas along the Cambodian border. He reported that "our field command in South Vietnam is convinced that the vast bulk of supplies entering Cambodia come in through Sihanoukville. . . . What we are doing about this is very limited. . . . The command in the field has made several requests for authority to enter Cambodia to conduct pre-emptive operations and in pursuit of withdrawing forces that have attacked us. All such requests have been denied or are still pending without action."

The importance of Sihanoukville was one of the disagreed issues in the NSSM 1 study. The U.S. military command in Saigon was convinced that between October 1967 and September 1968 some 10,000 tons of arms had entered Vietnam through Sihanoukville. The CIA and State disputed this. According to them, the flow of supplies over the Ho Chi Minh Trail in Laos was more than adequate to take care of the external requirements of *all* Communist forces in South Vietnam. At stake in this analysts' debate, of course, was whether the Cambodian sanctuaries were a crucial target that should be attacked; as happens frequently, intelligence estimates followed, rather than inspired, agency policy views. Those who favored attacks on the sanctuaries emphasized the importance of Sihanoukville; those who were opposed deprecated it. (When U.S. and South Vietnamese forces moved into these sanctuaries in April 1970, documents in Communist storage dumps indicated that shipments through Cambodia far exceeded even the military's highest estimates.)

Whatever the dispute about whether the matériel traveled through Sihanoukville or down the Ho Chi Minh Trail, there was no dispute about the menace of the North Vietnamese bases in Cambodia to American and South Vietnamese forces. On February 18, I attended a briefing by a two-man team from Saigon, together with Laird, Deputy Defense Secretary David Packard, General Wheeler, and Laird's military assistant, Colonel Robert E. Pursley. I reported to the President General Abrams's conviction that no Cambodian civilians lived in the target area. Nevertheless, I advised against the recommendation from our field commanders and the Joint Chiefs of Staff. We should give negotiations a chance, I argued, and seek to maintain public support for our policy. We could review the situation again at the end of March—the classic bureaucratic stalling device to ease the pain of those being overruled. Nixon approved that recommendation on February 22, the day before he was to leave for Europe.

• • •

On the very day of Nixon's decision to defer action against the sanctuaries, the North Vietnamese transformed vague contingency planning into a need to deal with a crisis. After weeks of preparation antedating the new administration, Hanoi launched a countrywide offensive. Americans killed in action during the first week of the offensive numbered 453; in the second week, 336, and in the third, 351. South Vietnamese casualties were far heavier, averaging over 500 a week. It was an act of extraordinary bad faith. No substantive negotiating sessions had been held in Paris; the new administration could not possibly have formed its policy. It ignored that Nixon had communicated with the North Vietnamese in the transition period, emphasizing his commitment to settle the war on the basis of the self-respect and honor of all parties involved. Without even testing these professions, the first major move of Hanoi was to step up the killing of Americans. Whether by accident or design, the offensive began the day before a scheduled presidential trip overseas, thus both inhibiting a response and humiliating the new President. I noted in a report to the President that the North Vietnamese had been "able to achieve a relatively high casualty rate among U.S. and South Vietnamese forces while not exposing their own main units."

Nixon received a military briefing on the enemy offensive in the Oval Office surrounded by piles of loose-leaf briefing books for each of the European countries he was about to visit. He was going through the books, committing them to memory, grumbling about the effort he had to make to do so. He was also seething. For years he had charged his predecessors with weakness in reacting to Communist moves. But he was eager also that his first foreign trip as President be a public success. American retaliation might spark riots in Europe; passivity might embolden Hanoi. He did not resolve this dilemma immediately. The only White House reaction on the day the offensive started was a phone call by me to Soviet Ambassador Anatoly Dobrynin at Nixon's direction. The President wanted Moscow to understand, I said, that if the North Vietnamese offensive continued, we would retaliate.

But the next day, on February 23, while in the air en route from Washington to Brussels, Nixon suddenly ordered the bombing of the Cambodian sanctuaries. It seemed to me that a decision of this magnitude could not be simply communicated to Washington and to Saigon from *Air Force One* without consultation with relevant officials or in the absence of a detailed plan for dealing with the consequences. I therefore recommended to Nixon that we postpone the final "execute" order for forty-eight hours, and I sent a flash message to Alexander Haig, then a colonel and my military assistant in Washington, to meet me in Brussels, together with a Pentagon expert, to go over the military plans and to work out a diplomatic scenario before Nixon would make a final decision.

Haig, Robert Haldeman (Nixon's Chief of Staff, who attended on behalf of Nixon since the President could not leave his residence without attracting attention), a Pentagon planning officer, and I met on board *Air Force One* at the Brussels airport in the early morning of February 24. In this setting, we worked out guidelines for the bombing of the enemy's sanctuaries: The bombing would be limited to within five miles of the frontier; we would not announce the attacks but acknowledge them if Cambodia protested, we would invite a U.N. inspection of the base areas and offer to pay compensation for any damage to civilians. In the short time available, we developed as best we could a military and a diplomatic schedule as well as guidance for briefing the press. Haig and the Pentagon expert left immediately for Washington to brief Laird. Later that day in London, Nixon gave Secretary of State William Rogers a cryptic account of his thinking but no details.

During the evening, Laird communicated reservations from Washington. He thought that it would be impossible to keep the bombing secret; the press would be difficult to handle, and public support could not be guaranteed. He urged delay to a moment when the provocation would be clearer. In retrospect, it is astonishing that during this entire period no serious consideration was given to resuming the bombing of North Vietnam; the bombing halt, entered to bring about constructive negotiations, was turning into an end in itself, even in the absence of any negotiation and in the face of a significant North Vietnamese offensive.

I agreed with Laird's conclusions about the need for delay. I also thought that a failure to react was likely to encourage further military escalation, as North Vietnam undertook to whipsaw Nixon as it had Johnson. But it was inappropriate to launch a new military operation while the President was traveling in Europe, subject to possible hostile demonstrations and unable to meet with and rally his own government. I said as much to the President. The following day, while in Bonn, Nixon canceled the plan.

The so-called mini-Tet brought home the precariousness of our domestic position. The enemy offensive surely must have been planned over many months. It occurred before the enemy could possibly know what the Nixon administration intended—since it did not know itself. Yet the *New York Times* on March 9 blamed the new administration for having provoked Hanoi by presuming to spend a month in studying the options in a war involving an expeditionary force of over 500,000 men: "The sad fact is that the Paris talks have been left on dead center while Ambassador Lodge awaits a White House go-ahead for making new peace proposals or for engaging in private talks out of which the only real progress is likely to come. Everything has been stalled while the Nixon Administration completes its military and diplomatic review." This theme was frequently repeated in Congress.

Nixon adopted a restrained posture in public while champing at the bit in private. At a news conference on March 4, he declared:

> We have not moved in a precipitate fashion, but the fact that we have shown patience and forbearance should not be considered as a sign of weakness. We will not tolerate a continuation of a violation of an understanding. But more than that, we will not tolerate attacks which result in heavier casualties to our men at a time that we are honestly trying to seek peace at the conference table in Paris. An appropriate response to these attacks will be made if they continue.

On March 4, I passed on to the President without comment a Laird memo recommending against proposals by the Joint Chiefs to attack North Vietnam. Laird was far from a "dove"; he would have preferred to aim for victory. But he was also a careful student of the public and congressional mood. He was a finely tuned politician who navigated with great care between his convictions, which counseled military reaction, and his political instinct, which called for restraint. He opposed bombing North Vietnam; he became a strong supporter of the attack on the Cambodian sanctuaries. (His only disagreement had to do with public relations policy; he did not think it possible to keep the bombing secret, on practical, not on moral, grounds.) The President, following a similar logic, ordered a strike against the Cambodian sanctuaries for March 9. On March 7, Rogers objected in order not to impair the prospects of negotiations in Paris.

Nixon retracted his order a second time. But each time he marched up the hill and down again, his resentments and impatience increased. Like

Laird, he kept saying that he did not want to hit the North, but he wanted to do "something." On March 15, the North Vietnamese fired five rockets into Saigon—a further escalation and violation of the understanding. There had been thirty-two enemy attacks against major South Vietnamese cities in the first two weeks of March. The day the rockets hit Saigon, I received a phone call from Nixon. He was ordering an immediate B-52 attack on the Cambodian sanctuaries. Capping a month of frustration, the President was emphatic: "State is to be notified only after the point of no return. . . . The order is not appealable." ("Not appealable" was a favorite Nixon phrase which, to those who knew him well—which I did not at that point, six weeks into the new administration—meant considerable uncertainty; this, of course, tended to accelerate rather than slow down appeals.)

I urged to give senior advisers an opportunity to express their views—if only to protect the President if it led to public controversy. No time would be lost. A detailed scenario would have to be worked out in any event, and to prepare instructions would require at least twenty-four hours. A meeting was therefore scheduled for the following day in the Oval Office. I consulted Laird, who strongly supported the President's decision. To prepare for the meeting, I submitted a memo to the President listing the pros and cons. The risks ranged from a pro forma Cambodian protest to a strong Soviet reaction, from serious Cambodian opposition to explicit North Vietnamese retaliation—though it was hard to imagine what escalation Hanoi could undertake beyond what it was already doing. Finally, there was the risk of an upsurge of domestic criticism and new antiwar demonstrations. I recommended that our Paris delegation ask for a private meeting on the day of the bombing so as to emphasize our preference for a negotiated solution. I urged the President to stress that the proposed bombing was a one-time decision, not a precedent. What my checklist did not foresee (what none of our deliberations foresaw) is what in fact happened: no reaction of any kind—from Hanoi, Phnom Penh, Moscow, or Beijing.

The meeting on Sunday afternoon, March 16, in the Oval Office was attended by Rogers, Laird, Wheeler, and myself. It was the first time that Nixon had confronted an international crisis since becoming President; it was also the first time that he would face opposition from associates to a course of action to which he was already committed. He approached it with tactics that were to become standard. On the one hand, he had made his decision and was not about to change it. On the other hand, he felt it necessary to pretend that the decision was still open. This led to hours of the very discussion that he found so distasteful and that reinforced his tendency to exclude the recalcitrants from further deliberations.

The Oval Office meeting followed predictable lines. Laird and Wheeler strongly advocated the attacks. Rogers objected not on foreign policy but on domestic grounds. He did not raise the neutral status of Cambodia; it was taken for granted that we had the right to counter North Vietnam's blatant violation of Cambodia's neutrality, since Cambodia was unwilling or unable to defend its neutral status.* Rogers feared that we would run into a buzz saw in Congress just when things were calming down. There were several hours of discussion during which Nixon permitted himself to be persuaded by Laird and Wheeler to do what he had already ordered. Having previously submitted my positive recommendations in a memorandum, I did not speak. Rogers finally agreed to a B-52 strike on the base area containing the presumed Communist headquarters. A month of an unprovoked North Vietnamese offensive, over 1,000 American dead, elicited after weeks of anguished discussion exactly *one* American retaliatory raid within three miles of the Cambodian border in an area occupied by the North Vietnamese for over four years.

After the meeting, the Joint Chiefs sought to include additional attacks on North Vietnamese troop concentrations violating the Demilitarized Zone. The proposal was not approved.

The B-52 strike took place on March 18 against North Vietnamese Base Area 353, within three miles of the Cambodian border. Originally the plan was for a single raid. Nixon ordered another single strike in April 1969 partly because there had been no reaction from either Hanoi or Phnom Penh to the first, but above all because of an event far away in North Korea, where an unarmed American reconnaissance plane had been shot down. Nixon had wanted to react by bombing North Korea. (He had severely criticized Johnson for his failure to take forceful measures in response to the capture by North Korea of the electronic ship *Pueblo*.) He had refrained, primarily because of the strong opposition of Rogers and Laird. But as always when suppressing his instinct for a jugular response, Nixon looked for some other place to demonstrate his determination.

In May 1969, Nixon approved attacks on a string of other Cambodian

---

* Under the Hague Convention of 1907, a neutral country has the obligation not to allow its territory to be used by a belligerent. If the neutral country is unwilling or unable to prevent this, the other belligerent has the right to take appropriate counteraction.[6]

base areas, all thinly populated and within five miles of the border. From April through early August 1969, attacks were intermittent; each was recommended by the Joint Chiefs of Staff and approved specifically by the President. Afterward, general authority was given: raids were conducted regularly at the discretion of the Joint Chiefs of Staff and the Secretary of Defense.

Periodic reports were sent to the President. In November 1969, he wrote on one, "continue them." In December 1969 and February 1970, he asked for an evaluation of their usefulness. Each time, Laird reported that General Abrams and Ambassador Bunker were convinced (as he reported on one occasion) that "the operation has been one of the most telling operations in the entire war." General Abrams credited the bombings with disrupting enemy logistics, aborting several enemy offensives, and reducing the enemy threat to the entire Saigon region. Laird endorsed the Joint Chiefs' and General Abrams's view that the strikes "have been effective and can continue to be so with acceptable risks."

The original intention had been to acknowledge the first strike when Cambodia or North Vietnam reacted, which we firmly anticipated. For example, the CIA predicted in memoranda of February 20 and March 6 that Hanoi would "certainly" or "almost certainly" seek to derive propaganda advantages from charging an American expansion of the conflict. The Defense Department doubted that the attacks could be kept secret; my own view on that subject was agnostic. In a conversation with Nixon on March 8, I said: "Packard and I both think that if we do it, and if silence about it doesn't help, we have to step up and say what we did." The President agreed. A formal acknowledgment was prepared if Cambodia protested. It offered to pay damages and asked for international inspection of the base areas to support the American position that they were being illegally used by North Vietnam.

Our initial reticence was to avoid forcing the North Vietnamese, Prince Sihanouk, and the Soviets and Chinese into public reactions. A volunteered American statement would have obliged Hanoi to make a public response, required Sihanouk to take a public stand and, given the balance of forces, obliged him to lean toward Hanoi as he tried to walk a tightrope of neutrality. It could have prompted reactions from the Soviet Union and China, complicating our beginning pursuit of triangular diplomacy.

But Hanoi did *not* protest. In fact, its delegation in Paris accepted Lodge's proposal for private talks on March 22, within seventy-two hours of our request and less than a week after the first American attack. And Sihanouk not only did not object; he treated the bombing as something that did not concern him because it occurred in areas totally occupied by North Vietnamese troops and from which Cambodians had been expelled—hence it was outside his control and even formal knowledge.

Sihanouk's subtle and skillful balancing act between domestic and foreign pressures had gone on for a decade. A hereditary prince, Norodom Sihanouk had managed to establish his country's independence and acquired the aura of indispensability. He had maneuvered to keep his country out of the wars of Indochina. After the Laos settlement of 1962, he had concluded that the Communists, whom he hated, would probably prevail in Indochina. He therefore adjusted to that reality. In 1965, he found a pretext to break diplomatic relations with the United States. Yet his collaboration with the Communists was reluctant; Hanoi was encouraging the Khmer Rouge (Cambodian Communists), who began guerrilla activity long before there was any American action in Cambodia; Sihanouk sentenced the Communist leaders to death in absentia. For all these reasons, I strongly supported a recommendation by Secretary of State William Rogers to the President in February 1969 that we approach Sihanouk with a view to improving relations.* These overtures were eagerly received. The U.S. embassy in Phnom Penh reopened, headed by a chargé d'affaires.

Sihanouk's acquiescence in the establishment of North Vietnamese base areas had always been reluctant. As early as January 10, 1968, during the Johnson administration, he had all but invited an American attack on them when he told presidential emissary Chester Bowles:

> We don't want any Vietnamese in Cambodia. . . . We will be very glad if you solve our problem. We are not opposed to hot pursuit in uninhabited areas. You would be liberating us from the Viet Cong. For me only Cambodia counts. I want you to force the Viet Cong to leave Cambodia. In unpopulated areas, where there are not Cambodians,—such precise cases I would shut my eyes.

---

* These diplomatic overtures to Cambodia were opposed by the Department of Defense and the Joint Chiefs of Staff, who feared that they might interfere with possibilities of bombing the Cambodian sanctuaries. I received a memorandum from Defense warning against such "diplomatic action which implies a restraint or inhibition in any expansion of current operating authorities designed to protect our forces in South Vietnam."

On May 13, 1969, nearly two months after the so-called secret bombing had begun, Sihanouk held a press conference, all but confirmed the bombings, emphatically denied any loss of civilian life, and to all practical purposes invited us to continue:

> Here it is—the first report about several B-52 bombings. Yet I have not been informed about that at all, because I have not lost any houses, any countrymen, nothing, nothing. Nobody was caught in those barrages—nobody, no Cambodians.
>
> I have not protested the bombings of Viet Cong camps because I have not heard of the bombings. I was not in the know, because in certain areas of Cambodia there are no Cambodians.
>
> That is what I want to tell you, gentlemen. If there is a buffalo or any Cambodian killed, I will be informed immediately. But this is an affair between the Americans and the Viet Cong—Viet Minh without any Khmer witnesses. There have been no Khmer witnesses, so how can I protest? But this does not mean—and I emphasize this—that I will permit the violation by either side. Please note that.

And on July 31, 1969, after four and a half months of bombing of North Vietnamese sanctuaries inside Cambodia, Sihanouk warmly invited President Nixon to visit Cambodia to mark the improvement of U.S.-Cambodian relations, which continued to improve until Sihanouk was unexpectedly overthrown.

Nor were the attacks all that secret. In addition to Sihanouk's press conference, accounts of B-52 or other air strikes against sanctuaries in Cambodia appeared in the *New York Times* (March 26, April 27) and *Washington Post* (April 27); a detailed story by William Beecher appeared in the *New York Times* on May 9; there was another in the *Wall Street Journal* on May 16; a widely disseminated UPI story appeared in the *Washington Post* on May 18; *Newsweek* reported it on June 2.

On August 22, 1969 (six months after the bombing started), Sihanouk told visiting Senator Mike Mansfield (according to a reporting cable):

> There were no Cambodian protests of bombings in his country when these hit only VCs [Vietcong] and not Cambodian villages or popu-

lation. He declared that much of his information regarding US bombings of uninhabited regions of Cambodia came from US press and magazine statements. He strongly requested the avoidance of incidents involving Cambodian lives.

Nixon and I briefed Senators John Stennis and Richard Russell, Chairmen of the Senate Armed Services and Appropriations Committees, in the Oval Office on June 11, 1969. Senate Minority Leader Everett Dirksen was also informed. In the House, Representatives Mendel Rivers and Leslie Arends, the Chairman and a ranking minority member of the House Armed Services Committee, as well as Minority Leader Gerald Ford, were briefed. Laird had earlier briefed key members of the Armed Services and Appropriations Committees of both houses. Not one raised the issue that the full Congress should be consulted. This was at that time the accepted practice for briefing Congress on classified military operations or intelligence operations. Obligatory standards for congressional consultation have since changed, and this is undoubtedly for the better.*

Nor is it true that the bombing drove the North Vietnamese out of the sanctuaries and thus spread the war deep into Cambodia. To the extent that North Vietnamese forces left the sanctuaries, it was to move back into Vietnam to be closer to the fighting, not deeper into Cambodia—until after Sihanouk was unexpectedly overthrown a year later. Then, North Vietnamese forces started to overrun Cambodian towns and military positions in order to isolate Phnom Penh and topple Sihanouk's successors, as I will describe in a later chapter, triggering an American incursion by ground troops.

The number of casualties for Cambodia in various accounts allegedly caused by American bombing appear vastly exaggerated when they are not outright inventions. Neither Cambodia nor North Vietnam ever claimed that there were significant civilian casualties from the so-called secret bombing. On the contrary, Prince Sihanouk publicly denied there were any casu-

---

* The double-bookkeeping the Pentagon had devised for the Cambodian bombing had a motivation much less sinister than that described in revisionist folklore. To preserve the secrecy of the initial (originally intended as the only) raid, Pentagon instructions were kept out of normal channels. The purpose was not to deceive Congress (where key leaders were informed) but to keep the attack from being routinely briefed to the Saigon press. The procedure was continued by rote when bombing became more frequent two months later. When congressional committees asked for data four years later, new Pentagon officials, unaware of the two reporting channels, unwittingly furnished data from the regular files. This was a bureaucratic blunder, not deliberate design.

alties; indeed, he claimed—as we too believed—that there were very few Cambodians living in these sanctuaries.*

Nixon confined his role to authorizing categories of attack invariably recommended by the Joint Chiefs of Staff. In a very few cases (especially in response to the North Vietnamese 1972 offensive) he ordered specific categories. For a period of two weeks between the conclusion of the Vietnam negotiations and the signature of the Paris agreement, I explained the meaning of the agreement for Cambodia to the Chairman of the Joint Chiefs. Afterwards, from February to August 1973, the actual targets were chosen by the Joint Chiefs or the local commanders who, in the vast majority of cases, had asked for the authorization in the first place. The military chain of command and the method of selecting of targets was identical to that which operated in every American war since the end of the Second World War, from the Korean war to the Gulf war to Afghanistan.

With this as a background, it is possible to divide bombing of Cambodia into three time periods. There was the so-called secret bombing of the sanctuaries described in the previous pages. It lasted from March 1969 to May 1970. After that, from May 1970 to January 1973, bombing in Cambodia was under the command of the Saigon military headquarters as part of the Vietnam operations and regularly announced. From February to August 1973, new rules of engagement were developed through existing procedures to reflect the changed political situation of the peace agreement. These required a recommendation by the appropriate military commander, coordination with the Cambodian government, validation by the U.S. ambassador in Phnom Penh, a distance of one kilometer from civilian dwellings, and careful pre- and post-strike photography. These rules of engagement are described in the Appendix in a memorandum prepared in 1979 for the State Department historian by the former ambassador to Cambodia, Emory Swank.†[8]

---

* The Historical Office of the Secretary of Defense cites an instruction from Nixon of May 21, 1970, to "avoid . . . tactical air strikes in heavily populated areas."

† The casualty estimates by revisionist writers are often set at 300,000. Since I am in no position to make an accurate estimate of my own, I consulted the OSD Historian, who gave me an estimate of 50,000 based on the tonnage of bombs delivered over a period of four and a half years.[7] I cannot reconstruct the scale of those attacks. They were subsidiary to the air operations in Vietnam. In a telephone conversation with Nixon in the fall of 1970, I estimated them at thirty tactical air strikes for that week.

Attempts at a Diplomatic Outcome

It would have been impossible to find two societies less intended by fate to understand each other than the Vietnamese and the American. On the one side, Vietnamese history and Communist ideology combined to produce an almost morbid suspiciousness and ferocious self-righteousness. This was compounded by a legacy from French colonialism of Cartesian logic that produced an infuriatingly doctrinaire technique of advocacy. Each North Vietnamese proposal was put forward as the sole, logical truth, and each demand was stated in the imperative (the United States "must"). By 1971, we had been so conditioned that when on one occasion the North Vietnamese substituted "should" for "must," we thought great progress had been made. On the other side, there was the American belief in the efficacy of goodwill and the importance of compromise—qualities likely to be despised by dedicated Leninists who saw themselves as the inexorable spokesmen of an inevitable future, absolute truth, and superior moral insight.

But the fundamental problem went deeper still. The North Vietnamese considered themselves in a war to the finish; they treated negotiations as an instrument of political warfare. Negotiations were a weapon to exhaust us psychologically, to split America from its South Vietnamese ally, and to divide American public opinion through vague hints of solutions just out of reach because of the foolishness or obduracy of the U.S. government. The North Vietnamese were concerned lest the Nixon administration use the fact of the negotiations to rally public support; in the public talks, they would not compromise on even the smallest issues because any appearance of "progress" might enhance American staying power. They preferred secret talks because this gave them an opportunity to reconnoiter the terrain and marginally adjust their positions without paying the price of the appearance of progress. When they settled an issue, their motive was to have a maximum domestic impact in the United States. The bombing halt occurred just before the 1968 election in order to commit both presidential candidates to it; the shape of the table was settled just before Nixon's inauguration to prevent the new administration from building support by beginning with a "success." Throughout the war, we were taunted by the appearance of great reasonableness by the North Vietnamese toward American visitors, especially those opposed to the Nixon administration. These guests were treated with great civility and a cat-

alogue of skillful and intriguing code words that permitted a variety of interpretations, none of them as clear or as meaningful as the visitor imagined. All
of them evaporated as soon as they were tested in a serious forum.

The Paris talks quickly fell into a pattern. In the conference room, the
North Vietnamese acted like a stern tutor berating a wayward pupil; the student was being graded on answers to questions he had no right to participate
in framing, by criteria determined exclusively by the professor. Outside the
conference room, the North Vietnamese created the impression that the negotiations were like a detective story. They threw out vague clues at whose
answers we had to guess; if we missed the riddle, the war would go on and the
administration would be accused of having "missed an opportunity." Many
of our critics fell in with this procedure. In our public debate, it was rarely
challenged; hardly anyone asked why Hanoi did not put forward an intelligi-
ble proposition and why they should proceed so allusively and indirectly. Of
course, when Hanoi was finally ready to settle (in October 1972), it proved as
capable of framing concrete proposals as it had previously been skillful in ob-
fuscation, and as impatient as it had previously been dilatory.

Between the hammer of antiwar pressure and the anvil of Hanoi, it was
the better part of a year before a settled strategy for negotiations emerged.

But the issue rarely came up as a debate about strategy. Rather, for several
months there was a dispute over the inherited policy of mutual withdrawal
embodied in the Manila formula, specifically whether American withdrawals
should begin only after the North Vietnamese had completed their own
withdrawal or simultaneously with it. The debate was absurd, first, because
Hanoi had no intention of withdrawing its own forces and, second, because
every key official knew that Nixon intended to start a unilateral withdrawal
of significant American forces in a few months, a policy which, due to domestic pressures, soon developed its own momentum quite separate from the
diplomatic necessities. A second issue concerned the residual force. All agencies agreed that a substantial residual force had to remain. This issue, too, was
soon overtaken by events and congressional pressures.

A third debate was over the possibility of unilateral de-escalation of the
fighting on the battlefield. The State Department and the Paris negotiating
team urged an offer to discuss the curtailment of B-52 strikes, of U.S. offensive operations, and of the use of artillery for interdiction. Both our commander in Saigon and the Joint Chiefs of Staff disagreed strongly, insisting
that such measures would cede the military initiative to the enemy and allow

him to rebuild his strength in the populated areas. That, too, turned out to be a moot issue, as Hanoi never showed the slightest interest in de-escalation, even as America implemented it unilaterally—often for budgetary reasons. The North Vietnamese were less interested in humanizing the fighting than in winning it.

Whatever the administration and regardless of the issue, American negotiators like to succeed. They deluge Washington with proposals to break deadlocks; they are tireless in thinking up initiatives. Animated by the high value they place on willingness to compromise or at least the appearance of it, they grow restive with deadlock. Imperceptibly, they tend to add their own pressures to the proposals of the other side. Since Washington's decisions as often as not are made by adversary proceedings, negotiators feel secure in urging far-reaching concessions, safe in the knowledge that other agencies holding opposite views will be equally one-sided in opposition. The President is left with seeking a compromise between contending pressures, not with developing a strategy. And if he is reluctant to dominate the process in detail, he runs the risk that each bureaucratic contender pursues its favorite course unilaterally.

So it was with the negotiations in Paris. During February and early March, there was constant pressure from our Paris delegation, headed by Henry Cabot Lodge, who had replaced Harriman, to initiate private talks with the North Vietnamese. When the first substantive private meeting finally took place, on March 22, it produced not a negotiation but North Vietnamese demands for the unconditional withdrawal of all American forces and for dismantling the Thieu-Ky-Huong administration.*

The various departments were pushing seemingly inexhaustible ideas for bringing about their preferred outcome. In a conversation with Soviet Ambassador Dobrynin on March 8, Rogers unilaterally abandoned the two-track approach of separating military and political issues. Rogers told Dobrynin that we were willing to talk about political and military issues simultaneously.

Laird contributed a unilateral step in the military field. On April 1, after several meetings on the subject, Nixon issued a directive prohibiting any pro-

---

* The only noteworthy occurrence at the first private meeting was the totally gratuitous and unexpected outburst by North Vietnamese negotiator Xuan Thuy to Lodge in Paris that the United States should not count on the Sino-Soviet split to help us settle the war in Vietnam, which, I must say, caused us to notice opportunities of which we had not been fully conscious.

posals on de-escalation except in the context of mutual withdrawal or of reciprocity. On that very day, the Pentagon announced publicly that, because of budgetary considerations, the U.S. was reducing B-52 sorties by over 10 percent, effective June 30. Laird explained privately that he could not pay for the higher rate beyond June 30 and that he was actually continuing the higher rate three months longer than had been planned by his predecessor. Neither the President nor I had been aware of that plan or of the announcement.

I had no fixed view as to the right number of B-52 sorties. But if we were going to de-escalate, it should be as part of a negotiation; the worst way to do it was unilaterally in response to budgetary pressures.

Nothing is more askew than the popular image of Nixon as an imperial President barking orders at cowed subordinates. Nixon hated to give direct orders—especially to those who might disagree with him. He rarely disciplined anybody. When he met opposition, he sought to accomplish his objective without the offender's being aware of it. This indirection might achieve the goal; it did little for discipline or cohesion. In the absence of a presidential willingness to confront his Secretary of Defense, I negotiated a rather ambiguous press statement with Laird: "It is the policy of the United States that reductions of military operations might be brought about by the phased mutual withdrawal of external forces. Budget planning figures will be brought in line with this policy on the basis of periodic review."

But the impact on the diplomatic process of such uncoordinated initiatives could not be undone. A journalist told me that he took the B-52 reduction as a signal to both Hanoi and Saigon, because "you do not do a thing like this for budgetary reasons." He said it could not be read by Hanoi as anything except a move toward the withdrawal of American forces, or by Saigon as a warning that there were firm limits to the commitment of the United States. He was right in both judgments, though he gave the administration too much credit for thoughtful design. Ultimately, we made a virtue of necessity. Ambassador Lodge was instructed to cite the B-52 cutback in his public presentation at the Paris peace talks as a commitment to de-escalation. The President referred to the reduction in sorties in his November 3 speech. Neither then nor later did the unsentimental leaders in Hanoi acknowledge these gestures. They did not pay for what they had already pocketed.

Peace Initiatives

By early April, the Nixon administration had been in office for two months. We had faced a North Vietnamese offensive and suffered nearly 2,000 casualties. We had attended weekly negotiating sessions that were totally stalemated. We had approved a private meeting at which Hanoi demanded unilateral American withdrawal and the overthrow of the political structure of our allies. It had ignored steps toward de-escalation.

To put an end to the seemingly endless dissipation of America's negotiating assets, I recommended to Nixon to bring matters to a diplomatic head. The concept was to make a comprehensive offer to Hanoi and empower a senior official to negotiate it. During the election campaign, Nixon had implied that he would find some way to involve the Soviet Union in ending the Vietnam war. The time had come to try the Soviet card. We would give the Soviets an incentive to negotiate by authorizing a representative to go to Moscow to open talks on the limitation of strategic arms side by side with negotiations with a senior North Vietnamese envoy. I suggested Cyrus Vance for the mission.

I had met Cy Vance, who later became President Carter's Secretary of State, when he was Deputy Secretary of Defense in the Johnson administration. Deliberate, soft-spoken, honorable, he was the epitome of the New York corporation lawyer, meticulously executing his assignments, wisely advising his clients. Beneath his controlled manner, there was a passionate streak in harmony with the liberal views widely held in the circles in which he moved. On the Paris delegation, he had come to share the ardent dedication of his chief, Harriman, to a negotiated settlement. When Vance left his position as Deputy Chief of the U.S. delegation to the Paris peace talks on February 19, 1969, Nixon sent him a warm cable of appreciation.

Nixon had instructed me to stress in conversations with Soviet Ambassador Anatoly Dobrynin that a fundamental improvement in U.S.-Soviet relations presupposed Soviet cooperation in settling the Vietnam war. Dobrynin had always evaded a reply by claiming that Soviet influence in Hanoi was extremely limited. We tried to link all the negotiations in which the Soviet Union was interested—the strategic arms limitation talks (SALT), the Middle East, and expanded economic relations. But we had never made a comprehensive proposal to the Soviets on Vietnam.

On March 18, I met with Vance to explore his general willingness to undertake a mission to Moscow. Vance was to begin discussions on the limitations of strategic arms and on the same trip meet secretly with a senior North Vietnamese representative. He would be empowered to make rapid progress in both areas, while seeking to keep them in tandem. The next day, Vance raised a number of sensible questions: How would the two negotiations in Moscow be related to each other; how could there be time to carry out both assignments adequately; how would his talks on Vietnam be kept secret from the team responsible for arms control?

On April 3, I formally proposed the Vance mission to the President. The negotiations proceeding in Paris had built-in dilemmas. We had to convince the American public that we were eager to settle the war, and Hanoi that we were not so anxious that it could afford to outwait us. The U.S. government had to be disciplined enough to speak with a single voice but maneuver with sufficient skill to avoid the charge of intransigence. Relations with Saigon had to be close enough to deprive Hanoi of the expectation that the negotiations could be used to demoralize the South Vietnamese government but not give Saigon a veto. I doubted our ability to fulfill all these conditions simultaneously. Budgetary pressures and unilateral withdrawals would reduce military options with no hope of reciprocity. Internal divisions made it unlikely that American negotiations could present a coherent policy or prevent oscillation between extremes.

For all these reasons, Nixon approved approaching Dobrynin with a proposal: the President was to make progress in U.S.-Soviet relations on a broad front. But the Vietnam war was a major obstacle. To resolve the impasse, Nixon was prepared to send a high-level delegation to Moscow, headed by Cyrus Vance, to agree immediately on principles for a negotiation on strategic arms limitation. While in Moscow, Vance would also be empowered to meet with a negotiator from North Vietnam and to agree with him on a military and political settlement for Indochina. On the military side, we proposed a cease-fire and mutual withdrawal. On the political side, we offered that the NLF, if it renounced violence, could participate in the political life of the country under international supervision. This would be coupled with agreement on a separate and independent South Vietnam for five years, after which there would be negotiations for unification. The President would give the effort six weeks to succeed. If the outcome of the Vance mission was positive, the President would also consider "other meetings at even higher levels" (that is, a possible summit). Vance was the right emissary because he would be meticulous in carrying out instructions and contribute to obtaining bipartisan support.

These peace terms went far beyond anything urged, at that time, by most doves. It included a cease-fire—at that point opposed by the Pentagon. It accepted complete withdrawal (without residual forces), and it agreed to a role for the NLF in the political life of Saigon. We did not yet understand that Hanoi's leaders were interested in victory, not a cease-fire, and in guaranteed political control, not a role in free elections. Least of all they wanted a negotiation in Moscow which implied Soviet tutelage and would strain their relationship with China.

On the morning of April 5 when I spoke with the President at Key Biscayne, he was dubious that the "Vance ploy," as he called it, would work. Nevertheless, he approved it with a few marginal notes in his handwriting, which extended the deadline to two months and were more explicit than my draft in holding out the prospect of economic cooperation to the Soviets.

Using a technique I was to employ occasionally later on, I let Dobrynin read these talking points together with the President's initials and handwritten amendments. Dobrynin took copious notes, stopping now and again to ask for an explanation. When he got through, he asked whether Nixon was making a Vietnam settlement a condition for progress on the Middle East, economic relations, and strategic arms. I replied that we were prepared to continue talking on those topics but that talks would move more rapidly if the preoccupation with Vietnam were removed. Also, if there was no settlement, we might take measures that would create "a complicated situation."

Dobrynin was voluble in emphasizing Moscow's desire to begin negotiations whatever happened in Vietnam. He speculated that China was attempting to produce a clash between the Soviet Union and the United States. An escalation of the war in Vietnam, he added, could only serve the interests of China. I said that if this were so, the Soviet Union had a joint obligation to avoid complicating matters. Dobrynin's parting words were that this was a "very important" conversation.

Yet no reply was ever received from Moscow—no rejection, no invitation, not even a temporizing acknowledgment. In June, Dobrynin mentioned in passing that the proposal had been transmitted to Hanoi but had not found favor there. The next time I heard from Dobrynin about the Vance mission proposal was eight months later, on December 22, when in the course of a global review he told me that Moscow had tried to be helpful with the Vance mission. Hanoi, however, had refused to talk unless the United States agreed ahead of time to a coalition government to be installed before any other steps were taken. Rather than return a negative reply, the Kremlin had preferred to say nothing. I answered coolly that some sort of acknowledgment, at least, might have been in order.

The aborted Vance mission showed that Moscow would not risk its relation with Hanoi—and the leadership of global Communism—to engage itself in ending the war. And in truth, its influence was limited. Hanoi would not circumscribe its freedom of action by negotiating in Moscow under Soviet tutelage with the risk that Moscow might sacrifice some of its interests for superpower relations.

On May 8, at the sixteenth plenary meeting in Paris, Hanoi, in effect, replied to the proposal inherent in the Vance mission. The Communists with great flourish put forward a ten-point peace program. Couched in the by now customary style of an ultimatum, the Ten Points listed what the United States "must" do to end the war. They demanded total, unconditional, and unilateral U.S. withdrawal, abolition of the South Vietnamese government, and American reparations for war damage. They proposed that the South Vietnamese government be replaced by a coalition government to include all "social strata and political tendencies in South Vietnam that stand for peace, independence and neutrality."

The proposal for a coalition government did not sound unreasonable; many unwary Americans read it as simply a demand for Communist participation in the Saigon government. But once we started exploring its meaning, we discovered that the Communists reserved for themselves the right to define who stood for "peace, independence and neutrality." In four years of negotiations, Hanoi never designated *one* individual, even from among the Saigon government's most explicit opponents, who would pass this test. The operational content of the Ten Points was that simultaneously with overthrowing the government of South Vietnam and total and unconditional withdrawal, we would then collude with the Communists to force the remaining non-Communist elements into a structure containing the NLF and whatever groups the Communists alone would define as acceptable. And that new coalition government was to be only interim; the definitive political structure of South Vietnam was to be negotiated between this unarmed Communist–dominated coalition and the all–Communist NLF, backed by

Hanoi's army. Such was Hanoi's definition of a "just" political settlement.* And when the Communists took over Saigon in 1975, not even a coalition government was established; in fact, even the NLF was excluded from any share in power.

Years later this proposal came to be described as a "missed opportunity" and its terms as similar to what was finally accepted four years later after additional sacrifices were described as "unnecessary." No serious examination would sustain that proposition. The Paris terms were quite different, as a later chapter will describe in detail, in that they provided for a cease-fire and the continued existence of the Thieu government, required Vietnamese withdrawal from Laos and Cambodia, permitted continued American military and economic aid to Saigon, and prohibited North Vietnamese infiltration and reinforcement into South Vietnam.

No responsible President could have accepted even the military terms of total unilateral withdrawal. The official position of the Johnson administration had been U.S. withdrawal after the North Vietnamese troops had been withdrawn and the guerrilla war had "subsided." Averell Harriman and Cy Vance had left memoranda for the new President recommending a residual U.S. force of up to 260,000. How was the United States to accomplish the withdrawal of 543,000 troops surrounded by nearly a million South Vietnamese troops, enraged at being betrayed, and hundreds of thousands of North Vietnamese troops and South Vietnamese guerrillas in the absence of any political structure in the South? Hanoi did not even dress up its Ten Points by offering a cease-fire. It was a proposal to turn American forces into hostages for extorting ever increasing demands for reparations and collusion with Hanoi to achieve its political program of overthrowing the government the Kennedy and Johnson administrations had helped establish.

The proposal was one-sided in content and insolent in tone. But the mere existence of a Communist peace plan, however extreme in nature, generated congressional, media, and public pressures not to pass up this "opportunity." If we were not going to be whipsawed, we clearly needed to elaborate a clear-cut American position. On April 25, I called the President's attention to a remark made by North Vietnamese negotiator Xuan Thuy: "If the Nixon

---

* In July 1971, with Le Duc Tho, a member of Hanoi's Politburo, I went over a list of Saigon politicians, including all known opposition leaders, who might prove acceptable as meeting the test of standing for "peace, independence and neutrality." Not *one* passed muster.

administration has a great peace program, as it makes believe, why doesn't it make that program public?"

On May 14, Nixon, on national television, elaborated for the first time the premises of his Vietnam policy, the steps that had been taken, concluding with a concrete new negotiating proposal. He reviewed the actions of his first four months in office: the blunting of the enemy offensive, the improvement of relations with the Saigon government, the strengthening of the South Vietnamese forces, and, above all, the development of a coherent negotiating position.

Nixon proposed an eight-point program that represented a major change in the American negotiating position. Specifically, he abandoned the Manila formula (Hanoi's withdrawal six months before America's) and proposed simultaneous withdrawal. Yet the North Vietnamese withdrawal could be de facto (by "informal understanding") rather than explicitly admitted by Hanoi.* The United States agreed to the participation of the NLF in the political life of South Vietnam; it committed itself to free elections under international supervision and to accept their outcome. The President offered to set a precise timetable for withdrawal and cease-fires under international supervision; it went far beyond the dove platform defeated at the Democratic Convention. In short, the May 14 speech provided every opportunity to explore the possibilities of an honorable political outcome. The only condition it did not meet turned out to be the Communist sine qua non: unconditional withdrawal of U.S. forces and the collusive installation of a Communist-controlled government.

Xuan Thuy initially raised hopes by a relatively mild reaction, delicately noting that there were "points of agreement" between the Ten Points of the NLF and the Eight Points of the President's May 14 speech. But in the formal negotiations, he adamantly refused to discuss them. Soon the negotiating sessions reverted to the sterile reiteration of standard North Vietnamese positions. The stalemate continued.

---

* I explained in a White House background briefing before the speech, "We do not care whether they acknowledge that they have forces there, as long as they make sure the forces leave there and we will settle for supervisory arrangements which assure us that there are no longer any North Vietnamese forces in South Vietnam."

The Beginning of Troop Withdrawals

After the May 14 speech outlining American proposals for negotiation was rejected, the administration turned to implementing as much of its program unilaterally as was compatible with the security of our allies. Nixon had inherited, in one of the less felicitous phrases of foreign policy, a general commitment to "de-Americanize" the war. The Johnson administration had begun the effort to strengthen the South Vietnamese army, but there were no plans for American withdrawals. As Secretary of Defense Clark Clifford had said on September 29, 1968, "the level of combat is such that we are building up our troops, not cutting them down."[9] In a news conference after Nixon's election on December 10, 1968, Clifford reiterated that there were no plans for any reduction.[10] The new Nixon administration started studying the withdrawals of American troops for two reasons: to win public support and give Hanoi an incentive to negotiate seriously by enhancing the staying power of our remaining forces. At the same time, if the South Vietnamese were strengthened sufficiently, withdrawals might gradually end American involvement *without* agreement with Hanoi.

Therefore, in a news conference on March 14, Nixon laid down three criteria for American withdrawals: the ability of the South Vietnamese to defend themselves without American troops; negotiating progress in the Paris talks; and a reduced level of enemy activity.

General Wheeler at the January 25, 1969, NSC meeting had said he thought President Thieu would probably agree to a small reduction of U.S. forces because it would help Nixon domestically and convey the image of a self-confident South Vietnam. Rogers thought we could buy an indefinite amount of time at home with a withdrawal of 50,000 troops. Laird and Nixon kept their own counsel. On February 6, Thieu expressed confidence publicly that a sizable number of American forces could leave Vietnam in 1969. General Goodpaster, then serving as deputy to General Abrams, attended an NSC meeting on March 28 and reported that the South Vietnamese improvement had already been substantial; we were in fact close to "de-Americanizing" the war, he said, but were not at the "decision point" yet. Laird spoke up: "I agree, but not with your term 'de-Americanizing.' What we need is a term like 'Vietnamizing' to put the emphasis on the right issues." The President was impressed. "That's a good point, Mel," he said. Thus

"Vietnamization" was born. And Laird carried it through with persistence and skill.

On April 10, the President ordered me to issue a directive on his behalf requesting the departments and agencies to work out a schedule for Vietnamizing the war. Nixon decided the time was ripe soon after his May 14 speech. A meeting was arranged for June 8 with South Vietnamese President Thieu to win his support. The site was to be Midway Island in the Pacific, chosen because of the fear that a visit by Thieu to the United States would provoke major demonstrations.

On the way to Midway, Nixon convened a meeting in Honolulu on the afternoon of June 7 with Rogers, Laird, General Wheeler, Ambassador Lodge, Ambassador Bunker, General Abrams, Admiral McCain and myself, in the conference room of the Kahala Hilton Hotel overlooking the Pacific. The meeting was to take the final decision on withdrawal strategy. It was clear that the military approached the subject with a heavy heart. Deep down they knew that Saigon would do well to defend what it had by its own effort; victory would become impossible. The process of withdrawal was likely to become irreversible. Henceforth, we would be in a race between the decline in American combat capability and the improvement of South Vietnamese forces—a race whose outcome was highly uncertain but which could at best achieve a stalemate.

The Midway meeting could not have had a more surrealistic setting. For the space of seven hours, this atoll of no more than two square miles was invaded by the presidential entourage of more than 500 officials, security men, communicators, journalists, and supernumeraries who considered themselves indispensable. The airport hangar was freshly painted; the commander's house, where the President was to meet Thieu, received new furniture and a fresh coat of paint, making this navy officer the one unambiguous beneficiary of the Midway meeting. All this was observed with beady eyes by the gooney birds, who are native to this island and have grown insolent after being protected by the Interior Department for generations. No one has yet discovered the mystic bond between that dismal island and these strange birds, which soar majestically but take off like lumbering airplanes after an extended run. On Midway, the only island they deign to inhabit, they squat arrogantly in the middle of the roads, producing traffic jams, secure in the knowledge that the Department of Interior will severely punish anyone who gives way to the all-too-human impulse to deliver a swift kick.

Thieu's position at Midway was unenviable. For days there had been reports that Nixon would announce the beginning of the withdrawals of U.S. forces and that this in turn would be intended as a warning to Thieu to put his house in order. By this, his critics generally meant the early installation of Western-style democracy, if not a coalition government. Just how democratic freedoms might be ensured in a country overrun by hundreds of thousands of hostile troops and guerrillas those critics rarely made clear. Thieu was expected to accomplish within months and amidst a civil war what no other Southeast Asian leader had achieved in decades of peace. He was being asked simultaneously to win a war, adjust his own defense structure to the withdrawal of a large American military establishment, and build democratic institutions in a country that had not known peace in a generation or democracy in its history. His legitimacy as a nationalist leader was to be enhanced by reforms undertaken under pressure from the great power that had connived in the overthrow of his predecessor and thereby left the country bereft of its civil administration.

It was a poignant scene as Nguyen Van Thieu, for whose country over 40,000 Americans had already died but who was not permitted to visit his powerful ally, stepped jauntily from his chartered Pan American plane. I felt sorry for him. It was not his fault that he was the focus of American domestic pressures; he was, after all, the representative of the millions of South Vietnamese who did not want to be overrun by the North Vietnamese army. He came from a culture different from ours, operating by different values. But all Vietnamese have an innate dignity, produced by the cruel and bloody history of their beautiful land. The Vietnamese have fought for centuries, against outsiders and against each other, to determine their national destiny. And difficult as they can be, they have survived by a heroic refusal to bow their necks to enemy or ally.

There were two sessions. The decisive one took place in the commander's refurbished house. It included Nixon and me, Thieu and his personal assistant. Thieu did not act as a supplicant. He conducted himself with assurance; he did not ask for favors. We had been concerned that the projected troop withdrawal would produce an awkward scene. Thieu anticipated us by proposing it himself. We suggested the initiation of private contacts with Hanoi at the presidential level. Thieu agreed, provided he was informed about any political discussions. Because the five-hour time difference with the East Coast put the media under pressure to file, the two Presidents stepped outside the commander's house after an hour-and-a-half discussion, and President Nixon announced the first American troop withdrawal.

Nixon considered the announcement a political triumph. He thought it would buy him the time necessary for developing a new strategy. His advisers, including me, shared his view. We were wrong on both counts. We had crossed a fateful dividing line. The withdrawal increased the pressures from families whose sons remained at risk. And it brought no respite from the critics, the majority of whom believed that since their demonstrations had already produced a bombing halt and now the initial decision to withdraw, more pressure could speed up the process. Most of them did not care if accelerated withdrawals produced a collapse in Saigon; many might consider it a bonus. As a result, the Nixon administration's commitment to unilateral withdrawal would come to be seen, at home, abroad, and particularly in Vietnam, as irreversible. The last elements of flexibility disappeared when the Defense Department began to plan its budget on the basis of anticipated troop reductions. Because henceforth to interrupt withdrawals would produce a financial shortfall affecting the procurement of new weapons, the services developed a vested interest in the program.

The North Vietnamese, on the other hand, were not interested in symbols but in the balance of forces on the ground. They coolly analyzed the withdrawal, weighing its psychological benefits to America in terms of enhanced staying power against the decline in military effectiveness represented by a shrinking number of American forces. Hanoi kept up incessant pressure for the largest possible withdrawal in the shortest possible time. The peace movement echoed these demands. The more automatic American withdrawal, the less useful it was as a bargaining weapon; the demand for mutual withdrawal grew hollow as the unilateral withdrawal accelerated. And the more rapid and extensive the withdrawal, the greater the possibility of a South Vietnamese collapse.

These realities dominated the withdrawal strategy. Laird had prepared five options for troop withdrawals in 1969. At the low end was a withdrawal of 50,000 troops, at the high end, 100,000. For the longer term, Laird put forward timetables ranging from eighteen to forty-two months and ceilings for the residual American force—those troops remaining until Hanoi's forces withdrew—ranging from 260,000 to 306,000. In a memorandum to the President on June 2, Laird offered a "feasible" timetable of forty-two months (stretching withdrawals to the end of 1972) and a residual force of 260,000.

He warned that in the absence of North Vietnamese reciprocity, a more rapid withdrawal would result in serious setbacks to the pacification program, a significant decline in allied military capacity, and the possibility of South Vietnamese collapse.

Within the bureaucracy, two trends quickly developed. Since implementing Vietnamization was largely a Pentagon responsibility, the State Department stepped up the pressure on the subjects in its jurisdiction, which included political reform in Saigon. It unleashed a flood of cables on the besieged Thieu to speed up the process of political and economic reform. In fact, a sweeping change in the system of land tenure was put into effect. Our advocacy, however, may have weakened Thieu by making his rather extensive reforms appear to result not from strength and growing self-confidence but from American pressure. On July 11, Thieu offered free elections in which the Communists could participate, supervised by a mixed electoral commission of Vietnamese, including the Communists, and a body of international observers. Rogers anticipated part of this program in a July 2 news conference, which led Thieu, out of pique, to delay sending us an advance draft.

In this atmosphere, it was decided to make a basic change in the battle-field orders for General Abrams. The existing "mission statement" for U.S. forces in Southeast Asia, inherited from the Johnson administration, declared the ambitious intention to "defeat" the enemy and "force" its withdrawal to North Vietnam. The new mission statement (which went into effect on August 15) focused on providing "maximum assistance" to the South Vietnamese to strengthen their forces, supporting pacification efforts, and reducing the flow of supplies to the enemy. As it turned out, the President at the last moment changed his mind and countermanded the new instructions. But Laird had already issued them, and they stood. I do not know whether the changed orders—which were quickly leaked—made any practical difference. Given the administration's commitment to withdrawal, they reflected capabilities, whatever the doctrine.

On July 30, Nixon, on an around-the-world trip, made a surprise stop in Saigon against the advice of the Secret Service. For security reasons, the Saigon stop was not announced until the last moment. Nixon was whisked from the airport to the Presidential Palace in a helicopter that seemed to go straight up out of range of possible sniper fire and then plummeted like a stone between the trees of Thieu's offices. I never learned how often the pilots had rehearsed this maneuver or how its risks compared with that of sniper fire. Nixon told Thieu that continued withdrawals were necessary to maintain American public support. He also argued that it was important that the reductions appear to be on a systematic timetable and at our initiative. We were clearly on the way out of Vietnam by negotiation if possible, by unilateral withdrawal if necessary.

A Secret Meeting

On June 24, we initiated another attempt at negotiations, through Jean Sainteny, in the 1950s French Delegate-General in Hanoi and familiar with North Vietnamese personalities. Sainteny saw the President in the Oval Office on July 15. Like many Frenchmen who had served in Indochina, he considered our enterprise hopeless; unlike many of his compatriots, he understood the importance of an honorable exit for America and for other free peoples. I did not doubt that he would report our contacts to his government. This was of secondary importance, since this knowledge could confer on France no unilateral benefit; it would satisfy curiosity, not affect policy. I trusted Sainteny's honor and reliability in doing what he had undertaken; he and his wife were friends of long standing. He was trusted by the North Vietnamese as well. No more can be asked of an intermediary. Sainteny indicated that he would be prepared to visit Hanoi and carry a message. Alternatively, he suggested a meeting between me and Le Duc Tho when he next visited Paris.

Nixon chose the first course. A private letter from Nixon to Ho Chi Minh was drafted to be delivered personally by Sainteny in Hanoi. The letter stressed America's commitment to peace; it offered to discuss Hanoi's plans together with our own. It concluded:

> The time has come to move forward at the conference table toward an early resolution of this tragic war. You will find us forthcoming and open-minded in a common effort to bring the blessings of peace to the brave people of Vietnam. Let history record that at this critical juncture, both sides turned their face toward peace rather than toward conflict and war.[11]

But the North Vietnamese refused to give Sainteny a visa. The letter was handed over to Hanoi's Delegate-General, Mai Van Bo. Determined to try for a breakthrough before taking other decisions, we asked Sainteny to arrange for me to meet North Vietnamese negotiators.

At the end of July, I accompanied the President on an around-the-world trip, beginning with the *Apollo 11* splashdown and visiting Southeast Asia, India, Pakistan, and Romania. I split off from the President's party to visit Paris and Brussels while the President flew home. My secret meeting was scheduled for Sainteny's apartment on August 4. Le Duc Tho having left Paris, my interlocutor was to be Xuan Thuy, Hanoi's plenipotentiary at the plenary peace talks. This, as I learned later, guaranteed that little would be said other than the stock formulas that had come to dominate the plenary sessions. For Xuan Thuy was not a policymaker but a functionary. Representing the Foreign Ministry and not the Communist Party, he had been sent by Hanoi to proclaim the official line at the public sessions. Tiny, with a Buddha face and a sharp mind, perpetually smiling even when saying the most outrageous things, he had no authority to negotiate. His job was psychological warfare. When Hanoi wanted serious talks, its "Special Adviser" to its Paris delegation, Le Duc Tho, the fifth-ranking man in the Politburo, would arrive from North Vietnam. He, too, could be described as flexible only by the wildest flight of fancy. But he, at least, had authority, and in the end it was he who concluded the negotiations.

My colleagues and I arrived at Sainteny's apartment a half-hour before the scheduled time. Sainteny ushered us into his living room and showed us where the refreshments were located. The apartment contained some valuable artifacts. "I hope if you disagree, you will not throw the crockery at each other," said Sainteny dryly and excused himself.

Xuan Thuy and Mai Van Bo arrived exactly on time. We were seated on sofas facing one another, the American group with its back to the Rue de Rivoli, leaving the view of the Tuileries Gardens to the Vietnamese. As in all my later meetings, I was impressed by their dignity and quiet self-assurance. Here was a group of men whose contact with the outside world had been sporadic and shaped by the requirements of their many struggles. But in meeting with the representative of the strongest power on earth, they were subtle, disciplined, and patient. Except for one occasion—when, carried away by the early success of the spring offensive of 1972, they turned nasty— they were always courteous; they never showed any undue eagerness; they never permitted themselves to appear rattled. They were specialists in political warfare, determined to move at their own pace, not to be seduced by eloquence or goaded by impatience. They pocketed American concessions as their due, admitting no obligation to reciprocate moderation. They saw compromise as a confession of weakness. They were impressed only by their own assessment of Hanoi's self-interest. They admitted to no self-doubt; they could never grant that they had been swayed, or even affected, by the arguments of adversaries. Their goal was total power in South Vietnam, or at least a solution in which their opponents were so demoralized that they would be easy to destroy in the next round. They deviated from their quest for victory only after the collapse of their Easter offensive in 1972 left them totally exhausted.

After an exchange of pleasantries, I turned to the purpose of the meeting. I expressed my respect for the courage and the suffering of the Vietnamese people. The United States sought a settlement compatible with the self-respect of both sides. The fact remained that, by November 1, the negotiations which had begun with the bombing halt would be a year old. In that period, the United States had made a series of significant unreciprocated gestures: We had stopped sending reinforcements, we had announced the unilateral withdrawal of 25,000 men, and we had projected further withdrawals. We had offered to accept the results of internationally supervised free elections in which the NLF could participate. There had been no response. I was in Paris, I said, to suggest from the highest possible level and in great earnestness that we make a major effort to settle the conflict by the time the negotiation was one year old—that is to say, by November 1. We were prepared to discuss the Ten Points of the NLF, but we could not accept the proposition that like the Ten Commandments they were graven in stone and not subject to negotiation. It was in the long term intolerable for us to be treated at every meeting like schoolboys taking an examination in the adequacy of our understanding of Hanoi's formal position.

I proposed intensifed negotiations and an effort to find common ground between the NLF's Ten Points and Nixon's Eight Points of May 14. Specifically, the United States was prepared to withdraw all its forces, without exception, as part of a program of mutual withdrawal. We were ready to accept the outcome of any free political process. We understood that neither side could be expected to give up at the conference table what had not been conceded on the battlefield; we believed that a fair process must register an existing balance of political and military forces. Successful negotiations required that each side recognize that its opponent could not be defeated without its noticing it. At the same time, if by November 1 no progress had been made, the United States would have to consider steps of grave consequence.*

Xuan Thuy listened impassively without so much as hinting that I had in fact presented the most comprehensive American peace plan yet. As was the North Vietnamese custom, he asked a few clarifying questions, especially about the procedures for intensified negotiations, and then launched himself into a long monologue. He first recounted the epic of Vietnam's struggle for independence through the centuries. I was to hear this tale many more times over the next four years. It became a ritual, like saying grace—except that it took much longer. The heroic saga of how the Vietnamese defeated all foreigners was impressive, even moving, although after constant repetition over many years this litany came to test my self-control. Turning to substance after about forty-five minutes, Xuan Thuy denied that the Ten Points were, as I had said, the Ten Commandments; they were, however, the only "logical and realistic basis for settling the war"—a distinction I lacked the subtlety to grasp.

According to Xuan Thuy, there were two problems, the military and the political. The military solution was the complete withdrawal of U.S. and what the North Vietnamese called "satellite" forces (troops contributed by allied countries). The United States had been very imprecise on that subject, he said—meaning that we had not given an unconditional schedule for their removal. The political solution required the removal of Thieu, Ky, and Huong (the President, the Vice President, and the Prime Minister of America's ally) and the establishment of a coalition government composed of the Communist Provisional Revolutionary Government† and the remnants of the Saigon administration as long as they stood for "peace, independence and neutrality." The two issues, military and political, were linked, said Xuan Thuy; one could not be solved without the other. In other words, not even a unilateral U.S. withdrawal would end the war or secure the release of American prisoners.

---

* Nixon had made the same point to various host governments on his global trip, and to various leaders on state visits to Washington, in the expectation that these warnings would filter back to Hanoi. They did. But no plans yet existed to implement the threat if no progress resulted.

† The "Provisional Revolutionary Government," or PRG, was after June 1969 the designation of the National Liberation Front.

Hanoi continued to insist that the United States decapitate the existing political structure while rendering it impotent through the withdrawal of the American forces and demoralized by the removal of its leadership. If the United States had the effrontery to withdraw without bringing about such a political upheaval, the war would go on and American prisoners would remain as hostages. Over the years, the Nixon administration moved from position to position, from mutual to unilateral withdrawal, from residual forces to complete departure. But Hanoi never budged. We could have neither peace nor prisoners until America did for Hanoi what Hanoi apparently no longer trusted itself to accomplish: the overthrow of the political structure in Saigon. And the longer the process stretched out, the more it was America that was being accused of intransigence by its domestic critics.

Though Xuan Thuy and I had achieved little except to restate established positions in a less contentious manner, we agreed that either party would be free to contact the other and that another meeting should take place. Xuan Thuy indicated that Hanoi did not like intermediaries from other countries and asked us to designate an American to receive or deliver messages in this channel. I named General Vernon Walters, American defense attaché in Paris, who had acted as interpreter for this session. A summary was sent to Ambassador Bunker in Saigon to inform President Thieu, who had authorized such private talks at the Midway meeting. In the absence of Ambassador Lodge from Paris, his deputy, Philip Habib, was briefed by me.

The newly established channel was not used again in 1969. Two days later, on August 6, there was a Communist attack on Cam Ranh Bay, which one could barely explain on the ground that it might have been planned well before the meeting with Xuan Thuy. On August 11, however, Communist forces attacked more than 100 cities, towns, and bases across South Vietnam, ending the eight-week lull in the fighting.

Another Reassessment

Nixon reacted to the new Vietnam attacks by announcing on August 23 from the San Clemente White House that he was deferring consideration of the next troop withdrawal until his return to Washington. There was an unusually tentative response from the North Vietnamese in Paris. The apparent delay in unilateral withdrawal had given Hanoi pause—a hint of its respect for American forces and of what might have happened had the domestic situation permitted us to sustain that course. But it did not. Though Nixon's decision was exactly in accordance with two of the three criteria for troop withdrawal he had announced in March and frequently repeated (reduction in enemy activity, progress in Paris, and improvement of the South Vietnamese forces), the decision was greeted with outrage by Congress and the media.

On August 25, Ho Chi Minh replied to President Nixon's letter of July 15. (Actually, the reply was received on August 30, three days before Ho's death.) Ho's letter, not reciprocating Nixon's salutation of "Dear Mr. President," reiterated North Vietnam's public position in a peremptory fashion:

> Our Vietnamese people are deeply devoted to peace, a real peace with independence and real freedom. They are determined to fight to the end, without fearing the sacrifices and difficulties in order to defend their country and their sacred national rights. The overall solution in the 10 points of the National Liberation Front of South Vietnam and of the Provisional Revolutionary Government of the Republic of South Vietnam is a logical and reasonable basis for the settlement of the Vietnamese problem. It has earned the sympathy and support of the peoples of the world.
>
> In your letter you have expressed the desire to act for a just peace. For this the United States must cease the war of aggression and withdraw their troops from South Vietnam, respect the right of the population of the South and of the Vietnamese nation to dispose of themselves without foreign influence. This is the correct manner of solving the Vietnamese problem.

Ho's reply once again made clear that Hanoi would be satisfied only with total victory. It counted on the exhaustion of the United States; it would tolerate no appearance of "progress" in negotiations that might enable us to rally public opinion. A very natural response from us would have been to stop bringing soldiers home, but by now withdrawal had gained its own momentum. The reductions were always announced for a specific period; it was inevitable that pressures, partly public, partly budgetary and bureaucratic, would build up as the end of each period approached. The August 23 riposte to Hanoi's belligerence was the last time Nixon tried to halt withdrawals.

Laird and he had become convinced of the paradox that the war effort could be sustained only by unilateral withdrawal.

On September 12, another NSC meeting was convened to discuss the next troop reduction. There was no longer any debate. On September 16, the President announced his decision to lower the troop ceiling by another 40,500 by December 15. The total reduction in the authorized ceiling now amounted to 65,500. This was 15,000 more than had been considered necessary by Rogers at the beginning of the year to convince the public that we were serious about ending the war. After the announcement on September 16, withdrawals became inexorable; the President never again risked the end of a withdrawal period to pass without announcing a new increment for the next. Hanoi was on the verge of achieving the second of its objectives without reciprocity: The seemingly unbreakable bombing halt was now leading to unilateral withdrawal. We had come a long way: We had accepted total withdrawal, started out of Vietnam unilaterally, and had de-escalated our military activities—all without the slightest response and all without mitigating the protest movement.

At the NSC meeting on Vietnam of September 12, I took little part in the discussion but exclaimed toward the end: "We need a plan to end the war, not only to withdraw troops. This is what is on people's minds." Two days before the meeting, I had sent the President a personal memorandum questioning some of the assumptions of Vietnamization. Withdrawals would become like "salted peanuts" to the American public; the more troops we withdrew, the more would be expected, leading eventually to demands for total unilateral withdrawal, perhaps within a year (this in fact happened). I argued that our military strategy could not work rapidly enough against the erosion of public opinion and predicted, unhappily rightly, that Hanoi would probably wait until the American withdrawal was nearly completed before launching an all-out attack. In short, there was a big risk that Vietnamization would not work. The full text of my memorandum of September 10 is in the notes at the end of this book.[12]

Therefore, just as the planning for the Vance mission had produced a detailed peace proposal, in September and October I formed a special task force to explore the military options should we conclude that negotiations had failed.

The planning was given the name Duck Hook, for reasons that totally escape me today. The Joint Chiefs of Staff devised a plan for mining North

Vietnamese ports and harbors and destroying twenty-nine targets of military and economic importance in an air attack lasting four days. The plan also anticipated periodic attacks of forty-eight to seventy-two hours if Hanoi continued to avoid serious negotiation. The target date to implement the planning was to be November 1, 1969, the first anniversary of the bombing halt understanding that had promised us "prompt and productive" negotiations.

As the scenario took shape, it became apparent that there was not enough consensus in the administration to pursue such a course. The President clearly did not have his heart in it. There was as yet no relaxation of tensions with the Soviet Union and no opening to China. And the European allies were certain to be opposed. Emphasis on a military solution thus risked the isolation of the United States. Recoiling before the bitter opposition and domestic turmoil which the alternative of trying to force a showdown with Hanoi would have evoked, Nixon never placed the plan before the National Security Council. In this atmosphere, on October 17, I recommended that Nixon defer consideration of this option until he could assess the rate of North Vietnamese infiltration for the remainder of the year.*

My doubts about Vietnamization persisted, reflecting the insoluble dilemmas of fighting both North Vietnam's army and domestic critics, of whom a significant percentage objected violently to the very concept of a coherent strategy. On October 30, I wrote a personal memorandum to the President, once again raising doubts about the assumptions on which Vietnamization was based:

> We have seen so many Vietnam programs fail after being announced with great fanfare, that I thought I should put before you in summary form my questions about the assumptions underlying Vietnamization. To believe that this course is viable, we must make favorable assumptions about a number of factors, and must believe that Hanoi as well will come to accept them.
>
> US calculations about the success of Vietnamization—and

---

* This was, actually, an evasion. The strategy implied by the Duck Hook plan should have had nothing to do with the rate of infiltration—in fact, on the basis of my own prognosis, infiltration would not pick up until we had reduced our forces much further. The plan should have been linked primarily to the progress of negotiations.

Hanoi's calculations, in turn, about the success of their strategy—
rely on our respective judgments of:

—the pace of public opposition in the US to our continuing
the fight in any form. (Past experience indicates that Vietnamization will not significantly slow it down.)

—the ability of the US Government to maintain its own discipline in carrying out this policy. (As public pressures grow, you
may face increasing governmental disarray with a growing
number of press leaks, etc.)

—the actual ability of the South Vietnamese Government and
armed forces to replace American withdrawals—both physically and psychologically. (Conclusive evidence is lacking here;
this fact in itself, and past experience, argue against optimism.)

—the degree to which Hanoi's current losses affect its ability to
fight later—i.e., losses of military cadre, political infrastructure, etc. (Again, the evidence is not definitive. Most reports of
progress have concerned security gains by US forces—not a
lasting erosion of enemy political strength.)

—the ability of the GVN* (Saigon government) to gain solid
political benefit from its current pacification progress. (Again,
reports of progress have been largely about security gains behind the US shield.)

Our Vietnamization policy thus rests on a series of favorable assumptions which may not be accurate—although no one can be certain on the basis of current analyses.

This memorandum foresaw many of our later difficulties. It was also
doomed to irrelevance. In Washington, ideas do not sell themselves. Authors
of memoranda who are not willing to fight for them are more likely to find
their words turn into *ex post facto* alibis than guides to action.

By the time Nixon took office, the available choices in Vietnam were
among unilateral withdrawal, escalation, and Vietnamization. They all had
unpalatable aspects. Unilateral withdrawal at a rate faster than was already
taking place would have led to political and military chaos. Nixon rejected escalation because it might risk America's social cohesion and its alliances. He

---

* Government of Vietnam, i.e., South Vietnam.

chose Vietnamization because he would not abandon America's postwar role or the millions of Southeast Asians who had relied on America.

The Unpacifiable Doves

A week before inauguration, on January 12, 1969, the distinguished diplomatic correspondent of the *Washington Post,* Chalmers Roberts, had perceptively outlined Nixon's dilemma:

> As a guess, the country and Congress will give the new President six months to find the route to disengagement with honor from the Vietnam war. But very probably six months, or any limited extension that public attitudes may grant, will not be enough. . . .
>
> President Nixon is bound, not so much by his own words as the national mood, to continue on the Johnson course. . . .
>
> The election campaign made it very evident that the big majority of Americans want to get out of Vietnam, but in a way that does not make a mockery of the loss thus far of more than 31,000 American lives.
>
> This combination of attitude restricts Mr. Nixon both as to the time and substance.

So it was. As the months went by in 1969, we were confronted by public protests and demonstrations and quickening demands in the media and Congress for unilateral concessions in the negotiations. They had one common theme: The obstacle to peace was not Hanoi but their own government's inadequate dedication to peace and Saigon's obduracy.

Starting in 1970, Vietnam critics pressed the administration to announce a final deadline for total withdrawal. But that was either a variation of Vietnamization or the equivalent of capitulation. If the deadline was arbitrary—that is, too short for the South Vietnamese to take over—everything would disintegrate and it was a formula for collapse. If the deadline was feasible in terms of our own planning for Vietnamization, the only difference was that it was publicly announced. The issue was the tactical judgment whether an announcement would help or hinder extrication from the war. For better or worse, our judgment was that a public announcement would

destroy the last incentives for Hanoi to negotiate; it would then simply outwait us. And how would any administration explain to American families
why their sons' lives should be at risk when a fixed schedule for total withdrawal existed? It is important to remember that most responsible critics at
first only asked for the withdrawal of *combat* troops by the end of 1970, leaving a large residual force behind.

As for the frequently heard argument that we should stop giving Saigon a
"veto" over the American negotiating position, it would be absurd to deny
that the government on whose territory American forces were located had
some influence over American policies. Its self-confidence, legitimacy, and
survivability were after all one of the key goals of the war; if we collapsed it by
pressures beyond its capacity to bear, we would in effect have settled on
Hanoi's terms. But America's influence on Saigon was much greater than the
reverse. There is no question that in response to our recommendations, the
Saigon government made extraordinary efforts to broaden its base and to
agree to a political contest with the Communists. Saigon's politics were more
pluralistic and turbulent than its American critics admitted—and vastly better in human terms than the icy totalitarianism of North Vietnam, which was
in fact the only alternative available. Too often attacks on Thieu were not so
much an advocacy of concrete reform as an alibi for abdication.

Future generations will find it difficult to reconstruct the domestic convulsion that the Vietnam war induced. On July 2, 1969, antiwar women destroyed draft records in New York. On July 6, members of Women Strike for
Peace flew to the University of Toronto to meet three women representing
the Vietcong. The mayors of two towns petitioned the President to stop
sending their sons to Vietnam. Demonstrators launched a mock invasion of
Fort Lewis on July 15. There were weekly demonstrations at the Pentagon,
including such gestures as pouring blood on its steps. On August 14, twelve
young soldiers from a base in Honolulu sought refuge in a church as an "act
of deep involvement against all the injustice inherent in the American military system." A group called Business Executives for Vietnam Peace called on
the White House on August 28 to inform the administration that "the honeymoon is over." While Nixon was on the West Coast in August 1969, he
was exposed to repeated demonstrations at his vacation residence in San
Clemente. On September 3, a group of 225 psychologists demonstrated outside the White House, protesting the Vietnam war as "the insanity of our
times." Protesters read lists of war dead at public rallies and had them in-

serted into the *Congressional Record*. A number of members of the previous administration joined this practice, even though most of the casualties they were reading had been suffered while they were in office. During August, leaders of the protest movement announced a series of monthly demonstrations starting October 15 to bring pressure on the government—the so-called Moratorium. All of this was conspicuously and generally approvingly covered by the media.

As the summer drew to a close and students returned to universities and Congress ended its recess, the pace of protest quickened. The death of Ho Chi Minh on September 3 was alleged to present a new opportunity for ending the stalemate in Paris, though whatever evidence was at hand indicated the opposite. There was clamor that we propose a cease-fire in deference to the leader who had caused us so much suffering, and hope that such a cease-fire would then become permanent, as if Hanoi might be made to slide without noticing it into an arrangement it had repeatedly rejected. In fact, we observed a cease-fire on the day of Ho's funeral; it was not extended by our adversaries.

On September 3, Senator Edmund Muskie of Maine complained that President Nixon's plan for ending the war was "very ambiguous"; he also questioned whether Nixon was in fact seeking a negotiated settlement rather than a military victory. ("Victory" was turning into an epithet.) On September 5, Senators John Sherman Cooper and Gaylord Nelson suggested that the President use the "opportunity" created by Ho Chi Minh's death to propose new initiatives to end the war; they did not describe what the opportunity consisted of. On September 6, Senate Majority Leader Mike Mansfield made the same suggestion. On September 25, a week after the President's announcement of withdrawal of 40,500 more troops, Congressman Allard Lowenstein of New York proclaimed plans to mobilize public support for another "dump Johnson"–style movement, this time with Nixon as the target. On the same day, Senator Charles Goodell of New York announced that he would introduce a resolution in the Senate requiring the withdrawal of all U.S. forces from Vietnam by the end of 1970.

As the October 15 Moratorium drew nearer, congressional critics from both parties grew more vocal. On October 2, Senator Mansfield called on the President to propose a standstill cease-fire. Senator Eugene McCarthy on the same day announced his support for the Goodell proposal. Senator Charles Percy on October 3 urged the administration to halt allied offensive operations as long as the enemy did not take advantage of the situation—the same formula that had started the discussions of the abortive bombing halt. Between September 24 and October 15, eleven antiwar resolutions were introduced in Congress. These included Senators Mark Hatfield and Frank Church's bill calling for a schedule for immediate withdrawal of all U.S. forces from Vietnam, and Senators Jacob Javits and Claiborne Pell's resolution for withdrawal of combat forces by the end of 1970 and for revocation of the 1964 Gulf of Tonkin Resolution under which President Johnson had first introduced American combat forces in Vietnam. On October 9, Kingman Brewster, president of Yale, called for unconditional withdrawal from Vietnam. On October 10, seventy-nine presidents of private colleges and universities wrote to President Nixon, urging a firm timetable for withdrawals. On October 14, North Vietnamese Premier Pham Van Dong fed the American public debate by an unprecedented open letter to American antiwar protesters in honor of the Moratorium, hailing their "struggle" as a "noble reflection of the legitimate and urgent demand of the American people . . . the Vietnamese people and the United States progressive people against United States aggression [which] will certainly be crowned with total victory."

The Moratorium demonstrations took place across the country on October 15. A crowd of 20,000 packed a noontime rally in New York's financial district and listened to Bill Moyers, President Johnson's former assistant and press secretary, urge President Nixon to respond to the antiwar sentiment. Thirty thousand gathered on the New Haven Green. Fifty thousand massed on the Washington Monument grounds within sight of the White House. The demonstration at the Monument was preceded by a walk around the city of several thousand people carrying candles. At George Washington University, Dr. Benjamin Spock informed a large gathering that President Nixon was incapable of ending the war because of "limitations on his personality." The demonstration in Boston, where 100,000 people converged on the Common, appeared to be the largest of all. The common feature of all these demonstrations was the conviction that the American government was the obstacle to peace; that it needed not a program for an honorable peace—a concept evoking condescending ridicule—but instruction on the undesirability of war. The impression was created that some magical concession stood between America and a solution, prevented above all by U.S. rigidity, if not by more substantial moral defects. The issue came to be defined in terms both wounding and misleading: who was for and who was against the war, who liked bombing and who opposed it.

In such an atmosphere, communication broke down between an administration which had inherited the war, and which by every reasonable criterion had made major efforts to liquidate it, and those elements that had formerly felt a stake in the presidency and the international role of the United States. Part of the reason was the demoralization of the very leadership group that had sustained the great initiatives of the postwar period. The war in Indochina was the culmination of a decade that had opened with the clarion call of a resurgent idealism and ended with assassinations, racial and social discord, and radicalized politics. The Vietnam dilemmas were very much a product of liberal doctrines of reformist intervention and academic theories of graduated escalation. The collapse of these high aspirations shattered the self-confidence without which establishments flounder. The leaders who had previously sustained American foreign policy were particularly upset by the rage of the students. The assault of these middle-class young men and women—who were, after all, their own children—was not simply aimed at policies; a major target were lifestyles and values heretofore considered sacrosanct. Stimulated by a sense of guilt and encouraged by modern psychiatry and the radical chic rhetoric of upper middle-class suburbia, these outbursts symbolized the end of an era of simple faith in the traditional values of mid-America. Ironically, the insecurity of their elders turned the normal grievances of maturing youth into an institutionalized rage and a national trauma.

There were other causes having to do with the structure of American politics. The Vietnam war toppled both Lyndon Johnson and Hubert Humphrey in 1968, not because the whole country shifted against the war (the Wallace vote and the Republicans, reflecting the majority view, were either pro-Vietnam or silent), but because the war split their base of power, the Democratic Party. Once out of the White House, the Democratic Party found it tempting to unite in opposition to a Republican President on the issue of Vietnam. Those who opposed the war but reluctantly supported Johnson and Humphrey were no longer constrained by party loyalty. On the Republican side, the right wing had given up on Vietnam during the inconclusive strategy of the Johnson years, and Richard Nixon was able to reconcile them to a withdrawal program and an inconclusive outcome. Thus there was no conservative counterweight to the increasingly strident protests. In

1969, I asked my friend William Buckley, at the request of Nixon, whether he could help mobilize conservative opinion behind a firm policy. "No," he replied. "That horse has fled the barn." The tranquilized and passive right liberated the protest movement from constraints; the center of gravity of American politics thus shifted decisively to the antiwar side even though the public had not changed its basic view significantly.

The challenge to the new Nixon administration was similar to de Gaulle's in Algeria: to withdraw without collapsing other national obligations. This was even more important for the United States, on whose self-confidence and credibility so much of international order depended. But de Gaulle had been fortunate in the nature of his opposition; it came from those who wanted victory and who thought he was conceding too much. This gave him a margin for maneuver with the Algerian rebels; they were bound to consider the alternative as worse than de Gaulle. By contrast, Nixon's opposition came from groups who wanted a more rapid liquidation of the war, if not defeat, and this destroyed our bargaining position. Hanoi would benefit from Nixon's domestic collapse. Thus—even though every opinion poll showed the majority of the American public eager for an honorable solution and firmly against capitulation—the momentum of American politics was in the direction of unilateral concessions. For the Nixon administration to have maintained the initiative for four years and brought off a settlement and a genuine opportunity for survival of Vietnam amidst these turbulent forces was no small feat.

There is no gainsaying, however, that the turbulent national mood touched Nixon on his rawest nerve. He had taken initiatives that reversed the course of his predecessor; he had withdrawn troops and de-escalated the war—all steps urged on him by the Establishment groups whom he simultaneously distrusted and admired. And instead of being acclaimed, he was being castigated for not moving more rapidly on the path on which his predecessors had not even dared to take the first step. It was not a big leap to the view that what he really faced was not a policy difference but the same liberal opposition that had sought to destroy him ever since the Alger Hiss case. Here were all the old enemies in the press and in the Establishment, uniting once again. And Nixon possessed no instinct for understanding the outburst of the young, particularly the university students. Having worked his own way through college and law school, he thought they should be grateful for the opportunity of a higher education. If what he was confronting was a political battle for survival, rather than a foreign policy debate, he believed himself justified in using the methods of all-out political combat. On international issues, Nixon was sensitive to nuance and comfortable with tactics of conciliation and compromise. In domestic political battles, he was a gut fighter; he turned to uses of presidential power that he never ceased believing—with much evidence—had been those of his predecessors as well.

Nixon was never able to transcend his resentments and his complexes. But neither did he ever receive from his critics compassion for the task his predecessors had bequeathed to him. There was a self-fulfilling obtuseness in the bitterness with which the two sides regarded each other: Nixon's belief in the liberal conspiracy, the critics' view that the Nixon administration was determined to pursue the war to fulfill psychological defects.

I agreed with the essence of Nixon's Vietnam policy. But because of differences in background, my attitude toward the protesters diverged from Nixon's. He saw in them an enemy that had to be vanquished; I considered them former students and colleagues to whom to build bridges. I understood the anguish of the nonradical members of the protest movement; humanly I was close to many of them. While convinced that their policies were wrong and their single-minded self-righteousness dangerous for America's world position and domestic tranquillity, I attempted to maintain a dialogue between the administration and its critics. I devoted a great deal of time and effort to meeting antiwar groups despite the opposition of Nixon's domestic advisers, especially Haldeman. My theme was constant, that the war had to be ended as an act of policy, not in response to demonstrations. The tragedy was that the administration and its critics could frustrate each other but, by doing so, neither could achieve what both sought: an early negotiated end to the war in Vietnam. All this time Hanoi stood at the sidelines, coldly observing how America was negotiating not with its adversary but with itself.

A Strategy Emerges

Nixon sought to reduce his opposition by various moves. On September 19, he and Laird—who had already asked Congress for a draft lottery—announced at a White House briefing that the withdrawals of 60,000 men from Vietnam enabled the Nixon administration to cancel draft calls for

November and December. Calls scheduled for October would be stretched out over the final quarter of the year. The Department of Defense began limiting induction to nineteen-year-olds; on November 26, the President signed into law a bill permitting a draft lottery.

A campaign on behalf of American prisoners of war in Vietnam was launched in August by demanding North Vietnamese compliance with the Geneva Convention and Red Cross inspection. This was followed by forceful American statements at the Paris peace talks and at the International Conference of the Red Cross in September 1969. Forty senators signed a statement condemning North Vietnamese brutality against American POWs on August 13; 200 representatives signed a similar statement in September. At the outset, these measures rallied support at home, though in later years it was turned against the Nixon administration, as the prisoners became an added argument for unilateral withdrawal and dismantling of the South Vietnamese government (though very rarely from the families of the prisoners).

But Nixon tried to play for higher stakes. In a number of his talks with foreign leaders over a period of months in late 1969, he created the impression that the anniversary of the bombing halt on November 1 was a kind of deadline on whether the constructive talks promised by Hanoi in return for the bombing halt had materialized. On his world trip, he dropped hints that his patience was running out and that if no progress had been made in Paris by November 1, he would take strong action. So far as I could tell, Nixon had no precise idea of what he had in mind. (Duck Hook developed later as the exploration of options regarding threats already made.) The first I heard of the deadline was when Nixon uttered it to Pakistan President Yahya Khan in August 1969. And because Nixon never permitted State Department personnel (and only rarely the Secretary of State) to sit in on his meetings with foreign leaders, few in the government even knew that a threat had been made by the President.

On September 27, Dobrynin called on me to explore an invitation for Foreign Minister Andrei Gromyko to meet with the President when visiting the United States for the United Nations General Assembly. During our conversation, Nixon—by prearrangement—called my office and asked me to tell Dobrynin that Vietnam was the critical issue in U.S.-Soviet relations, that "the train had left the station and was heading down the track" (a favorite Nixon phrase, used, for example, after the Oregon primary in 1968 to encourage wavering convention delegates). I repeated Nixon's observations and added that the next move was up to Hanoi.

On October 6, Nixon met with Rogers and prohibited any new diplomatic initiative on Vietnam until Hanoi responded in some way; for the first time, he mentioned his deadline of November 1. On October 13, the White House announced that the President would be giving a major speech to review Vietnam policy on November 3. (The date was chosen because November 2 would be the day of the New Jersey gubernatorial election, and Nixon did not wish to trigger a large turnout of protest votes against the Republican candidate—who, in the event, became the first Republican governor of New Jersey in sixteen years.) To announce a presidential speech so far ahead was a daring decision. It was intended to reinforce the threats even as it encouraged pressures to sway whatever decision he might be announcing.

In the interval, Nixon sought to elicit Soviet support. On October 20, he met with Dobrynin, who had just returned from consultation in Moscow. Nixon pointed out that the bombing halt was a year old; if no progress occurred soon, the United States would have to pursue its own methods for bringing the war to an end. On the other hand, if the Soviet Union cooperated in bringing the war to an honorable conclusion, we would "do something dramatic" to improve U.S.-Soviet relations. Dobrynin was not prepared with any North Vietnamese offers, but he did put forth a sort of Soviet concession. After months of sparring, we had indicated to the Soviets in June that we were prepared to begin strategic arms talks immediately. Characteristically, even though the Soviets had professed their eagerness for talks for months, once we were committed, they evaded a reply. On October 20, Dobrynin informed us that the Soviet Union would be prepared to start the talks by mid-November.

It was a shrewd move. Aware of the eagerness of much of parts of the U.S. government to begin SALT negotiations, the Kremlin correctly judged that Nixon could not possibly refuse. In the resulting climate of hope, any escalation in Vietnam would appear as hazarding prospects for a major relaxation of tensions with the Soviet Union; this inhibition would thus be added to the domestic pressures dramatized by the Moratorium just a few days earlier. The Soviet calculation proved to be correct. Despite White House efforts to hold up a reply on SALT until after the November 3 speech, Rogers insisted on announcing our acceptance on October 25.

As was his habit, Nixon sought to compensate for his unwillingness to face down his old friend by escalating the menace to the Soviets. He told me that I should convey to Dobrynin that the President was "out of control" on Vietnam. In serving Nixon, one owed it to him to discriminate among the orders he issued and to give him another chance at those that were unfulfillable or dangerous. This one was in the latter category. Based on his reaction to the Duck Hook planning, I knew that Nixon was planning to take no action on November 1. To utter a dire threat followed by no action whatever would depreciate our currency. So I waited to see whether Nixon would return to the theme. He did not.

Meanwhile Nixon isolated himself at Camp David to work on his November 3 speech. It proved one of his strongest public performances. Against the recommendations of all of his Cabinet, he drew the line and made no concessions to the protesters. He took his case to the people, thereby to gain the maneuvering room he needed for what he considered "peace with honor." The speech had a shock effect because it defied the protesters, the North Vietnamese, and all expectations by announcing no spectacular shift in our negotiating position and no new troop withdrawals. It appealed to the "great silent majority" of Americans to support their commander-in-chief. For the first time, a presidential statement spelled out clearly what the President meant when he said he had "a plan to end the war"—namely, the dual-track strategy of Vietnamization and negotiations. And it made the point that Vietnamization offered a prospect of honorable disengagement that was not hostage to the other side's cooperation.

Nixon listed the steps taken to withdraw U.S. troops, reduce air operations, and step up South Vietnamese training. He emphasized that Vietnamization envisaged "the complete withdrawal of all U.S. combat ground forces and their replacement by South Vietnamese forces on an orderly scheduled timetable." Nixon disclosed the secret correspondence with North Vietnam prior to the inauguration, the repeated discussions with the Soviet Union to promote negotiations, and the secret letters exchanged with Ho Chi Minh in July and August, the texts of which were released by the White House. He did not reveal my secret meeting with Xuan Thuy. But he explained candidly that "no progress whatever had been made except agreement on the shape of the bargaining table."

The response to the speech was electric. From the moment it ended, the White House switchboard was clogged with congratulatory phone calls. Tens of thousands of supportive telegrams arrived which rapidly overwhelmed the general critical editorial and television comment. No doubt some of the enthusiasm was stimulated by Haldeman's indefatigable operatives, who had called political supporters all over the country to send in telegrams. But the outpouring went far beyond the capacities of the White House public relations operatives. Nixon had undoubtedly touched a raw nerve. The polls showed a major boost in his support. The American people might be tiring of the war; they were not ready for capitulation.

Nixon was elated. Professing indifference to public adulation, he nevertheless relished those few moments of acclaim that came his way. He kept the congratulatory telegrams stacked on his desk and on the floor in such numbers that the Oval Office could not be used for work, and for days he refused to relinquish them.

As soon as the public mood became clear, organized pressures began to ease somewhat, so that for the first time since January the administration had some maneuvering room.

We would need more than this, however, to outwait and outmaneuver the hard and single-minded leaders in Hanoi. In 1969, those leaders engaged in no effort that by the most generous interpretation could be called negotiation. They refused to explore or even to discuss any compromise proposal—not free elections or mixed electoral commissions or a cease-fire. Unilateral withdrawals of men and airplanes did not improve the atmosphere; de-escalation did not speed up the negotiating process. Hanoi was determined to break America's will at home, and to achieve this it could permit not a flicker of hope or the appearance of progress.

In retrospect, the reasoning behind the Vance mission in April, the Duck Hook planning, and my criticism of Vietnamization in September and October was almost certainly correct. Time was not on our side, and piecemeal concessions and withdrawals did more to encourage intransigence than compromise. Analytically, it would have been better to offer the most generous possible proposal imaginable—and then, if rejected, to seek to impose it militarily. Nothing short of this could have produced Soviet cooperation, for in the absence of crisis there was no incentive for a concrete Soviet step. If we had offered at one dramatic moment all the concessions eventually made in three years of war, and if the military actions taken with steadily declining forces over 1970, 1971, and 1972, in Cambodia, Laos, and North Vietnam (even without the last bombing assault) had been undertaken all together in early 1970, the war might well have been appreciably shortened and the final settlement more sustainable.

But it is hard to tell at this remove whether Saigon would have been ready to carry the burden of going it alone after a settlement. Nor was the international environment propitious. Relations with the Soviet Union were still tense in the aftermath of the occupation of Czechoslovakia in 1968; no contact had yet been made with China; the NATO allies were restive. Laird, who managed the Vietnamization process with extraordinary dedication and skill, was convinced that escalation would contradict Nixon's campaign promises and undermine the remaining public trust. In the face of the domestic turmoil, the divisions within the administration, and the international situation, I reluctantly went along with the general view that, all things considered, Vietnamization was the best amalgam of our international, military, and domestic imperatives.

Once embarked on it, there was no looking back. I knew that it would be painful and long—I had outlined its dangers repeatedly to the President. I also believed that it was better than the alternatives that were being proposed by the domestic critics.

Vietnamization was a risky course, but it had the advantage of giving the American and South Vietnamese peoples a way of getting used to the inevitable American withdrawal. If, in the process of inexorably reducing the American forces, America succeeded in strengthening South Vietnam—and the Nixon administration meant to do just that—America's objective would be achieved. If it failed and unilateral withdrawal became the only remaining choice, the final extrication could take place after American forces had shrunk to a level which reduced the risks of chaos and humiliation.

And so it happened that the year ended with an assessment, on the correctness of which the outcome of the war would depend. The President's first foreign policy report to Congress, issued on February 18, 1970, summed up the Nixon administration's Vietnam policy in strikingly sober terms, giving the lie to the argument that Nixon deliberately deceived the American public. Rarely had a presidential statement been as candid in admitting doubts and raising questions:

> Claims of progress in Vietnam have been frequent during the course of our involvement there—and have often proved too optimistic. However careful our planning, and however hopeful we are for the progress of these plans, we are conscious of two basic facts:
> —We cannot try to fool the enemy, who knows what is actually happening.

—Nor must we fool ourselves. The American people must have the full truth. We cannot afford a loss of confidence in our judgment and in our leadership.

The report admitted the existence of problems not yet solved and offered a benchmark by which progress could be judged in the future. We admitted that the administration did not yet know the final answers to all the issues posed by the war—about enemy intentions, the prospects for Vietnamization, and the attitude of the Vietnamese people:

—What is the enemy's capability to mount sustained operations? Could they succeed in undoing our gains?

—What is the actual extent of improvement in allied capabilities? In particular, are the Vietnamese developing the leadership, logistics capabilities, tactical know-how, and sensitivity to the needs of their own people which are indispensable to continued success?

—What alternative strategies are open to the enemy in the face of continued allied success? If they choose to conduct a protracted, low-intensity war, could they simply wait out U.S. withdrawals and then, through reinvigorated efforts, seize the initiative again and defeat the South Vietnamese forces?

—Most important, what are the attitudes of the Vietnamese people, whose free choice we are fighting to preserve? Are they truly being disaffected from the Viet Cong, or are they indifferent to both sides? What do their attitudes imply about the likelihood that the pacification gains will stick?

This was not a clarion call for domestic or military confrontation; it was the sober reflection and analysis of leaders grown cautious by the disappointments of a decade, serious about basing their policy on reality, and willing to accept an honorable political outcome.

3

SECRET NEGOTIATIONS AND A WIDENING WAR

At the end of 1969 and the beginning of 1970, the Nixon administration engaged in a major attempt to answer the questions raised in the President's foreign policy report. An interagency committee was established chaired by Undersecretary of State Elliot Richardson and me called the Vietnam Special Studies Group. Its purpose was summed up in a memorandum by me to the President dated September 5, 1969:

> Looking back on our experience over the last years, it is remarkable how frequently officials have let their preconceptions about Vietnam lead them astray even though a careful and objective analysis of readily available facts would have told them differently.

The group met for the first time on October 20, 1969. Richardson, Deputy Secretary of Defense David Packard, CIA Director Richard Helms, and representatives of the Joint Chiefs of Staff and the Defense Intelligence Agency were in attendance. A working group conducted an intensive study of twelve of the forty-four provinces in South Vietnam to achieve an accurate assessment of the contest over control of the rural population.

I covered the 100-page paper, which reviewed the same issues as the NSSMI study had done a year earlier, with handwritten questions. What had changed? Did U.S. advisers know what they were looking at? "I have found," I wrote, "that the most incompetent ones are those most easily satisfied. . . .

If you have a lower level of incidents, does this mean you are doing well, or is it the enemy's deliberate intention? If it's the latter, is it a signal? How do we know what the infrastructure is that we've destroyed? . . . Everyone says land reform is important. It hasn't happened, yet we make progress in pacification. How can this be?" After a new draft incorporated answers to these questions, I summarized the paper's conclusions for the President on January 22, 1970. Thirty-eight percent of the population of South Vietnam lived in the cities, fairly securely under the authority and protection of the government (especially after the failure of the Tet offensive of 1968 decimated the Vietcong cadres). But a primary objective of the enemy's strategy remained to gain control of the 62 percent of the people that lived in the countryside, thereby to surround the cities so that they would "fall like ripe fruit." The conclusion of the study was that since September 1968 the Saigon government's control of the countryside had risen from 20 to 55 percent; that of the Communists had fallen from 35 to 7 percent. Some four million rural South Vietnamese lived in contested areas, during the day controlled by Saigon, at night by the Vietcong. We could not be sure that these percentages could be maintained, however, as we continued our troop withdrawals:

> (1) The North Vietnamese cannot have fought for 25 years only to call it quits without another major effort. This effort could come in many ways—through attacks on American forces, ARVN* forces or local forces. But if they had decided not to make the effort, they would presumably have been more forthcoming with regard to negotiations. [Here the President scribbled: "makes sense."]
>
> (2) We have not seen proof that ARVN has really improved. It may be that the enemy forces have been hurt rather than that ARVN is significantly better than it was in the past. It could be that when the enemy drew back its main forces and cut down its activity in August and September, perhaps because of our threat in Paris at the beginning of August, they under-estimated the effect this would have on their guerrilla forces.

For these reasons I recommended that the President send my then military assistant Alexander Haig (who later became my deputy and afterward NATO Commander and Secretary of State) and a team of analysts to tour

---

* ARVN, the Army of the Republic of Vietnam, that is, South Vietnamese forces.

South Vietnam. Between January 19 and 29, 1970, they surveyed nine key provinces and confirmed the results of our Washington studies. They also warned, however, that the rate of improvement had definitely slowed in the last months of 1969: "There is no sign that the enemy has given up. . . . The pressures on the GVN resulting from U.S. troop withdrawals may lead to . . . a deterioration of territorial security force performance and a loss of popular support for the GVN." Similar conclusions were reached by an independent CIA study that revealed a growing pessimism among South Vietnamese leaders deriving from fear of an overly hasty American withdrawal. When I sent this CIA report to Nixon, he wrote on it: "K—the psychology is enormously important. They must take responsibility if they are *ever* to gain confidence. We have to take risks on that score."

To be sure, there were contrary views. Sir Robert Thompson, the British expert on guerrilla warfare credited with devising the strategy that defeated the Communist guerrillas in Malaya, reported after a visit to Vietnam in November 1969 that Saigon held a "winning position" and would be able to maintain it unless the United States withdrew too rapidly and reduced its aid.

But no amount of study, however objectively or carefully conducted, could solve our basic dilemma. An enemy determined on protracted struggle could only be brought to a political outcome by being confronted by insuperable military obstacles on the ground. Once committed to the Vietnamization strategy, we would build up the South Vietnamese forces and seek to blunt every effort Hanoi made to interrupt this process. The strategy was certain to be bitterly contested by a dedicated, vocal, and growing minority. The November 3 speech bought some time for Vietnamization. But time is fickle; we had to use the breathing spell to strengthen the American position on the ground. Simultaneously, we were determined to probe the prospects for negotiations—the process by which the two sides tested their respective assessments of each other and we sought to shape a settlement from a seemingly intractable stalemate.

The Secret Negotiations

The optimum moment for negotiations is when things appear to be going well. To yield to pressures is to invite them; to acquire a reputation for limited staying power is to give the adversary a powerful incentive for protracting negotiations. When a concession is made voluntarily, it provides the greatest incentive for reciprocity. It is also the best guarantee for staying power. The best negotiating strategy is to define the most reasonable outcome—the outcome both parties have (or should have) the greatest incentive to sustain—and then get there rapidly in one or two moves.

In November 1969, our position seemed the strongest since the beginning of the Nixon administration. We had withstood a military offensive by Hanoi, as well as the domestic protest; the President had taken his case to the people and received substantial support. Nixon, to show his displeasure with the slow progress of negotiations, declined to name a successor to Henry Cabot Lodge, who had resigned as ambassador to the Paris talks in November for personal reasons. Hanoi, having stonewalled the Paris talks for a year, now began to clamor for the appointment of a new senior negotiator. I suggested to Nixon that we might use this period to make another attempt at secret talks. The North Vietnamese could not use the secret Paris channel for propaganda; if they refused to talk, their refusal could be used against them if we made it public; and if Hanoi was ready to settle—which I doubted—we would learn of it only in secret talks. However the talks turned out, we would be able to build a record to demonstrate that Hanoi was the obstacle to negotiations.

Nixon was skeptical for a variety of reasons. He did not believe that Hanoi would be prepared to settle for any terms we could live with without having suffered major military setbacks; in this he proved to be right. He was in general uneasy about any process of negotiation; he hated to put himself into a position where he might be rebuffed. And for that reason he always carefully constructed an alibi for failure. In every negotiation, my instructions included some expression that Nixon did not really expect success. But because Nixon, for all his bravado, genuinely wanted peace, he inevitably fell in with the argument that we owed it to the American people to explore the possibility of an honorable settlement, however unlikely the chances, and to establish a record of having done so.

Accordingly, toward the end of November 1969 we asked General Vernon Walters, the U.S. defense attaché in Paris, to request a private appointment with Xuan Thuy; it was quickly granted. It was the first time that the Nixon White House approached the North Vietnamese directly without a foreign intermediary. Walters proposed another secret meeting. But the North Vietnamese were not ready. On December 12, General Walters was called to the North Vietnamese compound. Mai Van Bo, the North Vietnamese Delegate-General in Paris, proclaimed Hanoi's unhappiness with the "warlike" speech of November 3 and the President's refusal to name a senior replacement for Henry Cabot Lodge. He called attention to Hanoi's proposal at the August meeting, which he described as "both logical and reasonable." Since we had already rejected that "logical and reasonable" offer, there was no point, Hanoi said, in a new secret meeting unless we had something new to say.

The constant attacks on his dedication to peace notwithstanding, Nixon authorized another approach exactly one month after Hanoi's rebuff. On January 14, General Walters suggested a meeting any weekend after February 8, "provided both sides were willing to go beyond the existing framework." Nixon was still skeptical. "I don't know what these clowns want to talk about," he said to me, "but the line we take is either they talk or we are going to sit it out. I don't feel this is any time for concession."

Hanoi did not respond for several weeks. But on January 26, we received the first indication that a negotiation might soon get under way. It was announced that Le Duc Tho, who was a member of the North Vietnamese Politburo (in fact, the fifth man in the hierarchy) would attend the forthcoming French Communist Party Congress. Then, on February 16, Walters was called to the North Vietnamese compound and informed that our insolent interlocutors accepted a meeting for February 20 or 21. After keeping us waiting for over a month, the North Vietnamese demanded our answer within twelve hours. I have regretted ever since that we accepted the date of February 21, within the deadline. To honor this unreasonable demand gave an unnecessary impression of eagerness; it enabled Hanoi to score one of the psychological points so dear to its heart. It surely got us off on the wrong foot.

Thus began the secret negotiations between Le Duc Tho and me. Three meetings were held between February 20 and April 4, 1970.

The house in the Paris suburb of Choisy-le-Roi where we met with the North Vietnamese probably belonged to a foreman in one of the factories in the district. On the ground floor there was a small living room connected to an even smaller dining room, which opened into a tiny garden. In the living room two rows of easy chairs, heavily upholstered in red, faced each other. The American group—I, Richard Smyser (my Vietnam expert), Winston Lord, who replaced Tony Lake as my executive assistant after the first series of meetings, and General Walters—would sit alongside the wall to the left of the door, the North Vietnamese delegation, numbering six, sat along the other wall. There were four or five feet of floor space and eons of perception separating us.

At the first meeting on February 21, 1970, Xuan Thuy greeted me and led me into the living room to meet the man whose conceit it was to use the title of Special Adviser to Xuan Thuy, although as a member of the governing Politburo he outranked him by several levels.

Special Adviser Le Duc Tho and the First Round of Talks

L e Duc Tho, gray-haired, dignified, rather short, invariably wore a black or brown Mao suit. His large luminous eyes only rarely revealed the fanaticism that had induced him as a boy of sixteen to join the anti-French Communist guerrillas. He was always composed; his manners, except on one or two occasions, were impeccable. He knew what he was about and served his cause with dedication and skill.

That cause was to break the will of the United States, to destroy the government in Saigon it was supporting, and to establish Hanoi's rule over a country that our predecessors had pledged to defend. Our private banter grew longer as our meetings progressed and some limited human contact developed; it revealed that Le Duc Tho's profession was revolution, his vocation guerrilla warfare. He could speak eloquently of peace but it was an abstraction alien to any personal experience. He had spent ten years of his life in prisons under the French. In 1973, he showed me around a museum of Vietnamese history in Hanoi, which he admitted sheepishly he had never visited previously. The artifacts of Vietnamese history—mostly assembled, ironically enough, by the French colonial administration—reminded Le Duc Tho not of the glories of Vietnamese culture but of prisons in the cities or towns where they had been excavated.

Le Duc Tho had been sustained through his exertions by a passionate belief in Leninist discipline and faith in the Vietnamese nation. His sense of national destiny made personal hatred of the United States irrelevant; the Americans were simply one of the hordes of foreigners whose congenital ignorance had, over the centuries, tempted them into Indochina, where it was Vietnam's mission to expel them (not, I often thought, without driving them mad first).

Le Duc Tho's Leninism convinced him that he understood my motivations better than I understood them myself. His Vietnamese heritage expressed itself in an obsessive suspicion that he might somehow be tricked. When the negotiation finally grew serious after three years, it would impel him to look for traps in the most innocent of our proposals. At the outset it led him into lectures, which in time grew tiresome, of his imperviousness to capitalist tricks.

Le Duc Tho considered negotiations as another battle. Any proposed settlement that deprived Hanoi of total victory was in his eyes a ruse by definition. He was there to wear me down. Hanoi's proposals were put forward as the sole "logical and reasonable" framework for negotiations. The North Vietnamese were "an oppressed people"; in spite of much historical evidence to the contrary, he considered them by definition incapable of oppressing others. America bore the entire responsibility for the war. Fashionable proposals to reduce hostilities, by de-escalation or cease-fire, were disdained by Le Duc Tho either as tricks or opportunities to sow confusion. In his view, the sole "reasonable" way to end the fighting was American acceptance of Hanoi's terms, which were unconditional withdrawal on a fixed deadline and the overthrow of the South Vietnamese government.

As a spokesman for the truth, Le Duc Tho considered trading concessions immoral unless a superior necessity supervened, and until that happened he was prepared to wait us out. He seemed concerned to rank favorably in the pantheon epic of Vietnamese struggles; he could not consider as an equal this barbarian from across the sea who thought to deflect the inexorable march of history with words. Le Duc Tho undoubtedly was of the stuff of which heroes are made. What we grasped only with reluctance—and many at home never understood—is that only in epic poems are heroes humanly attractive. More usually in real life their dedication makes them unrelenting; their courage makes them overbearing; they are out of scale and therefore not amenable to ordinary mortal intercourse.

Still half believing what was an article of faith among my former academic colleagues, that Hanoi's lack of trust in our intentions was a principal obstacle to a compromise peace, I opened the morning session with a prepared statement of our commitment to serious negotiations. I stressed that we sought to achieve a settlement which resolved the issues once and for all; we had no wish to repeat the experience of all previous agreements that had been mere armistices in an endless war. I pointed out that Hanoi's position had not improved since my meeting with Xuan Thuy in August. President Nixon had demonstrated his ability to achieve public support; the balance of forces on the ground did not warrant Hanoi's insistence on political predominance. Finally, it was our judgment "that the international situation has complications which may make Vietnam no longer the undivided concern of other countries and may mean that Vietnam will not enjoy the undivided support of countries which now support it"—an unsubtle reference to the Sino-Soviet dispute.

I then stressed that the United States intended to retain no bases in Vietnam; and that in arranging for *mutual* withdrawal we did not insist that North Vietnamese troops be placed on the same legal basis as American forces. We sought a practical, not a theoretical, end to the war. We did not insist that Hanoi formally announce its withdrawal so long as it in fact took place. On this basis I proposed that we set aside propaganda and work out some agreed principles. These could then be fleshed out in the plenary sessions taking place at Avenue Kléber; we were prepared to send a new senior negotiator to Paris to complete an agreement.

Since Le Duc Tho was technically only Special Adviser to Hanoi's Paris delegation, Xuan Thuy as formal head of the delegation made the first response. He could not bring himself to forgo such an opportunity to impress his superior with his rhetorical skill (the content had obviously been worked out in advance). He insisted that before any political negotiations the United States would have to set a deadline for unilateral withdrawal. The negotiations would then concern the modalities of our retreat; they could not affect its timing, which had to be unconditional. Thuy offered a cease-fire with the United States as a reciprocal concession. But the fighting against South Vietnam would continue until the Saigon government was overthrown; there was no mention of the release of our prisoners of war. Continuing its insistence on denying the significance of any American gesture, Xuan Thuy dismissed the announced departure of over 100,000 troops as "withdrawal by driblets." Our reduction of B-52 sorties by 25 percent and the change in military orders that severely curtailed offensive operations by American forces did not prevent absurd allegations that we were escalating the war.

In the afternoon it was Le Duc Tho's turn. He began by challenging my assessment that events had moved in our favor since August. "Only when we have a correct assessment of the balance of forces," said Le Duc Tho in his role as Leninist schoolmaster, "can we have a correct solution." He revealed the importance Hanoi attached to our public opinion by giving it pride of place in his presentation. He denied that Nixon's public standing had improved, citing a Gallup Poll which showed that the number of Americans favoring immediate withdrawal had risen from 21 to 35 percent. This, however, was "only" public opinion. "In addition, I have seen many statements by the Senate Foreign Relations Committee, by the Democratic Party, by Mr. Clifford, which have demanded the total withdrawal of American forces, the change of Thieu-Ky-Khiem,* and the appointment of a successor to Ambassador Lodge." I replied sharply that I would listen to no further discussions regarding American public opinion; Le Duc Tho was there to negotiate the Vietnamese position.

Le Duc Tho next attacked our military assessment. He cut to the heart of the dilemma of Vietnamization. All too acutely, he pointed out that our strategy was to withdraw enough forces to make the war bearable for the American people while simultaneously strengthening the Saigon forces so that they could stand on their own. He then asked the question that was also tormenting me: "Before, there were over a million U.S. and puppet troops, and you failed. How can you succeed when you let the puppet troops do the fighting? Now, with only U.S. support, how can you win?"

From this analysis, Le Duc Tho's conclusions followed inexorably. He insisted that military and political problems be dealt with simultaneously—a position from which he never deviated until October 1972. According to Le Duc Tho, the only military subject he was prepared to discuss was the unconditional liquidation of America's military involvement. Even if American forces withdrew unilaterally, Hanoi would stop fighting only if there was a political settlement. This, in Le Duc Tho's view, presupposed the immediate removal of the "warlike" President Thieu, Vice President Ky, and Prime Minister Khiem and the creation of a coalition government composed of people who stood for "peace, independence and neutrality." The NLF would have a veto over those who stood for "peace, independence and neutrality." This coalition government, loaded as it was in Hanoi's favor, was not, however, the final word. With one third of it composed of Communists, with the remainder approved by the Communists, with all anti-Communist leaders barred, it was then to negotiate with the fully armed NLF for a definitive solution. Tho comforted me by observing that this scheme would open hopeful prospects: "If you show goodwill and serious intent, a settlement will come quickly."

The next meeting took place three weeks later on March 16. I proposed

---

* Tran Thien Khiem, who had replaced Tran Van Huong as Prime Minister of South Vietnam.

that neither side exert military pressure in Vietnam or in "related" countries during the negotiations—in other words a mutual de-escalation of military operations throughout Indochina. This was contemptuously rejected with a pedantic lecture that every war had its high points with which it was impossible to interfere. At the April 4 meeting I repeated the proposal in the form of a formal cease-fire. Le Duc Tho spurned it without any exploration whatsoever. On March 16, I put on the table a monthly schedule for American withdrawal over a sixteen-month period. The North Vietnamese said it was unacceptable because it differed from the proposal of twelve months in the President's November 3 speech. (I had used sixteen months because it was the only precise schedule that existed in the Pentagon and reflected the technical assessment of how long it would take to withdraw nearly half a million remaining American personnel and their equipment.) When I explained that the schedule was illustrative only and that the deadline would of course be made to coincide with presidential pronouncements, it was turned down as being incompatible with the "correct and logical" deadline of six months put forward by the NLF. Above all, our schedule was defective because it would start to run only *after* the agreement was completed, while Hanoi insisted that American troops withdraw unconditionally. Furthermore, Le Duc Tho refused to discuss any political solution that preserved any member of the South Vietnamese government in office; he derided our proposal for mixed electoral commissions, including members of the Vietcong, which we proposed as a means to supervise free elections.

At the April 4 meeting Xuan Thuy summed up Hanoi's objections to our position once again. The deadline was "wrong" because it was longer than their demand of six months and depended on the settlement of other issues; mutual withdrawal was unacceptable; no settlement was possible as long as Thieu, Ky, and Khiem and other leaders "opposed to peace, independence and neutrality" remained in office; the American delegation in Paris still lacked a senior replacement for Lodge.

Vitriolic comments were reserved for Laos, where a North Vietnamese offensive had just been launched, and Cambodia. Le Duc Tho accused us of escalating the war in Laos. When I replied that one good test of who was doing what to whom was to see which side was advancing, Le Duc Tho argued that we had "provoked" the North Vietnamese offensive and that the fighting was being conducted by Laotian forces in any event. As for Cambodia, where Sihanouk was being attacked for permitting Vietnamese bases,

Le Duc Tho was implacable. I proposed an immediate agreement on the neutrality of Cambodia. Le Duc Tho ridiculed the offer. The wars in Indochina had become one, he insisted, and would be fought to the finish on that basis.

In short, the North Vietnamese rejected a schedule for mutual withdrawal, de-escalation, the neutralization of Cambodia, a cease-fire, or a mixed electoral commission for South Vietnam. When I asked Le Duc Tho whether his political program expressed a preference or a condition, he said flatly: "This is a condition." It was a condition to which Hanoi stuck until the fall of 1972.

The first series of secret negotiations with Le Duc Tho ended with his statement that unless we changed our position, there was nothing more to discuss.*

In going over the record with the perspective of time, I am astonished by our willingness to persist in them. The record leaves no doubt that we were looking for excuses to make the negotiations succeed, not for a pretext to escalate. Far from being determined on a military solution as critics have never tired of alleging, we went out of our way to give the benefit of every doubt to the pursuit of a negotiated settlement. Nor can Thieu be fairly charged with being an obstacle—except in the special sense that Hanoi objected to his existence.

I cabled reports after every session by back channel to Ambassador Ellsworth Bunker in Saigon, to brief President Thieu. Thieu interposed no objections, no doubt calculating that all our proposals were bound to be re-

---

* Typical of the never-never land of the public debate was an article that appeared the day after my first meeting with Le Duc Tho in the *Philadelphia Bulletin*. Its author, Roger Hilsman, had been director of Intelligence and Research at the State Department during the period of America's initial involvement in Vietnam and was later Assistant Secretary of State for Far Eastern Affairs under Johnson. He claimed that the President was "rebuffing a Communist offer of a more-or-less immediate Vietnam peace on terms that many Americans might find perfectly acceptable." Hilsman claimed to be supported in his view by a number of experts, including Averell Harriman. On the basis of an exegesis of Hanoi's Delphic declarations, Hilsman and his associates professed to have discovered the following peace offer:
  • No election but an old-fashioned political deal setting up a coalition government including representatives of all political factions, Communist and non-Communist;
  • Although their propaganda still calls for immediate total withdrawal of American troops, privately they have indicated the withdrawal could be phased over two or three years;
  • Postponement of the reunification of North and South Vietnam for a period of between five and ten years;
  • International guarantees of the territorial integrity of Laos and Cambodia.
Hanoi, of course, had explicitly rejected each of these points.

jected and that acquiescence in them was his best means of assuring American support for the conduct of the war.

The first round of negotiations with Le Duc Tho collapsed because diplomacy always reflects some balance of forces and Le Duc Tho's assessment was not wrong. His sense of public opinion in America—and especially of the leadership groups with which Hanoi identified—was quite accurate. The dilemmas of Vietnamization were real. In these circumstances Le Duc Tho could see no reason to modify his demands for unconditional withdrawal and the overthrow of the Saigon government. He would see none until two and a half years later, when the military situation left him no other choice.

Laos Interlude

In the northwest corner of Indochina, wedged between mountain ranges and the plain of the Mekong River, the tribes and peoples of Laos, ruled by a Buddhist king, had led a peaceful existence for centuries, essentially unaffected by the wars and struggles of their more bellicose neighbors. In the nineteenth century Laos was conquered by the French without recorded resistance and then governed by them from Hanoi along with the rest of Indochina.

By one of history's ironies, those struggling for national independence often adopt the imperial pretensions of their former colonial rulers. Thus the Leninist masters of Hanoi saw themselves as the natural heirs of all that had been ruled by France from the very headquarters they were now occupying. There had been efforts by Vietnam to dominate Laos and Cambodia in the eighteenth and early nineteenth centuries;[1] now there was added a proclivity to inherit the territories of French colonial rule. After the 1954 Geneva Agreement, which ended the French presence, the peace-loving peoples of Laos had the misfortune of being astride routes by which North Vietnam could invade the South while bypassing the Demilitarized Zone set up by that agreement.[2]

From the beginning the Pathet Lao (the Laotian Communists, dominated by Hanoi) retained control over two northeast provinces where the writ of the government in Vientiane never ran. By 1961, a three-cornered civil war was raging between the Pathet Lao in the northeast, neutralist forces in the center of the country on the fabled Plain of Jars, and a rightist group along the Mekong River bordering Thailand. By 1961, more than 6,000 North Vietnamese troops were involved. The conflict became sufficiently grave for President Kennedy to warn at a news conference on March 23, 1961: "Laos is far away from America, but the world is small. . . . The security of all Southeast Asia will be endangered if Laos loses its neutral independence." In May 1961, negotiations over the future of Laos opened in Geneva. Like all negotiations with Hanoi, they proved protracted; pursuing its normal tactic, Hanoi maintained military pressure until President Kennedy sent 5,000 U.S. Marines to neighboring Thailand in May 1962. Within two months of that show of force, a new Geneva Agreement was signed by fourteen nations, including North Vietnam and the Soviet Union, providing for neutralization of Laos. All foreign military personnel were to be withdrawn and a coalition government would be established, headed by the neutralist Prince Souvanna Phouma, in which all three factions would be represented.

North Vietnam flouted the accords from the day they were signed. All 666 American military personnel in Laos departed through international checkpoints; of the 6,000 North Vietnamese in the country only *forty* (yes, forty) left through the checkpoints; the rest remained.

In April 1963, the precarious coalition split apart. Fighting soon resumed. Southern Laos was in effect annexed by the North Vietnamese army. By 1970, over half a million North Vietnamese troops had moved south along the so-called Ho Chi Minh Trail. The number of North Vietnamese troops stationed in Laos had risen to 67,000—ten times the number that in 1961–1962 had precipitated a major crisis under President Kennedy.

The Kennedy and Johnson administrations extended increasing support to Premier Souvanna Phouma, the neutralist leader who had been recognized as the leader by all sides in the 1962 Geneva Accords. The purpose was to maintain a neutralist government and also to secure Souvanna's acquiescence in the ongoing efforts to interdict the Ho Chi Minh Trail. The Kennedy and Johnson administrations gave financial assistance to the Royal Laotian Army, to some irregular forces of Meo tribesmen led by General Vang Pao, and from time to time to Thai volunteers operating in Laos. American civilians (mostly retired military personnel) under contract to the CIA acted as advisers. The operations were financed largely out of CIA funds to avoid controversy about the Geneva Accords.

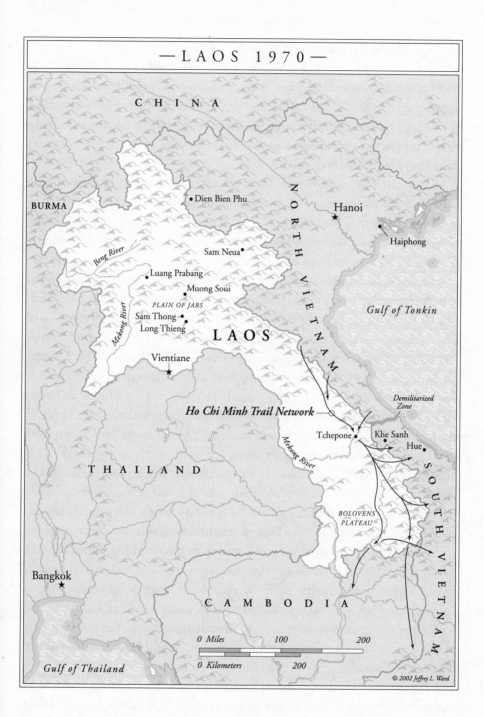

— L A O S   1 9 7 0 —

CHINA

BURMA

Dien Bien Phu

Hanoi

NORTH VIETNAM

Haiphong

Beng River

Sam Neua

Luang Prabang

Muong Soui

PLAIN OF JARS

Mekong River

Sam Thong

Long Thieng

LAOS

Gulf of Tonkin

Vientiane

Ho Chi Minh Trail Network

Mekong River

Demilitarized
Zone

Tchepone

Khe Sanh

Hue

SOUTH VIETNAM

THAILAND

BOLOVENS
PLATEAU

Bangkok

CAMBODIA

0 Miles   100   200

0 Kilometers   200

Gulf of Thailand

© 2002 Jeffrey L. Ward

The Nixon administration essentially followed the procedure it inherited. Most of these activities were occasionally reported in the press; by 1970 all of it was known to the Senate Foreign Relations Committee because of a number of classified hearings conducted by Senator Stuart Symington. But the U.S. government made no formal acknowledgment, so as to avoid giving Hanoi a pretext to compound its massive violations of the Geneva Accords by taking over all of Laos.

Early in 1970 Laos briefly became the focal point of our Indochina concerns and domestic debate. A North Vietnamese offensive was threatening to overrun northern Laos. Domestic critics used the occasion to cry havoc about the danger that we might slide into another "open-ended" commitment in Indochina without noticing it.

Hanoi was fighting essentially two wars in Laos, though both for the same objective of hegemony in Indochina. In the south, the Ho Chi Minh Trail was Hanoi's link to the battlefield of South Vietnam. In northern Laos, Hanoi supported the Pathet Lao but it was restrained by fear of American or Thai intervention. It sought to maintain just enough pressure on the Laotian army to prevent it from consolidating itself as an instrument of authority; it would be dealt with after victory in South Vietnam. We did not, for our part, seek to disturb this uneasy equilibrium. It would not make sense to expand the conflict into Laos, except for the minimum required for the protection of our forces in Vietnam, especially when we were withdrawing troops from South Vietnam. It was this position that the North Vietnamese challenged in late January 1970 when they suddenly sent 13,000 reinforcements and a great deal of extra equipment to the Plain of Jars, where the neutralists were holding back the Pathet Lao. That threatened Souvanna, and our relations with him; if he abandoned his acquiescence in the bombing of the Ho Chi Minh Trail, Hanoi's logistics problem would be greatly eased, exposing us in South Vietnam to growing peril. Worse, if the North Vietnamese troops reached the Mekong, the war would lose its point for Thailand. Bangkok would then be under pressure along the hundreds of miles of the vast river dividing a plain without any other obstacles. We would be denied use of the Thai airbases, essential for air operations in Vietnam.

The bombing of Laos is often mentioned as another violation of a neutral country by an arbitrary Nixon administration. The facts are these: Nixon inherited from the Johnson administration a systematic bombing campaign of the Ho Chi Minh Trail, through which most supplies moved to Vietnam, in the panhandle of Laos. It was largely unpopulated except for some 60,000 Vietnamese troops stationed there. These attacks were conducted under the command of the Commander of the Pacific Forces in the Johnson administration. Nixon continued this authority without modifications.

In the rest of Laos, every target had to be authorized by Souvanna Phouma and our ambassadors in Thailand and Laos. Nixon followed the same rules of engagement except that in the spring of 1970, he authorized the use of B-52s following the same chain of command described above. The White House was not engaged in the selection of targets unless there was a dispute between the different headquarters. Those cases were extremely rare—for bureaucracies prefer to settle among themselves rather than invoke higher authority.

On January 23, 1970, an enemy offensive imminent, the American ambassador in Laos, G. McMurtrie Godley, requested B-52 strikes against a major North Vietnamese concentration containing, it was believed, 4,000 troops; it would have been the first use of B-52s in northern Laos. This inspired a stately bureaucratic minuet in Washington that told much about the state of mind of our government. We were caught between officials seeking to protect the American forces, for which they felt a responsibility, and a merciless congressional onslaught that rattled these officials.

I scheduled a meeting of the Washington Special Actions Group (WSAG)—the crisis management group—for January 26 to consider Godley's request. Two hours before the meeting Mel Laird told me that he favored using B-52s against that target; on the other hand, he did not want it discussed in an interagency forum for fear of leaks. Laird urged approval in the same channels as the secret strikes in Cambodia. One hour before the meeting Rogers called to tell me that he was against using B-52s in northern Laos and that he had Laird on his side. I mumbled some doubts about this claim but suggested a meeting of the three of us with the President. Unfortunately, the President chose this moment to go into seclusion at Camp David to prepare his first veto message, rejecting a welfare appropriations bill. By the time he was again available all the principals were on record with some statement protecting themselves against all possible developments. Since it was now too late to obtain a consensus regarding this particular target, I recommended deferring the immediate decision but promised to get a clear-cut presidential decision on the principle of using B-52s.

On February 12, the long-feared North Vietnamese offensive finally broke on the Plain of Jars. The next day, Premier Souvanna Phouma made a formal request for B-52 strikes—the first of several such requests. By February 16 the North Vietnamese and Pathet Lao had driven government forces from most of the high ground that dominates the approaches to the Plain of Jars. The President called a meeting for the afternoon of February 16 with Laird, Acting Secretary of State Richardson, Helms, Admiral Tom Moorer (Acting Chairman of the Joint Chiefs), and me. I recommended that the President authorize B-52 strikes if the enemy advanced beyond Muong Soui, the farthest point of Communist penetration before the government counteroffensive of the previous summer. The President agreed. The Communists reached beyond Muong Soui within twenty-four hours. An attack with three B-52s was launched on the night of February 17–18. It had taken a month of discussion, a major North Vietnamese offensive, and the near collapse of the Laotian front to induce exactly one B-52 strike. I do not know to this day whether Laird favored or opposed the action; his stand was compatible with both positions. Wheeler was consistently in favor. Rogers moved from opposition to indifference.

But one B-52 strike was enough to trigger domestic furor. The next day, February 19, the *New York Times* reported that B-52s had been diverted from South Vietnam to attack North Vietnamese and Pathet Lao forces in northern Laos. Senators Eugene McCarthy and Frank Church deplored the involvement of American planes and pilots in Laos; they made no reference to the North Vietnamese offensive. Senator Mike Mansfield, also without mentioning the North Vietnamese onslaught, attacked American "escalation" on February 21. Reports appeared of "armed Americans in civilian clothes" supporting the Laotian command.[3] On February 25, Senators Charles "Mac" Mathias, Mansfield, Albert Gore, Symington, Cooper, and Percy attacked administration "secrecy" over what they termed a "deepening U.S. involvement." Senators Gore (the father of the later vice president and presidential candidate) and Mansfield on February 25 demanded publication of secret testimony taken by their subcommittee in October on U.S. involvement. Senator Symington sent a letter to Secretary Rogers urging that Ambassador Godley be brought back from Laos to testify. On February 27, the *Wall Street Journal* halfheartedly supported the use of B-52s but warned against further escalation. The *Washington Post* on March 2 weighed in with a stinging editorial entitled "Laos: The Same Old Shell Game."

This was the culmination of a campaign extending over many months in the Senate and in the media to get at the "truth" in Laos. The issue was not to obtain the facts—they were widely known—but to induce the government to confirm them publicly. The Senate Foreign Relations Committee had substantially full knowledge from its staff investigations as well as from its classified hearings. Similarly, the media had given the public a reasonably accurate picture. The issue for us was to what extent an official acknowledgment would wreck what was left of the 1962 Geneva Accords, give Hanoi an alibi for further stepping up its attacks in northern Laos, and fuel even more passionate controversy at home.

The American role in Laos had been "secret" in three administrations of two parties precisely because each President wanted to keep it limited. To spell out the limits publicly was as dangerous to this strategy as to spell out the extent of our involvement. Now we were being pressed to do both. From the critics' point of view the issue was useful for a challenge to the entire Vietnam enterprise. Some would even have considered it a bonus if a collapse in Laos had led to a collapse in Vietnam. They wanted not facts but ammunition.

I explained the issue in a memorandum for the President:

> The real issue in Laos is entirely related to Vietnam:
> —There is no question but that the North Vietnamese can overrun Laos at any point in time that they care to, providing they are willing to pay the political and psychological costs of upsetting the 1962 Accords.
> —Should North Vietnam overrun Laos, our whole bargaining with respect to the Vietnam conflict would be undermined. In fact, if North Vietnamese military operations in Laos succeed to the point that Souvanna believes he must succumb to their influence in order to survive, we could then anticipate that he would refuse to permit us to continue our interdiction of the Ho Chi Minh Trail and thus our military operations in South Vietnam would be catastrophically damaged.
> —These are the fundamental considerations with all the rest amounting to balderdash. . . .

The North Vietnamese offensive soon faced us with new decisions. The Communist advance reached the Long Thieng area, the last stronghold before the capital of Vientiane. It also threatened the headquarters of Vang Pao, the leader of the Meo tribesmen who were resisting Communist domination. With a Communist advance to the Mekong imminent, Thailand offered to send volunteers to Long Thieng if the Laotian government asked for them. This proposal was strenuously resisted by the State Department and received only lukewarm support from other agencies at two WSAG meetings. After we received a formal request from both the Laotian and Thai governments, the President overruled the agencies. He was convinced (and I agreed) that to refuse the offer would raise doubts in Thailand about America's commitment to its defense and might panic Souvanna.

The Laotian government launched a counteroffensive on March 27, aided by the Thai volunteers. The Thai intervention was decisive. On March 31, Laotian government forces recaptured nearby Sam Thong; its airfield was soon back in use and American planes began ferrying supplies. North Vietnamese forces pulled back from the Long Thieng area the next day. The Laos crisis thus subsided for the rest of the year; the political and military equilibrium in northern Laos was maintained. This turned out to be but a prelude to a more intense crisis in the neighboring country of Cambodia.

The Overthrow of Sihanouk

For nearly thirty years the political life of Cambodia had been identified with the tempestuous career and personality of Prince Norodom Sihanouk. Crowned King in 1941 at the age of eighteen, he abdicated the throne in 1955 to play an active political role as Prime Minister; in June 1960, by unanimous vote of the Cambodian National Assembly, he was elevated to chief of state. It was Sihanouk who had guided the kingdom of Cambodia to independence from France in 1953, shaped its political institutions, and dominated its policies.

In leading his country, Sihanouk skillfully walked a tightrope between East and West in global politics, between the Soviet Union and China in the emerging Communist schism, between the opposing sides in the battle over Vietnam, and between right and left in his own country. Voluble, erratic, fun-loving—"mercurial" is the word usually used—he dexterously kept his country a haven of peace amid the bloody wars that ravaged the rest of Indochina. Suddenly in 1970, the nimble tightrope walker slipped and fell, and thus catapulted his people to a hell far worse than even their neighbors had endured.

On January 7, 1970, Prince Sihanouk, with his wife, Monique, and a retinue of eleven, left their capital, Phnom Penh, for a two-month vacation at a clinic in Grasse on the French Riviera. It was his custom to "take the cure" there every two years to ease the discomfort of what he called his "obesity, blood disease, and albuminuria." In his absence his government was left in the hands of his own chosen leaders: Chairman of the National Assembly Cheng Heng (who became acting head of state); Prime Minister Lon Nol (whom Sihanouk had appointed in August 1969 and praised in September as "the only person I could trust because of his faithfulness to the Throne and Nation");* and Sirik Matak, Deputy Prime Minister.

From the point of view of the Nixon administration, the precarious political balance in neutral Cambodia under Sihanouk's skillful, if unpredictable, tutelage was the best attainable situation. To be sure, Hanoi's use of Cambodian sanctuaries for launching military operations against American and allied forces, in flagrant disregard of international law, was a continuing menace. But a certain equilibrium had been established. Sihanouk had acquiesced in, if not encouraged, the bombing of these sanctuaries; we desisted from ground operations across the border; Hanoi continued to use the sanctuaries, if at a higher cost. And we had some warning of how precarious the internal balance in Cambodia was. When President Nixon met with President Thieu in Saigon on July 30, 1969, Thieu cautioned prophetically that if the balance in Cambodia were upset by the overthrow of Sihanouk, the Communists would win in the end.

We agreed with this assessment. Cambodia's tragedy was that its internal stresses finally upset the delicate equilibrium that Sihanouk had struggled to maintain, unleashing precisely the forces which Thieu had foreseen. The precipitating issue was the Communist sanctuaries from which the North Vietnamese had tormented the free world forces in Vietnam. These increasingly aroused the nationalist outrage of Cambodians, who over the centuries have seen successive Vietnamese rulers colonize their ancestral lands; indeed, the area around Saigon was conquered by Vietnamese only in the early nine-

---

* Lon Nol was also Sihanouk's representative to China's National Day celebrations in Beijing on October 1, 1969, standing on Tiananmen with Mao Zedong.

teenth century. Had French occupation not supervened, it is quite possible that all of Cambodia would have suffered that fate. The antipathy of Cambodians for Vietnamese has ancient roots. Sihanouk's inability to dislodge the hated and feared North Vietnamese from Cambodian soil undermined his position with every passing month.

Sihanouk's public statements of the period leave no doubt as to whom he considered the primary threat to his country's independence. Repeatedly and publicly he protested North Vietnamese "aggression" and infringement of Cambodia's sovereignty. In June 1969—three months after the so-called secret bombing started—he complained at a press conference that Cambodia's Ratanakiri province was "practically North Vietnamese territory," and that "Viet Minh" (North Vietnamese) and Vietcong forces had heavily infiltrated into Svay Rieng province. In the October 1969 issue of *Sangkum*, a journal of which Sihanouk was editor, an article entitled "The Implantation of Viet Cong and North Vietnamese Along Our Borders" protested the North Vietnamese occupation at length; a map showed the location of 35,000 to 40,000 North Vietnamese and Vietcong troops occupying Cambodian territory (not unhelpful to our intelligence). In a signed article in the December 1969 issue, Sihanouk went so far as to pay tribute to the American role in Vietnam. He argued that "in all honesty and objectivity," the presence of American forces in Southeast Asia established a regional balance of power that permitted small nations like Cambodia "to be respected, if not courted, by the European, and even Asian Socialist camps." America's Asian allies could not compensate for a withdrawal of American power by turning toward the Communists because, wrote Sihanouk, like a bird before a serpent, "the bird, gentle or not, always ends up being swallowed up."

Sihanouk had no doubt which side had committed the fundamental aggression in Indochina. For example, in November 1969 the Vietcong had fired on a U.S. Special Forces camp in Vietnam from Cambodian territory; retaliatory—and publicized—American air attacks were said to have killed some twenty-five Cambodians. Sihanouk had protested this to the United States; we offered to pay compensation. Nevertheless, in a speech on December 15, Sihanouk placed the responsibility for this incident on the North Vietnamese:

> Who triggered the Dak Dam incident? It was the Viet Cong who
> fired at the Americans from our territory. When the Americans got

hit, they became angry and bombed us. Then the Viet Cong and the Viet Minh fled, and only Khmer inhabitants were left to become victims. That is the whole story. . . .

The big Red powers who claim to be our friends, the European Reds at the United Nations, have forbidden us to complain to the United Nations.

Sihanouk told his audience that he would not break diplomatic relations with the United States again, as some were urging, because if he did so, "we'll have to do the same thing with the Viet Minh and Viet Cong, because they still continue to commit aggression against our territory even after we established diplomatic relations with them."

On February 22, 1970, toward the end of his vacation in France, Sihanouk announced that on his way home in March he intended to visit the Soviet Union and China, "those great, friendly countries," to enlist their support to reduce or eliminate the North Vietnamese presence in his country. These statements—together with those quoted earlier—contradict the folklore, which has been elevated into historical truth by endless repetition, to the effect that Cambodia's tragedy was caused by the secret bombing which allegedly drove the North Vietnamese out of their sanctuaries and deeper into Cambodia. No statement of Sihanouk sustains this. The bombing at first caused the Hanoi forces to move toward Vietnam and keep close to the battlefield. They reversed fronts only when they decided to take over Cambodia.

For the first time in his career Sihanouk lost his grip on events. On March 8 villagers in Cambodia's Svay Rieng province demonstrated against the North Vietnamese occupation. On March 11, 20,000 young Cambodians sacked the embassies of the North Vietnamese and the Vietcong in Phnom Penh. (The Cambodian government clearly had a hand in organizing the demonstrations.) The two houses of the Cambodian Parliament held a special joint session and requested the government to reaffirm Cambodia's neutrality and to defend the national territory. The Parliament urged an expansion of the Cambodian army, which Sihanouk had kept deliberately weak because he feared that it might move against him.

From Paris, Sihanouk sent a public cablegram to his mother, the Dowager Queen, in Phnom Penh denouncing "certain personalities" in his government who were trying to "throw our country into the arms of an imperialist capitalist power." He announced his intention to return to Phnom Penh immediately "to address the nation and the army and ask them to make their choice." In an interview while still in Paris, Sihanouk warned the North Vietnamese and Vietcong that they had a choice between respecting Cambodia's neutrality or seeing a pro-American faction take over his government.[4] For reasons never fully explained, he hesitated in Paris, however, and the kettle in Phnom Penh began to boil over. On March 12, Deputy Prime Minister Sirik Matak announced suspension of a trade agreement with the Vietcong and the expansion of the Cambodian army by 10,000 men. New anti-Vietnamese riots took place in Phnom Penh with attacks on shops and churches of the Vietnamese community. On March 13, the Cambodian Foreign Ministry announced that it had notified the North Vietnamese and Vietcong embassies that all Vietnamese Communist armed forces were to leave Cambodian territory by dawn on March 15, 1970—two days later.

The same day, March 13, Sihanouk made his single most fateful decision. He left Paris, not to return to Phnom Penh as he had announced two days earlier, but to carry out his scheduled visit to Moscow. Attempting to regain the initiative on the issue of primary concern to his public, he announced in Paris: "I am going to Moscow and Peking to ask them to curb the activities of the Viet Cong and Viet Minh in my country." He reprinted a letter he had written in *Agence Khmer-Presse* that he would fight "against the Communist Vietnamese who, taking advantage of the military situation, infiltrate and settle our territory." Despite his earlier intention to return quickly to Phnom Penh, despite Soviet President Nikolai Podgorny's advice to fly home the next day, Sihanouk spent five crucial days in Moscow haggling over military aid—in a last-ditch effort to placate his military, who were chafing at being cut off from all new equipment. Even then, he headed not for Phnom Penh but for Beijing. In his own account, Sihanouk asserts rather defensively that he "needed more time to watch developments in Phnom Penh";[5] at several points he claims that Lon Nol and Sirik Matak would have blocked any attempt to return. But it was not until March 18 that his own legislature deposed him as chief of state and only then were the airports closed. Sihanouk learned of this startling turn of events from Premier Kosygin on the ride to Moscow's Vnukovo airport. He was stunned. For none of his aides had had the courage to tell him that earlier that day the ninety-two-strong Cambodian National Assembly and Council of the Kingdom, in another special joint session, had voted unanimously to remove him as chief of state.

Sihanouk arrived in Beijing to be embraced by Premier Zhou Enlai and feted by the Chinese as if nothing had changed; Zhou assured him that China still regarded him as chief of state. In Phnom Penh, meanwhile, the Cambodian Parliament named Cheng Heng, whom Sihanouk had left behind in his place, as interim—instead of acting—chief of state. It was not a military coup in the classic sense; it was Sihanouk's own government without Sihanouk.

Any attempt to assess the blame for propelling Cambodia into the maelstrom of bloody conflict must begin here. For Lon Nol and Sirik Matak, the crucial step was their act of bravado to take up the popular battle against the hated—and far superior—forces of the North Vietnamese and Vietcong. For Sihanouk, the crucial step was his week of hesitation, because what Lon Nol and Sirik Matak feared, and Podgorny advised, the United States also believed and preferred: that Sihanouk's bold reentry into Phnom Penh to face down his opponents would have turned the tide of events and was in everybody's best interest. Once returned to power, Sihanouk could have resumed his balancing role from his traditional position, which I described to Nixon on April 21 as one of "placing himself deliberately on the extreme left wing of the right wing." We would have cooperated with this effort. But by March 20 events were racing out of control.

The role of the United States through these events was primarily that of a spectator. Preoccupied with Laos for the first three months of the year, and with no intelligence personnel in Phnom Penh, our perceptions lagged behind events. For America, the status quo was quite acceptable. We neither encouraged Sihanouk's overthrow nor knew about it in advance. We did not even grasp its significance for many weeks, as is reflected in the memoranda I sent to Nixon. Though he received daily summaries of key events, an analysis of the first (March 11) demonstrations against Sihanouk was not forwarded until March 17, a week's delay that indicates that Cambodia was scarcely a high priority concern. Even more striking is the conclusion of the memorandum that it all could have been an elaborate trick by Sihanouk.

> Given the sharp competition between Sirik Matak and Sihanouk, it is possible that Sirik wanted to present Sihanouk with a fait accompli, or to challenge him to a test on grounds where Sirik Matak's position would be popular. On the other hand, nobody has challenged Sihanouk so directly in years, and it is quite possible that this is an

elaborate maneuver, to permit Sihanouk to call for Soviet and Chinese cooperation in urging the VC/NVA [Vietcong/North Vietnamese army] to leave, on the grounds that he will fall and be replaced by a "rightist" leader if the VC/NVA stay in Cambodia.

The motivations of the principal actors in Phnom Penh were obscure to our analysts, not least because Lon Nol had been among those profiting from the smuggling trade with the very Communist forces that his government was now challenging. On March 19, in another memorandum to the President, I still argued that Sihanouk might attempt to return to Phnom Penh and put some of the pieces back together.

> *The Implications for Foreign Policy and for Us.* Khmer nationalism has [been] aroused against the Vietnamese Communist occupation. Any future government will probably have to be more circumspect and covert about its cooperation with the Vietnamese. Lon Nol has chosen this issue, and he will need to be able to demonstrate publicly that he is taking action against the Vietnamese occupation. Similarly, Sihanouk will not for some time open himself to the charge of being "soft on the Vietnamese."

None of my reports to the President discussed any U.S. intelligence involvement or expressed any particular pleasure at the coup. Nor was CIA reporting more prescient, doubtless in part because the Agency had been banned from Phnom Penh. It was not until March 18—the day of Sihanouk's ouster—that a CIA report was circulated in Washington. Its burden: that the Lon Nol–encouraged riots were a precursor to a coup against Sihanouk if Sihanouk refused to go along with an anti-Hanoi policy. The information had been acquired the week before from an Asian businessman not otherwise identified. The delay in distributing this report and the CIA's failure to predict the overthrow of Sihanouk were later the subject of an investigation by the President's Foreign Intelligence Advisory Board. I do not recall any document predicting the coup that came to my attention before the event, and I have not unearthed one in my papers. Of charges of intelligence failure, it should be remembered that Sihanouk had a far greater incentive to know the truth in his country, and he failed to anticipate the plot.

On March 20, Nixon and I discussed a forthcoming press conference by him. I recommended that he not comment on Cambodia beyond urging respect for Cambodian neutrality. Nixon agreed, adding that Sihanouk "may come back and take it over again." At the news conference, which took place on March 21, Nixon called the situation in Cambodia "unpredictable" and "fluid" and expressed hope that the North Vietnamese would respect Cambodia's neutrality. He repeated publicly what he had told me privately, that he still expected Sihanouk to return to Phnom Penh.

Our priorities were reflected in a meeting of the WSAG on March 19 called to discuss Laos and Cambodia; most of the discussion concerned Laos. My staff's briefing papers showed as much concern for the *Columbia Eagle,* an American ship impounded by the Cambodians after two sailors mutinied and diverted it to Sihanoukville, as for the long-range implications of the coup. On the political situation the staff paper regarded the outcome as uncertain and still left open the possibility of Sihanouk's return. The briefing paper asked a key question: "Does the presumably more pro-Western orientation of Lon Nol make up for the assumption that Sihanouk's departure may lead to increased instability?"

Until the middle of April our capability to monitor or influence the situation in Cambodia was severely limited. By then, however, the issue was no longer a quarrel between Cambodian factions, the success of either of which would have been compatible with American interests. For Sihanouk made a second fateful decision. Ensconced in Beijing (with which we had no contact of any kind at that stage), Sihanouk threw in his lot with Hanoi and turned violently against the United States. His vanity did not permit him to accept that a revolution against his rule might have Cambodian roots. Or else he concluded that he would regain power only with Communist help. Whatever his motive, on March 20—two days after he was deposed—he declared war on the Lon Nol government. He issued a statement calling for a national referendum and denouncing his removal as "absolutely illegal." He blamed the "turbulence" in Cambodia on CIA collusion with the "traitorous group" that had deposed him; he defended the North Vietnamese in Cambodia on the ground that they were "resisting American imperialism." The next day, Sihanouk vowed a struggle "until victory or death" against the new government, which he denounced as "stooges of American imperialists." Henceforth, Sihanouk's return would have meant not a restoration of neutralism but the victory of his new Communist patrons, whom he had lost all capacity to control.

In retaliation, the Cambodian National Assembly on March 21 voted to arrest Sihanouk and to charge him with treason if he returned. Newspapers and broadcasts in Phnom Penh were filled with lurid accounts of his personal life and attacks on his years of leadership. On March 22, after three days of avoiding direct comment on Cambodian events, North Vietnam labeled Cambodia's new leaders a "pro-American ultra-rightist group." The authoritative Hanoi party newspaper, *Nhan Dan,* claimed that Sihanouk's ouster had been engineered by the United States and affirmed that "our people fully support the struggle of the Cambodian people" against the new leadership. On March 23, Sihanouk in a five-point statement promised formation of a "liberation army" and "national united front," lauding the anti-U.S. struggle of the Communist Vietnamese, Laotians, and Cambodians.

In early April the North Vietnamese and Vietcong forces began making good their pledge of "support." Communist forces left their base areas and started penetrating deep into Cambodia to overthrow the new government. By April 3, the North Vietnamese began attacking Cambodian forces in Svay Rieng province. By April 10, Cambodian troops were forced to evacuate border positions in the Parrot's Beak area. Communists started to harass Mekong River traffic. By April 16, the North Vietnamese and Vietcong troops launched raids on the capital of Takeo province, south of Phnom Penh.

On April 2, Sihanouk denounced the United States as "the principal and sole culprit responsible for the war and political instability in the three countries of Indochina." On April 3, he appealed to his compatriots to take to the jungles and join the "resistance zones already there." On April 4, Premier Zhou Enlai, while on a visit to North Korea, formally endorsed Sihanouk's resistance movement. On April 14, Radio Beijing reported the formal establishment on April 6 of the provisional committee of Sihanouk's "national united front" in Cambodia's Svay Rieng province. In short, by the middle of April, *before* we had undertaken any significant action, Sihanouk had irrevocably joined forces with the Communists, the Communists had dedicated themselves to the overthrow of the Phnom Penh government, and North Vietnamese units were attacking deep inside Cambodia.

Le Duc Tho's behavior in the secret talks removed any doubt that Hanoi had formally linked Cambodia to its war in Vietnam. He emphasized Hanoi's intention to overthrow the Phnom Penh government, to replace it with personnel acceptable to Hanoi, and to use Cambodia as a base for operations in Vietnam. At the secret meeting of March 16—two days before Sihanouk was deposed—Le Duc Tho accused us of having organized the riots in Phnom Penh five days earlier, a charge I vigorously denied.

Fears about Hanoi's overall intentions were reinforced by a sudden military "high point" in South Vietnam, which broke the lull that had lasted since September. On March 31, while negotiations with Le Duc Tho were still going on and in the face of our offer of de-escalation, the North Vietnamese launched scores of attacks throughout South Vietnam. American dead for the week were 138, nearly double the previous week's total.

This set the stage for our climactic secret Paris negotiating meeting of April 4. Le Duc Tho blamed us once again for the upheaval in Cambodia and effectively declared war on the new Cambodian government:

> You thought you could use a group of military reactionaries to overthrow Norodom Sihanouk and it would be all over. It is too simple thinking. It is precisely your actions there which make the whole people of Cambodia fight against the agents of the U.S. They have responded to the appeal of Prince Sihanouk and the National Front of Cambodia. The Khmer people have stood up with all their strength to defend freedom and neutrality.

I rebutted his charges emphatically but futilely:

> I despair of convincing the Special Adviser that we had nothing to do with what happened in Phnom Penh, although I am flattered of the high opinion he has of our intelligence services. If they knew I was here, I would tell them of this high opinion.
>
> Again, there is a simple test. Who has troops in Cambodia? Not the U.S. I am impressed again with the linguistic ability of the people of the Indochinese peninsula. We discovered that the Pathet Lao speaks Vietnamese, and now we find the same phenomenon in Cambodia.
>
> We have shown great restraint vis-à-vis the bases you maintain in Cambodia and which you use in attacking our forces in Vietnam.

I insisted that the United States sought no expansion of the war. To achieve this goal I proposed to discuss *immediately* specific steps to assure the neutrality of Cambodia:

We are prepared to discuss immediately concrete and specific measures to guarantee the neutrality of Cambodia and to make absolutely certain it does not become a pawn in any international conflict. We are willing to do this bilaterally with you or in an international framework. . . . We shall be prepared to entertain reasonable propositions to guarantee that Laos and Cambodia—especially Cambodia, as it is a new problem—remain neutral.

But Le Duc Tho dismissed any suggestion of neutralization or of an international conference. The conflicts in Indochina had now become one, he asserted; he would not even discuss confining the war to Vietnam. Cambodia had become a theater of operations and Hanoi would brook no discussion about maintaining its neutrality. Over three weeks *before* our incursions into the sanctuaries, Le Duc Tho said:

The three peoples of Indochina—the Vietnamese, Lao and Khmer people—have had traditional unity in the fight against colonialism. This cannot be broken by you. Now, faced with the extension of the war to Cambodia by the U.S., the three peoples will continue to fight to have victory, no matter how great the sacrifices may be.

According to Le Duc Tho, there could be no formal agreement on the neutralization of Cambodia. Instead, the regime that had seized power in Phnom Penh had to be overthrown: "We do not recognize the Lon Nol–Matak government. We support the Five Points of Norodom Sihanouk. We are convinced that so long as the Lon Nol–Matak government remains in Cambodia, then the Cambodian question cannot be settled."

In Cambodia, as in Vietnam, Hanoi had insisted on the overthrow of the established government (which most nations, including the Soviet Union, continued to recognize). A spokesman for United Nations Secretary-General U Thant declared on April 6 that the United Nations would "deal with the authorities which effectively have control of the situation in Cambodia," in effect recognizing the Lon Nol government.

The first official Cambodian request for U.S. military assistance came as we gradually and reluctantly perceived the impossibility of Cambodia's neutrality, owing to Hanoi's insistence on Communist domination of *all* of

Cambodia. On the evening of April 9, Commandant Lon Non, Lon Nol's younger brother and commander of the Phnom Penh gendarmerie, requested a meeting with an embassy official. Lon Non spoke of the expansion of the Cambodian army from 35,000 to more than 60,000 men; there was an immediate need for 100,000 to 150,000 weapons, and ultimately for 200,000 to 250,000, including ammunition.

The U.S. chargé, Lloyd Rives, considered these quantities exaggerated and the need impossible to assess, since no breakdown was given as to types desired. To Washington, Rives recommended "serious consideration of supplying weapons through a third party or parties, if such can be found." Lon Non's request was considered at first in intelligence channels because we still were eager to avoid direct intervention. Delivering arms clandestinely would avoid giving Hanoi a pretext for an all-out assault, and it also placed an inherent limit on the amount we could supply. The consensus was that American military forces and American arms should stay out of Cambodia. Our principal interest, it was agreed, was to prevent Cambodia's use as a supply base for Vietnam. We were even prepared to accept a degree of accommodation between Lon Nol and the Vietcong if this proved essential to the survival of the Cambodian government. To limit our involvement, we sought to arrange military assistance through third parties as Rives had recommended; to approach France to encourage more French assistance to Cambodia; to explore other possible intermediaries; and to have the Defense Department ascertain what captured *Communist* arms and ammunition were available in South Vietnam for transfer to the (hitherto Communist-equipped) Cambodian army. No American military assistance was authorized.

The Communists were not showing similar restraint. On April 13, a Cambodian military outpost in Kampot province near the South Vietnamese border was overrun. On April 13 and 14, several Cambodian military positions in Takeo province south of Phnom Penh were captured. The Cambodian government reported on April 14 an attack by "several hundred" Vietcong on Koh Rocar, Prey Veng province, about twenty-five miles to the northeast of Phnom Penh. On April 15, a Cambodian post at Sre Khtum in Mondolkiri province fell to the North Vietnamese, leaving the town of O Rang, farther east on Route 131, cut off. Also on April 15, a military outpost at Krek in Kompong Cham province was taken by the Communists, denying Cambodians access to the provincial capital of Mimot, astride Route 7. On April 16, the provincial capital of Takeo was attacked by Vietnamese Com-

munist forces, who were repulsed. But on April 16, they overran the town of
Tuk Meas in Kampot province. The same day a small enemy force attacked
an outpost north of Kratie and also the town of Chhlong south of the provincial capital (see the map on page 139). Hanoi's strategy clearly was to cut off
Phnom Penh from the provinces and to bring about the collapse of Lon Nol.

In a broadcast on April 14, Lon Nol responded that "because of the gravity of the situation, it is deemed necessary to accept from this moment on all
unconditional foreign aid from all sources." He accused the Communists of
mounting "an escalation of systematic acts of aggression." When I brought
this to the President's attention, Nixon said he was determined not to let the
new Cambodian government collapse under Communist pressure. I called a
meeting of the WSAG for April 14. The WSAG's composition was essentially the same as the earlier intelligence forum, but more staff personnel were
permitted to attend and its documents were handled in formal channels. The
shift from intelligence channels reflected that a major policy decision was
likely to be required in the near future.

The participants had not changed their reluctance to see America involve
itself. I asked the WSAG to recommend a level and type of military aid that
would provide psychological reassurance to Lon Nol without furnishing a
pretext for an even stronger offensive by Hanoi. The consensus was to send
up to 3,000 captured Communist AK-47 rifles from South Vietnamese
stocks and, to maintain our dissociation, to have them delivered through
South Vietnamese channels. Everyone, including myself, agreed that it was
"premature" to provide American M-1 rifles. For that reason, I reported to
the WSAG that the President was not yet prepared to approve the delivery of
1,000-man packs of American equipment (CIA packages of hand weapons
that were occasionally supplied to friendly forces on a covert basis). There
was no discussion of heavier equipment. The State Department was reluctant
to deliver even medical supplies overtly; it was finally agreed that the choice
of the mode of delivery should be left to the Cambodians. In short, three
weeks after the North Vietnamese had left their sanctuaries and were seeking
to isolate Phnom Penh, the United States made available exactly 3,000 captured Soviet rifles delivered clandestinely. We gave no other aid.

The next day the Cambodian government submitted a request for military and economic assistance to expand their army to 200,000 men. This request clearly went beyond the framework of existing policy; it also far
exceeded what in our judgment Cambodia could absorb. Another WSAG

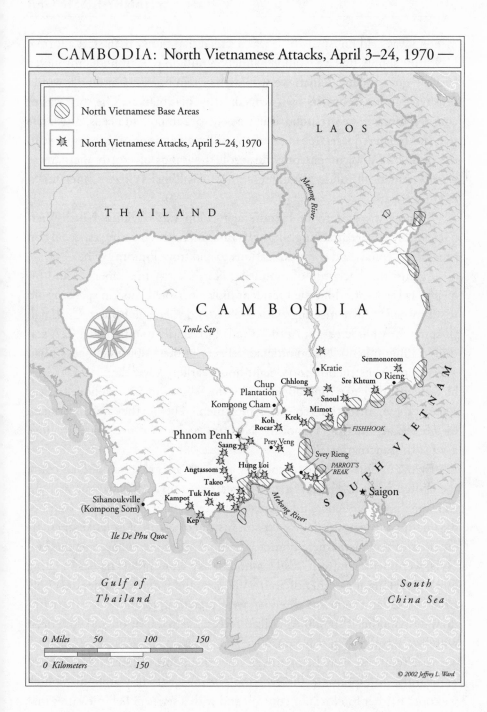

— CAMBODIA: North Vietnamese Attacks, April 3–24, 1970 —

North Vietnamese Base Areas

North Vietnamese Attacks, April 3–24, 1970

LAOS

THAILAND

Mekong River

CAMBODIA

Tonle Sap

Kratie

Senmonorom

O Rieng

Chup
Plantation

Chhlong

Sre Khtum

Kompong Cham

Snoul

Mimot

Koh
Rocar

Krek

FISHHOOK

Phnom Penh

Saang

Prey Veng

Svey Rieng

PARROT'S
BEAK

Hung Loi

Angtassom

Takeo

Tuk Meas

Sihanoukville
(Kompong Som)

Kampot

SOUTH VIETNAM

Saigon

Kep

Ile De Phu Quoc

Mekong River

*Gulf of
Thailand*

*South
China Sea*

0 Miles   50   100   150

0 Kilometers   150

© 2002 Jeffrey L. Ward

meeting was held on April 15. It was decided that rather than start a formal U.S. arms supply line we would channel $5 million to Cambodia through a friendly government (which we would then reimburse); Cambodia would thus have funds to buy its own arms on the open market. The sum was of course symbolic; it corresponded in no way to Cambodian needs, much less to Cambodian requests. It can hardly be called a heroic or urgent response to the pleas of a government on whose soil thousands of North Vietnamese were systematically undermining its authority, killing its citizens, and annexing its territory.

By now the pattern of Hanoi's aggression was obvious. North Vietnamese forces were attacking all over Cambodia, concentrating especially on provincial capitals and communications to and from Phnom Penh.

Against this backdrop of mounting North Vietnamese menace and his own growing frustration, the President took a personal hand in speeding aid to Cambodia. At a meeting with Helms and General Robert Cushman (Deputy CIA Director) on April 16 called primarily to establish a CIA station in Phnom Penh, Nixon ordered delivery of the 1,000-man packs I had rejected at his instruction forty-eight hours earlier. A few days later he doubled the contingency fund approved by the WSAG to $10 million. In fact, none of these instructions could be implemented before they were overtaken by more escalation from Hanoi and Nixon's decision two weeks later to move against the sanctuaries.

By the middle of April, then, over a month after the Cambodian coup, the United States had barely lifted a finger. The coup itself had come without warning; its consequences threatened not only the independence of Cambodia but our entire position in Vietnam. Instead of a strip of isolated sanctuaries close to the Vietnamese border we would, after the collapse of the Lon Nol government, confront *all* of Cambodia as a Communist base, stretching 600 miles along the border of South Vietnam and with short lines of supply from the sea at a moment when we were preparing to announce the withdrawal of another 150,000 American forces. Vietnamization and American withdrawal could then come unstuck.

As a result, we were being driven toward support of Lon Nol hesitantly, reluctantly, in response to the evolving circumstances in Cambodia, which we could neither forecast nor control, and with a series of half measures that always lagged behind the rapidly deteriorating situation. Of all the parties that made crucial decisions in that period—Hanoi, Lon Nol, Sihanouk, and the United States—the United States had the least freedom of choice. The record leaves no doubt that the North Vietnamese, also caught by surprise by the March coup, bear the heaviest responsibility for events in Cambodia. Their illegal occupation of Cambodian territory had torn apart the fragile unity of Sihanouk's neutralist country; they had created the Khmer Rouge as a force against Sihanouk well before his overthrow; they then used him to give credibility to that at first tiny band when he went into exile. On April 4, Le Duc Tho had rejected discussion not only of a cease-fire anywhere in Indochina, but of any scheme for the neutrality of Cambodia. It was the North Vietnamese, not America, who had decided on a fight to the finish on the bleeding body of a small neutralist kingdom which wanted only to be left alone.

But before the die was finally cast there was a brief interlude, during which to maintain America's position in Vietnam we felt obliged to take another unilateral step toward weakening it. In the midst of the escalating war in Cambodia, Nixon felt obliged to undertake another troop withdrawal.

Another Major Troop Withdrawal

On the surface, the issue was straightforward. The most recent withdrawal (announced December 15, 1969) had been 50,000 over a four-month period ending on April 15, 1970. With 115,000 troops already out, it was clear that the next increment would begin to cut sharply into our combat strength. The dilemma was obvious. Troop cuts poulticed public anguish at home, but they were destroying Hanoi's need to bargain about our disengagement. And if Vietnamization was not making good the defensive gaps created by our withdrawals, we hazarded South Vietnam's independence and the entire basis of our sacrifices.

Secretary Laird, the Cabinet member most directly involved in the withdrawal strategy, was the most politically astute of the President's senior advisers. He understood the public's ambivalence, shown by every poll. It opposed unilateral withdrawal, yet it wanted the war ended, and saw the reduction of our troop strength as a sign of progress. Laird aspired to stay in tune with this mood. He was prepared to give Vietnamization a real chance; for a long time he favored a residual U.S. force of several hundred thousand. But he wanted to reduce to that residual force rapidly, and to maintain public confidence he thought it important to make our withdrawal look as inexorable as possible. He also saw Vietnam as an obstacle to his plans to modernize America's armed forces; congressional pressures to cut his defense budget could be reduced, he thought, if he was identified with troop pullouts. He sought to guarantee his preferred course by gearing the withdrawal rate to the defense budget in such a way that any slowdown of withdrawals was bound to reduce procurement—thus enlisting the support of the services for rapid withdrawal by threatening their cherished new projects.

I had been the most wary of the President's senior advisers; it is difficult to conduct a strong policy while dismantling the means to implement it. The seemingly inexorable troop withdrawals were progressively reducing our diplomatic options. Had we been prepared to engineer Saigon's disintegration, we could have adopted any of the many proposals for setting a deadline for American withdrawal that had become staples of the public and congressional debate. But if we meant what we said about the global consequence of an American collapse, we had to give the South Vietnamese time to replace American forces without a catastrophe. And if we wanted to husband negotiating assets, our withdrawal strategy had to provide the President some discretion to accelerate it or slow it down in response to enemy actions. We were in danger, I thought, of adopting a withdrawal program too slow to satisfy our critics but too drastic to sustain military or political effectiveness. Nixon agreed with this as a concept but felt constrained by congressional and public pressures from acting on it.

These differences of perspective, some of nuance, some of substance, were given added sharpness because each chief actor strove for some of the credit for the withdrawal program; nobody volunteered to shoulder the blame for defeats it might produce. Memoranda proliferated, to be available for later reference; the authors assumed that history would deal kindly with those advocating large withdrawals—but history is more likely to judge outcomes than expedients. The President, eager to garner whatever favorable publicity could be made to come his way, warily kept his own counsel. He feared that if he were more confiding, his associates would leak higher withdrawal numbers than he was prepared to authorize and so place him at a disadvantage in the public eye.

This was a game in which Laird was not easily bested. He was a patriot whose every instinct was for his country to emerge from the war with honor;

he was also a politician to the core. He was perfectly prepared to support a strong policy so long as he was not identified as its principal author. In crises he was redoubtable. In the run-up to them he produced a blizzard of memoranda that would make it next to impossible to determine either his real intentions or—what was more important to him—his precise recommendation.

On March 11, I sought General Wheeler's views on the relative merits of one more four-month withdrawal increment (the largest period then being considered) or two withdrawals over two months each. Wheeler replied on March 20 in an unsigned memorandum, which he passed to the President through Haig, thus avoiding the inconvenience of Defense Department channels and the certainty of Laird's wrath. Wheeler recommended a "one-bite approach," because the longer period provided greater flexibility by making it possible to retain key units until the end of the period. However, Wheeler added that he preferred "no further redeployment" at all because of the uncertain "overall situation." He strongly urged holding the next withdrawal decision in abeyance for ninety days.

Laird entered the fray on April 4 with a long memorandum, the thrust of which was to remind everyone that our effort in Vietnam was "large and costly." He recommended a fixed monthly rate of withdrawal and a reduction in B-52 and tactical air operations in proportion to our withdrawals. Laird's military proposals all assumed that the enemy threat would decline in parallel with our withdrawals. The opposite was by far more probable.

Throughout the war there were many exhortations, from within and outside the government, to eschew a military solution and to seek a diplomatic one. But the raw truth was that this distinction not only was unacceptable to Hanoi; it was incomprehensible to it. There was no purely diplomatic alternative. Unless military and political efforts were kept in tandem, both would prove sterile. The attempt to postpone collapse at home might well make it inevitable in Indochina.

By April 8, General Abrams's assessment reached the White House. (It had actually been sent nearly three weeks earlier, but because its recommendations did not find favor, it had been held up in the Pentagon for "staffing.") It supported Wheeler's recommendation of a ninety-day moratorium on withdrawals. And it seriously challenged Laird's proposed reduction in tactical air operations and B-52 sorties. Abrams stressed that our withdrawals forced him to use the South Vietnamese forces in a static defense role. The

B-52s thus became his sole strategic reserve. On April 15, I sent the President a memorandum arguing that since Vietnamization gains were "fragile" and allied forces were "stretched nearly to the limit of their capabilities," the sharp cutbacks in air operations implied by the defense budget had disturbing implications. I recommended that the President order a study of what air operations were required to support Vietnamization. Such an order was issued on April 17. It put an end to reductions during the immediate crisis, but the cutbacks in air operations were resumed—almost imperceptibly—in the fall, forcing us to send substantial reinforcements when an all-out enemy offensive broke in 1972.

Abrams's and Wheeler's pleas to maintain troop levels, especially in the light of North Vietnamese offensives in Laos and Cambodia, had much merit. But so did the President's concern that to stop withdrawals for ninety days would trigger the same public protests as had occurred the previous summer and make the eventual resumption of withdrawals appear as a defeat. A primary flaw lay in the apparently immutable timetable. An announcement was expected every few months, always triggering a debate within the executive branch as well as in public and giving added confidence to Hanoi. These self-inflicted deadlines were sapping America's endurance and raising doubts about American purposes.

For these reasons, I proposed that Nixon announce a large withdrawal and stretch it over one year. After consultation with General Wheeler, I recommended a total reduction of 150,000 men. This represented a slight increase in the monthly rate of withdrawal; but to compensate for this I proposed that only a very small withdrawal take place over the next ninety days, with the bulk of withdrawals planned for 1971. Nixon understood the strategic discretion this gave him and the favorable public impact. But he was also convinced that if he revealed his intentions to his associates he would rapidly be embroiled in controversy on at least three fronts: They would seek to transform his plan into a fixed monthly rate; they would urge that the rate be increased; and there was in the end the near certainty of a leak arranged in such a way as to create the impression that others had recommended an even larger figure.

The result was a complicated bureaucratic poker game wherein Nixon moved toward a foreordained decision while playing his cards close to his chest.

On April 17, Nixon went to Hawaii to greet the returning *Apollo 13* astronauts. In order to keep an eye on Cambodia as well as the maneuvering over withdrawals, I did not accompany him. Admiral John McCain, our commander in the Pacific, briefed Nixon at length in Honolulu. This doughty, crusty officer could have passed in demeanor, appearance, pugnacity, and manner of speech for Popeye the Sailor Man. His son and namesake, later a United States senator and presidential candidate—and a treasured personal friend—had been a prisoner of war in Hanoi for years; this tragedy left the father undaunted. He fought for the victory that his instinct and upbringing demanded and that political reality forbade. McCain brought home to Nixon the danger in Laos and Cambodia; he reinforced Nixon's conviction that the withdrawal schedule had to be flexible.

Nixon and I rejoined forces in San Clemente on the evening of April 19. Separated from his Cabinet by 3,000 miles, Nixon announced to the press that he would make a speech the next evening on redeployment from Vietnam but declined to give any indication of its content. We were besieged with calls from Washington, especially from Laird. Nixon refused to take them.

Late that afternoon of April 20 in San Clemente—too late for leaks to the evening newscasts—I called Laird and Rogers with the President's decision: a withdrawal of 150,000 by the end of spring of 1971, with 60,000 to be withdrawn in 1970 and the remaining 90,000 in 1971. During 1970, the greater portion of the 1970 withdrawals would take place after August 1. Nixon made his surprise announcement on April 20. It was one of the tours de force by which he sustained our effort in Vietnam but also deprived it of symbolic quality. It met the political need for a withdrawal schedule and the military necessity to retain the largest possible number of troops during the next three critical months while Hanoi's forces were assaulting Cambodia and pressing forward in Laos. Whatever the bureaucratic maneuvers or the monthly fluctuations in the withdrawal rate, the fact remained that we had within one year projected a total reduction of 265,500 below the troop ceiling of 549,500 the Nixon administration had inherited.

Rogers supported the President's decision, regretting only that by forgoing more frequent announcements, the President deprived himself of periodic respites from public pressures. Laird wanted the withdrawals spaced more evenly; he insisted on an appointment with Nixon. I arranged it for the next day in Washington. Nixon flew back to Washington immediately after his announcement. When they met on April 21, Nixon explained to

Laird that "we must play a tough game" for the next two or three months and therefore had to postpone actual withdrawals. Laird demurred: "I want you to know you have a fiscal problem. You know that, don't you?" (a favorite Laird phrase, used whether or not one had any way of knowing what he had just communicated—especially when one had not). The President assured him he did know. Laird told the President that he had to take out 60,000 men by the time of the November congressional election or "you might just as well forget about the election." Nixon replied that he would be judged not by how many men left Vietnam in a given period but by how we left Vietnam in the end. Nixon said he would "think about" Laird's warning, meaning he would confirm his decision either through Haldeman or by memorandum, which he did the next day.

> Memorandum for the Secretary of Defense:
>   Following our discussion yesterday afternoon, I want to reiterate my decision that no more than 60,000 troops are to be redeployed this year. A plan to this effect should be submitted to me by May 1.
>   Until I have reviewed the plan, no further withdrawals should be scheduled.

Laird accepted the decision with apparent good grace. But he knew his chief well enough to return to the fray at a more propitious moment. In August he persuaded the President that he could dramatize the success of the military operation against the Cambodian sanctuary best by withdrawing 90,000 by the end of 1970 and 60,000 in 1971—the exact opposite of the President's original intention. Laird got his way. Nixon acquiesced, in part because he hated constant controversy, in part because congressional elections were imminent.

I have discussed the troop withdrawal at some length because of the insight it gives regarding the dilemmas of extricating America from a war it inherited whipsawed between an irreconcilable domestic opposition, a divided administration, an implacable Hanoi, and the Nixon administration's style of government.

The dilemmas of our Vietnam policy were reflected in the gulf between the perception of reality of the policymakers and the nature of the public debate. Our reality consisted of enemy offensives in Laos and Cambodia that threatened the American military position in South Vietnam and the possibility of an honorable extrication. Yet as the objective threats grew, a program of unilateral withdrawal was imposed by the near civil war conditions of the domestic protest. The public debate focused on the danger that we might slide into a new "commitment" in two other faraway countries. Our reality was that only by preventing a collapse of these countries could we strengthen the South Vietnamese sufficiently to take up the slack of withdrawal without turning it into a rout. The public debate challenged all military calculations on the assumption that military effort was futile and was either unrelated to or inconsistent with our diplomatic prospects. (This would have been news to North Vietnam's Defense Minister General Vo Nguyen Giap.) We had seen enough of Le Duc Tho to know that without a plausible military strategy we could not have an effective diplomacy.

As for Nixon's style of government, he was prepared to make decisions without illusion. Once convinced, he went ruthlessly and courageously to the heart of the matter; but each controversial decision drove him deeper into his all-enveloping solitude. He was almost physically unable to confront people who disagreed with him; and he shunned persuading or inspiring his subordinates. He would decide from inside his self-imposed cocoon, but he was unwilling to communicate with those who disagreed. It was the paradox of a President strong in his decisions but inconclusive in his leadership.

The Attack on North Vietnamese Sanctuaries

The first two weeks of April saw a wave of Communist attacks on Cambodian towns and communications. These soon escalated. On April 17, several Cambodian government posts near the provincial capital of Senmonorom were captured by the North Vietnamese. On the same day, a Cambodian military spokesman announced that the enemy had more than doubled its area of control in the preceding two weeks. On April 18, a Cambodian army battalion was badly mauled on the west bank of the Mekong twenty-five miles south of Phnom Penh. Farther south on the Mekong, a Cambodian army headquarters at Hung Loi was besieged for a week. On April 20, enemy forces unsuccessfully attacked Snuol in Kratie province. In Kandal province, Communist forces temporarily captured the town of Saang, some twenty miles south of Phnom Penh. On Tuesday, April 21, the day after the President's troop withdrawal announcement, Communist forces struck the town of Takeo and cut the road between it and Phnom Penh.

General William Westmoreland, Acting Chairman of the Joint Chiefs in General Wheeler's absence, reported that the Cambodian armed forces were only "marginally effective" against the superior North Vietnamese and Vietcong. He wrote: "The enemy objective may well be to isolate the city of Phnom Penh, bring military pressure to bear on it from all sides, and perhaps, ultimately, to bring Sihanouk back to regain political control at the appropriate time."

If these steps were unopposed, the Communist sanctuaries, hitherto limited to narrow unpopulated areas close to the Vietnamese border, would be organized into a single large base area of a depth and with a logistics system which would enable rapid transfer of units and supplies. I told a group of Republican senators on April 21 that we would have preferred the old Sihanouk government. But Sihanouk's pronouncements left little doubt that this option was no longer open. If Lon Nol fell, the Sihanouk who returned would not, as heretofore, balance contending forces to achieve neutrality but lead a Communist government. His necessities (as well as his outraged vanity) would force him to purge the moderate groups on which his freedom of maneuver between contending factions had previously depended; he would be reduced to a figurehead. Sihanoukville would reopen to Communist supplies. Security throughout the southern half of South Vietnam would deteriorate drastically.

By April 21, the basic issue had been laid bare; it was whether Vietnamization was to be merely an alibi for an American collapse or a serious strategy designed to achieve an honorable peace. If the former, neither the rate of withdrawal nor events in neighboring countries were important; in fact, anything that hastened the collapse of South Vietnam was a blessing in disguise. Some of the opposition, like Senator George McGovern, took this position. Though I considered it against the national interest, it was rational and honest. My intellectual difficulties arose with those who pretended that there was a middle course of action that would avoid collapse in Vietnam and yet ignore the impending Communist takeover in Cambodia.

Hanoi's unopposed conquest of Cambodia would likely have been the last straw for South Vietnam. In the midst of a war, its chief ally was withdrawing forces at an accelerating rate and reducing its air support. Saigon was being asked to take the strain at the very moment Hanoi was massively increasing reinforcements even over the level of the preceding year, which had seen a significant offensive. If Cambodia were to become a single armed camp, catastrophe was inevitable in South Vietnam. Saigon needed time to consolidate and improve its forces; the United States had to pose a credible threat for as long as possible; and Hanoi's offensive potential had to be weakened by slowing down its infiltration and destroying its supplies. It was a race between Vietnamization, American withdrawal, and Hanoi's offensives.

There had been no consideration of attacking the sanctuaries before April 21. The final decision was taken on April 28. It is important therefore to review the decision-making process in some detail.

No doubt Admiral McCain's briefing of Nixon on April 18 gave focus to the President's hitherto inchoate anxieties about Cambodia. He was sufficiently concerned to ask McCain to come to San Clemente and give me the same briefing on April 20. On the trip to San Clemente to rendezvous with him I had come to the same conclusion. I did not see how we could stand by and watch Cambodia collapse without thereby risking at the same time the collapse of all America had done in Vietnam. Nixon's insistence and McCain's briefing preempted a recommendation by me to the same effect.

On returning to Washington, Nixon's first step was to schedule a meeting with Helms and me for 7:00 A.M. on April 21. Helms's briefing showed that the North Vietnamese were attacking all over Cambodia and that Phnom Penh could not long withstand this assault. In discussing the status of our negligible response, Nixon discovered that the $5 million for arms for Cambodia approved by the WSAG on April 15 and doubled by him shortly thereafter was still being held up by bureaucratic foot-dragging. Nor had the communications equipment for the CIA, which he had ordered on April 1 and insisted upon on April 16, been delivered. Nixon was beside himself. He ordered an immediate transfer of the money. He called an NSC meeting for the next day to determine overall strategy.

In preparation, I asked General Westmoreland about the feasibility of military operations by South Vietnamese forces into the sanctuaries. Westmoreland thought they could be effective, but not decisive without American support. I also sent a back-channel message to Ellsworth Bunker, asking for his and Abrams's "candid judgment" of the military, political, and psychological consequences of Sihanouk's return or of a Communist victory in Cambodia. I also requested their suggestions of possible countermeasures.

Since February, the South Vietnamese had been urging occasional shallow cross-border operations—to a distance of about three miles—into the sanctuaries with American logistical support. A company or less in size, these were designed to discover caches of weapons. General Haig had reported after his January tour of South Vietnam that there were enemy supply caches a few miles over the Cambodian border that could not be safely targeted by B-52s because they were too near populated areas. Laird had authorized General Abrams to give logistical support to South Vietnamese forces for shallow penetrations when he visited Vietnam in February. A cross-border operation by South Vietnamese forces had taken place on March 27. It was reported by the press. A second operation took place the next day and was also reported. White House Press Secretary Ron Ziegler had declared on March 28 that American field commanders were now authorized to cross the Cambodian border in response to threats to American forces.

Upon learning of the first cross-border operation, I requested a temporary halt to them until we could reach a considered and coordinated judgment in light of the new situation and to avoid giving Hanoi a pretext for expanding the war. I did not want policy determined by the tactical decisions of field commanders. After issuing these instructions, I went on a long-scheduled vacation for a week—another indication that I thought no crisis was imminent. Haig therefore sent the implementing cable to Bunker on March 27:

> If these operations continue we will be subject to accusation that South Vietnamese Government is drawing US into expanded war.
>
> While recognizing that you are not a free agent in this respect, Mr. Kissinger hopes that you can encourage Thieu to refrain from these operations except in situations where current US rules of engagement would apply. Mr. Kissinger wants you to be aware that while President is understanding of South Vietnamese motives, he is concerned that short term military benefits of cross-border operations might be outweighed by the risks posed to our efforts to maintain our current levels of domestic support for our overall Vietnam policy.

On March 30, as instructed, Bunker met with Thieu and explained why cross-border operations should be held in abeyance. Thieu accepted the recommendation. On March 31, the *New York Times* warned that the Cambodian government's willingness to permit allied cross-border raids against Communist sanctuaries might draw the United States deeper into the war. The Cambodian government thereupon, on March 31, "faithful to its policy of strict neutrality," formally denied that the United States and South Vietnam were authorized to conduct such raids.

That same day, while I was on vacation, Laird called on the President to protest the suspension of cross-border operations. I had instructed Haig by telephone to try to delay a response until after my return and in any case not to authorize further cross-border operations before my meeting with Le Duc Tho scheduled for April 4. Nixon overruled my recommendations. He ordered Haig to instruct Bunker by back channel to reinstate cross-border operations, provided they were kept to the level of those carried out prior to the moratorium and were coordinated with the Cambodian armed forces. As far as I can determine now, four shallow cross-border operations took place during the first three weeks of April—all after my meeting on April 4 with Le Duc Tho, none lasting more than a day.

In the last two weeks of April, Communist forces stepped up assaults on Cambodian towns. On April 22, the border town of Snuol was attacked. The Cambodian government made a new appeal to the United Nations for help in fighting the invaders. It was ignored, as had been all others, though it would have been difficult to find a more flagrant case of aggression. In Washington, April 22 was the occasion of a major NSC meeting on Cambodia; it also saw a stream of messages from the President to me that reflected his mounting concerns.

In the first message, dictated at 5:00 A.M., Nixon stressed the need for a "bold move" in Cambodia, and expressed determination to "do something symbolic to help [Lon Nol] survive" even though he feared Lon Nol would not be able to do so. He thought we had "dropped the ball" by worrying that American help would destroy Lon Nol's neutrality and give the North Vietnamese an excuse to come in; the Communists never waited for an "excuse," as demonstrated in Hungary in 1956, Czechoslovakia in 1968, in Laos, and now in Cambodia. The President suggested sending a senior emissary to reassure Lon Nol. "In the event that I decide to go on this course," Nixon wanted me to stress with "some of the lily-livered Ambassadors from our so-called friends in the world" that their posture on this issue would show us "who our friends are."

A second missive in the day reiterated the same theme—that I should call in the Japanese, French, British, and other friendly ambassadors and stress that we counted on our allies to back us. A third memorandum commented on a recent letter from Sihanouk to Senator Mansfield. Sihanouk had compared the Lon Nol regime with Hitler and said that "the most severe ideology—as long as it is based on social justice—is infinitely preferable to a regime composed of greatly corrupted people and anti-popular reactionaries." Sihanouk said he was determined to liberate his country, even "at the price of an ideological change in Cambodia." Nixon suggested that Sihanouk "parrots the Communist line in every respect," and asked me to pass the letter to Rogers and Helms. A fourth message asked me to call in the Soviet chargé and warn him that the President had made a "command decision" to react if the Communists moved on Phnom Penh.

The pace of events gave me no opportunity to carry out these instructions. In a meeting with the President later in the morning of April 22, I advised against sending a senior emissary to Cambodia because it would trigger an enormous debate and would probably be overtaken by the decisions at the NSC. The President said, "Well, whatever, I want to make sure that Cambodia does not go down the drain without doing something." He went on: "Everybody always comes into my office with suggestions on how to lose. No one ever comes in here with a suggestion on how to win." The President ordered a replacement for the chargé, Lloyd Rives, in Phnom Penh and U.S. support for shallow cross-border operations. As with many Nixon orders to fire people, it was intended to show his displeasure; it was not meant to be carried out.

Meanwhile, we had received a long back-channel cable from Bunker and Abrams, which sketched dire consequences if Sihanouk returned to power as a Communist figurehead: Vietcong and North Vietnamese morale would be strengthened; Hanoi's capacity for protracted warfare would be enhanced; there would be shock waves in South Vietnam; Vietnamization would be jeopardized. Bunker and Abrams recommended both an immediate increase in shallow cross-border operations and combined U.S.–South Vietnamese operations against the key Communist sanctuaries.

The NSC meeting was presented with three options: doing nothing (the preferred course of the State and Defense Departments); attacking the sanctuaries with South Vietnamese forces only (my recommendation); and using whatever forces were necessary to neutralize all of the base areas, including

American combat forces, recommended by Bunker, Abrams, and the Joint Chiefs of Staff.

Two base areas were of special concern. The so-called Parrot's Beak, Cambodia's Svay Rieng province, jutted into Vietnam to within only thirty-three miles of Saigon. It had sheltered North Vietnamese armies attacking the Saigon area and the rice-producing delta region during all the years of the Vietnam war. Farther north was a second area, code-named the Fishhook. Our intelligence analysts believed that COSVN, the Communist headquarters for all operations in the South, was located there; it also was the staging area for the 7th North Vietnamese Division, which periodically threatened Saigon and always harassed the adjoining Tay Ninh province of South Vietnam. The Fishhook was well defended; we did not think the South Vietnamese army was strong enough to handle both operations simultaneously. Hence, to recommend that the actions be confined to South Vietnamese forces was tantamount to opting for operations against only one base area.

By the time an issue reaches the NSC it has been analyzed by so many lower-level committees that the Cabinet members perform like actors in a well-rehearsed play; they repeat essentially what their subordinates have already announced in other forums. As usual, there was also an ambivalence between taking positions compatible with their chief's designs and fear of the domestic consequences. There was a sinking feeling about anything that could be presented as escalation in Vietnam. No one around the table questioned the consequences of a Communist takeover of Cambodia. Their disagreements concerned how to strike the best balance between resisting the immediate challenge and maintaining public and congressional support for a long-term strategy. But everybody knew that, whatever the decision, another round of domestic acrimony, protest, and perhaps even violence was probable. If Cambodia collapsed we would be even harder pressed to pull out unilaterally; if we accepted any of the other options we would be charged with "expanding the war."

The initial decision to attack the sanctuaries was taken at a subdued and rather random NSC meeting. Rogers opposed substantial cross-border operations even by South Vietnamese but urged unrestricted bombing of Cambodia after the overthrow of the government in Phnom Penh. Laird had been the strongest advocate of shallow cross-border operations, but he opposed General Abrams's recommendation of destroying the sanctuaries altogether. Helms was in favor of any action to neutralize the sanctuaries. Nixon normally announced his decisions after, not during, an NSC meeting; he would deliberate and then issue instructions in writing or through intermediaries. He did this to emphasize that the NSC was an advisory, not a decision-making, body and to avoid a challenge to his orders. On this occasion Nixon altered his usual procedure. He approved attacks on the base areas by South Vietnamese forces with U.S. support. Since the South Vietnamese could handle only one offensive, Wheeler recommended that they go after Parrot's Beak. This led to a debate about American participation; Laird and Rogers sought to confine it to an absolute minimum, opposing even American advisers or tactical air support.

At this point Vice President Spiro Agnew spoke up. He thought the whole debate irrelevant. Either the sanctuaries were a danger or they were not. If it was worth cleaning them out, he did not understand all the pussyfooting about the American role or what was accomplished by attacking only one base area. Our task was to make Vietnamization succeed. He favored an attack on *both* Fishhook and Parrot's Beak, including American forces.

If Nixon hated anything more than being presented with a plan he had not considered, it was being shown up in a group as less tough than his advisers. Though chafing, he adroitly placed himself between the Vice President and the Cabinet. He authorized American air support for the Parrot's Beak operation but only "on the basis of demonstrated necessity." He avoided committing himself to Fishhook. These decisions were later sent out in writing.

The North Vietnamese, in any event, were free of inhibitions. On Thursday, April 23, North Vietnamese and Vietcong forces attacked the Cambodian towns of Mimot and Angtassom and captured an important bridge on Route 13 linking the town of Snuol and the capital of Kratie province. The Cambodian military headquarters at Hung Loi in Kandal province, under siege for several days, had to be abandoned on April 23 despite South Vietnamese air strikes. Two bridges west of Svay Rieng on Route 1 were captured by the enemy. Beginning on April 23 and continuing on April 24, Communist forces staged hit-and-run raids on the coastal city of Kep.

The Communists escalated politically as well. On April 24, a "Summit Conference of the Indochinese Peoples" was convened at an undisclosed location in the Laos-Vietnam-China frontier area, summoned at Sihanouk's initiative to coordinate strategy among the three insurgent groups. In attendance were Sihanouk, Prince Souvanouvong of the Pathet Lao, Nguyen Huu Tho of the Vietcong, and Pham Van Dong, Premier of North Vietnam. A lengthy Joint Declaration published by Sihanouk on April 27 in Peking pledged "reciprocal support" in the "struggle against the common enemy," that is, "U.S. imperialism." Sihanouk in his closing speech to the conference hailed the birth of "People's Cambodia."

As I reflected on the outcome of the NSC meeting, I was becoming increasingly restless with the decision that was in effect my recommendation: to have the attack on the sanctuaries carried out by Vietnamese forces. Agnew was right; we should either neutralize the principal sanctuaries by whatever means were available or abandon the project. It was hard to imagine how a limited operation into just one sanctuary, in which South Vietnamese forces had at best limited American air support, could make a decisive difference. We were in danger of combining the disadvantages of every course of action. We would be castigated for intervention in Cambodia without accomplishing any strategic purpose.

Before I could present these views to Nixon, there occurred another of those seemingly trivial events that accelerated the process of decision-making. Journalist William Beecher in the *New York Times* reported the contents of a highly classified cable informing our chargé in Phnom Penh that we had decided to provide captured Communist rifles to the Cambodian government. Nixon exploded. Leaks infuriated him in the best of circumstances; this one seemed to him a clear attempt by the bureaucracy to generate congressional and public pressures against any assistance to Cambodia. To make matters worse, at about the same moment Nixon found out that the signal equipment and CIA representative that he had ordered into Phnom Penh on April 1 and again on April 16 had still not been sent.

The internal debate accelerated the conclusions toward which Nixon was moving, in any event: to accept Agnew's advice and to proceed against Fishhook and Parrot's Beak simultaneously, using American forces against Fishhook. He called a meeting on the morning of April 24 with Admiral Moorer, Acting Chairman of the Joint Chiefs, and Helms and Cushman of the CIA. Nixon wanted to discuss the feasibility of a combined U.S.–South Vietnamese operation against Fishhook, in parallel with the Parrot's Beak operation. It was a reflection of his extreme irritation at bureaucratic foot-dragging that he excluded both Rogers and Laird, on the pretext that he merely wanted a military and intelligence briefing. Helms and Moorer were both strongly in favor of an attack on the Fishhook sanctuary. They felt it would force the North Vietnamese to abandon their effort to encircle and terrorize Phnom Penh. The destruction of supplies would gain valuable time for Vietnamization. But Nixon was not prepared to announce a decision yet. Instead, he helicoptered to Camp David to reflect further and to figure out a way to bring along his Cabinet.

Once he was launched on a course, Nixon's determination was equal to his tactical resourcefulness. At Nixon's request, I invited the Chairman of the Senate Armed Services Committee, Senator John Stennis from Mississippi, for a briefing. Stennis belonged to a generation of Senate leaders whose long years of service and accumulated experience embodied concern for the national interest. Many were Southerners, sons of a region that had known its own tragedy. They understood, as most other regions of the country did not, that irrevocable disasters are possible, that mankind is fallible, that human perfection cannot be assumed, that virtue without power is a pose. Courtly, wise, and patriotic, Stennis, like his distinguished colleague Richard Russell, was one of the legislators who made the separation of powers function despite its formal intractability. Presidents could rely on his integrity; Cabinet members could count on his respect for their efforts.

I saw Stennis on the afternoon of April 24 and explained to him that a United States–supported incursion into Cambodia was a military necessity if Vietnamization was to proceed. I showed him a map with the base areas, which were an integral part of the war in Vietnam. In the middle of our conversation Nixon called my office, by prearrangement. In Stennis's hearing I summed up my briefing and reported Stennis's generally favorable reaction. Stennis then took the phone and expressed his support personally to the President.

I urged Nixon to call an NSC meeting to give all parties an opportunity to state their views. As I told Helms, "It is my judgment and strong recommendation that any decision must be discussed with the two Cabinet members [Laird and Rogers]—even if the decision has already been made and an order is in the desk drawer. You can't ram it down their throats without their having a chance to give their views." The meeting was set for Sunday afternoon, April 26.

Its purpose was to enable Nixon to put the fundamental question: Could we in good conscience continue a gradual withdrawal from Vietnam with Sihanoukville reopened and all of Cambodia turned into one contiguous base area? How could we proceed with Vietnamization if the entire Cambodian frontier opened up to massive infiltration? Nor would inaction avoid our domestic dilemma. If we resisted, we would be charged with escalation; but if we acquiesced in the Communist takeover of Cambodia, American casualties started rising, and Vietnam began to disintegrate, we would be accused of needlessly prolonging the war.

On Saturday, April 25, Nixon called me to Camp David to review the planning. I walked along at the edge of the swimming pool while he paddled in the water. We discussed the NSC meeting scheduled for the next afternoon. Nixon was determined to proceed with the Fishhook operation; indeed, he began to toy with the idea of going for broke: perhaps we should combine an attack on the Cambodian sanctuaries with resumption of the bombing of North Vietnam, as well as mining Haiphong. The opposition would be equally hysterical either way.

Nixon dropped the subject after ten minutes and never returned to it. I do not believe that he was seriously considering the option. But in retrospect I believe that we should have taken it seriously. The bane of America's military actions in Vietnam was that successive administrations were always trying to calculate with fine precision the absolute minimum of force needed, encouraging the adversary to hold on until doubts overrode our efforts.

On Sunday, April 26, North Vietnamese and Vietcong troops gave urgency to our deliberations by attacking commercial shipping on the Mekong River route to Phnom Penh. Communist forces took the town of Angtassom. The rail line leading south from Phnom Penh was cut at several points in Takeo province. Press statements from Hanoi and Beijing rejected the proposal, advanced by Indonesia, of an Asian conference to restore the neutrality of Cambodia—a proposal we favored.

The President met that evening with his principal NSC advisers— Rogers, Laird, Wheeler, Helms, and me—in his working office in the Executive Office Building. Agnew was not included. Even though he was now taking his Vice President's advice, Nixon was still smarting from Agnew's unexpected sally and was determined to be the strong man of *this* meeting. From the outset, the meeting took an odd turn. Helms gave an intelligence assessment that Hanoi was expanding its base areas, linking them together and trying to create so much insecurity in Phnom Penh that the government would collapse. Wheeler described the proposed U.S. operation against the Fishhook complex and the possibility of expanding it to include other base areas. Nixon tried to avoid a confrontation with his Secretaries of State and Defense by pretending that we were merely listening to a briefing. He would follow with a written directive later. To my astonishment, both Rogers and Laird—who, after all, were familiar with their elusive chief's methods by now—fell in with the charade that it was all a planning exercise and did not take a position. They avoided the question of why Nixon would call his senior advisers together on a Sunday night to hear a contingency briefing.

Nixon was immensely relieved. He construed silence as assent; at any rate, he had managed to avoid controversy. As soon as the meeting was over he called me over to the family quarters and instructed me to issue a directive authorizing an attack by American forces into the Fishhook area. I had it drafted, and he signed it. Just to be sure, the President first initialed the directive and then, beneath his initials, also signed his full name.

This double-barreled presidential imprimatur by no means guaranteed compliance. I was chairing a meeting of the WSAG in the Situation Room the next morning to discuss implementation of the directive when I was called out to a phone call from Rogers. He wanted to know whether the directive, which had just reached him, meant that the President had ordered an American attack on one of the Cambodian sanctuaries. I allowed that there was hardly any other way to interpret it. Rogers said this would put him into a very difficult position with the Senate Foreign Relations Committee, since that very afternoon he was planning to testify that there was no American involvement in Cambodia. I suggested that he call the President.

I had no sooner returned to the Situation Room when the other senior Cabinet officer called. With his invariable tactic of raising the issue on which one was most vulnerable, Laird claimed that the combined Parrot's Beak and Fishhook operations could cost 800 men killed in action in a week. He argued that Abrams and Wheeler did not think both operations feasible. When Wheeler had spoken on Sunday afternoon of two sanctuary operations, he was, Laird insisted, referring to Parrot's Beak plus Base Area 704, a sanctuary far to the south (which, as it turned out, was completely waterlogged at this time of the year). I suggested that Laird, too, should call the President.

The WSAG meeting had barely resumed when I was called out again, this time by Haldeman, who told me that Rogers and Laird were both on their way to see the President. He invited me to attend, but reminded me to "let the President carry the ball."

The President's meeting with his senior Cabinet officers did not lack a surrealistic quality. Rogers was above all concerned with his appearance before the Senate Foreign Relations Committee that afternoon. He wanted to be able to testify that no Americans were involved in Cambodia; he therefore requested that the President withdraw his directive. Laird was more complicated. He repeated his fear of high casualties; he implied there had been a terrible misunderstanding about Abrams's recommendation, which really was for the waterlogged southern base area.

Nixon said little, and what he said was ambiguous—a sure sign to anyone familiar with his methods that he meant to stick with his decision. He adjourned the meeting, telling his Cabinet officers that they would hear from him shortly. No sooner had Rogers and Laird left than Nixon showered all his frustrations on me. He could not understand why his senior advisers never gave him a strategic argument and wasted his time on their personal political problems. He would not be deflected. I recommended that he delay execution of his directive for twenty-four hours; he might withdraw it temporarily if this eased Rogers's problems. In the meantime, I would query Bunker and Abrams in his name to verify their views; we had to make sure that there was no misunderstanding about either their recommendations or the casualties they were expecting. Nixon withdrew the directive, and I informed his Cabinet members that a final decision would be forthcoming within twenty-four hours.

In the meantime, Nixon asked me to send a back-channel cable to Ambassador Bunker asking his and General Abrams's views on a number of questions on a most urgent basis: the desirability of a combined U.S.–South Vietnamese attack on Fishhook; whether the Fishhook operation should coincide with the Parrot's Beak operation or follow it; whether comparable efforts within South Vietnam would bring better returns than in Cambodia; whether other base areas—like Base Area 704—would be more rewarding; what casualties would be expected. The cable concluded (in the President's name):

> I am concerned whether General Abrams really wants to conduct this operation on its merits or whether he favors it only because he assumes it represents my wishes. Therefore, please give me yours and General Abrams' unvarnished views on the foregoing questions and I will be heavily guided by them. Please show this message to General Abrams.

By early evening the memorandum from Laird and the reply from Bunker and Abrams had arrived. Laird restated his earlier position: he opposed the use of U.S. combat troops in Cambodia; but he favored the use of South Vietnamese forces against the Parrot's Beak, supplemented if necessary by an attack on Base Area 704, also to be carried out by South Vietnamese forces. It is to Laird's enormous credit that once Nixon decided irrevocably on an American combat role, he did not participate in the fashionable effort to dissociate himself; nor did this master leaker of trivialities ever publicly reveal that he had, in writing, opposed the operations in Cambodia.

As for Abrams and Bunker, they strongly recommended the combined allied attack on Fishhook as the "most desirable," preferably in parallel with the attack on Parrot's Beak, which was the second most important target. Base Area 704, Abrams confirmed, "does not rank in importance" with the other two. Bunker and Abrams did not believe that any operation within South Vietnam would produce comparable results. Abrams cagily gave no estimate of probable casualties but pledged to do all he could to keep casualties to "an absolute minimum."

As in most decisions with major political consequences, Nixon decided to call in Attorney General John Mitchell. The three of us spent until nearly midnight going over the memoranda and the pros and cons of the available options. In the end, Nixon decided to reaffirm his original decision to use American forces against the Fishhook base area and to tell Laird and Rogers in the morning, in Mitchell's presence.

The next morning, Tuesday, April 28, Nixon met with Mitchell and me from 9:30 to 10:20 to review the operations once again. Nixon asked me to leave by a side door before his meeting with Rogers and Laird; he generously tried to shield me from departmental criticism. In a twenty-minute meeting with Rogers, Laird, and Mitchell, the President then reaffirmed his decision to proceed with the combined U.S.–South Vietnamese operation against Fishhook. He noted that the Secretaries of State and Defense had opposed the use of American forces and that Dr. Kissinger was "leaning against" it. This was no longer true; I had changed my view at least a week earlier. Nixon assured them he would dictate a summary of events leading up to the decision that would make clear the contrary recommendations of his senior advisers; they would be on record in opposition; he would assume full responsibility. Mitchell's record of the meeting is in the notes.[6]

The final decision to proceed was thus not a maniacal eruption of irrationality, as the uproar afterward sought to imply. It was taken painfully and carefully, with much hesitation, by a man who had to discipline his nerves almost daily to face his associates and to overcome the partially subconscious, partially deliberate procrastination of his executive departments and the near constant assault from his critics. The decision was not made behind the backs of his senior advisers, as has been alleged. Nixon overruled some of his Cabinet members; he did not keep them in the dark. This is the essence of the presidency, the inescapable loneliness of the office.

After the meeting in the Oval Office, Nixon withdrew to his hideaway in the Executive Office Building, not to emerge until he delivered his speech of April 30 announcing the Cambodian incursion. I spent hours with him every day, bringing him up to date on the planning. Pat Buchanan drafted the basic speech from a rough outline supplied by my staff. But its major thrust was Nixon's. He supplied the rhetoric and the tone; he worked for hours each day on successive drafts. In the days before announcing this most fateful decision of his early presidency, Richard Nixon was virtually alone, the stereo softly playing classical music—reflecting, collecting material, and refining his argument. The Churchillian rhetoric that emerged reflected his undoubted sense of defiance at what he knew would be a colossal controversy over a decision he deeply believed to be right, and in the making of which he had received little succor from his associates.

Once a Cabinet department recognizes that a decision is irrevocable and cannot be altered by artful exegesis or leaks, it can become a splendid instrument, competent, efficient, thoughtful. The WSAG meetings, which in previous weeks had been dominated by evasion and foot-dragging, now turned crisp and precise. U. Alexis Johnson, the seasoned Undersecretary of State for Political Affairs, produced one of those masterful overall plans (called "scenarios" in bureaucratese) that were his specialty, an hourly schedule of tasks for every key individual and department down to and then for forty-eight hours after zero hour.

"Operation Rock Crusher," as it was labeled, or *Toan Thang* 42 ("Total Victory") for the South Vietnamese, was launched against the Parrot's Beak during the night of April 28. About fifty American advisers accompanied the initial wave, joined by twenty-two more in the first four days.

The evening of April 30 the President delivered his speech at 9:00 P.M., explaining that "the actions of the enemy in the last ten days clearly endanger the lives of Americans who are in Vietnam now and would constitute an unacceptable risk to those who will be there after withdrawal of another 150,000." He opened by explaining, with a map, that the North Vietnamese had begun to threaten Phnom Penh and expand their previously separated base areas into "a vast enemy staging area and a springboard for attacks on South Vietnam along 600 miles of frontier." We had three options: to do nothing; to "provide massive military assistance to Cambodia itself"; to clean out the sanctuaries. The decision he now announced was a combined U.S.–South Vietnamese assault on "the headquarters for the entire Communist military operation in South Vietnam." The action was limited, temporary, not directed against any outside country, indispensable for Vietnamization and for keeping casualties to a minimum.

Adding rhetoric out of proportion to the subject though not to the stresses of the weeks preceding it, the President emphasized that America would not be "humiliated"; we would not succumb to "anarchy"; we would not act like a "pitiful, helpless giant." Nor would he take "the easy political path" of blaming it all on the previous administrations. It was vintage Nixon. He had "rejected all political considerations":

> Whether my party gains in November is nothing compared to the lives of 400,000 brave Americans fighting for our country and for the cause of peace and freedom in Vietnam. Whether I may be a one-term President is insignificant compared to whether by our failure to act in this crisis the United States proves itself to be unworthy to lead the forces of freedom in this critical period in world history. I would rather be a one-term President and do what I believe is right than to be a two-term President at the cost of seeing America become a second-rate power and to see this Nation accept the first defeat in its proud 190-year history.

Afterward, there was much criticism to the effect that this was a divisive speech, apocalyptic in its claims, excessive in its pretensions. Nixon would not have to face another election for over two years; no doubt he personalized the issue. Certainly the speech was unsatisfactory to those for whom ending the war in Vietnam was the only aim and who identified this goal with withdrawing rapidly regardless of consequences. Nixon surely played into the hands of his critics by presenting an essentially defensive operation, limited in both time and space, as an earthshaking, conscience-testing event, lending color to the claim that he had exceeded presidential authority by "expanding" the war.

In their turn, the critics made little effort to go beyond Nixon's rhetoric to the realities of the decision. For the merits of the case were overwhelming. That Nixon's rhetoric was excessive did not change the reality that we had only the choices he outlined. If Hanoi succeeded in establishing a contiguous base area, either we would have to stop withdrawals or Vietnamization would become a subterfuge for dismantling an allied country. Doing nothing was the same as acquiescing in the collapse of both Cambodia and South Vietnam while 400,000 Americans were still in place. If we were serious about reducing our involvement in Vietnam and not leaving those who had relied on us to their fate, we had to thwart Hanoi's designs on Cambodia.

The Cambodian Incursion

American and South Vietnamese forces pushed into the Fishhook area at 7:30 A.M. Saigon time on May 1. The same day, Nixon visited the National Military Command Center at the Pentagon and—on the spur of the moment—ordered what he had long been considering, an incursion into all other base areas. As a result, twelve North Vietnamese base areas were attacked in the first three weeks. Some were combined allied operations; some were conducted by the South Vietnamese alone with U.S. air and logistics support. Some were brief (a week to ten days); some were for the duration of the campaign.

Two U.S. naval ships and naval patrol aircraft took up stations off the port of Sihanoukville (by then renamed Kompong Som) outside the twelve-mile limit. They were to watch the port and to effect a blockade if necessary. This terminated on June 13. On May 26, the secret bombing was formally ended; B-52 strikes continued as open operations in support of the U.S. ground forces in Cambodia on the general authorities described earlier. In addition, two days of air strikes were conducted in North Vietnam against three enemy supply bases just north of the Demilitarized Zone. General Abrams had called attention to this logistics complex in late April, considering it the hub of the enemy supply effort.

Nixon's speech had highlighted the presence of COSVN—the Communist headquarters for South Vietnam—in the Fishhook area and had listed it as one of the targets of our assault. The Cambodian Communists confirmed eight years later what some Americans would not believe when Nixon stated it: that COSVN was indeed located in the Fishhook area.[7] In my briefings to the press in advance of the speech, I emphasized that COSVN was highly mobile and that we did not expect to capture it intact. In fact, the assault into the Fishhook sanctuary severely disrupted COSVN's operations and captured or destroyed many of its personnel, supplies, and installations. On May 18, COSVN informed its subordinate units that it was being seriously threatened by allied attacks; it directed all its attendant radio stations to monitor closely because the headquarters would resume communications only briefly when needed. COSVN remained off the air for considerable periods while subordinates tried repeatedly to reestablish radio contact. But since we could not reveal intelligence information, we were naked before the media's merciless mocking of the pursuit of the elusive Communist headquarters.

COSVN aside, there was no doubt about the operation's success. By the end of the first month, five and a half tons of enemy documents had been captured, including vital documentation of the enemy order of battle in Vietnam, detailed plans for its campaign to overthrow the Phnom Penh government, and bills of lading for shipments through Sihanoukville that went beyond our highest estimates of Sihanoukville's importance. On May 22, the Defense Department estimated that 12,000 North Vietnamese troops were held up in the infiltration pipeline by the incursions. Communist communications lamented these troops' consumption of stocks, scheduled for later use during the rainy season. The number of defectors from the Communist side increased substantially. In his final report to the nation at the end of June, Nixon listed the quantities of matériel captured:

> —22,892 individual weapons—enough to equip about 74 full-strength North Vietnamese infantry battalions and 2,500 big crew-served weapons—enough to equip about 25 full-strength North Vietnamese infantry battalions;
> —more than 15 million rounds of ammunition or about what the enemy had fired in South Vietnam during the past year;
> —14 million pounds of rice, enough to feed all the enemy combat battalions estimated to be in South Vietnam for about 4 months;

—143,000 rockets, mortars, and recoilless rifle rounds, about
14 months' expenditures in South Vietnam;
—over 199,552 antiaircraft rounds, 5,482 mines, 62,022
grenades, and 83,000 pounds of explosives, including 1,002
satchel charges;
—over 435 vehicles and destroyed over 11,688 bunkers and
other military structures.

The military impact might have been even greater but for the decision to withdraw our forces in two months and limit the depth of their penetration to twenty miles.

Soon after his April 30 speech, Nixon started pressing for token, and then for substantial, withdrawals from the sanctuaries. The June 30 deadline began as an improvised and very approximate projection for congressional leaders of how long the effort might last; it was soon made sacrosanct. At another congressional briefing Nixon suddenly introduced a limit of thirty kilometers for U.S. penetrations (which was inexplicably translated by the Pentagon to mean twenty-one miles). The President was coming danger-ously close to the perennial error of American military policy in Vietnam: acting sufficiently strongly to evoke storms of protest but then by hesitation depriving actions of decisive impact. The limitations of time and geography placed on our forces' operations helped only marginally to calm the Congress and the media but certainly kept us from obtaining the operations' full ben-efit. The base areas by then extended over hundreds of square miles; hidden caches could not be discovered except by systematic searches; it then took some time to remove what was found. The time limit did not permit a thor-ough search. And the geographical restraints simplified the enemy's plan-ning: he merely withdrew his forces and some of his caches to areas declared safe by us. I doubt if we would have attracted much more public hostility by extending the stay of the American forces for the two or three additional months that a careful search needed. Still the restraints did not prevent us from achieving important goals. The attack on the sanctuaries deprived Hanoi of stockpiles for a sustained offensive for several years. In the areas of South Vietnam that had been most exposed to attacks from the sanctuaries, there was no significant combat for nearly two years thereafter. The Mekong Delta and the heavily populated areas were effectively secured. And when Hanoi launched a nationwide offensive in the spring of 1972, its major thrust came across the DMZ, where its supply lines were shortest; its attacks from Cambodia were the weakest and the most easily contained.

For Americans, of course, the key criterion was reduction of casualties. During the attack on the sanctuaries they rose briefly though they never reached more than a quarter of the 800 per week that Laird had feared. Afterward, the number of men killed in action dropped to below 100 a week for the first time in four years. They continued to drop with every month thereafter. For each month beginning with June 1970, the casualty figure averaged less than half that of the corresponding month of the previous year. By May 1971, a year later, it had fallen to thirty-five a week; in May 1972, ten a week. To be sure, the withdrawal of American forces was a factor, but we had several hundred thousand Americans in Vietnam through 1971, and had Hanoi possessed the capability, it could have inflicted substantially higher casualties than it did. That it did not do so was importantly due to the breathing space provided by the Cambodian operation.

In the international arena, the complications with other countries predicted by most critics did not materialize. The Soviet Union advanced ambiguous barbs, stopping well short of any specific threat. On May 4, Soviet Premier Kosygin held a tough press conference, asking what trust the Soviets could place in America's international undertakings given our "violation" of Cambodian neutrality. But he made clear that the SALT talks would continue. He did not pledge Soviet support to the "Indochinese Peoples' Summit Declaration," or even disavow the Lon Nol government. On May 18, Soviet Deputy Foreign Minister Nikolai Firyubin told one of our European allies that the Soviets planned to keep their embassy in Phnom Penh because "there is nothing else to do." Firyubin described the situation in Cambodia as confused and Sihanouk as a prisoner of Beijing, which was beginning to emerge as Moscow's principal obsession.

The Chinese were equally prudent, though with more colorful language. On May 19, a government statement "sternly" warned the United States against its "flagrant provocation." Reminding everyone of Chairman Mao's dictum that the United States was a "paper tiger," China asserted that the "three Indochinese peoples" would "surely" win if they stayed united. A *People's Daily* editorial the next day reiterated the same themes, comforting the Indochinese revolutionaries with the thought that "the vast expanse of China's territory is their reliable rear area." In other words, as I told the President, "the Chinese have issued a statement, in effect saying that they wouldn't do anything." On May 20, an unusual statement was issued in the name of Chairman Mao with the inflammatory title of "People of the World, Unite and Defeat the U.S. Aggressors and All Their Running Dogs!" Mao endorsed Sihanouk's new government in exile and the "Summit Declaration of the Indochinese Peoples," and pointed out again that "U.S. imperialism, which looks like a huge monster, is in essence a paper tiger, now in the throes of its deathbed struggle." My analysis, forwarded to the President on May 23, was that this also offered little to Hanoi except verbal encouragement.

Far from hurting America's relations with the two Communist giants, the Cambodia operations improved our position by adding another bone of contention between Moscow and Beijing. With Moscow recognizing Lon Nol and Beijing Sihanouk, the Sino-Soviet split was transplanted into Indochina. By June 10, Dobrynin and I were again exploring negotiations on SALT, the Middle East, and even a U.S.-Soviet summit. And by the end of June, we had received unmistakable signals from the Chinese that they were willing to reopen contacts with us.

The crisis was neither on the battlefield nor in our diplomacy, but at home.

The Domestic Travail

The domestic eruptions of the spring of 1970 turned the period of the Cambodian incursion into a time of extraordinary stress. The antiwar movement had been dormant since November, awaiting a new opportunity. In mid-April there were isolated protests, and the April 28 news of the purely South Vietnamese operation in the Parrot's Beak was widely criticized in the media as a major escalation two days before Nixon's speech. North Vietnamese forces had been roaming through Cambodia for well over a month, without a word of criticism of Hanoi. Yet the South Vietnamese response was denounced in the *New York Times* ("a virtual renunciation of the President's promise of disengagement from South East Asia"), the *Wall Street Journal* ("Americans want an acceptable exit from Indochina, not a deeper entrapment"), and the *St. Louis Post-Dispatch* ("a shocking escalation"). The South Vietnamese thrust was intended to assist an orderly withdrawal. But in Congress legal obstacles were being erected almost immediately against helping

Cambodia, itself suffering a savage invasion by the same enemies and indeed the identical units that were fighting us in Vietnam. Senator J. William Fulbright, Chairman of the Senate Foreign Relations Committee, told NBC News on April 27 after the briefing that had given Rogers so much anticipatory anguish that the committee was virtually unanimous in the view that assisting Cambodia in its resistance to North Vietnamese conquest "would be an additional extension of the war."

All the critical themes of the later explosion were present before the President's speech: America was escalating the war. No military action could possibly succeed; hence, claims to the contrary by the government were false. The Nixon administration was alleged to be so little in control of its decisions that the smallest step was seen as leading to an open-ended commitment of hundreds of thousands of American troops. The media greeted Nixon's speech on April 30 with a simple counterassertion: They did not believe him. It was "Military Hallucination—Again" according to the *New York Times*: "Time and bitter experience have exhausted the credulity of the American people and Congress." To the *Washington Post* it was a "self-renewing war" supported by "suspect evidence, specious argument and excessive rhetoric." To the *Miami Herald* "the script in Cambodia shockingly is the same as the story in Vietnam in the days of Kennedy and Johnson. We have heard it all before—endless times."

The President's statements, oscillating between the maudlin and the strident, did not help in a volatile situation where everything was capable of misinterpretation. His May 1 off-the-cuff comment about "bums . . . blowing up campuses," a gibe overheard by reporters during a visit to the Pentagon, was provocative, although he was referring to a tiny group of students who had firebombed a building and burned the life's research of a Stanford professor. When on May 4, four students at Kent State University were killed by rifle fire from National Guardsmen dispatched by Ohio Governor James Rhodes to keep order during several days of violence, there was a shock wave that brought the nation and its leadership close to psychological exhaustion.

The administration responded with a statement of extraordinary insensitivity. Ron Ziegler was told to say that the killings "should remind us all once again that when dissent turns to violence it invites tragedy."

The momentum of student strikes and protests accelerated immediately. Campus unrest and violence overtook the Cambodian operation itself as the major issue before the public. Washington took on the character of a besieged city. A pinnacle of mass public protest was reached on May 9, when a crowd estimated at between 75,000 and 100,000 demonstrated on a hot Saturday afternoon on the Ellipse, the park to the south of the White House. Police surrounded the White House; a ring of sixty buses was used to shield the grounds of the President's home.

At the same time, a Gallup Poll showed considerable support for the President's action. When people were asked, "Do you think the U.S. should send arms and material to help Cambodia or not?" 48 percent of those questioned responded yes, 35 percent no, 11 percent expressed no opinion, while 6 percent gave a qualified answer. When they were asked, "Do you approve or disapprove of the way President Nixon is handling the Cambodian situation?" 50 percent expressed approval; 35 percent expressed disapproval; 15 percent expressed no opinion. And 53 percent of those questioned expressed approval of the way President Nixon was handling the situation in Vietnam; 37 percent expressed disapproval; 10 percent had no opinion.

The tidal wave of media and student criticism powerfully affected the Congress. From not unreasonable criticism of the President's inadequate consultation, opposition escalated to attempts to legislate a withdrawal from Cambodia and to prohibit the reentry of American troops. On May 13, debate began in the Senate on the Foreign Military Sales Bill, to which Senators Frank Church and John Sherman Cooper proposed an amendment prohibiting the extension of U.S. military aid to, and U.S. military activities in, Cambodia after June 30. On the other hand, an amendment offered by Senator Robert Byrd would have granted the President authority to take whatever action he deemed necessary to protect U.S. troops in South Vietnam. This amendment was narrowly defeated, 52–47, on June 11, in what was seen as a trial heat. Senate debate and parliamentary skirmishing lasted seven weeks, until on June 30 the Senate approved the Cooper-Church amendment in a 58–37 roll call vote. The bill then went to a House-Senate conference. The entire Foreign Military Sales Bill remained in conference for the remainder of 1970, deadlocked over the House's refusal to agree to the Senate-passed amendment.

Whereas the Cooper-Church amendment focused on Cambodia, the McGovern-Hatfield amendment to the Defense Procurement Bill aimed at ending the Indochina war by cutting off all funds by the end of 1970, later extended to December 31, 1971. The move was finally defeated by the Senate on September 1, 55–39. But the pattern was clear. Senate opponents of the war would introduce one amendment after another, forcing the administration into unending rearguard actions to preserve a minimum of flexibility for negotiations. Hanoi could only be encouraged to stall, waiting to harvest the results of our domestic dissent.

The very fabric of government was falling apart. The executive branch was shell-shocked. Some 250 State Department employees, including fifty Foreign Service Officers, signed a statement objecting to administration policy. The ill-concealed disagreement of Cabinet members showed that the executive branch was nearly as divided as the country. Interior Secretary Walter Hickel protested in public. The *New York Times* on May 9 reported that the Secretary of State had prohibited any speculation on his own attitude— hardly a ringing endorsement of the President. A group of employees seized the Peace Corps building and flew a Vietcong flag from it. Robert Finch, Secretary of Health, Education, and Welfare, refused to disagree publicly with his President and old friend—as indeed he did privately—and a large number of his officials occupied the department's auditorium in protest.[8] The President saw himself as the firm rock in this rushing stream, but the turmoil had its effect on him as well. Pretending indifference, he was deeply wounded by the hatred of the protesters. He would have given a great deal to gain a measure of the affection in which the students held the envied and admired Kennedys. In his ambivalence Nixon reached a point of exhaustion that caused his advisers deep concern. His awkward visit to the Lincoln Memorial to meet students at 5:00 A.M. on May 9 was only the tip of the psychological iceberg.

Exhaustion was the hallmark of us all. I had to move from my apartment ringed by protesters into the basement of the White House to get some sleep. Despite the need to coordinate the management of the crisis, much of my own time was spent with unhappy, nearly panicky, colleagues.

All this accelerated the processes of disenchantment. Conservatives were demoralized by a war that had turned into a retreat, and liberals were paralyzed by what they themselves had wrought—for they could not completely repress the knowledge that it was two liberal administrations that had sent half a million Americans to Indochina: They were equally reluctant to face the implications of their past actions or to exert any serious effort to maintain calm. Extraordinarily enough, all groups, dissenters and others, passed the buck to the presidency. It was a great joke for undergraduates when one senior professor proclaimed "the way to get out of Vietnam is by ship." The practical consequence was that in the absence of any serious alternative the government was left with only its own policy or capitulation.

What we faced was a painful, practical decision: whether the use of American troops to neutralize the sanctuaries for a period of eight weeks was the best way to maintain the established pace and security of our exit from Vietnam and prevent Hanoi from overrunning Indochina. Reasonable men might differ; instead, rational discussion ended. The President's presentation that elevated his decision to the same level of crisis as some of the crucial choices of World War II was countered by the critics with the image of an out-of-control President acting irrationally, who had provoked the enemy and whose actions were immoral even if they *succeeded.*

But it was not the incursion into Cambodia that was the real subject of debate. It was the same issue that had torn the country during the Moratorium the previous year: whether there were any terms that the United States should insist on for its honor, its world position, and the sacrifices already made, or whether it should collapse its effort immediately and unconditionally. A political settlement as urged by Senator Fulbright—other than the quick imposition of a Communist government in Saigon—was precisely what Hanoi had always rejected, as Le Duc Tho had confirmed to me in the most unqualified terms not three weeks earlier.

What none of the moderate critics—who professed to support an honorable extrication—was willing to admit was that if we followed their recommendations of refusing aid to Cambodia we would soon have no choice but to accept Hanoi's terms, which none of them claimed to support. Our opponents kept proclaiming an assumption for which there did not exist the slightest evidence—that there was some unspecified political alternative, some magic formula of neutrality, which was being willfully spurned.

The Balance Sheet

The ultimate victims of America's domestic crisis have been the people of Cambodia. And the intervening decades have not eased America's internal divisions but set them in concrete. Perspective has not been gained. The bizarre argument has been invented that the Khmer Rouge victory was the product of five years of American and Cambodian efforts to resist them.[9] The aspiration to collective amnesia suppresses the root reality that it was Hanoi that invaded Cambodia in the middle 1960s, that organized the Khmer Rouge long before *any* American bombs fell on Cambodian soil; it was North

Vietnamese troops who were trying to strangle Cambodia in the month before our limited attack; and it was in the end North Vietnamese troops which have overthrown the Khmer Rouge in 1978–1979. Had we not invaded the sanctuaries Cambodia would have been engulfed in 1970 instead of 1975. If anything doomed the free Cambodians, it was war weariness in the United States.

Cambodia gradually turned into the butt of our national frustrations. Domestic critics, thwarted in their various schemes to legislate an end of the war in Vietnam, were more successful in imposing abdication in Cambodia. Even though the same enemy was using Cambodia as a base, even though Hanoi had no means of reinforcing beyond what it was already doing so that any increase in Cambodian strength was bound to weaken it or put it on the defensive, American advisers were barred by law from Cambodia, and American aid was tightly constrained. The Cambodians tied down much of Hanoi's manpower in the South, but American aid funds were doled out grudgingly, amounting to about $200 million in 1970, and they were encumbered with the restriction that they could not be expended to "maintain the Lon Nol government"—an astounding policy of helping a country without assisting its government.

Cambodia's dilemma touched even two staffers of the Senate Foreign Relations Committee, Richard M. Moose and James G. Lowenstein, whose annual visits to Southeast Asia had been the terror of our officials because the two opposed the war and were adept at turning up bureaucratic bungling. Their reports were a semiannual salvo in the congressional assault on the Nixon administration Vietnam policy. On a visit to Cambodia at the end of 1970, however, Moose and Lowenstein came to conclusions not very different from our own, and had the courage to state them. The thrust of their report was that the United States was really doing very little for Cambodia, that the Cambodian government had broad popular support, and that the United States was letting Cambodia down:

> It appeared to us that there is considerable support for the government of General Lon Nol among the youth and intellectuals, in marked contrast to the situation in South Vietnam, and among civil servants and members of the Senate and the Assembly. . . . There is an evident sense of national identity and purpose and a determination to defend the country without foreign troops. . . .

Cambodians find it difficult to understand the complicated and involved elements of the American dilemma in Southeast Asia today. Looking back at the pattern of American behavior in Asia over the past two decades, they seem mystified by the signs of American hesitancy in arming them to defend against an invading force armed by China and the Soviet Union.

Whereas the earlier Moose-Lowenstein reports, supporting prevalent preconceptions, had been printed in fancy booklets and widely distributed, this report was bottled up for several days in committee. Then, apparently under pressure from some members, it was released—but in as inconspicuous a way as possible. Senator Fulbright simply inserted it into the *Congressional Record* on December 16, 1970, along with a few newspaper editorials, without calling attention to it and without a public reading.[10]

Whether to attack the sanctuaries was a decision on which honest and serious individuals might well differ. But once the North Vietnamese forces had spread all over the country, once a "liberated zone" had been created under Communist control as a step toward overthrowing the non-Communist government in Phnom Penh (all antedating *any* American response), the die had been cast. Attacking the sanctuaries prevented an immediate collapse of Cambodia but could not remove the long-term threat. Those who had opposed the original decision now sought to undo it by blocking further assistance to the Cambodian government. But this neither undid the decision nor prevented an expansion of the war; all it accomplished was to give Hanoi and the Khmer Rouge a breathing spell to build up for the final assault. It doomed hope for an independent, free, and neutral Cambodia. The administration and critics were strong enough to block each other's goals and frustrate each other's policies, preventing any coherent strategy. From this mélange of North Vietnamese determination, Cambodian rivalries, and American internal conflicts, everything followed with the inevitability of a Greek tragedy until there descended on that gentle land a horror that it did not deserve and that none of us have the right to forget.

4

DIPLOMACY AND STRATEGY: FROM A CEASE-FIRE PROPOSAL TO THE INTERDICTION OF THE HO CHI MINH TRAIL

By the summer of 1970, the participants in the Vietnam debate were drained from the trauma of Cambodia. The administration had achieved its objective of reducing Hanoi's capacity for offensive operations. But it had done so at the cost of psychological exhaustion; the fear of another round of demonstrations permeated the thinking about Vietnam in the executive branch—even that of Nixon, who pretended to be impervious. And crises along the Suez Canal, in Cienfuegos, Jordan, and Chile of September 1970 absorbed most of the government's attention and focused public concern on other parts of the world.

America's military position had improved. The North Vietnamese supply system through Cambodia had been disrupted and enemy forces based there severely weakened. More important, the North Vietnamese troops in the southern half of Vietnam—the so-called Military Regions 3 and 4—would now have to be used to protect new base areas and to train Cambodian guerrillas rather than for offensive operations in South Vietnam; their capacity for offensive operations had been gravely undermined for at least a year. Allied casualties dropped correspondingly. In the twelve months before Cambodia, more than 7,000 Americans had been killed in action. In the year after, the figure was less than 2,500. The next year it fell to less than 500.

But the fundamental dilemma remained. Hanoi was not weakened to the point of abandoning hope for total victory. It had not modified its demands for unilateral withdrawal and overthrowing the Saigon government. Nor had U.S. domestic circumstances changed. By the end of August, the Senate was debating the McGovern-Hatfield amendment, which set a deadline for American withdrawal of December 31, 1971, allowing the President to extend the deadline by sixty days in an emergency. This scheme received wide editorial support. For the *Washington Post*,[1] it would "end the shell game." But once a final withdrawal date had been established by law, the already narrow margin for negotiations would evaporate. America would lose the capacity to bargain even for its prisoners, for there would be literally nothing left to offer except the overthrow of a friendly government and the abandonment of millions to a brutal dictatorship. To negotiate successfully, the administration needed to present Hanoi with the very margin of uncertainty about its intentions that our domestic opponents spent every effort to remove.

The defeat of the McGovern-Hatfield amendment on September 1, 1970, 55–39, was technically an administration victory. But that thirty-nine senators sought to prescribe the conduct of peace negotiations, in the face of administration warnings that they were legislating a debacle, dealt a serious blow to the psychological basis for a coherent strategy. Nor was that vote the end of the amendment. It would come back month after month in different variations with constantly increasing support, dramatizing to Hanoi the erosion of Nixon's domestic position and thus reducing the North's incentive for serious negotiation. And congressional pressures led to another self-defeating dilemma. In order to maintain public support, Nixon and Laird felt obliged to withdraw forces at a rate undermining the bargaining leverage inherent in offering withdrawals in return for a political settlement.*

I wrote to Nixon on July 20, 1970, warning him once again that a strategy relying on Vietnamization and withdrawals would not be compatible indefinitely with a strategy of negotiations. Each unilateral withdrawal tended

---

* For a splendid discussion of the impact of the withdrawal strategy on Abrams's command, see Lewis Sorley, *A Better War.*

to weaken our bargaining position. If troop withdrawals were already at the fastest rate consistent with Saigon's survival, the margin for speeding them up was limited or nonexistent. Somewhere down the road, probably by the middle of 1971, we might have to choose between Vietnamization and negotiation.

The concept of a free choice would have been hard to sell to the North Vietnamese in the best of circumstances, for they had never practiced even a semblance of it. They had seized power by the gun; they had expanded it by struggle. They were dedicated Marxist-Leninists. To them, political legitimacy resided in the militant elite that embodied the "real wishes" of the people; dissenters had to be reeducated or eliminated. Nor did Vietnamese history offer encouragement: Past rulers had governed by the mandate of heaven by which they maintained themselves in office by success. Schemes for impartial electoral commissions and free ballots were rejected disdainfully by Hanoi; they were accepted reluctantly by Saigon to indulge a domineering benefactor whose support was essential for survival, even while his naïveté constantly courted disaster. How in the light of Communist ideology and Vietnamese history it could ever have been supposed that all the Communists were fighting for was a coalition government—or that indeed any Vietnamese would genuinely accept it—can only be explained by the national American experience which had never encountered irreconcilable ideological hostility.

It was to try to explore possibilities for breaking the deadlock that during July and August 1970 the administration's thinking crystallized around the idea of a standstill cease-fire (or cease-fire in place), a proposal previously broached by Cyrus Vance after he retired as negotiator in Paris,[2] Averell Harriman, the *New York Times*,[3] and Senator Mike Mansfield. In 1969, a standstill cease-fire had become a favorite formula for moderate opponents of the war who did not wish to advocate American capitulation or a fixed deadline for withdrawal. Their views were shared by many senior officials, for various motives. Some in the Defense Department favored a cease-fire to ease budgetary pressures and free funds for weapons procurement. The State Department urged it in response to congressional and media pressures. Nixon was generally disdainful of all these schemes based on advice from Saigon. For in 1969, the South Vietnamese government, U.S. military commanders, and the Saigon embassy had all been convinced that a standstill cease-fire would precipitate the military collapse of South Vietnam because it would be unenforceable against guerrillas. The Vietnam Special Studies Group studied the impact of a cease-fire province by province. Its conclusions tended to confirm the Saigon judgment. This is why the day after his November 3, 1969, speech, the President wrote to his Secretaries of State and Defense, specifically rejecting any initiative for a cease-fire. Nevertheless, on November 8, Rogers urged that we support a resolution introduced by Senator Mansfield for a Vietnam cease-fire as a means of winning over the doves. On November 10, a formal State Department memorandum arrived at the White House proposing a cease-fire initiative.

All this kept the idea in play, on the theory that, if it were accepted in principle, we would insist on terms that gave the South Vietnamese a reasonable chance to survive. In February and March 1970, I had proposed to Le Duc Tho a cease-fire for Laos and Cambodia; I listed it among the subjects we were prepared to discuss for Vietnam.

But Le Duc Tho refused any such discussion. At every turn—until October 1972—he contemptuously lectured me about the impossibility of a cease-fire without a prior political settlement; and his terms for that were a thinly disguised Communist takeover. I do not know whether Hanoi was so disdainful because it thought its prospects in the countryside better than we did, or because it feared that we would keep our troops in Vietnam after a cease-fire, or because of a doctrinaire Marxist-Leninist mistrust of any concept of equilibrium. For whatever reason, Hanoi ignored the suggestion in Nixon's May 14, 1969, speech, paid no attention to its reiteration on November 3 (both of these were in the form of offering local cease-fires, but the hint could have been easily picked up), and rejected my proposal along these lines in the talks with Le Duc Tho.

In late May of 1970, a new study produced a variety of cease-fire options to be discussed at interagency meetings in June and July, including an NSC meeting on July 21. Everyone agreed that Hanoi would reject a cease-fire involving regroupment or withdrawal; the only cease-fire with any chance of being accepted was a cease-fire in place. The success of the Cambodian operation now made the risks tolerable; the North Vietnamese had regrouped their forces, withdrawing them closer to the border and using them to protect training bases for the Cambodian Communists. Nevertheless, our studies predicted that in a cease-fire in place, Saigon's control over the population would erode by at least 6 percent.

Nevertheless, during the summer, a consensus developed around putting forward a standstill cease-fire proposal. The idea of a cease-fire temporarily united all points of view in the government: those who thought it should be offered in order to preempt critics even though it was almost certain to be rejected; those who saw it as an opening wedge for more sweeping proposals that they were as yet reluctant to articulate; and those who sincerely believed that a cease-fire proposal would break the negotiating stalemate. At the same time, a bipartisan group of fourteen senators whom the *Washington Post* called "an unusual cross-section of hawks and doves"[4] sent Nixon a letter urging him to devote his efforts at the Paris peace talks toward "an internationally supervised standstill cease-fire throughout Vietnam." Sixteen more senators joined by September 18. At the same time, a nonpartisan Committee for a Political Settlement in Vietnam, led by Clark Kerr, head of the California university system, began pushing the proposal.

Even Nguyen Van Thieu went along; as was his tactic when facing the inevitable, he even recommended it. Only too aware of the growing war weariness in America, Thieu was in the near impossible position of being asked to replace ever decreasing American forces, to share power with an adversary that daily proclaimed its determination to destroy him, and to carry out political reforms. Any one of these tasks would have tested the fabric of a stable society; to succeed in them all in the midst of a civil war with hundreds of thousands of foreign troops on his soil was daunting. Thieu was well aware that he was a target for war critics, who vilified him as the obstacle to peace. Like almost all Vietnamese, he could not see how power might be shared. He knew he needed time and that it would be a close race under the best of circumstances. Thieu sought to purchase it by making what he considered the least damaging concessions to this strange ally who sought to induce flexibility on the part of an implacable opponent by unilaterally weakening his own position. So he went along with the proposal, partly because he thought it a tolerable gamble, partly because he suspected that Hanoi would reject it, and partly because it might avail him some relief from the incessant pressures for coalition government.

During the summer, Nixon had appointed David Bruce as ambassador to the negotiations in Paris. Scion of an old Maryland family, he had deep roots in both Maryland and Virginia and had been at different times a member of both state legislatures. He had written about the early Presidents, and his admirers found in him many of the same sturdy qualities. He devoted his life to the public weal. He had proved his courage in the OSS in World War

II. He had served as ambassador in London and Bonn. Handsome, wealthy, emotionally secure, he was free of that insistence on seeing their views prevail through which lesser men occasionally turn public service into ego trips. In the summer of 1970, Bruce proved a steadying influence. He asked to study the issue for two months before making proposals; he did not wish the impression to be created that he had received fresh instructions. Hanoi would settle only if it believed that it could not extract fresh concessions simply by digging in.

After David Bruce was well established in Paris, Nixon decided to offer a cease-fire. It proved to be a decision of profound long-term consequence. The standstill cease-fire was put forward as being provisional. If achieved, it was to be followed by a diplomatic conference to settle the war, at which the U.S. would presumably continue to put forward the demand for the withdrawal of North Vietnamese forces. However, it was not likely to be realizable. Even with a war going on, congressional pressures for the unilateral withdrawal of American forces were mounting; not a month passed without some sort of legislated deadline being considered before one of the houses of Congress. In such an atmosphere, it was inconceivable that Congress would permit us to keep troops in Indochina when a cease-fire had already been achieved, no matter what Hanoi did about its forces. The decision to propose a standstill cease-fire in 1970 thus implied the solution of 1972. That North Vietnamese forces would remain in the South was implicit in the standstill proposal; no negotiation would be able to remove them if we had not been able to expel them by force of arms.

Madame Binh's Eight Points

As was the administration's strategy after a military operation, I had sent a message to the North Vietnamese on July 5 through General Walters, suggesting a meeting with Le Duc Tho for any weekend after July 25. Characteristically, Hanoi did not reply until August 18, six weeks later, when it proposed a meeting with Xuan Thuy for August 29. This time we did not repeat the demonstration of eagerness of the previous February. The meeting finally took place on September 7, a week after the defeat of the McGovern-Hatfield amendment.

I traveled to Paris secretly by the now familiar route from Andrews Air Force Base to the military base in Avord near Bourges in central France. A French presidential jet took my party to Villacoublay Airport, where General Walters took us in hand. We met our Vietnamese interlocutors in the familiar simple house at 11 rue Darthé in Choisy-le-Roi on the outskirts of Paris. Xuan Thuy greeted us, his Buddha's face suffused by smiles, along with the familiar cast of characters: Mai Van Bo, the North Vietnamese Delegate-General in Paris; two other assistants; and the interpreter, who had become extremely skilled at delivering the same standard speech with the same intonation and emphasis on exactly the same phrases for three years—which had the effect of nearly undermining our sanity. Ours was the by now standard group: Lord, Smyser, and Walters comprised my team.

I had told Nixon that as a result of Cambodia I expected little but vituperation at this first meeting; progress was even less likely because Xuan Thuy was my interlocutor. If Hanoi wanted serious talks, they would be conducted by Politburo member Le Duc Tho. The major purpose of the meeting was to clean up the record and to probe for any opening, especially regarding cease-fire. As it turned out, there was no vituperation; Cambodia was barely mentioned; I was able to report to Nixon later that "the atmosphere was the friendliest of any of these sessions—indeed of any session with the Vietnamese." Xuan Thuy even permitted me to explain our proposal of mixed electoral commissions to supervise elections. Having negotiators from Hanoi agree to listen to an American proposal was considered progress. This, too, was to become standard. Contrary to the conventional wisdom, the North Vietnamese were generally more friendly after we escalated and more intransigent when we were under pressure.

But nothing had really changed—not the speech, nor Xuan Thuy's instructions. In this phase, when the negotiations were still sporadic, the first session in a series was always the friendliest. (Later on, when Hanoi got down to serious bargaining, the opposite applied; the opening position was invariably tough.) The North Vietnamese negotiators used it as a come-on to encourage us to put the largest possible number of concessions on the table. These would then become the starting point for the next round of talks.

We confined ourselves to bringing our private position into line with our public one. In April, I had given Le Duc Tho a sixteen-month withdrawal schedule. Because Nixon had already publicly offered to withdraw within a year, I now gave Xuan Thuy a schedule of twelve months. (We were still talking in the context of mutual withdrawal.) We proposed free elections supervised by a mixed electoral commission composed of representatives of Saigon, the Communists, and neutrals. We would not agree to determine their outcome in advance: "We have no intention of interfering with the political evolution produced by the process agreed upon here." International observers would offer additional guarantees.

The American domestic situation endowed these proposals with a surreal quality. Given the domestic pressures for unilateral withdrawal, which were accelerating by the month, we were telling the North Vietnamese that they had better agree to mutual withdrawal now lest we have Congress oblige us to withdraw unilaterally later. And we were seeking to persuade the most doctrinaire of Leninist regimes to rest the outcome of a lifetime's struggle on free elections such as they had never risked in their own country.

When the war was safely over, the American agreement to permit North Vietnamese forces to remain in South Vietnam was treated as the key concession. But as shall be discussed in a later chapter, this was implicit in the standstill cease-fire on which there was near unanimity in both governmental and public discussion. In my view, the key concession was the abandonment of the previous commitment to an American residual force. No other ally of the United States—not Europe, or Korea, or Japan—had been asked to defend themselves entirely by their own efforts. And South Vietnam faced the most implacable enemy over the most difficult frontiers. The absence of a residual presence would make the enforcement of any agreement much more difficult and place increasing reliance on the threat of air power.

Xuan Thuy, in any event, had no authority to modify even slightly the standing Hanoi position. He was opaque about Hanoi's six months' deadline for unconditional American withdrawal but only because, as we found out within ten days, Hanoi was about to unveil a new proposal, which, however, was no different in essence from that already on the table. Xuan Thuy did not spend much time on the withdrawal question; no one who followed our congressional debates or our media could doubt that the pressures for unilateral withdrawal had their own momentum. He dismissed our appointment of David Bruce as ambassador to the negotiations, despite the fact that at every meeting in February and March, Le Duc Tho had castigated us for failing to replace Henry Cabot Lodge with a man of comparable distinction. Now Xuan Thuy claimed that Bruce's appointment simply put an end to what we should never have done in the first place; it required no reciprocity.

What interested Xuan Thuy above all was the political structure for South Vietnam. Much as Hanoi wanted us to withdraw from Vietnam, it had assigned us a final role. There would be no agreement and hence no release of prisoners until we had overthrown all the leaders who had been our allies—President Thieu, Vice President Ky, and Premier Khiem, and, it soon appeared, almost any other South Vietnamese leader of prominence. If we did not overthrow this government, Xuan Thuy said, "no settlement can be reached." In defiance of past and current experience, Xuan Thuy informed me that "the Vietnamese love one another. It is always easy to find solutions among the Vietnamese themselves." Xuan Thuy strenuously denied that the presence of hundreds of thousands of North Vietnamese troops in the South (and substantial additional forces in Laos and Cambodia) was designed to exercise pressure; they were there through the free choice of the local population. All of this was highlighted by the perennial claim to epic stature: "We are afraid of nothing. We are not afraid of threats. Prolongation of negotiations doesn't frighten us. We are afraid of nothing." At the end of the meeting, we agreed to study each other's presentations and to meet again on September 27.

Before the next meeting could take place, however, the Communists published a new peace program. Ten days after the secret meeting, on September 17, Madame Nguyen Thi Binh, the representative of Hanoi's front group for the South, the NLF, unveiled a new eight-point "peace program" in Paris. Xuan Thuy had given me no advance word of this; clearly, Hanoi was more interested in propaganda than in negotiation. (Formally, all proposals were put forward by Madame Binh, the so-called Foreign Minister of the Provisional Revolutionary Government. This caused the negotiations to be conducted with a double set of mirrors. In the public talks, Madame Binh was the spokeswoman, though only Xuan Thuy had authority. In the private talks, Xuan Thuy was the spokesman, though only Le Duc Tho had authority.)

The eight points demanded total and unconditional U.S. withdrawal in nine months, specifically by June 30, 1971. Withdrawal would have to be completed even if the negotiations stalemated on all other issues. And that unconditional withdrawal had to be coupled with the installation of a provisional coalition government in Saigon composed along familiar lines of the Communist PRG; neutralists "standing for peace, independence, neutrality and democracy"; and members of the Saigon government other than Thieu,

Ky, and Khiem. The next year I was to find that no political figure known to us would prove acceptable. This totally stacked coalition, according to Madame Binh, was then to negotiate with the Communists to decide South Vietnam's future.

In return for the dismantling of the political structure in Saigon, Hanoi was prepared not to release our prisoners but to "engage at once in discussions on" that subject, during which it would no doubt think up additional demands. A cease-fire would take effect only after we had agreed to all the other conditions, starting with the betrayal of our allies.

Against this unpromising background, I met Xuan Thuy again on September 27, 1970. As the President was leaving for Rome that day, I had come to Paris openly the day before to consult with David Bruce and to have a talk with South Vietnamese Vice President Nguyen Cao Ky, who happened to be in the city. Ky had thrown Washington into a dither by indicating that he might visit us in October. It was a month before congressional elections. Hence many Republican congressional candidates, including those who had generally voted with the administration, were frantic about the visit of the Vice President of a country where over 40,000 Americans had already died. Some delicate footwork dissuaded Ky; a meeting with me in Paris was offered as a substitute.

As I had made the opening presentation at the previous session, it was Xuan Thuy's turn this time. He proved that he had indeed studied our twelve-month withdrawal schedule, and now put forward his own—it was Madame Binh's nine-month deadline, with withdrawals so arranged that all but about 20,000 Americans of the some 350,000 remaining would depart within the first six months. His terminal date remained inflexibly June 30, 1971, even if the negotiations on the remaining issues reached a complete deadlock. He elaborated slightly on the eight points. There would be a "cease-fire" between U.S. and Communist forces while we withdrew; the war against the South Vietnamese forces would continue. As for the political side, Xuan Thuy rejected any discussion of the mixed electoral commission. He insisted on the unconditional removal of Thieu, Ky, and Khiem. He threw in Huong, who had previously served as Prime Minister, for good measure.

The chief lesson of this series of meetings was another confirmation that, for Hanoi, even unilateral withdrawal was not enough; the United States was asked to engineer a political turnover before we left, or else the war could not end, we would have no assurance of a safe withdrawal of our remaining forces, and we would not regain our prisoners. We remained caught between an enemy unwilling to compromise and an antiwar movement in Congress refusing either to admit that Hanoi might be implacable or to countenance military action that might have induced Hanoi to alter its terms.

After the September 27 meeting with Xuan Thuy, it was obvious that the embryonic idea of a standstill cease-fire would be rejected out of hand. But so many in our government had invested so many hopes in it that the administration was governed by a rare unanimity as planning proceeded. All senior officials came to favor anything that might get the negotiations off dead center and their critics off the front pages, if only for a few days. Nixon met to consider his cease-fire speech with Rogers, Bruce, Habib, and me on Sunday, October 4, at Dromoland Castle, County Clare, Ireland, on the way home from his European trip. The meeting could not have been more optimistic. Habib was certain that the North Vietnamese would take the bait. From my conversations with Xuan Thuy (of which Bruce and, through him, Habib were fully informed), I knew better, but I thought the President's proposal would give us some temporary relief from public pressures.

Nixon's speech on October 7, 1970, in fact presented a comprehensive program that could well have served as a basis for negotiation except with an opponent bent on total victory. Nixon offered a standstill cease-fire, including a halt to our bombing *throughout* Indochina. He proposed a peace conference to bring an end to the wars in all the countries of Indochina. He expressed a readiness to negotiate an agreed timetable for the total withdrawal of American forces. He put it in the context of mutual withdrawal, but in language so deliberately fuzzy as to invite exploration. He invited Hanoi to join us in a political settlement based on the will of the South Vietnamese people. He offered to abide by the outcome of the agreed political process but rejected the "patently unreasonable" demand that we dismantle the organized non-Communist forces and guarantee in advance the victory of the Communists. Finally, he called for the release by both sides of all prisoners of war.

For once a speech on Vietnam received almost unanimous praise. The Senate adopted a resolution, sponsored by Senator Charles Percy and a number of others, calling the President's new peace initiative "fair and equitable." Senator Fulbright expressed his hope that the President's initiative might lead to a breakthrough. Senator Mansfield said the speech was excellent; he would do his "very best to support it." The media joined the chorus of praise. The

New York Times of October 9 called Nixon's approach a "major new peace initiative." The *Wall Street Journal* said: "However Hanoi finally responds, in fact, the President has put forth an American position so appealing and so sane that only the most unreasonable critics would object to it."

But it was a short-lived honeymoon. Xuan Thuy made a statement in Paris the next day rejecting Nixon's proposal out of hand; he refused even to talk about it at plenary sessions. The classic pattern of the Vietnam debate reappeared. Some proposal would become the subject of passionate advocacy; it would be urged as the key to a breakthrough. At last the administration would accept it, sometimes against its better judgment. Hanoi would refuse. The proposal would then immediately disappear from the public debate and some other scheme would become the national obsession. Within weeks critics would be back with demands for additional concessions, and the previously hailed proposal would gradually emerge as a sign of intransigence. The new gimmick was to urge setting a withdrawal deadline unilaterally, in the belief—against all evidence—that this was key to a settlement acceptable to Hanoi.[5] Another was coalition government. The *St. Louis Post-Dispatch* on November 5—less than a month after it had hailed the President's cease-fire offer—argued:

> The Communists demand some sort of coalition government, and since they have fought for so many years there is no reason to think they will settle for anything less. Why should they? It seems to us a coalition, which would give each side a certain responsibility and authority, is the logical way to avert the bloody post-hostilities revenge Mr. Nixon so often envisions.

The administration's critics were stirred up even more when, with simultaneous air strikes, a brave band of American commandos conducted a raid on an installation twenty miles from Hanoi—the Son Tay prison—thought to house sixty American prisoners of war. The incident illustrated a basic axiom of policymaking: A President, and even more his National Security Adviser, must take nothing on faith; they must question every assumption and probe every alleged fact. Not everything that is plausible is true, for those who put forward plans for action have a psychological disposition to marshal the facts that support their position. The Son Tay raid, carried out on November 20, was meticulously planned and heroically executed but was based on an egregious failure of intelligence: The prison had been closed at least three months earlier. We knew the risk of casualties, but none of the briefings that led to the decision to proceed had ever mentioned the possibility that the camp might be empty. *After* the failure of the raid, I was informed of a message sent in code by a prisoner of war that the camp was "closed" on July 14. This was interpreted by analysts to mean that the gates were locked; it had not been considered of sufficient importance to bring to the attention of the White House.

By January 19, 1971, Clark Kerr's National Committee for a Political Settlement in Vietnam, which had pressed so passionately for a U.S. cease-fire proposal, now urged a *unilateral* American cease-fire in Vietnam. Hanoi's rejection was attributed not to intransigence but to America's actions in the Son Tay raid, protective reaction strikes, and failure to extend the Christmas cease-fire—all this despite the fact that Xuan Thuy had already rejected our offer five weeks *before* these events. Hanoi's rigidity was to be overcome by further American concessions. "A diplomatic effort is essential in the coming months," Kerr's committee wrote the President, "if we are to break down the resistance of the other side to a cease-fire, and build pressures on them eventually to negotiate an agreement. . . . We remain convinced that such an agreement can be achieved eventually through vigorous diplomatic and political efforts and initiatives." The committee gave no evidence on which to base such a conviction. We had considerable proof to the contrary.

The Setting of a Strategy

By the end of 1970, we faced the certainty that a "political solution" was elusive and the danger that the domestic debate would turn on the rate of our unilateral withdrawal. Even within the administration there was tremendous weariness. The constant pressures that transformed even the most minor military action into a test of credibility, the endless testimony before congressional committees, the incessant probing for credibility gaps by the media—all tended to work against a political outcome. No negotiating scheme could possibly succeed with the cold-eyed planners in Hanoi unless it was related to some calculus of the balance of forces. Critics took it for granted that it was up to America to supply all the concessions and demonstrations of goodwill and flexibility; demands for ingenuity were never addressed to the other side. But the more the negotiating process degenerated into an accumulation of unreciprocated concessions, the greater was Hanoi's incentive to stonewall in order to see what further movement toward its position our growing psychological exhaustion would produce.

In this seeming lull, it became imperative to develop a strategy for ending the war. In November, reacting to a setback in the congressional elections, Nixon toyed with the idea of announcing an almost total withdrawal in 1971 and coupling it with a quarantine of North Vietnam and the resumption of heavy bombing. He conveyed this thought through Haldeman, which suggested it was made mostly for the historical record. I did not believe that such an attempt to force a rapid conclusion could work. The sudden withdrawal, even if it did not wreck the South Vietnamese government and the prospects of Vietnamization, would convey such a sense of impatience to Hanoi that it would simply buckle down and endure the bombing, counting on the domestic uproar to stop American military pressure. I told the President through Haldeman that even from the political point of view, his problem was less one of withdrawing in 1971 than of preventing a collapse in Vietnam in 1972.

But this obliged us to develop an alternative strategy. An end had to be put to the endless maneuvering over withdrawal rates. I recommended that when the current withdrawal increment was completed in May 1971, we should announce another substantial reduction, perhaps on the order of 100,000 over six months. This would still maintain security in South Vietnam through its presidential election scheduled for October. After that, when American forces would be down to about 180,000, we would announce fairly frequent smaller reductions until we had reached a residual force of about 50,000 volunteers by the summer of 1972. These would remain until there was a settlement. Sometime in 1971, depending on the situation, we would announce the end of American participation in ground combat operations. Sometime in 1971, too, we would offer the North Vietnamese a more rapid withdrawal in return for a cease-fire. If it was rejected, we would know that we would face an offensive in 1972. The outcome of the war would then depend on whether the South Vietnamese, aided only by American airpower, would be able to blunt the assault.

For this strategy to succeed, however, it was imperative to weaken the North Vietnamese as much as possible in the interval. The Cambodian operation had delayed Hanoi's logistics buildup for at least fifteen months; every month gained strengthened the South Vietnamese. We looked for ways to consume Hanoi's supplies, to postpone further its readiness for offensive operations, and to blunt the assault should it come. If Vietnamization was a serious policy, three concurrent efforts had to be managed until Saigon could stand on its own feet: American troop withdrawals; the rapid strengthening of South Vietnamese forces; and the progressive weakening of the enemy.

It was the pursuit of this strategy that led to the Laos operation of 1971.

The Laos Operation

That there was bound to be another test of strength was evident in the stridency of North Vietnam's public statements. For example, at the 100th plenary session of January 21, 1971, Xuan Thuy ridiculed our October 7 cease-fire proposal. Quoting liberally from American war critics, he demanded that we respond positively to Madame Binh's eight points. Reporting on a plenary session of the Central Committee, the North Vietnamese party newspaper *Nhan Dan* called for a relentless war effort no matter how "fierce" and "protracted" the war might be.

At the end of 1970, it was clear that Hanoi would need most of 1971 to protect, enlarge, and rebuild its supply system. Hanoi's big push was expected for 1972, in order to have a maximum impact on our presidential election. A meeting of the Senior Review Group—the deputies of the department sitting on the NSC—on January 15, 1971, tried to forecast more precisely the situation the South Vietnamese would face in 1972. The Communist strategy would rely on the traditional combination of guerrilla and regular (main-force) units to whipsaw the defenders. If we concentrated on guerrillas, the enemy's main-force units would occupy large parts of South Vietnam. If we dealt with the main-force units, the guerrillas would make gains in the countryside. Wherever the nexus between guerrilla and main-force units could be broken, enabling Saigon to concentrate on one or the other, Saigon gained the upper hand fairly rapidly. After the Cambodian operation, the war virtually ended in the southern half of South Vietnam until well into 1972, and even then never regained full force. The North Vietnamese divisions in Cambodia were absorbed with rebuilding and protecting their supply system; they were confined to shallow hit-and-run raids across the frontier. In the northern regions, the nexus between main-force units and guerrillas continued; North Vietnamese supply lines were short. Pacification progress was correspondingly slow. It was the most likely target for an offensive.

But statistics did not truly reflect the nature of the problem. The South Vietnamese army was organized on the basis of two divisions for each of four military regions, with an airborne division, a Marine division, and various Ranger and Special Forces units representing a strategic reserve. Thanks to the success of the Cambodian operation, there were excess troops for every foreseeable contingency in Military Regions 3 and 4, southern South Vietnam. In the northern regions, we expected a substantial deficit despite the military stalemate in Cambodia and Laos.

But the challenge could not be met by moving "surplus" southern troops into the "deficit" northern areas. Except for the strategic reserve, each division was tied to the military region in which it was stationed; and southern divisions were judged not to be useful for fighting in the northern Central Highlands and along the Demilitarized Zone. There were several reasons. Divisions were stationed where they were recruited. The dependents of the troops lived near their bivouac areas; and experience had shown that a division which was moved out of its home region would rapidly suffer desertions and loss of morale. (During the North Vietnamese offensive in 1972, the 21st Division, which had been outstanding in the Mekong Delta, was moved into the Saigon area not seventy-five miles distant; its performance was dismal.) Moreover, any such redeployment would be resisted by the generals commanding the affected military region; these were indispensable props of the Saigon government; they judged—correctly—that their political influence at the capital bore some relationship to the number of troops they commanded. South Vietnamese generals were also constrained in the number of casualties they could tolerate—especially in offensive operations that the nearby dependents might consider unnecessary. For all those reasons, statistical analysis understated the strategic problem. In practice, only the strategic reserve divisions were available to fill the gap in the north.

If this analysis was correct, two conclusions followed. The enemy had to be prevented from taking over Cambodia and Laos if Vietnamization was to have any chance of success. And the enemy's dry-season logistics buildup would have to be slowed down, or if possible interrupted. One obvious solution would have been to keep an additional American combat division in the country through the 1972 dry season as a strategic reserve. Behind its shield, pacification could have been accelerated in Military Regions 1 and 2, freeing the South Vietnamese divisions to resist an enemy main-force attack in 1973. This could never be considered, however, in the face of the domestic pressures. The problem thus became how to make up the deficit either by strengthening the South Vietnamese or by weakening the North Vietnamese, especially by disrupting their logistics buildup.

This is why thought turned to an *allied* dry-season offensive, which would disrupt the Communist logistics effort and enhance Hanoi's incentive to negotiate. The winter of 1970–1971 would also be the last that American combat troops would be available. While redeployments and the domestic situation precluded the use of American troops in offensive operations, American forces could assume static security functions and so free South Vietnamese troops for spoiling attacks.

Originally, my staff and I thought that the best place for a dry-season offensive was Cambodia. The idea was to commit Saigon's strategic reserve and one of the divisions guarding the border to wipe out North Vietnamese supplies and forces in Cambodia and to destroy the Cambodian Communist infrastructure in the process of being rebuilt. This would eliminate any residual threat to the southern half of South Vietnam; it would squelch the still developing Khmer Rouge and enable the Lon Nol government to control most of the country. Thieu would then be able to shift his strategic reserve to the north to repel a Communist attack in 1972, or perhaps to mount another spoiling offensive before North Vietnam's logistics preparations had run their course in the following year.

The advantage of the Cambodian operation was that it was almost certain to succeed. North Vietnamese forces in Cambodia were still substantially occupied with containing Lon Nol's forces; the Cambodian Communists were not yet strong enough to stand on their own. There were practically no North Vietnamese reserves available; in Cambodia, North Vietnamese units could not, as in Vietnam, hide in the population. Cambodia was at the end of the North Vietnamese supply lines; it could not be significantly reinforced. And a demonstrable success would strengthen the self-confidence of the South Vietnamese and lend a psychological boost for the almost inevitable showdown in 1972. The drawback of the concept was that it dealt only indirectly with our biggest strategic concern for 1972: a possible North Vietnamese attack in the Central Highlands and across the Demilitarized Zone.

With the President's approval, I sent Al Haig and a team of NSC staff members to Vietnam to study the prospects. Haig returned with a report that Bunker, Abrams, and Thieu thought a dry-season offensive imperative. However, they recommended a much more daring concept. They proposed to deal with the enemy's logistics buildup in one fell swoop by cutting the Ho Chi Minh Trail in Laos near the Demilitarized Zone.

On the territory of a sovereign state whose neutrality Hanoi had formally recognized in the Geneva Accords of 1962, the North Vietnamese over nearly a decade had built a complex system of more than 1,500 miles of roads in an elaborate trail network. At its hub was the small provincial town of Tchepone, on which all trails converged and from which supplies and men were then infiltrated into South Vietnam. The Ho Chi Minh Trail was defended by some 60,000 North Vietnamese logistics troops, together with supporting security forces. It operated each year from about October to May, when the onset of the rainy season made it impassable. At that point, North Vietnamese troops generally withdrew until the next dry season.

Between 1966 and 1971, the Communists had used the Ho Chi Minh Trail to infiltrate at least 630,000 North Vietnamese troops, 100,000 tons of foodstuffs, 400,000 weapons, and 50,000 tons of ammunition, or the equivalent of 600 million rounds, into South Vietnam. Since the overthrow of Prince Sihanouk and the closing of the port of Sihanoukville, Hanoi had become almost completely dependent on the Ho Chi Minh Trail for its logistics effort into South Vietnam.

It was General Abrams's view, as conveyed by Haig, that if the Ho Chi Minh Trail could be denied to the Communists, or effectively disrupted for even *one* dry season, Hanoi's ability to launch major offensive operations in the South (and Cambodia) would be significantly curtailed, if not eliminated, for an indefinite future. Abrams therefore proposed a bold plan. American forces would set up blocking positions along the DMZ in South Vietnam westward to the Laotian border. In the process, the important road junction and airstrip of Khe Sanh—scene of a bitter siege by North Vietnamese during the 1968 Tet offensive and since abandoned—would be reoccupied. American artillery would move up to the Laotian frontier. The crack South Vietnamese 1st Division would then cross into Laos along Route 9 and head for Tchepone, building defensive fire bases along its exposed northern flank. When it was about halfway to the objective, the airborne division would seize the Tchepone airfield and link up with a tank column coming overland. (See the map below.) The entire assault would take four or five days. The rest of the dry season would be spent in interdicting the trail and destroying the logistics complex assumed to lie along it, and especially around Tchepone. A successful campaign was expected to gain us at least two years, as the enemy would need one year to rebuild the logistics structure, perhaps longer if there were later South Vietnamese spoiling offensives.

It was a splendid project on paper. Its chief drawback, as events showed, was that it in no way accorded with Vietnamese realities. South Vietnamese divisions had never conducted major offensive operations against a determined enemy outside Vietnam and only rarely inside. They would be doing it this time without American advisers because these were barred by the Cooper-Church amendment from entering Laos. The same amendment proscribed even the American officers who guided our tactical air strikes, thus sharply reducing the effectiveness of American air support. Vietnamese

— LAOS OPERATION 1971 —

North Vietnamese Ho Chi Minh Trail Network

South Vietnamese Thrust

NORTH VIETNAM

LAOS

DMZ

Dong Ha

Quang Tri

Tchepone

Khe Sanh

SOUTH VIETNAM

0 Miles   10   20
0 Kilometers   20

© 2002 Jeffrey L. Ward

units had practically no trained ground controllers who could speak English; excessive amounts of time would be lost as requests for air support went up and down the entire chain of command of the two sides. The South Vietnamese divisions were simply not yet good enough for such a complex operation as the one in Laos. Finally, Tchepone was located at the precise point where Hanoi could most easily reinforce—its strategic location made it possible to bring up troops from both North and South Vietnam.

Instead of raising issues as these immediately—which is what the National Security Adviser's office is there to do—we allowed ourselves to be carried away by the daring conception, by the unanimity of the planners in both Saigon and Washington, by the memory of the success in Cambodia, and by the prospect of a decisive turn. Energies were soon absorbed in implementing a preconceived idea rather than testing the assumptions on which it was based.

Nixon was determined not to stand naked in front of his opponents, as he had the year before over Cambodia. This time he would oblige his key Cabinet officers to assume personal responsibility. But this determination did not extend to confronting both Rogers and Laird at the same time at an NSC meeting. To get around his reluctance to give direct orders to his subordinates, and judging Rogers to be the most likely recalcitrant, Nixon conceived the idea of first inducing Laird to propose what Nixon preferred, and then letting his Secretary of Defense become the advocate of the plan within the National Security Council. He therefore considered it time well spent to preside over a succession of meetings, each covering exactly the same topic. For each meeting, one more participant was added—someone whose view Nixon did not know in advance or who he judged to be potentially hostile.

Haig first reported to the President about his trip to Indochina in my presence. Nixon next added Tom Moorer, Chairman of the Joint Chiefs of Staff, to confirm that he supported the concept. On December 23, Haig presented the same report to Nixon in the presence of Mel Laird and Moorer. Nixon indicated that he favored an operation in Cambodia and that he was well disposed toward cutting the Ho Chi Minh Trail. He asked Laird to look into the concept during a trip he planned to take to Southeast Asia in early January.

Laird's attitude, as always, was complex. He was aware of the domestic pressures against the war; but he also favored moves that would reduce the risks of withdrawal. Almost certainly he had also already heard from Moorer and Abrams through his own channels about a possible Laos operation. Whatever the reason, Laird backed the concept of cutting the Ho Chi Minh Trail, arguing that it would buy us at least a year. He thought that the first major offensive operation by the South Vietnamese army without *any* U.S. ground support would provide clear-cut evidence of the success of Vietnamization. Vastly relieved, Nixon approved both plans in principle, subject to review after Laird's forthcoming trip.

Planning continued in the Pentagon and in Saigon during Laird's trip, which started on January 5, 1971. On his return, Nixon called another meeting in the Oval Office for January 18. Its participants were those of the December 23 meeting plus Rogers and CIA Director Richard Helms.

Laird spent a great deal of time on technical aspects of Vietnamization, the forthcoming presidential election in Vietnam, the performance of Thai forces in Laos, the need to monitor equipment deliveries in Cambodia. He covered, in fact, every conceivable subject except a dry-season offensive. After his audience was thoroughly anesthetized, Laird at last presented the concept of the Tchepone thrust, with the aid of maps. He indicated that the first phase, the movement by U.S. forces to take up blocking positions along Route 9 inside South Vietnam and to reoccupy Khe Sanh as a forward base, should start around January 29. Phase II—the leapfrogging to get Vietnamese units along Route 9 into Laos—would follow around February 8.

After reassuring himself that there would be no significant increase in casualties, Rogers supported the plan as presented by Laird. He insisted that it was crucial that the operation succeed; Laird and Moorer vehemently affirmed their complete confidence. Helms turned out to be the only adviser to raise serious questions. He pointed out that the proposed operation had been frequently considered in the past and had always been rejected as too difficult. Later I learned that four years earlier our then Vietnam commander, General William Westmoreland, had thought that such an operation would require two corps of *American* troops. Though he was now a member of the Joint Chiefs of Staff, no such view was submitted to the White House in 1971.

The die was cast. Nixon gave his tentative approval to proceed. I scheduled WSAG meetings starting January 19 to carry out detailed planning on a full interagency basis.

The governmental consensus of the December 23 and January 18 meetings began to evaporate as soon as Rogers was exposed to the passionate opposition of his staff. By January 21, it became apparent that State was dragging its feet. At WSAG meetings, Undersecretary Alex Johnson began to surface objections that did not challenge the decision but would have delayed its implementation indefinitely—a bureaucratic maneuver in which Johnson was superbly skilled. The device to procrastinate was to insist on the prior approval of the Laotian Premier, Souvanna Phouma.

It was a bizarre argument. The North Vietnamese had been occupying part of Laos for a decade, in flagrant violation of two Geneva Accords. They had in effect seized all of southern Laos as the logistics base for operations in Vietnam. No Laotian writ had run in southern Laos for years; whatever sparse Laotian population had lived there had been expelled by the North Vietnamese. We had been bombing the Ho Chi Minh Trail for at least five years with Souvanna's acquiescence but without his formal approval. Anyone familiar with Souvanna had to know that he would welcome our actions but possibly feared to endorse them publicly, lest he supply a pretext for further escalation to his ruthless neighbor.

In the event, days were consumed in exchanges with our embassy in Vientiane about how to approach Souvanna. To the acute disappointment of at least some of our officials, our ambassador in Laos, Mac Godley, reported that Souvanna's tacit concurrence was probable, provided we kept him informed. Godley was instructed to obtain a more specific endorsement. Once again, Souvanna, who knew very well that his country's survival depended on a North Vietnamese defeat, failed to live up to the hopes of the opponents of the operation. He gave qualified approval so long as it did not last more than three weeks. Godley was sent back with a yet more formal approach. But Souvanna, who understood his country's needs, refused to play: No matter how many opportunities he was given, he would not oppose the operation, which meant that he in fact welcomed it.

It was becoming clear that the State Department objections went beyond the procedural. Rogers was quite explicit in several conversations with me. I, therefore, recommended another meeting of the senior members of the NSC. It was scheduled for January 27.

Before that meeting, on January 25, I reviewed the military planning with Admiral Moorer. I raised a number of concerns. If cutting the Ho Chi Minh Trail was potentially as decisive as Abrams thought, it was certain that the North Vietnamese would fight. They might even welcome an opportunity to inflict a major setback on the South Vietnamese. And Tchepone at the hub of communications could be reinforced with North Vietnamese divisions redeployed quickly from both North and South Vietnam. How many casualties could the South Vietnamese stand? How long could they sustain operations? Given the immobility of the South Vietnamese divisions, where were replacements going to come from? How would these divisions react when deprived for the first time of American advisers and air controllers during the most bitter fighting of their experience? And were we sure that our air support would be adequate and timely under these novel command arrangements? If the objective was so important, should we reinforce our airpower? I submitted a memorandum to Nixon with questions along this line for use with Moorer and arranged for a meeting of the two for January 26.

Nixon did not, in fact, ask the questions with the explicitness that I had suggested, but in his indirect way he managed to touch on all the points. Moorer was emphatic in his reassurances. If the enemy fought—and probably it would—American airpower would isolate the battlefield and inflict heavy losses that would be difficult to recoup. If it did not, its supply system would be destroyed. The operation would ensure the success of Vietnamization, increasing our ability to withdraw forces more rapidly. It would help the Cambodian government in its struggle for survival by cutting off enemy supplies. In short, "decisive" results were probable.

Thus armed, Nixon met all his senior advisers—Rogers, Laird, Helms, Moorer, Haig, and me—on January 27. Moorer's presentation followed substantially his briefing of the President. When Moorer finished, Nixon had run out of stalling time; Rogers had to be given his day in court. In an extraordinarily effective presentation, Rogers argued that the risks were excessive. The enemy had intelligence of our plans. A battle was certain. We were asking the South Vietnamese to conduct an operation that we had refused to undertake when we had 500,000 troops in Vietnam because we thought we were not strong enough. If Saigon were set back, we would risk all the gains of the previous year and might shake Thieu's position in the process.

Rogers was right on target. Unfortunately, Nixon had heard similar objections the year before over Cambodia, and none of the predicted dire contingencies had materialized. He accepted Abrams's and Moorer's word as to military feasibility; he knew from Godley that Souvanna was sympathetic regardless of the public position he might take. He therefore ordered Phase I of the Tchepone operation to proceed immediately.

The onset of another military operation automatically generated congressional and media pressures. On January 21, having read reports of American air strikes in support of South Vietnamese operations in Cambodia, sixty-four members of the House of Representatives introduced legislation to ban the use of funds "to provide U.S. air or sea-combat support" for *any* military operations in Cambodia. On January 27, Senators McGovern and Hatfield, along with nineteen Senate colleagues, reintroduced the Vietnam Disengagement Act, which, to allow for the passage of time, now required the withdrawal of all American troops by December 31, 1971 (instead of June 30).

As Phase I of the Laos operation began, the Defense Department urged, and the WSAG agreed, that to protect security and prevent inaccurate and misleading reports, the press in Saigon be briefed on the military movements, but under an embargo. This proved to be a naive mistake. The official briefings accelerated a wave of leaks. The Saigon press corps might observe the embargo, but they were free to inform their colleagues in Washington of the basic facts and these were under no restraint. The Washington journalists and the TV networks not only dropped the broadest possible hints of an imminent allied operation in Laos; they also treated the embargo as a major story in itself, a sinister plot of deception and cover-up.

Editorial comment was not long delayed. On February 3, the *New York Times* and the *Los Angeles Times* expressed disquiet about the planned operation. On February 5, the *Wall Street Journal* joined in, and lest it be ignored, the *New York Times* added another editorial emphasizing that any attempt to choke off supplies through Laos was bound to fail because there was so little to choke off. Obviously the *Times* had different statisticians from the CIA's, who estimated that 18,000 tons had already passed through Tchepone in the current dry season. Many other journals joined the chorus. On February 1, the State Department briefed Republican Senator George Aiken on the same basis as the press corps in Saigon had been briefed by Abrams and with identical results; the story was out within twenty-four hours.

To Nixon, all this was only too reminiscent of his 1970 experience over Cambodia. And as in 1970, he withdrew into his shell and sought the support of those advisers who he thought backed his policy. On February 1, I briefed Vice President Spiro Agnew, Secretary of the Treasury John Connally, and Attorney General John Mitchell about the Laos operation. I gave them a detailed account of the pros and cons—allowing for my original bias in favor of the operation—including detailed notes of Rogers's presentation of January 27. Not surprisingly, they favored going ahead. Nixon met with Rogers, Laird, Helms, Moorer, Haig, and me at 5:00 P.M. that day. No new arguments emerged.

Late that evening, after a White House dinner, I saw Nixon again. I suggested he take another look at the proposed operation, whatever its undoubted military advantages. Surprise had been lost; our government was clearly divided.

Once launched on what he considered a strong course, however, Nixon was generally not to be deflected. On February 3, he told me that he had decided to go ahead, and to pay the price both domestically and with the Soviets. He then called in Mitchell and Connally, who urged him to proceed. From about 12:30 to 2:00 P.M., Admiral Moorer and I briefed Senator John Stennis in my office; Nixon wandered in and took the three of us back to his own office to continue the discussion. When Stennis agreed that the operation made sense, Nixon gave the "execute" order. I held it up a few hours to have a chance for one more review with the WSAG and one more discussion with the President. At 6:00 P.M., I informed the principals of the President's decision.

On February 8, South Vietnamese troops began Phase II by crossing the Laotian border. On February 9, Representative Thomas P. O'Neill and thirty-seven co-sponsors introduced legislation not only forbidding direct U.S. intervention in Laos but also American support of any kind for any military operation in Laos.

Lam Son 719: The Military Operation

The operation, conceived in ambivalence and assailed by skepticism, proceeded in confusion. It soon became apparent that the plans on which we had been so eloquently and frequently briefed reflected staff exercises, not military reality.

The Vietnamese staff plan, approved and reviewed several times by our military commanders, had impressively predicted a rapid interruption of the trail system to be followed by a systematic destruction of the logistics structure. But from the beginning, it became clear that the South Vietnamese divisions had not been trained for the daring thrust envisaged by Lam Son 719

—the Vietnamese name for the operation.* Their experience had been with static defense in South Vietnam; their offensive operations had been usually unopposed sweeps of the countryside in support of pacification. Here they were propelled into an alien landscape, deprived for the first time of American advisers and air controllers, and asked to take on the formidable North Vietnamese divisions close to their vital supply bases. They proceeded in so cautious a fashion as to invite the sort of set-piece battle in which, as I pointed out to Admiral Moorer on February 22, the North Vietnamese excelled. If the South Vietnamese continued their defensive tactics, I warned, they might well be run out of Laos.

As for the American side, General Abrams was one of the ablest soldiers, greatest patriots, and finest human beings it has been my privilege to meet. But he was being given tasks beyond human capability and perhaps endurance. By 1971, our command in Saigon had concentrated for nearly two years on preventing disaster while redeploying forces. Indeed, in its role as redeployment headquarters, it was being asked to reduce its forces by 60,000 even while the Laos operation was going on. It simply could not adjust to performing both of its missions: withdrawal and offensive operations. It remained silent while the Vietnamese headquarters for the battle remained in a comfortable permanent base over fifty miles from Tchepone. It did not set up a special command structure for what was described to Washington as a "decisive" operation. It assumed that Vietnamese air controllers could replace American ones; too late we found out that many of the Vietnamese air controllers spoke no English. The untested Vietnamese divisions were thus deprived of much of the air support on which the original plan had counted to control the battle. The Laos operation had to compete for resources with all the other requirements for Indochina, including redeployment.

With every passing day after Phase II started on February 8, it became more obvious that what was taking place resembled the original plan only in the briefings from a hapless JCS colonel every morning. The usual procedure when things go wrong is to try to avoid informing the highest levels of government in the hope that the problem will go away and on the theory that too many raw facts might induce panic. But the problem did not go away. Nothing could obscure the reality that the South Vietnamese units, after

---

* Lam Son was the place of a battle in northern Vietnam where the Vietnamese won an ancient victory against the Chinese.

penetrating only eight to twelve miles, simply stopped and dug in. We found it impossible to tell what they were doing, whether they were cutting supply routes, searching for caches, or simply awaiting a North Vietnamese assault.

In the face of a clearly stalled operation, the White House was given a new date for the promised movement into Tchepone on six different occasions between February 8 and 22. None materialized. On February 13, I began to press Admiral Moorer for an assessment by General Abrams, comparing "actual ARVN troop movements and time phasing with those originally planned, and reasons for any deviations therefrom." It was not until February 16 that General Abrams replied, giving some technical reasons primarily having to do with enemy antiaircraft fire. Abrams concluded optimistically: "I am confident that the task that was initially laid out will be done."

But not much changed over the next four days. Optimistic reports from the field did not square with the obvious stalemate on the ground. Not until March 18—after the operation was over—did Washington find out that on February 12—or four days after the start of the operation—President Thieu had ordered his commanders to be careful in moving west and to stop the operation altogether as soon as they had suffered 3,000 casualties. Given Hanoi's probable penetration of the South Vietnamese high command, this had to be known to the enemy, who therefore could organize a response designed to maximize casualties rather than contest territory. Nixon would never have approved the Tchepone plan had such a restriction been communicated to the White House.

On February 23, Moorer was absent from Washington, which made General Westmoreland Acting Chairman of the JCS on the basis of seniority. I used the occasion to ask for a briefing; in reality, I wanted Westmoreland's assessment. According to the protocol of the Joint Chiefs, the White House was supposed to deal with the Chairman, not individual chiefs.

Westmoreland looked like the beau ideal of an American officer: straight as an arrow, handsome, serious. Like so many of his colleagues, he had launched himself into Vietnam with self-confident optimism only to withdraw in bewilderment and frustration. Saddled with restrictions for which there was no precedent in manuals, confronted with an enemy following a strategy not taught in command colleges, he soon fell into a trap that has been characteristic of American commanders since the Civil War: substitution of logistics for strategy.

With rare and conspicuous exceptions like Douglas MacArthur or

George Patton, America's modern generals have preferred to wear down the enemy through the weight of matériel rather than the bold stroke, through superior resources rather than superior maneuvers. In this, they reflected the biases of a nonmilitary, technologically oriented society. But wars of attrition cannot be won against an enemy who refuses to fight except on his own terms. The Vietnam terrain, the nature of guerrilla warfare, the existence of sanctuaries—all combined to make it impossible for Westmoreland to wear down his adversary as he sought. Instead, the North Vietnamese hiding in the population and able to choose their moment for attack wore *us* down. And then the 1968 Tet offensive, though a massive North Vietnamese military defeat, turned into a psychological triumph by starting America on the road to withdrawal. (In fairness, it must be stressed that Westmoreland labored under political restrictions that barred any of the major maneuvers that might have proved decisive—sealing off the Ho Chi Minh Trail in 1968, for example.)

Whatever the reason for the failure, Westmoreland lived through the neglect suffered by those who have teetered on the edge of popular acclaim and whom the public then punishes for not living up to their assigned roles. Whoever is at fault, they are consigned to an oblivion all the more bitter for having been just one step away from being cast as hero. Westmoreland sat in the sumptuous office of the Army Chief of Staff, deliberating over weapons procurement, enjoying the deference of the uniformed service due to his position, but ignored by the policymakers. He was almost never consulted about the war he had conducted with gallantry, if not always ultimate success. His advice had not been sought individually about the proposed assault on Tchepone, though we were told that he had endorsed it together with the other Joint Chiefs of Staff.

When I saw Westmoreland on February 23, his assessment was bleak. He did not think that the forces assigned to the Laos operation were adequate; he himself had considered that four American divisions would be needed to seize and hold Tchepone; the South Vietnamese had allotted less than two to the operation. Nor did he think a frontal assault the best way to interrupt the trail system. He recommended hit-and-run raids by air-mobile units out of Khe Sanh to cut the trails at various points. This would throw the Communist supply system into a maximum of turmoil and achieve our objectives at much less risk. Even allowing for a natural bias against his successors, Westmoreland's comments made a great deal of sense.

They did not make sense to Laird and Moorer, who argued that Westmoreland had failed to object while the plan was under consideration. They were convinced Abrams would resent being second-guessed by his predecessor. They insisted on the principle of the autonomy of the field commander. But theories of command did not solve our basic problem: to find out whether we were achieving the objective of interrupting the Communist supply system. No doubt the operation was having *some* effect. The supplies being consumed in the battle would not be available farther south. Not all of the reports of caches found could be wrong—though one could not help noticing that the claims were much less exuberant than in the Cambodia operation of the previous year.

On March 1, I cabled the White House concerns directly to Bunker via back channel:

> Since the operation has been launched, the President has received reports on a wide range of modifications to the plan brought on by the host of very real difficulties with which the ARVN have been confronted, only to discover that events on the ground and subsequent operational reporting have not been consistent with the forecast. Specifically, we have found ourselves in the following position:
>
> (1) The President was initially briefed to the effect that ARVN forces would seize Tchepone four to five days after H-Hour.
>
> (2) On February 15, he was told that weather, supply problems, conditions on Route 9, and enemy resistance would delay achieving this objective for a period of 8 to 10 days.
>
> (3) Subsequently, the President was informed that Tchepone was less important because all routes going through Tchepone were being cut southeast of Tchepone.
>
> (4) Subsequently, the President was informed that a modified scheme of maneuver would be adopted which would place two regiments attacking on a northwest axis along Route 914 and the high ground to the north with the objective of seizing Tchepone.
>
> Since receiving information on these various conceptual approaches, events on the ground have not confirmed our ability to accomplish them. This has quite naturally resulted in concerns here as to the overall future outlook of the operation. An additional factor

which concerns me greatly is the limited ARVN strength which has been involved in this operation at a time when the enemy has obviously committed his full resources. . . .

We will do our best to hold the fort. But we must know what we are up against. There is no chance to keep panic from setting in if we are constantly outstripped by events.

But the Saigon command had seen too many hortatory cables from anxious civilians over six years of war. Bunker sent back a soothing telegram on March 3 describing the dedication of Thieu and General Cao Van Vien, the chief of the military staff, to success (which was not the issue): "In operations of this kind, one cannot be tied to preconceived ideas of what might be thought of as ideal procedures. A posture has to be maintained flexible enough to adapt to fluid conditions which may be governed by weather, terrain or changes in enemy tactics." This was unexceptionable, but it did not answer our fundamental concern, which was not procedural: to what extent, if any, were the South Vietnamese forces interrupting the enemy buildup by whatever plan. The conclusion seemed to put our fears to rest: "General Abrams and I are both confident that if we hold steady on our course, the Cambodia and Laos operations will have the impact on the enemy's activities in South Vietnam and our troop withdrawals which we originally contemplated."

And for a few days, things seemed to improve. In battles between South Vietnamese and North Vietnamese units, the North Vietnamese grudgingly gave ground (at least if reports were to be believed). A new assault was launched in the direction of Tchepone on March 3, and by March 6, the South Vietnamese were close enough to that objective to sustain the claim of having captured it. But soon the suspicion grew that they wanted Tchepone only so that they could withdraw from Laos altogether without loss of face. As early as March 8, Abrams informed us that South Vietnamese commanders, having occupied the Tchepone area, considered their mission accomplished and were eager to retreat.

This ran counter to any concept of the operation as the White House had understood it; the whole point of the exercise was to disrupt the North Vietnamese trail system for the better part of the dry season and to destroy as many caches as could be found. When I called this to Bunker's attention on March 9, he and Abrams paid another visit to Thieu, from which they emerged with a mystifying clarification: Thieu was not withdrawing from Laos but rotating his units. He would pull back elements of his strategic reserve but replace them with fresh units.

I insisted on sending Haig to take a firsthand look. By this time, Laird knew something was wrong; he acceded readily. In the meantime, I sent off another back-channel to Bunker on March 18:

> I hope Thieu understands that the President's confidence is an asset he should not lightly dissipate and that this may be his last crack at massive U.S. support.

By March 19, Haig's arrival in Vietnam put an end to all illusions. He reported that after three weeks of uninterrupted combat, the commanders of the two South Vietnamese divisions were no longer willing to continue the operation. "My visit to I Corps has convinced me that the issue now is not feasibility of reinforcing and remaining in Laos, but [the] urgent need to impress upon ARVN the necessity of moving out only with full concentration of US firepower in an orderly and tactically sound fashion."

Within a few days, the retreat from Laos was in full swing. On the whole, the South Vietnamese extricated themselves in creditable fashion, except for the unedifying and untypical television pictures of a few panicky soldiers clinging to the landing gear of the helicopters. It would have been difficult in the best of circumstances for the White House to give a balanced assessment; those pictures destroyed any such prospect. In any event, Washington was so badly informed and the operation deviated so much from the original plan that a convincing briefing was nearly impossible.

The dry-season offensive of 1971 was a watershed. It marked the last offensive operation in which American troops participated, even in a supporting role. It clearly did not realize our hopes; nor did it fail completely. As always in Vietnam, the truth lay somewhere between the claims of the administration and the abuse of the critics. The assault on Tchepone did not interrupt the North Vietnamese logistics buildup sufficiently to prevent an offensive by Hanoi in 1972. But it did consume enough supplies to delay that offensive for several months and to confine its maximum impact to the areas closest to North Vietnam. The major enemy thrust in 1972 came across the Demilitarized Zone, where Hanoi's supply lines were shortest and least affected by the operations in Cambodia in 1970 and Laos in 1971. The farther south the North Vietnamese attempted to attack in 1972, the weaker was their impact, because their sanctuaries and supply system had been disrupted by our operations in the previous two years. As it was, the combination of South Vietnamese ground forces and American airpower enabled us just barely to blunt the North Vietnamese offensive in 1972. Without the attrition caused by the incursions into Laos and Cambodia, this might well have been impossible.

At the same time, the Laos incursion fell far short of expectations. There were several reasons for this. The command in Saigon had been transformed by Washington pressures into a redeployment headquarters. Suddenly it was being asked to oversee complex offensive operations while adhering to a withdrawal schedule in which it did not believe. It was barred by law from having its own men on the ground with the advancing troops even to control our air operations; and it was in the straitjacket of limitations on air sorties mechanically imposed by budgetary cuts.

As for the South Vietnamese, Laos exposed many of their lingering deficiencies. Their planning turned out to be largely abstract. It formalistically imitated what was taught at our command and general staff schools without adaptation to local conditions. In retrospect, I have even come to doubt whether the South Vietnamese ever really understood what we were trying to accomplish. The objective surely was not Tchepone or any other geographic trophy. It was to slow up North Vietnamese resources and logistics throughout the dry season so as to pull the teeth of the 1972 offensive, when only residual American forces would be left. What Thieu seemed to want—it later emerged—was a quick success, not a long-range strategy. Above all, the South Vietnamese suffered from the flaws inherent in their military organization. They had few reserves; their tolerance for casualties was small, except in defensive battles. Each commander, aware that his political influence depended in part on the strength and morale of the units he commanded, was eager to husband his assets and reluctant to incur losses for what seemed a distant objective. The South Vietnamese had fought better than before; but there was no blinking the fact that the result had been inconclusive. The dry-season offensive of 1971 did not foreclose an assault by Hanoi in 1972, as we had hoped, though it almost surely lessened its impact. It was probable now that we would face another major military challenge the next year.

Finally, the Tchepone operation inspired melancholy reflections about what might have happened had it been undertaken in the early stages of the war when the U.S. combat divisions first arrived in Vietnam instead of relying on the bombing of North Vietnam which, given the state of technology then, did not sufficiently impede Hanoi's logistics. For at Tchepone, Hanoi could not have evaded battle as it did in South Vietnam in favor of hit-and-run raids. It would have had to defend the trail network or suffer the attrition of its main force units in the South; its units would have presented concentrated targets for airpower. It was the place to fight the war of attrition that Westmoreland sought and to deprive the South guerrillas of supplies for prolonged warfare.

Braving Domestic Opposition

After the withdrawal from Laos, both media and congressional pressures escalated. Between April 1 and July 1, there were seventeen House or Senate votes seeking to restrict the President's authority to conduct the war or seeking to fix a date for unilateral withdrawal (making a total of twenty-two for the year). On June 22, the Senate adopted, by 57–42, another resolution sponsored by Senator Mansfield that declared that "it is the policy of the U.S. to terminate at the earliest practicable date all military operations in Indochina and to provide for the prompt and early withdrawal of all U.S. forces not more than nine months after the bill's enactment subject to the release of American POWs." Though Sense of the Senate resolutions are not legally binding, the Mansfield resolution illustrated the Vietnam tragedy: The opposition was unwilling to accept ultimate responsibility for its views, but it would move heaven and earth to keep the administration from pursuing a coherent strategy.

The pervasive exhaustion reflected itself in ever more explicit assertions that no conceivable objective in Vietnam could outweigh the domestic controversy about the war. Vietnamization, urged two years previously as a means of ending our involvement, now was attacked as prolonging the war. On April 16, *Life* magazine criticized the refusal to set a withdrawal date: "Prolonged and open-ended withdrawal is too much like prolonged and open-ended warfare. . . . A country that finds the war intolerable will find such a prospect unacceptable." The *New York Times* proclaimed on April 25: "Mr. Nixon can be assured of broad public support if he will abandon the cruel delusion of Vietnamization and declare unequivocally his intention to withdraw all American forces from Vietnam by an early fixed date, contingent on agreement by the other side to release all United States prisoners and to guarantee the safe exit of American troops."

Former officials of the Johnson administration, having had no plan for even a limited withdrawal when they were in office and who, as late as November 1968, had recommended a residual American force of 250,000 to President-elect Nixon, now professed to be convinced that the promise of a total, unilateral withdrawal would guarantee an early peace. Clark Clifford and Averell Harriman never missed an opportunity to press this view; other ex-officials led delegations to lobby Congress for a fixed deadline. Praise for the cease-fire initiative of the year before had completely disappeared amid unrelenting castigation of the administration for not making another proposal, which we knew from the private talks had no attraction for Hanoi whatever.

Weariness was not confined to the critics. Nixon persisted in his course and I in my defense of it, because we knew a deadline was not enough; we would have to overthrow a friendly government (put into office by a coup organized by our predecessors) and mock the sacrifice of millions who had relied on us, as the price for getting out. And we did not know how to explain to American mothers why their sons should be at risk when a deadline for unilateral withdrawal had already been established. Nixon found it difficult to articulate this essentially moral issue in a generous manner. But he made valiant efforts in press conferences and speeches: "The issue very simply is this: Shall we leave Vietnam in a way that—by our own actions—consciously turns the country over to the Communists? Or shall we leave in a way that gives the South Vietnamese a reasonable chance to survive as a free people?"[6]

The fact that most critics were bored with the question—or ridiculed it as an "open-ended" commitment—did not make it any the less valid and central. America, the bulwark of free people everywhere, could not, because it was weary, simply walk away from a small ally, the commitments of a decade, 45,000 casualties, and the anguish of their families whose sacrifices would be retroactively rendered meaningless. Nixon certainly did not help matters by inflated claims and ungenerous comments. But it is not possible to understand the tragedy of Vietnam without a willingness to admit that some of the best people in our country thought they could serve peace best by discrediting their own government. I summarized this, our deepest problem, at a background briefing on April 8:

> I remember three years ago it used to be considered the height of enlightenment to believe that negotiations were a useful way of ending the war.
>
> Today, it is considered by many the height of obtuseness to believe that negotiations can still be a means of ending the war.
>
> There used to be a time when it was said that we should substitute Vietnamese for Americans. Now that is under attack. . . .
>
> We believe that we have to give the South Vietnamese a reasonable chance to stand on their own feet, and that what would happen to the American body politic if an American President, after seven years of war and 40,000 casualties, consciously turned the country over to the Communists, would be something from which we would suffer for many years, even if there is a temporary feeling of relief in the immediate aftermath of such a settlement.

It was rhetorically easy to speak of an abrupt unilateral withdrawal; practically, nearly impossible to accomplish it. We would settle for minimum terms. But we would not dishonor our country by joining our adversary against our friends. And if we would not accept Hanoi's terms, only two possibilities existed: Either we would negotiate a compromise compatible with our values, or else there would be another military test in 1972.

The Negotiations Are Resumed

After Laos, we first assessed the military prospects for 1972, and, second, considered how we could continue negotiating with Hanoi. The military conclusions of my systems analysis staff under Wayne Smith proved remarkably prescient. They considered that the Laotian incursion had gained a respite of a year. They predicted that, as a result of the Cambodian and Laotian operations, the North Vietnamese would retain the capacity for major offensives only in the northern part of South Vietnam across the DMZ in Military Region 1 and, to a lesser extent, the Central Highlands of Military

Region 2. Because of the Cambodian incursion, Hanoi's offensive operations in Military Region 3 would be deprived of guerrilla support; conventional attacks could not be sustained there for a long period. There was no main-force offensive threat to Military Region 4 at all. Because the Laos operation had disrupted Hanoi's logistics system, an offensive was unlikely before the second half of the dry season, probably not before early March 1972. (The estimate was off by only three weeks; the offensive, in fact, started at the end of March.) The question was whether Hanoi had made the same calculations and, if so, whether it would gamble on the outcome of an offensive in 1972 or attempt a serious negotiation in 1971.

With these questions in mind, we initiated another round of secret talks. While the Laos operations were taking place, negotiations inevitably had languished. In mid-April 1971, Xuan Thuy at a plenary session challenged the United States to set a withdrawal date; in return, Hanoi would guarantee the security of our retreat (but not of South Vietnamese forces) and "discuss" prisoners of war. We did not take up these schemes at the plenary meetings because we had heard them the year before and because a separate Washington-Hanoi cease-fire was unthinkable. We also knew that if Hanoi had anything new and significant to say, it would save it for the next secret meeting. On April 24, General Walters contacted the North Vietnamese in Paris, proposing May 16 as the date for a renewal of discussions "on the basis of new approaches." Hanoi accepted on May 14, but offered May 30 instead. We countered with May 31, partly so as not to accept Hanoi's date, but also for logistic and security reasons. (It was the last day of a long weekend; my absence was therefore less likely to be noted.)

Before the meeting, I submitted to Nixon a proposal for a new seven-point peace program. Though basically skeptical, and afraid that Hanoi would try to string us along, Nixon authorized it as a "final offer." It was, in fact, the most sweeping plan we had yet offered, cleared by Bunker, and approved by Thieu. It sought to bring our negotiating proposals into line with our actions.

The seven-point plan recognized that since we were withdrawing most American forces unilaterally, we could not use them to bargain for total Hanoi withdrawal. We would try to turn the residual force into a bargaining counter while recognizing that the mounting congressional pressures for deadlines—reflected in the ever-increasing votes for the McGovern-Hatfield type of amendment—would sooner or later make even this potential concession irrelevant. The first point set a date for total withdrawal. It gave up the demand for mutual withdrawal, provided Hanoi agreed to end all infiltration into all the countries of Indochina. The proposal sought to get away from the treadmill of demanding mutual withdrawal while in fact carrying out a unilateral withdrawal; it would, in effect, trade the residual force for an end of infiltration into South Vietnam. Theoretically, North Vietnamese forces would wither away if they could not be reinforced. To be sure, Hanoi might violate the prohibition against reinforcement, but in that case they would ignore a provision for withdrawal as well, as in fact it had done in Laos a decade earlier and were to do in Laos and Cambodia a few years later. Whatever the agreement, it would depend on America's willingness to enforce the agreement. The third point proposed a cease-fire in place throughout Indochina (not only in Vietnam) to become effective at the time when U.S. withdrawals began, based on a final agreed timetable under international supervision (point 5). The sixth point called for guarantees for the independence, neutrality, and territorial integrity of Laos and Cambodia, with both sides renewing their pledge to respect the 1954 and 1962 Geneva Accords. The final proposal was for the immediate release by both sides of all prisoners of war and innocent civilians on humanitarian grounds and as an integral part of the U.S. withdrawal timetable (point 7). The political future of South Vietnam was to be left to the South Vietnamese to settle (point 2). The proposal was made public by Nixon in a speech on January 25, 1972, and incorporated in our public position. In its essence it was accepted sixteen months later by Hanoi.

Xuan Thuy was too competent not to recognize immediately that we had made a major change on the military issues, though he pretended to have difficulty understanding it. He still argued that the "correct and logical" solution was for us to set a deadline for unilateral withdrawal unrelated to any other aspect of the negotiation. He refused to move from the position that Hanoi would only "discuss," not guarantee, the release of our prisoners, even if we set a withdrawal date; clearly, the prisoners were to be used as a lever to induce us to overthrow the Saigon government. Nor could he refrain from lecturing me on our precarious domestic situation, leading to a sharp exchange:

> KISSINGER: We'll take care of our public opinion and you of
> yours.

XUAN THUY: Since your public opinion speaks on the situation,
   therefore we must give an interpretation.
KISSINGER: I won't listen to it at these meetings.

Xuan Thuy maintained Hanoi's political terms: the replacement of Thieu,
Ky, Khiem, and other "warlike leaders." He even tried to be helpful in this effort; drawing on a lifetime of experience in rigged elections, he pointed out
that the imminent South Vietnamese presidential election provided a great
opportunity to get rid of Thieu and his colleagues in a "natural" way.

Even though I adamantly refused to embrace his loaded political proposals, Xuan Thuy was clearly eager to keep the discussion of our new military
proposal alive, which suggested that Hanoi might be in the process of recon-
sidering its political demands. On the whole, Xuan Thuy treated our propositions with more care than usual. He did not, for once, denounce them as
"nothing new." He said again and again that Hanoi would study our offer seriously. At one point, he even said that "in case your proposal is accepted in
general, then next time we should be prepared to discuss all concrete questions." He stressed Hanoi's desire to negotiate. He did not repeat the usual
insistence that a cease-fire was impossible in the absence of a full political settlement. He repeatedly asked for another meeting. For the first time, he
showed impatience, suggesting a date well before July. We settled on June 26.
Soon word was received that Le Duc Tho had left Hanoi, stopping in Beijing
and Moscow on the way to Paris. A serious negotiation seemed in the offing
for the first time, and there were other hints of a breakthrough. We were also
engaged in putting the finishing touches on my secret trip to Beijing (the definitive invitation reached Washington on June 2), and we were still exploring a summit with the Soviet Union. It was a moment of extraordinary hope.

All the while Xuan Thuy in Paris threw out tantalizing public hints to encourage congressional pressures to fix a withdrawal deadline. At the June 3
plenary, while he repeated that the political and military issues were "the two
crucial and inseparable questions," he added ambiguously that the withdrawal deadline was "the immediate crucial point." Former Secretary of Defense Clark Clifford, addressing a June 8 dinner meeting of lawyers lobbying
against the war, declared that he had "reason to believe" that a withdrawal
deadline of December 31, 1971, would secure the release of American prisoners. But under sharp probing by a journalist, Xuan Thuy himself refuted
this. Chalmers Roberts concluded, after an interview published in the *Wash-*

ington Post of June 10: "The central issue between the United States and North Vietnam at the Paris peace talks has always been the political future of the South, despite the recent concentration in Congress and elsewhere on American troop withdrawal and the release of prisoners of war."

June, too, was the month in which for the first time a house of Congress voted to override the administration's Vietnam policy by legislation. On June 22, to the editorial acclaim of the leading journals, the Senate passed by a vote of 57 to 42 the Mansfield amendment calling on the President to withdraw all American forces from Vietnam within nine months if Hanoi agreed to release all our prisoners. The practical effect was to make irrelevant five of the seven points in the secret negotiations. Hanoi now knew that there was a floor under its risks; if these pressures mounted, it would not need to negotiate about a cease-fire anywhere in Indochina, or pledge to cease infiltration, or promise to respect the neutrality and independence of Laos and Cambodia. If it agreed to release our prisoners, there was a good chance that Congress would impose an unconditional total withdrawal of American forces.

June, finally, was the month the Pentagon Papers (a compilation of some 10,000 classified documents from the Kennedy and Johnson administrations) were leaked. The intensity of the administration's reaction cannot be understood except in the context of our China initiative and Vietnam negotiations. Nixon believed, rightly or wrongly, that Hanoi was approaching a fundamental decision on whether to end the war before the Vietnamese presidential election in October. At the very moment these decisions were being made in Hanoi, thousands of documents suddenly appeared in the press, leaked by those whose motive was to discredit all U.S. efforts in Vietnam. Moreover, I was about to embark on the still secret trip to China. The publication of 10,000 classified documents at so sensitive a moment would, in our view, weaken our bargaining position by undermining our reputation for reliability. None of the documents concerned the Nixon administration; they were a compilation of records assembled at the direction of Secretary of Defense Robert McNamara to learn from the mistakes of the Kennedy and Johnson administrations. Thus Nixon's stance was on principle; insofar as the documents reflected on governmental actions, they indicted his Democratic predecessors. What concerned Nixon was that, if Hanoi concluded that our domestic support was eroding, for whatever reason, it was bound to stonewall. I do not believe now that publication of the Pentagon Papers made the difference in Hanoi's decision not to conclude a settlement in 1971. But neither those who leaked the papers nor the government could know this at the time.

Le Duc Tho, whom I met on June 26, could not have been more cordial. He took the American negotiating team into the tiny dining room, which had been equipped with a green-covered conference table. Le Duc Tho was so determined to create a friendly atmosphere that he even permitted me to interrupt his epic poem on American perfidy in Cambodia. When I again emphasized that we had nothing to do with Sihanouk's overthrow, Le Duc Tho's reply added a new dimension to epistemology (the philosophy of knowledge). With a maximum effort at generosity, he said: "I *temporarily* believe that you had nothing to do with the coup in Phnom Penh." Lest I be carried away by this unprecedented—if limited—declaration of faith in America, he immediately added that it was an assertion based on politeness rather than on conviction.

When we got around to the subject of the meeting, Xuan Thuy, being technically the chief negotiator, opened with some pointed questions about the May 31 proposal. Le Duc Tho, playing the role of Special Adviser to Xuan Thuy, followed with a lengthy, generalized statement about the history of negotiations, and alleged that allied military moves had interfered with a negotiated settlement. Both were very careful to avoid saying anything that suggested rejection. And their tone quickly became more conciliatory whenever I made a sharp reply.

After two hours of sparring, there was a tea break. Xuan Thuy went upstairs, presumably to work on his next statement, but Le Duc Tho for the first time joined me for a social chat in the small garden behind the house. I invited him to Harvard after the war to give a seminar on Marxism-Leninism. Le Duc Tho delicately suggested that his views might be strong medicine for a capitalist country. I assured him that he was more likely to be received cordially by my Harvard colleagues than I.

After the break, the probing resumed, until I said: "We have made our proposal. If you have no other proposals of your own, I have nothing more to say." This triggered Xuan Thuy into a long recital of the saga of Vietnamese history that turned out to be preliminary to a new North Vietnamese nine-point proposal. Since Hanoi felt obligated to demonstrate its moral superiority at every turn, the fact that he had put forward two more points than we, argued Xuan Thuy, showed "our desire is more earnest than yours to end the war."

Hanoi's new plan put forward a deadline for American withdrawals of December 31, 1971—or six months away, a retrogression from Madame Binh's eight points of the previous September, but matching the most recent versions of the McGovern-Hatfield amendment. It explicitly agreed, for the first time, that American prisoners of the Vietnamese would be released— instead of merely "discussed"—simultaneously with our withdrawals, thus also fulfilling the Mansfield amendment. A standstill cease-fire would be instituted on completion of the agreement and would be subject to international supervision and guarantees. Though still linked to the withdrawal issue, the political proposals were more ambiguous. Hanoi had understood that we would never agree to its version of coalition government. Therefore, we were now being asked to "stop supporting" Thieu, Ky, and Khiem so that "a new administration standing for peace, independence, neutrality and democracy" could be set up. To "stop supporting" our allies could mean anything from withdrawing our forces to ending all economic and military aid, or even conniving in their overthrow.

The obligation to respect the neutrality and independence of Laos and Cambodia (our sixth point) was referred to in one paragraph saying that the problems between Indochinese countries should be settled by them on the basis of mutual respect for their sovereignty. This was acceptable so far as it went, but adding that Hanoi was "prepared to join in resolving such problems," implied that Hanoi had a special status in determining the future of the countries of Indochina. And there was a demand—which I rejected out of hand—that the United States pay reparations "for the damage caused by the U.S. in the war zones of Vietnam." The proposals were put forward as an "integrated whole"; in other words, Hanoi would not countenance the withdrawal-for-prisoners exchange that was the staple of our domestic debate.

In the strange atmosphere of Vietnam negotiations, after two years of Communist stonewalling and domestic flagellation, my colleagues and I were optimistic because for the first time Hanoi presented its ideas as a negotiating document and not as a set of peremptory demands. Le Duc Tho repeatedly stressed that these were subjects for negotiation; we were invited to make counterproposals. In dealings with Le Duc Tho, one was grateful for small favors. The fact that the North Vietnamese used the phrase "the United States should" rather than the traditional peremptory "the United States must" was considered by the Hanoi demonologists on my staff as a significant advance. Le Duc Tho offered to stay in Paris until the negotiations were completed.

In fact, Hanoi's military proposals were negotiable. The demand for reparations and the ambiguity with respect to the political outcome were the stumbling block. If the latter masked the old demand that we overthrow the Saigon government, we were once again at a dead end. But if it marked a stage in the retreat from that position, a settlement might be possible. I reported to Nixon:

> The real meaning of their counter-proposal and their discussion is as of now unclear. There remains the strong possibility that there can be no negotiated solution except on terms which we cannot accept. Their position and approach were consistent with an attempt on their part to gain time. It was also consistent, however, with moving toward our approach, for if they are to do that they must first go through the exercise of fighting for their political demands and showing that we were unyielding. Also, they do not need to send Le Duc Tho to Paris to string us along, and in any event, it is not clear what that tactic really buys them; there is nothing we lose by waiting right now; their proposal had some positive as well as tough elements, and they were clearly eager to negotiate further and concretely.

My colleagues and I had never experienced a procedure by which Hanoi offered to reconcile parallel points in comparable documents. I proposed to Nixon—and he agreed—that on July 12, at the end of my trip around the world (including Beijing), I would submit a counterproposal seeking to merge Hanoi's document and ours. But before that meeting could take place, the North Vietnamese undertook another of the acts of bad faith that so heightened our distrust, especially when, in our domestic debate, it was we who were accused of bad faith. On July 1, Madame Binh, the principal negotiator for the NLF, published a new seven-point plan that partly duplicated Le Duc Tho's nine points, spelled out some of them in greater detail, omitted others altogether, and added some new ones.

Madame Binh's plan was clearly geared to the American public debate, dangling the prospect of a simple withdrawal-for-prisoners deal by grouping together the provisions on withdrawal and prisoners and creating the impression that the two were linked and perhaps could be separated from the rest of the package. The other points omitted any reference to Cambodia and Laos and were more vaguely expressed on some issues and more intransigent on others. For example, Madame Binh's proposals were sharper in spelling out a coalition government along familiar lines; they also deferred a cease-fire until such a government was formed, rather than its going into effect when the agreements were signed, as Le Duc Tho had had it.

Almost concurrently, Le Duc Tho strongly implied to Anthony Lewis of the *New York Times* on July 6 that Madame Binh's point 1—withdrawal for prisoners—could indeed be settled separately from the other provisions. This was a flat untruth; it was contradicted by the secret nine points, which explicitly linked all the provisions, calling them "an integrated whole." Similarly deceptive interviews were given to prominent antiwar Americans, including Senator George McGovern. Neither journalists nor legislators hesitated to take for granted the truth of Hanoi's claims and the deceit of ours. Le Duc Tho, in great form, reached new heights of cynicism when he suggested to journalists that he would be ready to meet if I asked him to do so.

Madame Binh's plan had its intended effect. Congress and the media were at one that the administration was passing up yet another unparalleled opportunity for peace. A *Baltimore Sun* editorial of July 3 spoke of an "opening in Paris." The *Washington Post* on July 8 saw "New Possibilities in Vietnam." The *Chicago Daily News* on July 9 detected a "faint scent of peace." *Newsweek* on July 12 headlined: "A Way to End the War?" Averell Harriman weighed in on July 15 with an article in the *New York Times* to the effect that Madame Binh had given us a "reasonable chance" to end the war. *Life* on July 23 had few doubts: "We hope President Nixon seizes the chance."

We were constrained from demonstrating that the "chance" was bogus and at variance with the entire record of the secret—and the public—negotiations, for precisely the opposite of the reason alleged by the critics. It was our eagerness to score a breakthrough that made us preserve a secrecy which enabled our adversaries to whipsaw the Nixon administration between a deceptive public position and a private record it could not publish.

No wonder that Nixon, always skeptical of negotiations, bombarded me with missives on my round-the-world trip to toughen up our stance in Paris and bring matters to a head. On almost all the negotiations I conducted, I was faced by this ambivalence. Nixon invariably approved the very detailed negotiating plan that I submitted to him. Then, when I was under way, he would deluge me with tough-sounding directives not always compatible with the plan, and some incapable of being carried out at all. The reason may have been his unease with the process of compromise or the fear of being rejected even in a diplomatic forum. A contributing cause was undoubtedly his highly developed sense of the historical record, which tempted him to ensure that he appear tougher than his associates; he was thus protected, whatever happened.

Ambivalence was compounded in this instance by the wish to be out of Vietnam before the presidential election of 1972, yet without having Saigon collapse. When the secret visit to Beijing succeeded, the first flush of euphoria caused Nixon to harden his Vietnam stand. Even the idea of suddenly announcing a total withdrawal coupled with an all-out air assault resurfaced in a Haig cable on July 12:

> You should be aware that he is seriously considering the alternative plan which he has mentioned previously of moving out precipitously and concurrently undertaking [a] major air effort against North. Obviously this message is characterized by overkill and instructions must be interpreted in the light of your discussions at previous stop [Beijing]. I did feel you should have the benefit of atmosphere here.

That afternoon, I was again face-to-face with Le Duc Tho and Xuan Thuy across a rectangular table covered with a green cloth. But the negotiating framework would never be the same again; it had been fundamentally changed by the trip to Beijing, though Le Duc Tho did not yet know this. Xuan Thuy again spoke first for Hanoi. His role was that of the picador in a bullfight. When serious exchanges began, Le Duc Tho would take over with his own monologue of Hanoi's view.

Not unexpectedly, the July 12 meeting began testily. I accused the North Vietnamese of bad faith in publishing Madame Binh's seven points, and Xuan Thuy answered with a grab bag of accusations, mostly about military actions within South Vietnam. However, the North Vietnamese were eager not to push these matters too far. They seemed anxious to engage in negotiations. Not yet knowing of my trip to Beijing, they thought they had us on the run; they probably wanted to see whether we would buckle.

"Negotiations," however, was a relative term. Le Duc Tho and Xuan Thuy would characterize their proposals as "concrete" and "factual"; ours by contrast were "unrealistic" and "vague" and "abstract," no matter how specific they might be. "Realism" was measured by correspondence with Hanoi's point of view. Le Duc Tho would treat his presence as a concession, his will-ingness to discuss our points—if only to reject them—as a sign of goodwill. He would introduce each new demand with the proposition that it was based on reason, fact, and history, which he would then explain at excruciating length—causing me on one occasion to remark that if he would emphasize reason and go easier on history, we would all be better off.

But with all these qualifications, the July 12 meeting did turn into a real negotiating session. We took the individual points of both documents, laying them side by side. It was apparent that agreement was within reach on most of the points (the principle of total U.S. withdrawal, release of POWs, reaffirmation of the Geneva agreements of 1954—which, among other things, established the DMZ—and 1962, an internationally supervised In-dochina-wide cease-fire at the end). There were two basic disputes: the de-mand for reparations, and Hanoi's insistence on the overthrow of the Saigon government. In spite of my previous rejection of it, the reparations question was not beyond compromise: It was primarily a matter of form, not sub-stance. We had said repeatedly in the private talks, and Nixon had stated publicly (as had President Johnson before him in several public pronounce-ments), that we would contribute to the economic rehabilitation of all of In-dochina, including North Vietnam, after the war. But we would do it of our own accord, not as an obligation.

Inevitably, it was the political issue that turned into the bone of con-tention. Le Duc Tho repeated: "I tell you in a serious way that you have to replace Thieu. . . . You have many means [to do this]." For one, he repeated, the forthcoming presidential election presented us with a perfect opportu-nity. Though phrased in terms of a single individual, it soon transpired that the demand included everyone not considered "peaceful" by Hanoi. And since Hanoi proposed to fight until it achieved its goals, anyone opposing it was causing war, hence was not peaceful, therefore had to be replaced. With every major non-Communist political figure thus disposed of, Le Duc Tho and Xuan Thuy took turns in seeking to cajole me into accepting their pro-posal. If this were done, we would have made a "big step forward" and "fa-vorable conditions will be created for a settlement." (Hanoi carried caution to the point of paranoia. It did not believe in making unconditional prom-ises. Even if we accepted its demand to overthrow Thieu, that would merely create "favorable conditions"; Hanoi left itself running room to put forward additional demands.)

Le Duc Tho disposed definitively once again (and would many times during the next year) of the argument of our critics that we should settle only the military issues and then withdraw. The dour and heroic men from Hanoi had not spent their lives fighting just for the chance to stop fighting. As Le Duc Tho told me on June 26: "There is no war without political goals. Military means are only the instruments to reach political ends." Clausewitz was alive and well in North Vietnam.

For some weeks, my colleagues and I were seduced by having settled in effect seven of the nine points; we hoped that Le Duc Tho's impassioned pleas to dismantle the Saigon government were a last-ditch effort to prove to his colleagues in Hanoi that we had reached the limit of our concessions and that they had better settle now for what was attainable. No doubt he assessed our conduct the same way. He must have thought it worth his while to persist in the negotiations with uncharacteristic flexibility to see whether, with all other issues solved, we would then throw the non-Communist South Vietnamese government to the wolves.

The talks had lasted four and a half hours. We set a new date for a meeting two weeks later, on July 26, indicating that we would in the meantime review each other's positions.

Before the July 26 meeting, I submitted a memorandum to Nixon indicating that we had narrowed differences to one issue—the political arrangements in Saigon:

> It is obvious that we cannot do their political work for them. For all his faults, Thieu has been a loyal ally. Moreover, the recent publication of the Pentagon Papers with their revelations about American complicity in the coup against Diem would make our involvement in Thieu's removal even more unpalatable. Last but not least, I am not even sure we could remove Thieu if we wanted to, unless we were prepared to engage in a major confrontation whose only certain result would be the destruction of South Vietnam's political fabric and everybody's self-respect.

We would not make peace at the price of overturning the South Vietnamese government. I continued to think that there was a chance that Le Duc Tho would drop his political demands.

I was wrong. At the meeting on July 26, we made further progress in meshing the formulations on all points save the political one. But it was becoming increasingly clear that these concessions were only come-ons to induce us to overthrow Thieu. Even with respect to the issues on which we seemed to be making progress, the wily Vietnamese had left themselves innumerable loopholes. No Martian observing the negotiation could have concluded that the men from Hanoi were representing an underdeveloped country inexperienced in world diplomacy. They were patient, disciplined, and superbly skillful in nuances of formulation. They had earned their place at the conference table by ruthless struggle; they would not give up its fruits for bourgeois notions of compromise, sentimental invocations of goodwill, or liberal ideas of free elections. It was our misfortune to stand in the way of Hanoi's obsessive drive for hegemony in Indochina. They fought us as strenuously and ably as they contemptuously used the sentimental misconceptions of so many of their supporters, our critics.

Le Duc Tho and Xuan Thuy had no interest in a free political process that they disdained. They would not hear of agreed limits on military aid by the United States; they wanted to cut off Saigon from *any* military supplies. For the third straight meeting, they zeroed in on the theme that having put Thieu into office, we had "the capability" to replace the "warlike and fascist" Nguyen Van Thieu. This time Xuan Thuy offered a secret understanding on the removal of Thieu: "We do not ask you to make a public statement. You should do that secretly." When I suggested that it would become obvious, Thuy persisted: "This understanding is between us only. It is not divulged." At an earlier point in the meeting, he made clear that a mere change of personalities would be insufficient: "If you change the person," he said, "and not change the policy . . . there is no change at all." Le Duc Tho was eager to be helpful. He even offered me the benefit of his professional advice as a revolutionary. During a break, he took me aside and suggested that if we did not know how to replace Thieu by means of the presidential election, assassination would do admirably. The vehemence of my refusal produced one of the few occasions when I saw Le Duc Tho temporarily flustered. He obviously had trouble understanding what I was getting so excited about. But he soon regained his aplomb. As we returned to the table, I summed up my problem with Hanoi's political "solution":

> What we cannot do is what you ask, to make a secret agreement
> to replace the leader of a country which is still an ally; which would

then lead to endless debate, moreover, as to what exactly a peaceful administration is, in which you have a veto because you are the only one who knows what is meant by peaceful. . . .

We want to end the war. We do not want to stand in the way of the people of South Vietnam. We are not permanent enemies of Vietnam. But you must not expect us to do impossible things.

So the issue was left at the meeting of July 26. Peace was as far away as ever.

The South Vietnamese Presidential Election

In the meantime, attention was increasingly focused on the presidential election scheduled for October 3 in South Vietnam. Hanoi had already shown that it was alive to the pretext the voting offered for removing Thieu. In the United States, there were many sincere and concerned individuals who thought that a fair democratic process in South Vietnam would unlock the door to negotiations. Why this should be so was never explained. The so-called Democratic Republic of Vietnam permitted no alternative political parties, had never held an election, and ridiculed the notion of free choice. With the self-assurance of experts who knew whereof they spoke, Xuan Thuy and Le Duc Tho never ceased explaining to me that the concept of a free election was meaningless: Whoever controlled the government would win.

Yet with all these handicaps, considerable progress had been made in developing democratic institutions in South Vietnam. Whereas Britain, in much less complex circumstances, had postponed elections for the duration of World War II, several elections had been held in South Vietnam while hundreds of thousands of North Vietnamese troops continued to despoil the country. In August 1970, in elections for the upper house of the National Assembly, sixteen slates competed, and opposition Buddhists won the most votes. In August 1971, in elections for the lower house, 1,200 candidates representing twelve major political parties and groups contended for the 159 seats and, again, opposition Buddhists won the most seats. Elections for local chiefs and councils had been held in over 95 percent of the country's villages; province chiefs and mayors were to be chosen by vote in November 1971.

The constitution of the Republic of Vietnam, promulgated in April

1967 and drafted with American advice and assistance, provided for a four-year presidential term. In the first presidential election, on September 3, 1967, Nguyen Van Thieu won with 35 percent of the vote. The second presidential election was scheduled for Sunday, October 3, 1971. Thus, at a crucial point in the history of America's involvement in Vietnam, an event imposed on Vietnam essentially by America turned into a new source of turmoil and uncertainty.

On May 19, the State Department issued elaborate instructions to American personnel in Vietnam to be neutral "in word, deed or act." On my visit to Saigon in July, I ostentatiously called on Ky, Minh, and the leader of the Buddhist opposition to emphasize our interest in a contested election. In August, I sent several back-channel messages to Ellsworth Bunker, reinforcing the formal instructions of the State Department, to explore the possibility of finding other opposition candidates or fixing a new date for an election for which they could qualify. I cabled Bunker that Thieu should not doubt the depth of the public reaction in America to high-handed methods. But neither Nixon nor I was prepared to toss Thieu to the wolves.

The premise of American neutrality in a South Vietnamese election made sense only if there was a real political contest with at least two authentic candidates. The U.S. government thus wound up in the curious position of searching for opponents to a President who was conducting a war as our ally. The two most likely prospects were Vice President Nguyen Cao Ky and General Duong Van Minh. Less than a year before, Ky had been considered so unpalatable to American critics that a visit to Washington was thought inopportune. But now there was a great effort to keep him in play as a candidate. When Minh headed the junta that overthrew President Diem, it was in part in order to prevent Diem and his brother Nhu from pursuing a coalition government. Minh now became the hope of many critics because his opaque comments lent themselves to the interpretation that he would accept Communists into his administration. He was believed to be the preference of Hanoi; Xuan Thuy implied on one occasion that he might be acceptable as a replacement for Thieu. But if Xuan Thuy's Delphic utterances meant what they implied, the reason was surely that all Vietnamese who knew Minh were agreed on one point: Minh was the most lackadaisical of the principal figures. If Hanoi accepted him—which was unclear—it would be because he was the easiest of all candidates to overthrow should he become President. (Minh finally became President when the Communists were about to take over Saigon in 1975. He was led out of the Presidential Palace by two North Vietnamese soldiers and was not seen again for years.)

Finally, there was Nguyen Van Thieu. He had not become President by accident. He was unquestionably the most formidable of the military leaders of South Vietnam, probably the ablest of all political personalities. Like most men who reach high office, he represented an amalgam of personal ambition and high motive. Those who do not find the exercise of power a tonic rarely aspire to it and almost never gain it. Equally, those without strong values cannot withstand the ambiguities, pressure, and anguish that are inseparable from great responsibility. Thieu clearly enjoyed his office; in this attribute, he was hardly alone among the world's chief executives. But he was also a man of principle; strongly anti-Communist, deeply religious and patriotic, highly intelligent, defending his people with great courage against an onslaught from within and without South Vietnam. He did not deserve the obloquy that those who sought excuses for our abdication insisted on visiting on him. He inherited a civil administration torn apart by the reckless coup against Diem, a guerrilla army threatening to overwhelm his country through systematic terror, and an invasion along a trackless border of 600 miles. He was saddled with an ally who first flooded his country with hundreds of thousands of troops and trained his army for a war not relevant to Southeast Asia; and then, while withdrawing at an accelerating rate, urged on him escalating concessions to an implacable enemy. He knew he could not possibly handle all these matters simultaneously without collapsing his government. But he did as many as he thought feasible, and more than many would have thought possible, including a major land reform. It was not his fault that our domestic critics proved insatiable and that, to many, he became a convenient scapegoat. He was not an obstacle to negotiations until the end, and—as I shall explain—he was in a terrible predicament even then. Periodically, Haig would visit Saigon to make a survey and to bring Thieu up to date. Though he must have had serious misgivings, Thieu conducted himself toward us— that eviscerating ally—without whining, with aloof dignity not untinged with contempt.

Thieu was convinced that South Vietnam could not afford a protracted period of ambiguous authority in the middle of a bitter war. His army had just suffered severe casualties in Laos. His ally had accelerated its withdrawals. He knew I was negotiating with Hanoi. And while he was familiar with the main outlines of our proposal, and had indeed approved them, he understood that

Hanoi would be insisting in all our meetings in Paris on his overthrow. His morbid suspiciousness—a quintessential Vietnamese trait—no doubt led him to fear that the offer might prove tempting. Nor was he ready to step down. Reminded repeatedly after 1967 that he had won with only 35 percent of the vote, he was determined this time to secure a bigger mandate. He therefore used the resources of incumbency without excessive delicacy.

His opponents, in turn, had no interest in participating in an election they were certain to lose even if it were conducted fairly. Minh easily collected the signatures required to qualify for the race but was uncertain about running. Ky, who wanted to run, had difficulty accumulating signatures because of Thieu's heavy-handed tactics. The Supreme Court of South Vietnam reinstated Ky in the race, but by then both he and Minh had chosen to withdraw. Ambassador Bunker tried in vain to persuade both to run. But they wanted in effect the same as Le Duc Tho: an American guarantee of their success. With Ky and Minh unwilling to run, the election turned into a referendum on Thieu. In the event, South Vietnam's voters, given the option of voting for Thieu, defacing their ballots, or boycotting the election, turned out 87 percent strong, of which 94 percent voted for Thieu. It would be preposterous to maintain that Hanoi lamented the absence of a fair election in Saigon. What bothered it was the American refusal to use the election as a pretext to decapitate the leadership of the non-Communist political structure in South Vietnam.

I met with the North Vietnamese again on August 16. Le Duc Tho was in Hanoi, which guaranteed that no breakthrough was possible. I opened the meeting by giving Xuan Thuy some unclassified technical material about the *Apollo* moonshots since Le Duc Tho had asked about them at the previous session. Xuan Thuy could not resist a wisecrack that although we had sent men to the moon, I had been a half-hour late to the meeting. (This was due to a private session I had had with the Chinese Ambassador to Paris, Huang Chen.) But when we got down to business, it became evident that this series of talks had deadlocked. Both sides knew that the military issues were capable of fairly rapid resolution. Each regularly made minor adjustments in its position to bring the formulations on those issues even closer together, and to tantalize the other side into concessions on the intractable political problem. We modified our original proposal that all our prisoners be released two months *before* our final withdrawal; we agreed that it could be simultaneous. We gave Xuan Thuy a rough estimate of economic assistance to all of Indochina after the war, though not as part of the agreement or as reparations. Hanoi agreed that all our prisoners throughout Indochina would be released and not only those held by the Vietnamese, as had been their original position.

But nothing could obscure our incapacity to settle the political issue. We would not make peace on Hanoi's terms of overthrowing an allied government. And for our principles, we were willing to brave domestic turmoil—focused irrelevantly on the essentially settled schedule for our withdrawal.

For some reason, Xuan Thuy insisted on another session a month later. His eagerness gave us another flicker of hope that maybe the Hanoi Politburo was using the time to review its position. Though Nixon was eager to break off the increasingly sterile contacts, I managed to persuade him that to meet would improve our negotiating record, that it gave Hanoi one more opportunity to modify its position, and that we had "nothing to lose, except my 36 hours of inconvenience." The absence of Le Duc Tho could leave no further doubt that we had run out the string on this series of meetings. Xuan Thuy made no effort to say anything new, in effect reading a propaganda speech of the kind put forth repetitively in the plenary sessions of Avenue Kléber. The meeting adjourned after two hours, the shortest session ever. At the end of one particularly bitter exchange, I summed up the impasse, not without some barbs at Xuan Thuy's subordinate status, and with a bravado implying that time (contrary to much of the evidence) was on our side:

> Now Mr. Minister, I know you have your instructions. And I know you are not authorized to be convinced by me. And you will make a reply that everything that happens is our fault. It is a pity. . . . The tragedy is that if we continue the war, then a year from now we will be at about the same point, and one day we will arrive at an agreement more or less on the terms we are discussing now. . . . But it is obvious from what you have said that you are not now disposed to do this. I have enough experience to know that nothing I can say can change your conviction, and even more, your instructions. . . . The only thing that remains for me to say is to express the hope that someday Hanoi will approach us with an attitude that we will make peace. If there is that attitude I know the Minister and I can find formulas to make peace. Until then, until we can find that attitude, we will stay as we are.

And this is what happened. Fourteen months later, we were to meet and set-tle essentially on the terms we had presented in the 1971 talks.

All that was left of the debates and negotiation of the summer was to per-mit our domestic critics to catch up with reality. Senator George McGovern had the opportunity of meeting with Xuan Thuy for four hours on Septem-ber 11. He left with the firm impression that the Communists were offering peace on the basis of a fixed date for U.S. withdrawal in exchange for the re-lease of prisoners. Though I knew such a deal was clearly inconsistent with Hanoi's nine points, Ambassador William Porter, who had taken over as the principal American negotiator, was instructed to explore it at the 129th ses-sion of the formal Paris peace talks, in order to put an end to the speculation once and for all. Porter told reporters after the meeting: "We spent the day trying to get them to confirm or deny officially things they have said in inter-views. They refused." In fact, the North Vietnamese shortly eliminated the previous ambiguity of their public position and announced yet again that the release of American prisoners was conditional on a political settlement. In the process, they left McGovern and several journalists high and dry. The *Washington Post* reported the next day:

> North Vietnam toughened its peace terms today, thereby scut-tling its carefully nurtured efforts over the past two months to appear more accommodating.
>
> Hanoi delegate Xuan Thuy made clear that the United States must "simultaneously" announce the end of its support for South Vietnamese President Thieu and total United States troop with-drawal before American prisoners could be released. . . . More opti-mistic impressions voiced by antiwar Sen. George McGovern (D-S.D.) and a hitherto unquestioned statement by Le Duc Tho, a Hanoi politburo member, were left in shreds.

The *Post* correspondent, Jonathan Randal, had for months been reporting the opposite on the basis of innuendos assiduously fostered by the North Vietnamese. Randal pleaded with the North Vietnamese press spokesman after the September 16 plenary meeting:

> You have known me for almost three years. Don't you under-stand why we no longer understand anything, and do you not under-

stand the confusion in our minds? Either things are not clear or I am a fool. . . . What you have said today contradicts not only the significance but maybe even the literal meaning of what we understood and filed. I feel like a fool.

Revealing the Secret Talks

Xuan Thuy's reaffirmation of Hanoi's rigid negotiating program meanwhile had had amazingly little effect on the American domestic debate. Even so staunch a figure as Senator Henry M. Jackson on September 10 urged a cutoff of aid to Vietnam unless Thieu arranged for a contested election. The *New York Times* of September 18 castigated Nixon for stating that we would stay until Saigon was able to defend itself against a Communist takeover. On September 30, the Senate voted a new version of the Mansfield amendment, making it national policy to pull all U.S. forces out in six months, dependent only upon return of prisoners. Hanoi, ironically, showed more faith in Vietnamization and the strength of the South Vietnamese resistance than our own senators or editorial writers. Its insistence that *we* overthrow the South Vietnamese government betrayed Hanoi's uncertainty whether it could accomplish the objective by itself after American withdrawal.

In this atmosphere, I submitted an analysis to Nixon on September 18, summing up where we stood on Vietnam diplomacy. I reiterated that if we overthrew the political structure of South Vietnam either by precipitate withdrawal or by excessive political concessions, friends and adversaries would conclude—after a brief moment of relief—that America's post–World War II leadership was giving way to a post-Vietnam abdication. An ignominious end in Vietnam would also leave deep scars on our society, fueling impulses for recrimination and deepening the existing crisis of authority.

I urged Nixon to authorize a new negotiating proposal on the political issue, which would go the limit of what was compatible with our obligations, our international position, and our honor. I proposed that we put forward a provision for a new presidential election in South Vietnam within six months of signing the final agreement. The election would be run by an electoral commission representing all the political forces, including the Communists, under international supervision. One month before this election, President

Thieu would resign, and his function would be assumed by the President of the Senate. Thieu would be free to stand for election. At that point, the small residual American force would be withdrawn. We would also shorten our withdrawal deadline from nine months to seven to allow for the time elapsed since our original proposal.

Nixon approved this offer on September 20. Haig left for Saigon on September 21. Thieu accepted it on September 23, telling Haig that he was prepared to announce also that he would not even be a candidate in a new election once peace was achieved. This we thought would go too far; we recommended he keep his options open. But Thieu announced in a public speech three days before his November election that if peace were achieved, he would return to civilian life. In light of Thieu's stubborn resistance to America's position in the final negotiations a year later, the speed of his accepting this proposal (which in retrospect I find demeaning) is difficult to explain. Perhaps Thieu knew the North Vietnamese well enough to be confident any proposal requiring free elections would be refused.

In the past, we had always handed Hanoi any new proposals at a meeting. Now we decided to submit it in writing along with a request for a meeting. We wanted to have the proposal on record in case Hanoi refused to meet and instead launched the now all but certain offensive. On October 11, General Walters called on Mai Van Bo, the North Vietnamese Delegate-General in Paris, to request a meeting with Le Duc Tho for November 1. Walters read a message saying we were responding to Minister Xuan Thuy's statement on September 13 that the North Vietnamese side would be forthcoming if a general proposal were made by the U.S. side. Our proposal was "one last attempt" to reach a just settlement before the end of 1971.

But Hanoi's grim and implacable leaders would compromise only as a last resort; protracted warfare was their profession. If they were to compromise, they had to prove to themselves that they had no other choice, and they were not yet at that point. They were determined on another military test of strength. Hanoi replied on October 25—with customary arrogance, only six days before the date suggested for the meeting. There was no expression of goodwill, no comment on our proposal, no reference to an eagerness to settle in any particular time frame. It coldly proposed November 20, giving as a reason that "Special Adviser Le Duc Tho has at the present time activities under way in Hanoi and furthermore Minister Xuan Thuy is still under medical treatment." Hanoi did not even deign to characterize the activities in Hanoi as "important."

We accepted the date in a curt note of November 3, and afterward expected the usual report that Le Duc Tho had left Hanoi. It never came. On November 17, or less than forty-eight hours before I was supposed to leave for Paris, Hanoi informed us that Le Duc Tho would not be present because he had "suddenly become ill." No alternative date was offered; no expression of readiness to settle accompanied the message; there was still no comment on our major new proposal over a month after we had transmitted it. The only grace note—which was also a sign of disdain—was that Xuan Thuy was "still agreeable" to meet. But it was clear from the whole record of previous meetings that Xuan Thuy had no authority to negotiate.

On November 19, we returned a reply summing up the status of the negotiations and stating we would meet only with Le Duc Tho or any other member of the Hanoi leadership in order to bring a rapid end to the war on a basis just for all parties. We never received a reply. The North Vietnamese, in the late stages of planning their major military offensive of 1972, were bending all their energies toward one culminating confrontation.

As the dry season began, the large North Vietnamese logistics buildup left little doubt that a Communist military offensive was approaching. It was essential that we seize the initiative. On December 23, we bombed supply complexes in North Vietnam south of the 20th parallel for two days, to editorial and congressional outrage. We sent strong notes to both Beijing and Moscow—with which summits had been scheduled—summarizing our exchanges with Hanoi and warning that an offensive would evoke the most serious retaliation. We did not think that either capital would prove helpful in the negotiation, but we considered it probable that they had their own objectives to protect at the forthcoming summits and that they would therefore prefer to avoid a crisis. No reply was received from China cautioning us—in itself a significant sign of dissociation by what had been considered until then the capital of world revolution. Dobrynin's answer contained a novel twist. As part of one of our periodic global reviews, he tried to blame Hanoi's intransigence on China. My secret visit to Beijing had become known in Hanoi only thirty-six hours before it was announced, he said. This had so infuriated Hanoi it had put the negotiations on ice to show that peace had to be made with it and not imposed by the great powers.

As a U.S. election year approached, and as a North Vietnamese offensive grew imminent, our domestic position was under assault again. It became imperative to enable the American public to understand that we had made every effort to negotiate an end to the war. Critics (including presidential candidates) were taking up Hanoi's theme that we had not responded to Madame Binh's seven points. We had kept secret the entire negotiating process and a series of forthcoming American proposals in the hope of making a breakthrough. We had been willing for the sake of peace to pay the price in domestic and world opinion. But with Hanoi's military planning and intransigence becoming ever more ominous, Nixon decided to place his negotiating record before the American people on January 25, 1972.

Nixon's speech was one of his most dramatic and impressive. He laid out the negotiating record of twelve private meetings with the North Vietnamese. He revealed that we had offered on May 31, 1971, to set a deadline for withdrawal but had been turned down. An annex to the speech published the seven points we had put forward in May, including the substitution of a prohibition of infiltration for mutual withdrawal. (Thieu had no reason to be surprised by our terms when Hanoi accepted them eight months later. What surprised him is that he had not expected Hanoi to do so.) Nixon reaffirmed our proposal of October 11, 1971, which spelled out a political settlement—internationally supervised free elections, with Communist involvement, and Thieu's willingness to step down a month before the election. Nixon reiterated that the "only thing this plan does not do is to join our enemy to overthrow our ally, which the United States of America will never do. If the enemy wants peace it will have to recognize the important difference between settlement and surrender."

The reaction was stunned surprise both at our long record of efforts and at the sweep of our proposals. The various presidential contenders responded with cautious support. The front-runner, Senator Edmund Muskie, called the plan "a welcome initiative." Hubert Humphrey reacted with characteristic ebullience: "So what, there are plenty of other issues"—implying that the speech had removed Vietnam as a political issue.[7] The *New York Times* on January 27 briefly abandoned its years-long carping and indicated cautious support, if not for every provision, at least for the overall approach. Most editorial comment followed this line.

Within a week, many of the critics were back in chorus. Once again the deadlock—Hanoi's rejection of America's proposals—was treated as entirely the administration's fault. But this time the criticisms demonstrated that we had won the psychological battle. The only alternatives left for critics to offer were unilateral withdrawal tied only to release of prisoners (already rejected by Hanoi) and the overthrow of the South Vietnamese government. Senator

Muskie responded in a speech on February 2 with a new turn: The United States should cut off all aid to Thieu, even after our unilateral withdrawal, unless he reached a settlement with the Communists. (Since the only terms available from Hanoi called for his overthrow, Thieu was being given the choice between execution and suicide.) This program became the new platform of antiwar protests and editorials. But the base of opposition support was narrowing. The war was deeply unpopular. Yet it seemed plain that however weary the public might be, it was not prepared to join an enemy in overthrowing an ally.

Meanwhile we sent the text of the President's speech to Moscow and Beijing with another emphatic warning that we would react strongly to a new offensive. Communist Party General Secretary Leonid Brezhnev replied in soothing fashion that he thought peace was still possible. Beijing, no doubt stung by Hanoi's charges as reported to me by Dobrynin, returned a tart reply on January 30 accusing us—not unjustly—of seeking to enmesh China. We responded sharply. The exchange had no effect on the Beijing summit three weeks later.

As for the North Vietnamese, we found them off stride. This was new in our experience. For a second time in six months, we had outmaneuvered them (the first time being the secret trip to Beijing). On January 31, they responded in Paris by publishing their side of the correspondence, including the nine-point peace plan that Le Duc Tho had presented to me on June 26, 1971.* Hanoi's spokesman, Nguyen Thanh Le, contrasted the two sides' peace plans, whose differences, he said, were "fundamental—like night and day." Le alleged that Hanoi had always wanted the substance of the negotiations to be public, but it had refrained "as wished by the U.S. party." Yet, in an effort "to shift onto the DRV side the responsibility for the deadlock of the negotiations," he said, the United States "has broken its engagements and created serious obstacles to the negotiations." He did not explain how the publication of positions that Hanoi had always wanted to publish could create obstacles to negotiations.

It was obvious that Hanoi sensed that it had offered thin gruel and was on the defensive, because soon afterward, on February 2, it published a two-point "elaboration" of its nine points. It was a slightly reworked version of the

---

* I had indicated in a January 26 briefing that we would not publish Hanoi's documents but would "have no objection" if Hanoi did.

old plan. Hanoi now explicitly agreed that American prisoners would be released on the date that our last troops withdrew. But this was linked to a political program that called for Thieu's immediate resignation, coupled with the dismantling of the "machine of oppression," meaning the police, the army, and the pacification program. So emasculated, the remaining South Vietnamese government was to negotiate with the fully armed Communists for setting up a coalition government containing the familiar tripartite structure. Not even the most ardent peace groups could find much sustenance in these propositions. It was no accident. After we had initialed the agreement a year later, I asked Le Duc Tho to tell me what exactly the two points had elaborated. "Nothing," he replied; they were advanced simply to have some "new" North Vietnamese position available to answer ours.

5

HANOI THROWS THE DICE: THE VIETNAMESE SPRING OFFENSIVE

Four weeks after Nixon's return from China, the long-awaited offensive in Vietnam finally took place. On March 30 of 1972, North Vietnamese artillery and infantry units launched coordinated attacks against South Vietnamese bases in northeast Quang Tri province. In violation of the understandings associated with the bombing halt four years earlier and the Geneva Accords of 1954, three North Vietnamese divisions poured across the Demilitarized Zone supported by more than 200 tanks and large numbers of new 130mm recoilless artillery, all furnished by the Soviet Union. Fresh units were poised to invade the northern part of South Vietnam from Laos along Route 9, reversing the direction of the South Vietnamese thrust into Laos the previous year, and to attack through the Ashau Valley toward Hue. There were ominous troop concentrations in the Central Highlands threatening the cities of Kontum and Pleiku. Three North Vietnamese divisions from Cambodia were moving into Military Region 3, which included Saigon. An enemy offensive was expected there at any moment. The pretense that the Vietnam conflict was a "people's war," a guerrilla uprising in the South, was over; this was an invasion by the North Vietnamese regular army in multi-division strength.

In Washington, as is usual at the onset of events, it was hard to find out exactly what was taking place. As early as March 31 (Good Friday), Secretary

Laird reported that the enemy offensive was a major one. But accounts from the Pentagon were initially soothing. General Abrams, we were told, did not consider that the attack had yet reached a critical stage; South Vietnamese fire-support bases seemed to be holding. There was no need for decisions at the highest level. For two days the attacks were treated as a major enemy probe.

On April 1, Nixon authorized American air attacks against military concentrations in North Vietnam, limited to within twenty-five miles north of the DMZ. But we encountered one of the perennial frustrations of the Vietnam war: Bad weather prevented air operations. Since the ceiling was constantly below 2,500 feet, very few missions could be flown.

On April 2, the South Vietnamese were forced to evacuate fourteen bases just south of the DMZ. There was no longer any doubt that a major offensive was under way. The next two months would be a decisive test of Vietnamization. We would now find out whether the effort and agony of the past three years had been productive or would vanish like a wisp of smoke in a breeze.

I was convinced that, whatever the outcome of the offensive, it would end the war. This was Hanoi's last throw of the dice. One way or another, there would now be serious negotiations; their substance would depend upon which side prevailed on the battlefield. If South Vietnam collapsed, the war would have ended in a debacle. If Saigon, with our help, held back the entire North Vietnamese army, Hanoi would have no choice but to come to terms.

The enemy offensive of 1972 had long been anticipated. The North Vietnamese had demonstrated in 1968 that they understood the impact of a major blow in a presidential election year. Now its onslaught coincided with the critical moment in the process of Vietnamization when our own forces had been reduced to a residual level, tempting Hanoi to determine whether in fact the South Vietnamese could take over their own defense.

Starting on January 4, 1972, General Abrams had warned of an imminent offensive. In a dispatch of January 20, he predicted that the enemy would attempt "to face us with the most difficult situation of which he is capable." Abrams predicted an offensive for as early as the first part of February, just before Nixon's trip to Beijing. He requested authority to disrupt the enemy's preparations by air attacks north of the DMZ. He concluded with a reminder that this would be the decisive battle and that he, as field commander, needed the maximum flexibility in advance. "In the final analysis," Abrams added perceptively, "when this is all over, [the] specific targets hit in the southern part of North Vietnam will not be a major issue. The issue will be whether Vietnamization has been a success or a failure."

I convened a meeting of the Senior Review Group on January 24 to consider General Abrams's requests. No one was eager to renew attacks on the North. The White House thought it would interfere with the trip to Beijing; the State Department feared it would ruin the prospects of negotiation with Hanoi; Defense was loath to assume new budgetary burdens. Everybody dreaded the public outcry sure to be unleashed by resuming the bombing of the North, even in a limited area. Some took refuge in minimizing the threat we faced, a not infrequent device to evade the need for decision. The consensus of the group was that the assault would come in the Central Highlands; there was disagreement over General Abrams's concern with the enemy's concentrations just above the DMZ. On January 26 Mel Laird found a classic compromise. He recommended that the President let Abrams have part of his cake but not the bombing of the North. He approved instead stepped-up air activity in the South and the placing of more sensors in the DMZ. Of course, the sensors would tell us whether an attack was taking place; they did not prevent it or increase our capability to resist it. I went along with Laird's refusal to authorize new attacks on the North for two reasons: It seemed unwise in the two weeks before Nixon's visit to China; and I thought that bombing made sense only if it were sustained, which it could not be except in reaction to an overwhelming provocation. I therefore favored delaying authority for resumed bombing until the offensive's dimensions became clearer. (We had come a long way since President Johnson and his associates in 1968 had sold the bombing halt as leading to "constructive negotiations" and had threatened immediate resumption of the bombing if the understandings were violated.)

Nixon called an NSC meeting on February 2 to which he invited Treasury Secretary John Connally, as he did in all cases where opposition to a strong course was likely and support was needed. I cannot find a record of the meeting, but the talking points prepared for the President read as follows:

> I will not accept any failure which can be attributed to a lack of available US support or shortcomings in our own leadership or decisiveness. We must do all we can to assist the South Vietnamese and to ensure that they have both the means and the will to meet Hanoi's challenge this year.

In the final analysis we cannot expect the enemy to negotiate seriously with us until he is convinced nothing can be gained by continuing the war. This will require an all out effort on our part during
the coming dry season. I can think of no more crucial period in this
painful conflict and I expect each of you to bring promptly to my attention any proposal you might have for additional steps which
might be taken to guarantee success.

Meanwhile, we were confronted with the contradictory necessities of our
domestic situation. These undercut at least part of our readiness measures.
On January 13, even while North Vietnamese forces were massing, Nixon
thought it necessary to announce a withdrawal of another 70,000 American
troops by May 1. In less than three years he had withdrawn 480,500 of the
545,000 troops that he had found in Vietnam when we entered office. He
had done so while improving the military situation and extending the area
controlled by the government in South Vietnam. But the appetite for withdrawals was insatiable; retreat had become an end in itself. And so, by early
March, with a decisive offensive clearly approaching, we found ourselves in
the anomalous position of augmenting with forces that did not count against
the troop ceiling—B-52s, aircraft carriers—while continuing the promised
withdrawals of ground troops and planning the announcement of the next
round of withdrawals, which would be expected about May 1. Nobody, not
even General Abrams—who, it was clear, was silent because he thought it
useless to protest—argued for the most sensible decision, which would have
been to halt withdrawals when a major offensive was imminent.[1]

March thus turned into a period of waiting and of decisions that reflected the national schizophrenia: Withdrawals were combined with reinforcements; threats of retaliation alternated with fleeting moments of hope
that maybe for once Hanoi was bluffing. We were neither anxious nor confident, but rather resigned to events. General Abrams, expecting simultaneous
attacks across the DMZ and in the Central Highlands, began to contemplate
the further possibility of a third concurrent enemy thrust from across the
Cambodian border facing Military Region 3. On March 10, I told Nixon to
expect an attack within ten days on three fronts in South Vietnam. I urged
him to stay his hand against the North until any fair-minded person could
see that it was not we who had sought a test of arms; then we should
respond in great force. In the meantime, the recently arrived air reinforce-

ments should be used to interrupt the enemy buildup within South Vietnam, Laos, and Cambodia and inhibit the launching of the offensive for as long as possible.

Diplomatic Maneuvers

As the North Vietnamese military preparations threatened three fronts in Vietnam, so we were active on three diplomatic fronts—with Hanoi, Moscow, and Beijing. We continued the strategy initiated by Nixon in his January 25 speech, when he revealed the secret negotiations with Hanoi, to bring home to the American people that their government had explored every avenue toward peace and to make clear to Hanoi that the negotiating option was still open. As I told a White House press conference on January 26, the day after the President's speech revealing the private talks:

> Now the question is: Is there to be another round of warfare? We believe that we can contain the offensive, and it is even possible, maybe even probable, that the reason they make the offensive is as a prelude to a subsequent negotiation. This at least has been their pattern in 1954 and was their pattern in 1968. So this is an attempt to say to them once again, "It is not necessary. Let's get the war over with now."

In my view, diplomacy was an essential element of military strategy. But also I favored preceding or at least accompanying any military move with a diplomatic one, even when I rated the chances of success as low. If rejected, a conciliatory offer would help sustain our military effort with the American public. By preempting critics' charges that we had somehow missed opportunities, we would enhance our endurance in holding out for honorable terms—which was the name of the game in Vietnam.

Therefore I generally advised Nixon to keep some offer before Hanoi— even if only an offer to meet. This would enable us to deal with the periodic new Communist proposals (the eight points, the seven points, the two-point elaboration, and so on) from a stance of having an alternative program. It furnished an opportunity to test whether Hanoi was willing to settle and a program in the name of which to resist if honorable terms remained unavailable. On the occasions we gave up this posture—by canceling plenary meetings or refusing to send an ambassador to the peace talks, for example—we soon found ourselves buffeted by the North Vietnamese and media and congressional critics in a public debate over procedural issues. We therefore coupled Nixon's January 25 speech with a private message to Hanoi suggesting the resumption of private meetings. The message was sent on January 26.

At the same time, we communicated with Moscow and Beijing. Nixon sent a letter to Brezhnev; a note was delivered by General Walters to Huang Chen, the Chinese ambassador in Paris—a former general in the Chinese Civil War and close associate of Mao and Zhou. Huang Chen had been designated as our principal conduit to Beijing—diplomatic relations not having been formally re-established. Both communications made essentially the same point: We had gone to the limit of what could honorably be offered. We would react strongly if Hanoi responded with a military offensive.

Both Beijing and Moscow were becoming restless. Neither wanted to be perceived as derelict in its duty to its North Vietnamese ally, lest it lose support in the rivalry within the Communist world. Yet both feared that Hanoi's intractability might thwart major objectives with America that had matured over a period of years. And they feared that a military reaction by America would sharpen their dilemma. By threatening serious reprisals if Hanoi challenged us, we did our best to foster nervousness in Moscow and Beijing.

Beijing's reply—in the private channel used whenever China (or Moscow, for that matter) sought to avoid a public row—disclaimed all knowledge of the Vietnam negotiations; it asserted no national or ideological interest, only its moral obligation toward a beleaguered people to which it owed a historical debt. China had never asked the United States to make any commitments over Vietnam, the note stated significantly; nor had China made any, which was true. China rejected any effort to "enmesh" it in Indochina. Beijing was in effect washing its hands of the whole affair; Hanoi was on its own. Since its material support for Hanoi was marginal because of its limited resources, a posture of indifference did not conflict with our strategy. And we did not press China further.

Moscow was more assertive, though its basic thrust was the same. It was not secure enough to admit ignorance of the negotiations; nor could it plausibly do so, given my periodic briefings of Dobrynin regarding them. The

Soviets flaunted their familiarity with the negotiating record, though I noticed that Hanoi, to discourage mediation, always kept them one cycle behind where the negotiations actually stood. In general, Moscow supported Hanoi's position but without fervor. On February 7, Dobrynin, in conveying Brezhnev's reply to Nixon's message, took care to point out that the arguments made against our latest proposal were not put forward in Moscow's name; they were all ascribed to the North Vietnamese. Moscow could not stick to this complex position forever. But the Soviet Union procrastinated for an uncommonly long period—well over a week—before finally endorsing Hanoi's negotiating position. Even that endorsement was elicited only after the North Vietnamese ambassador had called on Premier Kosygin. That meeting was described by *Pravda* as having taken place at the ambassador's request—which indicated a Soviet effort to dissociate from its client. And their talk took place in a spirit of "friendship and comradely frankness," which in Communist parlance generally means some disagreement. The TASS commentary was noticeably cool.

But we would not let Moscow disengage as easily as the Chinese. Almost all of the weapons being assembled for Hanoi's assault were Soviet. If Moscow did not encourage Hanoi's military effort (as it constantly claimed), it surely made it possible. We had long since decided, therefore, to press Moscow if an offensive developed. I warned Dobrynin repeatedly that the Moscow summit would be jeopardized if Hanoi sought to force a military decision. To give Moscow an additional incentive to press its ally, Nixon accepted early in the year the Kremlin's repeated invitation that I go to Moscow to help prepare the summit with the Soviet leadership. However, the visit was made conditional on some move by Moscow to end the war, preferably a North Vietnamese negotiator in Moscow empowered to settle.

There matters rested with the Soviet Union while Nixon visited China. After returning, we received low-key protests from Beijing and Moscow about alleged American bombing attacks against North Vietnam. Apparently Hanoi was giving its allies the same misinformation it used to influence our public opinion as a pretext to delay negotiations. There was in fact no basis for the charge, because we had deliberately held our fire against North Vietnam during Nixon's visit to Beijing, despite the increasingly ominous North Vietnamese buildup. And we restrained our air operations in March to avoid the perennial debate as to whether we had "provoked" the Communist assault. Hanoi had obviously urged its "fraternal" Communist allies to make their démarches; they could not refuse, but they showed their discomfort by essentially going through the motions.

These complicated maneuvers must be seen in the context of the evolving triangle in American-Soviet-Chinese relations. Both of the Communist major powers had, for their own reasons, opted for better relations with the United States. Each was deeply suspicious of the other. Neither wanted to forego its claim to leadership in the Communist world by visibly abandoning its ally in Hanoi. But neither did they want singleminded fanatics in Hanoi to disturb their greater designs. They compromised—each in its own way—by limiting their diplomatic support for Hanoi's offensive to tame rhetoric and by not interfering seriously with our retaliation.

While all the major powers—the United States, China, and the Soviet Union—were painting on a canvas larger than Indochina, there was one group of men with only one concern and a monomaniacal passion: the Politburo in Hanoi. Not used to being on the defensive, they responded on February 14 to our note of January 26, which had proposed another meeting with Le Duc Tho. To our astonishment Hanoi accepted. It broke with precedent by proposing a date for any time convenient to us after March 15.

The excessively conciliatory tone, so out of keeping with past North Vietnamese practice, was a kind of alert as were the frantic military preparations going on north of the Demilitarized Zone. Never before had Hanoi proposed a date so far ahead. (Thieu, being Vietnamese, spotted this last feature immediately when we informed him.) Never had it left the date to our convenience. It clearly was gearing the resumption of negotiations to the timing of its forthcoming offensive, scheduling talks to take place under conditions of maximum pressure and discomfiture for us. But we had our own reason for waiting, both with negotiations as well as with retaliation. Delaying a counterblow against North Vietnam until *after* the offensive had started would put the United States into the best political and psychological position to overcome the approaching onslaught and to sustain our retaliation publicly.

On February 16, the eve of our departure for China, we responded to Hanoi by proposing March 20 for the meeting with Le Duc Tho. We warned that "the attempt to place one side under military duress by escalating the level of military activity is inconsistent with the purpose of these meetings." On February 29 (after Nixon had left China), Vo Van Sung, Hanoi's delegate in Paris, summoned General Walters to inform him that Hanoi was "of course agreeable to a meeting on the 20th of March at 11:30," as the United States had proposed. That genteel formulation, too, was unusual. It was far from a matter of course that Hanoi would accept a date we proposed for this far ahead; it was downright unprecedented.

On March 6, Hanoi made an about-face; it informed us that March 20 was no longer suitable; it wanted to postpone the meeting to April 15. The pretext was weak, that the United States had engaged in extensive aerial attacks just before and just after the President's trip to Beijing. Not only was the charge untrue, it was absurd, for Hanoi had accepted the March 20 date two weeks after some of the fictitious air attacks were alleged to have taken place. As for attacks after Hanoi had replied, they would have been totally inconsistent with our strategy. We were staying well clear of the North precisely to avoid this sort of accusation.

By now it had become evident that it was the forthcoming offensive which controlled the timing of North Vietnamese diplomacy. Hanoi's leaders would launch the assault that they were so frenetically preparing and then use my meeting with Le Duc Tho to inhibit our military response; they thought we would hesitate to attack while a "negotiation" was going on. The delay showed that it had taken considerably longer than originally anticipated to prepare their blow. But the maneuver was too crude; Hanoi had overplayed its hand. The better our public record for having sought a negotiated alternative, the better our position to respond violently to an offensive—as we were determined to do.

So we reacted only verbally. On March 13, a very sharp note was returned going over the record of the exchanges. We "utterly rejected" Hanoi's charges: "A careful rechecking of the facts makes clear that the allegations of U.S. aerial attacks in the period March 1 to March 6 is totally unfounded." In diplomatic language we were calling the leaders in Hanoi liars. We declined the offer to meet on April 15 and suggested April 24. We used the occasion to repeat our warning against escalation of military activity.

All this time the plenary sessions in Paris were proceeding across the round table at Avenue Kléber. Starting them had rent our country in 1968. But they already had achieved a great distinction in the annals of diplomacy. In four years of negotiation and more than 140 meetings, not even the most minor issue had been settled; it was the only regular conference of such length that could not point to a single accomplishment, however trivial. (Nor was this record ever to be broken; the settlement was achieved in a different forum—the secret talks between the White House and Le Duc Tho; the conference's only role in the peacemaking process was the final signing ceremony of the accords after 174 fruitless meetings.) Each week the plenipotentiaries assembled in the Hotel Majestic. Each ambassador read a set speech and made one rebuttal; then they adjourned. Afterward each briefed the press separately about his or her presentation. For Xuan Thuy and Madame Nguyen Thi Binh, the press conferences were clearly more important than the meetings.

Three distinguished ambassadors had represented the American side during this charade: Henry Cabot Lodge, David Bruce, and now William Porter, since Bruce had from the beginning agreed to serve only for one year. Not enough can be said for the dedication with which they acquitted themselves. Each was backed up by one of the most extraordinary foreign service officers I have known: Phil Habib, an energetic and indomitable deputy, who held our delegation together and buttressed his superiors until he was appointed ambassador to Korea in 1971. To endure weekly harangues without any hope for a breakthrough, which they knew must come in the private channel, required unusual reserves of patience, devotion, and self-discipline. They were all now briefed about my meetings with Le Duc Tho, and I often sought their advice. (I had even invited David Bruce to sit in, but since his South Vietnamese colleague would not be attending, Bruce thought it best to be informed rather than to participate. William Porter finally sat in on the last stage of the negotiations in 1972.)

Nixon had never liked the plenary sessions at Avenue Kléber. He considered that they gave the North Vietnamese a weekly forum on television to undermine our domestic support. And he constantly sought ways to diminish their importance. In 1969, he had refused to name a replacement for Lodge for seven months. Now he seized the occasion again.

When Hanoi did not respond to the March 13 note for a week, Nixon suspended the Paris public sessions. In his March 24 news conference he had said that we were trying to "break a filibuster"; the enemy was using the Paris forum for propaganda, and on this basis, "there was no hope whatever." On March 27, with its offensive preparations nearly complete, Hanoi accepted the proposed date of April 24 for a private meeting—on the condition that the public talks were resumed before then.

To avoid the propaganda disadvantage if the secret meetings failed because of an American refusal to attend plenary sessions, Ambassador Porter was instructed to propose on April 6 a plenary session for April 13. If the secret meeting on April 24 proved sterile, we could then interrupt the plenary sessions again. By then we would know more about the scale of the offensive. Our purpose, as I informed Bunker, was to "write an impeccable record of reasonableness" and to give Hanoi a last warning that we were reaching the outer limits of restraint. We told Hanoi on April 2 that Porter would propose a plenary session for April 13 in expectation of a secret meeting on April 24. The message to Hanoi concluded with another grave warning:

> The U.S. side points out that the military operations launched by the North Vietnamese in recent days near the Demilitarized Zone and elsewhere and the firing of missiles from North Vietnamese territory into South Vietnamese airspace are inconsistent with the purpose of these meetings. The U.S. side has been showing great restraint in its response in order to give negotiations every chance to succeed but it cannot remain indifferent if the step-up of military operations continues.

The diplomatic minuet was about to be overwhelmed by the fury of the battle. The day our message was delivered to the North Vietnamese, the full extent of the offensive became clear, including its blatant violation of the 1968 "bombing halt understandings" to respect the Demilitarized Zone. But this time we had prepared our ground with good effect. We were in a strong psychological position to resist; and militarily we were determined to prevail.

What Strategy?

Once the scale of the offensive became apparent, several schools of thought developed within our government. An important group of officials thought that we should let events take their course, continuing our existing level of assistance but not augmenting it for dealing with the crisis. This view—held by the civilian officials in Defense, much of the State Department, and the systems analysis experts on my staff—rested on the proposition that the conclusive test of Vietnamization was at hand. Therefore, we should strengthen South Vietnam's capacity to defend itself; we should not increase our own effort. "We all recognize," said a summary memorandum submitted to me by my staff, "that the key is not what we do but what the South Vietnamese do."

But neither Nixon nor I accepted such reasoning. North Vietnam had brutally and cynically chosen a test of arms. It had played with us for months, using negotiations as a smoke screen for a massive invasion. For three years it had rejected all efforts to negotiate seriously. On March 20, ten days before the offensive, North Vietnamese Premier Pham Van Dong in a public speech rejected the very concept of compromise. "Now, as in the past, the U.S. aggressors are indulging in this contention: 'Each side must go half way in negotiation, the Seven Points must be conciliated with the Eight Points, and so on.' This is the logic of a gangster." Peace could come only if the United States ceased "all its support and commitments to the Nguyen Van Thieu puppet régime." Now, as before, we were given only one way out of the war—to dismantle our ally and withdraw unconditionally. We had rejected surrender at the conference table; we would refuse it on the battlefield.

Starting on April 2, Nixon and I reviewed the situation several times a day. The Washington Special Actions Group met every day—sometimes several times. On April 3, I told the President that the attack would now precipitate matters; we would get no awards for losing with moderation. If we defeated the offensive, a negotiated settlement was probable. The North Vietnamese had thrown everything into their effort; if it failed, they would have no choice except to negotiate seriously. If they waited until after the election, they might have to face a President who was freed from any electoral pressures during his second term.

Nixon needed no encouragement. He had warned for years that he would react strongly to a North Vietnamese offensive. And he was as good as his word. Against intense bureaucratic opposition, he ordered repeated augmentations of our air and naval forces in Southeast Asia. He removed all budgetary restraints on air sorties. He directed naval attacks extended twenty-five miles up the coast of North Vietnam. On April 4, he authorized tactical air strikes up to the 18th parallel in North Vietnam. Twenty additional B-52s, four more squadrons of F-4 fighter-bombers, and eight more destroyers were sent to Southeast Asia. On April 4, I told the WSAG that the President was determined to defeat the offensive. Hanoi had committed so many resources to the effort that, once stopped, it would almost certainly be obliged to settle. I asked every agency to give absolute priority to defeating the offensive.

But it proved difficult to translate this determination to the battlefield. One reason was the foul weather, which, to our frustration, grounded most of our planes during the first week. More fundamental was the frame of mind that had developed during a decade of restraints and three years of withdrawal. "Our impression," I told the WSAG on April 5, "is that our commanders have had it drilled into their heads that we want a minimum of activity and that they will receive rewards for getting out fast. They are not aggressive enough."

Even after the message had gotten across, serious differences developed between the field commander and the White House. For four years General Abrams had performed, with dignity and skill, one of the most thankless jobs ever assigned to an American general. He took over a force of 540,000 men in 1968 but was immediately shackled by mounting restrictions. He was continually given assignments that made no military sense. Starting in the middle of 1969, he was asked to dismantle his command at an ever accelerating rate while maintaining the security of South Vietnam and putting the South Vietnamese forces into a position from which they could undertake their own defense. He succeeded to a remarkable degree. By the time Hanoi struck in 1972, more of the countryside than ever before was under Saigon's control; most of the South Vietnamese units had vastly improved. Still, deep down, General Abrams knew that he was engaged in a holding action in a battle for which even a small strategic reserve of American ground forces would almost surely have been decisive. For three years his command had been turned into a withdrawal headquarters. Now he was being urged to win the crucial final battle with only skeleton American forces.

A dispute had developed between the command in Saigon and other decision-makers over whether our air campaign should be confined to the battle in the South or whether we should start bombing North Vietnam, as Nixon was determined to do. Now that there were more airplanes available than Abrams—or the Pentagon, for that matter—had ever requested, the command in Saigon focused wholly on the local situation; it wanted *all* of them targeted on South Vietnam. Laird supported Abrams because he thought this would best prove the validity of Vietnamization. Nixon (as did I) feared that course as leading to a stalemate. It would not generate enough pressure on Hanoi or its Soviet and Chinese patrons; Hanoi could simply halt its advance and sit on its newly conquered territory; Moscow and Beijing would have no decisions to make. North Vietnam would get a free ride despite its cynical disregard of the 1968 bombing halt understandings and the Geneva Accords of 1954. Now that the gauntlet had been thrown down, Nixon was determined on a showdown. He saw no point in further diplomacy until a military decision had been reached.

This left the question of how to treat the two Communist major powers before a military showdown. Should we lump Hanoi, Moscow, and Beijing together and confront them as a group? Or was it wiser to adopt a differentiated approach to isolate Hanoi and to magnify the strain in Sino-Soviet relations? In the event, it turned out to be a theoretical choice. Neither Moscow nor Beijing was eager to identify itself with Hanoi. Each in its own way made it clear that it would not risk its relationship with the United States on behalf of an obstreperous ally.

To give Moscow an incentive to dissociate from North Vietnam, we emphasized the larger interests it was jeopardizing. On April 3, I saw Dobrynin in the Map Room of the White House and accused the Soviet Union of complicity in Hanoi's attack. If the offensive continued, America would be forced into measures certain to present Moscow with difficult choices before the summit. In the meantime, we would link the Soviet interest in a German settlement to our interests in Vietnam. Moscow had asked us to urge West German parliamentary leaders to ratify a treaty with the Soviet Union recognizing the status of the East German satellite, scheduled for a vote in about a month's time. Under current conditions, I told Dobrynin, we could not be active in Bonn. Moscow could not ask for assistance in Europe while undermining America's position in Southeast Asia.

That same day, I sent Winston Lord to New York to see Huang Hua, the Chinese U.N. ambassador. We used Huang Hua to underline the urgency of the message; we did not want to waste time by going through the channel established in Paris. The pretext for the message was to reply to a Chinese protest (conveyed, it should be noted, privately) at the intrusion of American vessels into what China claimed as territorial waters around the Paracel Islands (a chain of islands off the coast of Vietnam). It was partly a dispute over the definition of territorial waters. Beijing claimed twelve miles; America's historical position had been three miles. Lord, known to the Chinese because he had been on every trip to China and had attended every meeting with Chinese leaders, handed over an "oral note" informing Huang Hua that, without prejudice to our legal position on territorial waters, the U.S. navy would be instructed to stay at a distance of twelve miles from the islands. But the main portion of our note was a reminder to Beijing of the American stake in Vietnam. In the sharpest language ever used in any message to the Chinese, we protested China's public backing of the North Vietnamese invasion. The note pointed out that Beijing could be under no misapprehension about the profound importance of the issue for the United States. It warned that "major countries have a responsibility to use a moderating influence on this issue and not to exacerbate the situation." Attempts to "impose a military solution upon the US can only lead to unfortunate consequences." It repeated that we attached "extreme importance" to the improvement of America's relations with China—implicitly warning that Vietnam was an obstacle.

On the following day, April 4, we began to hold the Soviet Union *publicly* accountable for the offensive. Robert McCloskey, the State Department press spokesman, pointed out at his regular briefing that the North Vietnamese invasion of the South was made possible by Soviet arms. McCloskey, perhaps the ablest press officer I have known, carried off the assignment so well that he triggered a series of confirming comments from other agencies, raising speculation that the entire U.S.-Soviet relationship, including the summit, was in jeopardy.

On the same day, we also decided to bring home to Hanoi that we meant business. We had informed it that we would resume plenary sessions of the Paris conference on April 13. Following the elaborate procedures that were in inverse proportion to the significance of the agenda, this would normally have required a formal proposal to be submitted a week before, or by April 6. With the offensive mounting in fury by the day, it had become absurd to request a plenary session. Therefore, a message was delivered on April 6 in Paris, informing Hanoi that the plenary session was being canceled.

> The Government of North Vietnam has intensified military operations against the territory of the Government of South Vietnam to include the most flagrant violations of the understandings of 1968. Because of this grave escalation of military activity, and the flagrant violation of the Geneva Accords and the understandings of 1968, Ambassador Porter will not now propose a Plenary Session for April 13, 1972. A decision about the Plenary Session for April 20 will depend on the circumstances existing at that time.

Nothing was said about the secret meeting of April 24; we put the onus on Hanoi to cancel that if it chose.

As it happened, the note of April 6 crossed a North Vietnamese message that illustrated what Hanoi promised itself from the secret meeting. In the midst of an offensive that violated every previous understanding, our self-confident interlocutors made their agreement to a private meeting conditional on America keeping its "engagement" to halt the bombing of the North. In fact, we had not yet really resumed bombing because of the weather. Nevertheless, it took extraordinary gall to try to hold the United States to an "engagement," every provision of which North Vietnam had already broken.

On April 6, too, I had another meeting with Dobrynin. I told him the present situation was intolerable. As I had warned him in January, a North Vietnamese offensive would force us to bring the war to a decisive military conclusion. As for the Soviets, either they had had a hand in planning it or their negligence had made it possible. Either interpretation raised unpleasant prospects. I briefly reviewed the status of preparations for the summit, to give Moscow a sense of what it stood to lose. We would now insist, I stressed, on ending the war by negotiation if possible, by force if necessary.

While putting on the diplomatic pressure, we continued the buildup of our forces. On April 9, twenty-eight more B-52s were sent to Guam. On April 10, a fifth aircraft carrier was ordered to Vietnam. The cruiser *Newport* and another carrier were moved from the Atlantic to Southeast Asia. By the end of the first week of April, the weather had lifted enough to begin bombing of tactical targets in North Vietnam. Authority was given to attack as far north as the 19th parallel.

Antiwar critics who depicted the military establishment as champing at the bit to sow death and destruction would have been amazed that almost all reinforcements occurred over the opposition of at least the civilian leadership of the Pentagon. Concerned by the budgetary pressures, eager to use the offensive to demonstrate the efficacy of Vietnamization, the Pentagon civilians on the whole maintained that the forces in the field were already sufficient. This might have been accurate by the sophisticated calculations of systems analysis; it was not adequate for the political goal of bringing matters to a head and overawing outside intervention. If we wanted to force a diplomatic solution, we had to create an impression of implacable determination to prevail; only this would bring about either active Soviet and Chinese assistance in settling the war or else Soviet and Chinese acquiescence in mounting military pressures.

As the new forces were being assembled in Southeast Asia, the NSC staff prepared contingency plans for their use. A planning paper by Al Haig dated April 6 outlined courses of action should South Vietnamese forces fail to halt the offensive. It provided for the bombing of all military targets throughout North Vietnam (except in a buffer zone along the Chinese border) and for the mining of all North Vietnamese ports.

Nixon briefly played with the idea of going on television to report on the offensive to the American people. William Safire was assigned to write the speech.[2] The project was abandoned as premature after a few days, around April 10. If the South Vietnamese held, there was no need to create a crisis atmosphere. If the North Vietnamese assault gained momentum, we would have to take drastic measures; that would be the right moment for a presidential speech. But as I told the President, if we failed and South Vietnam collapsed, not even ten speeches would do any good. We had a somber, philosophical conversation. Nixon mused that if we failed, it was because the great forces of history had moved in another direction. Not only South Vietnam but the whole free world would be lost. "No," I replied, "if it fails, we'll have to tighten our belts and turn the forces around."

We kept up the diplomatic pressure. On April 8, I sent a note to Egon Bahr, West German Chancellor Willy Brandt's adviser, warning him that we were reassessing our entire Soviet policy. Two military offensives against American interests made possible by Soviet arms within the space of six months was too much. (The first was the Indian attack on East Pakistan in December 1971.) We doubted the value of a policy of détente in these circumstances. Bahr, with the ratification of Brandt's Eastern treaties hanging in the balance, was certain to convey these sentiments to the Soviet ambassador in Bonn. And Moscow would be reminded that America was not without means of pressure. An American confrontation with the Soviet Union would surely risk ratification of the treaties by which the Federal Republic recognized the status quo in Eastern Europe.

On April 9, in a heavy-handed exercise of triangular diplomacy, I invited Anatoly Dobrynin to the White House to watch Chinese-made films of the President's Beijing visits, which he had expressed an interest in seeing. At the end Dobrynin complained that the American buildup in Southeast Asia was growing ominous. "Anatol," I replied, "we have been warning you for months that if there were an offensive we would take drastic measures to end the war once and for all. That situation has now arisen." Dobrynin volunteered that

Moscow was extremely interested in a successful outcome of my projected private meeting of April 24 with Le Duc Tho and had informed Hanoi accordingly.

Clearly, Moscow was getting nervous. I warned Dobrynin that we would no longer agree to talk while the fighting was going on. We would insist on an end to the offensive or we would take ever more serious measures. He did not bristle at this threat. The Soviets rarely bullied when they believed the opponent to be strong and serious. Dobrynin replied that he would transmit this warning to Moscow; he was certain there would be an early response.

Once engaged in confrontation, it is more dangerous to stop than to proceed. A pause in one's moves causes the other side to wonder whether it has seen the limit of the response and to test whether the status quo can be sustained. Confrontations end when the opponent decides that the risks are not worth the objective, and for this the risks must be kept high and incalculable. We therefore continued to raise both the diplomatic and military stakes.

On April 10 the President attended a State Department ceremony at which he signed a multilateral convention banning biological weapons. Dobrynin was present, Nixon took the occasion to remind the Soviet Union that a "great responsibility particularly rests upon the great powers" not to "encourage directly or indirectly any other nation to use force or armed aggression against one of its neighbors."

I spoke to Dobrynin an hour later to elaborate on the President's remarks. We would not stand still for the tactic by which Hanoi had whipsawed us in the last two series of secret talks. If Hanoi once again published new proposals in the middle of negotiations, the secret channel would be at an end. Dobrynin used this occasion to mention that we could take a hundred reporters to the summit in Moscow. Clearly, nothing had yet happened to change the Kremlin's priorities.

We stepped up military pressure in Vietnam. Even before the President put the Soviets on notice at the State Department ceremony, twelve B-52s had struck supply dumps near the North Vietnamese port of Vinh, about 150 miles north of the Demilitarized Zone. It was the first use of B-52s in North Vietnam by the Nixon administration.* It was a warning that things might get out of hand if the offensive did not stop.

April 10 was a busy day. The Chinese Foreign Ministry issued a rare pub-

---

* B-52s had been used against North Vietnam by the Johnson administration in 1967.

lic criticism of our air attacks on North Vietnam and hailed Communist victories in the South. Despite its polemic tone, we considered the statement to be minimal for the occasion. Its condemnation of our bombing demonstrated ideological solidarity; the catalogue of Communist victories forestalled any claim on additional Chinese resources. We noted that the Chinese statement failed to pledge the standard "resolute" support nor did it demand—as previous statements had—that the United States accept Hanoi's terms. Throughout the spring and summer, China confined most of its protests to the private channel, and even there, in almost every case, protested only instances when American aircraft or vessels impinged on *China's* sovereign airspace or territorial waters.

By now the offensive was in full swing on all three fronts. Several Communist divisions were crossing the DMZ deep into Quang Tri province in Military Region 1. An attack was developing in the Central Highlands, and farther south against the provincial capital of An Loc. We responded on April 11 by canceling the plenary session scheduled for April 20. We told Hanoi: "In light of the continued flagrant violation of the Demilitarized Zone by the North Vietnamese and the extension of military operations into Military Regions 3 and 4 of South Vietnam, no useful purpose would be served by the holding of a plenary session of the Paris Conference on April 20." The note offered to proceed with the secret meeting of April 24 and to resume plenaries should that meeting prove successful.

The pressure was beginning to tell on Hanoi. Though its offensive was now in high gear, it faced an American buildup that was as menacing as our bombing was unexpected. The South Vietnamese, though gradually being driven back, were still holding. Too cautious in attack, they were fighting adequately when on the defensive. On April 15, Hanoi turned down the proposed private meeting with Le Duc Tho for April 24 until we agreed to resume the public sessions. But it did so in an uncharacteristically halfhearted way that showed profound confusion. It suggested April 27 for resuming the plenaries and May 6 for the secret meeting; May 6 was chosen, the note said, to give Le Duc Tho time to travel. Rarely before had Hanoi answered so rapidly or offered an explanation for any of its decisions.

We decided to stick to our strategy. On April 16, we proposed that the secret meeting take place as scheduled on April 24, *after* which we would attend the plenary meeting on April 27. The North Vietnamese replied on April 19—again with unprecedented speed. After condemning the "atrocious" intensification of the air and naval war against North Vietnam, including the B-52 raids against Hanoi and Haiphong, Hanoi added a slight sweetener to its previous proposal. It stuck to April 27 for a plenary and May 6 for a secret meeting, but said that if the United States announced its willingness to return to the plenaries, Le Duc Tho would leave immediately for Paris.

Both sides were clearly shadowboxing, half wanting a private meeting, half not, careful above all to avoid the onus of canceling. In effect, both sought to keep the possibility open until the opportune moment. The North Vietnamese wanted to time a meeting for the moment of our maximum discomfiture in the wake of a massive defeat. We wanted to hold it only after the Soviets had been brought fully into the game. It would have been a simple matter to find some formula for simultaneous agreement on secret and plenary meetings; this would quickly have resolved the matter. But we wanted to play that card with Moscow.

A great deal now depended on the exchanges with the Soviet Union. The Soviets had begun to engage themselves in earnest on April 12. During a luncheon to review summit preparations, Dobrynin let it be known that my planned (but shortly to be canceled) meeting with Le Duc Tho was crucial. He assured me that his leadership was not interested in a showdown. I replied that the Soviets had put themselves into the position where a small ally could jeopardize everything that had been negotiated for years. The Soviet Union must have known when it signed two supplementary aid agreements during the year that it was giving the North Vietnamese the wherewithal to launch an offensive. What did the Soviet leaders expect? Did they think the President would run the risk of being defeated and having 69,000 Americans taken prisoner? Dobrynin objected that the North Vietnamese had often offered to repatriate all Americans immediately. I said, "Anatol, this is not worthy of comment, and that situation will not arise. There must be a meeting this month. It must lead to concrete results, and if it does not there will be incalculable consequences."

Dobrynin replied that it seemed to him that a visit by me to Moscow, which had been discussed since early in the year, was now urgent. The agenda could be Vietnam, as well as accelerated preparations for the summit. I told Dobrynin I would put this idea to the President.

The proposition evoked the most diverse emotions in Nixon. He was eager for the summit. To be the first American President in Moscow stimulated his sense of history; to go where Eisenhower had been rebuffed would fulfill his ambition to outstrip his mentor. To be sure, he often spoke of canceling the summit. But anyone familiar with his style knew that such queries, like occasional musings about his dispensability,[3] were really meant to elicit reassurance. On the other hand, Nixon did not want to go to Moscow in a position of weakness, and he was suspicious of a Soviet maneuver to delay or complicate our planned military campaign against North Vietnam by means of negotiations in Moscow. Not the least of Nixon's concerns was how he would explain to Rogers yet another secret mission by his National Security Adviser, this time to Moscow, which he had prevented his Secretary of State from visiting for nearly four years. (Rogers had wanted to make an advance trip to Moscow to match my advance trips to Beijing; Nixon had turned him down.)

Nixon had little to lose and much to gain from a preparatory visit to Moscow. For the first time Moscow had offered to engage directly in discussions on Vietnam at a high level and without conditions. That mere fact was bound to disquiet Hanoi. The Kremlin could not string us along; it could gain no more time than the days I spent in Moscow. As for the summit preparations, they provided the vehicle by which to separate Moscow's interests from Hanoi's; the summit was Moscow's incentive either to press Hanoi toward compromise or to acquiesce if we forced the issue by military means. If my trip advanced the prospects for the summit—as was likely—it would help neutralize a Soviet response to our retaliation; Moscow would then know clearly what price it would pay by reacting against us. It was, of course, possible that Moscow was playing the same game. But we had more to lose in Vietnam than Moscow stood to gain by our humiliation. Thus in an odd way the American bargaining position was stronger; our threats were more plausible.

On April 12, Nixon authorized me to inform Dobrynin that I would arrive in Moscow April 20. I even resurrected the proposal to meet a senior North Vietnamese official in Moscow, an offer unlikely to be accepted but useful in keeping the Kremlin on the defensive and us in the position of being ready to negotiate. But Nixon's mood fluctuated. On April 12, he urged me to discuss not only Vietnam in Moscow but also the summit. However, by April 15 he was worried that Brezhnev would "filibuster" me and our hands would be tied militarily for a week. The summit was sure to go down the drain if we played our "hole card" of blockade against the North. Perhaps we should preempt by canceling the summit ourselves, he told me. I assured him that even while I was in Moscow we could bomb all over North Vietnam except in the area of Hanoi and Haiphong. Moreover, my trip to Moscow would itself be a "hole card" to neutralize domestic critics and Soviet responses. Nor did I believe that cancellation of the summit was a certainty. Nixon then agreed that my trip was "a good thing to do. . . . I think it's right; you've just got to go," he said. He now was sure that "the strategy, which you and I both agree on, is the right one"—but he clearly wanted reassurance. At any rate, Nixon's memoirs leave no doubt that by the end of the day on April 15, he came back to the conclusion that I should proceed.[4]

To make sure that both Hanoi and Moscow understood our determination, Nixon had approved a dramatic two-day B-52 attack on fuel storage depots in the Hanoi-Haiphong area together with a shore bombardment by naval gunfire. It took place on the weekend of April 15–16. By chance, April 15 was the day that Hanoi turned down our proposal for a meeting on April 24, a decision which—allowing for transmission time for its messages—it clearly had made before the attack. This postponement gave us the opportunity to assume the offensive. When one is running risks, it is almost always preferable to be bold. A strong message was sent to the Soviets on April 15 questioning whether any progress could be made on Vietnam during my visit to Moscow if the Soviet Union could not bring about even one meeting on an agreed date.

That evening Dobrynin came to my home to discuss the message and to urge me to go ahead with the plan to visit Moscow. Dobrynin, who must have known from the news tickers of the B-52 attacks, did not mention them. In an extremely friendly manner he suggested that great powers must be able to put local differences aside to settle fundamental issues. I said, "Anatol, for us it isn't just an international problem; it has now become a major domestic problem. We cannot permit our domestic structure to be constantly tormented by this country ten thousand miles away. The war must now be brought to a conclusion, and we will do it either together with the other great powers or alone."

The next morning, April 16, Dobrynin read me a message from the Soviet leadership stating that they had brought my complaint about the aborted secret meeting to the attention of Hanoi. Hanoi "could agree" to a secret meeting on April 24 if the plenary meetings were also resumed; this was puzzling since Hanoi the day before had rejected a meeting on April 24.

There was also an implication that its agreement was dependent on a halt to the "expanded" bombing of North Vietnam. Hanoi had not yet responded to my suggestion to meet with North Vietnamese representatives in Moscow. Hanoi was clearly thrashing around. Its conduct lacked the self-assurance of previous years.

Finally, a formal Soviet protest arrived. Four Soviet merchant ships had been accidentally hit in Haiphong harbor, with loss of life. Like the Chinese, the Soviet protests about the bombing of North Vietnam took on a grave tone only when Soviet lives or property were in jeopardy. About the B-52 attacks, Moscow confined itself to an expression of regret because it "seriously complicates the situation." Nevertheless, the Kremlin assured us that our views were being conveyed to Hanoi. What was significant was not that the criticism stopped well short of a protest but that Moscow maintained its invitation even in the face of an unprecedented assault on its client.

As for Beijing, on April 12, we had received a stiff reply to the note of April 3 in the private channel. China expressed solidarity with North Vietnam and warned us that we were getting bogged down further. But the note made no threats and concluded with a reaffirmation of Chinese interest in the normalization of relations with the United States.

As I departed on my secret trip to Moscow, we had not been panicked by the offensive; we had assembled massive power to blunt it should Hanoi refuse negotiations. We were in the process of separating Hanoi from its allies. The next weeks would tell whether there would be a negotiation or another test of arms.

6

THE SHOWDOWN

B rezhnev spoke from notes when he opened the first session of our meeting in Moscow on April 21—a departure from what we had learned of his practice in encounters with foreign leaders, where he had relied on prepared statements. Brezhnev effusively expressed his commitment to the success of the summit planned for May 22. There would be agreements, he insisted. "We have no wish to bring about a quarrel in the [summit] meeting. That is something we could easily do by staying in Washington and Moscow." He referred only tangentially to Vietnam. In an uncharacteristically delicate reference to the B-52 bombing of Hanoi and Haiphong four days before my arrival, he observed: "Unfortunately it so happens that events in the recent period—shortly before this private meeting between us— dampened the atmosphere somewhat." It was not much of a statement of support for an ally being bombed daily. And even this was immediately qualified by a reassurance: "I am not saying this will reduce the prospects for our meeting." The next day Brezhnev said that he controlled neither our peace proposals nor our bombers, offering no suggestions for the former and uttering no threat with respect to the latter. His priority was clearly the summit and U.S.-Soviet relations, not Vietnam.

All of the first day, however, was to be devoted to Vietnam. On behalf of the President I expressed our commitment to a successful summit. We wanted to improve not only the atmosphere but also the substance of East-West relationships. This set the stage for an exposition of North Vietnamese duplicity and of our determination to bring matters to a head in Vietnam. I said bluntly that Hanoi's offensive threatened the summit. I asserted that the

Soviets had an interest in preventing a North Vietnamese victory; I doubted that the President would come to Moscow if America suffered a defeat there. Even if the outcome were still in doubt by then, the American people would be aware that it was Soviet equipment which had made Hanoi's offensive possible; hence the President's freedom of action would be severely limited. "I must in all honesty tell the General Secretary that if developments continue unchecked, either we will take actions which will threaten the summit or, if the summit should take place, we will lose the freedom of action to achieve the objective which we described." I insisted that there had to be a private meeting with Le Duc Tho before May 6—the date suggested by Hanoi for initiating secret discussions—and that it would have to be conclusive: "We are not interested in talks. We are interested in results."

Brezhnev's response was mild in the extreme. He did not dispute my characterization of the North Vietnamese. He did not answer my thinly veiled threats. He read instead a note from Hanoi refusing to send an emissary to meet me in Moscow. He proudly showed me the cable, which I was of course unable to read, to demonstrate that he alone was listed on the distribution. The North Vietnamese were now insisting on resumption of the plenary sessions on April 27 to be followed by a secret meeting on May 6. They added two minor concessions, however; Le Duc Tho would leave Hanoi as soon as we had accepted a plenary session, and we could propose an earlier date provided we gave Le Duc Tho a week to reach Paris. (He usually traveled via Beijing and Moscow, stopping for consultations in each "fraternal" capital.) The North Vietnamese, who trusted no one, not even their principal supporter, forty-eight hours earlier had sent us directly the very proposal Brezhnev read to me. They had felt no need to remind us, however, of their long-standing refusal to meet me in Moscow.

As was already clear before I went to Moscow, a private meeting required some formula to preserve everyone's face. For this we did not need Soviet assistance. What we had to accomplish in Moscow was to convey our determination to bring matters to a head; to estimate our host's likely response if we proceeded unilaterally; and to engage the Kremlin in a manner most likely to bring home to Hanoi its increasing isolation. Above all, we were determined to bring matters to a head by shortening the deadline before a meeting. I told Brezhnev ominously: "So we have two requirements. The first is that the meeting cannot take place on May 6; first, because I am occupied on that day, and secondly, because that is too late; as I told your Ambassador, May 2 is the latest date I can attend and on which private talks still make sense." I warned that at the next meeting Le Duc Tho had to change his negotiating habits. We would no longer hold still for a recital of ultimatums in which Hanoi's demands were treated as the sole revealed truth: "If this process is maintained we will act unilaterally at whatever risk to whatever relationship."

It was a measure of Brezhnev's commitment to the summit that he listened to these provocative remarks without demur. Only the Chinese, he said, opposed the summit: "You should bear in mind that powerful forces in the world are out to block the summit meeting. It would be quite a big gift to the Chinese if the meeting did not come off. It would only help China." In other words Brezhnev would go to great lengths to avoid canceling the summit. Nothing could have revealed better the Soviet fixation with China than Brezhnev's apparent assumption that something that helped China would by definition be anathema to us. The "Chinese menace" had become second nature; it supplied its own justification even when cited to an American who, not two months previously, had drafted a communiqué in Beijing in which the agreed opposition to hegemony was clearly aimed at the Soviet Union. This obsession also accounted for the compulsive manner in which the Soviet leader kept raising China, oscillating between seeming uneasiness and the unshakable conviction that sooner or later—if the Soviets only kept long enough at warning us—we would join them in a joint effort to stifle what they considered the overwhelming threat from the East.

The next day, April 22, involved another five-hour session. I began by presenting a compromise proposal to break the deadlock over the sequence of plenary and private meetings with the North Vietnamese: We would attend a plenary session on April 27, provided Hanoi agreed in advance of it to a private meeting on May 2. I pointed out that this was the last practicable date before we had to make "other decisions"; results therefore had to be achieved at that meeting. Brezhnev hailed my proposal as "constructive." As far as I was concerned, its major utility was to make the Soviets share responsibility for the meeting's outcome and to put the onus on Hanoi for its failure.

I next put forward a substantive proposal that had been approved by the President on April 19: withdrawal of those North Vietnamese units that had entered South Vietnam since March 29, respect for the DMZ, immediate exchange of prisoners who had been held for more than four years, and a serious effort to negotiate a settlement within an agreed time period. In return, the United States would halt the bombing of North Vietnam and withdraw the air and naval forces we had introduced since March 29.

Brezhnev responded in an extraordinarily conciliatory manner. He mumbled something about the difficulty of withdrawing North Vietnamese divisions in the midst of an offensive. "Just by listening by ear"—assuring me he did not want to "raise any conditions"—he wondered if we could "perhaps" exclude that provision. What would I think of a cease-fire along existing lines with all units staying in place? I said that three weeks earlier we would have seized such an opportunity. Now that Hanoi had put its entire army into the South, it would no longer do:

> But now we have a situation where North Vietnam has violated the understanding we had with them in 1968. You know very well in this room that there was an understanding to respect the Demilitarized Zone. Therefore, it is imperative, if we are to stop the bombing, that they withdraw the divisions that crossed the DMZ, and that henceforth the DMZ be respected.

I doubted that Hanoi would accept a cease-fire in place—a proposal that had been on the table since May 31, 1971. If Hanoi should be interested, we would surely hear about it on May 2. That would be the time to make the decision; it was not an issue to be settled in Moscow. And my Soviet hosts were in no mood to debate Vietnam proposals. Brezhnev was obviously eager to get on to other business. He therefore agreed to submit our proposals to Hanoi. And, in fact, the head of the Soviet Central Committee section dealing with foreign Communist Parties, Konstantin Katushev, left on a special plane for Hanoi shortly afterward. Moscow was now engaged.

(Lest this account give an incorrect impression of Soviet pliability, it must be stressed that it covers only the Vietnam portion of the dialogue with Brezhnev. Much of the time was spent on completing the preparations for the Moscow summit visit of Nixon. Brezhnev's eagerness to achieve this—in part as a counterweight to our opening to Beijing—represented the "carrot" to achieve Soviet acquiescence in our policy on Vietnam.)

Hanoi accepted our proposal for a private talk on May 2, but on April 24, the very day that it accepted the proposal, it launched a military offensive in the Central Highlands. A powerful assault threatened the provincial capitals of Kontum and Pleiku, in the process destroying about half of the South

Vietnamese 22nd Division. Attacks also multiplied against An Loc, another provincial capital, sixty miles north of Saigon. Clearly, the North Vietnamese did not believe in the utility of gestures of goodwill so incessantly urged on us by our critics. They wanted us in a position of maximum military disadvantage when the talks resumed; they hoped to bring about a South Vietnamese collapse before our pressures, political or military, could work.

Nevertheless, we went through with the meeting of May 2 with Le Duc Tho, however painful it was to wait before responding to the new offensive. Our challenge was as much psychological and political as military. We needed to keep our domestic, diplomatic, and military moves in tandem. When we retaliated, it had to be clear that it was Hanoi that had chosen a test of strength rather than a negotiated settlement. And the closer to the summit we could act, the more the Soviet leadership would be committed to its success and the more incentive it would have to acquiesce in any countermeasures we might take against Hanoi.

At first, everything seemed to fall into place. On the morning of April 25, my secret trip to Moscow was made public; in the evening the resumption of the Paris plenaries was announced. The next morning, April 26, Nixon announced the next slice of troop withdrawals. This was imposed upon us once again by the completion of the 70,000-man withdrawal announced three months earlier, and with it came the dilemma that intensified with every increment of America's retreat. The fewer troops there were left, the deeper would be the impact of constant withdrawals. At the current rate there would soon be no residual forces left as negotiating counters. But if withdrawals were slowed, congressional and media critics would proclaim Vietnamization a failure and add another domestic complication to the growing uneasiness about the outcome of the North Vietnamese offensive. And indeed not a single congressman, senator, or commentator called attention to the anomaly of withdrawing forces in the midst of an enemy offensive.

Nixon finally settled on a figure of 20,000 over two months, having reached another understanding with General Abrams that most of the withdrawals would occur at the end of the period; by then, the North Vietnamese offensive was likely to have run its course. The major advantage of announcing the withdrawals was that Nixon could report about the military situation on television in a context that offered hope, rather than in the crisis atmosphere that would have surrounded a presidential speech addressed solely to the North Vietnamese offensive. In the event, Nixon, speaking from the Oval Office, mixed determination with conciliation. He contrasted our record of peace proposals with the enemy's steady buildup for a new offensive. This "invasion" was "a clear case of naked and unprovoked aggression across an international border." Twelve of North Vietnam's thirteen regular combat divisions were in South Vietnam, Laos, or Cambodia. The South Vietnamese forces were doing the ground fighting, with United States air and naval forces engaged in support. Nixon announced the 20,000-man withdrawal. His instruction to Ambassador William Porter to attend the plenary session the next day (announced by press secretary Ron Ziegler the day before) was a sign of our readiness to negotiate. Nixon could take justifiable pride in the record:

> By July 1 we will have withdrawn over 90 percent of our forces that were in Vietnam in 1969. Before the enemy's invasion began, we had cut our air sorties in half. We have offered exceedingly generous terms for peace. The only thing we have refused to do is to accede to the enemy's demand to overthrow the lawfully constituted Government of South Vietnam and to impose a Communist dictatorship in its place.

Hanoi answered the withdrawal announcement by launching another offensive, this time in the far north, against Quang Tri. On April 27, five days before I was to meet with Le Duc Tho, the North Vietnamese attacked with the heaviest artillery barrage of the war and large numbers of tanks. In the next few days the South Vietnamese 3rd Division was destroyed. The North Vietnamese captured their first provincial capital when Quang Tri fell on May 1, and most of the province was occupied as well. Many South Vietnamese units panicked. We estimated 20,000 South Vietnamese casualties, a large percentage of them civilians.

Nixon grew increasingly restive. We were bombing up to the 20th parallel, but refrained from attacking Hanoi and Haiphong pending my May 2 meeting with Le Duc Tho. In the face of Hanoi's renewed offensive, Nixon was eager to do something. On April 30, he told me that he had "decided" to cancel the summit "unless we get a settlement." As usual, it was part of the assistant's task—expected by Nixon—to winnow out those "decisions" that he really did not mean to have implemented. I urged Nixon to defer any escalation until after the May 2 meeting. We would know within forty-eight hours whether Hanoi was seeking a showdown or a negotiation.

Nevertheless, on the same day, Nixon sent me a long memorandum ordering a three-day B-52 strike against Hanoi and Haiphong for the following weekend (May 5–7), apparently regardless of the outcome of my meeting with Le Duc Tho. He was determined, he said again, to cancel the summit unless the situation improved.[1] Speaking to the press at John Connally's ranch in Texas that evening, Nixon warned that Hanoi was "taking a very great risk" if it continued its offensive in the South.

On May 1, Brezhnev wrote to Nixon suggesting that prospects for negotiations would improve if we exercised restraint. This was damaged merchandise; it was exactly the same argument used to obtain the bombing halt in 1968, but a bit shopworn after 147 fruitless plenary sessions. Brezhnev, trying a little linkage in reverse, suggested that such a course would also enhance the prospects for the summit.

Nixon saw in the letter a confirmation of all his suspicions that Hanoi and Moscow were in collusion.[2] To me, however, Brezhnev's intervention seemed no more than standard rhetoric. His letter made no threat; it spoke of the impact of bombing on the "atmosphere" of the summit; it made no hint at cancellation. Since I was leaving that evening for Paris, it was idle to speculate. Our course would have to turn on Le Duc Tho's attitude, not on what the Soviets said. There was no doubt that if the meeting failed, some new, fundamental decisions were in order.

The May 2 Secret Meeting

My meeting with Le Duc Tho was brutal. Contrary to the mythology of the time, the North Vietnamese were never more difficult than when they thought they had a strong military position—and never more conciliatory than when in trouble on the battlefield. Unfortunately for our emotional balance, Tuesday, May 2, was a day on which Le Duc Tho was confident he had the upper hand. Quang Tri had fallen the day before. Pleiku was in peril. An Loc was now surrounded. For all Le Duc Tho knew, a complete South Vietnamese collapse was imminent. Le Duc Tho was prone to boast that Hanoi was impervious to military pressure; he clearly did not believe that we were.

Le Duc Tho immediately went on the offensive. He opened by accusing the United States of having interrupted the private meetings—an extraordinary effrontery given the record of Hanoi's canceling the November 20 meeting on three days' notice, not responding for two months to our offer to meet on an alternative date, and then postponing several scheduled sessions to fit in with the plans for the North Vietnamese offensive. Having arrived directly at the meeting from an overnight transatlantic flight, I was testy and made no effort to be diplomatic. "I don't know what world you live in, but I'm under the illusion that you postponed the private meetings. In fact, a man who says he is your representative was giving us notes, so we have it in writing."

Le Duc Tho was not to be put off. He resumed his attack with the argument that Hanoi's offensive was not in fact an offensive since it had been provoked by the United States, which was the real aggressor. He proceeded to quote statements from our American critics to support his argument, which led to a testy exchange:

> KISSINGER: I won't listen to statements by American domestic figures. I have told this to the Special Adviser.
>
> LE DUC THO: I would like to quote a sentence from Senator Fulbright to show you what Americans themselves are saying.
>
> KISSINGER: Our domestic discussions are no concern of yours, and I understand what the Senator said.
>
> LE DUC THO: I would like to give you the evidence. It is an American source, not our source. Senator Fulbright said on April 8 that the acts of the liberation forces in South Vietnam are in direct response to your sabotage of the Paris Conference—
>
> KISSINGER: I have heard it before. There is no need to translate. Let's get on to the discussion.
>
> LE DUC THO: I would like to quote—
>
> KISSINGER: I have heard it before. Please go ahead.

When we finally got down to business, I stated our position, hinting that we had discussed it with the Soviets:

> We are meeting with you today in the expectation that you have something constructive to say. There are three requirements for effec-

tive negotiations. First, your offensive must stop. Second, the 1968 Understandings must be restored. Third, there must be serious, concrete and constructive negotiations leading to a rapid conclusion of the conflict.

We are prepared to make our contribution to this last point. We are willing to work with you to bring about a hopeful opening towards a peaceful settlement. But I don't want to underrate the seriousness of the point at which we meet and your side, which has chosen to launch a major offensive while pretending to prepare for private meetings with us, now has the responsibility to put forward concrete suggestions.

That is all I have to say at this moment. Besides, I understand your allies have already told you some of the ideas we have.

But Le Duc Tho had no suggestions, concrete or otherwise. He simply went through the motions. Hanoi had never responded to our proposal of October 11, 1971, regarding procedures for a free presidential election in South Vietnam, or its amplification in Nixon's speech of January 25, 1972. Le Duc Tho took the occasion to drop it without further discussion. Quoting a statement by Secretary Rogers that our eight points were "not an ultimatum," he suggested that we should begin the negotiations with our fallback position: "Now show us what flexibility you have and I am prepared to discuss your new flexibility, the new position you will express. We know that time is not on your side."

We had never been given an explanation of what Hanoi found inadequate in an American proposal that offered a cease-fire, total withdrawal, and the resignation of an allied head of government a month before an internationally supervised free election in which the Communists could participate. We were given no explanation now, nor was there the slightest hint of North Vietnamese flexibility. All Xuan Thuy would do was to read me the published text of their "two-point elaboration," issued three months before. Since major decisions flowed from this meeting, it is important to catch its flavor:

> KISSINGER: What's new about that? I have read it. I know what
> it says. What do we have to answer? We went through the
> seven and nine points. Is there anything there that we did
> not discuss last summer?

XUAN THUY: It says that—[continues to read from point 1 of the two-point elaboration].

KISSINGER: I have read it. There is no need to read it again. That's not my question. This is what we discussed last summer. We gave an exhaustive answer last summer. What additional answer is needed?

XUAN THUY: You don't set a specific date for withdrawal of your forces. You put only a six-month period.

KISSINGER: I know you are asking for the same thing we refused to do last summer [a deadline that would run independent of any agreement]. I'm asking whether you said anything new that requires an additional answer.

XUAN THUY: But since you refused, we have to continue our demand. The more you refuse, the more we have to continue our demand.

The second point of the two-point elaboration deals with the political problem in South Vietnam.

KISSINGER: I have read it. I know the words very well.

XUAN THUY: You don't respond.

KISSINGER: We rejected it not because we don't understand it but because we understand it only too well.

XUAN THUY: Since you still refuse to answer, it shows you have not understood. So if you want us to present it again, I will.

KISSINGER: You don't have to present it again.

My first private meeting with the North Vietnamese in nearly eight months, the object of so many weeks of effort, thus consisted of nothing more than Hanoi's reading its public position to me without explanation, modification, or attempt at negotiation. I suggested that there was really nothing left to discuss. Le Duc Tho thought otherwise. In his view I had been deprived for too long of his epic poem of American treachery and Vietnamese heroism, and he now made up for this neglect. I suggested that perhaps one way to start the discussions would be to return to the situation of March 29, before the North Vietnamese offensive, in which case we would end our bombing and also withdraw our reinforcements. Le Duc Tho contemptuously dismissed this as to our unilateral advantage. I summed up where we now stood:

> Mr. Special Adviser and Mr. Minister, much as I enjoy this conversation about the history of the war, I don't see that you are ready to talk seriously about bringing about a rapid solution to the war. Since that is not the case, much as I regret coming a long distance for a very brief meeting, I propose that we adjourn the meeting and meet again when either side has something new to say. . . .
>
> I want to make it perfectly clear that we notified you in February that we were prepared to discuss our eight points and include discussion of your points. You have refused to discuss our eight points at all. Since you are prepared to discuss only your points, points which we already explored last summer, there is no basis for discussion. We have invited you to make counter-proposals to our suggestions. But they have not been made. We have asked you whether there was anything new in your proposals and you simply read me your proposal. We told your Soviet allies last week what we wanted to discuss and they said they would transmit them to you. I find it difficult to understand why you meet with us at all since you knew what we wanted to discuss.
>
> I want to make it absolutely clear, so that there is no misunderstanding, we are prepared to discuss any political process which genuinely leaves the political future of South Vietnam open. We are not prepared to discuss proposals which have the practical consequence of simply installing your version of a government in Saigon. We told you this last summer. We tell you this again.

At this point, Xuan Thuy, evidently thinking the record was not yet complete, responded by reiterating the demand for the immediate resignation of Thieu—"the sooner the better. If . . . tomorrow, it would be better." After that, the remaining "Saigon Administration" should change its policy, abolish the system of repression, abandon Vietnamization. When I asked him to explain why a Vietnamese government should abandon a policy of Vietnamization, he reverted again to Hanoi's unchanging demand for a tripartite coalition government in which the anti-Communist government, decapitated and deprived of its police and army, was supposed to join a coalition with "neutralists" (approved by Hanoi) and the fully armed Communists backed by the North Vietnamese.

As my interlocutors were in such a feisty mood, I decided to use the occasion to nail down once and for all an issue that had rent our public debate for over a year. All that time Hanoi had given in public the impression that the military and political issues could be separated, that if we withdrew our forces, our prisoners would be released, while in all meetings with me, it consistently and totally rejected the notion. As I have already pointed out, media and congressional urgings in that direction were unending. The following exchange settles the issue:

> KISSINGER: All last summer—you know well—there was a whole succession of journalists and senators who came to see you. They came away with the impression that you were prepared to discuss a military solution only. It is true that you never said so explicitly, but with great skill you left that impression. . . . Let me sum up where we go from here. We are prepared to reopen these talks either on the military issues alone, that is the complex of issues on withdrawal and prisoners of war. But my impression is that at this moment you are not prepared to discuss this. I want to make sure I learned my lessons properly.
>
> LE DUC THO: So you have correctly learned this lesson because I never separated these two questions. And when I talked to newspapermen I did not tell them this. The newspapers were just speculating.
>
> KISSINGER: But you didn't do much to discourage them.
>
> LE DUC THO: They speculate too much.

The die was cast. I had advocated delaying an all-out military response until we had explored every diplomatic avenue. We had used the time to assemble power for a massive blow. We had striven to bring about the greatest possible diplomatic isolation of Hanoi. Now there was no question that the back of the North Vietnamese offensive had to be broken militarily. We might obtain Soviet acquiescence in what was necessary, but Moscow clearly either could not or would not affect Hanoi's decisions until the outcome of the offensive was clear. Perhaps Moscow would cancel the summit, but the summit was not worth having if Saigon collapsed under the weight of Soviet arms. The point of decision had arrived.

The Mining and Bombing of North Vietnam

On my way home from Paris on May 2, I cabled the White House and Saigon to begin preparing for the crucial choices. Haig informed me that the President had received my preliminary report calmly and with resignation. Haig had passed on to him my recommendation that he withhold any decision until we had analyzed the implications of the meeting. It seemed to me that we needed not a spasm produced by disappointment but a long-range plan of action. Haig's cable also brought the news that a South Vietnamese base on the perimeter of Hue had been evacuated under heavy enemy assault. If the old imperial capital fell, the rout might well be on; South Vietnam could be on the verge of disintegration.

A little later another report arrived from Haig. Nixon was adamant about ordering a two-day B-52 strike on Hanoi, starting Friday, May 5. He thought this essential for public opinion, for South Vietnamese morale, and as a signal to the Soviets and North Vietnamese. Again Nixon had mused about canceling the summit, referring to it as a "political" question—meaning that it was outside my sphere of competence. Haig knew my views; he repeated that he had told Nixon to be careful not to pursue a course "which will cost us both the summit and not achieve what we are seeking with respect to Southeast Asia." Haig urged me to reflect on our options on the way back. He and a helicopter would meet me at Andrews Air Force Base and take me to the Washington Navy Yard and the presidential yacht, *Sequoia,* where Nixon would discuss the strategy to be adopted.

Nixon's journey to a decision was often tortuous. He would put forward propositions disguised as orders that he expected to be challenged. Until the last possible moment he would put forward several often contradictory options. But when the moment of decision was reached, the nervous agitation would give way to a calm decisiveness. At moments of real crisis, Nixon would be coldly analytical. He might shrink his circle of advisers to a very few; he would surely withdraw to his hideaway in the Executive Office Building. He would sit there with a yellow pad, feet on a hassock, working out his choices. He would call in his close associates for endless meetings, going over the same questions again and again until one almost began to hope that some catastrophe would provide a pretext for going back to one's own office to get to work. But once launched on the process, he would—in foreign policy matters at least—invariably get to the essence of the problem and take the course dictated by his view of the national interest, rather than his political advantage.

So it was on this occasion. I described my meeting with Le Duc Tho. Its significance was not that the North Vietnamese had been unyielding, even bloody-minded. That had been true of previous meetings. What the May 2 meeting revealed was Hanoi's conviction that it was so close to victory that it no longer needed even the pretense of a negotiation. It would have been easy for Le Duc Tho to sound conciliatory, to advance some ambiguous formulation that would have put us in the dilemma of whether to escalate the conflict in the face of a possible diplomatic opportunity. An offer of a cease-fire in place, for example—with Communist forces at the outskirts of Hue, encircling An Loc, and threatening Kontum and Pleiku—would have demoralized Saigon had we accepted it, and shaken our domestic support if we refused. Le Duc Tho's disdain of any stratagem indicated that in Hanoi's judgment the rout had begun, beyond America's capacity to reverse. Our action had to provide a shock that would give the North pause and rally the South.

Nixon was still eager for B-52 strikes against Hanoi and Haiphong starting Friday, May 5. I did not believe a one-shot operation would meet our needs; I urged Nixon to wait until a plan for sustained operations could be developed. In addition, I knew that General Abrams was opposed because he wanted to throw all B-52s into the ground battle in the South. How specifically to react was primarily a tactical question. But Nixon, Haig, and I were all agreed that a major military move was called for and that we would decide on its nature within forty-eight hours.

What concerned Nixon most was the imminent Moscow summit. Haunted by the memory of Eisenhower's experience in 1960, when Khrushchev canceled a planned summit on short notice—after a U-2 spy plane was shot down over the Soviet Union—he was determined that any cancellation or postponement should come at his initiative. My view was that we had no choice; we would have to run whatever risk was necessary. If Le Duc Tho was right and the collapse was at hand, we would not be able to go to

Moscow. We could not fraternize with Soviet leaders while Soviet-made tanks were rolling through the streets of South Vietnamese cities. We had sought to give Hanoi every opportunity for compromise and the Soviets the maximum incentive to dissociate from Hanoi. That strategy would now have to be put to the test. We would have to break the back of Hanoi's offensive, to reestablish the psychological equilibrium in Indochina. Whether to preempt the expected cancellation or leave the decision to the Soviets seemed to me a matter for Nixon's political judgment.

Nixon was adamant that a cancellation by Moscow would be humiliating for him and politically disastrous; if it had to be, we must cancel the summit ourselves. He ordered preparation of a set of severe retaliatory military measures against the North Vietnamese. He would address the nation early the following week to explain whatever military moves he finally decided on, and announce his cancellation of the summit. SALT—the talks on the limitation of strategic arms—would go forward, however; it could be signed in a low-key way at a lower level.

Our first move was to warn the Soviet leaders that grave decisions were impending. On May 3, Nixon wrote to Brezhnev informing him of my fruitless meeting with Le Duc Tho. Hanoi was attempting to force us to accept terms tantamount to surrender. We would not permit this. After our experience at the Paris meeting, we would communicate no further proposals; in the light of Hanoi's conduct, there was no reason to believe they would have any positive effect. The letter spoke of "decisions" about to be made. It implied that the Soviet Union was at least partly responsible. It asked coldly for Brezhnev's "assessment of the situation" on an urgent basis.

The rest of May 3 was spent in preparing the military plans. They included various levels of air attacks north of the 20th parallel—that is, the Hanoi-Haiphong area—as well as the option of blockading North Vietnam that had been considered as part of the Duck Hook planning in 1969. Nixon went over the options with me late at night in the Lincoln Sitting Room without, however, making any decisions. Haldeman sat in on some of these meetings. He had no views on the military operations, but he strongly opposed cancellation of the summit, and said so. He saw no benefit in taking the initiative; it would, on the contrary, damage the President by making him appear impulsive. Nixon suggested that Haldeman and I solicit John Connally's views.

We called on Connally at the Treasury Department around noon on

Thursday, May 4, in the elegant office of the Secretary of the Treasury. We explained that the President was determined to resume bombing in the Hanoi-Haiphong area, beginning with a three-day B-52 strike, and had decided to preempt Moscow's probable reaction by canceling the summit. Haldeman said that he disagreed with the latter option. Connally resoundingly seconded Haldeman. He would hear nothing of cancellation; it would gain us nothing domestically. Either way we would be charged with jeopardizing East-West relations; if we took the initiative in canceling, the accusation of rashness would be added to the usual barrage of criticisms. We should do what we thought was necessary and leave the dilemma to the Soviets, whose arms had made it all possible. Anyway, Connally did not think it a foregone conclusion that the Soviets would cancel.

Connally's second contribution was to stress that while *we* should not cancel the summit, we also should not refrain from doing what we thought necessary out of fear of the Soviets' doing so. Whatever measures we took had to be decisive. Challenging the Soviet Union was, in fact, safer if we showed no hesitation. The principal issue, he said, was simply what would be the most effective military response.

I told Connally that we needed a military step that would at once shock Hanoi sufficiently to change the course of events in Vietnam and could be in terms of American public opinion. A three-day B-52 attack on Hanoi and Haiphong would give the shock but would be too brief. In the sustained longer term it might be negated by the public outrage that it would probably generate at home; it would be a godsend for our critics. (It also had to contend with the reluctance of General Abrams, who, even though his air forces had been augmented far above his recommendations, still insisted that he needed all his assets for the crucial battle in South Vietnam.) My preferred strategy was the plan first developed in 1969 and resubmitted on April 6: the blockade of North Vietnam, to be accomplished by mining.

I favored a blockade because it would force Hanoi to conserve its supplies and thus slow down its offensive at least until reliable new overland routes had been established through China. Since most of the supplies would be Soviet, this would be far from automatic. I preferred mining because it did not require the repeated confrontations of a blockade enforced by intercepting ships. Even though the brunt of stopping the offensive would still have to be borne by the forces in South Vietnam, the mining would create strong pressures for negotiations as enemy supplies in the South were running down. I agreed with bombing north of the 20th parallel, including Hanoi and Haiphong, especially concentrating on road and rail links to China by which Hanoi might try to circumvent the blockade. Connally strongly supported the blockade and expressed no objection to the bombing strategy.

When I reported Connally's views, Nixon's ready acceptance of them demonstrated how reluctant, despite all the bravado, had been his "decision" to cancel the summit. He scheduled a meeting for 3:00 P.M.; he, Haig, Haldeman, and I were to be the sole participants. In the meantime, I asked Admiral Moorer about the Joint Chiefs' view of the mining option and the timing of its implementation. Moorer was enthusiastic, having repeatedly recommended it in the 1960s; he had also participated in the Duck Hook planning in 1969 as Chief of Naval Operations and had been consulted by Haig on the subject in early April. He thought that the mining could be carried out as early as May 9, Indochina time, or the evening of May 8 in Washington.

We met in Nixon's hideaway in the Executive Office Building at the appointed hour. The President was calm and analytical. The only symptom of his excitement was that instead of slouching in an easy chair with his feet on a hassock as usual, he was pacing up and down, gesticulating with a pipe on which he was occasionally puffing, something I had never previously seen him do. On one level he was playing MacArthur. On another he was steeling himself for a decision on which his political future and the position of America in the world would depend. Playacting aside, he was crisp and decisive, his questions thoughtful and to the point.

Nixon did not again mention canceling the summit. Whether persuaded by Connally's argument or by his own long-standing desire to carry out Eisenhower's plan to visit Moscow, he proceeded with a much stronger military response than any previously considered, and yet he was willing to put the burden of abandoning the summit on the Soviets. Nixon then and there decided upon the mining of North Vietnamese ports. He would speak to the nation on Monday evening, May 8, or as soon thereafter as the mining could be implemented. He would convene the National Security Council that morning to give his advisers a last opportunity to express their opinions. The decision on holding the summit would then be up to the Soviets.

It was one of the finest hours of Nixon's presidency. He could have taken the advice of his commander in the field, supported by his Secretary of Defense, and concentrated on the battle in South Vietnam. He could have temporized, which is what most leaders do, and then blamed the collapse of South Vietnam on events running out of control. He could have concentrated on the summit and used it to obscure the failure of his Vietnam policy. Nixon did none of these. In an election year, he risked his political future on a course most of his Cabinet questioned. He was willing to abandon the summit because he would not go to Moscow in the midst of a defeat imposed by Soviet arms. And he had insisted on an honorable withdrawal from Vietnam, because he was convinced that the stability of the post–Vietnam world would depend on it.

We no longer sought to hide that major decisions were imminent; the less surprising they were, the less likely that Moscow would react emotionally. On May 4, one of the regular plenary sessions took place in Paris; they had been resumed only the week before. At its end, Ambassador Porter, as instructed, refused to schedule another meeting, by reason of "lack of progress in every available channel." On May 5, Hanoi violated the secrecy pledge on which it had itself insisted and disclosed that Le Duc Tho and I had met on May 2. It did not characterize the meeting or reveal that I had refused another date. Instead, it floated rumors that I had agreed to a coalition government. Such crude duplicity could be explained, if at all, only as an attempt at psychological warfare, to create an impression that would compound the demoralization of Saigon. The ploy was too transparent and cynical. It actually played into Nixon's hands by enabling him to use Hanoi's intransigence at the May 2 meeting to explain the actions that would now be inevitable. We advised Thieu to ignore Hanoi; we were on course and would not be deflected. He was free to deny the rumors of a coalition government in any manner he saw fit.

On May 5, I stressed again to Dobrynin that grave decisions were in train. The President was not angry, I said, he was preparing our actions coldly and deliberately. We were no longer asking Moscow to do anything. We would look after our own needs. We asked of Moscow only understanding of what had brought us to this point. To make sure that the command in Saigon was under no misapprehension about the President's determination, a back channel was sent to Ambassador Bunker on the President's behalf:

> To put it in the bluntest terms, we are not interested in half-measures; we want to demonstrate to Hanoi that we really mean business and we want to strike in a fashion that maximizes their diffi-

culties in sorting out what their priorities should be in responding to these retaliatory actions.

There should be no question in either your or General Abrams' mind that we want to devote the necessary assets to this action. If in your judgment the assets required for operations in the North lead you to conclude that more air is needed to meet tactical exigencies in the South, then that air should be promptly requested and we will get it to you.

Abrams responded through Bunker that his forces were sufficient. Bunker added his own personal appreciation for the President's courage.

My conversation with Dobrynin triggered a rapid reply from Brezhnev to the President's letter of May 3. On the afternoon of Saturday, May 6, Dobrynin delivered a letter distinguished by its near irrelevance to the real situation. In defiance of all evidence, Brezhnev insisted that our "pessimism" about my meeting with Le Duc Tho was "unjustified." On the basis of Katushev's visit to Hanoi, he could assure us that North Vietnam was ready to seek a political settlement; of course, he added, this required a coalition government. In other words we could have peace by accepting Hanoi's terms; for this insight Brezhnev was not needed. Brezhnev tactlessly mentioned the Pentagon Papers among the reasons that Hanoi allegedly had to mistrust the actions and intentions of the United States—a gaffe hardly likely to elicit a calm reaction from Nixon. Brezhnev cautioned us against attempting to exert military pressure on Hanoi, hinting darkly that this could "entail serious consequences" for peace and for Soviet-American relations.

Brezhnev's letter served only to reinforce our determination. He threatened no specific responses; the danger to peace he foresaw was stated hypothetically and as arising "even irrespective of our wishes." In any event, the United States could not delay because of vague Soviet predictions and elliptical threats. We did not answer the letter until we had already acted.

In Vietnam, meantime, a lull had settled over the battlefronts. An Loc remained surrounded; the North Vietnamese were still moving up supplies for the attack on Hue and Kontum. Sunday, May 7, was spent in preparing for the NSC meeting. In contrast with the Cambodian operation two years earlier, the mood was one of resigned determination, not incipient hysteria. Seeing the President toasting Brezhnev while we were being defeated by Soviet arms in Vietnam would not be understood by Americans whose sons had risked or given their lives there or were on the verge of being taken prisoner. Lord and I spent the beautiful spring day at Camp David working with the President on the speech he proposed to deliver the next evening. The imminence of a television appearance had its usual electric effect on Nixon. While every public appearance made him nervous, once he had leaped the psychological hurdle toward decision, momentum took over. Though technically the decision to proceed was not to be made until the NSC meeting the next morning, every succeeding speech draft made its outcome more certain.

Publication of Nixon's office tapes in 2002 from the period shows the President's determination to examine all options to bring matters to a decision. Between April 25 and May 5, he asked for an exploration of an attack on the dikes controlling floodwaters in the North, the use of nuclear weapons, and more extensive bombing of urban centers. I strongly advised against each of these options, and, characteristically, Nixon did not persist. I mention these discussions not to demonstrate any moderating influence on my part but to illustrate Nixon's method of decision-making. I am convinced that Nixon would never have implemented these measures even had my advice been more accommodating. They were his way of conveying his determination, not his tactics.

No such ideas were advanced at the NSC meeting on Monday, May 8. All present knew that Nixon had arrived at a final decision. They therefore had much less interest in considering the options than in positioning themselves for the certain public uproar. Nixon, with his back to the wall, was at his best: direct, to the point, with none of the evasions that often characterized his style when facing opposition. He led off the meeting with a long monologue emphasizing his determination not to let South Vietnam fall. He was convinced that "there will be no summit"—whichever course we took. If we took strong action, this would "jeopardize" the summit; if we did nothing and Vietnam was collapsing, he could not go anyway.

Admiral Moorer presented the mining plan and the campaign to interdict railroads. Helms presented an intelligence appraisal. The CIA's assessment was that Moscow "would almost certainly move to cancel the summit" and perhaps bring pressure to bear on Berlin; China would "probably" provide direct support to Hanoi analogous to the 90,000 support troops it had sent during the pre-1968 American bombing and since withdrawn; the overland routes would effectively replace the sea route. Helms concluded with the noncommittal prediction that Hanoi would wait for the outcome of the military test before deciding its course. Laird argued that the most critical supplies came in by rail and in any case the North Vietnamese had four to five months of stocks in reserve. He expressed confidence that the South Vietnamese "can make it. Hue may go but it will not be as bad as 1968." His conclusion was that the mining and interdiction campaigns were unnecessary. The cheaper solution from the budgetary point of view was to send more equipment to South Vietnam. Nixon interjected: "Suppose we are wrong? Suppose Vietnam falls? How do we handle it? You don't assess the risks for our policy."

John Connally and Vice President Agnew rejected Laird's analysis altogether. Agnew was unequivocal that we simply could not afford to let South Vietnam collapse; it would have disastrous international consequences, especially in the Middle East and around the Indian Ocean. We were "handcuffing ourselves" by being "compulsive talkers"; the President really did not have a choice. Connally agreed: "If Vietnam is defeated, Mr. President, you won't have anything."

Rogers was ambiguous, agreeing that a failure in South Vietnam would be "disastrous for our policies" but pointing out the risk that the proposed actions might not be effective and would only compound our problems. We had to rely on the military's judgment of how effective it would be. On the other hand, couldn't we wait a few weeks, rather than torpedo the summit? He reassured the President that even if we did nothing and lost, the American people would support the President, knowing he had done all that was possible. Connally emphatically rejected that proposition. A collapse of Vietnam discredited the President's entire foreign policy; no excuse would be accepted.

I then answered the analyses that disparaged the effect of mining. The North Vietnamese would have to find alternative routes for their annual more than 2.1 million tons of seaborne imports. Sihanoukville was closed. They could use railroads only by night for fear of air interdiction: "You can't throw these figures around without a better analysis. It is easy to say that they have a four months' [reserve] capacity and could go all out and end the war, but they would end with zero capacity. . . . One thing is certain, they will not draw their supplies down to zero."

Nixon summed up:

> The real question is whether the Americans give a damn anymore. . . . If you follow *Time, The Washington Post, The New York*

Times and the three networks, you could say that the U.S. has done enough. "Let's get out; let's make a deal with the Russians and pull in our horns." The U.S. would cease to be a military and diplomatic power. If that happened, then the U.S. would look inward towards itself and would remove itself from the world. Every non-Communist nation in the world would live in terror.

The meeting ended at 12:20 after three hours and twenty minutes. Nixon announced that he would make a decision at two o'clock—the last moment, according to Moorer, to issue the "execute" order if the mining was to coincide with the President's speech. Nixon invited Connally and me to join him in the Oval Office immediately. He asked us whether anything had happened at the NSC meeting to change our minds. We both told him that the discussion had reinforced our conviction to proceed. Nixon calmly said that he would go ahead. I should bring the necessary "execute" order to his Executive Office Building hideaway at two o'clock.

The Summit in the Balance

I immediately passed the order to a jubilant Moorer. It was what he had been recommending for five years. He guaranteed that there would be no repetition of Laos; the effort would not fail because the military devoted inadequate resources or attention to it. I called all the other principals. As always in the face of great events, they seemed relieved that the uncertainty was over. I knew from past experience that whatever Laird's attitude at the meeting, he would be staunch and imaginative in defending and carrying out the decision. Rogers would keep a low profile. Helms would act like the superb professional he was. And so it proved to be.

On Sunday Undersecretary of State Alex Johnson worked on the obligatory scenario: which country was to be notified by whom at what time. The NSC office would take care of the Soviets and the Chinese; the State Department would handle all the others. Contrary to past practice, I would give no press briefing *before* the speech; it would carry its own message. I would hold an on-the-record news conference the next day explaining the decision. There was never any contest over White House preeminence where taking the heat over Vietnam was concerned; the other departments were only too eager to leave the inevitable public buffeting to the NSC staff. The President would brief the congressional leaders at eight o'clock in the evening. I would see Dobrynin at the same time. One of my principal aides, Peter Rodman, would go to New York to inform the Chinese at their U.N. mission.

With these preparations completed, all was quiet for a few hours.

At 8:30 P.M. the lull was over. While the President briefed the congressional leadership,[3] I saw Dobrynin, whom I had called away from a dinner. In a crisis, Dobrynin exhibited none of the camaraderie with which he normally eased the processes of diplomacy. He began by telling me that whenever I saw him before a speech, he knew it would not be good news. I joked that normally he was out of town in a crisis and let his deputy Yuli Voronstov bear the brunt; we had obviously caught him unaware. I handed him a letter from Nixon to Brezhnev. At once firm and conciliatory, it pointed out that Brezhnev's message of May 6 did not change the situation; indeed, it confirmed it. There had been no indication, however minimal, that Hanoi would halt its offensive and resume negotiations on any acceptable basis. The letter then outlined the measures that would be announced.

Nixon's letter followed the same strategy as my trip to Moscow in April: putting forward the prospect of a successful summit as an incentive for Soviet restraint. It tantalizingly summarized what had already been agreed on SALT, the Declaration of Principles, and expanded trade, and waxed eloquent about the possible accomplishments of "our forthcoming meeting." The onus was now squarely on Brezhnev if he chose to cancel.

Dobrynin was all business. He asked what precise measures were implied in the blockade. He lost his cool only once, when I asked him how the Soviet Union would react if the 15,000 Soviet soldiers in Egypt were in imminent danger of being captured by Israelis. Dobrynin became uncharacteristically vehement and revealed more than he could have intended: "First of all, we never put forces somewhere who can't defend themselves. Second, if the Israelis threaten us, we will wipe them out within two days. I can assure you our plans are made for this eventuality." His temper quickly subsided as he asked for a copy of the President's speech. It was quite literally still being typed a half-hour before it was to be delivered because Nixon was making revisions until the last moment. Dobrynin did not believe this for one second. He said it was sad that I did not trust him to keep a secret for even fifteen minutes. At last a copy arrived. Dobrynin noted a sentence to the effect that my meeting with Le Duc Tho on May 2 had been based on Soviet assurances;

this would be taken very ill in Moscow. I excused myself for a few minutes and went to the Oval Office, already crowded with cameras and technicians. I met with Nixon in a small office off the formal room. He agreed to delete the offending phrase; by some miracle, Ron Ziegler managed to correct the press copy in time. When I told Dobrynin, he said resignedly that at least he had achieved something in his dealings with the Nixon administration.

At 9:00 P.M. Nixon addressed the nation. In a restrained and powerful speech he stressed that we would not accept Hanoi's terms but that a negotiated outcome was still our preference. He explained the sequence of our most recent negotiating effort: my April trip to Moscow, the disappointing May 2 meeting with Le Duc Tho. He repeated his willingness to settle the war. But the North Vietnamese "arrogantly refuse to negotiate anything but an imposition." The only way to stop the killing, therefore, was "to keep the weapons of war out of the hands of the international outlaws of North Vietnam." He recited the military actions he was taking; he stated our negotiating position in the terms he had outlined in his speech of January 25 and repeated in his letter to Brezhnev: a standstill cease-fire, release of prisoners, withdrawal from Laos and Cambodia, and total American withdrawal within four months. As did the proposal of May 31, 1971, and of January 25, 1972, it dealt with the issue of North Vietnamese forces by proscribing future infiltration. All this was accepted by Thieu, giving lie to the argument that the settlement four months later incorporating these terms took him by surprise. What Thieu was not expecting was the North Vietnamese acceptance; heretofore he had gone along with American positions to stay in step with his dominant and, to him, incomprehensibly naive ally.

That same evening Peter Rodman delivered a letter from Nixon for Zhou Enlai to the Chinese U.N. mission in New York. Ambassador Huang Hua read the letter somberly but made no comment; its content did not prevent him from making pleasant small talk and from offering Rodman several cups of jasmine tea. Nixon's letter to Zhou Enlai characterized our negotiating proposals as fair and reminded him of our repeated warnings that we would react strongly to an enemy offensive.

I briefed the press the next morning in the East Room of the White House. Important though explanations to our public were, they also served a vital diplomatic function. Every statement was part of an effort to persuade Moscow and Beijing to acquiesce in our course and thus to move Hanoi, by isolating it, to meaningful negotiations. Our most important concern, of course, was the summit, now less than two weeks away. I adopted a posture of "business as usual." I explained that we had not heard from Moscow—nor could we have—but that we were "proceeding with the summit preparations, and we see at this moment no reason from our side to postpone the summit meeting." We recognized that the Soviet leaders would face "some short-term difficulties" in making their decision, but we, for our part, still believed that a new era in East-West relations was possible. Because I did not want to embarrass the Soviets, I sidestepped a question about whether on my visit I had forewarned Brezhnev of our intended actions. I simply stated that after my visit, the Soviet leaders could not have been "under any misapprehension of how seriously it would be viewed if this offensive continued."

For the moment, the explanations and the signals were overwhelmed by congressional and media outrage. Senator William Proxmire denounced the President's action as "reckless and wrong." Senator Mansfield was convinced that our decision would protract the war. Senator McGovern called for congressional action: "The President must not have a free hand in Indochina any longer. . . . The nation cannot stand it. The Congress must not allow it. . . . The political regime in Saigon is not worth the loss of one more American life." Senator Muskie thought the President was "jeopardizing the major security interests of the United States."[4]

The media's outrage was nearly uniform. The *New York Times*'s first reaction was relatively mild: "The many dangers that lie ahead in Vietnam are exceeded only by the threat to the peace of the world if a new Soviet-American crisis blocks the strategic arms limitation accord that is virtually assured in Helsinki."[5] After further reflection the *Times* decided to raise the decibel count, denouncing the President's "desperate gamble." The *Times* called upon Congress to cut off all funds for the war to "save the President from himself and the nation from disaster." The *Washington Post* declared that Nixon "has lost touch with the real world. . . . The Moscow summit is in the balance, if it has not yet toppled over. . . . The only relief in this grim scene is that Mr. Nixon is coming to the end of a term and the American people will shortly have the opportunity to render a direct judgment on his policy." The *Christian Science Monitor* found that "the wisdom of that decision and the rightness of it are clearly open to question."[6]

If the critics had paid closer attention, they would have noted that the Communist reaction was much more restrained than their own. They could not have known, of course, that Dobrynin and I spoke early on May 9, when

I told Dobrynin of an accord worked out between West German Chancellor Brandt and opposition leader Rainer Barzel that could lead to ratification of treaties normalizing relations between the two German states now before the Bundestag—the German parliament. The linkage was obvious. Although I told Dobrynin soothingly that at least outside of Southeast Asia we would continue to do business as usual, I was implying that if the Soviets got tough, so could America. Clearly the treaty, which in the event was passed by but two votes, would not pass against U.S. opposition or even in an atmosphere of U.S.-Soviet tensions. Dobrynin said that since this was a holiday in the Soviet Union (V-E Day), the official reaction to the President's speech might be somewhat delayed—an extraordinary explanation in the midst of an international crisis. If Soviet leaders were not prepared to interrupt a holiday, they could not be viewing the crisis as all that serious. He assumed that a statement or message could be expected sooner or later, however. I told him I would send a copy of my press conference remarks, which spoke positively about U.S.-Soviet relations.

The critics were, of course, unaware of these exchanges. But there were many public Soviet signals that the response might be low-key. Hanoi fulminated against the "insolent challenge" and asked for increased support from its Communist backers. But there was no rush to the barricades in either Moscow or Beijing. The Soviet SALT negotiators in Geneva continued their work. (We had instructed our delegation to proceed as if nothing had happened—but to refuse to discuss Vietnam.) A Soviet commercial delegation headed by Trade Minister Nikolai Patolichev was in Washington on a visit reciprocating that of Commerce Secretary Maurice Stans the preceding November. It missed sessions for one day but stayed in Washington. The only Soviet public comment was a TASS article on May 9 summarizing the President's speech and, significantly, calling attention to Nixon's assurance that America's efforts were not directed against any other country.

The Chinese response was more subtle still. A public statement on May 9 protested attacks on Chinese ships on May 6, 7, and 8 (before the President's speech), thus maintaining the distinction of recent months: Beijing might complain of American actions against North Vietnam, but it would "protest" (implying some governmental sanction) only when Chinese lives or property was involved. We immediately notified the Chinese U.N. mission in New York that special care would be taken to avoid Chinese ships; the point was in any case moot, since the North Vietnamese ports were now closed. That evening the Chinese gave us another lesson in indirection. Their embassy in Paris—the point of contact for routine business—matter-of-factly inquired about technical arrangements for the trip to China of House leaders Hale Boggs and Gerald Ford, which was to take place at the end of June, nearly two months away. Beijing was telling us that the trips were still on; the improvement of our relations was not affected by the President's action.

On the afternoon of May 10, Dobrynin came to the Map Room of the White House to hand me a brief Soviet note of protest. Like Beijing's, it was confined to damage caused to Soviet ships by our bombing, including the loss of life. The note asked for assurances against a recurrence. It said nothing about the mining. The fact that it came through our private channel indicated the Soviet desire to avoid a public confrontation. Dobrynin even gave us his "personal view"—an unlikely possibility—that Moscow's decision to move this way was "encouraging," but it was perhaps "premature" to draw final conclusions. Playfully, he asked me what I thought the Politburo would decide. I replied that I would place my answer in a sealed envelope for both of us to look at when the crisis was over. I reminded him of the President's interest in a new era in our relations. Dobrynin asked detailed questions about our cease-fire proposal. We both spoke delicately about the discussions that would take place "if" the two leaders met.

Dobrynin was a good chess player. At the end of the meeting, he inquired, as if it were a matter of routine, whether the President had as yet decided on receiving Trade Minister Patolichev. The request could only mean that the Soviet leaders had decided to fall in with our approach of business as usual. Trying to match the ambassador's studied casualness, I allowed that I probably would be able to arrange a meeting in the Oval Office. Playing a little chess myself, I mentioned that it was customary on these occasions to invite the media for a photo opportunity. Dobrynin thought this highly appropriate.

In almost every crisis tension builds steadily, sometimes nearly unbearably, until some decisive turning point. The conversation with Dobrynin, if not yet the turning point, marked its approach. We knew that the summit was still on. In that case Hanoi would be isolated; we would have won our gamble. I quickly scheduled a meeting between the President and Patolichev for the next morning.

We awoke on May 11 to the first official statement released by TASS. It was both belated and mild. The Soviet Union considered our action "inadmissible" and "will draw from this appropriate conclusions." The United States was advised to return to the conference table in Paris. The Soviet government "resolutely" insisted that the American military measures be "cancelled without delay," which Moscow knew was technically impossible; and that freedom of navigation be respected, which was irrelevant, since we were not interrupting ships at sea. As for the aid for the North Vietnamese, TASS employed some strange language. It noted that the Soviet "people" would continue to give the Vietnamese people "the *necessary* support" (not "increased" support, as Hanoi had asked). The statement reeked of procrastination and hesitation.

That was not the attitude of Nikolai Patolichev when he appeared for his thirty-minute courtesy call in the Oval Office. Press and photographers were ushered in to witness what has been called "the usual contrived cordiality."[7] But in this case, contrived or not, the smiling pictures conveyed the Soviet message and it unambiguously spelled summit. Even the banter for the press was symbolic and by Soviet standards extremely subtle; the subject (I cannot recall why) was the differing pronunciation in Polish and Russian of the word "friendship." Lest anyone miss the point, Patolichev was all smiles when he left the White House. A television reporter asked him if the summit was still on. "We never had any doubts," replied the Soviet minister, wide-eyed at the seemingly inexhaustible obtuseness of Americans. "I don't know why you asked this question. Have you any doubts?"—implying that if there was any obstacle to the summit, it was in Washington.

The last remaining uncertainty was removed when Dobrynin and I met over lunch the same day to continue our regular discussion of summit preparations. Dobrynin claimed that the United States was "making too much" of the Soviet role in Vietnam; I stressed that the important thing was to settle the war. In the middle of the luncheon, one of Dobrynin's aides brought in a message from Brezhnev in Russian replying to Nixon's letter of May 8. Usually the Soviet embassy supplied a written translation: In this case Dobrynin's assistant did the honors in a way which might well have defeated its purpose. But even a rough oral translation left no doubt that Brezhnev was avoiding any hint of confrontation, despite the letter's conventional bluster warning against the consequences of our actions. I asked innocently whether Brezhnev's warning referred to new actions or to steps that had already been taken. Obviously, replied Dobrynin, his patience apparently tried by my denseness, the General Secretary could only have meant *additional* measures to those announced on May 8.

The crisis was over.

On May 11, Beijing, too, was heard from. A *People's Daily* commentator expressed "resolute" support for the people of Vietnam and "extreme indignation and strong condemnation" of the mining of North Vietnam. But the author neither denounced Nixon nor indicated any Chinese response to the interdiction campaign. China was Vietnam's "reliable rear area"—a phrase used before, implying that China did not consider itself on the frontline and would take no action. Even more astonishing, the *People's Daily* printed the entire text of the President's speech. Probably the Chinese leaders wanted their people to learn of our challenge to the Soviet Union. Whatever the motive, it was the first time the Chinese "masses" had seen an account of Hanoi's intransigence and details of an American peace program. The North Vietnamese Politburo could only interpret it as dissociation by their two major allies.

From then on, summit preparations continued with Dobrynin. On May 12, he and I were already discussing protocol points, such as the gifts to be exchanged. After that the emphasis was on SALT and other summit topics.

On May 11, we judged Hanoi sufficiently isolated to resume contact. I sent Le Duc Tho, who was still in Paris, an extract from my press conference of May 9, which stressed our readiness to resume negotiations. Le Duc Tho replied by sending me an extract from *his* press conference of May 12; he had repeated the insistence on a coalition government, though in language much more moderate than he had used to me on May 2. Once more this demonstrated the fallacy of the popular myth that Hanoi would be conciliatory only when we showed "goodwill." The opposite was in fact true. On May 12, Le Duc Tho affirmed an unconditional readiness to resume talks:

> If Mr. Nixon really desires serious negotiations, as far as we are concerned, faithful to our serious attitude and good will, we are disposed to seek together with the American side, a logical and reasonable solution to the Vietnamese problem. During the course of the last two decades, in its fight for independence and liberty, the Vietnamese people negotiated for a peaceful solution to the Vietnamese problem with the French Government in 1954, and participated in the peaceful solution of the Laotian problem with the United States

in 1962. Consequently at present, there is no reason not to arrive at a negotiated solution to the Vietnamese problem. This question, of course, depends on Mr. Nixon's attitude.

In other words, serious negotiations would resume once Hanoi's offensive had run its course.

And the offensive stalled. The North Vietnamese attack on Hue never developed full steam. Kontum did not fall; neither did besieged An Loc. The South Vietnamese counteroffensive to relieve An Loc developed with excruciating slowness. But the tactical use of B-52s in the South was clearly disrupting the North Vietnamese buildup, and after some months the mining would make it increasingly difficult for the North Vietnamese to accumulate supplies for another big push.

For the rest of the time before the summit, Vietnam disappeared as a point of contention in our dialogue with the Soviet Union. On May 12, Dobrynin handed me a note—in the private channel—that grudgingly accepted the President's expression of regret at the harm to Soviet ships and seamen and his assurance that care would be taken to avoid such incidents in the future. Nothing was said about the blockade of North Vietnam. On May 14, we returned a conciliatory reply repeating our assurances with respect to Soviet shipping. We also informed Moscow that while the President was in the Soviet Union, Hanoi would not be attacked. By implication bombing would continue against all the rest of North Vietnam, including Haiphong. This was done.

Later in the day of May 14, Dobrynin delivered a note that urged a resumption of the Paris negotiations. If it were possible to announce this in advance of the summit, "that would in many ways be favorable to the Soviet-American meeting." The Soviets proposed that neither side set preconditions and that the plenary and secret meetings proceed in tandem. These were presented as Soviet suggestions "on our own behalf" and not from Hanoi. However, the Kremlin was prepared to pass our response on to the North Vietnamese.

Clearly, someone had blinked. Less than a week after the resumption of full-scale bombing and the blockade of North Vietnam, efforts were being made to resume negotiations "without preconditions"—a far cry from Hanoi's previous insistence on the "correctness" of its terms. If Moscow presented these propositions on its own—which it claimed but I doubted—the isolation of Hanoi had proceeded more rapidly than any of us had dared to hope. If Hanoi was using Moscow as an intermediary, it had at last begun its retreat toward a more negotiable position.

We thought it premature to announce a return to the plenaries. It would confuse our public; it might generate demands for military restraint when the best chance for a rapid solution was to convey our implacability. On May 15, I handed an unsigned note to Dobrynin that agreed in principle to the reopening of the plenary sessions. However, to avoid raising false expectations, it should be preceded by a private meeting with Le Duc Tho. If we made progress, plenaries could resume. Originally, our note had included a tough paragraph warning of "the most serious consequences" if there was further military escalation by the North Vietnamese. When Dobrynin balked at being asked to pass on a threat, I had the offending paragraph typed on a separate sheet of paper and called it an "oral note." Dobrynin withdrew his objections and accepted it in this form.

On May 17, Dobrynin told me that Moscow had urged our procedural proposal on North Vietnam in the strongest language. No reply was ever received from Hanoi—perhaps because its planners lacked a strategy for the new challenge, perhaps because they feared that failure of a new meeting would lead to another round of escalation, perhaps they did not want to encourage Soviet mediation.

Meanwhile, I met almost daily with Dobrynin to work out the summit agenda and schedule. The SALT negotiators were putting their text into final shape. The various subsidiary negotiations were making rapid progress. On May 17, Dobrynin was invited to spend the night at Camp David. After breakfast with the President, he told me that Moscow would spare no effort to make the summit a success. However, because of Vietnam the public welcome in Moscow could not be as warm as had originally been planned, Dobrynin suggested, giving an insight into the "spontaneity" of the Soviet masses.

Beijing, too, demonstrated that it had its priorities straight. In a conversation with me in New York on May 16, U.N. ambassador Huang Hua repeated the official line that China stood behind its friends. But he did not demur when I pointed out that we had warned Beijing at least half a dozen times of our determination to react strongly if Hanoi sought to impose a military solution. Nor did our actions in Vietnam prevent Huang Hua from encouraging a visit by me to Beijing in June. We had not only achieved a free hand in Vietnam; we would be able to continue at the same time the larger design of our foreign policy.

The media and Congress soon shifted their position, retreating to the familiar attacks on "indiscriminate" bombing and demands for a legislated deadline to end the war. Some praised the Soviets for their restraint; praise for Nixon's courage was sparse.

It was my fate throughout the Vietnamese war to be in the middle of the crossfire between my former associates and my new chief. A poignant and frustrating encounter occurred with seven presidents of Ivy League universities who came to the Roosevelt Room of the White House on May 17, three days before we left for Moscow. These men, heads of the most prestigious American universities, had come to tell me, in effect, that rational judgment was no longer relevant to the war in Vietnam. One of them complained of destruction being inflicted "for reasons that are not clear and for a cause that no one seems willing to defend." When I tried to explain the issues posed by the North Vietnamese invasion and above all by Hanoi's insistence that we collude with them to impose Communist rule, my interlocutors took refuge in the passions of the students: "Be that as it may, it is turning large numbers of young people away from their country." I replied that I was aware of the students' view, but "we in government have an obligation not only to register what the students say but also to put it into the framework of the longer term." We were willing to take "any reasonable step," but turning Vietnam over to Communism was not a reasonable step. Another of the group asked how he should explain the cost of the war to the students. I could only respond by asking how he would explain it if, after eight years of war, we did for Hanoi what it could not do for itself.

But it was a dialogue of the deaf. The distinguished Ivy League presidents were not interested in the merits of the issues in dispute between America and North Vietnam. They were there as spokesmen of an emotion. One of them stated that none of the students would really care if Saigon fell. Another allowed that our principles might be "persuasive," including the principle of "not letting one group dominate another," but since we did not help people in similar circumstances elsewhere, why did we have to do it in Vietnam? In other words, unless we defended every moral purpose everywhere, we had no right to defend any principle anywhere. But the real problem boiled down to a more practical concern. One of them admitted: "I don't see how we can continue to run our universities if the war escalates. . . . What will we face in September?"

From the other side of the barricades, I was the recipient of frequent missives from Nixon, berating me for the military's insufficient audacity and toughness in the prosecution of the war. On May 9, a memorandum descended on me, urging me to look for new ways of hurting the enemy with airpower:

> We have the power to destroy his war-making capacity. The only question is whether we have the *will* to use that power. What distinguishes me from Johnson is that I have the *will* in spades. If we now fail it will be because the bureaucrats and the bureaucracy and particularly those in the Defense Department, who will of course be vigorously assisted by their allies in State, will find ways to erode the strong, decisive action that I have indicated we are going to take. For once, I want the military and I want the NSC staff to come up with some ideas on their own which will recommend *action* which is very *strong, threatening* and *effective*.[8]

Nixon was entitled to some release for his nervous tension. He had acted boldly and won a brilliant gamble. He had challenged the Soviet Union and to a lesser extent China and in the end improved relations with both. He had prevented the military collapse of South Vietnam, which (in 1972) would have undercut these relationships and the entire postwar design of American foreign policy. After weeks of impatient musings about canceling the Moscow summit, he had settled on the wiser strategy of using the Soviet stake in a successful summit to restrain a Soviet response, to gain a free hand in Vietnam, and eventually to bring to fruition our patient efforts to build a more constructive U.S.-Soviet relationship.

Conscious of its own vulnerabilities, the Kremlin cut loose from its obstreperous small ally on the other side of the globe. By proceeding with the summit, Moscow helped neutralize our domestic opposition, providing the freedom of action to break the back of North Vietnam's offensive. The strategy of détente—posing risks and dangling benefits before the Soviets—made possible an unfettered attempt to bring America's involvement in the Vietnam war to an honorable close. Nixon could leave for Moscow with dignity, for he had not sacrificed those who had put their trust in America; with confidence, since the interlocking design of our foreign policy had withstood extraordinary stress; and with hope that he was laying the foundations of a global equilibrium which could bring safety and progress to an anxious thermonuclear world.

7

FROM STALEMATE TO BREAKTHROUGH

The first formal discussion of Vietnam between Nixon and Brezhnev was scheduled for the second day of the summit, Tuesday, May 21. The occasion was a dinner meeting at Brezhnev's dacha attended by the other two members of the Soviet triumvirate, Prime Minister Alexei Kosygin and President Nikolai Podgorny. The evening began convivially enough when Brezhnev took his guests on a speedboat ride on the Moskva River—perhaps to soften them up for what was to follow. When talks finally started around a square table in the living room, it appeared for a while that the subject of Vietnam would never be raised, the two leaders circling each other like prizefighters waiting for the opponent to strike the first blow. Reviewing the status of various negotiations, Brezhnev suggested that Foreign Minister Andrei Gromyko and I agree on some joint instructions for the delegations negotiating the Strategic Arms Limitation Treaty (SALT) in Helsinki. Nixon fell in with the spirit of the exchange and listed some other issues on which progress seemed possible. Finally, Brezhnev mentioned in passing that the Middle East and Vietnam might be worth discussing at some point. Just as it seemed as if the shadowboxing might go on all night, Nixon decided to put Vietnam squarely on the table.

He began by arguing that the "collateral issue" of Vietnam should not interrupt the basic progress in our relations that was being achieved. He then gave a concise and firm summary of our position. He was aware that the Soviet Union had an ideological affinity with Hanoi. But we did not choose this moment for the "flare-up" in Vietnam. Hanoi, aided by Soviet equipment, had. Once the offensive took place, "we had to react as we did." We could not reconsider our policy unless Hanoi indicated new flexibility in its negotiating stance. Moscow, he needled, should use the influence it acquired through supplying military equipment to make Hanoi think again. As for us, we were determined to bring the war to a conclusion, preferably by negotiation, if necessary by military means.

Now that the subject of Vietnam had been formally introduced, the easy camaraderie vanished. Each of the three Soviet leaders in turn unleashed a diatribe; Nixon, except for two one-sentence interruptions, endured it in dignified silence. Not only was the substance tough, the tone was crudely hectoring.

Brezhnev led off. He complained not only about our "cruel" bombing but about the entire history of our involvement in Vietnam, which seemed to him designed to embarrass the Soviet Union. He recalled that North Vietnam had first been bombed in 1965 while Prime Minister Alexei Kosygin was visiting Hanoi. He denied that military actions were needed to end the war. Hanoi was eager to negotiate; all we had to do was to get rid of Thieu and accept Hanoi's "reasonable" political program. There were several not too subtle allusions that stopped just short of comparing American policy with Hitler's. Confirming the validity of our strategy, Brezhnev then explained the Soviet reasoning for going ahead with the summit:

> It was certainly difficult for us to agree to hold this meeting under present circumstances. And yet we did agree to hold it. I want to explain why. We felt that preliminary work prior to the meeting warranted the hope that two powers with such economic might and such a high level of civilization and all the other necessary prerequisites could come together to promote better relations between our two nations.

In a non sequitur that revealed again the Soviets' raw nerve about China, Brezhnev assailed the Chinese for an immoral foreign policy and cited the Shanghai Communiqué (that had ended Nixon's visit to Beijing earlier that year) as supporting evidence; in his view, the fact that each party had stated its own position without defining a common stand made the whole document unprincipled.

Before we could penetrate the logic of this curious attack on a document we had participated in drafting, it was Kosygin's turn. Where Brezhnev had been emotional, Kosygin was analytical; where Brezhnev had pounded the table, Kosygin was glacially polite. He recalled his conversations with Lyndon Johnson, who had also predicted victory and then failed. He implied the same fate for Nixon. He complained bitterly about damage to Soviet ships and loss of Soviet lives in Haiphong harbor. He hinted that Hanoi might reconsider its previous refusal to permit forces of other countries to fight on its side—prompting Nixon to retort that we were not frightened by that threat. Kosygin turned this into a dig at China by volunteering that Beijing had been prepared to send in troops in 1965 but had been rebuffed by the North Vietnamese. Kosygin suggested that we get rid of Thieu; the Moscow summit was a logical place to come together on such a proposal; he was reasonably sure it would be accepted by Hanoi. So, of course, were we.

President Nikolai Podgorny concluded the presentations. The third leader in a row now demonstrated the Soviet insecurity about China. He was in Hanoi, he said, when he learned of my secret trip to China. He was able to reassure the North Vietnamese by telling them that Nixon was planning to visit Moscow, too—as if a double sellout and isolation was better for Hanoi. While Podgorny was talking, his tone milder than that of his colleagues, Brezhnev marched up and down behind his back, muttering to himself. It was not entirely clear whether he was trying to lend emphasis to Podgorny's remarks or was getting bored.

Suddenly the thought struck me that, for all the bombast and rudeness, we were participants in a charade. While the tone was bellicose and the manner extremely abrupt, none of the Soviet statements had any operational content. The leaders stayed well clear of threats. Their so-called proposals were the slogans of the Paris plenary sessions, which they knew we had repeatedly rejected and which we had no reason to accept now that the military situation was almost daily altering in our favor. The Soviet leaders were not pressing us except with words. They were speaking for the record, and when they had said enough to have a transcript to send to Hanoi, they would stop.

Nixon, who behaved with great dignity throughout, replied calmly but firmly. He noted coldly that the U.S.S.R. had been "instrumental" in April in getting the private talks restarted; we were then "somewhat disappointed" when the North Vietnamese were "more intransigent than ever before." He referred pointedly to Brezhnev's cease-fire offer, which we had accepted but

Hanoi had rejected out of hand. He proposed that we take up Vietnam again later in the week. We would continue to negotiate with the North Vietnamese, but it was pointless if they were not willing to make peace. We were not expecting the Soviets to solve the problem, but, he said, "maybe you can help us." Kosygin commented sharply that a new proposal was needed, and the President replied equally sharply that the discussion had already gone on too long.

At this point, Brezhnev obviously decided that the record was complete—though it had taken the better part of three hours to make it (including translation). He allowed that we had had a "most serious discussion on a problem of world importance," as if it were an academic debate among professors. He said he drew the conclusion from Nixon's remarks that the United States was prepared to look for a reasonable solution—a proposition hard to argue with. Kosygin chimed in that not a single ship carrying military equipment was on the way to Vietnam, "only flour and foodstuffs, no armament whatever." And, on that note, Brezhnev suggested that we repair to dinner.

The fact was that, except for their bullying tone in this session, the Soviet leaders treated Vietnam as a subsidiary issue during the entire summit. The top leaders reverted to Vietnam only once more, when Brezhnev asked Nixon whether we could modify our proposal of January 25 by having Thieu resign *two* months before a new election rather than one, as we had proposed. Nixon hinted that he might be willing to suggest this if Hanoi would accept our other terms.

By the time we returned home from Moscow, Hanoi's offensive had run out of steam. Several factors had contributed. The North Vietnamese did not follow up the capture of Quang Tri with an assault on the old imperial capital of Hue, whose fall might have been decisive. As in 1968, Hanoi opted for psychological rather than military impact by launching a countrywide offensive, which, as then, led to its military defeat. Three fronts proved too difficult to synchronize and even more complicated to supply; hence Saigon was able to switch its small strategic reserve to meet each threat as it developed. The dispersal of effort also meant that the North Vietnamese needed nearly three weeks to bring up reinforcements for the attack on Hue. By then, part of the South's strategic reserve had moved in. Saigon's airborne division fought both at An Loc and near Hue. The marines were used in both the Central Highlands and in Military Region 1. And the South Vietnamese divisions fought better than in any previous battle. Our massive reinforcement of B-52s, raising the total to over 200 by the end of May, exposed the attacking forces to a formidable concentration of firepower, making mass attacks increasingly difficult. Hanoi's problems multiplied further because its commanders were not experienced in handling large units. Attacks by tanks, artillery, and armor frequently bogged down as the various elements lost contact with one another. So, by the middle of June, with our bombing and mining making themselves felt, the North Vietnamese army was stalled.

On June 9, in an appraisal for the President of what the blockade and intensified bombing begun on May 8 had achieved, I described the prospects for South Vietnam as "substantially brighter." The blockade had forced all supplies to North Vietnam to come by rail, and the railroad lines were being cut by air attacks. More than 1,000 railroad cars were backed up on the Chinese side of the border. As a result, supplies had to be transferred to trucks, which required time-consuming loading and unloading and encountered extreme difficulties during the rainy season. Enemy communications spoke of ammunition shortages; our pilots reported a noticeable reduction in surface-to-air missile firings, indicating that Hanoi might be rationing its stocks. Radio Hanoi lamented "a number of difficulties" in providing labor for agriculture, industry, and transport. North Vietnamese public statements attacked corruption and black marketeering.

The twin summits with Moscow and Beijing had undoubtedly engendered a sense of isolation in North Vietnam. And they had greatly strengthened Nixon's domestic position, thus removing Hanoi's key leverage on us. In June, we received the first inconclusive hints that Hanoi might be engaged in cease-fire planning. During the summer, the evidence became clearer. By the middle of September, it was unmistakable.

Morale in South Vietnam had reached its nadir after the fall of Quang Tri. Wild rumors that the United States had agreed to turn over the northern part of the country to Hanoi—almost certainly disseminated by Communist cadres—had been ended by Nixon's decision to mine North Vietnamese harbors. Thieu rallied his population with revived hope and purpose. We were in a strong position to resume talks.

Many consider negotiations as a sign of weakness. I always looked at them as a weapon for seizing the moral and psychological high ground. Some treat willingness to talk when there is no pressure as an unnecessary concession; in my view, it is a device to improve one's strategic position because the interlocutor is aware that one faces no necessity to make concessions. It was, however, not for theoretical but for practical reasons that Nixon approved an approach to Hanoi on June 12. We proposed a private meeting with Le Duc Tho for June 28, when I had a weekend free between a trip to China and a sojourn in San Clemente. Our message avoided a repetition of the maneuvers of the previous spring by suggesting that the secret talk should *precede* a plenary session. Nixon suggested the timing to deprive the Democratic Convention's opening on July 10 of the ability to charge us with a deadlock.

While we were waiting for Hanoi's reply, two events underscored North Vietnam's isolation.

On June 8, I asked Dobrynin what had happened to Podgorny's mission to Hanoi, mentioned to Nixon by Brezhnev in Moscow. He said the Soviets were still waiting for an official invitation—an explanation that, given my knowledge of the Kremlin's prickly clients, was quite plausible. Finally, on June 11, while I was paying a brief visit to Japan, Dobrynin told Haig that Podgorny would leave for Hanoi on June 13 and requested that we stop the bombing of North Vietnam while he was there. We replied, as Nixon had indicated to Brezhnev, that, during Podgorny's stay, we would not bomb within ten miles of Hanoi and within five miles of Haiphong; no other restrictions would be observed. On June 22, Brezhnev reported to Nixon that Hanoi's leadership had listened with "an attentive attitude" to Podgorny's exposition of the American negotiating position; they were prepared to resume negotiations on a businesslike basis; they did not insist on discussing only North Vietnamese proposals. If accurate, this was a tone we had never heard from North Vietnam. Previously, Hanoi had dismissed any deviation from its various "points" as not "reasonable and logical." Brezhnev's letter concluded with the suggestion that the United States should propose a date for the resumption of negotiations.

This was puzzling since we had made precisely such a proposal to Hanoi on June 12. Was Hanoi keeping Moscow in the dark? Or was Brezhnev urging us to reply promptly to a message from Hanoi that reached us on June 20? That reply had turned out to be much milder than usual. Contrary to the predictions of our critics, bombing and mining had greatly improved Hanoi's manners. After perfunctorily cataloguing grievances—the bombing and mining and the suspension of plenary sessions—it got to the heart of the problem in near-biblical language: "The DRV side, clothed by its goodwill, agrees to private meetings." Its goodwill did not, however, extend to abandoning its insistence on a prior plenary session. Hanoi's message claimed that

Le Duc Tho and Xuan Thuy, being "engaged in work previously scheduled in Hanoi," could not attend a plenary before July 13. This was another interesting sign; Hanoi was not in the habit of giving explanations for its refusal of a proposed date. July 15 was proposed for the private meeting. Since plenary sessions were always announced a week in advance, this meant that the resumption of negotiations would become known July 8, two days before the Democratic Convention. This would represent a boost to Nixon, which Hanoi, finely tuned to American domestic politics, would surely have avoided had it felt stronger.

Hanoi's isolation was dramatized also by the fact that this message reached me in Beijing, where from June 19 to 23 I briefed the Chinese leaders on the Moscow summit. The visit brought no new developments on Vietnam. As always, Zhou Enlai showed more interest in a cease-fire than in a political settlement. He understood well enough that a cease-fire was the easier to arrange, and he was eager to remove the irritant of Vietnam from U.S.-China relations. Unlike Moscow, Beijing had no interest in a demonstration that the United States was prepared to abandon its friends; in its long-range perspective of seeking a counterweight to the Soviet Union, Beijing in fact had a stake in our reputation for reliability. And there was always an undercurrent of Chinese uneasiness about Hanoi's hegemonic aspirations in Indochina. Zhou asked pointed questions about Nixon's May 8 proposal, repeated the standard line of China's historical debt to Hanoi, avoided any implication of any Chinese national or ideological interest in the war, and implied that most of China's supplies to Vietnam were foodstuffs. This paralleled what Kosygin had told us about Soviet deliveries four weeks earlier. Given China's more rudimentary armaments industry, Zhou was the more likely to be telling the truth. Hanoi was not in a brilliant position when its two patrons were, in effect, telling its adversary that they were no longer supplying military equipment.

On the day of my return (June 23), we replied to the North Vietnamese. We accepted July 13 for the resumption of plenary sessions and suggested July 19 for the private meeting. We dismissed Hanoi's complaints curtly: "In order to help create the proper atmosphere for these discussions, the US will not respond to the allegations in the DRV note of June 20." On June 26, Dobrynin came to the White House to discuss my visit to Beijing. In the process, he inquired about Vietnam. Our four-day postponement of the private meeting would, he said, arouse profound suspicions in Hanoi. This implied a new sense of urgency in our adversary, which earlier in the year had procrastinated for four months before setting a date. Dobrynin guessed that Hanoi might be waiting until American electoral prospects were clearer before making a final decision on whether to conclude the war.

It was a prescient remark. Hanoi was indeed watching our election campaign, though it was not yet apparent whether it would hold out on negotiation until after the election in November or opt to negotiate seriously just before. It would not decide, I told Nixon in a memorandum on June 26, "until it believes it has a clearer picture of whether or not you will be re-elected." I sent him a summary of a June 10 article in the Hanoi party newspaper that spoke favorably of McGovern but refrained from predicting his victory. North Vietnam's anger at its own allies was thinly concealed in the denunciation of Nixon for having remained a hawk even when he "borrowed dove's wings for distant trips."

The "hawk" was meanwhile faced with another troop withdrawal decision. Our numbers were now so low that, when the deadline came up at the end of June, there was no room for any dramatic reductions. But Nixon decided to announce the withdrawal of 10,000 troops over two months—and told Ziegler to add that no more draftees would be sent unless they volunteered. The draft, which had been at the heart of so much campus unrest, no longer threatened students with Vietnam service; when schools reopened in the fall, the student protest ended. Nixon enjoyed announcing the resumption of plenaries at a press conference on June 29, one day after the troop withdrawal news, a week and a half before the Democratic Convention. The *New York Times* complained that this coincided with the political calendar. In fact, Hanoi had picked the date. Hence only two conclusions were possible: either Hanoi wanted to promote the reelection of Nixon, an unlikely prospect; or else Hanoi wanted to preserve the option of a settlement *before* the election.

Testing the Stalemate

The resumption of negotiations was of considerable symbolic importance. If Hanoi had been confident of winning, it would have timed the negotiations to coincide with some spectacular new offensive. If it had believed that it could bring about the political defeat of Nixon, it would have stonewalled and published ambiguous peace proposals to stir up our domestic opposition and paint the administration as an obstacle to peace—as it had done before the Easter offensive. That Hanoi insisted on resuming plenaries, even though they would coincide with the Democratic Convention, was a demonstration of Hanoi's growing doubt that total victory was possible or that Nixon's electoral defeat was likely. And if Nixon won the election, they would face a President who had resisted all their previous pressures and, freed of concerns about another election, might even step up military operations.

My private prediction was that, if Nixon was more than ten points ahead in the public opinion polls by September 15, Hanoi would seek an immediate settlement and substantially change its negotiating strategy. But to maintain that option, Hanoi would have two tasks: It would have to reconnoiter our intentions; and it would have to try to narrow the differences in the interval so that a final agreement could be put together quickly in the few weeks remaining until the election.

If Hanoi's position was militarily precarious, ours was difficult psychologically. The President had gained some maneuvering room with his bold decision to bomb and mine, but if it did not bring results fairly quickly, it would be increasingly attacked as a "failure." The demands for "political" alternatives would mount—in practice, pressure to accept Hanoi's demand for a coalition government and a fixed deadline for withdrawals, conditional at best on the release of prisoners of war. May, June, and July saw the height of the favorable public reaction to the combination of the successful summit and the bombing and mining. Nevertheless, in that same period, there were nineteen votes in the House and Senate on a series of end-the-war amendments. All were variations on offering withdrawal for the return of our prisoners. In Congress, the difference between supporters and opponents of the war had narrowed to one issue, whether we should insist on a cease-fire or settle simply for the return of our prisoners in conjunction with our withdrawal.

There were three schools of thought in the Senate on that issue. A growing minority (about thirty senators) favored setting an unconditional deadline for American withdrawal in the "expectation" that this would lead Hanoi to free our prisoners. About forty senators favored making withdrawal contingent only on release of our prisoners. A dwindling minority favored making our withdrawal depend also on a cease-fire. None—not one—argued for mutual withdrawal. By the end of 1971, a majority on behalf of the withdrawal-for-prisoners option had developed; it grew through 1972. Requiring a cease-fire before withdrawal had become the *conservative* position; amendments including it in a settlement were consistently defeated in both houses. Thus, the dominant "peace" position in the Senate now was to get out of Vietnam even while the war among the Vietnamese continued. We would end ten years of war in return for our prisoners, while leaving our allies to their fate. Sentiment for cutting off aid to Thieu unless he agreed to a coalition government was growing as well.

We managed to block the various demands for unconditional withdrawal but by ever smaller margins. On July 24, a John Sherman Cooper–Edward Brooke amendment insisting on a withdrawal in return only for the release of prisoners passed in the Senate by five votes; the same day, an attempt by Senator James Allen of Alabama to make our withdrawal contingent on a supervised cease-fire as well was *defeated* by five votes. Sooner or later, one of the amendments to cut off funds would pass. At a minimum, Hanoi had every reason to believe that it had a guaranteed safety valve: If it offered to release our prisoners, Congress would probably stop the war. Whatever the parliamentary arithmetic, all of the recurring resolutions, differing as they did from our negotiating position, obviously weakened us for the bargaining that was now inevitable. And we would not go along with the Senate view. We were committed to tying withdrawal to a supervised cease-fire. It remained our view that it would be inhuman, ignoble, and destructive of larger interests elsewhere to withdraw while fighting continued against allies that had relied on us. But there was not *one* senator nor *any* newspaper editorial nor *any* senior official asking us to insist on mutual withdrawal— which analysts are, at this writing, advocating as an option retrospectively.

Still, we entered the negotiations in the best position ever. If the public opinion polls on the election during September would tip the balance, no concessions on our part in July were likely to affect Hanoi's calculations. And, in fact, our margin for concession was by now severely circumscribed. If we remained true to our principles, we could not, except cosmetically, go beyond our public military proposals of May 8, 1972 (or May 31, 1971), and our public political proposals of January 25, 1972. So I prepared for the negotiations in an optimistic and relaxed frame of mind; the fundamental decisions would have to be made by Hanoi, not by Washington. Until Hanoi had analyzed the likely electoral outcome, our best strategy would be to stay cool, offer nothing significantly new, and thus hope to intensify the pressures on Hanoi. The critical moment would come only after Hanoi had made its final judgment of Nixon's electoral prospects.

Later on, the myth developed that Nixon, for domestic political reasons, was eager to end the war before the election. Nothing could be further from the truth. As I have repeatedly shown, Nixon was exceedingly wary of negotiations in general (unless he had a nearly ironclad guarantee of success) and especially with the North Vietnamese. As his election prospects improved, he saw no domestic reason to pursue them. In July, he still saw some benefit in keeping his Democratic opposition off balance by periodically announcing private meetings with Le Duc Tho. But after the debacle of McGovern's vice presidential nominee, Senator Thomas Eagleton—forced off the Democratic ticket because of undisclosed health problems—Nixon lost interest even in that. As the weeks went by, he became convinced that he had narrowed McGovern's support to a fringe that would oppose him regardless of what he did on Vietnam. On the other hand, settling even on the terms we had put forward publicly might well displease some of the conservative groups he considered his base. Nixon saw no possibility of progress until *after* the election and probably did not even desire it. Even then, he preferred another escalation before sitting down to negotiate.

I urged negotiations because I did not think our bargaining position would improve after the election—quite the contrary. If things broke right, our election would serve as an immutable deadline, the equivalent of an ultimatum. Hanoi's fear of what Nixon might do with a new mandate for four years might lead it to make major concessions before the election. Contrary to both Hanoi's probable analysis and our own conventional wisdom, I thought that we would actually be *worse* off after the election. All the polls suggested that the composition of the new Congress would be substantially the same as of the old or even slightly less favorable—a prospect reinforced by Nixon's decision to separate his campaign as much as possible from the congressional race in order to obtain the largest presidential electoral margin in history. Thus, the pressures for ending the war by legislation were certain to resume after November. And the opposition would have a convenient target because the administration would have to submit a supplementary budget of $4 to $6 billion in January to pay for the costs of reinforcements during the offensive. Nixon already had before him a proposal by Laird to withdraw the augmentation forces sent to Indochina to repel the offensive after January 1, 1973, to keep the supplementary costs from growing un-manageable. Specifically, Laird proposed withdrawing ninety-eight B-52s and three squadrons of F-4s as of January. Once Hanoi understood that our forces were declining, it could revert to waiting us out. And once the composition of Congress became clear, Hanoi would resume its psychological warfare. If this was true, we had a window of about three months.

Decades after the events described in these pages, it became fashionable to describe a scenario of one-sided American concessions moving in a frantic effort to achieve a rapid settlement before the American election.[1] It is the exact opposite of the truth, which will be shown in describing in detail the steps that led to the final settlement. Once negotiations resumed, virtually all the significant concessions were made by Hanoi.

By the end of June 1972, no progress had been made in the negotiations in 174 plenary sessions and eighteen private meetings between Le Duc Tho and me. The positions of the two parties were as follows:

Hanoi insisted on a deadline for a unilateral American withdrawal. The deadline would have to be observed regardless of whether there was agreement on other issues. The United States was to overthrow the existing government in Saigon and replace it with a coalition government, one-third of which would be Communist and over the remainder of which the Communist element would have a veto. That government, deprived of American military assistance, would then negotiate a final outcome of the war with the Communist NLF, backed by Hanoi. After the political terms had been met, there would be a cease-fire with the American forces, but the war against the South Vietnamese army would continue. American prisoners would be discussed only after the political terms were agreed upon. Laos and Cambodia were declared outside the purview of the negotiations. No military resupply or economic aid to Saigon would be permitted.

The American position—expressed in presidential speeches of January 25 and May 8—was that there had to be an Indochina-wide cease-fire. American prisoners throughout Indochina had to be released on a fixed time schedule starting with the implementation of a cease-fire. North Vietnamese troops had to withdraw from Laos and Cambodia; in Vietnam, no further infiltration of men and matériel would be permitted. American economic and military aid to South Vietnam would continue. All this was to be supervised by an International Control Commission.

On the political side, the American position rejected any kind of coalition government. It provided for free elections to be supervised by an Electoral Commission on which the Communists could be represented. One month before the election, President Thieu would resign, but he was free to present himself as a candidate.

All of these proposals were public; all of them had been approved by Thieu and his government. The American position was widely attacked in Congress and the media as being too intransigent and as a subterfuge for continuing the war. I can think of no objection—within the administration, Congress, the media, or from Saigon—that the terms were too generous or accommodating. None had been accepted by Hanoi. With this as a background, the reader can determine which side moved toward the other in the negotiations that began on July 19.

Our basic strategy in the private meetings starting July 19 was to stand pat until Hanoi's intentions became clearer. If serious negotiations started, we would try to drain Hanoi's political proposals of operational content by countering their coalition government with an anodyne scheme for a joint electoral commission. If Hanoi went along, we would then gradually emerge with the dual-track approach we had offered originally: settling the military issues and leaving the political issues essentially to future negotiations among the parties.

Early in July, Haig was sent to Saigon to assess the situation and to consult with Thieu about the positions we proposed to take. Haig saw Thieu on July 3, but he encountered a different leader from the one we had dealt with thus far. Thieu's army had now been tested in battle; he thought that Hanoi would no longer be able to defeat him, certainly so long as our airpower was available. Through all the years of the Nixon administration, the real reason he had never challenged any of our negotiating proposals was that he calculated that they would be rejected by Hanoi. He considered these formal concessions the price he had to pay for continued American support. But, in 1972, he grew increasingly convinced that a serious negotiation was imminent and that he was no longer defenseless.

The prospect of a compromise confronted Thieu and America with diametrically opposite problems. A compromise would be the beginning, not the end, of massive problems for South Vietnam. We would withdraw; South Vietnam would remain. Hanoi would never give up its implacable quest for victory; sooner or later, South Vietnam would have to fight alone. Going on to total victory seemed more sensible to Thieu and probably no more costly than the compromises now achievable.

Unfortunately, we no longer had such a choice. If Hanoi did not soon accept our proposals, the new Congress would force us to settle on worse terms—withdrawal for prisoners—than those we would seek to negotiate. (Our bargaining edge was that Hanoi, focused on the presidential election, did not yet grasp this.) It was understandable that Thieu would continue to demand victory, which would have required several years of further American as well as South Vietnamese exertion. But we had no margin at home for such a course. It would require much effort and discipline even to obtain the terms Nixon had put forward publicly on January 25 and May 8 before Congress voted us out of the war essentially unconditionally.

The looming tensions emerged only indistinctly during Haig's visit, like the first rumbles of a distant storm. On July 3, Haig briefed Thieu on the Vietnam discussions of the Moscow summit and my June trip to Beijing. He described our new proposal—a cease-fire, the return of POWs, a four-month withdrawal, and Thieu's resignation two months before a new presidential election. The sole difference from previous proposals was the earlier timing provided for Thieu's resignation, as Nixon had promised Brezhnev.

Thieu's response showed that he was not on our wavelength. He did not make this explicit because, according to him, Hanoi's leaders did not feel the pressure to negotiate that Haig was predicting. They would not settle, he argued, unless they obtained a coalition government. A permanent cease-fire would guarantee their defeat because they would never be able to start the war up again—two points Thieu forgot when Hanoi accepted precisely such a cease-fire without insisting on a coalition government three months later. Thieu seemed concerned that we might press for a temporary cease-fire during the election period; this, he argued, must be rejected (we had no such intention). He said nothing about mutual withdrawals. Of course, the Senate would soon go on record for a total American withdrawal in return for prisoners without any cease-fire whatsoever. Thieu had no problem over offering to resign two months before a new election in South Vietnam; he was willing to step down even four months before, if that helped the negotiation. He seemed at one with his brethren in Hanoi in the conviction that whoever controlled the election machinery would win in the end.

As I left for Paris on July 19, the differences among the principals on our side lay not only in nuances of formulations but in an as yet unrecognized gulf in motivations. At that point, Nixon pursued the negotiations largely for their utility in confusing his domestic opponents. Thieu believed that the refusal of a coalition government offered a safe haven from the risks of negotiation and the uncertainty of defending South Vietnam without the presence of American forces. I expected a breakthrough—but not until the second half of September. Thus all principals rallied around a negotiating strategy that essentially held to established positions and sought to garner whatever concessions Hanoi might offer in seeking to narrow the gap before making its final decision.

Le Duc Tho and I met on July 19 in the dingy residence at 11 rue Darthé, which had been the site of all but the first of our previous fourteen meetings. I began with an analysis of why our previous talks had failed, proceeding at a very deliberate pace and in largely philosophical terms to remove any thought that we felt under the pressure of the approaching election. I warned that any attempt to manipulate the negotiations to influence our elections would lead to an immediate rupture. My opening remarks concluded with a statement of general principles. Hanoi's refusal to distinguish between what could be settled by negotiation and what had to be left to history guaranteed a war to the end. We were willing to coexist with Hanoi after the war. We had no desire to retain permanent bases in Southeast Asia. We would not impose our preferences on a freely elected government in Saigon. I withheld any concrete proposals.

Le Duc Tho conducted most of the conversation for the North Vietnamese, an indication that they were serious. This was a different Le Duc Tho—one I had seen only once before, the previous July, when he had tried to convince us to jettison Thieu prior to the South Vietnamese election. Now he was all conciliation. He laughed at my sallies; he flattered my academic credentials. We were spared the epic poem of Vietnam's heroic struggle for independence. Instead, Le Duc Tho insisted that Hanoi was eager to settle the war during Nixon's first term. He asked repeatedly if we would respect whatever agreements were reached, signed or unsigned. He would make a "great effort" to have this meeting become a turning point, he said, provided *both* sides reexamined their positions—an unprecedented disclaimer of infallibility; Hanoi, he averred, would keep in mind our responsibilities in other parts of the world even though these were of no direct concern to the Vietnamese themselves—another startling departure. He dwelt only briefly and perfunctorily on the bombing and mining; amazingly, he did not even ask us to stop them, resorting instead to the refrain of 1968 that ending these activities would create a "propitious" atmosphere for negotiations.

After sparring for a while, I put forward Nixon's public proposal of May

8—omitting, however, the part about extending the time limit for Thieu's resignation. Le Duc Tho turned it down, though much less polemically than in the past. He reiterated Hanoi's standard proposal of a three-part provisional coalition government, modified, however, in one respect: He gave up the insistence on a Hanoi veto over the composition of the Saigon segment; indeed, he implied that once Thieu resigned, the rest of the government could stay and even receive American help, pending a final negotiation with the Communist NLF. Our meeting had lasted for six and a half hours—the longest ever. We agreed to meet again on August 1.

As I left, I told Le Duc Tho that my movements were too well observed now to have the meetings remain secret. There would be too many journalistic inquiries to which we would have to reply either evasively or untruthfully. So I suggested that we announce each meeting after it had been held but give no details. When Nixon had revealed the secret talks in January, Hanoi had declared with bravado that it had only reluctantly agreed to keep them confidential. Now, when put to the test, Le Duc Tho grumbled. Obviously, he was loath to give up the advantage of probing our position secretly while demoralizing the American public by stalemating the visible diplomacy. I gave him no choice now. The fact of the talks would be made public. For the remainder of the negotiations, we blunted one of the psychological weapons in Hanoi's arsenal by announcing each meeting. Symptomatic of the widespread cynicism about peace prospects, no serious attempt was made by the media to cover the negotiations or to follow either my movements or Le Duc Tho's. Two announced private meetings in eleven days, coupled with a trip to Saigon, did little to shake the widespread conviction that it was all an electoral maneuver. No one explained why Hanoi would cooperate in playing such a game.

Upon my return, I briefed both Dobrynin and Huang Hua. In the interval, we also had an exchange with Thieu that proved an omen of things to come—though once again we took for a tactical misunderstanding what turned out to be a fundamental disagreement. We had told Thieu routinely that we would present during the next plenary session what we had withheld on July 19: Thieu's proposed resignation two months before a new election. We also proposed to insist that the cease-fire go into effect on the signature of an agreement in principle, contrary to Hanoi's previous insistence that a cease-fire be deferred until political issues had been resolved—in other words, until Thieu had been overthrown. We wanted to avoid a trap in which an agreement in principle would turn into a swap of prisoners for our with-drawal, leaving Hanoi free to pursue the war against South Vietnam.

Though Thieu had agreed once again to the resignation proposal in his conversation with Haig on July 3 (suggesting that he could even agree to re-sign sooner) and though the provision for cease-fire seemed to us entirely to his benefit, he now objected to both. He said that we could indicate the two-month resignation interval informally but not in writing. He tied the cease-fire to a withdrawal of all North Vietnamese forces within three months—a point he had never raised in the two years that the cease-fire proposal had been on the table.

Thieu's new proposal was unfulfillable. After having based our public position on an unconditional cease-fire for two years, we would never be able to sustain a continuation of the war on the issue of a Hanoi withdrawal; a majority of the U.S. Senate was opposed even to making unilateral with-drawal conditional on a cease-fire. On May 31, 1971, we had put forward a proposal prohibiting further infiltration into South Vietnam after a cease-fire to be supervised by international machinery. Nixon had repeated it publicly with Thieu's public concurrence on January 25 and May 8, 1972. This would have the practical consequence of causing the North Vietnamese forces in the South to atrophy owing to normal attrition. Even this position had next to no public support in the United States, but we were determined to stick to it.

The option of escalation—implied in going for broke after the elec-tion—was dramatic but not realistic for any extended period. Our military possibilities would not then be different from now; American military prospects might, in fact, decline. General Abrams was to tell me during my August visit to Saigon that, due to the limited offensive capabilities of South Vietnamese forces, another year of fighting would not significantly improve the territorial balance. And shortly after our election, Hanoi would rediscover not only our domestic fragility but also the budgetary pressures that would force us to reduce our forces unilaterally, in line with Laird's fiscal planning. We would then have to settle disagreements with Hanoi by testing each other's military endurance through a series of additional deadlocks—a process that would further divide our country and make ending the war as searing as its conduct. But we did not pursue the disagreement with Thieu, since it seemed irrelevant to the deadlocked negotiations.

The August 1 meeting in Paris with Le Duc Tho turned out to be the longest yet, lasting eight hours. I described it in a memorandum to the President as "the most interesting session we have ever had." Le Duc Tho was not yet so eager for a settlement as to give up his tactic of opening with an assault on our good faith, concentrating his fire this time on our announcements of the private meetings. Then, after an hour-long wrangle, Le Duc Tho yielded to the inevitable. He knew very well that there was no way of keeping the fact of the meetings secret if we were determined to publicize them—unless, of course, he was prepared to threaten to break off the conversations.

And this, it transpired, he was not at all willing to do. For on August 1, Le Duc Tho continued the retreat that he had begun on July 19. I presented our new "plan," but Le Duc Tho realized that it consisted mainly of cosmetic modifications. For once, his charge that I was offering "nothing new" was accurate. After we had consumed nearly three hours, first in haggling and then in going over familiar ground, Le Duc Tho asked for a recess. It lasted an hour and a quarter, the longest interruption yet.

After the recess, Le Duc Tho read me a little lecture on the mining and bombing. When I showed impatience, he finally came to the point. He had a whole new set of North Vietnamese proposals.

For two and a half years, Hanoi had been taunting us with the demand for unconditional withdrawal whereby we were asked to commit ourselves to a schedule of withdrawals that would have to be carried out regardless of what else happened in the negotiations and while the fighting would go on against our South Vietnamese allies. Hanoi's one-sided proposal had been gaining momentum within the United States. Several Senate resolutions embodied it; it was McGovern's campaign position. Now Le Duc Tho abandoned it. He was willing to settle for less than he was being offered by the American opposition candidate—a pretty clear indication of how Hanoi was reading the forthcoming election. Le Duc Tho agreed that whatever schedule we agreed upon would not start running until *after* all issues were settled; the unconditional deadline, which had rent our domestic debate, was dead.

Le Duc Tho began also to modify his political demands. He still insisted on a coalition government, but he put forward two concessions. Hanoi up to now had demanded a *provisional* coalition government in which the Communists appointed a third of the members and had a veto over the other two thirds. Le Duc Tho now proposed making the tripartite coalition government in effect the *definitive* government; it would not have to engage in additional negotiations with the NLF. Reflecting Hanoi's sense of urgency, Le Duc Tho gave up, in addition, the veto over the composition of the non-Communist segments of his proposed structure. In the three-part coalition, the Communists and Saigon would each appoint their third and also one half of the allegedly "neutral" third. In other words, the tripartite coalition had become a fifty-fifty split—with Saigon thus having a veto—rather than a grab for total power. We were opposed to any form of coalition government, but we were certain that we had not seen the last of Hanoi's flexibility.

Once Le Duc Tho started making concessions, he proved as inventive as he had been obnoxious while stonewalling. He next submitted a procedural proposal for speeding up the negotiation, so complex that it required an advanced degree to understand the bewildering series of forums he was now putting before us. Saigon and the South Vietnamese Communists would negotiate on political issues—something we had been proposing in vain since 1969; the three Vietnamese parties would discuss subjects affecting all of Vietnam; all four parties (including the United States) would treat the questions relating to the cease-fire. To us, the significant feature of this procedural cornucopia was that, in each of the forums, the *existing* South Vietnamese government, *including* Thieu, could participate as an equal. Hanoi was obviously in full retreat from its hitherto unyielding position that Thieu would have to resign *before* anything else happened.

I thought Le Duc Tho's proposals sufficiently serious to send the whole voluminous text to Bunker and Thieu for their consideration. In a memorandum to the President—on which Nixon wrote skeptical marginal comments about the tedium of the exercise—I pointed out that Hanoi's new formulations could be a first step toward separating the military and political issues, which had been our position since he took office. But if North Vietnam was indeed beginning to change course, the military issues such as cease-fire, prisoner exchange, and withdrawals would be settled definitively while the political issues would be left to prolonged, and in all likelihood inconclusive, negotiations among the Vietnamese parties.

We were, of course, entering dangerous waters. As long as Hanoi asked us to overthrow an allied government, we were on moral high ground in rejecting it. But with Hanoi now moving toward the gray area of accepting a genuine political contest, the dividing lines would begin to blur. Symbolism and substance would merge. And the former might be more dangerous to our precarious allies in Saigon, who would have to remain to defend their freedom after we had withdrawn 10,000 miles away. As the private talks—still unnoticed by the media—grew progressively more serious, what emerged more and more as the key issue was something intangible: the psychological resilience of Saigon.

For the time being, we were not compelled to decide. Hanoi had not yet moved far enough to test our consistent position that the principal obstacle to a settlement was our refusal to overthrow an allied government. Nixon would just as soon have put the whole negotiating process on ice until after the election. I agreed we should sit tight because I wanted to conserve for the final push the marginal adjustments in our position we were still capable of making. Hanoi would not make the final decision until well into September, when Nixon's prospects would be unambiguous. This assessment was shared by Dobrynin, who seemed well informed on our negotiations.

To coordinate policy, Nixon agreed that I should visit Saigon immediately following the next private meeting in Paris, scheduled for August 14. This had the additional advantage of supporting our strategy of procrastination; it gave me a pretext to delay a reply to Hanoi's August 1 proposals for at least another two weeks. If my assessment of the pressures posed by our election deadline was correct, Hanoi would find itself forced to disclose its hand soon thereafter. For the first time in the war, it was our opponents who were under time pressure.

As it turned out, Le Duc Tho, too, was going to travel; he told us that he had been called back to Hanoi. This confirmed that fundamental decisions were in the offing. As a result, the meeting on August 14 turned into a holding action on both sides. We agreed to meet again on September 15 on my way back from a long-planned trip to Moscow.

After three meetings, then, there had been significant movement, entirely by Hanoi; it was moving in our direction but not at a pace that would keep it from reversing course later. Hanoi had given up the demand for Thieu's immediate removal. It had agreed to negotiating forums in which the Saigon government would participate, thus in a sense recognizing its legitimacy. It had abandoned the demand for a unilateral deadline for the withdrawal of American forces. The proposed coalition government, heretofore a transparent front for a Communist takeover, had been reduced to a fifty-fifty split of power.

I reported to the President after the August 14 meeting:

> The North Vietnamese will be watching the polls in our country
> and the developments in South Vietnam and deciding whether to
> compromise before November. They have an agonizing choice. They

can make a deal with an administration that will give them a fair chance to jockey for power in the South, but refuses to guarantee their victory. Or they can hold out, knowing that this course almost certainly means they will face the same administration with a fresh four-year mandate that reflects the American people's refusal to cap ten years of sacrifice with ignominy. . . . During this process we have gotten closer to a negotiated settlement than ever before; our negotiating record is becoming impeccable; and we still have a chance to make an honorable peace.

Nixon's attitude was reflected in the notes he wrote to Al Haig on the margin of my report:

> Al—It is obvious that no progress was made and that none can be expected. Henry must be discouraged—as I have always been on this front until after the election. We have reached the stage where the mere *fact* of private talks helps us very little—if at all. We can soon expect the opposition to begin to make that point.
>
> Disillusionment about K's talks *could* be harmful politically—particularly in view of the fact that the Saigon trip, regardless of how we downplay it, may raise expectations.
>
> What we need most now is a P.R. game plan to either stop talks or if we continue them to give some hope of progress.

Clearly, Nixon would not have been unhappy if I had recommended halting all negotiations until after the election. I did not do that because my analysis was different.

A Visit to Saigon

In this mood of expectancy, I arrived in Saigon on August 17, after having spent a day in Switzerland to celebrate my parents' fiftieth wedding anniversary with them and my children. It was a peaceful respite from the fanatics of Hanoi and the desperate men in Saigon, each groping for a maneuver that would open the road to destroying his adversary.

Saigon was teeming with rumors that I had come to impose a settlement.

The city wore its incongruous, characteristic air of hysterical lassitude, noisy with motorbikes and military vehicles, flaunting its desire for the good life so ostentatiously as to raise the question whether it could ever mobilize the dedication to prevail against enemies whose only profession, perhaps even avocation, was war. Ambassador Bunker greeted me at Tan Son Nhut airport, unflappable as always. He was convinced that Thieu felt stronger than ever but also that his newfound strength would make him more difficult to deal with. Since Thieu was convinced that South Vietnam held the upper hand militarily, he now was wary of concessions to which he had agreed in less promising times. According to Bunker, Thieu seemed genuinely afraid of peace. All his life, he had known only war; his entire career had been based on American support. A world in which the South Vietnamese would have to stand on their own was full of terrors that his pride would not let him admit.

My first meeting with Thieu did not support Bunker's forebodings. We met in the modernistic Presidential Palace, flung into the center of Saigon at the juncture of two broad boulevards as if to defy the legacies of both French colonialism and a Vietnamese past. Thieu was accompanied by Nguyen Phu Duc, who was more or less my equivalent on his staff, and Hoang Duc Nha, his nephew, press assistant, and confidant. Duc, a splendid product of the French educational system, moved from abstract definition to irrelevant conclusion with maddening, hairsplitting ingenuity. America had to take some responsibility for Nha. He was in his early thirties; he had been educated in the United States and, in the process, had seen too many movies of sharp young men succeeding by their wits; he came on like the early Alan Ladd. He was dressed in the fanciest Hollywood style, spoke American English fluently, and had retained from his Vietnamese background primarily an infinite capacity for conspiracy. Both Bunker and I were convinced that he did much mischief in exacerbating every misunderstanding.

Thieu greeted us with his unvarying dignity and courtesy. His sparkling eyes gave no clue to his inner thoughts, which could not have been free of contempt for a superpower eager to settle for compromise when total victory seemed within reach. I assured him that the United States would not culminate its long Vietnam effort with dishonor.

In this spirit, I submitted for Thieu's consideration the draft of a counterproposal to Le Duc Tho on September 15. We would not change the military provisions except to reduce our withdrawal deadline from four to three months. This did not make much difference, as over four months would have elapsed since we had offered the four-month deadline on May 8. On the political side, we would reject a coalition government. But we would spell out the composition of the joint electoral commission we had been offering for three years, since May 14, 1969.

Every American plan since that time had proposed an electoral commission on which the Communists would be represented, together with all other political forces. The new proposal would finish off the scheme of coalition government once and for all by renaming the electoral commission a Committee of National Reconciliation, without changing its function. However, each side would appoint half of its membership; the renamed electoral commission would make decisions on the principle of unanimity. Thus Saigon had a double veto in the proposed scheme: in the composition of the committee and in its operation. To underline further that the committee had no function beyond supervising the election, another provision in the new plan permitted the Communists to participate in the government emerging from the election only in proportion to the votes they polled. We estimated that this might give the Communists two out of twenty seats. As I explained to Thieu: "In our country, political opponents are taken into the cabinet not to be given influence but to be deprived of it." That particular argument Thieu understood.

A new and important dimension of Thieu now emerged. He had never been obliged to deal with an American offer that he thought had any chance of being accepted by Hanoi. But with a serious negotiation approaching, his views and ours began increasingly to diverge. Schemes that only slightly modified proposals to which he had already agreed, he now treated as major deviations; what we considered tactical maneuvers, he escalated into confrontations. He was, in effect, looking for retroactive justification to undo the negotiating record of the past three years.

We did not grasp what was happening right away. We still thought we were operating in tandem with Thieu and therefore blamed his reserve on drafting difficulties and shortsighted advisers. We were prepared to be patient in finding a solution. And Thieu confused us further by applying to us the elusive tactics Vietnamese reserve for stymieing foreigners: He never actually made an issue of anything; he simply kept his agreement tantalizingly close but always out of reach. I should have recognized the methods from Le Duc Tho. Thieu raised no immediate objections to my presentation. Following a pattern with which we were to become only too familiar, he heard us out with seeming sympathy, asked penetrating questions, suggested modifications, discussed details of implementation. Thieu doubted that Hanoi would offer a cease-fire. A cease-fire worked too one-sidedly in our favor, he said. It would be a "gift" to President Nixon's campaign, and it would be a psychological set-back to the morale of the Communists, since they would be laying down their arms without any political achievement (arguments he would bitterly reject five weeks later). I agreed that Hanoi would probably not give up its political demands, but I reminded him that we were, in fact, committed to what we had proposed publicly: "If they come back—I don't want to mislead you— and say that there should be a cease-fire, we must accept it."

Thieu handed me an eight-page memorandum criticizing Le Duc Tho's August 1 proposal. It had been crafted in meticulous, nitpicking detail. After skimming it, I said with irony that I was left with the unavoidable impression that Saigon was not accepting every detail of Hanoi's proposal, but then nei-ther would we. At the end of the conversation, I noted again—for the third time—that, if Hanoi accepted our May 8 proposal, we would have no choice but to go along.

The next day, August 18, again at the Presidential Palace, Thieu handed me a new memorandum, this one of four pages, containing some twenty proposed changes in our plan. About fifteen of these were easily assimilated; others presented greater difficulty. Thieu wanted to alter the phrase "stand-still cease-fire" to "general cease-fire" for reasons never made clear unless it was that the South Vietnamese forces had no intention of standing still after a cease-fire. Thieu objected to the tripartite Committee of National Recon-ciliation even in our fifty-fifty version. I responded that we had always stated publicly that all elements including Communists would be represented on the electoral commission. We were, in effect, burying the concept of coali-tion government. On the other hand, I pointed out, for yet a fourth time, that if Hanoi proposed an unconditional cease-fire, we would have to accept. Thieu reiterated his belief that the North Vietnamese were afraid of a cease-fire because "once they accept a cease-fire, they can never start again, and we will prolong the political talks forever." Thieu seemed above all afraid that we might make political concessions; the timing of the cease-fire seemed to concern him less. This turned out to be a misapprehension; Thieu opposed whatever aspect appeared close to a solution. In any event, we finally decided not to alter the existing language on the cease-fire.

But there was a deeper reason for Thieu's ambivalence. He had no difficulty pointing out ambiguities in negotiating documents designed to bridge the gap between mortal enemies. But none of these drafting changes went to the heart of the problem, which for Thieu was domestic and ultimately involved the survival of the non-Communist political structure in South Vietnam.

The root fact was that Thieu and his government were simply not ready for a negotiated peace. They were not satisfied with survival; they wanted a guarantee that they would prevail. They preferred to continue the military contest rather than face a political struggle. As Bunker said on August 31 when he, the President, and I met in Honolulu to review the bidding: "They fear that they are not yet well enough organized to compete politically with such a tough disciplined organization."

But we had our own imperatives. I sympathized with Thieu's concerns, but there were limits to our capacity to meet them. We had accepted nearly unbearable fissures in our society to maintain the solemn pledges of our predecessors and our perception of the national honor. We had sustained our effort by convincing our public that the one issue on which we would not compromise was to impose a Communist government on an ally. But if Hanoi were to accept our offer of a cease-fire and abandon its demand for a coalition government, we would not be able to withdraw the terms we had publicly offered. If Nixon decided otherwise, Congress would make our nightmare real and vote us out of the war without any significant conditions, undermining the authority of the American presidency in every corner of the globe.

This was all the more the case because neither Thieu—nor General Abrams, for that matter—could come up with a military strategy to change the basic balance of forces in Indochina should negotiations break down. Abrams argued that, after another year of fighting, the territorial balance would be roughly the same as it was. And this did not take into account the withdrawal of the forces sent to resist the North Vietnamese offensive. Nor did Thieu's crystal ball show a better alternative. He expressed the view that by December 1973—fifteen months away—"if we don't sign anything . . . they will have less supplies, less manpower and less regular units in December 1973 than they had in December 1971 or March of 1972." In other words, after another long stretch of fighting presumably backed by unimpaired American airpower, we could look forward to a territorial balance similar to that which had produced only stalemates in the past. We did not think that either the American public or Congress would hold still for this prospect. And I knew that budgetary stringency would soon force us to reduce our air and naval forces by 30 percent.

But Thieu did have a case. In the process of meeting the demands of our insatiable opponents in the media and Congress, we had already reduced our terms to a level far below that which had been thought necessary to maintain the security of South Korea under much more favorable circumstances. Whereas 50,000 American combat troops were still stationed in Korea over twenty years after the end of the Korean war and 200,000 in Europe thirty years after VE Day, we proposed to withdraw *all* our troops from Vietnam, which had much longer and much less easily defended frontiers and an even more implacable enemy. (And in the next two decades, we retained forces in the Persian Gulf and in the Balkans after military operations ended. Vietnam has remained the only war which was ended with a total U.S. withdrawal.) Even though we were obtaining better terms than had been thought possible, for Thieu, everything depended on America's ability to enforce them with uncertain domestic backing against an enemy that had observed no agreement since 1954.

Altogether the cultural gap between American and Vietnamese perceptions was unbridgeable. A primeval hatred animated the two Vietnamese sides. They had fought each other for a generation. They had assassinated each other's officials, tortured each other's prisoners. The chasm of distrust and mutually inflicted suffering was not amenable to acts of goodwill or the sort of legalistic compromise formulas toward which diplomats incline. Each Vietnamese party saw in a settlement the starting point of a new struggle sometime in the not too distant future. Every formula put forward was designed in part to inflict a humiliation on the hated adversary. Every American proposal was tested for its suitability for such a purpose. And both sides were marvelously subtle and ingenious in finding phraseology for such taunts, particularly in the Vietnamese language with its finely shaded meanings quite beyond our grasp.

The dialogue between Saigon and Washington thus developed like a Greek tragedy in which each side in pursuit of its own necessities produces what it most dreads. For in essence both sides were right. Thieu was a patriot and a highly intelligent man. He had seen his country through a searing war with ability and dedication. He did not deserve the opprobrium American opponents of the war heaped on him as an outlet for their frustration and as an alibi for the surrender they wanted to force on their government. But the imperatives on him were almost diametrically the opposite of ours.

He was, in his view and ours, the legitimate head of the government of South Vietnam. For him to accept the potential legitimacy of those seeking to subvert it was to weaken the psychological basis of his rule. Yet their acceptance in some form was inherent in even the most attenuated compromise proposal on how to supervise elections put forward for three years. Thieu's domestic imperatives imposed intransigence. We could sustain domestic support for him only by a show of conciliation. Our goal was honor; we could (as the phrase went) run a risk for peace. But Thieu's problem was survival; he and his people would be left indefinitely after we departed; he had no margin for error.

I left Saigon with a false sense of having reached a meeting of the minds. Thieu and I had decided that we would settle the apparently few remaining disagreements over our draft proposal by exchanging messages through Bunker. There was plenty of time—nearly four weeks until the next meeting on September 15.

We soon learned better. Almost immediately, Thieu enveloped himself in silence; we heard absolutely nothing from the palace. And Nha began to play games with the media. After what we had endured in our domestic debate on behalf of Saigon, we were perhaps overly sensitive to the attacks on our motives that found their way increasingly into the Saigon newspapers. Certainly the treatment of Ellsworth Bunker, who, then in his seventies, had sustained Saigon for five years, verged on the outrageous. Bunker's requests for appointments with Thieu went unanswered or were granted after so much delay that their subject matter had become moot. For example, we had invited Bunker to come on August 31 to Honolulu where Nixon was meeting with the new Japanese Prime Minister, Kakuei Tanaka. The purpose was to review the negotiations with Le Duc Tho. Bunker was to consult with the South Vietnamese beforehand. We were hoping to use the occasion to complete the draft proposal to be submitted on September 15. But despite repeated efforts, Bunker failed to obtain an appointment with Thieu. Nor would the palace reply to our comments on the memorandum handed to me by Thieu, which we had sent from the plane on August 19.

Bravado is the armor of the weak; it is a device to muster courage in the face of one's own panic. On September 13, after a month of trying to elicit a reply from Thieu and forty-eight hours before my meeting with Le Duc Tho,

Thieu again rejected our proposal for the composition of the committee even though it gave him an absolute veto over substance and composition (indeed, since it operated by unanimity, it was almost certain never to function at all). After a month of exchanges, Thieu had dug in on a point so peripheral to the final result that we would never be able to justify to the Americans breaking up a negotiation over it. If we simply stonewalled on September 15 and Hanoi went public, we would start from a much worse position. If we accepted Thieu's conduct, we would have reached the condition that our domestic critics had accused us of permitting: Thieu would have an absolute veto over our policy.

Moreover, we were again locked into the withdrawal treadmill. On August 29, Nixon announced another withdrawal of 12,000 men, which reduced our forces in Vietnam to 27,000 (well below what we still had in South Korea). The President and I wanted to leave open the possibility that this might be a permanent residual force which Hanoi could get us to remove only by making concessions. But the Pentagon immediately leaked that it did not consider this the end of the withdrawals. As soon as Congress returned in January, we would be faced with a new flood of resolutions setting a terminal date for our involvement, on terms far less favorable than those we might be able to achieve in Paris, and enforced by budgetary cuts. We would then confront again Hanoi's maddening mixture of procrastination, ambiguous concession, and occasional military "high points" interspersed with congressional unilateral withdrawal schemes.

Thus if Hanoi decided to settle before the election, we had, in my view, an opportunity unlikely to return. After November 7, whichever course we chose—endurance or escalation—would have to be pursued without a deadline on Hanoi; instead *we* might well be worn down by congressional and media pressures. We might not be able to count on Soviet and Chinese acquiescence indefinitely, or we might be asked to pay some price for it. I thought it wiser to exploit a unique conjunction of domestic, military, and international circumstances to extract major concessions from Hanoi.

These were the reasons that induced me to recommend to Nixon that, on September 15, we submit a proposal that included the provision on the composition of the electoral commission which we had been proposing publicly since Nixon's first speech on the subject over three years earlier and which we now called the Committee of National Reconciliation. Thieu had not accepted the new name. I cabled Nixon from Moscow, requesting his approval:

If the other side accepts our proposal, which we believe quite unlikely, then the fact that GVN was not totally on board to the last detail will be obscured by myriad other complexities in what will essentially be a new ballgame. In such an eventuality, it is inconceivable that [the] GVN would find it in its interest to surface what few differences we may have had. . . .

If on the other hand [the] other side rejects our offer, as we think far more likely, [the] GVN will have absolutely every incentive to go along with us. We cannot imagine that they would want to publicly intimate the existence of any past divergences with us once our reasonable offer is out in the open, Hanoi has declined it, and we are in an excellent position to counter any public efforts by the other side by pointing to negotiating initiative of our own.

Nixon was far from enthusiastic. He was bolstered by a Lou Harris public opinion poll published on September 11, which showed that a substantial majority of American voters (55 to 32 percent) supported the continued heavy bombings of North Vietnam, and a 64-to-22 majority supported the mining of North Vietnamese harbors. A 47-to-35 plurality was opposed to a coalition government in South Vietnam (the widest plurality ever on that question). By 51 to 26 percent, a majority of the public disagreed with McGovern's charge that "Henry Kissinger's travels to Paris and Saigon were no more than a publicity stunt that falsely raised hopes for peace." And by 51 to 33 percent, more voters agreed with President Nixon's approach to bringing home American forces from Vietnam than with McGovern's approach. (Twelve days earlier, on August 30, the Gallup Poll had shown the following election preferences: Nixon, 64 percent; McGovern, 30 percent; undecided, 6 percent.)

Though Nixon perceived no domestic political advantage in proceeding with the negotiations, he accepted the foreign policy rationale though not without reminding me that it was really against his political interests. Haig cabled me in Moscow on behalf of Nixon:

He [the President] stated that the NSC does not seem to understand that the American people are no longer interested in a solution based on compromise, favor continued bombing and want to see the United States prevail after all these years. I pointed out that this very attitude was fragile and had been accomplished simply because we had been able to carefully blend a series of strong and forthcoming measures in a way that reestablished presidential credibility. . . . The President finally agreed but insisted that in conveying his approval to you that I emphasize to you his wish that the record you establish tomorrow in your discussions be a tough one which in a public sense would appeal to the Hawk and not to the Dove. I again told the President that the record thus far of these meetings was unassailable and that I was confident that it would remain that way following tomorrow's meeting.

Interlude: Meetings of September 15 and 27

In the event, on September 15, Le Duc Tho made the American internal debate irrelevant by presenting the third new North Vietnamese proposal in the four meetings since July.

In the mild, almost pleasant tone that he had displayed since the July 19 meeting, indeed, almost plaintively, Le Duc Tho repeatedly inquired whether we were willing to settle rapidly. I was vaguely reassuring in principle and tabled our plan, including the paragraph to which Thieu had objected. Le Duc Tho dismissed it as nothing basically new, which was close to the mark. But instead of militantly sticking to Hanoi's previous position, he tabled a new ten-point proposal. Its major feature was to deprive the Government of National Concord, which he had outlined at the last session, of some of its power. Whereas on August 14 Hanoi had argued that the Saigon government could continue but only until a Government of National Concord was formed, Tho now proposed that the two existing administrations continue even *after* a settlement. The Government of National Concord would be confined to supervising compliance with the provisions of the agreement and the conduct of foreign policy.

As Le Duc Tho must have expected, I rejected his proposal. We would accept no coalition government in any guise, I told him. Contrary to his previous practice, he responded with only ritual complaints about our "sincerity" and even seemed to redouble his efforts. Was I prepared to aim for an agreement in principle by a certain timetable, he suddenly wanted to know. After such an agreement, the various forums proposed in his August 1 draft would begin to negotiate its implementation. I saw no harm in agreeing to a target date so long as we were making no additional concessions. We settled on October 15. The various forums would still leave plenty of room to refine aspects of the basic agreement.

To gain more time and thereby bring more pressure on Le Duc Tho, I proposed that we devote the next meeting to nailing down language on the already agreed points. The agreements were largely confined to military questions. Tho was uncharacteristically agreeable. Though pointing out that progress on the political question (code word for the removal of Thieu) would "facilitate" the solution of the military issues, he dropped it as a precondition. He next proposed a *two-day* meeting, preferably *within a week's time*. I accepted this unprecedented request but pushed the date back to September 26. The more we squeezed Le Duc Tho against what was more clearly than ever his self-imposed deadline of our presidential election, the more forthcoming he was likely to be. In a summary memorandum prepared for Nixon immediately after the meeting, I wrote:

> Their dilemma is that further talks strengthen our domestic position and negotiating record without in any way restricting our military flexibility, while if they break them off, they have no hope of settling before November, which I sense from our meeting is their strong preference.
>
> My surmise is that they are deeply concerned about your re-election and its implications for them but, with their collective leadership, they may be having deep difficulties coming to grips with the very political concessions they will have to make to move the talks off dead center. They continue to pose unacceptable demands, perhaps because they lack imagination, perhaps because they wish to defer the necessary concessions to the last possible moment.

We were, in fact, in the strongest bargaining position of the war. September 15 was the day that South Vietnamese forces recaptured Quang Tri, the one provincial capital taken by Hanoi in its offensive. It was the week of polls showing growing public support for Nixon's handling of the war and the widest Nixon lead over McGovern ever. And it was the time (we learned a few weeks later) that COSVN Directive 06 informed Communist cadres that an effort would be made to "force" Nixon to settle the war before election day—which was Hanoi's way of preparing its people for an agreement on terms that had heretofore been publicly rejected.

I left the September 15 meeting convinced that Hanoi, having come this far, would sooner or later table its rock-bottom position. This same prospect filled Thieu with renewed dismay. Bunker was unable to obtain an appointment with Thieu to report on the meeting. But Bunker gave me his own assessment that our "patience and persistence seems to be paying off." He added: "I think we have been understanding and very forbearing in deferring to his [Thieu's] views and I believe that we should now be firm in making clear that we also have imperatives."

Bunker was given no opportunity to implement his recommendation. Thieu would not see Bunker on September 16 to receive a report on the meeting with Tho. Instead he was handed a letter from Thieu to Nixon ostensibly in reply to Nixon's letter of August 31. Characteristically, it voiced no appreciation for our having held the line on the key issues of coalition government, supervised cease-fire, and no further infiltration; rather, it warned that no further concessions should be made.

The next day, September 17, Thieu finally deigned to receive Bunker's briefing on the meeting with Le Duc Tho. Thieu saw two possibilities: The North Vietnamese might be preparing to reach an agreement in principle prior to the American elections or else they were uncertain about our strategy. Still half believing that Thieu's lack of cooperation must reflect a misunderstanding, I sent Bunker an even more detailed report of the September 15 session. But Thieu's intransigence was heightened not so much by the fear of failure as by the prospect of success. On September 20 in a speech in Hue, he pointedly declared: "No one has a right to negotiate for or accept any solution" except the people of South Vietnam. On September 23, I made one more effort to heal the breach, wiring Bunker:

> If Thieu is genuinely worried that we might settle prematurely, he must understand that the appearance of differences between Washington and Saigon could have the practical consequence of influencing Hanoi toward a rapid settlement in the secret talks so as to exploit what they might perceive as a split between the U.S. and GVN and the resulting political disarray in Saigon . . . Therefore it is essential

that Thieu stay close to us so that we demonstrate solidarity to Hanoi.

For the session of September 26–27, the North Vietnamese chose the quiet country town of Gif-sur-Yvette, in a white stucco house with a large garden behind a high green wooden fence, the former home of the cubist painter Fernand Léger. Surrounded by striking reproductions (and perhaps some originals) of Léger's abstract paintings and tapestries, we began a round of increasingly concrete negotiations to end the war.

Le Duc Tho and Xuan Thuy continued to display the same sense of urgency for an early end to the war as at the previous meeting. They spent two hours laying out a work program (a "shed*yule*," according to Nguyen Dinh Phuong, the North Vietnamese interpreter)* designed to complete a settlement *within the month*. This "shedyule" soon took the place of the epic poem of Hanoi's struggle for liberation as the opening ritual of our talks. Tho would put forward his recommendations for accelerated negotiation like an opening prayer. I would respond. We would haggle, since I considered this as good a subject as any other on which to waste time so as to push Hanoi against its own deadline. At last I would agree to the "shedyule." Tho would write it down personally in a little notebook whose pages were lined with blue squares, thereby conferring additional formality on it. The next time we met, the process would be repeated. The "shedyule," however, would be delayed by the interval that had since elapsed. Once in exasperation, Tho called out: "I am writing it down, but I want you to know that I don't believe it."

Le Duc Tho's new plan—which he called his "final" offer—stripped away further layers from the Communist demand for a tripartite coalition government and moved again toward the mixed electoral commission of the long-standing American proposal. He still called for a Provisional Government of National Concord without Thieu, but once again he had reduced its functions; the Government of National Concord was to be *advisory* to the existing governments with a vague responsibility to mediate between the two sides, and with neither enforcement powers nor the right to conduct foreign

---

* Far be it from me to make fun of anyone's accent—he was an excellent interpreter. But the schedule that Le Duc Tho insisted on became a crucial point in the breakdown of the negotiation in October. The word "schedule"—pronounced in the British way but with the stress oddly on the last syllable—was repeated so many times by Le Duc Tho that it remains indelibly in our memory in Phuong's pronunciation.

policy. It would "operate in accordance with the principle of unanimity"—
that is, any member had a veto, guaranteeing its impotence even for its limited functions. It remained unacceptable, but "from Hanoi's perspective it
represents major movement," I later reported to the President. It was "not inconsistent," I observed, "with their eventually turning their coalition government into an irrelevant committee in order to give a face-saving cover to a
standstill cease-fire and de facto territorial control by both sides."

An even more significant concession was Le Duc Tho's offer that, after a
settlement, Hanoi's troops would withdraw from both Laos and Cambodia
and that our prisoners in Laos would be released. (He said there were no
American prisoners in Cambodia; we had never had any intelligence to the
contrary.) It was a breakthrough. We had insisted on an Indochina-wide
cease-fire; we had pressed for the release of all our prisoners held in Indochina; we had demanded North Vietnamese withdrawal from the other
countries of Indochina. None of these proposals had been accepted before.
None of these terms, except the return of prisoners, had much domestic support in America; yet all were on the way to being realized—though the gap in
achieving acceptable terms and seeing them carried out was wide.

Since our strategy seemed to be working, I confined myself to handing
over short drafts on such questions as international guarantees, the technicalities of international supervision of a cease-fire, and the exchange of prisoners. As Le Duc Tho pressed harder and harder for rapid progress, he expressed
irritation that I was only inching forward and concentrating on peripheral
issues—which was true as far as Hanoi was concerned. To us, of course, the
return of prisoners was a key issue.

I told Le Duc Tho that the continuing requirement that Thieu would
have to leave office after the signature of a final agreement remained unacceptable. I emphasized again that we would never overthrow our allies, directly or by some subterfuge. Le Duc Tho stressed the "finality" of their offer.
I reiterated that the American people would never stand for our ending a war
which had cost so much by imposing a Communist government. The final
outcome would have to be left to the free decision of the people, a concept
that Tho had great difficulty in grasping. Despite all these rejections, Le Duc
Tho proposed a *three-day* session for next time. He suggested October 7—
ten days away. He said that the meeting would be "decisive." To step up the
pressure slightly, I accepted for October 8.

All this made it increasingly obvious that we were approaching a crucial
point. We had in principle settled all military issues: cease-fire, ban on infil-

tration, withdrawals, release of prisoners, international supervision, Laos. We lacked agreement on Cambodia; Le Duc Tho insisted that Hanoi did not have influence on the Khmer Rouge to decide on a cease-fire for them. He was still pushing political formulas designed to undermine Saigon. But his eagerness for a three-day meeting in early October left little doubt that we had not yet heard the last word. That might prove unacceptable and, when we came to putting what had been agreed in principle into formal language, the entire process might evaporate. But we had come a long way. The next meeting would bring either a breakthrough or a commitment to another military test.

I had no doubt what Thieu preferred. Defiant leaks from Saigon were multiplying. Appreciation for services rendered was not Thieu's distinguishing characteristic; Thieu took our dogged rearguard action on behalf of his country for granted, or else he wanted to shift the onus for any concessions onto our shoulders. But as we approached this climactic moment, another consultation with Thieu was clearly necessary.

Nixon was campaigning on the West Coast. Within hours of my return from Paris on September 27, I reached Haldeman in Los Angeles and proposed that we send Al Haig to Saigon to review with Thieu the various contingencies that might arise during my next meeting with Le Duc Tho. Nixon agreed.

As it turned out, Haig could have saved himself the trip. A great admirer of Thieu, Haig this time found himself exposed to the by now standard insolence. When the two men met first on October 2, for two hours and forty minutes in the Presidential Palace, Thieu was calm and conciliatory, asking thoughtful questions designed to elicit as much information as possible. Haig argued that Hanoi had, in fact, made a "dramatically revised proposal." Haig assumed that Thieu was reassured. He reported that Thieu's frame of mind was "as constructive as we could have hoped for and he will be inclined to be more cooperative than otherwise would have been the case."

He was soon to learn otherwise. His scheduled appointment with Thieu for October 3 was abruptly canceled. In the meantime, Nixon had met with Gromyko at Camp David on October 2. Under the impact of Haig's optimistic report, Nixon had told Gromyko that we would make our final offer at the meeting of October 8. If it was rejected, there would be no further negotiation during the election period. Afterward, we would turn to "other methods."

On October 4, Thieu dropped the other shoe. He confronted Haig with his entire National Security Council and bitterly attacked almost every aspect of the American proposal, including those he had supported for several years. He would discuss none of the variants we had put before him. Thieu was in tears at some moments. (I was to be subjected to the identical procedure less than three weeks later.)

On the morning of October 4, Nixon told me that Haig had made a mistake returning home as had always been planned; he should have stayed to work over Thieu. Bunker had better have another "cold turkey" talk with Thieu; Thieu had to be made to understand that Nixon refused to be placed in so untenable a position. Nixon authorized me to proceed with the October 8 meeting, consoling himself that Hanoi would probably turn down our proposals anyway. He wanted to stall until after the election. "And we're just going to have to break it off with him [Thieu] after the election, I can see that. You know, if he's going to be this unreasonable, I mean the tail can't wag the dog here." I warned Nixon that there was a fifty-fifty chance that Hanoi would finally accept our September 15 proposal (in turn a combination of our proposals going back sixteen months). I thought this was the best chance we would get: "We can't improve that by another year of bombing." Nixon said he agreed. I repeated my view of the strategy: We had "the clock running on the North Vietnamese." I wondered aloud whether Thieu did not really *want* to be pressured by us so that we would bear the onus for an agreement he knew to be necessary but did not want to be perceived by his hard-liners as having made.

The upshot was a decision that I would stick with our September 15 position and not present any new proposals. Hanoi would be asked to be more specific about military issues before we could offer any new political program. If Hanoi accepted our September 15 proposal, I would ask for a recess to go to Saigon. Nixon told me that then I was to "cram it down his [Thieu's] throat."

In the meantime, our task was to prepare the context of the October 8 meeting as well as possible. We had to prevent Thieu from making our disagreements public, for this would undermine both our negotiating position with Hanoi and our domestic position with Nixon's constituency on the right. But we also had to put Thieu on notice that the evolving negotiations might force us to return to some of the political proposals that Haig had discussed with him. On October 5, I drafted a message to Thieu, promising consultation before any final decision. The next day, I cabled Bunker that

Thieu should study the political proposals—for a presidential election or election for the Constituent Assembly—left by Haig "so that he cannot complain that he has not had sufficient time to consider the various aspects of these proposals should it be necessary to do so."

In preparation for the October 8 meeting, I asked Undersecretary of State Alex Johnson and Deputy Assistant Secretary for East Asia William Sullivan to produce working papers on international supervisory machinery and cease-fire implementation. Their contribution proved invaluable. On the morning of Saturday, October 7, we set off for Paris for what turned out to be the climax of four years of negotiations with Hanoi to end the war.

The Breakthrough: The October 8 Meeting

This time my entire party stayed at Ambassador Arthur Watson's residence, a newly renovated mansion on the fashionable Rue du Faubourg St. Honoré. It was expected to be a three- or four-day session. Al Haig accompanied me because he had a recent, firsthand sense of Saigon and because he would be able to help sell any possible agreement to Thieu. Richard T. Kennedy of my staff was left to run the NSC office.

Sunday, October 8, was a crisp, clear autumn day. The meeting started in the still secret white stucco house at Gif-sur-Yvette at 10:30 A.M. After opening pleasantries, I noticed two big green folders in front of Le Duc Tho and asked him whether he wanted to read them to me. Xuan Thuy invited me to speak first—obviously to see whether I had brought an offer better than what they were prepared to concede. I replied that we found some positive elements in Le Duc Tho's latest political proposal, such as the principle of unanimity for the proposed Committee of Reconciliation, but it still had major drawbacks:

> You would remove the incumbent President upon signature of an agreement; you would abolish the present constitutional structure; you would create new quasi-governmental organs from Saigon right down to the village level. . . .
>
> The cumulative impact of these various elements is clear. Even if

any particular one would not necessarily prove decisive, the combination of them all occurring simultaneously has to give us concern.

I then turned to the military issues, which, I stressed, had taken on "a particular urgency." There were many unresolved problems in Hanoi's latest proposal, particularly in the modalities of a cease-fire, the withdrawal of North Vietnamese forces from Laos and Cambodia, an end of infiltration through Laos and Cambodia into South Vietnam, and the release of U.S. prisoners in Laos and Cambodia. There had been hints but no concrete proposals. We would insist on cease-fires throughout Indochina, although we were open-minded as to the specific arrangements. Even if the cease-fires in Laos and Cambodia had to be arranged separately, they should go into effect simultaneously. I handed over a series of short explanatory papers on all the technical topics—substantially what Alex Johnson and Bill Sullivan of the State Department had drafted.

I also handed over a "new" peace proposal, which offered in reality only a slight cosmetic change by spelling out somewhat more specifically the functions of the Committee of National Reconciliation; it was to supervise elections and anything else the committee might agree on, which was not likely to be much because of Saigon's veto. The nature or the timing of the elections it was to supervise was not specified; it was left open to negotiation among the parties. If this was our "last offer," as Nixon had told Gromyko, then it could only have signaled to Le Duc Tho that we were standing fast on our position of maintaining the existing structure in Saigon and were making no further political concessions.

Apparently Le Duc Tho drew the same conclusion. Instead of exploding as he would have at any point during the previous three years, he said: "I propose now a break and afterward I shall express my views." The meeting broke up at 12:38 P.M. A generous array of luncheon snacks was available while the North Vietnamese disappeared upstairs. At 1:00 P.M., Le Duc Tho reentered the room and chatted with me near the snack table. "When the war ends, some day I will show you the Ho Chi Minh Trail," he joked. He left again for a few moments to rejoin his colleagues. Then he returned to say that since I had given them "so many papers," the North Vietnamese preferred to have a longer break. He suggested that the meeting resume at 4:00 P.M. I agreed.

My staff and I strolled a bit in the clear autumn air in the garden, whis-

pering softly (in case the bushes were bugged). Then, to pass the time, someone suggested a visit to Rambouillet, the forest and château about fourteen
miles away. I agreed, and the seven members of the team piled into two
cars and headed westward down Route Nationale 306. We never reached
Rambouillet. After ten minutes' drive, restless and wanting to confer more
privately with Haig, I asked to stop the car at a place where Haig and I could
take a walk. We pulled over at a picnic area in a woods fronting a small
lake. Families were spreading out their food on checkered tablecloths; cou-
ples were lying under the trees. The sky had the mellow blue of the early
French autumn. None of these Parisians paid the slightest attention to this
group of self-absorbed Americans walking part of the way around the lake.
Haig and I reviewed the bidding, then turned and headed back. The delegation was equally preoccupied and tense over what was to come in two hours'
time.

The meeting resumed on schedule. Le Duc Tho did not beat around the
bush. He turned immediately to his green folders. "I think we cannot negotiate in the way we are doing now," he said, if we were going to keep the
schedule that had been agreed upon and rapidly settle the war. All the procedures and multiforum scenarios that he had introduced into the negotiation
at the previous meeting Tho now described as inadequate. They were "very
complicated" and would take "a long time for these discussions, many
weeks." Therefore: "In order to show our goodwill and to ensure a rapid end
to the war, rapid restoration of peace in Vietnam, as all of us wish for, today
we put forward a new proposal regarding the content as well as the way to
conduct negotiations, a very realistic and very simple proposal."

Le Duc Tho suggested that the United States and North Vietnam sign an
agreement settling the military questions between them—withdrawal, prisoners, cease-fire. On the political problems of South Vietnam, "we shall only
agree on the main principles. After the signing of this agreement, a cease-fire
will immediately take place." The political problem—"that is the most
thorny, the most difficult problem"—would not be allowed to prolong our
negotiations. Le Duc Tho no longer demanded the formation of a coalition
Government of National Concord before the cease-fire. Indeed, he dispensed with the entire concept of a coalition government. It was now only an
Administration of National Concord, to be set up within three months by
the two South Vietnamese parties and charged with implementing the
signed agreements, achieving national concord (whatever that meant), and

"organizing" unspecified general and local elections. The two "administra-tions" in South Vietnam—the Saigon government and the Communist PRG—would continue in existence, with their armies. This Administration of National Concord might never even be set up at all, since it required the approval of the two South Vietnamese parties; its functions were yet to be ne-gotiated by the two mortal enemies, and afterward it would operate on the principle of unanimity.*

This barely visible vestige of Hanoi's former demands for a coalition gov-ernment was not much to show for a decade of exertion and suffering by the North Vietnamese. I was sure I could further reduce the importance of this "administration" in the negotiations yet to come. After four years of implaca-ble insistence that we dismantle the political structure of our ally and replace it with a coalition government, Hanoi had now essentially given up its polit-ical demands. In fact, the Administration of National Concord never came into being.

Le Duc Tho's other new provisions also moved toward our proposals. For three years, Hanoi had insisted that an end of American military aid to South Vietnam was an absolute precondition of settlement. Le Duc Tho now scrapped this proposal. "Replacement of armament" (that is, military aid) was permitted; while Hanoi said nothing about withdrawing its troops (in-deed, not even admitting that they were there), it accepted the American pro-posal of May 31, 1971, repeated publicly on January 25 and May 8, 1972, that infiltration into South Vietnam cease; if observed, this would bring about the gradual erosion of Hanoi's strength in the South. Le Duc Tho ac-cepted international control and supervision—although he considered this "not a pressing question" and proposed to discuss it *after* the cease-fire. There were, inevitably, still some gaps. Le Duc Tho was as yet silent about North Vietnamese troops in Laos and Cambodia (although he had conceded their withdrawal previously); he would not commit Hanoi to cease-fires there be-cause this was contrary to the principle of noninterference in these countries. "But so is the presence of your troops," I observed. But if Le Duc Tho was sincere in his profession that he would now work as resolutely for peace as he had previously fought the war, these issues could be settled in the next few

---

* This element of unanimity was, in fact, not in Le Duc Tho's October 8 written plan, but he men-tioned it in his oral presentation, and I was sure he would accept it, since it had been in his proposal of September 27. He did.

days. He knew there would be no agreement otherwise. At the end of his presentation, Le Duc Tho handed me the text of a draft agreement.

Time and again, Le Duc Tho insisted that his plan represented an acceptance of our own proposals.

> And this is what you yourself have proposed, the same proposal. . . . So our proposal has shown our good will, our real desire to rapidly end the war. And it is the same proposal made by President Nixon himself—ceasefire, release of prisoners, and troop withdrawal. . . . As to the internal political and military questions of South Vietnam we agree on principles and the South Vietnamese parties will discuss. . . . We do this with a view to reducing the thorny questions. So our aim is to do what you proposed previously: ceasefire and cessation of hostilities, troop withdrawal, release of prisoners. . . . And it is your proposal, and we met it with great good will, in order to end the war. . . . Because this new proposal is exactly what President Nixon has himself proposed: ceasefire, end of the war, release of the prisoners, and troop withdrawal . . . and we propose a number of principles on political problems. You have also proposed this. And we shall leave to the South Vietnamese parties the settlement of these questions.

My colleagues and I understood the significance of what we had heard at once. In the immediate recess I asked for, Winston Lord and I shook hands and said to each other: "We have done it." Haig, who had served in Vietnam, declared with emotion that we had saved the honor of the military men who had served, suffered, and died there. Le Duc Tho's paper still had unacceptable elements, to be sure. And others of my colleagues, especially John Negroponte, focused on the reaction of Saigon in the half-hour break after our interlocutor finished his presentation. But its essence was an Indochina-wide cease-fire, withdrawal of U.S. forces, release of prisoners, no further North Vietnamese infiltration, the right to resupply the South Vietnamese forces up to existing levels, and above all, the recognized continuation of the existing political structure in Saigon, eligible for U.S. economic and military aid—the basic program we had been offering since May 1971 and that had consistently been rejected.

I have participated in many dramatic events, but the moment that moved me most deeply has to be that cool autumn Sunday afternoon, while the shadows were falling over the serene French landscape and that large quiet room, hung with abstract paintings, was illuminated only at the green baize table across which the two delegations were facing each other. At last, we thought, there would be an end to the bloodletting in Indochina and the turmoil in America. We stood on the threshold of what we had so long sought, a peace compatible with our honor and our international responsibilities.

But negotiators must not betray emotion; to do so becomes a weapon in the hands of the other side. When we resumed, I confined myself to saying: "I of course have not had an opportunity to study your paper. From your presentation I believe that you have opened an important new chapter in our negotiations and one that could bring us to a rapid conclusion." I warned Le Duc Tho that whatever was negotiated would have to be approved first by President Nixon, then by Saigon. Only then could we speak of a visit by me to Hanoi as he urged. I asked to spend the evening and the next morning studying the paper and to meet again at 2:00 P.M. on Monday, October 9. Le Duc Tho assented. At the embassy residence, Winston Lord and John Negroponte redrafted Le Duc Tho's document, weakening the political provisions, strengthening our right to assist South Vietnam, tightening the provisions against infiltration with language drawn from earlier American proposals, and insisting on North Vietnamese withdrawal from Laos and Cambodia.

In the last analysis, I had three choices. I could reject Le Duc Tho's plan as inadequate in principle; I could accept it in principle and negotiate its improvement; I could stall, perhaps by returning to Washington and Saigon for consultations.

I was aware, of course, that Nixon on the whole preferred to string out the talks until after our election and then go for broke with both Hanoi and Saigon. But this option was not, in fact, available. Procrastination would force Hanoi into the public arena, with a proposal in effect going beyond our public proposals. We had no possible basis for refusing. The offer was much more favorable than anything imagined by Congress, the media, and the public to be achievable. If Hanoi did publish its proposal, public opinion and Congress would force us back to the conference table *without* the improvements I was practically certain I could achieve in three or four days of intensive secret negotiations under the pressure of a deadline. And

Congress would legislate one of the many proposals for unilateral withdrawal before it.

I have since often anguished over whether I should have suspended the talks and returned home for consultation. And, in normal circumstances, I would have. But neither Haig nor I doubted that Nixon would approve the evolving terms, since they were far better than what he had already authorized. From talking to Johnson and Sullivan, I knew that the State Department experts doubted that our terms were achievable. And we were in the midst of a presidential campaign, during which Nixon was constantly traveling, while all those familiar with the details of the negotiation were with me in Paris.

So I decided to proceed. The political provisions of the new proposal were better than what Nixon had offered on January 25, 1972. The general elections provided for in Tho's plan were so vague as to be unachievable in practice (as compared with our proposal of presidential elections within six months and Thieu's withdrawal two months before). The Administration of National Concord had less power than even the joint electoral commission which we had been urging for over three years, because there was no agreed election to supervise. And I was certain that in a rapid negotiation we could water down the political provisions even further.

As for the military terms, the offer of the cease-fire in place in Vietnam was unqualified. Le Duc Tho had hinted that it could be extended to Laos and Cambodia. The draft he handed over included a provision requiring the withdrawal of all foreign forces from Laos and Cambodia; I would have to try to pin down the timing and make certain that Le Duc Tho considered North Vietnamese forces "foreign." And Hanoi was prepared to return our prisoners as our remaining forces left. There was, admittedly, no provision for the withdrawal of North Vietnamese troops from the South. But we had abandoned this demand—with Thieu's concurrence—in our cease-fire proposal of October 7, 1970; in our secret seven-point plan of May 31, 1971; and in Nixon's public offers of January 25, 1972, and May 8, 1972. Starting in June 1969, we were in the process of withdrawing unilaterally. By October 1972, our forces had been reduced from 543,000 to 25,000. On the basis of what balance of forces could we insist on mutual withdrawal? The modification of the concept of mutual withdrawal did not occur on October 8, 1972. It was imposed on us by the unilateral withdrawal judged necessary to maintain any effort to save Vietnam. Once the unilateral American withdrawal started in

1969, it created its own momentum. The more we withdrew, the more was demanded—as I warned Nixon in my memorandum of September 1969. To argue a generation after the event that we should have achieved with a residual force of 20,000 and air assets diminishing for budgetary reasons what our predecessors had failed to bring about with half a million men is to give a higher priority to enshrining the divisions of a sad period than to learning from them. Nobody—hawk or dove or Thieu, for that matter—objected when the earlier proposals without this provision were put forward. On the contrary, our terms, including this provision, were generally attacked as too intransigent.

We had a moral duty to our allies in Saigon not to abandon millions who had put their trust in our word. Hundreds of thousands of Americans and billions of dollars of equipment had been sent to South Vietnam, and we had endured social upheaval for ten years. We had bought time while strengthening South Vietnam's capacity to defend itself. But, finally, we had a moral obligation as well to our own people: not to prolong their division beyond the point demanded by honor and international responsibility; to end the war in a manner that would heal rather than divide.

Thus I assumed the responsibility of concluding a draft agreement but giving Nixon every opportunity to stop the process or recall me.

Well past midnight I sent a cryptic message to Haldeman: "Tell the President that there has been some definite progress at today's first session and that he can harbor some confidence the outcome will be positive." While giving no details, it enabled Nixon to call a halt or to request additional information if delay was what he wanted. There was no response. Simultaneously, a short message was sent to Ellsworth Bunker to forewarn President Thieu that "the other side may surface a cease-fire proposal during these meetings," and therefore it was "essential that Thieu instruct his commanders to move promptly and seize the maximum amount of critical territory."

I delayed the next session with Le Duc Tho until 4:00 P.M. because we needed the time to prepare a counterdraft. When the meeting of October 9 began, I handed Xuan Thuy a regimental necktie as a reward for having worked on Sunday. He said he would wear it when the agreement was completed. (He did.) I opened the meeting by stressing that Le Duc Tho had given us "a very important document, which I believe will bring us to an agreement." I handed over our new proposal and went over its provisions point by point. We accepted some provisions, reformulated others, dropped some, and added new ones, tightening the provisions on infiltration, replacement of military equipment, and Laos and Cambodia. Le Duc Tho reserved his position until he could study the document but vocally protested his eagerness to settle with the same intensity that had previously marked his procrastinations.

After two hours, we adjourned. This time the North Vietnamese needed the morning to study our draft. The next meeting was set for 4:00 P.M. the following day.

I sent another terse cable to Haldeman:

> At this juncture I believe we have chance to obtain significant progress by maintaining firm position and anticipate progress at tomorrow's session. The essential aspect of issue is to be sure now that no public statements are made which would suggest either anxiety or concern for the current rounds of talks. It is even more important to be silent as to substance. We are at a crucial point.
>
> We will have firm prognostication at the end of tomorrow's session.

Again there was no reply nor a request for further information.

There were two principal reasons for our sparse reporting. There was no Vietnam expert left in the White House who could have analyzed the various provisions for the President. The members of the NSC staff who would normally do this were all with me in Paris. The President distrusted the State Department too much to consult it. In any event, I was sure that I was operating well within presidential guidelines. From my talks with Johnson and Sullivan, I was convinced they would be enthusiastic about the emerging terms. And the supervisory machinery was based on State Department drafts. The October 8 draft was much more favorable to us than what Haig had taken to Thieu, with Nixon's approval, less than a week before.

To avoid misunderstandings in Hanoi, I told Le Duc Tho that all our negotiations were *ad referendum* until they were approved by the President. And to prevent uneasiness in Washington, I sent the President a personal cable:

> The negotiations during this round have been so complex and sensitive that we have been unable to report their content in detail

due to the danger of compromise. We know exactly what we are doing, and just as we have not let you down in the past, we will not do so now. Pending our return and my direct report to you it is imperative that nothing be said in reply to McGovern or in any other context bearing on the current talks.

I added a postscript for Haldeman's eyes only: "Please hold everything steady. I recognize the uncertainties there but excessive nervousness can only jeopardize the outcome here." There was no reply.

The two delegations convened again on Tuesday, October 10, at 4:00 P.M. at Gif-sur-Yvette. Overnight I had had a message delivered to Le Duc Tho enumerating our requirements about security and Laos and Cambodia. This was designed to press him to be as forthcoming as possible when he presented his counterdraft. Tho grumbled that they "complicated" matters and that I was bringing "pressures"—as if such a procedure were foreign to the tender hearts of the men from Hanoi. But we then got down to cases and, in a six-hour session, started the tedious process of comparing the two drafts, reconciling them, temporarily putting aside insoluble issues, and starting the negotiation of separate written understandings on topics, such as Laos, that did not fit into a Vietnam peace agreement.

The next day, October 11, we launched ourselves into a marathon session that lasted sixteen hours, from 9:50 A.M. until after 2:00 A.M. the following morning. We quickly agreed on a cease-fire, an American withdrawal in two months, and a simultaneous release of prisoners. Our principal objective was to drain the political provisions of any vestiges of coalition government and to phrase the remaining political obligations of both sides in such a way that failure to fulfill them would give Hanoi no pretext for resuming hostilities. We therefore changed Hanoi's provision that the two South Vietnamese parties had to agree on a political settlement within three months to a weaker formulation—they would "do their utmost" to reach such a settlement—transforming an objective obligation into a subjective promise to make an effort. We added the principle of unanimity. (The political paragraph in Le Duc Tho's draft of October 8 and the end result as of October 11 are given in the notes.)[2]

We had achieved one of our key goals. For four years, Hanoi had insisted that the peace process had to start with the overthrow of the Saigon government and its replacement by a coalition government in effect nominated by

Hanoi. All that was left of Hanoi's original program was a committee charged with supervising elections, over the holding of which Saigon had a veto and which, in the event, never met. When Saigon finally collapsed, it was not because of the political provisions of the agreement but due to the demoralization caused by the attrition of American aid.

The reverse side of success on the political provisions was, of course, that Hanoi bargained all the more tenaciously about military issues. It was only after great effort that we were able to achieve Le Duc Tho's agreement that all infiltration of personnel into South Vietnam would cease and that equipment could be replaced on a one-for-one basis under international supervision. (Tho had asked for "equality," meaning that the Communists would have the right to introduce weapons in the South equal to what we were giving to Saigon. Since Saigon's army was much larger, we insisted on our formulation, which meant that existing equipment could be replaced but not augmented.)

We settled the ban on infiltration and dealt with withdrawal by a formulation that, after the cease-fire, the two South Vietnamese parties would discuss "steps to reduce the military numbers on both sides and to demobilize the troops being withdrawn." I had no illusions. Whenever either we or Hanoi were looking for an elegant way to bury an issue, we left its resolution to the two South Vietnamese parties, who we knew would probably never agree on anything.

Much time was spent on Laos and Cambodia. There were three issues: in what legal form to express the obligations being undertaken; the status of foreign forces, including North Vietnamese; and how to establish a cease-fire. The first issue arose because Tho claimed that internal Laotian and Cambodian matters could not be dealt within a Vietnamese peace treaty. We settled that by reflecting our understanding in separate written documents. Le Duc Tho accepted that the withdrawal of foreign forces from Cambodia and Laos *should* be part of the Vietnam agreement; after much debate, he accepted that all foreign troops would be withdrawn from Laos and Cambodia and that Vietnamese troops would be considered foreign for that purpose. On the cease-fires in Laos and Cambodia, we insisted that these be established by a fixed date that would precede our complete withdrawal. Le Duc Tho agreed to a cease-fire in Laos within thirty days after signing the agreement; he insisted that Hanoi's influence on the Cambodian Communists was not decisive. We were skeptical. As subsequent events made clear, it turned out to be an occasion when Le Duc Tho was telling the truth. The Khmer Rouge deeply distrusted Hanoi.

A major bone of contention was the alleged 30,000 civilian prisoners in South Vietnamese prisons, about 10,000 of them Vietcong cadres. Le Duc Tho's October 8 draft required that they be released together with all prisoners of war. I saw no possibility of Saigon's releasing the core of the Vietcong guerrillas. I proposed that this issue be left to the two South Vietnamese parties, who would "do their utmost" to settle it. Le Duc Tho objected, as well he might, since it in effect left all South Vietnamese Communist prisoners in Saigon's jails. Yet it was totally unacceptable for us to allow the release of American POWs to be made conditional on our ability to persuade Thieu to release Vietcong prisoners. A week later, the North Vietnamese agreed to the unconditional release of American prisoners, in effect leaving the Vietcong cadres in Saigon's detention centers—an example of a major concession we extracted by making a rapid conclusion of the agreement depend on it.

Finally, Le Duc Tho and I agreed to put into the agreement a general statement reflecting what had first been offered by President Johnson in 1965 and repeated by Nixon explicitly on January 25 and May 8, 1972; that, after the war, America would contribute to the economic reconstruction of Indochina, "to heal the wounds of war" as the document phrased it somewhat more poetically. I made clear that we would do this as in our own interest, for humane reasons, and to increase the prospects for improved bilateral relations between our countries (and in turn to give Hanoi a greater incentive to honor the agreement). But we rejected then, and continually thereafter, any principle of guilt or reparation; I also made clear that Congress would have to approve—a concept nearly impossible for Le Duc Tho to grasp.

There were extended technical discussions about other issues, including international control machinery and the participants at an international peace conference. But at last, at 2:00 A.M. on October 12—after having negotiated nonstop for sixteen hours, and twenty-two out of the last thirty—Le Duc Tho and I were prepared to call it a day. We had settled all principal Vietnam issues except the formulation on the right of the United States to replace military equipment for South Vietnamese forces and the question of civilians detained by Saigon. We also still needed to formulate a more precise commitment to a cease-fire in Laos and Cambodia. But we had come so far that a conclusion was now inevitable. We were doomed to success, even if it took time. I joked—presciently—that it might achieve no more than to unite all the Vietnamese parties in their opposition to me.

There came over us at last the relief of the end of strenuous exertions accompanied by excruciating tension. For over three years, Le Duc Tho and I had tested each other's endurance, tried to break down each other's defenses, sought to deprive each other of options. Diplomacy can be a deadly business, all the more so for being clothed in conciliatory forms. Both sides generally had been obliged to put aside the objectives with which they had entered the struggle; both were gambling on the future. We were not so naive as to believe that Hanoi's dour leaders had abandoned the aspirations of a lifetime. But having fought for the freedom and independence of those who had relied on us and joined their efforts to ours, we expected that we would not shrink from the exertions required to preserve the peace.

This was the mood we carried back to Washington. Winston Lord and David Engel (our able interpreter) stayed behind to make certain the North Vietnamese and we were working from the same texts and to clear up some technical points. After our just completed marathon, having averaged about three hours sleep a night for four days, they were to spend ten straight hours the following afternoon and evening on painstaking, nitpicking technical and linguistic issues.

I had heard nothing from Nixon during the entire period though my cables left little doubt that the end might be in sight. At the conclusion of the session of October 10, I had sent another cryptic message indicating that a breakthrough was imminent: "Please pass following message to Haldeman for the President: We have decided to stay one more day in expectation that we may score a major breakthrough. Either way we will return tomorrow afternoon. In my judgment we are sufficiently close to a breakthrough to run the risk of another day here." Immediately after returning from the sixteen-hour negotiating session, I sent another message to Haldeman: "Have just completed extremely long session here. It is essential that I have ample time with President tomorrow for thorough review of situation since careful game plan is now required." Haldeman replied that the President was on a campaign trip and that therefore I should not arrive before 5:00 P.M., after which Nixon wished to have dinner with Haig and me.

We had not been much more explicit with Saigon, except to stress with increasing urgency the probability of a cease-fire. I had decided to defer sending the complete text of our agreement to Thieu partly for security reasons; because of our growing distrust of his entourage; because we thought (correctly) that further improvements were possible; and, above all, because we wanted to wait for Nixon's approval and instructions. Haig and I believed, indeed, that Thieu would be so delighted at our success in laying the ghost of a coalition government and legitimizing his continued rule that his acceptance of a standstill cease-fire would be a formality. The biggest obstacles, in our view, would be the outrageous Nha and the pedantic Duc, who would nitpick the agreement to death and would not understand that it represented the best outcome available. John Negroponte was considerably more worried about Thieu's reaction. He proved to be more attuned to the Saigon psychology than the rest of us.

Decades later, it is still being claimed by some that we settled in 1972 for terms available in 1969. Not even the slightest acquaintance with the record sustains that argument. Never before October 8, 1972, had Hanoi agreed to abandon its demand for the overthrow of the Saigon governmental structure, agreed to the continued existence of a South Vietnamese army, continued American military and economic aid to Saigon, North Vietnamese withdrawal from Laos and Cambodia, a cease-fire in Vietnam and in Laos, the end of infiltration, and several other major concessions which emerged only in the negotiations starting on October 8.

Others argue that all the Nixon administration sought was a decent interval before it would acquiesce in a Communist takeover. In terms of the formal diplomatic positions, Nixon (and I) repeatedly affirmed that the United States would accept a political outcome based on free elections. In that sense, we were negotiating for an interval before these elections. But Hanoi at no point showed any interest in such a process. Analysts decades later approaching their task with prosecutorial zeal may be able to twist phrases into meanings not held at the time and, above all, never practiced. Throughout the negotiations, the refusal of an imposed political solution was the key given in the American position. And the nearly desperate effort to overcome congressional restraints on adequate aid to Vietnam gave the lie to any notion of a search for an alibi for abdication.

All of us who negotiated the agreement of October 12 were convinced that we had vindicated the anguish of a decade not by a "decent interval" but by a decent settlement. We thought with reason that Saigon, generously armed and supported by the United States, had been given a decent opportunity to sustain itself; that it would be able to overcome moderate violations of the agreements with its own forces; that the United States would stand by to enforce the agreement and punish major violations by the use of air and naval power; that Hanoi might be tempted also by economic aid into choosing reconstruction of the North if conquest of the South was kept out of reach; that we could use our relations with Moscow and Beijing to encourage Hanoi's restraint; and that, with our aid, the South Vietnamese government would grow in security and prosperity over the time bought by the agreement and compete effectively in a political struggle in which it had the loyalty of most of the population. And so we landed in Washington, suspended between euphoria and exhaustion.

8

THE TROUBLED ROAD
TO PEACE

Nixon received us in his hideaway in the Executive Office Building.
It was a two-room suite. The outer office contained a round table
and some chairs; its walls were covered with originals of cartoons having
Nixon as their subject. There was no desk or receptionist. I never saw the an-
teroom used for any purpose. One was not invited to the hideaway except by
direct presidential command, transmitted either by Nixon or by Haldeman;
there was no need therefore of a waiting room. Nixon's office was a rather
long rectangular room with a fireplace at the far end. Its windows opened on
a porch overlooking West Executive Avenue, a narrow fenced-off street separating the White House from the Executive Office Building. Almost invariably the blinds were drawn. There was a very large desk in front of the
window and, in the corner next to it, an easy chair with a hassock in front. To
its right, as one stood facing it, were a smallish round table and a number of
wooden chairs with armrests.

Nixon generally sat in the easy chair with his legs on the hassock, even
when working. His aides sat in the wooden chairs. They could grow uncomfortable if the meeting was prolonged, as it frequently was when the President was in a ruminating mood.

But that was not the case on October 12. Affecting nonchalance, Nixon
asked Haig and me to report. Somewhat exultantly, I told him that it looked
as if we had achieved all three of our major goals for 1972—the first two
being the visit to Beijing and the Moscow summit. I then went through the

provisions of the Vietnam agreement in detail, explaining the differences between the agreement and Nixon's January and May proposals, all in America's favor. Nixon's principal concern was Thieu's reaction. I was—naively— optimistic, for we had done better than what we had jointly proposed over the years. Nixon remembers Haig as worried;[1] he gave no such indication in my presence, though he may have done so privately.

Nixon ordered steak and wine to celebrate the event. I outlined the tentative "shedyule" I had agreed to with Le Duc Tho. I would return to Paris on October 17 for a meeting with Xuan Thuy to try to make progress on the two remaining issues of civilian detainees in South Vietnam and replacement of military equipment for the South Vietnamese armed forces. We would also need to work out the understandings on cease-fires in Laos and Cambodia. I would then fly from Paris to Saigon, where I would stay from October 18 through the twenty-second. On the evening of October 22, I would go to Hanoi, returning to Washington on October 24. The agreement would be announced on October 26 and signed on October 31. It was a tight schedule and, as it turned out, a wildly optimistic one. The basic purpose was to use Hanoi's impatience and a short deadline to force it into rapid agreement on disputed issues.

The President agreed, and we began immediately to squeeze Hanoi. Winston Lord, who was still in Paris collating the Vietnamese and American texts, was instructed to tell Xuan Thuy that Nixon consented to the basic draft provided Hanoi agreed to four changes "without which the US side cannot accept the document." These changes included more precise formulations of the ban on infiltration, on continued U.S. military aid to South Vietnam, and two provisions weakening the powers of the National Council of Reconciliation even further. We had had these texts ready in Paris before I left; and they could have been submitted there. They were sent from Washington to add a sense of urgency, to give them presidential authority, and to make the "shedyule" work for us.

A word is in order here about the messages that passed between Washington and Hanoi during this period. Drafted by my staff and me, some were sent as unsigned notes; when we wanted to lend emphasis, they were dispatched in the name of the President. As in all other negotiations I conducted on his behalf, Nixon was given a copy of everything; he certainly had the possibility to countermand any message. He never did so. Once he had given general guidelines, he had no desire to involve himself in the process of

negotiating. Nor would the text of documents interest him. He would sometimes comment on my oral account of a document, but the fine points and
the specifics of language and nuance held no interest for him. At this stage in
the Vietnam negotiations, he did not intervene; the stories leaked at the time
that his sharp legal eye spotted loopholes were pure fiction. He endorsed the
draft agreement without any change. He understood that the viability of the
agreement depended on the vigor with which it was enforced.

What worried Nixon most was the possibility of a blowup with Saigon.
This he was determined to avoid at almost all costs. If Thieu balked, I was to
back off and conclude the agreement after the election. The instruction was
more easily issued than implemented, for Hanoi could still force us to take a
stand by publishing the texts. Nor did I think matters would reach that
point. As yet I was under the illusion that Thieu would happily go along with
an agreement better in almost all essentials than the terms we had been offering with his concurrence for two years—above all, one in which his continued rule was legitimized—and the existing structure in Saigon was preserved.

Nixon was quite positive that an agreement was unnecessary for the election; its benefit would be too marginal to warrant any risks. Haldeman,
whom I saw directly after Nixon, went further. He thought that an agreement was a potential liability; he was certain that McGovern's support had
been reduced to fanatics who would not vote for Nixon even if he arranged
the Second Coming. On the other hand, an agreement might disquiet conservative supporters and thus shrink Nixon's margin of victory. The Vietnam
negotiations, in short, were not used to affect the election; the election was
used to accelerate the negotiations. It performed the role normally carried
out by an ultimatum—except that it raised no issue of prestige and, being
fixed by the Constitution, was not subject to alteration.

With Haig, I briefed Rogers over breakfast on October 13. He was enthusiastic; he considered the agreement a complete vindication of the U.S.
position. Given our strained professional relations, this was high praise indeed—and magnanimous. With a cease-fire in sight, I realized that we were
reaching the limit of my small staff's resources. Many technical protocols
would have to be prepared that required specialized competence. I asked
Rogers for help, something I was not in the habit of doing but should have
been. Rogers agreed and assigned Deputy Assistant Secretary William Sullivan and State Department Deputy Legal Adviser George Aldrich for that
purpose. A former Ambassador to Laos, then head of the Department's Vietnam Working Group, Sullivan had carried out many thankless assignments

with skill, daring, and an unusual willingness to assume responsibility. He performed on my staff with panache. He accompanied me on my October around-the-world trip as my deputy. He briefed the Laotian and Thai leaders on our negotiations. And he headed the technical discussions with the Vietnamese in the last phase. Sullivan's and Aldrich's contributions to the final round of negotiations were indispensable.

That day a cable arrived from Ellsworth Bunker with a warning that, whatever the agreement, we might be sailing into stormy seas in Saigon. As had become customary, Thieu was unavailable to be briefed; his stalling was now part of every exchange—last time the excuse had been a tetanus shot, now it was an upset stomach. Nha helpfully supplied another reason: Thieu was surprised that the American embassy was open on Friday the thirteenth. Bunker replied dryly that he had cleared the problem with his astrologer. He warned me, however, that Thieu was settling into a siege mentality reminiscent of 1968. He would almost surely try to stare us down, whatever we brought him. He seemed convinced that, if the war continued, he would be "in position to make a better settlement a year or two years from now," but he gave no idea in what respect it would be better or how we could sustain a war with no goal the American public could understand after Hanoi had accepted our own proposals—that Thieu had publicly endorsed—on October 8.

I told Bunker to give Thieu an accurate summary of where we were heading.

> Prior to my arrival in Saigon, now tentatively scheduled for Wednesday night, I will be seeing Minister Xuan Thuy and anticipate that the other side will propose a political formula which will require far less of Thieu than the alternate arrangements outlined to him by Haig during his recent visit. This would be combined with a cease-fire in place to go into effect as early as two weeks from the time that an overall agreement in principle is arrived at. In view of this likelihood, it is essential that Thieu understand now that we could have settled the conflict long ago under terms which would have removed him from power. Therefore, he cannot approach his upcoming meeting with me in the context of a confrontation but rather with a positive attitude in which we can confirm arrangements which will consolidate and solidify his future control. I am confident that such political arrangements are in the offing from Hanoi and Thieu

must be put off his current confrontation course with us and at the same time be prepared, in return for Hanoi's political concessions, to show a reasonable flexibility on the modalities of a cease-fire in place.

Bunker conveyed this outline to Thieu on October 14. He never received a response.

On both October 14 and 15, I stressed to Dobrynin the importance we attached to the outstanding issues. I asked for a Soviet assurance of restraint in arms supply after a settlement. Dobrynin, who had received the text of the draft agreement from Hanoi, evaded the point. A Nixon letter to Brezhnev asking for a similar assurance was also evaded. Even more worrisome was the fact that Hanoi had obviously played games with the translation of the agreed draft. The Vietnamese version of the draft agreement, according to Dobrynin, called the proposed National Council of National Reconciliation and Concord a "political structure." Le Duc Tho and I had spent hours in Paris agreeing to denote it in English as an "administrative structure" to emphasize its nongovernmental character; the Vietnamese translation was unsettling.* I impressed on Dobrynin that Hanoi's version was totally unacceptable.

We also sent a note asking for weapons restraint to Beijing; there was no reply. But then the Chinese contribution to Hanoi's arsenal was too marginal to affect the outcome in the South.

On October 16, I breakfasted with Haig, who would run the NSC office while I was gone, and Undersecretary of State Alex Johnson, who was in charge of the State Department back-up. I then saw the President for forty-five minutes. At 11:00 A.M., I left for Andrews Air Force Base on the mission on which all hopes had been concentrating for four years: the end of the war in Indochina. On the plane, a handwritten note from Nixon was waiting for me. It read:

> Dear Henry, As you leave for Paris I thought it would be useful for you to have some guidance that we were talking about on paper. First, do what is right without regard to the election. Secondly, we

---

* In the October agreement, Le Duc Tho and I settled on a phrase committing the parties "to set up an administrative structure called the National Council of National Reconciliation and Concord." Hanoi sought to translate "administrative structure" in Vietnamese by a phrase implying a governmental authority. In the technical meeting in Paris on October 12, Lord and Engel had explicitly rejected this Vietnamese translation and insisted on a weaker phrase with no governmental connotations.

cannot let a chance to end the war honorably slip away. As far as the elections are concerned, a settlement that did not come unstuck would help among young voters, but we do not need it to win. A settlement that became unstuck would hurt, but would not be fatal. At all costs we must avoid the fact or the impression that we have imposed or agreed to a coalition government. In sum, getting back to my original instruction, do what is right to secure an honorable peace, but do not let the timing be affected by the election.

Interlude in Paris

The meeting with Xuan Thuy on October 17 lacked the drama of the previous week's sessions with Le Duc Tho. We improved the political provisions further by making explicit that the National Council of National Reconciliation and Concord could supervise elections; it had no authority to order them. The parties would "do their utmost" to agree on any new election—the all-purpose formula for burying an issue. The National Council not only gave a veto to Saigon; it was deprived of anything to do. Hanoi's political program was dead.

With respect to replacement of military equipment, Xuan Thuy insisted on the principle of equality and we on the principle of a one-for-one replacement for worn-out equipment. Xuan Thuy finally accepted our formulation but made it contingent on the release of civilian detainees in South Vietnam. I rejected the proposition; Saigon would never accept it; the issue of civilian detainees was a political matter to be settled between the Vietnamese parties. Moreover, we found Hanoi's assurances regarding a cease-fire in Laos and Cambodia unsatisfactory. I told Xuan Thuy that I could not go to Hanoi unless we had settled the text of the agreement as well as the associated understandings. And his leaders should be clear that we could not proceed except with the approval of Saigon. It might thus be necessary for me to return from Saigon to Paris for another round of negotiations. Alternatively, it might be desirable to meet with Le Duc Tho again, say, in Vientiane after completing my Saigon stop. Xuan Thuy grumbled but clearly had no authority to give a definitive reply.

On the way to Saigon, I sent a message to Hanoi in my name reiterating what I had said to Xuan Thuy: that a visit to Hanoi could take place "only in the context of an agreement." I included our proposed texts for the disputed points. For emphasis, another message was sent to Hanoi later that day, October 18—this time in the President's name—repeating the impossibility of visiting Hanoi while any points were outstanding and proposing a meeting between Le Duc Tho and me, preferably in Vientiane, if necessary in Paris. Hanoi's cherished "shedyule" would thereby slip by another three or four days.

Consultation with Thieu

Ellsworth Bunker always had a soothing effect in a crisis. When one saw at the foot of the ramp that tall, erect, thin figure, immaculately dressed as if no suit on him would dare rumple even in the tropical heat of Saigon, one knew there was no risk of failure from either excess of impetuosity or lack of dedication. Ellsworth came to government service relatively late in life after a distinguished business career; he had no need to prove anything to himself or to others. His ambition was to make a contribution to the foreign policy of his country, whose well-being he identified with the security and hope of all free peoples. He was a quintessential American in the optimism that made him appear youthful even then, in his late seventies. For five years he had been in Saigon, serving two Presidents of different parties and earning their unqualified trust and admiration. Through the worst of our domestic travails, he never flinched. For all his years of service, he had stood by the South Vietnamese government to which he was accredited, defending it within official councils and in public against the charge that it was the principal obstacle to peace. Nobody deserved less the shoddy treatment to which Thieu was subjecting him—the endless waiting, the postponed appointments, the evasive if not downright deceptive answers. Throughout all this, Ellsworth Bunker never uttered a word of complaint. He had nursed matters to this point; no one who knew him could doubt that he would interpret the requirements of honor strictly.

Bunker, his deputy Charles Whitehouse, General Abrams, and I met soon after our arrival in the small library of the ambassador's modest residence, selected not for its elegance but for its location on a dead-end street, which eased the security problem. It was the first time Bunker and his associates had seen the full draft of the agreement. Bunker said that it exceeded what he had thought attainable; less would still have been practically and morally justifiable. His opinion was shared by General Abrams, who reiterated what he had told Nixon and me: that there was nothing to be gained by fighting another year on the present scale—adding that, if we reduced our effort by withdrawing the augmentation air and naval forces—as Laird insisted—conditions might well deteriorate. Our choice was escalation or settlement. He reported that the North Vietnamese had launched a "high point" of offensive activities, especially around Saigon, obviously trying (as I was urging Saigon to try) to seize as much territory as possible before a cease-fire. Abrams thought this offensive would be troublesome but also that it could be defeated without significant loss of territory.

Charles Whitehouse was the only one present to raise a word of caution. He shared his colleagues' judgment of the quality of the agreement, but he doubted that Thieu would accept it before the American election. For Saigon to cut the umbilical cord with the United States would be a wrenching psychological blow. No matter what the terms, Thieu would need many weeks to prepare himself and his people for it.

The next morning, I consulted Phil Habib, newly appointed as ambassador to Korea, whom I had asked to join me in Saigon. Habib's opinion meant a great deal to me. Born in Brooklyn of Lebanese origin, educated at the University of Idaho, he was the antithesis of the public stereotype of the elegant, genteel Foreign Service officer. He was rough, blunt, direct, as far from the "striped-pants" image as it is possible to be. He had served in Vietnam or dealt with Vietnam problems for nearly ten years. He had been the one element of continuity as deputy to a succession of ambassadors at the Paris peace talks. He had selected most of the young Foreign Service officers who had been posted in the provinces of South Vietnam. He had ridden the roller coaster from hopeful idealism to bleak despair. He wanted us to leave the graveyard of so many hopes, but with dignity. He had always urged flexibility but also realism, serious negotiations but no surrender, disguised or otherwise. He would have to sell the agreement to South Korea, an ally that had sent 50,000 troops to Vietnam and whose security depended on confidence in America's reliability. He would be a fair judge of what had been negotiated. Habib proved enthusiastic; the draft agreement exceeded his highest hopes. It would be considered a victory by our Korean allies. With that, every American senior official familiar with the negotiations and with Vietnamese affairs had endorsed our effort.

Had Thieu been able to bring himself to say, even privately, what White-house had outlined, much of the turmoil of the next few weeks would have been avoided. Had we understood immediately that Thieu objected not to specific terms but to the *fact* of a rapid agreement, we would certainly have maneuvered differently. However unreasonable Thieu's position, I was clear in my mind that Nixon did not want a blowup before the election. But Thieu never engaged in a conceptual discussion. Instead, he fought in the Viet-namese manner: indirectly, elliptically, by methods designed to exhaust rather than to clarify, constantly needling but never revealing his actual concerns. One cannot say that it has not worked; unfortunately, it inspires little confi-dence; it is especially tough on allies. But then no Vietnamese, North or South, would believe that trust in foreigners is decisive. They have survived foreigners for centuries not by trusting but by manipulating or fighting them.

The first meeting on October 19 reflected this attitude. On arrival at the Presidential Palace, I was kept waiting for fifteen minutes in full view of the press. Then Thieu's aide Hoang Duc Nha appeared to usher Bunker and me into the presidential presence. Thieu extended no greetings. Impassively, he accepted a letter by Nixon, which stated, *inter alia:*

> Dr. Kissinger will explain to you in the fullest detail the provisions of the proposed agreement which he carries with him and I will there-fore not provide further elaboration in this message. I do, however, want you to know that I believe we have no reasonable alternative but to accept this agreement. It represents major movement by the other side, and it is my firm conviction that its implementation will leave you and your people with the ability to defend yourselves and decide the political destiny of South Vietnam. . . .
>
> Finally, I must say that, just as we have taken risks in war, I be-lieve we must take risks for peace. Our intention is to abide faithfully by the terms of the agreements and understandings reached with Hanoi, and I know this will be the attitude of your government as well. We expect reciprocity and have made this unmistakably clear both to them and their major allies. I can assure you that we will view any breach of faith on their part with the utmost gravity; and it would have the most serious consequences.

To the typed text, Nixon had added the following handwritten note:

> Dr. Kissinger, General Haig and I have discussed this proposal at great length. I am personally convinced it is the best we will be able to get and that it meets my *absolute* condition—that the GVN must survive as a free country. Dr. Kissinger's comments have my total backing.

If ever, this was the time for Thieu to state his real concerns and to have a heart-to-heart talk with the emissary of a President who had, after all, staked his country's credibility and his political future on supporting South Vietnam. Instead, Thieu read the letter and, without comment, invited me into the next room where, just as during Haig's trip three weeks earlier, his National Security Council was assembled, augmented by the South Vietnamese ambassadors to Washington and the Paris peace talks. The American side included Bunker, Whitehouse, Abrams, Sullivan, Lord, and the interpreter, David Engel. The confrontational mood was established immediately when Thieu, without a word of introduction, opened the session by announcing that Nha would serve as interpreter. Considering that every Vietnamese present at least understood English, this indicated that Thieu was not going to make things easy. Nha proceeded to mock his role by condensing all my remarks to about half their length. This caused me to point out that either Vietnamese was a more concise language than English or else Nha was abbreviating (in which case it would have been interesting to know what he was leaving out). "I am a master of contraction," said Nha tauntingly.

I began by outlining our strategy. The American Vietnam effort, I argued, had been held together by a very few people against massive domestic pressures, which were seeking to liquidate our involvement in exchange for only the return of American prisoners. Our concern was not the two weeks before our elections but the months that would follow. The additional costs of the military augmentation after the offensive—amounting already to $4.1 billion—would have to be submitted to Congress in January. The supplementary budget would provide a convenient pretext for cutting off support. For over two years, we had made a clearly defined set of proposals with Saigon's concurrence; these had been accepted by Hanoi. Our supporters in Congress would never understand refusal to make peace now that these terms had been met and, in some respects, exceeded. That was the real deadline against which we were working.

In response, Thieu repeated the tactic from his previous encounters with Haig and me. He asked a number of intelligent questions, none of them going to the heart of the agreement. Thieu wanted to know to what extent I thought the terms compatible with our May 8 proposal; he inquired into the modalities of signing the agreement, when the international supervisory machinery would go into operation, what schedule I recommended—all of which suggested that, if the answers were satisfactory, he would go along. Suddenly he asked whether the agreement was needed for Nixon's reelection. I responded by reading the handwritten note from Nixon that was given to me on the plane as I left Washington.

We agreed to resume the discussion with his full NSC the next morning. Another meeting was scheduled for the afternoon with Thieu, Abrams, General Cao Van Vien (Chairman of the South Vietnamese Joint General Staff), and me to discuss the additional military supplies foreseen by Enhance Plus, a massive airlift of military equipment into South Vietnam before the agreement went into effect to establish the highest possible base line for the permitted resupply. My colleagues, Bunker, and I were at this point very optimistic. Thieu's questions and his eagerness to discuss Enhance Plus suggested that he was moving toward a settlement. I sent off a report to Nixon outlining prospects cautiously:

> It is too early to tell Thieu's reaction; we have learned from past trips that he doesn't show his hand until the second meeting. My instinct is that we face the difficult task we all predicted. In sum I made emphatically clear that we considered this an excellent agreement that would redeem years of sacrifice and fully protect both the GVN and Thieu. It was a much better settlement than anyone could have expected and resulted from our firm military and diplomatic support.

At the meeting on the afternoon of October 19, Abrams described to Thieu the matériel we would leave for the South Vietnamese forces and the additions we would provide through the Enhance Plus program before the cease-fire. This included over 150 additional planes, to be delivered in a fourteen-day period. Once again Thieu asked perceptive questions; to our unsubtle minds, it sounded as if he was moving toward agreement.

Before the next meeting, the other Vietnam was heard from. Hanoi's messages to me now had to travel to Saigon—only 800 miles away—over a distance of 20,000 miles. Hanoi delivered them in Paris to Colonel Georges R. Guay, our air attaché, who had replaced General Walters as our point of contact. From there, they went to Haig in Washington through White House channels. Haig retransmitted them—again in White House channels—to Saigon. When we contacted Hanoi, the procedure was reversed.

A message that came late on October 19 showed Hanoi's eagerness. Replying within twenty-four hours, it rejected another meeting either in Vientiane or in Paris. Instead, Le Duc Tho suggested that we stick to the original schedule. To enable us to do so, he *conceded* the two remaining points on civilian prisoners and replacement; Hanoi accepted not only our position but also the text we had put forward. A cease-fire would free all prisoners *except* 10,000 Vietcong cadres in South Vietnamese jails. And the one-for-one replacement provision, coupled with the massive augmentation of South Vietnamese forces even then under way, permitted what amounted to unlimited American military assistance to Saigon.

When Haig cabled the North Vietnamese reply, he added accurately: "I recognize this message adds immeasurably to your burdens at today's meeting." It was indeed ironic that Hanoi's complete acceptance of our demands was thought to add to my burdens. But indeed it did. Hanoi's military offensive would make it much harder to persuade Thieu to go along; Hanoi's message would make it nearly impossible for us to sustain our position domestically if he did not.

Thieu was in no hurry. As for me, once launched on the journey, I had no choice except to go forward. We had used the "shedyule" to exact concessions; in the process, we had given up scope for procrastination. Until our election, delay, if judiciously used, could improve our bargaining position. Afterward, procrastination would work increasingly in Hanoi's favor. As it became apparent that our military and political position would not improve after November 7, Hanoi would turn the tables on us and push us up against our own deadline of a returning Congress and our need for a $4 to $6 billion supplementary appropriation.

I therefore sent a cable to Hanoi "on behalf of the President" through the White House Situation Room. It declared the text of the agreement regarding Vietnam "complete" but also pointed to unsolved issues remaining in three areas: American prisoners in Laos and Cambodia; an end to the war in Laos; and the future of Cambodia. A proposed text for each of these topics was sent to Paris for transmission to Hanoi. It asked for the release of prisoners in the rest of Indochina on the same schedule as in Vietnam. It demanded that a cease-fire in Laos would follow within thirty days of that in Vietnam. With respect to Cambodia, where Hanoi insisted—as it turned out, truthfully—that its influence was not decisive, we asked for confirmation in writing of statements by Le Duc Tho that offensive operations would be stopped, North Vietnamese troops withdrawn, and infiltration ended.

Saigon was not eager to meet any timetable. What was success for us, including the withdrawal of American forces and the return of prisoners, was a nightmare for our Vietnamese allies; even with a cease-fire, they simply could not imagine how they would be better off without America. The meeting scheduled with Thieu and his National Security Council for October 20 was delayed from 9:00 A.M. to 2:00 P.M. The session lasted three and a half hours. The composition of the Vietnamese side was the same as the day before. The American delegation was also identical except for Bill Sullivan, who had gone to Bangkok and Vientiane to brief the Thai and Laotian leaders.

Thieu opened the meeting, once again without a word of grace, by expressing profound skepticism about Hanoi's motives and the danger of what he called "ambushes." Nha then went through a list of extremely intelligent questions that centered on the North Vietnamese forces in the South, on clarification of the arms replacement provision, on the composition and functions of the National Council of National Reconciliation and Concord, and on the American attitude if the agreement were violated. I replied in detail, repeating the arguments of the previous day that the ban on infiltration should cause the attrition of the North Vietnamese forces; that the replacement provision would mean, in effect, unlimited American military aid because of Saigon's large inventories, augmented by Enhance Plus; that the operations of the National Council were to be negotiated after the cease-fire and that Saigon would have a veto over its composition and operation.

As to the American response to violations, I reiterated Nixon's assurance that, in the event of massive North Vietnamese violations, the United States would act to enforce the agreement.

The argument was later advanced that it was not within the President's power to give such assurances without explicit authorization by Congress, and also that we should have known that Congress and the media would never tolerate military enforcement. This idea not only did not occur to us; it would have struck us as inconceivable that the United States should fight for ten years and lose over 55,000 men and then stand by while the peace treaty, the achievement of their sacrifice, was flagrantly violated. It was not a position the United States has ever taken—not in Korea, not in the Balkans, and not in Iraq, where the U.S. is bombing ten years after a cease-fire. Diplomacy could not survive such casuistry. Any peace negotiations so constructed would become surrenders; no agreement would ever be maintained. In Vietnam, a refusal to enforce the agreement would have turned the negotiations into a subterfuge for abandonment. We could have done that earlier and with much less pain. What else could be the meaning of a solemn compact ending a war, ratified by an international conference? The point was made privately to Thieu and his associates. It was also made publicly by Nixon, Elliot Richardson (when he was Secretary of Defense), me, and other officials.[2] It seemed to us then the least controversial of the issues raised by the agreement.

Rumblings

The members of the American team were becoming frustrated by Thieu's seeming dilatoriness. Even General Abrams, normally so taciturn, intervened to urge that Thieu accept the draft agreement:

> I am confident that the structure here as it stands today is capable of securing this country and this government. I echo the sentiments of Dr. Kissinger that no agreement will secure this country— only vigilance and determination will secure it.
>
> When President Nixon on Monday afternoon of this week called me to his office with Secretary Laird and asked me what I thought about this . . . I told him I thought it was time to take the next step. It was a difficult step to make the first withdrawal and each subsequent one, but as confidence and capabilities and skill developed, it became practicable. So more and more as time has gone on the defense of South Vietnam has been by the South Vietnamese people themselves. I have always had great respect and admiration for the South Vietnamese people and military, but I have always believed from the beginning that the day had to come for you and for your own pride and your people when the security and the political strength was all yours, with eventually our air power standing in the wings and our equipment and supplies coming into your ports.

Unfortunately, the real cause of Thieu's anxiety was not the agreement but a lack of the self-confidence Abrams had defined as so essential. Abrams had urged Thieu not to overestimate Hanoi because the North Vietnamese had made grave errors; they had misjudged the situation repeatedly. Had they moved the two divisions that besieged Khe Sanh in 1968 to Hue, we would never have been able to relieve the city. Similarly, Hanoi "stupidly" dispersed its forces during the 1972 offensive: "They are making an offer because they have lost and they know it. This is the first time they have gotten smart about the war." But Thieu drew the opposite conclusion and turned Abrams's argument against him: "This fact, General Abrams, about how they could have dispatched two divisions from Khe Sanh toward Hué, the fact they didn't means that this is due to the talent of our generals, and the fact that the Communists have lost is due to the talent of our generals." This apparent avowal of self-confidence in fact masked a deep doubt; Thieu refused to accept Abrams's claim of Communist ineptitude. Listing North Vietnamese failures did not reassure him if success derived not from South Vietnamese skill but from luck.

That was the problem which no systems analysis or proclamations about Vietnamization could erase. After eight years of American tutelage, the South Vietnamese simply did not feel ready to confront Hanoi without direct American involvement. Their nightmare was not this or that clause but the fear of being left alone. Saigon's leaders could not believe that Hanoi would abandon its implacable quest for the domination of Indochina. In a very real sense, they were being left to shape their own future; deep down, they were panicked by the thought and too proud to admit it. And they were not wrong. America has considered the presence of American forces in Korea essential for the military and psychological balance on that peninsula for fifty years after the peace agreement. American troops have never left Europe. American forces have remained in the Gulf and in the Balkans since these conflicts ended a decade before this writing.

It was not Thieu's fault that America had simply come to the end of the road—largely as the result of its domestic divisions. But even if Thieu had understood our position intellectually, he could not, as a Vietnamese patriot, bring himself to accept it publicly. The terms we had obtained were the best possible; they were indeed better than what we had publicly put forward for two years; theoretically they gave South Vietnam the means to survive. But they did not of themselves provide the sinews of confidence and cohesion in

Saigon essential to maintain the equilibrium which had, in fact, been achieved on the battlefield.

At the end of the three-and-a-half-hour discussion with Thieu, I reported to Washington:

> It was clear from the sober, somewhat sad, mood of the session that they are having great psychological difficulty with cutting the American umbilical cord. They probably realize that the deal is a good one by American standards, but their focus is on remaining North Vietnamese forces and the likelihood of violations of the agreement. While they showed pride in the talents of their generals, they continued to exhibit awe of Communist cunning and a lack of self-confidence. They undoubtedly feel they need more time, but one senses they will always feel that way. They know what they have to do and it is very painful. They are probably even right. If we could last two more years they would have it made. . . .
>
> I have the sense that they are slowly coming along and are working themselves into the mental frame of accepting the plan, but their self-respect requires a sense of participation.

Suddenly I found that the difference in time zones from Washington made an effective exchange of views extremely difficult and, as events speeded up, produced escalating misunderstandings, compounded by the pressures of deadlines. Saigon was thirteen hours ahead of Washington. My evening reports of meetings would thus arrive in Washington during the morning. For security, we had a complicated system of double-coding at each end that required two sets of communicators. Because of Saigon's curfew, our messengers had to arrange for a special escort each time we sent or received a message. All this caused additional delay, so that Washington lagged far behind our deliberations. By the time Haig could discuss our messages with the President, draft a reply for Nixon's consideration, and send it off, the Washington working day was usually over. I would get Washington's reaction during the morning of the next day, generally while I was already involved in another meeting. Thus each end of the communication cycle was continually commenting or reporting on events or recommendations already largely overtaken by events.

It was hardly surprising that I began to develop the classic sense of feeling abandoned that comes sooner or later to diplomats who work in the field. There were times when Washington seemed to me more interested in positioning itself with respect to what had already happened than in sharing responsibility for critical decisions yet to be made. For instance, after my relatively hopeful report of October 19, Nixon instructed me to tell Thieu that:

> I have personally studied in great depth the draft agreement which has been worked out with Hanoi, and I am convinced that it is in the best interest of the government and the people of South Vietnam that this proposal be accepted. Also advise President Thieu in the strongest terms that for the four years I have been in office and, indeed, for the period before that when I was out of office, no American public figure has stood up more staunchly for the proposition that there can be no Communist government imposed on the people of South Vietnam. Furthermore, no U.S. public figure has been a stronger supporter of President Thieu himself. You should assure the President that he can unreservedly rely on the continuation of that support in the days ahead.

But the next day, Nixon, as part of his consultation with senior advisers, met with General William Westmoreland, on the verge of retiring as Army Chief of Staff, who suddenly surfaced objections to the very concept of a cease-fire in place. This was amazing, since a standstill cease-fire had been part of our position since October 1970 and had been endorsed then, as had all its evolutions, by the Joint Chiefs of Staff, of whom Westmoreland was one. Without telling me of that conversation, Nixon now sent me yet another cable, for the fifth time in four days, telling me not to pay any attention to the forthcoming election and to emphasize solidarity with Thieu:

> As I outlined yesterday we must have Thieu as a willing partner in making any agreement. It cannot be a shotgun marriage. I am aware of the risk that Hanoi might go public but am confident that we can handle this eventuality much easier than we could handle a preelection blow-up with Thieu or an agreement which would be criticized as a pretext for U.S. withdrawal.

The first time I had heard this injunction, I was impressed and agreed with it; now I began to be nagged by the perhaps unworthy notion that I was being set up as the fall guy in case anything went wrong. Of all of Nixon's assistants, I was the least involved in the election campaign. I had been out of the country almost constantly since early September. I never participated in meetings dealing with political strategy. On the principle that foreign policy was bipartisan, I had refused to attend any fundraising functions. I had turned aside repeated requests by John Ehrlichman, Nixon's primary adviser on domestic policy, who alleged that he was transmitting orders from Nixon, to declassify documents embarrassing to previous administrations to help in the campaign. (This was before the Freedom of Information Act made such matters routine.) My strategy—explained in innumerable memoranda—had been to take advantage of Hanoi's expressed desire to settle before our election, using it as an inflexible deadline with which to extract concessions. Never either orally or in writing had I argued the reverse, that concluding the agreement would help our electoral prospects. Exhausted by two weeks of working fifteen to eighteen hours a day, testy from jet lag, and touchy from being assailed by two monomaniacal groups of Vietnamese, I returned a sarcastic reply to Haig:

> I am grateful for the helpful comments that I have been receiving. It must be kept in mind that any settlement will at best be precarious and usher in a messy period. Nor in the best of circumstances can the South Vietnamese be expected to be enthusiastic since they are losing our military presence and then have to adjust to a situation they have not faced since 1962.
>
> If I am being told to stop this process, then this should be made unambiguous. On the other hand, it is everyone's judgment here—including Bunker, Abrams, Habib and Sullivan—that this is the best deal we are ever going to get. We have to weigh the electoral considerations against the fact that I cannot imagine the prisoner issue being settled in less than a matter of weeks under normal conditions.
>
> In any event I am prepared to stall this operation if I receive a clear signal to do so.

No such signal was forthcoming, nor in fairness could one have been issued. For events in Saigon began to accelerate beyond the capacity of our communications system to handle.

Showdown with Thieu

On October 21, as I have indicated, we still supposed that we were inching to an understanding with Saigon, if with pain and little grace on the part of Thieu. In the morning, I met with the South Vietnamese team of experts headed by Foreign Minister Lam to go over their suggested changes in the draft.

There were twenty-three. Some were of major significance. Saigon wanted to delete the phrase describing the National Council of National Reconciliation and Concord as an "administrative structure" in order to avoid haggling about translation. It urged that the reference to the Demilitarized Zone be strengthened to emphasize its character as a dividing line and to make assaults across it illegal. It insisted that there be no reference in the text to the Provisional Revolutionary Government (Hanoi's political arm in the South). Other changes were seemingly minor, though the notoriously unsubtle Western mind might well not grasp the nature of apparently insignificant phrases. My associates and I had no illusions about the difficulties of obtaining that many changes. But we promised Saigon we would try, in good faith. We spent the morning seeking to discover the rationale behind the proposed changes so that we could determine some priority when we took up Saigon's proposals with Hanoi. The atmosphere was professional, marked by a serious attempt to assess the attainable and calculate the practical.

I had lunch with Bunker. We both were quite optimistic as we repaired to his office shortly before 2:00 P.M. to await the summons to the Presidential Palace for a scheduled meeting with the South Vietnamese National Security Council. No call came at the appointed hour. About an hour later, Nha called Bunker to say that we should stand by; the meeting had been moved to 5:00 P.M. We would be notified when Thieu was ready. There was no apology for the delay nor an explanation. Nha simply delivered his message and hung up; he must have seen Humphrey Bogart do this in some movie. At 4:30 P.M.—or two and a half hours after our scheduled meeting—Thieu's motorcade passed the embassy with sirens at full blast. By 5:30 P.M., we had not yet had a word from the palace, giving rise to a historic occasion: a show of temper by Bunker. He tried to reach Thieu by telephone and was told the President was in a Cabinet meeting. When he asked to speak to Nha, he was told that the press secretary had left the building also and was unreachable. An hour later, or nearly five hours after the scheduled meeting time, Thieu called Bunker to tell him that he would see us right after the Cabinet meeting, which was still taking place. After another three quarters of an hour, Nha telephoned to say that Thieu would see Bunker and me at 8:00 A.M. the next morning. When Bunker remonstrated that the time difference would now mean a delay of at least twenty-four hours in Washington decision time, Nha simply hung up.

We returned to Bunker's residence. Seated in his small library, we tried to understand what was happening. Clearly, the South Vietnamese needed time to deliberate over major decisions. But their insolent manner implied an imminent confrontation. But over what? Thieu had not yet stated a position; he had confined himself to asking questions. The experts' meeting in the morning seemed to have gone well. We had promised to raise all of Saigon's points in Hanoi; we could not, of course, guarantee the outcome. Neither Thieu nor any of his associates had as yet invoked any issue of principle though the provisions regarding the continued presence of North Vietnamese troops obviously bothered them, even though it had been agreed to by Thieu as part of our public proposals since January. Thieu knew very well that we could not proceed without him; the more his indispensability was brought home to us—however outrageous the conduct—the more he could humiliate Hanoi, the more he could appeal to Vietnamese nationalism, and the better would be his bargaining position.

The emotional frenzy in the Presidential Palace quickly revealed itself. Around 9:00 P.M.—or seven hours after our original appointment—Thieu phoned Bunker. Nearly hysterical, he complained bitterly that Haig's mission three weeks earlier had been to organize a coup against him; members of my team were now continuing the effort. He demanded that we desist. Bunker and I had been among Thieu's principal supporters for years, resisting demands from Hanoi and from antiwar critics that we do away with the Saigon government. It was a bitter pill to be accused of trying to overthrow a leader for whose survival we had undergone no little travail. Bunker came as close to indignation as his gentle nature permitted in rebutting Thieu's charges. But we had no option except to endure—as Thieu had correctly calculated. The phone calls from the palace could leave no doubt that the mood was turning hostile and, in the absence of specific objections, we did not even know how to resolve matters or what there was to resolve. We began to hope that Hanoi might make the issue academic by refusing the texts on Laos and Cambodia that we had communicated on October 20. I reported to Washington:

> A familiar pattern is beginning to emerge. This puts us into an enormously precarious position. If Hanoi caves again on our latest message and I then refuse to make the trip, they will clearly know what the difficulty is. They would then have every incentive to go public and demand that we sign a settlement to which we have already agreed.

My prediction proved correct. On the evening of October 21, Hanoi once again *accepted* all our demands. The North Vietnamese agreed to all American formulations with respect to Laos and Cambodia. They informed us that there were no American prisoners in Cambodia, but that the prisoners in Laos would be released together with all Americans held in North and South Vietnam. They agreed, too, to the new "shedyule" I had transmitted on October 20. Our strategy was working everywhere with dazzling success—except with our allies in Saigon. The fact was, as Haig pointed out in a cable, that "we are now at the hard point, and your meeting with Thieu this morning becomes crucial."

Fortunately (given the circumstances), Hanoi made one mistake that provided a pretext for procrastination. The distinguished journalist Arnaud de Borchgrave suddenly had been offered a visa to visit Hanoi. What made the event even more remarkable was that he had not asked for it. Once there, he was granted an interview by Prime Minister Pham Van Dong, which he had not requested. The interview was to be published on October 23, while I was still in Saigon, when Hanoi knew I would be in the process of obtaining South Vietnamese concurrence.* The interview was an act of bad faith. For Pham Van Dong in his interview put forth a tendentious North Vietnamese interpretation of the draft agreement at variance with the text of what had been negotiated. Thieu was described as "overtaken by events"; a "three-sided coalition of transition" would be set up; all detainees on both sides (including civilians) would be released; America had to pay reparations.

---

* We received an advance text on October 21; de Borchgrave traded his unexpurgated version for Ambassador Godley's permitting him to use embassy communications in Vientiane to transmit his story to New York, no other quick and reliable cable facilities being available.

De Borchgrave reported that Hanoi was already informing foreign diplomats of the completed agreement and was preparing festivities that looked to him like "victory celebrations." The Pham Van Dong interview was bound to provoke the South Vietnamese and compound their gravest suspicions. It also put us on notice that Le Duc Tho's recent flexibility had been imposed by necessity, not a change of heart. But the interview exhibited weakness as well as duplicity. Pham Van Dong admitted that Thieu would stay after a settlement. Underneath the tendentious phraseology, he had made it clear that the agreement was essentially a standstill cease-fire, heretofore contemptuously rejected by Hanoi. The "two armies and two administrations" would remain in existence in the South.

At about the same time, a telegram arrived from Nixon instructing me for what we all agreed would be the decisive meeting with Thieu on the morning of October 22. I was to push Thieu to the limit without causing a blowup. I was to do the same with Hanoi. The best solution would be to defer the final agreement until after the election and to keep the two Vietnamese parties quiet until then.

In a letter from Nixon to Thieu, drafted by the President himself, Nixon repeated that he considered the agreement as it stood fully acceptable. And he added a grave warning that must have been extremely painful after all we had done to support Thieu:

> Were you to find the agreement to be unacceptable at this point and the other side were to reveal the extraordinary limits to which it has gone in meeting demands put upon them, it is my judgment that your decision would have the most serious effects upon my ability to continue to provide support for you and for the Government of South Vietnam.

Nothing in Vietnam works as expected. The meeting with Thieu at 8:00 A.M. the next morning—Sunday, October 22—did not, after the ominous preliminaries, produce a confrontation. Indeed, it almost seemed as if Thieu had staged the melodrama of the previous day to establish a posture of independence that would make it possible for him to go along with us at the last moment. Thieu and Nha were on the Vietnamese side, and Bunker was with me. Thieu restated his by now familiar objections to the agreement. He focused on the continued presence of North Vietnamese troops, a part of our proposals approved by Thieu for over a year, and on the composition of the National Council—which had no functions, in which he was to have a veto, and which, as it turned out, never came into being. I answered Thieu's concerns point by point and gave him Nixon's letter. Thieu responded with some dignity that for us the problem was how to end American participation in the war, for him it was a matter of life and death for his country. He had to consider not only the terms of the agreement but the perception of it by the people of South Vietnam. He was therefore consulting with the leaders of the National Assembly. He also wanted to hear a full report from his advisers on our reaction to the changes they proposed. He would meet Bunker and me again at 5:00 P.M. to give us his final reply.

Bunker and I left the meeting encouraged. "I think we finally made a breakthrough," I optimistically cabled Washington. I asked Bunker to send a fuller report to Washington, since I was leaving for the airport to visit Phnom Penh. Bunker cabled that "we both left with the impression that we had finally made a breakthrough. . . . We both left the meeting more encouraged that Thieu will be trying to find a way through his problems." While Bunker was at it, he also pointed out that Hanoi's attempt to seize as much territory as possible before the cease-fire was a complete failure. There was a large gap, he reported, between the enemy's capabilities and his intentions. "Our conclusion is that despite Communist instructions and efforts by the enemy to carry out these instructions, he has been unable to do so effectively and has suffered casualties in the effort."

Now that the war was coming to a close, the arrangements for the rest of Indochina proved the most complex of the settlements.

Laos and Cambodia were being dealt with in two sets of documents. Hanoi took the position that, in the draft Vietnam agreement, it could obligate itself only with respect to its own actions. Thus it could commit itself to withdraw its own troops from Laos and Cambodia. As for cease-fires between the belligerent parties, or securing pledges of releasing American prisoners, Le Duc Tho could only promise Hanoi's best efforts to persuade its allies. And it would promise these best efforts in written private understandings with us, not in the text of the Vietnam agreement. Thus, under Article 20 of the Vietnam agreement, Hanoi pledged to withdraw its forces from Cambodia and Laos and to refrain from using the territory of Cambodia and Laos for military operations against any of the signatories of the agreement— that is to say, South Vietnam.

The private understandings proved more complex. Hanoi was confident of its influence with its ally in Laos, the Pathet Lao. Le Duc Tho therefore promised to bring about a cease-fire in Laos within thirty days of the Vietnam cease-fire and to sign an understanding to that effect. He also promised to return the prisoners from Laos on the same schedule as those from Vietnam. He asserted that there were no prisoners in Cambodia. With respect to Cambodia, Le Duc Tho claimed to have less influence over the Khmer Rouge. He gave only general oral assurances that once the war stopped in Laos and Vietnam, "there is no reason for the war to continue in Cambodia." After repeated efforts to secure a more explicit commitment to a cease-fire in Cambodia, I could achieve no more than Hanoi's written acknowledgment of what Le Duc Tho had told me orally. I decided to urge Lon Nol to offer a cease-fire unilaterally as soon as the Paris Agreement was signed (which he did), and I warned Le Duc Tho that if the Khmer Rouge responded with a new offensive, this would be "contrary . . . to the assumptions on which this Agreement is based."[3] We gambled that Lon Nol's forces with modest support from America would be able to contain the indigenous Cambodian Communists if North Vietnamese troops were withdrawn and North Vietnamese infiltration ended—as the draft agreement required. Indeed, we had little choice. There would have been no support whatever at home for refusing an agreement in Vietnam that returned our prisoners and led to the withdrawal of the North Vietnamese from the countries of Indochina simply because the cease-fire in Cambodia was less than airtight.

I had sent Bill Sullivan to Bangkok and Vientiane because he knew the leaders of Thailand and Laos, having worked with them when he had served as ambassador to Laos. He had returned with their enthusiastic endorsement. According to Sullivan, Souvanna Phouma had exclaimed: "They are totally defeated." The reaction of the Thai leaders was similar. But because of our limited aid and the ambiguous settlement provision for Cambodia, I thought I owed it to Lon Nol to brief him personally.

It was a shaming encounter. Though Lon Nol had genuine cause for uneasiness, there was none of the nitpicking of Saigon or the insolence. The Cambodians, who had received such a microscopic fraction of the annual aid given to Saigon, continued to place their trust in us. Lon Nol understood that his was the one country in Indochina not given a specific date for a cease-fire though the North Vietnamese were firmly obligated to withdraw.

The trip to Phnom Penh was therefore painful in a way exactly the opposite of my Saigon sessions. Of all the victims of North Vietnam's quest for hegemony in Indochina, none had been left so much to their own devices as the people of Cambodia. In a very real sense, Cambodia bore the heaviest burden of the irreconcilability of the American domestic debate. After American troops had withdrawn from the sanctuaries, those who had denounced the 1970 incursion did their utmost to forestall any effective assistance to the beleaguered country, as if to punish the free Cambodians for not living up to the role of victim to which they had been consigned. The argument not to get bogged down in Cambodia had caused Congress in 1971 and 1972 to limit all aid to Cambodia to the paltry sum of around $300 million (about 3 percent of our expenditures in Vietnam), to place a ceiling on the number of military attachés to be posted in our Phnom Penh embassy, and to prohibit the sending of military advisers. Indeed, even American military attachés were prevented by law from visiting Cambodian troops. The argument about getting bogged down in Cambodia was based on a false parallel with Vietnam. The North Vietnamese forces in the South were overextended as it was; Hanoi was in no position to reinforce them; any improvement of Cambodian capabilities was bound to press them hard. And the Khmer Rouge were insignificant at first. All that America's self-denial accomplished was to leave Cambodia to its own meager resources against its implacable enemy in Hanoi and to give time to the murderous indigenous Khmer Rouge to build up their forces for their final conquest.

In the event, Lon Nol magnanimously endorsed the agreement, declared a unilateral cease-fire, and called for negotiations. His genocidal enemies ignored the appeal, and the American Congress within a year legislated a prohibition against using American airpower to assist him and, within two years, cut off all funds for Cambodia.

It was characteristic of Vietnam that a simple failure never seemed to satisfy the vengeful gods; they had to break one's heart as well. With Lon Nol and the Laotian and Thai leaders in accord, I thought we were in the homestretch. Bunker and I saw Thieu and Nha at 5:00 P.M., as scheduled, for nearly two hours. At the end of the talk, I telegraphed Haig with the news: "Thieu has just rejected the entire plan or any modification of it and refuses to discuss any further negotiations on the basis of it."

It had been a bizarre encounter. Thieu, who spoke English fluently, refused to use it. While talking, he frequently burst into tears—of rage rather than sorrow, Bunker and I thought. Nha translated, and, at the appropriate passages, he, too, wept.

The meeting began with my briefing Thieu on our successful consultations in Phnom Penh, Bangkok, and Vientiane. Thieu dismissed this with the comment that he was not surprised; those countries had not been "sacrificed." He said that the United States had obviously "connived" with the Soviets and China to sell out South Vietnam. He would not be a party to it.

I replied:

> I admire the courage, dedication and heroism which have characterized your speech. However, as an American, I can only deeply resent your suggestion that we have connived with the Soviets and the Chinese. How can you conceive this possible when the President on May 8 risked his whole political future to come to your assistance? When we talked with the Soviets and Chinese, it was to pressure them to exert pressure on Hanoi. We genuinely believed that the proposed agreement preserved South Vietnam's freedom—our principles have been the same as yours and we have defended them. You have only one problem. President Nixon has many. Your conviction that we have undermined you will be understood by no American, least of all by President Nixon.

I pointed out that we now had a practical problem: "We have fought for four years, have mortgaged our whole foreign policy to the defense of one country. What you have said has been a very bitter thing to hear." Obviously the negotiations could not continue without his agreement. I would return to Washington. It was in the interest of both our countries to avoid a confrontation if we were not to mock all we had sacrificed. I suggested that I pay a farewell call before my departure. We set the time for eight the next morning, Monday, October 23.

If October 8, when Hanoi had finally yielded on all its political demands, was the most moving moment of my government service, this was perhaps the saddest—at least to that point. Whatever happened now, Thieu's reaction guaranteed that the war would not end soon, or in a way that would heal the divisions of our country. Thieu's conduct made it more likely that the negotiation of the peace would haunt our future as the conduct of the war had mortgaged our past. Hanoi would certainly attack us publicly for having reneged on the peace agreement. If Hanoi published the peace terms, which it undoubtedly would, our critics—who had been asking us to settle for far *less*—would accept no excuses for our failure to sign. Hanoi could point to the repeated concessions it had made, beginning on October 8 and continuing up to October 21. If we did not settle on close to the terms now available, we would be forced out of the war by Congress.

And yet I had no leverage. Maddening as Thieu's conduct was in rejecting terms he had repeatedly approved publicly, it did not annul the principle that America did not betray its friends. Our duty was to avoid letting matters slide into chaos. Thieu bore a heavy responsibility for luring us deeper and deeper into the bog over four days. Had he revealed his real attitude the day I arrived, we would surely have sent different messages to Hanoi. Still, we could not abandon, out of personal irritation, everything for which millions of Americans had endured and suffered for ten years. Nor could we risk allowing Thieu's hysteria to turn into such despair that he would make our split public, tempting Hanoi into a new cycle of intransigence. But neither could we let him believe that he had stared us down and that we would be deflected from our larger objectives. We had to leave no doubt in his mind that any delay now was tactical, to give him a chance to paper over our differences and to exact marginal improvements but not a strategic reversal.

A similarly fine line had to be walked with Hanoi. We had to convince the North Vietnamese Politburo that we were determined to conclude the agreement on substantially existing terms. But we also had to make Hanoi understand it would not be able to use our differences with Saigon to jockey us at the last moment into doing what we had refused for four years: overthrowing the political structure in South Vietnam.

Immediately after my disastrous meeting with Thieu on Sunday, around 8:00 P.M. Saigon time, I cabled Haig that we now had two options. I could proceed to Hanoi as originally scheduled, present Saigon's changes, and go back and forth (the term "shuttle diplomacy" did not yet exist) until I had gained the concurrence of both sides. The second option was for me to return immediately to Washington; Haig meanwhile would tell Dobrynin that we had encountered major obstacles in Saigon which we were bound to present to the other side in another meeting with Le Duc Tho. I summed up: "Obviously I favor the second course, but have offered the first [trip to Hanoi] only for intellectual completeness."

The more I thought about it, the less appealing a trip to Hanoi became. I would be trapped there in almost certainly inconclusive meetings; communications with Washington would be difficult; it was hard to foretell to what harassments we would be exposed. It was important for me to return to

Washington as quickly as possible. The irony—it transpired—was that, while Nixon in Washington began to worry that I might proceed to Hanoi, I began to grow anxious that *against* my recommendation he might accept the first of the two options and order me to go there. Therefore, before I had received a reply to my first message, I sent off another cable: "I have thought the situation over and there is no viable route except the Soviet Union option which must be taken immediately in order to get ahead of the following message which has to be delivered in Paris at 11:00 P.M., today, Sunday, Paris time."

The message—in the President's name—to be delivered in Paris was for Hanoi and was designed to stall for enough time to enable me to get back to Washington before Hanoi blew up. It read:

> The President notes with appreciation the message from the Prime Minister of the Democratic Republic of Vietnam which satisfied all his points with respect to Laos and Cambodia as well as U.S. prisoners.
>
> As the DRV side knows, the U.S. side has made strenuous efforts in Saigon, Vientiane, Phnom Penh and Bangkok to secure an agreement. As the DRV side also knows, the U.S. side has always taken the position that it could not proceed unilaterally. Unfortunately the difficulties in Saigon have proved somewhat more complex than originally anticipated. Some of them concern matters which the U.S. side is honor-bound to put before the DRV side.
>
> The President wishes the Prime Minister to know that under these circumstances he has asked Dr. Kissinger to return to Washington immediately to consult on what further steps to take.
>
> The President must point out that the breach of confidence committed by the DRV side with respect to the Arnaud de Borchgrave interview bears considerable responsibility for the state of affairs in Saigon.
>
> The President requests that the DRV side take no public action until he can submit a longer message with his considerations which will be transmitted within the next 24 hours.
>
> The U.S. side reaffirms its commitment to the substance and basic principles of the draft agreement.

To Washington I cabled:

In the period now before us I think it is absolutely imperative that we not show any nervousness. Everyone should exude optimism and give the impression that we may be very close to an agreement. If we are hard-pressed by questions we should simply say that technical details always arise in the last stage of negotiations. And if we are really pressed to the wall we should concentrate on the question of North Vietnamese forces in the South. At all cost we must avoid letting Thieu become the object of public scorn, not for his sake but for our own. If Thieu emerges as the villain, even if we finally overcome his objections, everything that we have done for the past eight years will be thrown into question.

During my farewell call on Thieu, accompanied by Bunker, at 8:00 A.M., Monday, October 23, I tried to remove the bitterness. Thieu, for all his faults, was a patriot who had fought courageously for his country's independence. And it was important not to push him over the brink by rash acts and public confrontation. I informed Thieu that I had requested another meeting with Le Duc Tho to present Saigon's proposals. I hoped that Thieu would not engage in open debate with us in the meantime. There would be no public criticism of Thieu from our side. We would try to obtain as many of the changes proposed by Saigon as possible, but we would not abandon the basic draft. I concluded by stressing my respect for the redoubtable South Vietnamese President as a patriot and as a soldier. Still, I had to tell him "in anguish" that, if the war went on at the present scale for another six months, Congress would cut off our funds:

> What is important is that all the sacrifices that have been made should not have been made in vain. If we continue our confrontation you will not win victories, but we will both lose in the end. It is a fact that in the United States all the press, the media and intellectuals have a vested interest in our defeat. If I have seemed impatient in the last days it is because I saw opportunity slipping away. . . . I am not trying to convince you, but I want you to understand what we have attempted to do. Had it not been for the importance we place on our relationship, we would not have to make new plans—that is why I leave with such a sense of tragedy. We will do our best and Bunker will be in touch with you.

Thieu, much calmer now, reviewed his objections to the agreement once more. They had been softened slightly. He now concentrated on strengthening the provisions regarding the Demilitarized Zone (important because they affected infiltration and reinforcements) and the composition of the impotent National Council of National Reconciliation and Concord (essentially frivolous). He argued that the question of North Vietnamese troops in the South could be settled on a de facto basis by unannounced North Vietnamese withdrawals.

After making it clear to Saigon that we would proceed with the agreement, we had to convince Hanoi of the same thing without tempting it to exploit the rifts between Saigon and Washington. Just before leaving Saigon, I asked the Situation Room to send a message in the President's name to Colonel Guay in Paris for transmission to Hanoi's representatives (Haig would discuss it with the President). The time selected was 3:00 P.M. Paris time, which was 9:00 P.M. in Saigon, or when I was well on the way back to Washington. Allowing time for transmission, I might with luck reach Washington before Hanoi could respond. The message read in its key passages:

> The United States has proceeded in good faith to implement the general principles and substance discussed with the DRV in Paris. The DRV must certainly have been informed of the strenuous efforts made by Dr. Kissinger and his associates in Laos, Cambodia, Thailand and above all in Saigon.
>
> At the same time the DRV side is aware of the fact that the constant U.S. position has been that it will not impose a unilateral solution on its allies and that it will move ahead only on the basis of consultation. . . .
>
> The President reiterates his firm belief that an agreement is obtainable in the very near future. It is essential that the DRV and U.S. sides mutually explore existing difficulties in the same spirit of good will which has characterized discussions thus far.
>
> To this end the President proposes that special advisor Le Duc Tho and Dr. Kissinger meet again at the earliest opportunity in Paris, to reconcile the remaining issues. Dr. Kissinger will come to Paris on any date set by the DRV. In the present circumstances it is impossible for Dr. Kissinger to go to Hanoi until these additional discussions have been completed.

In order to demonstrate its good faith, the U.S. side will maintain the current restrictions on the bombing until the negotiations are concluded.

The U.S. side must warn that any attempt to exploit the present, temporary difficulties publicly can only lead to prolongation of the negotiations.

It is inevitable that in the war that has lasted so long and has generated such deep passions there should be some temporary obstacles on the way to a final resolution.

The Journey Home

On the trip home, I was determined to do my utmost to preserve the prospect of peace against the passions that would soon descend on us—against the pressure of Hanoi to sign the existing text; against the demand of Saigon to abandon the agreement; and against proclivities in Washington to reverse course, the result of which would be to lose control over events. I had had an inkling of those inclinations in a cable from Haig on October 21 in reaction to the first news of Thieu's rejection. Haig suggested that, in case of a blowup, we should attack the agreement as an effort by Hanoi to improve its security while giving nothing but fuzzy reassurances. I considered this course inconceivable. We had been offering less favorable terms for years. Nixon had approved a worse draft on October 12. Hanoi had just accepted the American language on all disputed sections. I sent a sharp reply on October 23:

> As for your characterization of the content of the agreement I would like to recall your view that it was a good agreement when we concluded it. It has since been greatly improved with respect to Cambodia, Laos, the International Conference, American prisoners, South Vietnamese prisoners and the replacement provision. As for asking Thieu to give up sovereignty over his territory just what has a cease-fire always added up to? We proposed this way back in October 1970 and again in January 1972 and May 1972. What else were these plans going to lead to except precisely the situation we now have? . . .

I cabled Washington from the plane that, if Hanoi went public, I should hold a press conference, acknowledge the agreement, indicate that it represented major progress, but insist that some details remained to be worked out free of any artificial deadline. I would put Hanoi on notice that the basic agreement was not being dropped, but that some changes were necessary; I would put Saigon on notice that we would give it more time and seek some changes, but that the basic structure was not subject to modification.

Nixon accepted this strategy, and it was to propel me after my arrival home into my first appearance at a televised press conference: the dramatic event summed up in the phrase "peace is at hand."

9

"PEACE IS AT HAND"

Returning to Washington from Saigon on October 23, my colleagues and I were absorbed in reviewing the detailed provisions of the stalled draft peace treaty; it was the last thing Nixon wanted to hear about. He was in the final phase of the reelection campaign, the concluding campaign of an improbable twenty-five-year career. His ambition—indeed obsession—was to win with the largest majority in American history. He thought this certain so long as nothing unexpected was allowed to happen in the last two weeks of the campaign. Therefore, he strove to prevent a fresh electoral issue arising out of Vietnam. He wanted the deadlock in Saigon to go away for two weeks so that he could deal with it right after the election. His instructions to me were to try to keep things quiet. This, I was certain, neither our enemies in Hanoi nor our allies in Saigon would allow.

By October 23, my colleagues and I had been in motion for over two weeks—Paris, Washington, Paris again, Saigon, Phnom Penh, and back to Washington, rarely getting more than four hours of sleep and riding an emotional roller coaster from hope to frustration, from elation to despair. A somewhat plaintive note from Moscow was waiting for me, suggesting that if I went to Hanoi, we would still be able to "complete the whole matter." That was clearly impossible, but at least it indicated that the North Vietnamese were still eager to proceed. I also briefed China's U.N. ambassador, Huang Hua, in New York, reminding him of the final negotiation of the Shanghai Communiqué during a night session in Hangzhou after the text had seemingly been concluded the previous day. Zhou had permitted us to reopen the communiqué then and thereby guaranteed its widespread acceptance in the

United States. If China used its influence with Hanoi to resume negotiations with the same wisdom, the result would be the same. On October 25, Beijing weighed in with a message—obviously drafted before it could have received Huang Hua's report of my conversation—urging us to seize this "extremely opportune time to end the Vietnam war." The Chinese explicitly blamed Saigon for the difficulties, affirmed their confidence in America's good faith—an unusual gesture—but asked rhetorically: "How can the world be forbidden to have its doubts?"

Meanwhile, Hanoi had rejected our message of October 23, accusing us of being not "really serious." It added ominously:

> If the U.S. side continues to use one pretext after another to pro-long the negotiations, delay the signing of the agreement, the war in Vietnam will certainly continue, and the U.S. side must bear full re-sponsibility for all the consequences brought about by the United States. . . . This statement of the DRVN side is a very serious one. The U.S. side should pay full attention to the views of the DRVN side expounded in this message.

Though firm, the message fell short of the fire-breathing tone of previous communications. It stayed well clear of threatening to abrogate the agreement. Hanoi had requested a reply during the day of October 24, Hanoi time—which was impossible, since by the time we received their message, it was already October 25 in North Vietnam. We nevertheless returned an immediate reply on October 25. The constant repetition of unfounded charges, we said, could only make things worse. We proposed another meeting during the week of October 30; I would attend "with instructions to bring about a final settlement."

A copy of the note was sent to the Chinese via courier the same day. I kept Dobrynin informed. In any case, our message affected no decisions in Hanoi. For during the night of October 25, before my message could have reached there, Hanoi went public.

I was awakened around 5:30 A.M. on Thursday, October 26, to learn that Radio Hanoi had been broadcasting its version of events for hours, first in Vietnamese, then in French, finally in English. Radio Hanoi revealed the negotiating record of the preceding month: On October 8, in a secret meeting, North Vietnam had taken "a new, extremely important initiative" by offering a new draft peace agreement. The broadcast accurately summarized the key points of the draft agreement. "The DRV side proposed that the Democratic Republic of Vietnam and the United States sign this agreement by mid-October 1972"—acknowledging that it was Hanoi that had pushed for signing before the election. It quoted me as admitting that the new proposal "was indeed an important and very fundamental document." It described the U.S. messages of October 20 and October 22 in which the President had called the text of the agreement "complete," and expressed satisfaction with Hanoi's concessions. It next recited the "shedyule" and the continual slippage to which Hanoi had agreed at American behest. But the United States had failed, on various "pretexts," to keep the schedule. Therefore Hanoi "strongly denounces the Nixon administration's lack of good will and seriousness," and demanded that the agreement be signed by October 31. It ended with a rather defensive exhortation to its "fighters throughout the country" to persevere in the face of "all hardships and sacrifices."

Once Hanoi had gone public, we had no choice except to state our case. The press conference of October 26—briefly notorious for the phrase "peace is at hand"—came to be denounced as a Nixon electoral ploy to raise hopes for peace during the last stages of the presidential campaign. Nothing could be further from the truth. As late as mid-September I could see no way to conclude the negotiations rapidly. It was Hanoi's October 8 proposal in Paris, abandoning its demand for a coalition government, and indeed its entire political program, that had unlocked the negotiations. It was Hanoi that had insisted on a signing by October 31 as a condition for a settlement; we had gone along with it in order to exploit Hanoi's eagerness to extract concessions considered unattainable earlier. Now it was Hanoi, not the United States, that announced the peace agreement and urged us to sign it. Nixon at this point clearly would have preferred keeping the agreement secret until *after* the election and before undertaking the final round of negotiations.

The purpose of my press conference was to explain to the American public what had happened and to rescue from Vietnamese hatreds a fragile agreement that might end a decade of agony. Nixon decided that I had to reply to Radio Hanoi's broadcast because I was most familiar with the substance of the document. I sought to achieve two objectives: One was to reassure Hanoi that we would stand by the basic agreement, while working for some of the changes urged by Saigon. The second was to convey to Saigon that we were determined to proceed toward agreement and that it would not have a veto. At the same time, we did not wish to have the South Vietnamese appear as

the obstacle to peace, thus triggering renewed assaults on the political structure of an ally. Nixon and I did not discuss the domestic political implications.

To achieve this balance, I appeared for the first time on national television at the very end of Nixon's first term. Until December 1971, except for
the announcement of my secret China trip, all my press briefings had been
on a background basis, which meant that I was identified as either a White
House or administration spokesman but never by name. During the India-
Pakistan crisis in December 1971, the *Washington Post* had broken the background rules. After that, most of my press conferences were on the record.
The White House public relations people, however, convinced that my accent might disturb Middle America, permitted pictures but no sound at my
on-the-record press conferences. On October 26, Nixon finally took a
chance on my accent. The only trouble was that he had not bothered to tell
me. He simply ordered Ziegler to have the cameras turned on.

The press conference is now remembered, if at all, for the phrase "peace is
at hand." And in some accounts, the impression is created that I came out from
behind a curtain, uttered the fateful words, and then ducked behind the curtain again. In fact, the essence of the press conference was a detailed description of the terms of the agreement—as the reader can determine by looking it
up in the backnotes.[1] Everyone who heard or read the contemporary media accounts had an opportunity to draw his or her own conclusions regarding the
imminence of peace and the substance of what had been negotiated.

My words reflected accurately the prevailing mixture of elation at the approaching end of the conflict, determination to complete the process, and
uneasiness masquerading as bravado at possible failure so close to the goal of
four years. In my opening remarks, I uttered the phrase ("peace is at hand")
that was to haunt me from then on:

> We have now heard from both Vietnams, and it is obvious that a
> war that has been raging for ten years is drawing to a conclusion, and
> that this is a traumatic experience for all of the participants. . . .
>
> We believe that peace is at hand. We believe that an agreement is
> within sight, based on the May 8th proposal of the President and
> some adaptation of our January 25th proposal which is just to all par-
> ties. It is inevitable that in a war of such complexity . . . there should
> be occasional difficulties in reaching a final solution, but we believe

that by far the longest part of the road has been traversed and what
stands in the way of an agreement now are issues that are relatively
less important than those that have already been settled.

I defended the right of the people of South Vietnam, "who have suffered so
much . . . who will be remaining in that country after we have departed," to
participate in the making of their peace. In that spirit, we would ask for
changes in the text to be achieved in a brief period of time. As for the American people, we were conscious of the anguish the war had caused:

> We have been very conscious of the division and the anguish that the
> war has caused in this country. One reason why the President has
> been so concerned with ending the war by negotiation, and ending it
> in a manner that is consistent with our principles, is because of the
> hope that the act of making peace could restore the unity that had
> sometimes been lost at certain periods during the war, and so that the
> agreement could be an act of healing rather than a source of new di-
> vision. This remains our policy.

And, after describing the provisions of the agreement, I ended with a warning to both Hanoi and Saigon:

> We will not be stampeded into an agreement until its provisions are
> right. We will not be deflected from an agreement when its provi-
> sions are right. And with this attitude, and with some cooperation
> from the other side, we believe that we can restore both peace and
> unity to America very soon.

Our overwhelming concern was to hold the agreement together. At that
point, we were not sure whether either Vietnamese party would return to the
conference table. And no doubt the press conference gave hostages to for-
tune. The drama of the phrase "peace is at hand" provided a handy symbol to
attack the administration. Despite all the opprobrium heaped on it later, the
"peace is at hand" statement was essentially correct—though clearly if I had
to do it over I would choose a less dramatic phrase. Negotiations resumed on
November 20 (Hanoi stalled nearly four weeks). The breakthrough that settled all issues of principle occurred on January 9, 1973; the agreement was

initialed on January 23. Semanticists may argue whether a six-week negotiation stretches the meaning of "at hand." The statement that one more session could conclude the negotiation in fact was to cause more trouble than the phrase "peace is at hand." For it established a deadline against which Le Duc Tho was bound to try to push, and his attempt to do so led to one more convulsion.

The immediate problem was to get the parties back to the negotiating table. Just before the press conference I had cabled Bunker to urge Thieu not to attack the agreement as a whole; Thieu should keep his comments compatible with ours. I informed Dobrynin of our intentions. He seemed to think—allegedly without instructions—that after a cooling-off period negotiations might resume.

We now embarked on several days of exchanges with Hanoi, complicated by Nixon's frequent absences on campaign trips. A rather mystifying note on October 26 from the North Vietnamese sought to explain why they had gone public. It seemed to refuse another meeting, though without the usual combative rhetoric. It proposed that the "best" (but not the "only") procedure was to sign the text of the agreement as it stood. But it concluded with two paragraphs that strongly suggested that Hanoi might be prepared to continue negotiations after all.

But the next day, October 27, the North Vietnamese spokesman in Paris, Nguyen Thanh Le, seemed to pull back. He told newsmen that Le Duc Tho and Xuan Thuy would see me again only if the United States was prepared to sign the October agreement: "If the date of signature is the 31st, then if on the 30th Kissinger wants to meet Le Duc Tho or Xuan Thuy to drink champagne while awaiting the signature, I think the response would be positive." Instead of "peace is at hand," Le offered "peace is at the end of a pen." We responded instead to Hanoi's note of the previous day, reiterating our proposal for a final negotiation and promising a full bombing halt forty-eight hours after a settlement. I sent a copy to the Chinese.

Now Thieu was heard from. On October 28, a lengthy and querulous memorandum by Nha pointed out alleged discrepancies between Hanoi's broadcast and my press conference on the one hand, and on the other, what Saigon had been told. He repeated Saigon's objections to the phrase "administrative structure," which he claimed proved that the National Council of National Reconciliation and Concord was a "disguised coalition government" even though Saigon had a veto over its creation, composition, and operation. We learned that Thieu had sent emissaries to America's other Asian allies to set out his objections to the agreement. This produced another Nixon letter to Thieu, in the drafting of which the President took a personal hand. Nixon gallantly pointed out that my press conference of October 26 reflected his own views. He emphasized that he would not change course after the election, and he used very tough language:

> Just as our unity has been the essential aspect of the success we have enjoyed thus far in the conduct of hostilities, it will also be the best guarantee of future success in a situation where the struggle continues within a more political framework. If the evident drift towards disagreement between the two of us continues, however, the essential base for U.S. support for you and your Government will be destroyed. In this respect the comments of your Foreign Minister that the U.S. is negotiating a surrender are as damaging as they are unfair and improper.
>
> You can be assured that my decisions as to the final character of a peace settlement are in no way influenced by the election in the United States, and you should harbor no illusions that my policy with respect to the desirability of achieving an early peace will change after the election.

On October 30, it was Hanoi's turn: Our proposal for another round of negotiations was being studied very carefully and would receive a reply later. Hanoi clearly did not want to agree before its own publicly proposed deadline of October 31 had passed. I told Haldeman, who was traveling with the President, that there were three possibilities: Hanoi would cancel the agreement and break off all talks; it would stand on the agreement but refuse any renegotiation; or it would resume talks. I considered the last most likely, a suitable interval after the proposed signing date.

Next day—October 31—Beijing weighed in, though with the usual nuance of difference from its North Vietnamese friends. Whereas Hanoi had put the blame squarely on the United States, the Chinese reserved their angriest rhetoric for Saigon, demanding that we "put a firm stop" to Saigon's behavior. More challenging was a reference hinting that America's relations with China were to some degree affected by our conduct in Vietnam. If we prolonged the war and protracted the negotiations, the note read, "then how are people to view the U.S. statements about its preparedness to make efforts for the relaxation of tension in the Far East?"

Committed as we were to bringing Beijing into the international system, we would not permit this objective to be used for blackmail. We therefore sent a firm reply:

> The Chinese side, considering all the conversations it has had with the U.S. side about respecting basic principles, must surely understand that the U.S. cannot treat an ally as a puppet. This would accord neither with reality nor principle. The constant assumption and public reiteration by the DRV that the U.S. has complete mastery over its friends has been one of the root causes of present difficulties. The U.S. side would like to remind the Chinese side of the many conversations between Dr. Kissinger and the Prime Minister in which Dr. Kissinger expressed understanding and respect for the Chinese meticulous treatment of Prince Sihanouk, a friendly leader who was a guest on Chinese soil. The U.S. side points out that its problems with its friends are no easier and its principles no different.

While we struggled to hold the agreement together, the American public debate heated up. After a moment of stunned surprise, the disclosures of October 26 produced jubilation nationally; the vast majority of the public felt enormous relief. At the same time, the bitterness of a decade was not stilled by the prospect of the end of hostilities. Two main lines of attack developed: that the whole thing was a fraud to help Nixon win the election, which, on the evidence of all the polls, was nonsense; and that the same terms had been attainable four years earlier, which was totally untrue. Some antiwar critics without embarrassment made a 180-degree turn and repeated Thieu's criticism of the inadequacy of the accords, especially regarding the disposition of North Vietnamese troops. The overwhelming majority of administration critics had been pressing for unilateral American withdrawal. They had long given up on a cease-fire; on North Vietnamese withdrawal from Laos and Cambodia; on a ban on infiltration into South Vietnam; on continued aid to Saigon; on the continuation of the Thieu government on international supervision. They had denounced these terms as examples of intransigence and worse.

George McGovern adopted the first approach. On October 29, he alleged on *Meet the Press* that he was "puzzled as to why the settlement comes in the closing hours of this campaign. . . . It is really not clear to me what fundamental change has taken place in the last few days which enables Mr. Nixon to announce, now, that we have a settlement just before we go to the polls." McGovern ignored that Hanoi had made the announcement. He was sterner with Thieu than he was with Hanoi; he would reserve the right to renegotiate any agreement that committed the United States to aid Thieu after the war ended.

The *Washington Post* in its first reaction on October 27 implied—without a shred of evidence—that similar terms might have been available in 1969 in the light of Hanoi's "post-Tet military prostration." By the first week of November, the phrase "peace is at hand" was being contrasted with the amount of time it took to arrange a cease-fire; the fact that Hanoi was refusing to talk was not known but should have been apparent from Hanoi's public statements. On November 6, the *New York Times* gave editorial expression to its impatience and implied that the promised peace might be a cover for new escalation. By November 9, Murrey Marder in the *Washington Post* had discovered unnamed administration officials willing to pretend to supposed knowledge that Nixon had never intended to consummate the agreement before the election; it would have been too "messy"; Nixon had therefore decided to risk Hanoi's rebuke despite firm promises and had refused to sign on October 31. On November 10, the *Post* wrote an editorial castigating the Nixon administration for misleading the American people.

On November 4, three days before the voting, I accompanied Nixon to San Clemente, stopping off in Albuquerque for the last stage of his campaign. That day we received Hanoi's acceptance of our offer to resume negotiations in an unusually mild tone, which made clear that Hanoi expected Nixon's reelection. It suggested November 14 or "another date which may be proposed by the U.S. side." Hanoi reaffirmed that it would abide by the text of the agreement—in other words, that it would seek no changes of its own. No North Vietnamese message could be complete without a reference to its legendary "consistent good will and seriousness," to the export of which the peoples of Indochina had been unremittingly exposed for over a decade and would be again in subsequent years.

In order to avoid further exchanges before the election, we replied on November 7, proposing November 15 to enable Haig to go to Saigon to concert our approach with Thieu. We also warned Hanoi that we expected it to desist from "tendentious public comment or selective releases from earlier documents of the negotiations which can only complicate the task of arriving at a final agreement." On November 8, Hanoi replied, suggesting a postponement to November 20 because Le Duc Tho was "ill." (There can be little doubt that it must have been a rough time for him. All the Communist forces that had geared up for land-grabbing operations in the pre-cease-fire period were now being decimated.) Because it would take Le Duc Tho a week to reach Paris, Hanoi asked for a reply "as quickly as possible." We accepted the proposed date on November 9. Negotiations were once again in train.

Election Interlude

The strangest period in Nixon's presidency followed his overwhelming victory on November 7, 1972. He had achieved a series of spectacular successes in 1971 and 1972: the Berlin agreement, the Beijing summit, the Moscow summit, the imminent end of the war in Vietnam. The outcome of the election promised to be the biggest landslide in our history. And yet as his hour of triumph approached, Nixon seemed seized by a strange premonition of catastrophe.

The morning after the election, on November 8, Nixon's long-stored-up resentments came to the surface. The White House staff had been awake much of the previous night celebrating his victory, though even then the festivities I attended seemed to lack spontaneity. The President was too withdrawn and shadowy a figure; very few of the celebrants had actually met him. His achievements were associated more with solitary discipline and remote courage than with personal inspiration; his support was based more on admiration for stern competence than personal affection. And yet there was great pride in an administration that had steered the country through crisis into a period of hopeful tranquillity, perhaps even of national unity.

The good feeling was shattered within twelve hours. The White House staff had been asked to assemble at 11:00 A.M. in the Roosevelt Room. At the hour, Nixon strode in through the door closest to the Oval Office. He seemed not at all elated. Rather, he was grim and remote as if the most fateful period of his life still lay ahead. Nothing in his demeanor betrayed that he was meeting associates from perilous and trying times; he acted as if they were from a past now irrevocably finished. Without sitting down, he thanked the assembled group in a perfunctory manner. After about five minutes, he turned the meeting over to Haldeman and left.

Haldeman wasted no time getting to the point. Every member of the White House staff was to submit his resignation immediately; they were to fill out a form listing the documents in our possession. The President would announce his personnel decisions for the new term within a month. The audience was stunned. It was the morning after a triumph, and they were being, in effect, fired. Victory seemed to have released a pent-up hostility so overwhelming that it would not wait even a week to surface. The same performance was repeated with the Cabinet an hour later.

What propelled Nixon into a course so degrading to his closest associates has never been satisfactorily explained. I had heard him frequently express his regret that the narrow margin of his 1968 victory and the pressures of Vietnam had prevented him from accomplishing a thorough housecleaning of the bureaucracy, which he mistrusted. Had Nixon waited a few weeks, it is certain that all assistants and Cabinet members would of their own accord have followed custom and submitted their resignations. Nixon could then have proceeded at his leisure, retaining or removing as suited his plans. But to ask for everybody's resignation within hours of being elected, to distribute forms obviously prepared during a campaign in which many of the victims had been working themselves to a frazzle, made removal from office appear to be not the result of presidential reflection about the future but as a settling of scores. (I was not directly affected, having been told by Haldeman right after the Roosevelt Room meeting that my letter of resignation would be a formality.)

The afternoon of November 8 I flew with Nixon, Haldeman, and Ehrlichman to Key Biscayne. Again, I was struck that triumph seemed to bring no surcease to this tortured man. He fretted that his popular margin had been a shade less than Johnson's over Goldwater. Above all, he occupied himself with planning the removal or reshuffling of most of his Cabinet, with the exception of George Shultz, who had recently replaced Connally at the Treasury. Rogers was slated to resign in the summer, tentatively to be replaced by Kenneth Rush. Now that he had achieved the overwhelming electoral approval which had been the ambition of a lifetime, Nixon was restless and distracted. It was almost as if standing on the pinnacle, Nixon no longer had any purpose left to his life.

As soon as we arrived in Key Biscayne, Nixon withdrew into his compound. From there he went to Camp David with Haldeman and Ehrlichman to plan his new administration. I saw him only twice in the next nine days, including a session on November 17, when we talked briefly at Camp David before I left for the resumed negotiations with Le Duc Tho. We spoke occasionally on the telephone. To others he was totally inaccessible. The leader who had just won 61 percent of the popular vote cut himself off from his own entourage. At a moment when, by reaching out, he might have engraved himself in America's heart, as he already had left his mark on its mind, he withdrew into a seclusion even deeper and more impenetrable than in his years of struggle.

Ever since the secret trip to China, my own relationship with Nixon had grown complicated. Every president carefully nurtures his own image; the pursuit of it, after all, brought him to where he is. No chief executive would take kindly to an appointee who is cast by the media as the fount of all constructive actions. In Nixon's case, resentment was compounded by his conviction that he faced a lifelong conspiracy of the old Establishment determined to destroy him. He had a point. In a way I had become the media's alibi for their dislike of Nixon.

To counterbalance this, during the last phase of the Vietnam negotiations, the White House public relations machinery avoided few opportunities to cut me down to size. And Nixon himself grew testy. His cables to me sometimes seemed written more for a record of dissociation in case of failure than for conveying instructions. In fact, Nixon and I never differed on the substance of our negotiating position. Our only difference, if any, was his desire to avoid bringing the negotiations to a head before election day and my conviction that, however desirable, Hanoi would not permit this. The publicity I received caused Nixon to look for ways of showing that he was in charge, even while endorsing the strategy we had jointly devised. One had to deduce these latent tensions from vague clues; they were never made explicit in our personal contacts, which were unfailingly courteous and in which no disagreement surfaced. (Of course, I had seen enough of Nixon with others to realize that this was no proof of presidential favor.)

Haig Visits Saigon Again

With negotiations about to resume, the immediate problem was in Saigon. We had committed ourselves to the American public to settle the agreement in one more session—which, in retrospect, was a mistake. Of course, Thieu felt no such compulsion. The longer he could keep American forces in the war, the further he put off the nightmare of being left alone.

On November 10, Xuan Thuy gave an interview that for a change was helpful: He confirmed that the National Council of National Reconciliation and Concord was not a coalition government in disguise. The National Council "will not yet be a government," he told Agence France Presse; the two existing governments would continue to exist until new elections. Thieu was not visibly appeased. In an effort to enlist his support, we sent Haig to Saigon carrying a letter from Nixon, dated November 8. The letter expressed disappointment with Thieu's public statements; it affirmed that we considered the draft agreement sound. We promised to improve on some provisions. For example, we would ensure that the Vietnamese translation of the phrase "administrative structure" was changed to remove any implication that the National Council was a governmental body. We would also make explicit what was now implied, that each side would appoint an equal number of the council members, giving each side a veto and ensuring that the council would be unlikely to function. We would attempt to strengthen the provisions to respect the Demilitarized Zone in order to emphasize the separate character of South Vietnam even more. "We will use our maximum efforts," wrote Nixon, "to effect these changes in the agreement. I wish to leave you under no illusion, however, that we can or will go beyond these changes in seeking to improve an agreement that we already consider to be excellent." Nixon urged Thieu to "take the political and psychological initiative by hailing the settlement and carrying out its provisions in a positive fashion." He asked for an unambiguous answer.

But absence of ambiguity was precluded by Vietnamese culture and Thieu's personality. Thieu followed the by now standard procedure. He met with Haig on November 10, listened attentively to his explanation of the President's letter, asked thoughtful questions, and promised to think about it overnight. Then on November 11, he confronted Haig and Ambassador Bunker with his entire National Security Council and flatly turned down our suggestion to establish priorities among the textual changes he sought. He insisted on all of them; he demanded the withdrawal of North Vietnamese forces, which, as I have repeatedly mentioned, had not been part of any of our joint agreed proposals since 1970. He toughened even this unattainable demand by spelling out how the withdrawal should take place and what weapons had to be taken along. He gave Haig a letter to Nixon restating these demands, as well as requiring changes in the proposed composition of the international supervisory machinery.

Between the two meetings, I had sent Haig a cable: "You should point out composition of our new Senate to Thieu. No matter what happens, there will be fund cutoff if we do not move in this direction." Haig made the point, but Thieu was either playing chicken or was on a deliberate collision course.

On November 14, Nixon answered Thieu's letter. He explained how we proposed to deal in the peace document with the problem of North Vietnamese forces in the South. We would do our best to obtain changes, but it would be "unrealistic" to expect to obtain what Thieu wanted. Nixon continued:

> But far more important than what we say in the agreement on this issue is what we do in the event the enemy renews its aggression. You have my absolute assurance that if Hanoi fails to abide by the terms of this agreement it is my intention to take swift and severe retaliatory action.

This letter was later released by South Vietnamese officials in April 1975 in a desperate attempt to obtain American aid to prevent the fall of South Vietnam. They had a right to consider that they had relied on these assurances when they signed the agreement. In 1972, we had every intention of carrying them out. We believed that an honorable agreement earned at the cost of more than 55,000 American lives was not signed in order to give Hanoi a free hand in Indochina. We did not intend to surrender. These assurances will be discussed in relation to enforcement of the agreement later in this volume. We considered that we had a right to enforce a solemn agreement signed by Hanoi and confirmed at an international conference by twelve nations in March 1973. Nixon said so when meeting with Thieu on April 3, 1973. Secretary of Defense Richardson said so to the press and testified to that effect before Congress until, under the impact of Watergate, it passed a law prohibiting us from exercising what international law recognizes and what the United States formally adopted in conjunction with the end of the Gulf and Balkan wars: the right to enforce a peace agreement. That reckless act destroyed the balance of risks on which the agreement rested.

To avoid any misunderstanding and to show good faith, I sent Bunker on November 17 another summary of the changes we would seek that took into account Thieu's comments to Haig. As was becoming habitual, Bunker could not get an appointment to present them for twenty-four hours. Finally, on November 18, the day before I was to leave for Paris, Thieu had Nha submit another memorandum. It showed that three strong presidential letters and the visit of two presidential emissaries had made no impression whatever. Instead of establishing priorities among its original twenty demands, Saigon now proposed sixty-nine modifications, leaving almost no paragraph of the draft document untouched. Thieu offered to send a representative to Washington to explain the proposed changes to Nixon—a slap at me and another blatant stalling tactic because there was no way an emissary could arrive before I had to leave for my meeting with Le Duc Tho. We returned an icy presidential letter warning again that these changes could not possibly all be achieved, and refusing to receive an emissary until the next round of negotiations with Hanoi had been completed. Nearly four weeks of exchanges had failed to narrow the gap between Washington and Saigon. Thieu knew that he would have to yield but would do so only at the last moment. He would force us to put pressure on Hanoi, hoping perhaps that Hanoi would break off the talks, in the meantime exploiting our reluctance to have a public rupture.

On November 13, I had dinner with Chinese Deputy Foreign Minister Qiao Guanhua, who was heading the Chinese delegation to the U.N. General Assembly. If Le Duc Tho stopped in Beijing on the way to Paris, I said, the Chinese leaders should use their influence in the direction of moderation. Qiao gave no such promise. But neither did he support Hanoi's point of view. He urged us to make concessions because great powers could afford a generous attitude: "One should not lose the whole world just to gain South Vietnam." On the other hand, no one should be humiliated. Qiao's line was an even softer version of what we had come to recognize as the standard Chinese position: sympathy for Hanoi, but no expenditure of Chinese capital on its ally's behalf. (Except for slightly cruder tactics, this was exactly Moscow's attitude.)

About Cambodia Qiao was more specific. I emphasized that American and Chinese interests in Cambodia were congruent because we both wanted a neutral, independent Cambodia free of the domination of any one country. He did not dispute this. Instead, he asked whether I would be prepared to meet Sihanouk on my next visit to China (then scheduled for January 1973). I evaded the specific question but replied in general terms that we were not opposed to Sihanouk provided he was able to establish an independent country.

> I can tell you now on a confidential basis it would be possible to arrive at an understanding with the Prime Minister that does justice to the concerns of Prince Sihanouk. If the war continues in Cambodia, then we have to maintain our present position. But what we want in Cambodia, to be very blunt, is . . . to preserve it from becoming an appendage of Hanoi. Whoever can best preserve it as an independent neutral country, is consistent with our policy, and we believe consistent with yours.

The next day, when I reported the conversation to Nixon, I repeated my view that after a cease-fire in Cambodia, Sihanouk would become a factor again and "could come back at the right moment."

A genuine solution involving Sihanouk's return required a balance of forces and the prospect of a cease-fire—as it had in Vietnam and Laos. There was no way Sihanouk could resume his pre-1970 balancing role unless there were several parties to balance. Paradoxically, Sihanouk needed the non-Communist forces to survive in Phnom Penh. With total victory in sight, the murderous Khmer Rouge would have no need for him. Starting in the spring of 1973, we sought to bring about Sihanouk's return based on a cease-fire.

The Meetings with Le Duc Tho Resume

The meeting with Le Duc Tho on the morning of Monday, November 20, was the first since the sixteen-hour marathon of October 12 and its emotional conclusion. The interval had not been kind to either of us. To his morbidly suspicious colleagues in the Hanoi Politburo, Le Duc Tho must have appeared guilty of the unforgivable sin of having been tricked by a wily capitalist. Relying on our acceptance of the draft peace treaty, the North Vietnamese had started land-grabbing operations. So had the South. The North had suffered fearful punishment and serious losses when it surfaced its cadres. We had used Hanoi's own October 31 deadline to extract concessions that, had Hanoi followed its usual negotiating style, would not have been made for many months, if ever, and we had done this only to confront the North Vietnamese at the end of the process with yet another series of demands of unspecified magnitude. I believed Dobrynin when he told me that the North Vietnamese were angry.

On the other hand, our situation was not exactly brilliant either. Once the agreement was public, what was left of congressional support for continuing the war evaporated. On November 27, Laird told me that it was impossible to "keep that thing going right now." He based his judgment on meetings with senators and House members during the preceding weekend. Laird repeated this conclusion in a meeting which Nixon convened with the Joint Chiefs of Staff on November 30. It was not contested by any of the Chiefs; it was confirmed by Nixon, who thought that the aid cutoff would take place within two weeks of the return of Congress. John Lehman, responsible for congressional liaison on my staff, estimated that the new Senate elected in November represented a net loss of three votes to Nixon, which would grow in significance because of the declining influence of Southern chairmen of key committees. We were facing the nightmare we had dreaded since the summer: negotiating against the deadline of the return of Congress with no additional leverage on Hanoi.

In this unpromising context, Le Duc Tho greeted me on November 20 at the door of the residence at Gif-sur-Yvette. Since our meeting had been announced on November 17, the press was fully alerted. They had staked out both the U.S. embassy residence and the North Vietnamese compound. I managed to shake off the pursuit with the aid of a death-defying French motorcycle escort. It was in vain. Le Duc Tho had made no effort to avoid pursuit, so when I arrived I found journalists and photographers of many nationalities camped across the street. They were to remain for the entire six hours of the meeting and to return for all subsequent meetings—five more days in November, thirteen days in December, and four days in early January. Léger's house stood alone; it was surrounded by a large garden bounded by a high wall. The journalists set up a scaffolding across the road from the house so the photographers could peer over the wall into the garden and—hopefully but in vain—into the house itself. Through the cold, rain, and snow of the Parisian winter, they kept a lonely vigil, never given any concrete information, never able to see much more than arrivals and departures, or occasionally Le Duc Tho or me walking in the garden during a break. There were no briefings and few pictures of Le Duc Tho and me together because we were usually greeted at the door by a lower ranking member of the delegation, and the two teams arrived and departed separately.

Le Duc Tho led off with a long recitation of Hanoi's goodwill and U.S. duplicity in failing to keep the "shedyule." Reading from a prepared statement, he warned against attempts to coerce North Vietnam; he complained that while North Vietnam had been deceived many times by the French and Japanese and Americans, never had it been deceived as it had this time.

I replied that Hanoi's previous four years of stonewalling had not prepared us for the suddenness of Hanoi's willingness to settle in October. I read to Le Duc Tho my many previous caveats that the agreement required the concurrence of both Washington and Saigon. I cited the difficulties caused by the de Borchgrave interview. It was time to look to the future and to conclude the agreement.

The impact of my presentation was immediately vitiated by the sixty-nine changes requested by Saigon, which I now put forward. This proved to be a major mistake. The list went so far beyond what we had indicated both publicly and privately that it must have strengthened Hanoi's already strong temptation to dig in and push us against the congressional deadlines. I put them forward in order to avoid the charge that we were less than meticulous in guarding Saigon's concerns—and to ease the task of obtaining Thieu's approval. As often happens when one negotiates for the record, we achieved neither objective. Since there was no possibility of obtaining this many changes—as we had warned Thieu—every one we abandoned was used in Saigon to demonstrate our lack of vigilance and in Hanoi as another incentive for recalcitrance. And once we started the process of retreat, we tempted Hanoi to delay in order to see what other concessions might be forthcoming.

Le Duc Tho's first reaction was predictable. He stated that if these changes were presented as an ultimatum, the war would go on another four years. He then asked for an overnight recess to study our proposals. One day of negotiation had elapsed without any progress whatever and with the clock now running against us.

When we met again in the afternoon of November 21, Le Duc Tho emphasized the obvious: The changes I was demanding were not just "technical" but substantive, not few but many. He rejected the overwhelming majority; he accepted a few technical ones. More worrying, he began demanding changes of his own. He withdrew the vitally important concession that American prisoners would be released unconditionally without linkage to Saigon's release of Vietcong civilian prisoners. Press reports had appeared, based on leaks from the Pentagon, that civilian technicians might be assisting the South Vietnamese after our military left; Le Duc Tho therefore now added a demand that all American civilian technicians be withdrawn along with our military forces. He insisted on the North Vietnamese translation of "administrative structure." All this was old-fashioned hard bargaining; it was also the stuff of which deadlocks are made. Obviously, this was not the Le Duc Tho of the late summer, relentlessly driving toward a settlement. On the other hand, his conduct was not yet the all-out political warfare of the previous three years. At a minimum, Le Duc Tho kept his options open. He could settle quickly, but he could also stonewall indefinitely.

The latter prospect gave no pain to the three South Vietnamese diplomats whom Thieu had assigned to keep an eye on the talks: Saigon's ambassadors to Washington, London, and the Paris talks were all in Paris. I briefed them every evening at the U.S. embassy residence. Their instructions were simple. They were authorized to accept Hanoi's surrender on all the sixty-nine changes proposed by the inventive Nha. They had no authority to consider less, to discuss any compromise, or to entertain any alternative language. Hanoi meanwhile was keeping open the option of insisting on the October text, knowing that whatever its merit, Thieu would be severely damaged by the humiliation of obtaining no changes whatever.

At the three-and-a-half-hour session of November 22, therefore, I returned to essentials, in the process separating from Saigon's position—and running the risk of returning to the dilemma we faced in October. In the guise of going through the agreement paragraph by paragraph, I dropped many of Saigon's less important nitpicks and reduced our demands to those Nixon had declared essential in his letter to Thieu of November 8.

Le Duc Tho played cat and mouse. In response to my requests, he agreed to a looser clause on replacement of weapons. It had read that weapons "worn out or damaged" could be replaced. He now permitted us to add the phrases "destroyed" and "used up," as in the 1954 Geneva Agreement. The practical consequence was, in Le Duc Tho's words: "It means that you will have a free hand to introduce armaments." But the flexibility was more apparent than real, for Le Duc Tho maintained his demands that Vietcong civilian prisoners be released at the same time as American POWs and that American civilian technicians be withdrawn along with U.S. forces. At this rate, we would be in Paris all winter.

Meanwhile, Washington was heard from. Ensconced at Camp David, surrounded only by public relations experts, Nixon was still deep in the bog of the resentments that had produced the darkest frame of mind of his presidency. Nixon now dispatched a tough-sounding instruction explicitly marked "not a directive—for possible use with the North Vietnamese." It read:

> The President is very disappointed at the tone as well as the substance of the last meeting with Le Duc Tho. Under the circumstances, unless the other side shows the same willingness to be reasonable that we are showing, I am directing you to discontinue the talks and we shall then have to resume military activity until the other side is ready to negotiate. They must be disabused of the idea they seem to have that we have no other choice but to settle on their terms. You should inform them directly without equivocation that we do have another choice and if they were surprised that the President would take the strong action he did prior to the Moscow summit and prior to the election, they will find now, with the election behind us, he will take whatever action he considers necessary to protect the United States' interest.

Another message from Haldeman recommended that I should present a sterner appearance in the television pictures with Le Duc Tho. The directive seemed unaware of the fact that it was our side which was demanding sixty-nine changes.

On November 23, in another six-hour session, I concentrated on strengthening the provision regarding the DMZ in order to enhance the legal barrier to infiltration from the North. Le Duc Tho offered a semiconcession on the DMZ in return for altering other parts of the agreement, especially the political sections, prisoners, and American civilian technicians. Le Duc Tho suggested that we settle for a de facto withdrawal of some of their forces

from the northernmost part of South Vietnam in return for the release of political prisoners. He refused to tell us how many would withdraw, rejected my
proposal of 100,000, and would not put the promise in writing. I thought
this package a significant degradation of the October document, because the
alteration of the prisoners provision was balanced only by a nebulous assurance—in the form of an "understanding"—of the removal of an unspecified
number of North Vietnamese troops a short distance across the DMZ.

It was Thanksgiving Day, and the North Vietnamese served a lavish
lunch of roast beef and chicken in honor of the occasion. Afterward I cabled
Nixon that while we had achieved some marginal improvements, the North
Vietnamese had pulled back somewhat, leaving the overall agreement
slightly worse than the one negotiated in October. I gave the President two
options: break off the talks and resume bombing north of the 20th parallel
(in effect, the course he had asked me to put to Le Duc Tho twenty-four
hours before); or else settle for the improvements in the draft agreement already achieved on the DMZ and weapons provisions, plus a few changes in
the political sections as a face-saver for Saigon; the rest of the agreement
would remain as it stood in October. I had, of course, no way of knowing
whether Hanoi would accept this; I was certain Saigon would refuse.

Nixon cabled back that "because of expectations that have been built up
in this country" (translation: the "peace is at hand" press conference), the
break-off of the talks, which he had instructed me to put forward twenty-
four hours earlier, was no longer possible. He chose the second option, asking me to play the hand as hard as I could:

> In my view the October 8 agreement was one which certainly
> would have been in our interest. You should try to improve it to take
> account of Saigon's conditions as much as possible. But most impor-
> tant we must recognize the fundamental reality that we have no
> choice but to reach agreement along the lines of the October 8 prin-
> ciples.

Rather than pressure Hanoi, Nixon preferred now to put the heat on Saigon:

> You should inform the Saigon representatives that all military
> and economic aid will be cut off by the Congress if an agreement is
> not reached. Inform them also that, under these circumstances, I will
> be unable to get the Congressional support that is needed.

The next morning, Nixon had second thoughts; I do not know what changed his mind. He sent another cable suggesting that I interrupt the talks after all, on the pretext of giving the negotiators an opportunity to consult their principals. In that case, he would authorize a massive air strike against North Vietnam during the recess.

> In giving [sic] this direction, we all must realize that there is no
> way whatever that we can mobilize public opinion behind us as in the
> case of November 3 [1969], Cambodia [1970] and May 8 [1972].
> But at least with the election behind us, we owe it to the sacrifice that
> has been made to date by so many to do what is right even though the
> cost in our public support will be massive.

The net result of all these instructions was to leave the decision up to me. All this time the Saigon contingent of ambassadors had taken an adamant stand, not budging from their demand for the sixty-nine changes. On November 23, we learned that Thieu's aide, Nguyen Phu Duc, was coming to Paris to reinforce the Saigon team. If Saigon were to show any flexibility, we would have to await his arrival. I also judged that it would be a mistake for the American and North Vietnamese delegations to keep meeting on the established pattern, formally working our way through the agreement. In the absence of new instructions for Le Duc Tho or flexibility from Saigon, we would merely confirm the deadlock.

I therefore proposed to Le Duc Tho that he and I, each accompanied by just one adviser, meet at our old place at Rue Darthé in Choisy-le-Roi. He agreed. Haig and I met him and Xuan Thuy for one and a half hours on November 24 for a philosophical discussion. I read to my interlocutors the strongest of Nixon's telegrams, especially those emphasizing his willingness to run military risks. I stressed that we would in no circumstances accept provisions weaker than those already published—thus rejecting Le Duc Tho's request for changes in Hanoi's favor.

Le Duc Tho maintained his position. After this meeting, I cabled Nixon that I leaned toward a week's postponement. It would show Hanoi that we were not excessively anxious. It would give us another week to work on Saigon unless Duc brought a fundamental change. As it stood, whatever was negotiable in Paris could not be sold in Saigon. I would wait for my meeting with Nguyen Phu Duc before recommending a final decision.

Duc brought nothing. Nixon's cable describing congressional attitudes impressed Duc but obviously could not change his instructions. I decided to ask for a week's recess the next day. In these circumstances, a meeting of the two delegations again seemed unwise. Le Duc Tho and Xuan Thuy thus met Haig and me for two hours on the morning of November 25 at Rue Darthé. Le Duc Tho granted a recess grudgingly; I did not have the impression that he was prepared for additional serious talks. We agreed to announce December 4 for a resumption.

This first round of talks thus ended with twelve improvements—some marginal—in the text, balanced against three or four demands by Hanoi for major changes in its favor. We were not clear about Hanoi's ultimate intentions. Le Duc Tho's tactics might be tough negotiating, or they could reflect a growing confidence that the psychological tide was running in Hanoi's favor. The North Vietnamese might calculate that we would try to force Saigon to go back to the October text if they held on long enough, shattering the morale of Thieu's government. Or else they might wait for Congress to force America out of the war. Nixon meanwhile had changed his mind again. He now thought I should keep the talks going.

An experienced negotiator—which, by this time, I was—develops a sixth sense for when the other side is ready to settle. The signals are usually matters of nuance: Some issues are not pressed to the absolute limit; some claims are marginally modified; the door to compromise is always kept tangentially ajar. None of these indicators appeared in the November round of talks; indeed, all the signs were contrary: Hanoi's concessions were marginal and inconclusive; they kept the goal of a settlement always tantalizingly out of reach.

One telltale sign was Tho's persistent refusal to let experts from both sides discuss the protocols—documents that were to spell out in detail the arrangements for implementing general clauses in the main agreements, such as the timing and supervision of the cease-fire, and the composition and authority of the international control machinery. I repeatedly asked for North Vietnamese drafts or ideas on these protocols and said that our experts headed by Ambassador Sullivan were ready to negotiate on them immediately. Tho evaded each of our requests with the excuse that the North Vietnamese drafts were not ready. This was amazing in light of Hanoi's insistence three weeks earlier that we sign the basic agreement by October 31.

Failure in Washington requires a sacrificial offering. I was the logical candidate. The media regularly reminded their audiences of the "peace is at hand" statement, though they treated me compassionately at this stage. The same could not be said of some White House aides who began to take precautions to dissociate the President from a possible collapse of the negotiations. Stories began to appear that I had exceeded my instructions in October, that Nixon had spotted drafting flaws in the original agreement, that Nixon was siding with Thieu against me. Most of it was self-serving nonsense. I had had no instructions to exceed in October; Nixon had not raised a single objection to any provision of the agreement. His private view of Thieu was, if anything, less charitable than mine, though he was worried about offending the Republican right wing. But in Washington, the fact of such leaks is often more interesting than their truth; they indicate, if not presidential displeasure, at least that some aides consider it safe to attack a close associate of the President. And foreign governments will draw their own conclusions from an appearance of division in high councils.

The Breakdown of the Negotiations

Upon my return, Nixon was calm and analytical. But there was no doubt we were caught in a vise. Thieu, on one side, was determined to give us no leeway; Hanoi, on the other side, saw the divisions looming between Saigon and Washington—as well as within our own government—as an opportunity to delay to see what benefits might be squeezed out of continuing deadlock. We decided to bring matters to a head, first with Saigon.

On November 26, I asked Bunker to tell Thieu yet again that our minimum conditions remained unchanged. To reinforce our position, we now accepted Thieu's earlier suggestion that he should send an emissary and requested the immediate dispatch of Nguyen Phu Duc to Washington from Paris so that Nixon could go over our final position with him. (The point was to disabuse Thieu of any hope that he could play on a Nixon-Kissinger split.) Bunker endorsed the approach; he shared our conviction that Thieu would do nothing to ease our task, would assume no responsibility for the negotiation, and yet would accept the result.

Duc arrived on November 29 to meet a determined Nixon. The President, in fact, thought my proposed talking points were somewhat "too soft." He wanted to show me how to achieve a clear-cut result. Having no experience with the Vietnamese negotiating style, he did not appreciate that it avoids showdown, that its pliant obtuseness often makes it impossible to determine the precise nature of the issue or what exactly has been agreed.

Duc carried an extremely long and eloquent letter from Thieu to Nixon. It recounted all the concessions extracted from Saigon over the years with the promise—broken, it alleged—that no other sacrifice would be demanded. Thieu had a point, of course; the tragedy was that what Thieu considered intolerable pressure by us had been regarded by our critics as abject yielding to Saigon.

Nixon succinctly explained to Duc the impossibility of such a course. We could not now abandon peace proposals we had jointly put forward for nearly three years. It was absurd to describe as a coalition government an organization operating by unanimity, selected jointly, and with no specified functions. Nixon would proceed whatever Saigon's attitude; the latter would determine not the outcome of the negotiation but our ability to provide help afterward and to enforce the agreement. It was strong stuff but not strong enough to elicit a clear-cut reaction. Duc denied any desire for a confrontation. On the contrary, his aim, he said, was close cooperation. On the other hand, he had no authority to go beyond the settled views of his President. Nixon grandly suggested that Duc and I sit down to work out a practical solution; his decision had been made. In other words, we were right back where we had started. Duc had no authority to settle, and Thieu would never yield to me.

The result was stalemate. I met Duc twice in my office, and in between our two sessions was another brief meeting with Nixon. Nixon stressed to Duc yet again that his ability to enforce the agreement was more important than any changes in the clauses, though he was prepared to seek some further improvements. He told Duc he was confident we could detect infiltration; he told him of contingency plans he had discussed that very morning with the Joint Chiefs. Nixon informed Duc, finally, that if the agreement failed, Congress would probably cut off funds by mid-January. All this fell on the stolid Duc without any noticeable effect. When it was all over, Nixon remarked resignedly to me that Thieu was playing chicken and that we had probably no choice except to turn on him.

On the morning of November 30, as he told Duc, Nixon had met with Laird and the Joint Chiefs of Staff. Laird estimated that Congress would surely vote to cut off funds.

We had sent a message to Hanoi on November 27 saying that we would make a maximum effort on December 4, and to show our goodwill, we were reducing air operations over North Vietnam. The President ordered a cut of 25 percent in our sorties. It was a mistake; I can remember no instance where the North Vietnamese reciprocated gestures of unilateral restraint. More likely, they saw such moves as impelled by weakness. Hanoi's response of November 30 in any case pocketed the gesture while dismissing it. We returned a tart reply on the same day.

Amid looming congressional disenchantment, caught between the two implacable Vietnamese sides which specialized in tormenting each other and us, stung by leaks at home that my position as negotiator was not all that secure, I was not in a brilliant position from which to resume the negotiation on December 4.

I had proposed by cable that Le Duc Tho and I should begin with another "open-hearted" private discussion. Hanoi accepted and suggested the original meeting place at 11 rue Darthé. What took place between Le Duc Tho and Xuan Thuy on one side and Haig and me on the other deserves many appellations, but "open-hearted" is not likely to be one of them. Contrary to his usual insistence that I speak first, Le Duc Tho launched into an opening statement harking back to the fiery rhetoric of our early encounters. He accused us of seeking to strengthen what he called the "puppet administration" of Saigon. He criticized the refusal to release Vietcong political prisoners—which he had accepted in October. He repeated the epic tale of North Vietnamese imperviousness to military pressure.

My reply tried to put before Le Duc Tho a road to peace—an enterprise that had always proved futile in the past and was to do so again. The plan was to settle the remaining issues within two days, that is by the evening of December 5. The morning after Le Duc Tho and I concluded an agreement, Vice President Agnew, accompanied by General Haig, would leave for Saigon to brief Thieu. Within forty-eight hours, we would stop all bombing of North Vietnam. We would sign the agreement no later than December 22. And I presented the minimum changes for which we would settle.

But Le Duc Tho was a specialist in the balance of power, and he saw the balance tilting toward him. As a result, he indulged in one of his maddening verbal games. He called on me to make a "great effort"; he promised that he would make an "effort." When he had said it often enough, I asked whether he was not entitled to an adjective for himself. No, replied that stalwart from

Hanoi's Politburo, because recently he had made "great efforts," and I had only reciprocated with "efforts." Lest I miss the point, he repeated: "We have already made great efforts and exhausted the possibilities. There remains only little effort [for us] to make."

On the afternoon of December 4, the two delegations met again—this time in a new location picked by the North Vietnamese, in Sainte Gemme, about an hour's drive west of Paris. Le Duc Tho did not even make little efforts; he made none at all. He seized the floor for a violent denunciation of our tactics. He then rejected all proposals from the morning's private session. While he was at it, he also withdrew nine of the twelve changes he had accepted during the previous sessions in November. At the same time, he maintained all his demands for changes in the October agreement.

I did not believe that Le Duc Tho would have dared to put forward such propositions unless he was willing to risk a break-off in the talks. Back at the embassy residence, my associates and I spent hours poring over the records of the meetings, seeking to distill flexibility from some arcane formulation. We could not find any. We had taken over the entire residence, since Ambassador Watson had resigned and his successor (John Irwin) had not yet taken up his post. Staff members were frantically rewriting documents; secretaries were collating materials. The dining room stayed open the better part of each night serving meals that were consumed in deepening gloom.

That first night I concluded that the only hope of averting a collapse would be messages to Moscow and Beijing informing Hanoi's Communist backers of the prospects before them. I asked Dick Kennedy, manning the NSC office in Washington, to tell Dobrynin that we were approaching a situation comparable to that of last May, requiring the same kind of reaction. To give Moscow time to make its influence felt, I asked Le Duc Tho on December 5 for a twenty-four-hour postponement of the meeting scheduled for that afternoon "because of the grave situation resulting from the December 4 meeting."

My report to Nixon made clear that I did not see how we could accept returning to the October text (not to speak of one even worse, as Hanoi proposed). Though I considered the agreement good then, intervening events would turn acceptance of it into a debacle. If we could not bring about a single change requested by Saigon (or worse still, accepted a less favorable agreement), it would be tantamount to wrecking the South Vietnamese government. Worst of all, "it would deprive us of any ability to police the agreement, because if the Communists know we are willing to swallow this backdown, they will also know that we will not have the capacity to react to violations."

I considered a breakup probable, and I recognized my own responsibility in having forced the pace since October: "If this happens, I will talk to you upon my return about my own responsibility and role. The immediate task now, of course, is to save our national honor and position ourselves as best we can with our people and the world so as to pursue a principled policy in Southeast Asia." I added another paragraph to the effect that if the President accepted my recommendation, he should explain the decision in a television address to the American people. Nixon, on December 5, approved the proposed course with one proviso. He agreed that in case of a breakup, we would have to step up military pressure. Indeed, he was eager to order an attack by B-52s on the Hanoi-Haiphong complex even before the talks resumed on December 6. He asked my judgment on whether he should order Admiral Thomas Moorer, Chairman of the Joint Chiefs of Staff, to increase the readiness of our forces and also whether I wanted to buy more time by returning to Washington for consultation. My idea of a presidential television address, however, found no favor at all. A message from the White House Chief of Staff made explicit what Nixon only hinted at. If the talks stalemated, Haldeman suggested, they should be recessed rather than broken off. In that case, I was to give a low-key briefing. He offered no clue as to how to give a "low-key" briefing on the collapse of Vietnam peace efforts.

Nixon may have been right in his judgment that there was no public opinion left to rally; if so, and if Hanoi shared the judgment, the negotiations were doomed, and prolonging the talks was useless. On December 6, I replied to Haldeman:

> Thank you for your message of December 5. We had better face the facts of life. If there is no agreement in the next 48 hours, we may be able to pretend that the talks are in recess long enough to permit me to give a briefing after my return. But soon after, there will be no way to keep either of the Vietnamese parties from making the stalemate evident. Furthermore if we resume all-out bombing this will be even more true. Thus in the event of a stalemate we have only two choices: to yield or to rally American support for one more effort, which I do not believe the North Vietnamese can withstand. If we are

to attempt to rally the American people only the President can adequately do that eventually. But if it is your judgment that I should go on first, I will of course be glad to attempt it.

The meeting with Le Duc Tho on December 6 brought no change. Both sides reviewed their positions. There was some tinkering with individual clauses, but we were simply treading water.

Nixon's reply directed me to open the next meeting with a series of questions much in the style of a prosecuting attorney, to try to pin Hanoi to a series of intransigent positions to strengthen the record in case the talks should recess or break up. I was then to invite Hanoi to make its final offer.[2] Nixon's approach had merit, though I thought he vastly overrated my ability to pin down Le Duc Tho to unambiguous answers.

On December 7, I asked Haig to instruct Richard Kennedy, who was the daily contact with the President, as to the nature of the advice he should give. The temptation to evade admitting that there was a deadlock, I was convinced, would make it much harder to manage the now nearly inevitable recess of the talks. Hanoi was likely to make its final concessions only if it was convinced that we were willing to risk failure and take the consequences. No one had more to lose from such an eventuality than the author of "peace is at hand." But there was no way of hiding a deadlock indefinitely and no chance of overcoming it if we were not willing to brave its implications. Haig's message to Kennedy on my behalf read in part, in his best army prose:

> Henry recognizes that you have been in a difficult position this week and therefore felt you should have the benefit of his personal views on the situation as it now stands. I would emphasize that his experience with the President during crisis periods confirms the fact that most of the President's counsel in the absence of Dr. Kissinger would come from elements within the White House whose orientation and background would cause them to focus primarily on public relations considerations which, while perfectly understandable, can leave a serious substantive gap during vital deliberations. . . . You, of course, must be the sole source of substantive counsel. Henry hopes that you will not make any other kind of assessments or join in any comments [on] Congressional attitudes or public opinion which are available to the President from people whose tasks are precisely that.

Your counsel must therefore always be in terms of national security substance. In this context it is now evident that we will need some time to position the public opinion at home in the event the talks break down. But there is no need to allow these considerations to affect our strategy vis-à-vis Hanoi. Hanoi has known for some time what the issues are and what minimum needs of ours they must meet. The question is simply: can they bring themselves to do so? Tactical ploys from our side indicating that we are inclined to avoid facing up to the fact of their intransigence can only make matters worse and their resolve to hang tough even firmer. . . .

Hanoi knows exactly what they have to do. If they meet our minimum demands the management of the agreement itself is going to take the most determined and decisive Presidential leadership to enforce an agreement which we are now convinced both sides will enter into with a minimum of good will. If, on the other hand, the talks break down because Hanoi could not accept even our minimum demands, there is little doubt that we can succeed only as a result of the most courageous and determined national leadership which is not dominated by PR considerations but rather the same realistic assessments of the national interest which have brought us to this point.

The four-hour meeting on December 7 made evident Hanoi's apparent calculation: that we were hopelessly cornered. Le Duc Tho changed his style somewhat. He abandoned the obvious stonewalling of the previous sessions. He started giving some ground—but always made sure to keep the conclusion of the text just out of reach. He adamantly refused to allow the experts to discuss the protocols; this gave him another means to prevent a conclusion and also added a surrealistic abstractness to the main negotiations. And a bullying tone crept into his presentations, indicating that he thought Hanoi was gaining the upper hand psychologically.

Le Duc Tho's "concessions" were of a peculiar kind. On the first day he had reneged on nine of the twelve changes he had agreed to in November, he now gave back six; he also dropped the crucial demand for the release of civilian prisoners in South Vietnam (which Hanoi had conceded in late October and reneged on in November). On the other hand, he raised ominous concerns on the DMZ provision. In November, he had accepted an important change strengthening the obligation to respect the Demilitarized Zone as the demarcation line between North and South Vietnam. Le Duc Tho now wanted a sentence to the effect that North and South Vietnam would discuss the legal status of the DMZ. This had the effect, as I told Nixon, of "placing into question the whole status of the DMZ," not to mention the ban on infiltration. The number of unsettled issues in the agreement was somewhat smaller than the day before, but we had not yet recovered all the November concessions that Le Duc Tho had retracted four days earlier. I cabled Nixon that we might well achieve one or two of our minimum additions in another session, but it was also true that this was precisely where Le Duc Tho wanted us: tantalizingly close enough to an agreement to prevent us from using military force, but far enough away to maintain the pressure that might yet at the last moment achieve Hanoi's objectives of disintegrating the political structure in Saigon. I reported to Nixon:

> We can anticipate no lasting peace in the wake of a consummated agreement, but merely a shift in Hanoi's modus operandi. We will probably have little chance of maintaining the agreement without evident hair-trigger U.S. readiness, which may in fact be challenged at any time, to enforce its provisions. Thus we are now down to my original question: is it better to continue to fight on by scuttling the agreement now; or be forced to react later, vindicated by the violation of a solemnly entered agreement?

I recommended the latter course, but Le Duc Tho was rapidly draining the prospect of peace of its exhilaration.

Nixon accepted the recommendation; his reply indicated that he would prefer almost any agreement to a recess. I should seek "some" (unspecified) improvement over the October draft. The message followed a meeting at Camp David of the President, Deputy Secretary of Defense Kenneth Rush, and Admiral Moorer to review contingency plans for a step-up of military operations. Rush and Moorer agreed that the October agreement was sound and that Congress would cut off funds, certainly after June 30, if it were not implemented.

The four-and-a-half-hour session of December 8 saw Tho's continuing refusal to discuss the protocols, coupled with grudging but not quite conclusive concessions. We were now down essentially to two issues: the DMZ and American civilian technical personnel for Saigon's armed forces. Compared with what had already been settled, these could be dealt with in one session provided there was a will to do so. On this assumption, I asked Haig to return to Washington. If we settled on December 9, I wanted him ready to leave for Saigon the next morning with the Vice President to obtain Thieu's concurrence.

But Le Duc Tho proved as wily in achieving delays as he had been ferocious in producing deadlocks or, briefly, flexible in moving toward a settlement in October. A three-and-a-half-hour meeting on December 9 seemed to produce further progress. But each apparent success confirmed the sinking feeling that our interlocutor was leading us through an endless maze, for no matter what was settled, Le Duc Tho managed to keep alive at least one more issue at each session. And he always had the implementing protocols available as a stalling device, for, in their absence, the terms of the agreement were only statements of principle. And these protocols Le Duc Tho refused to discuss at all.

On this occasion, Le Duc Tho "gave" us what had already been conceded in October: the right to have American civilians service sophisticated South Vietnamese military equipment. But he hung firm on the DMZ because he knew that permitting military movement through it vitiated the ban on infiltration, which was so important a part of the agreement. He now made a claim novel in our experience with Communist negotiators. He said that the Politburo in Hanoi had overruled him when in November he had agreed to the clause that the DMZ must be respected. He was still awaiting new instructions, he said; he could go no further. It was unprecedented for a member of any Communist Politburo to claim that he had exceeded instructions. Given our knowledge of North Vietnamese procedures, it was also highly improbable.

With the DMZ issue now remaining as the principal dispute, there was still a chance that we might finish at the next meeting on Monday, December 11. But I again underestimated Le Duc Tho. The experts' meeting of the day before had gone reasonably well, though it took seven hours to conform texts that had already been agreed half a dozen times. There was a cloud on the horizon when the North Vietnamese sought to change the provision in the agreement which stated that the parties "shall strictly respect" the 1954 and 1962 Accords on Cambodia and Laos. The North Vietnamese proposed to drop the "shall," thus turning the sentence not into an obligation but into a statement of existing fact—an extremely unsettling proposition when one reflected on the over 100,000 North Vietnamese troops even then fighting in these two countries.

The happiest group in Paris was the Saigon ambassadorial delegation assigned to keep an eye on the peace process. Their only duty was to listen to my briefings each evening; their instructions were to hold fast to each of Saigon's sixty-nine changes and to listen to no compromise—clearly to test whatever Le Duc Tho had left of my emotional equilibrium. There were no compromises to discuss. The increasing depression of the American delegation caused scarcely concealed elation among the South Vietnamese.

In any event, Le Duc Tho was one step ahead of us when we met on December 11. He wanted no agreement, at least on this round. The possibility that we might give in had obviously occurred to him as well; he therefore moved decisively to escape the potentially embarrassing situation. First, he rejected signing procedures that we had assumed settled. (This was a complex arrangement by which Saigon could sign without recognizing the Communist Provisional Revolutionary Government for South Vietnam.) Next, forty-eight hours after conceding the issue of American civilian technicians assisting South Vietnamese armed forces, he insisted that this applied only to the public text of the agreement to avoid embarrassing us. He now asked for a written private understanding that our technicians would be withdrawn. He also was not yet ready to discuss any of the protocols. And his instructions on the DMZ would not arrive until the next day. Le Duc Tho, in short, made it clear that he would not settle that day, nor (given the outstanding issues) was a settlement likely on the morrow. This behavior was doubly insulting since Le Duc Tho was well aware that for the last forty-eight hours, the Vice President had been poised to leave Washington to impose a negotiated agreement on a recalcitrant ally.

All the December meetings now alternated between the Communist meeting place in Gif-sur-Yvette (the Léger house) and the elegant villa of an American businessman in Neuilly, which the American embassy had procured. Every day we sped to the appropriate site in a hair-raising motorcade with a heroic French police escort. Wooden stands had been thrown up at both places from which the assembled journalists could observe the negotiators pacing during breaks. Ironically, the grimmer the situation inside, the more cordial now was the demeanor of the North Vietnamese welcoming us and bidding us farewell outside the house; no doubt they wanted to give enough of an impression that progress was being made to forestall any military escalation on our part.

A cable I received from Haig after the December 11 meeting further clarified Washington's frame of mind. The President wanted me to stay as long as there was any hope of a settlement; to return for consultations if I judged the deadlock to be unbreakable; to recess but not to adjourn the talks; and to brief the press if he decided to resume bombing. At my request, Haig told Dobrynin about the status of our negotiations and let him know that the promised Soviet intercession was clearly ineffective. Dobrynin made ambiguously helpful noises. I briefed the Chinese ambassador to Paris, Huang Chen. He did not even pretend that Beijing was doing anything, though he could not have been friendlier. Before my next meeting with Le Duc Tho, I learned of a very tough speech by Thieu to his National Assembly that rejected once again the existing framework of negotiations.

As I think about the events of that period, I admire the courage of that dauntless South Vietnam leader who, assaulted by hundreds of thousands of enemy troops and pressed by his only ally, most of whose leadership groups were vilifying him, nevertheless persevered in his complicated game of maneuvering between contending necessities. He sought to demonstrate to his own people simultaneously that he was a genuine Vietnamese nationalist and not a puppet of the United States; that he was capable of providing the leadership even in peace to resist the Communist invaders (under whose rule the vast majority of the population did not wish to live); and to the world that he was not an obstacle to peace. He navigated these shoals with skill and determination, on the whole to the benefit of his people, even while he was attacking the few American leaders who had been sustaining him for four years.

Nixon armed me for the meeting of December 12 with a message to read to Le Duc Tho that contradicted his instruction of the previous day to cave in as a last resort and that showed that whatever his maneuvers, once he had analyzed the problem, Nixon would do what was right. Written in expectation of a recess, it instructed me to tell Le Duc Tho that in no circumstances would we make the wrong kind of settlement and that until there was an end to North Vietnamese intransigence, there would be no further American concessions.

On December 12, the experts, headed by Sullivan on our side and Vice Foreign Minister Nguyen Co Thach on the other, met again in the morning. The North Vietnamese still refused either to discuss our draft protocols or to give us versions of their own. Le Duc Tho had meanwhile received instructions on the DMZ. He had a proposal that omitted the phrase "civilian" from the formula for permitted movement across the DMZ. In other words,

Hanoi wanted to leave open the right of military transit through a Demilitarized Zone—one of the neater tricks of diplomacy, and one that raised even further doubts about the ban on infiltration. To balance matters, Tho finally produced protocols for the cease-fire and international control machinery. He informed me that he had decided to leave Paris for Hanoi on Thursday, December 14, taking four or five days to get there. He would not be able to , settle unless he could personally convert the recalcitrants in the Politburo who were constantly giving him a hard time, especially on the DMZ. He offered to return if necessary, but thought we could settle the remaining issues by an exchange of messages—a patent absurdity given the many technical details still requiring attention. The idea of a pacific Tho constrained by his bellicose peers from making concessions was mind-boggling, but it served Tho's purpose of stalling without (he hoped) giving us an excuse to retaliate. Le Duc Tho agreed to meet once again the next day and to review the conclusions of the experts who would be at last reviewing the protocols.

Overnight we studied the North Vietnamese drafts of the protocols. They were "outrageous," as I reported to Nixon. The one spelling out the size, composition, and functions of the International Commission of Control and Supervision (ICCS) left the supervisory machinery subject to so many multiple vetos that it was inconceivable how it could possibly inspect anything. In case a loophole had been left unintentionally, the number of ICCS inspectors would be limited to 250, including support personnel, to inspect infiltration across 700 miles of jungle and an even longer shoreline. Hanoi's draft foresaw that the two-party Joint Military Commission (consisting of the Vietcong and Saigon), conceived as having primarily liaison function, would be as strong as the international inspection machinery was weak. This body was to have subgroups down to the district level, thus intruding a Communist presence into every area of South Vietnam in the guise of liaison machinery. I explained our objection sarcastically to Le Duc Tho the next day:

> We feel that your draft exaggerates the traditional Vietnamese hospitality to a point where these [ICCS] teams will find it almost impossible to observe anything, finding themselves surrounded as they are by their Vietnamese hosts at every moment. [Laughter.] As we analyze it, there are about four times as many liaison officers as there are Commission members, and Westerners not used to your

standards of hospitality may confuse it with being taken prisoner. [Laughter.] So I believe that some greater possibility for initiative should be given to these members. Secondly, as we understand your draft—and I am afraid we understand it—it provides for all communications and support of the Commission to be furnished by the party in whose area the Commission operates. Now the Special Adviser has already pointed out that they may have to move by buffalo cart. But our basic concern is the purposes of the Commission, and its incentive to find violations may be higher than that of the party committing the violation. And you have set it up not only that the party has to agree to the investigation to begin with but that it has to supply all the communications and transportation.

The cease-fire provisions were equally absurd. They provided for the grounding of every South Vietnamese airplane and the immobilization of every military vessel in South Vietnamese waters. On the pretense of defining the cease-fire, Hanoi proposed to deprive the South Vietnamese of any capacity for self-defense.

On December 13, the negotiation finally exploded. It was the first meeting with Le Duc Tho attended by the head of our delegation to the peace talks, Ambassador William Porter. It made him yearn for the calmer if equally sterile atmosphere of the plenary sessions. That morning the language experts had met again to ensure that both sides were working from the same texts of what had been agreed. Whereas earlier experts' meetings had been more or less businesslike, in this meeting, the North Vietnamese threw in seventeen brand-new gratuitous phrases which in effect reintroduced earlier North Vietnamese demands that had been dropped by Le Duc Tho in his talks with me ostensibly for the purpose of linguistic clarification.

I reported to Nixon:

> I have come to the following conclusion. Hanoi has decided to play for time, either because of the public split between us and Saigon; or because they have a pipeline into the South Vietnamese and know about our exchanges; or because their leadership is divided and they are still making up their minds on whether to conclude the agreement. Their consistent pattern is to give us just enough each day to keep us going but nothing decisive which could conclude an agree-

ment. On the other hand, they wish to insure that we have no solid pretext for taking tough actions. They keep matters low-key to prevent a resumption of bombing. They could have settled in three hours any time these past few days if they wanted to, but they have deliberately avoided this. . . .

They have reduced the issues to a point where a settlement can be reached with one exchange of telegrams. I do not think they will send this telegram, however, in the absence of strong pressures.

I concluded the December 13 meeting with a warning to Le Duc Tho of the growing impatience in Washington. We agreed to tell the press we would stay in contact about when to meet again. Experts from both sides would continue to meet on the protocols.

It was a somber trip back to Washington. No VIP aircraft being available, we had to use an airborne command post. It was an uncomfortable and noisy plane, with no windows, crammed with communications equipment—none of which, it turned out, could be made to communicate with the White House. Encapsuled in that gloomy cocoon, cut off from the world practically and symbolically, we could reflect on the ups and downs of the past two months. We had been negotiating for ten days on matters that with any goodwill could have been settled in two. Hanoi had quite simply decided that the split between Washington and Saigon, the evident divisions within our government, and the imminent return of a Congress even more hostile to the administration than its predecessor provided too good an opportunity to pass up. Hanoi, recently so eager for a settlement, had returned to its previous tactic of psychological warfare. There was no intractable substantive issue separating the two sides, but rather an apparent North Vietnamese determination not to allow the agreement to be completed. This was the dilemma which Nixon decided to resolve with the so-called Christmas bombing five days later.

The Christmas Bombing

My description of the December negotiations can leave little doubt that Hanoi had in effect made a strategic decision to prolong the war, abort all negotiations, and at the last moment seek unconditional victory once again. Nixon and I returned with the utmost reluctance to the consideration of military actions.

For me, December 1972 was a melancholy period. Whatever happened now, it was likely that the end of the war would parallel the conduct of it in divisiveness. If we took no decisive step, the two Vietnamese parties would drift further apart; the brief near-agreement of October would unravel; we would not again be able to get such terms except through military exertion of a scale and duration which Congress and the public would never sustain or which, if they did, would tear our country apart. We could, in my view, overcome the dilemma only by an immediate showdown simultaneously with both Hanoi and Saigon.

During the December round of negotiations, I had tried to impress on Nixon that a breakup (or a recess) would oblige us to step up military pressures on Hanoi if we did not want either an endless war or an unenforceable peace likely to wreck Saigon. Preoccupied with the negotiations, I had no time to think through what kind of military measures I would recommend when the time came. Haig had requested planning papers from the NSC staff that concentrated mostly on lifting our self-imposed bombing restrictions of the previous October; in other words, to confine B-52s to south of the 20th parallel and to attack the populated areas with fighter-bombers. I made no specific recommendation from Paris.

Nixon's attitude was more complex. Though I frequently received bellicose-sounding general instructions intended to be read to the North Vietnamese, operational recommendations were much softer. I was told to keep on negotiating, which, given the situation, could only confirm the deadlock. Had Hanoi in December given us one or two compromise propositions on the DMZ or civilian technicians, Nixon would probably have accepted them. He was not anxious to resume bombing. He had a horror of appearing on television to announce that he was beginning his new mandate by once again expanding the war.

But Hanoi had become overconfident. Encouraged by the evident discord between Washington and Saigon, anticipating that the new Congress would cut off funds in January, the North Vietnamese thought that they could make us cave in and demoralize Saigon. The North Vietnamese committed a cardinal error in dealing with Nixon: They cornered him. Nixon was never more dangerous than when he seemed to have run out of options.

He was determined not to have his second term tormented like the first by our national trauma—especially when a settlement had seemed so near.

There was another person not quite of the inner circle but getting ever closer to it who played a significant role: my deputy Al Haig, who was soon to be promoted to Vice Chief of Staff of the Army. He had originally supported the negotiations and had played a significant role in the drafting of the October agreement. But he had become more skeptical as Thieu balked and Hanoi stalled. The December round had convinced him that only massive military pressure could overcome Hanoi's disdainful obstruction. He favored large-scale B-52 raids in the North and made these views clear to me at Andrews Air Force Base on Wednesday evening, December 13, on my return from Paris.

Nixon, Haig, and I met on the morning of December 14 to consider the best course of action. We were agreed that if we did nothing, we would wind up in effect prisoners of whatever maneuver Hanoi might choose to inflict on us. There was no reason to expect Hanoi to change its tactics if talks did resume in January. Pressures on us to settle for the October draft would mount. That, of course, was precisely the reason for Hanoi's contemptuous behavior. Saigon, for its part, would see no point in flexibility; with Congress heading for a cutoff of funds, it would run no additional risks by sticking to its course. And given the President's reluctance to explain his case personally to the public, this was bound to erode whatever popular support was left. While I was on the way back from Paris, Laird had sent a memorandum to Nixon opposing a military response; he claimed to be supported in this judgment by Rush and Moorer. Haig, checking with Moorer, found that the Chairman considered his views "misunderstood."

All of us at the December 14 Oval Office meeting agreed that some military response was necessary. But we were not at first in accord about what kind, and it is difficult to reconstruct now because there seem to be no written records. Nixon remembers that I urged intensified bombing south of the 20th parallel and in southern Laos[3] but no bombing at all in the populated areas. I have no such recollection; my memory is that I favored resuming bombing on the scale of that before the October self-imposed restrictions, using fighter-bombers over the Hanoi-Haiphong areas because their greater accuracy involved a smaller risk of civilian casualties. Haig, on the other hand, favored B-52 attacks, especially north of the 20th parallel, on the ground that only a massive shock could bring Hanoi back to the conference table. Nixon accepted Haig's view. I went along with it—at first with reluctance, later with conviction. For Nixon and Haig were essentially right. We had only two choices: a massive, shocking step to end the war quickly, or letting matters drift into another round of inconclusive negotiations, prolonged warfare, bitter national divisions, and mounting casualties. There were no other options.

Nixon chose the road of forcing a conclusion—resuming heavy bombing and using B-52s on a sustained basis for the first time over the northern part of North Vietnam. The choice of B-52s was partly for shock effect but also because most of our fighter-bombers had no all-weather capability. About half our planned missions over North Vietnam to resist Hanoi's offensive in the summer of 1972 were aborted because of weather. Moorer estimated that weather difficulties would be even worse in December. (As it turned out, during the two-week period that B-52s were used over North Vietnam, there were only twelve hours when fighter-bombers could have operated.) Nixon reasoned, correctly, that he would pay a serious domestic price for lifting the self-imposed bombing restrictions, but it would become unmanageable only if he failed. He preferred a massive brief effort to a prolonged inconclusive one.

Later there were stories of a rift between Nixon and me over the use of B-52s. They were false. The fact is that I had repeatedly recommended stepping up military pressure if the talks failed. What I had in mind was the previous scale of bombing. But I was persuaded by Nixon's and Haig's arguments regarding the use of B-52s and concurred once Nixon had made the decision. I implemented it with pain and regret over the receding prospects of peace, but without hesitation, as the best of difficult alternatives.

The necessity of military measures was being powerfully reinforced in our mind every day by the conduct of the North Vietnamese at the experts' meetings continuing in Paris. Sullivan had stayed behind to negotiate on the protocols concerning the release of POWs, psychologically perhaps the most important documents for us. The North Vietnamese stalled all day on December 14; they finally submitted a Vietnamese-language text too late in the day to permit any negotiation. Their draft followed the pattern of the previous sessions of putting back into the protocols objectionable clauses Le Duc Tho had agreed to delete from the basic agreement. Thus the release of South Vietnamese civilian detainees appeared once again as a specific obligation, after having been dropped by Le Duc Tho on at least three previous occasions, the last time five days earlier. Sullivan reported sarcastically: "We expect to receive an English language text of this horror when we meet at Gif tomorrow and will transmit it immediately through this channel. At Gif, we will make a great effort" (Tho's code phrase).

Sullivan then returned to Washington, and Ambassador William Porter, head of our Paris peace delegation, was left to negotiate with Xuan Thuy on both protocols and understandings. They met on December 16; Xuan Thuy carried Le Duc Tho's arrogance to new heights. Instead of stalling on substance, he refused to discuss it with respect to any subject, on the Catch-22 pretext that he could not discuss any of the outstanding problems until he had dealt with all of them. (And of course he could not deal with *all* of them except by addressing the parts.)

This was the context in which I stepped into the White House press room on December 16 to explain the stalemated negotiations. I had been given detailed guidance by Nixon, who had sent me two personal memoranda on December 15 and December 16; the first took up five, the second two single-spaced pages. Their essence was that I should not try to defend the October 26 "peace is at hand" briefing; there were various subtle digs blaming that briefing for our difficulties. Nixon's advice was to stress the President's consistency, firmness, and farsightedness in carrying us through this difficult period.

The aim of the briefing was to place the blame where it belonged—on Hanoi—and again to leave no doubt in Saigon of our determination to conclude the agreement and our willingness to enforce it once concluded. I explained the reasons for the breakdown in some detail, stressing that Hanoi had raised one frivolous issue after another. "We will not be blackmailed into an agreement," I said. "We will not be stampeded into an agreement, and, if I may say so, we will not be charmed into an agreement until its conditions are right." Again I had two principal audiences—Hanoi and Saigon—but I also knew the hopes of the American people were riding on the outcome of the present impasse:

> So, we are in a position where peace can be near, but peace requires a decision. This is why we wanted to restate once more what our basic attitude is.
>
> With respect to Saigon, we have sympathy and compassion for the anguish of their people and for the concerns of their government.

But if we can get an agreement that the President considers just, we will proceed with it.

With respect to Hanoi, our basic objective was stated in the press conference of October 26th. We want an end to the war that is something more than an armistice. We want to move from hostility to normalization and from normalization to cooperation. But we will not make a settlement which is a disguised form of continued warfare and which brings about, by indirection, what we have always said we would not tolerate.

The first reaction by the media was measured and balanced if not overly generous. Few neglected to contrast it to my earlier "peace is at hand" statement. They now had another word to play with; I had said that I was speaking to avoid a "charade." The *Baltimore Sun* of December 18 titled an editorial: "End of the Vietnam 'Charade' "; the *Washington Post* ("The Great Peace Charade," December 19) concluded that at a minimum the administration had been "taken for a long hard ride by the North Vietnamese." The *New York Times* of the same date was more explicit, heading its editorial "Deception or Naivete?" and on the whole leaning to the former interpretation of the administration's motivation.

Questions such as these were rapidly submerged in mounting rage over the bombing that resumed on December 18 and lasted for twelve days, the so-called Christmas bombing. The *Christian Science Monitor* of December 20 expressed the common view that bombs not having worked before, they could not possibly lead to results now. The *St. Louis Post-Dispatch* of December 19 urged us to drop the "contemptible" President Thieu of South Vietnam and urged Congress to legislate us out of the war.

The moral indignation rose with each day. The proposition that the United States government was deliberately slaughtering civilians in a purposeless campaign of terror went unchallenged. Charges of immorality and deception were thrown around with abandon; "barbaric" was a favorite adjective. It seemed to be taken for granted that North Vietnam was blameless and that we were embarked on a course of exterminating civilians.

Congressional criticism, though more muted, was also mounting and bipartisan. Democratic Senator Muskie called the bombing "disastrous" and said he would "demand an explanation." Republican Senator Javits threatened a cutoff of funds, warning that White House freedom of action was measured in weeks; Republican Senator William Saxbe suggested that Nixon appeared to have "taken leave of his senses." Senate Majority Leader Mansfield called it "a Stone Age tactic" and promised to introduce legislation for a terminal date of the war. Representative Lester Wolff echoed the sentiment. "Monstrous outrage," said Representative Don Riegle. There was no doubt anymore that Congress would move rapidly toward a cutoff in aid.

Foreign criticism based on the same assumptions was equally vocal. The Swedish government compared the Nixon administration with the Nazis. The Danish, Finnish, Dutch, and Belgian governments castigated the alleged bombing of cities. The French Foreign Minister made allusively critical comments. Not one NATO ally supported us or even hinted at understanding our point of view—especially painful from countries who were basing their own defenses on a strategy involving massive American attacks on civilian targets. Interestingly, Beijing and Moscow, while critical, were more restrained. In Beijing, a Foreign Ministry statement and a commentary from the New China News Agency denounced the "new barbarous crime" because the bombings had occurred just when "the talks were about to enter their final stage"—a far cry from the allegations rampant in the West that the negotiation was a fraud. Moscow, too, in its formalistic denunciations, emphasized the need to conclude the agreement. If our tea-leaf reading was correct, Moscow and Beijing were telling Hanoi that it would not be able to use our bombing to extract another open-ended commitment for continued warfare.

"Indiscriminate carpet bombing of heavily populated areas" was the principal accusation. Once the phrase caught on among commentators, it took on a life of its own. The facts were otherwise. The targets were airports, antiaircraft defenses, industrial plants. As it happened, most of these were on the other side of the Red River from Hanoi's residential areas. There was next to no damage in Hanoi proper except that caused by a few stray bombs. The atrocity picture of the burning Swedish hospital widely used at the time in television coverage—and still occasionally shown in retrospectives— neglected to mention that it stood at the edge of a runway at the principal airport on the far side of the Red River.

A respected scholar who examined the evidence wrote:

> The North Vietnamese themselves at the time claimed between 1,300 and 1,600 fatalities, and even though both Hanoi and Haiphong were partially evacuated, such a number of victims—re-

grettable as any civilian casualties always are—is surely not indicative of terror-bombing. Attacks explicitly aimed at the morale of the population took place against Germany and Japan during World War II and killed tens of thousands. According to an East German estimate, 35,000 died in the raid on Dresden in February 1945; the official casualty toll of the bombing of Tokyo with incendiaries on 9–10 March 1945, stands at 83,793 dead and 40,918 wounded. The Hanoi death toll, wrote the London *Economist,* "is smaller than the number of civilians killed by the North Vietnamese in their artillery bombardment of An Loc in April or the toll of refugees ambushed when trying to escape from Quang Tri at the beginning of May. This is what makes the denunciation of Mr. Nixon as another Hitler sound so unreal." Part of the death toll was undoubtedly caused by the North Vietnamese themselves, for they launched about 1,000 SAMs, some of which impacted in the cities of Hanoi and Haiphong and took a toll on their own people. . . .

Malcolm W. Browne of the *New York Times* was greatly surprised by the condition in which he found Hanoi and wrote that "the damage caused by American bombing was grossly overstated by North Vietnamese propaganda. . . ." "Hanoi has certainly been damaged," noted Peter Ward of the *Baltimore Sun* on 25 March 1973 after a visit, "but evidence on the ground disproves charges of indiscriminate bombing. Several bomb loads obviously went astray into civilian residential areas, but damage there is minor, compared to the total destruction of selected targets." [4]

Negotiations Resume

The prediction that the bombing was destroying all prospects for negotiation was as common and as false as the accusation that it was a massacre of civilians. Exactly the opposite happened. On the morning of December 18, coincident with the resumption of bombing, we sent a message to Hanoi accusing North Vietnam of "deliberately and frivolously delaying the talks." We proposed both a solution to the negotiating impasse and a date for resuming talks. We suggested returning to the text as it stood at the end of the first round of resumed negotiations on November 23, including the changes to which Le Duc Tho had agreed, and retaining from the December round the deletion of the phrase "administrative structure" and the proposed signing procedures. I would be prepared to meet Le Duc Tho anytime after December 26.

The first North Vietnamese reaction to the resumed bombing surfaced on December 20 at the technical meetings in Paris where Heyward Isham (sitting in for Porter, who had influenza) was still trying futilely to make progress on the protocols with Hanoi's Vice Foreign Minister Nguyen Co Thach. Thach read a protest that by Hanoi's standards was extremely mild. He "firmly" rejected the allegation of frivolity and adjourned the technical meeting to December 23, a minimum gesture under the circumstances.

On December 22, we used Thach's protest as the occasion for another message to Hanoi. We did not back off; we added the charge of misrepresentation to that of frivolity. Matters had reached a watershed, and we therefore proposed another meeting—this time under a deadline:

> The choice is whether to slide into a continuation of the conflict or to make a serious final effort to reach a settlement at a time when agreement is so near. The U.S. side, preferring the latter course, proposes a meeting between Special Adviser Le Duc Tho and Dr. Kissinger January 3, 1973—Dr. Kissinger could set aside three days for the purpose of concluding the settlement.

If Hanoi agreed to a meeting on these terms, we said that bombing north of the 20th parallel would stop as of midnight December 31 for the duration of the negotiations.

Thach showed up as promised at the December 23 meeting of the experts; he read another protest and called for another adjournment, this time not setting a new date but inviting us to propose one—a minimal "escalation" of protest, dramatically revealing Hanoi's reluctance to be charged with breaking off the talks.

On December 26—the day of one of the biggest B-52 raids—we heard directly from Hanoi. It rejected the "ultimatum language" of our previous message—while accepting its terms. It went on for a few pages, summarizing its version of events since October in—for Hanoi—a nonpolemic manner. It then agreed that talks between experts could resume as soon as the bombing stopped. It pleaded that Le Duc Tho could not attend a meeting before January 8—because of his health. Hanoi affirmed "its constantly serious negotiating attitude" and its willingness "to settle the remaining questions with the U.S. side." We had not heard such a polite tone from the North Vietnamese since the middle of October.

I informed Nixon, who was in Key Biscayne. He wanted to make sure we would stay one jump ahead of the returning Congress. He therefore pressed for an announcement of resumed meetings at the same time as the ending of the bombing. I suggested that we, first, demand that the experts resume meetings on January 2; second, reaffirm our proposal of December 18; and third, insist on limiting my meeting with Le Duc Tho to three or four days. We would continue bombing until we had received a reply from Hanoi. Nixon agreed.

How eager Hanoi was for a bombing halt was shown the next day, when we received another message expressing readiness to resume technical talks as soon as bombing stopped and reaffirming Le Duc Tho's willingness to meet me on January 8.

We replied on December 27, stating the conditions I had outlined to Nixon: Technical meetings would have to resume on January 2; Le Duc Tho and I would meet on January 8; a time limit would be set on the talks. We warned against introducing into the protocols "matters adequately covered by the basic agreement." The resumed negotiations would be announced coincident with the end of the bombing. In order to give Hanoi the maximum incentive to reply speedily (and to meet Nixon's cherished aim of announcing the resumption of negotiations before the return of Congress on January 3), we offered to stop bombing within thirty-six hours of receiving the final confirmation of these procedures.

Hanoi's reply took less than twenty-four hours—an amazing feat considering the time needed for transmission to and from Paris and the time differences. On December 28, it confirmed our proposals as well as its "constantly serious negotiating attitude."

The next day, we told Hanoi we were stopping the bombing north of the 20th parallel as of 7:00 P.M. Washington time. The announcement was made on December 30. We had won our bet.

No foreign policy event of the Nixon presidency evoked such outrage as the Christmas bombing. On no issue was he treated more one-sidedly. It was not a barbarous act of revenge. It did not cause large civilian casualties by

Hanoi's own almost surely exaggerated figures; it cost much less than would have the continuation of the war, which was the alternative. A decade of frustration with Vietnam and a generation of hostility to Nixon coalesced to produce a unanimity of media outrage that suppressed all judgment in an emotional orgy. Any other course would almost certainly have witnessed an endless repetition of the tactics of December. Faced with the prospect of an open-ended war and continued bitter divisions, Nixon chose the only weapon he had available. His decision speeded the end of the war and saved lives.

There remained the recalcitrant ally in Saigon. On December 17, Nixon had asked me to prepare a draft letter for General Haig to deliver on another mission to Saigon: "I don't want him to take any heart from the fact that we are hitting Hanoi . . ."

I submitted a very firm draft to Nixon. Nixon toughened it nearly to the point of brutality. The letter was his "final" considered judgment; it was his "irrevocable" decision to proceed; he did not want Thieu "under any circumstances" to gain the mistaken impression that the military actions against Hanoi signaled a "willingness or intent to continue U.S. military involvement if Hanoi meets the requirements for a settlement which I have set." Nixon drafted the final sentence in his own hand:

> I have asked General Haig to obtain your answer to this absolutely final offer on my part for us to work together in seeking a settlement along the lines I have approved or to go our separate ways. Let me emphasize in conclusion that General Haig is not coming to Saigon for the purpose of negotiating with you. The time has come for us to present a united front in negotiating with our enemies, and you must decide now whether you desire to continue our alliance or whether you want me to seek a settlement with the enemy which serves U.S. interests alone.

Haig flew to Saigon and met with Thieu on December 19. Haig had sent a message beforehand insisting on a private meeting with Thieu and refusing to meet with his entire National Security Council. Whatever one's views of Thieu's attitude, one had to admire his courage. Nha attended with Thieu; Bunker accompanied Haig. Thieu orchestrated a replay of the previous dramas. He listened to Haig and commented perceptively. He said (correctly) that Haig's mission came down to a negotiation for continued American support. He predicted that after all American forces were withdrawn, Hanoi would resume its guerrilla warfare, keeping its provocation below the level that would justify American retaliation (which also proved to be totally correct). He characterized Nixon's letter as an ultimatum and promised a reply for the next day.

In the meantime, Haig visited Lon Nol, who expressed confidence as long as the North Vietnamese kept to the agreement and withdrew their forces from his country. He reaffirmed his willingness to offer a unilateral cease-fire designed to put the onus for continuing the war on the Khmer Rouge.

The next day, December 20, Haig cabled: "I am delighted to join the same club that you were initiated into in October." He had had a tentative appointment with Thieu for 11:00 A.M. It was canceled, and Haig was asked to stand by. At 3:30, he was finally received and handed a letter that looked to us like a rejection of Nixon's proposal. Thieu withdrew his objections to the political provisions, but he could not accept the continued presence of North Vietnamese forces in the South. Haig and I both recommended to Nixon that we proceed with the negotiations with Hanoi anyway. If Thieu still refused to come along, we would make a bilateral agreement with North Vietnam to withdraw in return for our prisoners. I believe now that Thieu's message was more subtle than we gave him credit for. At no point did his letter say he would refuse to sign an agreement. He rejected what he considered—correctly—a derogation of his sovereignty; he was willing to yield to *force majeure,* but not become part of it. From his point of view, he was right; and he was in effect giving us—though we did not understand it—the go-ahead for the final act.

The January Round of Negotiations

The renewed negotiations started inauspiciously. On January 2, 1973, the majority House Democratic caucus voted 154 to 75 to cut off all funds for Indochina military operations contingent only upon the safe withdrawal of American forces and the release of our prisoners. There was no provision for a cease-fire for any of the countries of Indochina, including

Vietnam, nor for respecting the maintenance of the DMZ, nor for an end to infiltration, nor for any supervisory machinery, nor for continued military and economic assistance. Congress was threatening to abandon *all* our allies in Indochina. On January 4, the Senate Democratic caucus passed a similar resolution by 36 to 12. It was a measure of the extremity in which Hanoi found itself that it proceeded with the negotiations, even in the face of the imminent congressional cutoff of aid to Vietnam.

The technical talks on the protocols reconvened on January 2, chaired by William Sullivan on the American side and Vice Foreign Minister Nguyen Co Thach for Hanoi. The mood at the outset was "deeply somber," Sullivan reported, but eventually the two teams got down to business. Over the next few days, Thach and Sullivan settled four contentious issues, leaving four others to me and Le Duc Tho. All of this was mildly encouraging. Obviously Hanoi would not show its full hand until Le Duc Tho was on the scene.

On January 4, Nixon met with Rogers, Moorer, Laird, and me. Most of the time was spent on a briefing by Laird and Moorer on the recent bombing, using pictures that showed the success of "smart bombs" against military targets. The rest concerned public relations, with each participant riding his own hobbyhorse: Nixon stressed the hypocrisy and double standard of the media, especially the TV networks; Laird wanted to talk about bombing results; Rogers was looking for material for congressional briefings; I urged that everyone should avoid statements of eagerness that might undermine a negotiation about which I was now quite optimistic.

On January 5, there was another exchange of letters between Nixon and Thieu. Thieu replied evasively, on January 7, urging Nixon to instruct me to put forward his concerns and stopping far short of endorsing our program. On the other hand, he did not say he would refuse to sign.

On January 6, Nixon and I met at Camp David to review final strategy. He urged me to settle on whatever terms were available. Belying his image-makers, he even said he would settle for the October terms. I demurred, pointing out that whatever their merit—and I thought them adequate—the October terms would now inevitably lead to Saigon's collapse. The South Vietnamese had to have something to show for their confrontations with Hanoi and Washington. At any rate, I was sure it would not come to that. The same day, Le Duc Tho arrived in Paris, issuing a bloodcurdling statement whose apparent intransigence actually enhanced our optimism. Tho announced grandly that he had come to Paris to make a "final" effort for a "rapid" settlement. Since this was the precise condition under which we had agreed to resume negotiations, he was simply putting as an ultimatum what we had insisted on as a precondition. He also adamantly rejected any "unreasonable" changes in the October draft, leaving open the door for "reasonable" changes.

And so on January 8, Le Duc Tho and I met again at Gif-sur-Yvette for what we both had promised would be our last round of negotiations. On the surface, nothing had changed; it was like a movie that had been restarted after the film had broken. The ubiquitous journalists were perched on their improvised bleachers, and there was the same confusion between appearance and reality. In December, when he was stalling, in order to place the onus for the deadlock on me, Le Duc Tho had been ostentatiously cordial with me in sight of journalists while being obnoxious at the conference table. Now, to play to the media's outrage at the bombing, he avoided any joint public handshakes with me. In fact, no Vietnamese appeared to greet me at the door. It was simply opened from the inside by an unseen factotum. All this evoked many media stories of a chilly atmosphere after our bombing. In fact, relations on the inside, out of sight of the press, were rather warm. All the North Vietnamese were lined up to greet us. Le Duc Tho was brisk and businesslike on the first day, escalating the cordiality when we began to approach agreement.

The first day's meeting, lasting four and a half hours, was inconclusive. Tho condemned our bombing along standard lines and in a perfunctory manner; the tone was much milder than his airport statement. After my brief rebuttal, we got into a procedural wrangle about which issues remained to be settled. Both sides having restated their proposals, we adjourned. Though obviously not yet prepared to reveal how far he was willing to go, Le Duc Tho took pains to foreshadow flexibility. As the meeting broke up, he stressed that he would take our requirements into account when speaking the next day— something we had never heard before. (During the lunch break, he had taken me aside to stress again that he was having difficulty with his colleagues in the Politburo who thought him too flexible. If this was true, it was beyond my imagination what his hard-line colleagues might be like.)

The breakthrough came at the next session on January 9. As in December, the meetings now alternated between a Vietnamese and an American location. Colonel Guay had discovered the residence of an American businessman located on a golf course in Saint-Nom-la-Bretèche, not too far from Versailles. There, in verdant surroundings where we could stroll in relative tranquility during breaks, it quickly became apparent that Tho had come to settle. He proposed that Thach and Sullivan be assigned to work full-time on the protocols and not participate in our main talks. I agreed. He then said:

> In order to prove our seriousness and good will to find a rapid solution, we should adequately take into account each other's attitude. Naturally, there should be mutual concession and there should be reciprocity. If one keeps one's own stand then no settlement is possible. Do you agree with me on these lines?

In fact, my goodwill was scarcely tested, for Le Duc Tho in effect accepted our proposal of December 18. He agreed to the draft as it stood on November 23 at the end of the first session after the election, including the twelve changes he had conceded during that session. He agreed to our formulation on the Demilitarized Zone, which he had adamantly rejected in December. It was Nixon's sixtieth birthday. I reported to Washington:

> We celebrated the President's birthday today by making a major breakthrough in the negotiations. In sum, we settled all the outstanding questions in the text of the agreement, made major progress on the method of signing the agreement, and made a constructive beginning on the associated understandings. . . .
>
> The Vietnamese have broken our heart several times before, and we just cannot assume success until everything is pinned down, but the mood and the businesslike approach was as close to October as we have seen since October.

Nixon flashed back: "I greatly appreciated your birthday greetings and your report. . . . If the other side stays on this track and doesn't go downhill tomorrow, what you have done today is the best birthday present I have had in sixty years."

Great events rarely have a dramatic conclusion. More frequently, they dissolve into a host of technical details. So it was in Paris in January. After the DMZ issue was settled, there remained primarily the theological issue of how to sign the documents so that Saigon did not have to acknowledge the Communist-front Provisional Revolutionary Government. After several days of haggling, we devised a formula according to which the PRG was not mentioned in the document; the agreement to end the war in Vietnam has the distinction of being the only document with which I am familiar that does not mention all of the main parties. Nor was it signed on the same page by the parties making peace. The South Vietnamese Communists signed together with Hanoi on one page, Saigon and the United States on another. The negotiations had begun in 1968 with a haggle over the shape of the table; they ended in 1973 with a haggle, in effect, over the same problem.

Once the deadlock was broken, the tension all but vanished. Barring a sudden change in signals from Hanoi, a settlement was now inevitable, and Le Duc Tho held course. He now agreed that Hanoi would bring about a cease-fire in Laos within fifteen days of the Vietnam cease-fire. Only Cambodia had to be satisfied with verbal assurances. Le Duc Tho repeated Hanoi's difficulty with the Khmer Rouge:

> I told you on many occasions that we want peace, we want peace in Vietnam and in Laos, and after peace is restored in Vietnam and in Laos we also want peace to be restored in Cambodia. Therefore I told you that when peace is restored in Vietnam then the objective conditions, partly, and our subjective desire on our part, will contribute to the peace in Cambodia. But practically speaking, when discussing with our allies in Cambodia it is not as easy as when we discuss with our allies in Laos. But I am firmly convinced that the restoration of peace in Vietnam and in Laos will create favorable conditions for the restoration of peace in Cambodia, some objective conditions for that. But as far as we are concerned when we have a peace in Vietnam and when our allies in Laos have peace in their country, it is illogical that we still want war in another place.

As we approached a conclusion, there was no longer in our group the elation which accompanied the breakthrough in October. The December negotiations had brought home to us the abiding mutual hatred of the two Vietnams. We knew that a bitter struggle with Thieu still lay ahead. We had learned how thin was the veneer of affability of Hanoi's leadership, whose single-minded quest for hegemony, we were certain, would continue after a settlement.

My colleagues and I—Bill Sullivan, Winston Lord, John Negroponte, David Engel, and Peter Rodman, joined toward the end by George Aldrich, Deputy Legal Adviser at the State Department—worked fifteen hours a day in negotiating sessions, reviewing drafts, briefing the South Vietnamese, exchanging cables with Washington. It was agreed that Haig would leave for Saigon within twenty-four hours after we completed all texts in Paris. Within forty-eight hours, all bombing of the North would stop. About January 18, it would be announced that I would return to Paris around January 23 to complete the agreement. The White House, liberated from the nightmare of failure, turned with a will to the public relations scenario. Frantic cables went back and forth; inauguration festivities complicated the problem of finding a time for an announcement both pregnant with meaning and sufficiently low-key not to tempt the North Vietnamese into another fit of stonewalling. Saigon perversely solved the problem by withholding its concurrence until January 20; Nixon judged wisely that he should not risk the prestige of the presidency until all parties were irrevocably signed up.

At last on Saturday, January 13, at the American venue for meetings in Saint-Nom-la-Bretèche, the draft agreement was once again complete, together with all understandings and protocols. The two delegations had never had any social contact except for brief bantering during breaks. In the first meetings, little food was served. Afterward each delegation served meals at its place but in separate dining facilities, even for the Thanksgiving dinner. On January 13, 1973, we ate for the first time as a group. Vietnamese and Americans sat alternately around the table. Tho and I made toasts to a lasting peace and friendship between our peoples.

In the negotiations since November 20, a number of changes had been achieved. The provision for continued military support for Saigon had been expanded to permit in effect unrestricted military assistance. The phrase "administrative structure" to describe the National Council of National Reconciliation and Concord had been dropped, underlining its advisory role. The functions of the council had been further reduced, by taking away from it any role in "the maintenance of the cease-fire and the preservation of peace" that had been in the earlier draft. The Demilitarized Zone was explicitly reaffirmed in the precise terms of the provisions that established it in the Geneva Accords. Military movement across it was prohibited and civilian movement allowed only with the agreement of the two Vietnamese parties giving Saigon a veto. A provision had been added that the parties undertook to refrain from using Cambodia and Laos "to encroach on the sovereignty and security of one another and of other countries." This provision prohibited the establishment of base areas and reinforced the earlier one requiring the withdrawal of foreign forces. The international control machinery, now expanded to 1,160 people, was ready to begin operating on the day the agreement was signed. A few additional technical improvements were made; all the protocols and understandings essential to implementing the agreement effectively were completed.

Was it worth it? Were the changes significant enough to justify the anguish and bitterness of those last months of the war? Probably not for us; almost surely for Saigon, about whose survival the war had, after all, been fought. Obviously, we thought the agreement of October adequate or we would not have proceeded with it. But the viability of any agreement depends on the willing cooperation of the parties. Once Thieu balked, the crises of the next two months were unavoidable. Had we attempted to impose a settlement in the last two weeks before the election, we would have been justly accused of playing politics. And it was appropriate for Saigon to play a major role in shaping an agreement as to its future. As it was, it required nearly three months, about twenty changes in the text of the agreement, and the threat of an American aid cutoff to obtain Thieu's acquiescence.

Peace involving American withdrawal was a traumatic event for the South Vietnamese. It could not be imposed on a people who for over a decade had suffered from Communist terrorism and the ravages of war. Thieu had to prepare it carefully and in such a way as to stamp himself as a Vietnamese patriot. Thieu had to inure his people to our physical absence, and he had to steel them to their psychological independence by a show of defiance. That his methods were often egregious, that in the process he nearly wrecked our own internal cohesion, does not alter the reality that he fought valiantly, that he was right by his lights and the realities of what he knew of Hanoi's purposes.

I have wrestled with the question in my own mind whether if I had dealt with Thieu in a more forthcoming way in October, the problems would have been avoided. Perhaps if I had brought him into the process earlier, he would have had one less grievance against me. But had I brought the original proposal of October 8 to Thieu, his reaction would have been no different, and since the draft was not yet improved, he would have resisted even more fiercely. Saigon's guerrilla warfare against the agreement would have started immediately; the improvements we extorted in return for accepting a "shedyule" would have evaporated. Hanoi would have published its text earlier. We would have been under enormous pressure to accept, and our bargaining position would have eroded. Hanoi's December performance would have come sooner, and we would have had no base from which to negotiate or to escalate. Paradoxically, therefore, a more deliberate pace would almost surely have produced a much worse agreement, not changed Saigon's attitude, increased our domestic division, and magnified the risk of collapse. Nailing down the agreement in October was indispensable to holding the pieces together later through what was bound to be a chaotic denouement of a bitter war.

Thieu Relents

I returned to the United States on January 13, stopping in Washington to pick up Haig for the trip to Key Biscayne.

Despite the latent tensions in my relationship with Nixon during this period—which I could deduce from the attitude of his associates and which found their way into most of their memoirs—we dealt with each other in a most cordial manner. That strange man who could be so ruthless, fierce, and devious was capable of considerable gentleness in his personal dealings. I reported to Nixon around midnight; we met for over two hours until 2:30 A.M. (it was 8:30 A.M. by my inner clock), reviewing the negotiation and the long ordeal that had brought us to this point. I felt an odd tenderness toward Nixon. He had seen our country through perilous times. He had reached his decisions by arcane processes. But when the balance sheet was drawn up, he deserved recognition for sustaining America's honor and dignity, and he had revolutionized international diplomacy. Much intelligence and knowledge lay behind his accomplishments. He was entitled in an hour of triumph to the limelight that had so pitilessly beaten down on him through all his adversities. And in this mellow mood, we reviewed where we stood and how to proceed toward the peace that was now so near. We spoke to each other in nearly affectionate terms, like veterans at a reunion, even though we both sensed that, after the end of the war, we would probably not make the rest of the journey together.

Haig would leave the next evening (January 14) for Saigon with an ultimatum that we would sign the document, if necessary, without Thieu. On January 15, the White House would announce the end of bombing; on January 18, it would be announced that I would return to Paris on January 23 to "complete the agreement." Nixon would address the nation that evening. The formal signature by foreign ministers would take place in Paris on January 27.

But we still did not have the agreement of that doughty little man in Saigon, President Thieu. Nixon was determined to prevail. "Brutality is nothing," he said to me. "You have never seen it if this son-of-a-bitch doesn't go along, believe me." Haig delivered a scorching letter from Nixon to Thieu on January 16. It summed up all the advantages of the agreement and listed the improvements which had been achieved in the November and December negotiations. Its crucial paragraph read:

> I have therefore irrevocably decided to proceed to initial the Agreement on January 23, 1973 and to sign it on January 27, 1973 in Paris. I will do so, if necessary, alone. In that case I shall have to explain publicly that your Government obstructs peace. The result will be an inevitable and immediate termination of U.S. economic and military assistance which cannot be forestalled by a change of personnel in your government. I hope, however, that after all our two countries have shared and suffered together in conflict, we will stay together to preserve peace and reap its benefits.

Haig, as instructed, demanded an answer by the evening of January 17.

But Thieu would not yield yet. He complained that the draft still lacked "balance." He now conceded that his forces would be able to handle the North Vietnamese remaining in the South; but their continued presence was a psychological challenge that he was duty-bound to resist. Haig thought, as we had so often before, that faced with the President's determination, Thieu would yield.

Thieu once again surprised us. On January 17, he handed Haig a letter to Nixon asking for one more effort to bring about some changes, this time in the protocols. But it was futile, as Thieu must have known. The texts were now frozen; no further negotiation could take place. Nixon replied the same day. The letter summed up once again all the arguments and threats of the previous message. It demanded a reply by the morning of January 20—inauguration day—when Haig would return to Saigon after having briefed the other countries of the area. Failure to answer by that time would be treated as a refusal. "The responsibility for the consequences rests with the Government of Vietnam."

On January 18, at Nixon's suggestion, Senators John Stennis and Barry Goldwater, both staunch supporters of Saigon, warned publicly that if Saigon blocked the agreement, it would imperil its relations with the United States. We heard from Thieu right on the deadline of January 20. He was sending Foreign Minister Lam to Paris, he said, to take personal charge of the final round of negotiations, almost certainly a face-saving formula indicating that he would sign. He still demanded a few textual changes, a gesture that again he must have known was only for the record. Nixon replied that he would need Thieu's agreement by noon the next day or else he would brief legislative leaders that Thieu had refused to go along, with all the attendant consequences. On January 21, Thieu relented with dignity, requesting only some unilateral statements by the United States that we recognized Saigon as the legal government of South Vietnam and that Hanoi had no right to maintain troops there. This was consistent with our interpretation of the agreement; the treaty gave no sanction to foreign troops and referred in several places to the "sovereignty of South Vietnam." We gave these assurances. And we had also given private assurances that American power would be available to resist major North Vietnamese violations—a subject I will treat in a later chapter.

I believed then, and I believe now, that the agreement could have worked. It reflected the existing equilibrium of forces on the ground. We had no illusions about Hanoi's long-term goals, as I had emphasized in several of the cables cited in this chapter. Nor did we go through the agony of four years of war and searing negotiations simply to achieve a "decent interval" for our withdrawal. We were determined to do our utmost to enable Saigon to grow in security and prosperity so that it could prevail in any political struggle. We were convinced that Saigon was left strong enough to handle the enemy forces that remained in its country; that we would resist other violations of the agreement; that we would be able to distill from the Moscow-Beijing-Washington triangle and the possibility of economic reconstruction for Indochina additional incentives for restraint. We sought not an interval before collapse, but peace with honor.

Peace at Last

R ichard Nixon's second inaugural took place on a day much like his first, cold and clear and blustery. I sat on the platform behind the Cabinet with my eighty-six-year-old father. The war would now soon be over, and hope was pervasive. Senators and Cabinet members came over to chat and to congratulate; my father, whose life's work had been destroyed when Nazism took over his native land, could barely believe that he was sitting in as an honored guest at a presidential inauguration.

There was a blare of trumpets, and Nixon appeared to the tune of "Hail to the Chief." He, too, seemed as if he could not really believe it had all happened; a term in office had not abated his sense of wonder at being there. And he seemed, if not really happy, quite detached.

Two days later, January 22, I left for Paris for the final meeting with Le Duc Tho. It was to take place for the first time on neutral and ceremonial ground in a small conference room at Avenue Kléber, the scene of 174 futile plenary sessions since 1968. Even now it would be used for only a symbolic event. Sullivan and Thach had spent several days checking all the texts. In a final paranoiac gesture, the North Vietnamese insisted that, on completion, each text be bound by string and the string sealed—to prevent the American delegation from deviously slipping in new pages overnight.

When I arrived in Paris, I learned that Lyndon Johnson had died that day. He was a casualty of the Vietnam war, which he had inherited and then expanded in striving to fulfill his conception of our nation's duty and of his obligation to his fallen predecessor. There was nothing he had wanted less than to be a war President, and this no doubt contributed to his inconclusive conduct of the struggle. In retirement, he had behaved with dignity not untinged by melancholy, burdened with the terrible truth that the only pursuit he really cared about, that of public service, was now closed to him—like a surgeon who at the height of his powers is barred forever from entering a hospital. Haldeman had phoned him on January 15 to tell him that the bombing would stop. I had sent him a copy of the peace agreement, with a warm note. It was symbolic that this hulking, imperious, vulnerable, expansive, aspiring man should die with the war that had broken his heart.

The meeting started at 9:35 A.M., Tuesday, January 23. Le Duc Tho managed even on this solemn occasion to make himself obnoxious by insisting on ironclad assurances of American economic aid to North Vietnam. I told him that this could not be discussed further until after the agreement was signed; it also depended on congressional approval and on observance of the agreement. Finally, at a quarter to one, we initialed the various texts and improvised brief closing statements.

After this, Le Duc Tho and I stepped out on the street in a cold misty rain and shook hands for the benefit of photographers. I lunched with Foreign Minister Lam of South Vietnam. He behaved with dignity and courage, giving no hint of the bitter dispute of recent months.

America's Vietnam war was over.

Postlude

On January 23, Washington was, as always before great events, consumed in technicalities. I returned to my office around 6:35 P.M. the same day, a few hours before Nixon was to announce the agreement and the cease-fire.

I sat alone in my office, waiting for Nixon's speech to the nation. It was the culmination of all we had endured and endeavored throughout four years. Over two million Americans had devoted parts of their lives to that distant land. Over 55,000 had died for it; several hundred thousand had been wounded. Their families could now take some solace that it had not all been in vain. And the peoples of South Vietnam, Laos, and Cambodia would perhaps attain at long last a future of tranquillity and security, a future worthy of their sacrifices.

Nixon spoke at 10:00 P.M. briefly and with conciliation. He paid tribute to Lyndon Johnson, who had yearned for that day, and he asked Americans to consecrate themselves to "make the peace we have achieved a peace that would last."

I called Nixon immediately afterward, as I had done after every major speech, to congratulate him. He seemed incapable of resting on any achievement. He was already worrying about the congressional briefings that would start the next day.

Mrs. Nixon took the phone to congratulate me. It took stout hearts to see it through, she said. What a gallant lady she had been. With pain and stoicism, she had suffered the calumny and hatred that seemed to follow her husband. Unlike the President, she was not capable of the fantasy life in which romantic imaginings embellished the sometimes self-inflicted daily disappointments. She was without illusions and insistent on facing her trials in solitude. Her dignity never wavered. And if she seemed remote, who could know what fires had had to be banked in her stern existence. She made no claims on anyone; her fortitude had been awesome and not a little inspiring because one sensed that it had been wrested from an essential gentleness.

Around midnight, when I was at home, Nixon called from the Lincoln Sitting Room, where he was brooding alone. He was wondering whether the media would appreciate what had been done; probably not. But that was not what he really had on his mind. He knew that every success brings a terrific letdown, he said. I should not let it get to me. I should not be discouraged. There were many battles yet to fight; I should not weaken. In fact, I was neither discouraged nor did I feel let down. Listening to him, I could picture the scene: Nixon would be sitting solitary and withdrawn, deep in his brown stuffed chair with his legs on a hassock in front of him, a small reading light breaking the darkness, and a wood fire throwing shadows on the wall of the room. The loudspeakers would be playing romantic classical music, probably Tchaikovsky. He was talking to me, but he was really addressing himself.

What extraordinary vehicles destiny selects to accomplish its design. This man, so lonely in his hour of triumph, so ungenerous in some of his motivations, had navigated our nation through one of the most anguishing periods in its history. Not by nature courageous, he had steeled himself to conspicuous acts of courage. Not normally outgoing, he had forced himself to rally his people to its challenge. He had striven for a revolution in American foreign policy so that it would overcome the disastrous oscillations between overcommitment and isolation. Despised by the Establishment, ambiguous in his human perceptions, he had yet held fast to a sense of national honor and responsibility, determined to prove that the strongest free country had no right to abdicate. What would have happened had the Establishment about which he was so ambivalent shown him some love? Would he have withdrawn deeper into the wilderness of his resentments, or would an act of grace have liberated him? By now it no longer mattered. Enveloped in an intractable solitude, at the end of a period of bitter division, he nevertheless saw before him a vista of promise to which few statesmen have been blessed to aspire. Having established a new relationship with China, eased tensions with the Soviet Union, and ended a debilitating war, he could envisage a new international order that would reduce lingering enmities, strengthen friendships, and give new hope to emerging nations. It was a worthy goal for America and mankind. He was alone in his moment of triumph on a pinnacle, which was soon to turn into a precipice. And yet with all his insecurities and flaws, he had brought America by a tremendous act of will to an extraordinary moment when dreams and possibilities conjoined.

10

A VISIT TO HANOI

O n January 24, 1973, I concluded a White House briefing on the Paris
Agreement by extending an olive branch to our critics:

> It should be clear by now that no one in this war has had a monopoly
> of anguish and that no one in these debates has had a monopoly of
> moral insight. And now that at last we have achieved an agreement in
> which the United States did not prescribe the political future to its al-
> lies, an agreement which should preserve the dignity and the self-
> respect of all the parties, together with healing the wounds in
> Indochina we can begin to heal the wounds in America.

As I was speaking, I did not realize that Watergate, the extent of which I was
still unaware of, was foreclosing the hopes for healing in the United States
while, in Vietnam, Hanoi's implacable determination to prevail was turning
the peace agreement into a brief respite before a renewed onslaught.

It did not take long for the relief of the end of the war to begin to turn
into foreboding. The date can be precisely noted: It was February 10, 1973,
when I paid my first and only visit to Hanoi. In the capital of our ferocious
adversaries who had brought war to Indochina and upheaval to America, I
intended to discuss with the North Vietnamese leaders the observance of
the Paris Agreement that I had negotiated with Le Duc Tho and, on that
basis, gauge the possibility of a more positive relationship between our two
countries.

For four years, I had read every scrap of information about the North

Vietnamese, at once so self-absorbed and so bellicose, so brave and so overbearing. What is the blend of qualities that lifts a people to dominion over
neighbors of roughly comparable endowments? What had given Rome preeminence in the world of city-states or Prussia in Germany or Britain in Europe? No doubt many physical factors were involved. But material elements
needed the impetus of intangibles of faith and dedication. These—unfortunately for us—Hanoi had in obsessive abundance.

The Vietnamese had lived through centuries of Chinese rule without losing their cultural identity, a nearly unheard-of feat. They had outlasted
French occupation, all the time nurturing the conviction that it was their
mission to inherit the French empire in Indochina. Lacking the humanity of
their Laotian neighbors and the grace of their Cambodian neighbors, they
strove for dominance by being not attractive but single-minded. So all-
encompassing was their absorption with themselves that they became oblivious to the physical odds, indifferent to the probabilities by which the
calculus of power is normally reckoned. And because there were always more
Vietnamese prepared to die for their country than foreigners, their nationalism became the scourge of invaders and neighbors alike.

More than passion, the Vietnamese had an invincible self-confidence
and a contempt for things foreign. This disdain enabled them to manipulate
other peoples—even their foreign supporters—with a cool sense of superiority, by an act of will turning their capital for over a decade into a center of international concern. What we considered insolent deception was, to them,
another definition of truth; whatever served Hanoi's purposes represented
historical necessity. Like a surgeon wielding a scalpel, Hanoi dissected the
American psyche and probed our weaknesses, our national sense of guilt, our
quest for final answers, our idealism, and even the values of its sympathizers,
whom it duped no less cold-bloodedly than its adversaries. Our misfortune
had been to get between these leaders and their obsessions.

The American Indochinese nightmare would be over; Hanoi's neighbors
were not as fortunate. Propinquity condemned them to permanent insecurity. Our relief that the war had ended was matched by their foreboding
that their freedom would end if we equated peace with withdrawal. The relief of Washington was matched by the uneasiness of those who depended
on America, which was the more intense the closer one approached the
borders of that implacable country conducting its aggressions in the guise
of victim.

We had wrung a tenuous compromise from these idealogues, but it took a greater act of faith than I was capable of to believe that they would abide willingly by an inconclusive outcome. The purpose of my journey to Hanoi in February 1973 was to encourage any tendencies that existed to favor peaceful reconstruction over continued warfare, to stabilize the peace insofar as prospects of American goodwill could do so, and to warn of the serious consequences should these hopes be disappointed.

The Boeing 707 of the presidential fleet landed at Noi Bai military air-field, about fifty miles north of Hanoi. It was a gray, misty morning. The landscape around the airport was flat and desolate, pockmarked from our B-52 bombing that had destroyed most of the buildings and cratered the runways, though they had been patched up well enough to permit the plane to come to a bouncing stop.

Le Duc Tho greeted me almost affectionately. He took me by the hand to a shabby little barracks beside the tarmac, its windows blown out. After light banter over tea, we boarded a Soviet An-24 light transport aircraft for the twenty-minute flight to Gia Lam International Airport nearer Hanoi, an-other landmark familiar to me from years of military briefings. (The 707 could not land at Gia Lam because its runways were not long enough.)

Gia Lam was heavily damaged; B-52s had scored a direct hit on its main runway. Only the front facade of the control tower was standing; one could look up through its windows and see the sky behind. We were greeted by other officials and set off in a motorcade of Soviet Volga sedans to the city. As it turned out, these were virtually the only automobiles I saw during my visit.

Both airports were on the north side of the Red River. Hanoi lay on the south side looking like a sleepy French provincial town. The river could be crossed only by pontoon bridges; the famous steel-girdered Paul Doumer (or Red River) Bridge, so frequently cited as proof of the ineffectiveness of Amer-ica's air campaign, had finally collapsed under the onslaught of the Christmas bombing.

The north side of the river was heavily cratered by U.S. bombing, resem-bling photographs of a lunar landscape. Once we reached Hanoi proper, however, the scene could not have been more peaceful. It was immediately obvious (and confirmed by surprised journalists a few weeks later)[1] that the city itself was practically undamaged by our bombing. Along the streets we traveled, the only destruction we saw was the shattered house of the French Delegate-General, hit accidentally several months earlier in the midst of our negotiations in Paris—endearing us neither to our interlocutors nor to our French hosts. Totally absent too was the frantic bustle of Saigon. A visitor from another planet would never have known that the same people inhabited both cities. Nor would he have guessed correctly which of the capitals had sent forth the invading armies that had terrified every neighbor and absorbed the world's attention—proving that faith and discipline, not material strength alone, create their own advantage.

The wide tree-lined avenues were filled with cyclists. There was an occasional Soviet-built truck but no private cars. The streets were not crowded; the authorities had not yet brought back all who had been evacuated during the previous year. The people looked solemn, serious, aloof, indifferent. How incongruously the heroic presents itself! Whatever had motivated these unprepossessing men and women to fight and endure so tenaciously was not to be read in their faces. They glanced at our motorcade with no visible interest, though its length must have made it evident that something important was taking place.

I drove into Hanoi with strange detachment. My visit was the end of a long journey, but it had no self-evident purpose. Ever since the climactic phase of the negotiation, Le Duc Tho and the Politburo had been eager for me to visit their capital. Their motive was elusive. It could not be the hunger for equal status with China, which had made Brezhnev press to receive me in Moscow after my secret visit to Beijing: Hanoi's leaders were too self-contained for that; psychological insecurity was hardly their most notable feature. Did they seek to tranquilize America before launching a new wave of conquest? It was possible, but it was a double-edged tactic. From our perspective, the demonstration that we had explored every opportunity for conciliation was a necessary condition in America for defending the Paris accords by military means if it came to that. Might Hanoi be content to rest on the frenzied exertions of a lifetime of struggle and begin meeting the needs of its people? That was what Le Duc Tho had been saying and what we were prepared to explore.

In any event, our choices were circumscribed. I had come to Hanoi in part to symbolize a commitment to national reconciliation at home—a subject of no interest to the North Vietnamese. We hoped to convince Hanoi's leaders of the futility of resuming military operations by insisting on a strict performance of the Paris accords. But deep down I knew, with a sinking feeling, that ultimately words would not impress them. Somewhere along the line we would be tested. We would have to show our mettle. At the same time, I had to attempt to provide inducements for peaceful endeavors in the shadow of two imponderables: Could Hanoi adjust its scale of values to give building its economy a higher priority than it had in all previous periods in its history? And would Congress support us?

I understood that, as the representative of a superpower, I was at a strange disadvantage in this city so devoid of all the appurtenances of modern life. America had been obsessed by Vietnam, but in the long run it was for us only a small corner of a world for whose security we had become at least partly responsible. On the other hand, the epic poem the leaders in Hanoi were acting out was their sole cause. They had the capacity to damage America out of any proportion to what we could gain, by resuming the war or their assault on American domestic tranquillity. But they could do little positive for us. They were too egotistical to think of foreign policy in terms of an international system, too arrogant to believe in goodwill, too ambitious to restrain their purposes by ideas of concord. And so I drove into Hanoi uneasily aware that the best outcome would be the avoidance of a loss and the best hope that Vietnam might recede into oblivion in our national consciousness.

I was housed in an elegant two-story guest house in the center of Hanoi that had once been the residence of the French Governor-General of Tonkin. Most of my staff stayed in the Reunification Hotel, a shabby old structure diagonally across the street, whose walls were covered with graffiti, mostly in Russian, the cultural contribution of various Soviet aid missions. Service there was based on the proposition that all foreigners were potential spies whose stay could be cut short by showing no mercy to any aspiration to elementary comfort.

Le Duc Tho accompanied me to my own room and then politely excused himself, to prepare for my first meeting with Prime Minister Pham Van Dong. Having some time, my colleagues and I decided to take a walk, much to the discomfiture of both the North Vietnamese protocol officials and my Secret Service protectors. For once, North Vietnamese pedantry deserted them. This possibility had not been foreseen; hence no instructions had been left, and the flustered guards at the gate did not impede our departure. We strolled along streets that the dearth of motor traffic made appear both old-fashioned and serene, crowded with people calmly performing their chores. Two little lakes form the center of Hanoi. We walked along them, the first American officials to move freely in Hanoi in two decades, while a few hundred yards away other Americans, our prisoners of war, still languished in a cruel captivity.* Passersby stared at us with no evident emotion. They displayed neither hostility nor friendliness, treating us as if we were some strange mutation of no possible relevance to them. In front of one of the buildings stood a huge billboard with a map showing what Hanoi's rulers were pleased to consider the "liberated areas" of the South. Though somewhat generous to Hanoi, it was not inaccurate. I wondered how the people of North Vietnam reacted to it; it was precious little to show for their twenty years of sacrifice.

We strolled back to my residence. And here North Vietnamese addiction to formal regulations took its revenge for our flirtation with the unexpected. At the gate, everyone was asked to show a pass in order to regain admittance. This was easy enough for my colleagues, who had been handed identity cards at the airport. Unfortunately, I had been given no such document. Bureaucratic rules in any totalitarian Communist state are not treated casually; in Hanoi, they were an obsession. I was refused admittance. The North Vietnamese guard had never heard of me. An officer showed up, but he too hesitated to bend the regulations. A twenty-minute argument ensued. It finally took Le Duc Tho's intervention to keep me from having to sleep in the streets. One of my staff later raised the matter with a North Vietnamese protocol official. He, nervously apologetic, explained that the head of a delegation was never given a pass; it was a mark of special status! Obviously, neither had any head of a delegation ever taken a walk. Eventually they provided me with a pass, to which I held on for dear life.

I had requested some time for sightseeing, especially of cultural sites, as I usually did in visiting a country for the first time. Le Duc Tho graciously accompanied me on these excursions. He found them quite educational since he claimed never to have seen them himself. We first visited Hanoi's History Museum, a collection of historical relics assembled mostly by the French. As reorganized by the North Vietnamese, the museum told of ancient battles against the Chinese or against smaller neighbors, great migrations and rebellions. Each artifact was labeled with its place of excavation. Le Duc Tho found the exhibits fascinating, mainly because the excavation sites reminded

---

* The Paris Agreement of January 27 provided for the release of all our POWs in stages, in parallel with the withdrawal of all U.S. troops from South Vietnam, within sixty days. The process had begun but would not be completed until March 27.

him of nearby prisons where the French had confined him as a guerrilla leader. The old revolutionary was clearly more interested in his fight to create a new culture than in celebrating an ancient one. He gave me a detailed account of the relative merits of solitary confinement in various prisons, and unhelpful hints on how to disguise myself as a Vietnamese peasant.

Pham Van Dong

A s we turned to serious talks, we soon found ourselves in the position of survivors of an ancient vendetta who have reluctantly concluded that their inability to destroy each other compels an effort at coexistence—though without conviction or real hope. We were both aware of the dictates of prudence, but neither side could shake off its memories, nor could Hanoi abandon its passions. The attempts to behave in a friendly manner were so studied and took so much exertion that they created their own tension; the slightest disagreement tended to bring to the fore the underlying suspicion and resentment.

Hanoi's leaders soon showed that they had lost none of the combativeness that for years had set our teeth on edge. My opposite number in these talks was Pham Van Dong, Prime Minister of the Democratic Republic of Vietnam for nearly twenty years. But the change of personality brought no alteration in the familiar style of condescending superiority or of deception masquerading as moral homily.

Pham Van Dong had come to my attention in January 1967, when he had given a brilliant interview to Harrison Salisbury of the *New York Times,* explaining why Hanoi was confident of winning against the mightiest power in the world. Dong had argued that the disparity in strength was illusory since more Vietnamese were willing to die for Vietnam than Americans. They would simply outlast us.[2] Pham Van Dong turned out to be right—aided not a little by an American military strategy massive enough to hazard our international position yet sufficiently inhibited to guarantee an inconclusive outcome.

Pham Van Dong, implacable and incisive, had stalked our consciousness, and occasionally our consciences, during the intervening years. His periodic Delphic pronouncements had both raised public expectations and dashed official hopes. In early 1972, he had denounced all talk of compromise as "the logic of a gangster."[3] In the last stages of the negotiation, it was Pham Van Dong in whose name the most important communications from Hanoi were addressed to President Nixon.

Pham Van Dong was wiry, short, wary, his piercing eyes watchful for the expected trickery and at the same time implying that the burden of proof of any statement by an arch-capitalist would be on the speaker. He greeted me on the steps of the elaborate structure now called the President's House. From here French colonial administrators had ruled all of Indochina and established in the minds of their all-too-receptive Vietnamese subjects the conviction that the strategic boundaries of Vietnam should coincide with those of the French colonial empire. We entered a large reception hall and seated ourselves in a semicircle for the introductory informal conversation—as in China. Also as in China, this was an occasion for subtle hints to establish the mood.

The meeting started pleasantly enough with Pham Van Dong and me protesting our eagerness to begin a new relationship, and pledging perseverance to that end. But then the Premier introduced a jarring note; less than two weeks after signature of the Paris Agreement, he dropped an ominous hint of renewed warfare. If a new relationship did not develop a solid basis of mutual interest, he averred, the just-signed Paris accords would be "only a temporary stabilization of the situation, only a respite." He immediately qualified this slightly by adding that such was not Hanoi's preference. As a devout Leninist, he happily fell in with my somewhat irrelevant response that we based our new relationship on the existing facts. Pham Van Dong could not resist returning to the theme of his earlier interview with Harrison Salisbury: "We Vietnamese living in this area will remain forever. But you are from the other side of the ocean. Should we take account of this fact, too?" In other words, when would America abandon South Vietnam?

Pham Van Dong did not take long to dash my dim hope that he might prove to be another Zhou Enlai and become a partner in transforming old enmity into new cooperation. After the initial thrust-and-parry, Pham Van Dong and I walked with our colleagues into a formal conference room of heavy furniture and drawn curtains, where we faced each other across a table and immediately ran into another squall. The North Vietnamese Premier made a little speech greeting me formally and graciously, expressing the hope for good results:

[We] should, in the spirit we have just mentioned outside and
we continue in this room, shift from war to peace, . . . shift from
confrontation to reconciliation as stipulated in the Agreement, and
. . . bring a new relationship, a solid relationship, on a basis agreed
upon by the two parties and aiming at the long-term goals as Dr.
Kissinger has just mentioned. As far as we are concerned, we will
firmly follow this direction—that is to say to implement the signed
Agreement, to implement all the provisions of the Agreement.

Unfortunately, Pham Van Dong's eloquence was not matched by his
country's actions. Our agenda consisted of three items: observance of the
Paris Agreement, normalization of relations, and economic reconstruction.
No sooner had we turned to the first agenda item than we realized that Hanoi
had no intention of making the Paris accords the first agreement on Indochina it had ever observed.

The cease-fire established by the Paris Agreement had gone into effect at
midnight Greenwich Mean Time on January 27. There were immediate reports of violations as both sides sought to seize as much territory as possible
in the hours before the cease-fire went into effect; some battles continued for
days afterward. In that early period, both sides were guilty of stretching the
letter as well as the spirit of the agreement. Saigon, still the stronger side, gave
as good as it received: it expanded its control over more hamlets than it lost.
But from then on, North Vietnam showed itself capable of uniquely gross
challenges to the solemn undertaking it had just signed.

The international supervisory machinery immediately ran into Communist obstruction. Hanoi would not designate the official points of entry
through which alone, according to the agreement, military equipment was
permitted to enter South Vietnam under international supervision. Hanoi
seemed to feel that refusing to comply with the provision for international
control also removed the inhibitions of another clause that limited new
equipment to one-for-one replacement. In flagrant violation, Hanoi's resupply efforts down the Ho Chi Minh Trail, freed of American bombing, proceeded massively and at an ominously more rapid rate than during the war.

As for the political provisions, Saigon was clearly in no hurry to set up
the National Council for National Reconciliation and Concord envisaged by
the agreement; Hanoi, for its part, thwarted any discussion of elections—to
be supervised by that council—which it knew it would lose. But while nei-

ther Vietnamese party was distinguished by concern for the political obligations, there can be no doubt that Hanoi's illegal infiltration of military equipment and personnel started almost immediately, proved decisive, and antedated all the alleged breaches of the Paris accords by Saigon cited later by Hanoi's apologists.

To make our point, I had brought along a compilation of North Vietnamese violations in the two weeks since the signature of the Paris Agreement. The list left no doubt that Hanoi observed no constraints of *any* of the provisions it had signed so recently. We had incontrovertible evidence of 200 major military violations. The most flagrant were the transit of the Demilitarized Zone by 175 trucks on February 6 and the movement of 223 tanks heading into South Vietnam through Laos and Cambodia. Transit of the DMZ by military vehicles violated Article 15(a), on the wording of which we had spent nearly two months and which banned all military traffic, as well as requiring the concurrence of Saigon for civilian traffic. It also violated the explicit stipulation that new military equipment could be introduced into South Vietnam only on the basis of one-for-one replacement through previously designated international checkpoints (Article 7). The movement of tanks through Laos and Cambodia violated Article 20, according to which all foreign troops were to be withdrawn from Laos and Cambodia and the territory of those countries was not to be used as a base for encroaching on other countries. When the tanks reached South Vietnam, they would also be violating Article 7's prohibition of the introduction of new matériel.

Pham Van Dong and Le Duc Tho were not fazed. With the casual brazenness I remembered so well from my encounters in Paris, they explained the violations in terms that were irrelevant to the issue but served marvelously to confuse it.

There is the story of a law professor who taught his students how to take advantage of every possible defense. If one's client is accused of stealing a black pot, the tactic should be to reply: "My client did not steal anything. In any case it was not a pot that he stole, and the pot was not black." Le Duc Tho followed the same approach. There had been no violations, he said. And in any case, the trucks crossing the DMZ were carrying civilian goods. This, of course, still violated the provision according to which civilian traffic required the assent of Saigon. And the resupply restrictions of Article 7 would become absurd if Hanoi could avoid international control by the simple device of declaring all supplies civilian. As for the tanks, Le Duc Tho and Pham

Van Dong halfheartedly denied the truth of my allegations but promised to look into them. They then suggested that perhaps the tanks had been en route when the agreement was signed. This was, of course, quite irrelevant to the prohibition of their entry into South Vietnam. Vice Foreign Minister Nguyen Co Thach, who had negotiated the technical protocols in Paris with Ambassador William H. Sullivan, had the cleverest idea. Probably, he averred, such was the urgency of the need of civilians that the tanks, too, were carrying civilian goods to the civilian population.

Equally frustrating were our discussions of the American soldiers and airmen who were prisoners of war or missing in action. We knew of at least eighty instances in which an American serviceman had been captured alive and had subsequently disappeared. The evidence consisted of either voice communications from the ground in advance of capture or photographs and names published by the Communists. Yet none of these men was on the list of POWs handed over after the agreement. Why? Were they dead? How did they die? Were they missing? How was that possible after capture? I called special attention to the nineteen cases where pictures of the captured had been published in the Communist press. Pham Van Dong replied noncommittally that the lists handed over to us were complete. He made no attempt to explain discrepancies. Experience had shown, he said, that owing to the nature of the terrain in Indochina, it would take a long time, perhaps a year, to come up with additional information, though he did not amplify what the terrain had to do with the disappearing prisoners. We have never, even at this writing, received an explanation of what could possibly have happened to prisoners whose pictures had appeared in Communist newspapers, or to the airmen who we knew from voice communications had safely reached the ground.

To calm the atmosphere, Le Duc Tho offered to release twenty prisoners of war ahead of schedule, ostensibly in honor of my visit, and gave me the opportunity to pick them from the POW list. While grateful for the early release, I refused to select the names. I had no basis for making individual selections among those who had already suffered so long. (Prisoners held the longest were being released earliest in any case.) This was one promise Hanoi kept; twenty additional prisoners were released with the first group.

The North Vietnamese were at their most adamant about Laos and Cambodia. Article 20 of the Paris Agreement explicitly stipulated that "foreign countries" should end all military activities in Cambodia and Laos and totally withdraw all their forces there.[4] In a separate written understanding, Le Duc Tho and I had agreed that Vietnamese as well as American troops were "foreign" within the meaning of this article. If words meant anything, this required immediate North Vietnamese withdrawal from Laos and Cambodia and an end to the use of Laotian and Cambodian territory for base areas, sanctuaries, or infiltration.

My conversations with Pham Van Dong had not proceeded far before it became apparent that the North Vietnamese proposed to drain Article 20 of all meaning. They took the position that the required withdrawal, unconditional on its face, would have to await not only a cease-fire in Laos and Cambodia but also a political settlement in *both* those countries. Hanoi would withdraw only after negotiations with the new governments there. Since Communist political demands were for what amounted to Pathet Lao predominance in Laos and a total Khmer Rouge victory in Cambodia, North Vietnamese withdrawal would take place, if at all, only after it had become irrelevant and the issue had been decided in favor of the Communist side. Hanoi was proposing in effect to negotiate with itself, or at best with its Cambodian and Laotian allies, about implementing provisions of an undertaking with us. The achievement of political settlements in Laos or Cambodia could not possibly be made a precondition for the fulfillment of obligations that made no reference to it whatsoever and, by their plain import, were without qualification.

In fact, we have since learned from Sihanouk's memoirs that the Khmer Rouge, considering the Paris Agreement a betrayal, had asked the North Vietnamese troops to quit Cambodia.[5] They stayed in violation of Article 20 *and* against the wishes of both their enemies and their own allies, whom they used as an alibi in their talks with us.

Needless to say, my response to Pham Van Dong was sharp. It was all very well, I said sarcastically, to note Hanoi's fastidious regard for the sovereignty of its allies. But it was bizarre to maintain that Hanoi could not make a unilateral decision to remove troops it had introduced unilaterally, in compliance with an agreement to which it had pledged itself barely two weeks earlier. Its soldiers were not prisoners in these countries. Hanoi, having introduced its forces without the approval of the legitimate governments, could certainly withdraw them on its own.

It cannot be said that my arguments left a deep impression. On the other hand, experience had taught that Hanoi did not always hold to the original version of its position; it had, after all, abandoned a similar position over South Vietnam. The only immediate "concession" we elicited was a promise by Le Duc Tho to use his "influence" to bring about a rapid cease-fire in Laos—the third time they had sold us that particular item. The Laotian cease-fire finally came about on February 22, but not without the spur of one more U.S. B-52 strike on North Vietnamese troop concentrations in Laos, to the accompaniment of outraged media and congressional protests that once again the administration was "expanding" the war. Despite the cease-fire, Hanoi withdrew no troops from Laos.

North Vietnamese stonewalling doomed Cambodia, however, to prolonged agony. Pham Van Dong and Le Duc Tho claimed that Vietnam was not involved in Cambodia—another flagrant misrepresentation; hence they needed to take no position with respect to the de facto cease-fire that Lon Nol had proclaimed. They spurned Lon Nol's offer to talk to Hanoi or to the Khmer Rouge; they maintained their position of 1970—demanding the overthrow of the Cambodian government. As in the long negotiating stalemate over Vietnam, they insisted that the political structure in Phnom Penh be disbanded *before* any talks, after which, of course, the talks would have had no purpose. In fact, Hanoi did not even pretend to want a coalition in Cambodia; it insisted on an undiluted Communist takeover. Le Duc Tho in an offhand manner suggested that I talk to Sihanouk, but he was curiously vague about the Prince's status or even his whereabouts, implying strongly that the Khmer Rouge would be the decisive element in the future of Cambodia. Le Duc Tho—clearly the Politburo's expert on the other countries of Indochina—was quite condescending about Sihanouk. He made fun of a visit Sihanouk had recently paid to Hanoi and the Prince's love of personal luxury. He showed a propaganda film about Sihanouk's visit to Communist-controlled territory in Cambodia, the clear implication of which was that Sihanouk was there on the sufferance of the Khmer Rouge. The primary use that Le Duc Tho seemed to see in Sihanouk was as a means to demoralize and undermine the Lon Nol government.

Where Le Duc Tho miscalculated was in his estimate of the pliability of the Khmer Rouge, who refused to be Hanoi's tools on the model of the Pathet Lao. But perhaps he was willing to pay the price of temporary Khmer Rouge autonomy because the immediate consequence of a Khmer Rouge victory would be the undermining of the government in Saigon, which could not long survive the communization of Cambodia. Hanoi also, as it later transpired, had its tried and true remedy for Khmer Rouge independence if it got out of hand. Less than four years after the Khmer Rouge victory in 1975, North Vietnam sent its troops to invade and occupy Communist Cambodia with no more scruple than it had shown toward Sihanouk's neutral Cambodia in the mid-1960s and Lon Nol's Cambodia in 1970.

As for a political settlement in Laos, the North Vietnamese leaders remained evasive. At one point, Pham Van Dong suggested that it might occur no more than ninety days after a cease-fire; then, amazingly, he was disavowed by Le Duc Tho, who sought a private meeting with me to suggest that henceforth Cambodia and Laos be discussed by him and me alone since his Prime Minister was not familiar with all the nuances. In the event, a political settlement was not reached in Laos until September 14, 1973. The newly constituted coalition government held together tenuously for two years until it was finally engulfed in the general debacle of 1975. And no more than in 1962 did North Vietnam pay even token obeisance to its pledge to withdraw its troops. Between 40,000 and 50,000 North Vietnamese troops remained in Laos even after Hanoi's own absurd interpretation of the Paris Agreement had been fulfilled.

Economic Aid

The one subject about which Pham Van Dong was prepared to observe the agreement was something on which we alone needed to perform: economic aid from the United States. He almost made it seem that Hanoi was doing America a favor in accepting its money. Not that its eagerness would reach the point of modifying its peremptory negotiating methods: American assistance was requested as a right. Any reminder that it was linked to Hanoi's observance of the other provisions of the Paris Agreement was indignantly rejected as interference in North Vietnam's domestic affairs or as an unacceptable political condition.

How we reached the point where a voluntary American offer became transmuted into a North Vietnamese "right" shows at the least the degree to which the two societies were doomed to mutual incomprehension and at most the ability of the North Vietnamese to turn single-mindedness into an art form. On the American side, the offer of economic aid grew out of a contradictory mixture of idealistic values and a materialistic interpretation of history according to which economic motives are thought to dominate political decisions. Perhaps no major nation has been so uncomfortable with the exercise of vast power as the United States. No other society has considered it a national duty to contribute to the rebuilding of a defeated enemy; after the Second World War, America made it a central element of its foreign policy. In Vietnam, successive administrations thought it a device to induce an undefeated enemy to accept compromise terms.

For years, all these strands had been woven through our Indochina policy. America had just begun to build up its forces in South Vietnam when President Lyndon Johnson in April 1965 offered Hanoi a program of postwar economic reconstruction. We do not know whether North Vietnam saw in this offer the first symptom of our declining resolution (so that it had an effect contrary to that intended), or evidence of bourgeois incapacity to grasp revolutionary dedication. The offer, in any event, was not taken up.

The Nixon administration did not wait long to follow in the footsteps of its predecessor. On September 18, 1969, in a conciliatory speech before the United Nations General Assembly, Nixon renewed the offer of economic aid to North Vietnam as well as the rest of Indochina, to no better effect than Johnson. Nixon reiterated the offer publicly as part of a comprehensive proposal on January 25, 1972. Briefing the press the next day, I explained that we were prepared to contribute several billion dollars to the reconstruction of Indochina, including North Vietnam. The President's Foreign Policy Report issued on February 9, 1972, was even more specific: "We are prepared to undertake a massive 7½ billion dollar five-year reconstruction program in conjunction with an overall agreement, in which North Vietnam could share up to two and a half billion dollars." In the "peace is at hand" press conference of October 26, 1972, I repeated this theme. And I did so again in a press conference on January 24, 1973, as did Nixon on January 31, 1973.

By then Hanoi's interest in the proposition had quickened. It would not admit that it would end the war for economic reasons. But once it had decided on a cease-fire out of military necessity, it was ready, if not eager, to extract the maximum aid from us. Nor were Hanoi's ideas of the appropriate aid level characterized by excessive modesty; Le Duc Tho simply demanded for Hanoi the entire package of $7.5 billion that we had earmarked for *all* of Indochina. We were prepared to accept neither of these propositions. We were willing to extend aid because it had been promised by two administra-

tions and especially because we thought it useful as one of the inducements
to encourage observance of the agreement. But we insisted that our offer was
an application of traditional American principles; it was a voluntary act, not
an "obligation" to indemnify Hanoi. It may have been hairsplitting, but to us
it involved a point of honor. Through weeks of weary haggling, we managed
to reduce Hanoi's demand to $3.25 billion, which was put forward as a target
figure subject to further discussion and congressional approval.

The relevant documents were the Paris Agreement and a presidential
message. Article 21 of the Paris Agreement stated:

> The United States anticipates that this Agreement will usher in
> an era of reconciliation with the Democratic Republic of Vietnam as
> with all the peoples of Indochina. In pursuance of its traditional pol-
> icy, the United States will contribute to healing the wounds of war
> and to postwar reconstruction of the Democratic Republic of Viet-
> nam and throughout Indochina.

It was a promise given in the expectation that the war was ending and an era
of reconciliation would then be possible. And I repeatedly emphasized to Le
Duc Tho that any aid presupposed both congressional approval *and* Hanoi's
living up to the Paris Agreement.

America's intention to extend aid and even its order of magnitude were
well known and had been stated many times on the public record. What was
kept secret at the time was a cabled message from Nixon to Premier Pham
Van Dong spelling out the procedures for implementing Article 21. In order
to underline the fact that it was voluntary and distinct from the formal obligations of the agreement, Le Duc Tho and I had agreed that the message
would be delivered on January 30, 1973, three days after the agreement was
signed, in exchange for a list of American prisoners held in Laos. When on
the appointed day the North Vietnamese failed to provide a list of the American prisoners of war held in Laos, we instructed our representative in Paris to
delay handing over the note. This produced immediate action: The Laotian
POW list was handed over on the afternoon of February 1; as agreed, we gave
the Nixon message to the North Vietnamese at the same time.

Nixon's message outlined the procedures for discussing economic aid.
On my visit to Hanoi, there would be a general discussion of principles, leading to the setting up of a Joint Economic Commission. Its purpose would be

to work out a precise aid program. (The Joint Economic Commission actually began its discussions in Paris on March 15.) The Nixon message spoke of an amount "in the range of $3.25 billion" over five years as an appropriate "preliminary" figure, subject to revision and to detailed discussion between the two countries. (Food aid was included in the total.) Whatever emerged from the deliberations of the Joint Economic Commission, the Nixon message stressed, would have to be submitted to Congress, as is any foreign aid program after discussions with a foreign government. A separate paragraph emphasized this point: "It is understood that the recommendations of the Joint Economic Commission mentioned in the President's note to the Prime Minister will be implemented by each member in accordance with its own constitutional provisions."

The Politburo's confidence that they could use our domestic pressures to push us from one position of disadvantage to another—not unreasonable in the light of a decade of experience—caused them to shrug off another important qualification, one that was equally real and equally explicit in my discussions with them. When I briefed the press about the agreement on January 24, 1973, I stressed that we would discuss aid to North Vietnam only after its "implementation is well advanced."

As it happened, the end of the war also reduced the fervid pressures against the administration to make concessions to Hanoi; indeed, many who had urged an offer of economic aid as a means to end the war became notably less enthusiastic when it came to voting for it in Congress. Nor was public opinion hospitable to the proposition that the U.S. should extend aid to a government whose brutality was becoming vividly clear through the tales of returning prisoners of war. Nixon was thus on safe ground when he instructed me to reiterate to my interlocutors in Hanoi that aid depended on strict observance of the Paris Agreement, with special reference to withdrawal from Cambodia. The North Vietnamese could not expect otherwise. If the war did not end, the "postwar" period could not begin, and the time for postwar reconstruction aid could hardly be said to have arrived.

Pham Van Dong rejected this argument. He advanced the startling view that asking Hanoi to observe a signed agreement was to attach "political conditions." Our aid was to be "unconditional." In other words, Hanoi was to be free to use American economic aid to complete its long-standing ambition of conquering Indochina in violation of the very agreement that it claimed obliged us to provide those resources.

What roused the North Vietnamese to genuine outrage was America's constitutional requirement of congressional approval. I had brought with me to Hanoi a voluminous set of documents to educate the North Vietnamese in our constitutional processes. It was a compilation of some fifty-seven single-spaced pages outlining the American budgetary procedure in both the executive and legislative branches; the various types of bilateral and multilateral aid programs in which the United States had participated; the texts of all relevant legislation (including congressionally mandated restrictions on aid to Hanoi); an outline of various projects that might be included in an aid program for Vietnam; and a list of pungent comments by leading congressmen and senators expressing growing skepticism about foreign aid in general. I handed over these documents to Pham Van Dong. He brushed them aside, pretending not to fathom these legislative matters (this despite the fact that he had shown great skill in manipulating congressional opinion *against* the administration while the war was still going on). He also suspected a trick:

> First of all, I would like to express my suspicion. . . . I will speak very frankly and straightforwardly to you. It is known to everyone that the U. S. had spent a great amount of money in regard to the war in Vietnam. It is said about $200 billion, and in conditions that one would say that the Congress was not fully agreeable to this war. When the war was going on then the appropriation was so easy [laughs], and when we have to solve now a problem that is very legitimate . . . then you find it difficult.

It was finally agreed, as anticipated, that a Joint Economic Commission would be set up to consider how to develop our economic relations and to work out an aid program that would be submitted later to Congress.

There were some inconclusive exchanges about normalizing diplomatic relations between Hanoi and Washington, and about the pending international conference that was to be held in Paris to lend international endorsement to the Paris Agreement. Hanoi was not yet ready to establish any formal ties, not even offices that fell short of full diplomatic status. We proposed a number of schemes; they rejected them all. With typical self-absorption, Hanoi meant to use the prospect of permitting some American diplomats to join the ostracism and general discomfort of their colleagues from Western Europe—and probably the Soviet Union—in Hanoi as a boon that we first had to earn. As for the international conference, Hanoi's preoccupation was to reduce the participation of the Secretary-General of the United Nations to a minimum, if not eliminate him altogether. We found an honorific role that preserved his dignity as well as took account of North Vietnam's touchy view of national sovereignty.

At a final banquet, Pham Van Dong expressed "delight" at my visit, as well as at its results—although as I reread the transcripts at this remove, the source of his pleasure is not self-evident. My mood was somber, but I had not yet given up hope.

After ten years of bitter warfare, perhaps not much more could be expected. Hanoi and Washington had inflicted grievous wounds on each other; theirs were physical, America's psychological and thus perhaps harder to heal. Our hosts had been courteous, but they were clearly applying to the implementation of the agreement the methods by which they had conducted the war: pressing against its edges, testing our tolerance, violating key provisions tentatively to see where the new balance of forces would be established. One could draw some hope from the prospect that Hanoi's nationalism might cause it to seek better relations with Washington to gain some margin of maneuver between its Communist patrons, Beijing and Moscow. Perhaps Pham Van Dong's dour insistence on economic aid might be a sign that Hanoi's rulers were considering the option of building their own society rather than conquering their neighbors. In that case, we were prepared to cooperate. But I left Hanoi with determination rather than optimism. The soggy weather, the Spartan austerity, the palpable suspiciousness combined in Hanoi to produce the most oppressive atmosphere of any foreign capital I have ever visited. I reported to Nixon on the Paris Agreement:

> They have two basic choices which I frankly pointed out to them. They can use the Vietnam Agreement as an offensive weapon, nibbling at its edges, pressuring Saigon, confronting us with some hard choices. In this case they would carry out the release of our prisoners and wait till our withdrawals were completed before showing their real colors unambiguously; they would keep their forces in Laos and Cambodia through procrastination of negotiations or straightforward violations; and launch a big new attack soon. They would calculate that we would not have the domestic base or will to respond.

Their other option is to basically honor the Agreement and seek their objectives through gradual evolution. They would welcome a more constructive relationship with us, seek our economic assistance and concentrate on reconstruction and building socialism in the north. Their Indochina allies would be told to pursue their objectives by political and psychological means. They would, in short, adhere to a more peaceful course and let the forces of history work their will, at least for a few years.

The North Vietnamese naturally proclaim the second option as their settled course, but this means nothing. I could not judge from my talks whether their enormous losses, isolation from their allies, and the prospect of aid mean they are ready for a breather. For them the ideal course would be to follow both options at once: violating the Agreement to pursue their objectives and improving relations with us so as to get economic aid. Our essential task is to convince them that they must make a choice between the two.

To navigate this passage successfully would have proved very difficult in the best of circumstances. It required a united country and a strong, purposeful, disciplined American government capable of acting decisively and of maintaining the delicate balance of risks and incentives that constituted the Paris Agreement. Watergate soon ensured we did not have either.

11

ENFORCEMENT AND AID

We had hoped—naively, as it turned out—that the Paris Agreement would unite the American people because the peace movement would be able to find fulfillment in the ending of hostilities, and the advocates of "peace with honor" could take pride in having extricated the United States without breaking faith with the people that had relied on America's commitment to their freedom. Former adversaries, we had hoped, would unite after the withdrawal from Vietnam behind the proposition that the embattled peoples of South Vietnam, Laos, and Cambodia were entitled to the continued economic and military assistance permitted by the agreement.

It was not to be. After all that had happened, perhaps it could not be; the wounds on both sides cut too deep. Watergate provided the pretext, but it was the legacy of a decade of civil conflict that furnished the impulse. The peace movement had evolved from seeking an end of the war to treating America's frustrations in Indochina as symptoms of moral degeneration that needed to be eradicated root and branch. The animating principle of post-1945 American foreign policy—that the United States had an obligation to protect and sustain free peoples—had become transmogrified in the hands of the new counterculture into a symbol of the arrogance and presumption of a corrupt society.[1] The collapse of non-Communist Indochina, which five American administrations of both parties had striven to prevent in the name of national security and honor, was, for this group, a desirable national catharsis.

This philosophical, cultural, almost obsessive crusade explains why the passions amounting to hatreds of the Vietnam period have been husbanded and nurtured in the decades since. With the passage of time, a rewriting of

history has taken place along two lines: that America made too many concessions, especially with respect to the continued presence of North Vietnamese
forces,[2] and that the Nixon administration should have known that Congress
and the public would never stand for the use of American airpower to enforce
the agreement.

None of this will stand up to serious scrutiny. Sooner or later, American
scholars will conduct a dispassionate analysis of the available material, unem-
barrassed by the possibility that serious men and women were dealing with a
perhaps intractable problem. A brief recapitulation of the negotiations is
therefore in order.

South Vietnam was being asked to defend its freedom under more
daunting conditions than any of America's other allies. American troops have
remained in Europe for over half a century after the end of the Second World
War; in Korea, for nearly as long; in the Gulf, for over a decade; and, at this
writing, in the Balkans for five years after the end of military operations. That
they were withdrawn from South Vietnam sixty days after concluding the
agreement was the principal weakness of the Vietnam agreement, far more
significant than the continued presence of North Vietnamese forces. And
this decision was not a result of negotiation; Nixon and I would have far preferred to keep a residual force as a bargaining counter and a nucleus force to
police the agreement. We were driven in the direction of unilateral withdrawal by domestic pressures, and we paid the price reluctantly—as I have
shown—to be able to arrange an honorable peace, albeit under the most adverse circumstances. No commentator or member of Congress—liberal or
conservative—gave support to the concept of a residual force with which the
administration started. A flood of congressional resolutions was urging ever
faster and more total withdrawals; indeed, Nixon was vilified for withdrawing too slowly and too conditionally. The protest movement, the media, and
Congress moved from a halt of the augmentation of our forces, to partial
withdrawal, to total withdrawal, to unilateral withdrawal, with ever shorter
deadlines. The principal difference was between those urging withdrawal in
return for the release of prisoners and others demanding unconditional withdrawal.

No one was more uneasy about the continued presence of North Vietnamese forces than those of us who faced the North Vietnamese across the
conference table for four years; we had no illusions about Hanoi's long-range
purposes. But our choice was circumscribed. It was between terms which

gave us a chance of ending America's role without abandoning the millions who had relied on us or being voted out of the war by Congress on terms that amounted at best to American withdrawal for prisoners and the abandonment of all local populations to Communist rule and reprisals. And even had we achieved, by a bombing campaign the country would not have tolerated, a promise of North Vietnamese withdrawal—as we did in Laos—we would have faced the same problem of enforcement. North Vietnam did not withdraw its forces from Laos after the Geneva agreement of 1954, nor from Cambodia and Laos as required by the Vietnam accords of 1973. Nor did Hanoi honor the commitment not to augment its forces or infiltrate new matériel into South Vietnam as stipulated by the 1973 agreement. In the event, Congress paralyzed enforcement when, in June 1973, it proscribed enforcing either the withdrawal from Laos or the ban on infiltration into Indochina. That, and not the legal terms of the agreement, ensured the collapse of Indochina.

The Nixon administration sought to manage these pressures by withdrawing gradually while at the same time strengthening South Vietnamese forces. In these conditions, it was impossible to achieve at the bargaining table what we did not bring about on the battlefield. Therefore, the American negotiating position moved step-by-step not to accommodate Hanoi but to gain time to build up Saigon and to hold out for terms that gave the South Vietnamese political structure a chance to survive. The key steps in this process were not secret; they were all contained in public presidential speeches—even when they had first been put forward in secret talks. The comprehensive proposal of May 1969, the cease-fire proposal of October 1970, the nine-point private proposal made public in January 1972, the President's speeches of January 25 and May 8, gradually replaced the demand for mutual withdrawal by an Indochina-wide cease-fire, a ban on infiltration, and a ban on using Laos and Cambodia as bases, thereby prohibiting the continued use of the Ho Chi Minh Trail. The withdrawal of North Vietnamese forces was not part of any American proposal after October 1970. All these proposals were turned down by Le Duc Tho and castigated as being too tough by the domestic opposition; none was criticized from any quarter— liberal or conservative—as being too accommodating. It was Le Duc Tho who, on October 8, abandoned Hanoi's heretofore intransigent rejection of these terms. And from then until the end of the negotiations, all the significant concessions were made by Hanoi.

Even so, with all the gains, it was a precarious agreement. The reason American troops had been left in other erstwhile combat zones was to serve notice of American determination to enforce what it had fought for. In Vietnam, the sole means left to enforce the agreement was American airpower. And the more tenuous the American presence in Indochina, the more dependent enforcement was on the willingness to resort to that threat quickly.

Neither Nixon nor I had illusions that Hanoi's fanatical leaders had abandoned their lifetime struggle. I had warned Nixon during the final phase of the negotiations in November 1972 that Hanoi would press against the edges of any agreement and that the peace could only be preserved by constant vigilance:

> As I have consistently told you since mid-September, this is a very high-risk operation. The eventual outcome of any settlement will essentially turn on the confidence and political performance of the two sides. Having seen the total hatred and pathological distrust between the Vietnamese parties, and knowing as well that Hanoi has no intention of giving up its strategic objectives, we must face the reality that this agreement may lack the foundation of minimum trust that may be needed. Thus it could well break down. It will certainly require from us a posture of constant readiness and willingness to intervene to keep Hanoi and its South Vietnamese allies from nibbling at the edges.

In early 1973, we thought that we were in a position to fulfill these requirements. Provided Saigon received adequate military and economic assistance, the military balance would leave South Vietnam strong enough to resist Communist pressures from the forces in the country—short of an all-out attack by the North Vietnamese regular army across the DMZ. Should North Vietnam betray the agreement and its prohibition against infiltration by launching such an all-out invasion, we intended to defend with air- and seapower what over 55,000 Americans had died to achieve. Too, we would give a chance to a program of assistance for all of Indochina, including North Vietnam, promised by two Presidents of both parties. If the new realities took hold for a sufficient period of time, this might possibly even turn Hanoi's attention (and manpower) to tasks of construction. Hanoi was indeed instructing its cadres in the South to prepare for a long period of *political* competition.

But no foreign policy is stronger than its domestic base. Nixon took it for granted that the conclusion of the Paris accords implied the right to enforce them—as has been the case in every previous and subsequent conflict in which Americans have sacrificed their lives. But Watergate undermined what was left of national cohesion and altered the previous equilibrium between the executive and legislative branches. The Paris Agreement did not so much end the controversy as give it a new focus.

But were Nixon (and I) entitled to make that assumption? But what else could the President do? If he had no ability to enforce any agreement, unconditional abandonment was the sole alternative. If Nixon had made any point, it was that he would never do so. And he had just won an overwhelming electoral victory in a campaign in which these issues had been drawn with rare ideological clarity. Watergate prevented this mandate from being carried out.

Throughout 1973 and 1974, enforcement of the agreement became as controversial as the war itself had been, and the arguments against it were identical. The antiwar movement would not accept the premise that America had achieved peace with honor, for to do so would contradict its basic theme that American power was itself a source of evil in the world.[3] The same groups that had opposed every measure that had enabled us to end the war now rejected any policy either to enforce the agreement or to sustain with American aid the peoples on behalf of whom the war had been fought.

The critics justified this post-agreement surrender with the proposition that there was no legal "obligation" to assist Vietnam or to uphold the Paris Agreement, only "secret" presidential letters expressing the intention of doing so. The accusation came with special bad grace from members of previous administrations who should have been well aware of presidential letters during their period in office which at least paralleled and at times exceeded what Nixon had promised to President Thieu.[4]

Presidential letters are not legal commitments but expressions of the intent of the incumbent President with respect to foreseeable contingencies. They impose a moral, not a legal, obligation on his successors (which inevitably declines with the distance from the presidency). And, of course, no President is able to commit Congress by a unilateral declaration. But if a President has no right to defend an agreement for which Americans have died, any settlement turns into a disguised surrender. It is on this basis that three administrations of both parties have used airpower in Iraq for over a decade.

In the case of Vietnam, the President's letters were written in the inter-regnum between the election and inauguration. Thieu therefore had every reason to expect that Nixon, just overwhelmingly elected after a campaign in which his Vietnam policy was a principal issue, would have four years to carry out statements of his intentions totally compatible with his previous record. Moreover, the President's associates repeatedly avowed the administration's determination to enforce the agreement publicly, as can be seen from the Nixon administration public statements in the notes.[5] Sometimes this took the form of refusing to rule out the use of force, as I did in my press conference on January 24, 1973, explaining the terms of the agreement, and as Secretary of Defense Elliot Richardson avowed even more explicitly in a television interview on April 1, 1973, and in remarks to newsmen on April 3, 1973. Sometimes it was stressed that there was no formal inhibition on our use of airpower, as Deputy Assistant Secretary of State William Sullivan pointed out on television on January 28, 1973, and as I reaffirmed in a television interview on February 1, 1973. There were ominous assertions that we had resorted to force before and could do so again, as Nixon warned in a news conference of March 15, 1973: "I would only suggest that based on my actions over the past four years, that the North Vietnamese should not lightly disregard such expressions of concern, when they are made with regard to a violation." (These and other warnings are quoted more fully in the notes.)[6] However indirectly phrased any one statement may have been, their overall impact was correctly summed up in the President's annual foreign policy report published on May 3, 1973: "Such a course [massive violations] would endanger the hard won gains for peace in Indochina. It would risk revived confrontation with us. . . . We have told Hanoi, privately and publicly, that we will not tolerate violations of the Agreement."

The media's reaction—especially to Nixon's scarcely veiled threat at his March 15 press conference—is the clearest possible evidence that there was nothing secret about the President's intentions. For example, the *Washington Post* editorialized on March 18, 1973:

> We do not doubt at all that, if he chose, the President could re-sume the bombing—even now, B-52s continue to rain death daily on Cambodia and no one seems to mind. More than that, we don't doubt at all that President Nixon is "tough" enough to bomb; nor do we know of anyone else who doubts it. Given his overwhelming mar-

gin of victory over Mr. McGovern; given his evident determination to run the government in a way avoiding the need to depend on or cooperate with the Congress; and given the new associations he has forged with Moscow and Peking [Beijing], we would not even argue that a resumption of bombing would significantly undercut his political or diplomatic plans for his second term. He is in an enviable position to conduct his Vietnam policy on the merits alone.

The same interpretation was put forward by the *New York Times* of March 17, 1973:

> The President left little doubt that he regarded resumption of bombing and harbor mining as a viable option against North Vietnam. Hanoi's leaders recently tried to test Mr. Nixon's resolve on the cease-fire terms by delaying the process of releasing American war prisoners, and when they saw the Administration's firmness they returned to the agreed upon schedule. A similar response is looked for now.

The President's determination to use force was thoroughly understood; and his right to do so early in 1973 was unimpaired. The issue, at bottom, is not really a legal question but turns on one's perception of the national interest. Our determination to enforce the agreement came up against all the passions unleashed by the Vietnam war. Those who had always wanted us to wash our hands of the non-Communist peoples of Indochina sought to vindicate their course upon the war's conclusion. Letting free Indochina go as the result of an agreement seemed to them no more pernicious than their previous insistence on unilateral withdrawal. They saw the Paris Agreement not as the honorable compromise it was, but simply as a fulfillment of their old prescription to disengage unconditionally. It was inevitable, and just as predictable, that the Nixon administration could not accept this. It had opposed unconditional surrender during the war. All the reasons that impelled it to pursue the war to an honorable settlement argued for maintaining the agreement's terms. We had no intention of abandoning by inaction what over 55,000 Americans died to achieve, or of abandoning the millions who in relying on America's promises had fought at its side for a decade. Convinced that the impact on international stability and on America's readiness to defend free peoples would be catastrophic if a solemn agreement were treated as unconditional surrender, Nixon refused simply to walk away from it.

How was the Paris Agreement then to be maintained? "By diplomacy," the favorite answer of critics, was no answer at all. It was diplomacy, after all, tedious years of it, that had produced the very agreement that was being violated. But it had not been diplomacy in a vacuum. Military pressure had been an important component. Effective diplomacy depends on other countries' assessment of incentives and penalties, not on the eloquence of negotiators.

The Thieu Visit

B efore turning to the events which marked this tragedy, it is important to record one of the saddest experiences of my period in office: the visit of America's ally, President Thieu, to the United States. Thieu visited the U.S. from April 2 to 5, 1973, while American policymakers were debating how to react to Hanoi's buildup and Watergate was gaining momentum. There was little about the visit of which America can be proud. Throughout the war, though his countrymen fought side by side with ours, it had been impossible to receive Thieu in Washington for fear that his presence might spark civil disorders. He had met American Presidents furtively in Guam, in Hawaii, and at Midway. He had never been permitted to set foot on the continental United States.

Thieu's 1973 visit to America was intended to make up for that, to symbolize a new peacetime relationship and our dedication to a free South Vietnam. It turned into almost the exact opposite. The end of the war had not ended the risk of public disturbances. It was therefore decided to receive the leader of an allied country, for whose freedom tens of thousands of Americans and their allies and several hundred thousand Vietnamese had given their lives, at the Western White House in San Clemente. The arrival and departure ceremonies could be held inside the well-guarded presidential compound. Even the State dinner was dispensed with and transformed into a small family gathering. The pretext was that Nixon's dining room could seat no more than twelve guests; the real reasons were doubt that we could generate a representative guest list and fear of hostile demonstrations.

To fulfill the promise of a visit to Washington, Vice President Spiro Agnew was chosen to act as the host in the nation's capital. The atmosphere there was revealed by a telephone conversation I had with Agnew shortly before Thieu's plane touched down. Agnew complained that only one Cabinet member—Secretary of Labor Peter J. Brennan—had been willing to join him for Thieu's arrival ceremony. The guests ready to attend the dinner tendered by the Vice President were appallingly few. Most senior members of the administration had found some excuse for being out of town. In my days in Washington, several Communist leaders had been received with honor. Senior officials had vied to attend State dinners in honor of neutralist leaders who specialized in denouncing the United States. But the staunch President of a friendly country was a pariah. His alleged failings as a democrat were, for a decade, used as an excuse—by those who wished to abandon his people to the enemies of democracy. There were no boat people fleeing from Vietnam while Thieu was there. Vietnamese by the millions voted with their feet during his rule, pouring into areas under his control and away from Communist-held territory. Conventional wisdom blamed this on the bombing; since it continued after bombing ended, it was surely a reaction to the brutality of Communist rule. Thieu took steps to liberalize his government—however inadequately—even in the midst of Communist terrorism of which his best officials were the primary targets. None of this benefited him with his critics.

To be sure, South Vietnam was hardly a democracy in the American sense. There were justified criticisms of harshness and corruption. But when Thieu's disgruntled opponents in Saigon's turbulent pluralistic politics expressed these to the media, no contrast was drawn with Hanoi, where no opposition was tolerated, the press was controlled, and access to foreign media was prohibited. It was not, in short, a fastidious assessment of degrees of democracy that was at work on American emotions about Thieu. He was the victim of a deeper, more pervasive confusion that manifested itself in double standards in all the democracies. When our European allies were sounded out about a visit by Thieu either in connection with his trip to the United States or separately, the response was an embarrassed silence. Neither he nor his Foreign Minister was ever received in allied capitals, except in Paris, which was the site of the negotiations; the process of delegitimizing the Thieu government—the first stage toward abandonment—was well advanced from the beginning. Meanwhile, Madame Nguyen Thi Binh, the so-called Foreign Minister of the phantom Communist Provisional Revolutionary Government, which could not boast even a capital, was lionized in Eastern Europe.

I had little personal affection for Thieu, but I had high regard for his courage as he continued his struggle in the terrible loneliness that followed America's withdrawal. He received scant compassion or even understanding. It did not dent his dignity. Though the sole head of state to have his reception ceremony in the absence of the public, he acted as if this were the most natural thing in the world. At the San Clemente arrival, Nixon made a polite speech that referred to South Vietnam's capacity to defend itself—a dubious proposition if Hanoi launched an all-out attack with Soviet weapons. Thieu fell in gracefully with this fairy tale, not, however, without contrasting South Vietnam's position to that of Europe, which still required 300,000 American troops a quarter-century after the end of World War II.

This ritual completed, the two leaders repaired for their private talks. There was, in fact, not much to discuss. Thieu did not whine about the task we had left him or Hanoi's malevolence. He gave a matter-of-fact account of North Vietnamese violations. Nixon assured him privately—as he had already done publicly on March 15 and elsewhere—that he would resist blatant violations by force if necessary. At the same time, he urged Thieu to lean over backward to carry out South Vietnam's obligations under the agreement. If there was to be a breakdown of the Paris accords, Nixon advised, the onus must fall unambiguously on Hanoi. Thieu pointed out that the main obstacle to assembling the National Council for National Reconciliation and Concord, as required by the agreement, was Hanoi's refusal to hold the elections that the Council was to supervise. The "political contest" so passionately advocated by some in America during the war would never be undertaken by Hanoi in peacetime. It would not risk a generation of struggle on ballots that it disdained in its own country.

Nixon's and Thieu's second day of discussion mostly concerned aid for South Vietnam. It had a slightly unreal quality because the American participants knew that congressional support even for economic development assistance was eroding fast. Liberals were losing interest because they had little commitment to the survival of South Vietnam, the conservatives believed that they had discharged their obligations by supporting the war to an honorable conclusion. Both reflected the war-weariness of the nation. Nixon promised to use Saigon's aid request as a target figure; the final result would depend on congressional consultation. Thieu did obtain a pledge in the final communiqué that the two allies would maintain "vigilance" against "the possibility of renewed Communist aggression after the departure of United States ground forces from South Vietnam." Furthermore, "actions which would threaten the basis of the Agreement would call for appropriately vigorous reactions"—yet another clear *public* statement of Nixon's intention to enforce the agreement.

Watergate and Enforcement

The assumptions about America's readiness to sustain the agreement had been based on ignorance of the most important factor affecting this undertaking. On April 17, 1973, President Nixon publicly acknowledged the possibility that Watergate, the name given to the break-in at the headquarters of the Democratic National Committee in the capital's Watergate apartment and office complex in June 1972 and the ensuing scandal, might have involved high levels of his administration. The burglars and two coconspirators, arrested at the scene or shortly thereafter, were indicted on charges of burglary, conspiracy, and wiretapping in September, and found guilty on all counts in January 1973. Granted leniency by the court in exchange for information not uncovered at the trial, they had disclosed past links to the CIA and the Committee to Re-elect the President; some of Nixon's closest aides then began talking to federal prosecutors.

I had begun to suspect the gravity of the situation following a March 13 meeting of the Washington Special Actions Group (the crisis management body of the NSC) which reviewed contingency plans regarding the situation in Indochina. After reviewing gross violations of the agreement, it concluded:

> The best military option appears to be a resumption of bombing the trails in Laos as soon as possible after the third tranche of POWs is released, possibly followed later by bombing of the DMZ and the area between the DMZ and the South Vietnamese lines, if necessary. The final decision will be made by the President.

At the end of February, there had been two brief tests of strength that validated this reasoning. The first was over Laos. Despite the fact that, during my visit to Hanoi, it had been agreed that a cease-fire for Laos would go into effect within days, the Pathet Lao—Hanoi's Laotian clients—continued what Premier Souvanna Phouma called a "general offensive." On the very first day of the truce, the Communists broke it no fewer than twenty-nine times. Souvanna therefore requested American B-52 strikes against the Pathet Lao. The President and I discussed it on the evening of February 22. Nixon was reluctant because he feared Hanoi would use it as a pretext to delay the release of American prisoners of war. I argued that Hanoi would refuse the release of our prisoners—our most insistent demand—only if it was prepared for a showdown for other reasons. Nixon authorized an immediate B-52 strike. Within forty-eight hours, the cease-fire in Laos was established.

The second mini-confrontation in late February was over the release of American prisoners of war. Hanoi failed to produce, on February 26, a list of the POWs who were due to be released the next day. It gave no explanation, though it hinted that the release of POWs was dependent on Saigon's release of its political detainees—a linkage we had spent weeks of negotiation to avoid. This happened at almost the same time that Washington and Saigon were protesting the appearance of three SAM-2 surface-to-air missile sites at Khe Sanh in violation of the standstill cease-fire.

We responded very sharply by suspending American troop withdrawals and mine-clearing operations in North Vietnamese harbors. A terse message was sent to Hanoi informing it of our actions. In addition, White House Press Secretary Ron Ziegler was instructed to read at his noon briefing a tough statement making clear that the release of American prisoners was an unconditional obligation of North Vietnam not linked to any other provision of the agreement. The POWs were released on schedule.

But, overall, the President approached the problem of the egregious North Vietnamese violations in an uncharacteristically desultory fashion. The single-mindedness that had been his hallmark in previous crises was lacking. In retrospect, we know that, by March, Watergate was coming to a head, though Nixon's advisers in the foreign policy field were not aware of it. On March 6, for instance, Nixon had ordered a bombing strike of one day's duration on the Ho Chi Minh Trail—timed for the following weekend. The illegal bumper-to-bumper military truck traffic coming down the trail promised profitable targets. The next day, March 7, he canceled the order. He said he did not want to give the North Vietnamese a pretext for delaying the scheduled release of the American prisoners. On March 14, I submitted a memorandum to the President urging acceptance of the WSAG recommendations for an air strike. It outlined the North Vietnamese leaders' possible motivations. They might believe that we would not react to their violations so long as they held American prisoners; they might simply be testing the limits of American tolerance; they might have decided to resume offensive operations as soon as their resupply operation was completed. Whatever their purposes, the future of the Paris Agreement depended on action now to enforce it:

> [T]he North Vietnamese are exposed both in the trail area of the Laotian Panhandle and in the northern reaches of South Vietnam's MR-I. In both areas they are operating in daylight and the traffic is so heavy as to be congested. They clearly are taking advantage of the fact that all air action against them has ceased. A series of heavy strikes over a 2 or 3 day period in either of these areas would be very costly to them in both personnel and matériel.

To meet Nixon's concern about the American prisoners of war, I recommended that an attack be launched on March 24–26, after the third but before the fourth group of prisoners was due for release. If we waited much longer, the rainy season would close down the Ho Chi Minh Trail.

Nixon temporized. He approved contingency planning but told me again that he was worried about risking delay in the release of POWs. On March 15, he issued a warning to Hanoi in his news conference, but failed to act on the March 14 memorandum.

Intelligence briefings, meanwhile, revealed that the North Vietnamese, in complete violation of the agreement, had built up an extensive complex of surface-to-air missiles south of the Demilitarized Zone, especially around Khe Sanh, where activity had been noted before, and in the Ashau valley threatening the old imperial city of Hue. The result was that the Joint Chiefs of Staff now insisted on three days of bombing for antiaircraft suppression before we could attack the North Vietnamese supply complex in Laos.

I returned to the charge in a memorandum on March 21:

> There is one principal argument for conducting the strikes at this time and that is to make it clear to the North Vietnamese that we may do something totally unexpected if pressed in defense of the agreement.

That same day, Nixon asked Brent Scowcroft, who had replaced Haig as my deputy, to query me again. Obviously I was not giving the desired advice. Nevertheless, I repeated my view on March 22:

> The operation is likely to cause considerable though not decisive damage. If they do not react to our strikes it will be seen as a sign of weakness on their part but I do not see what action they can take.

Nixon responded by ordering an immediate one-day strike on the Ho Chi Minh Trail. This combined every disadvantage. It was too short to be effective, too blatant to be ignored, and too hesitant to have the desired psychological impact on Hanoi. But Nixon's order achieved the effect he desired. It induced me to recommend postponing the decision until we could discuss matters after the final release of our prisoners.

On April 2, I outlined in a memorandum to Nixon further possible responses, both diplomatic and military, to the increasingly massive North Vietnamese violations of the agreement. The memorandum was labeled "information," meaning it asked for no decision but obviously not precluding one, as it almost surely would have a year earlier. Nixon was in San Clemente with Haldeman and Ehrlichman. They were under siege by the Senate committee investigating a possible Watergate cover-up, and the committee chairman, Sam Ervin, threatened to arrest any White House aide who refused to give testimony in public. Nixon simply placed a check mark on my memorandum to indicate that he had noted it. The paper was returned with none of the underlinings and marginal comments that normally showed he had studied a paper carefully.

To bomb for the better part of a week as the Joint Chiefs recommended, diplomatic preparation was necessary. Hanoi, pursuing its own stratagems to head off bombing, provided an opening by replying to our protests with a hint that it might be ready to talk about violations. In a message of March 31, Hanoi suggested that private meetings between Le Duc Tho and me could "resolve difficulties or snags which may arise in future in the implementation of the Agreement." Our response left no doubt that our patience was approaching its end:

> The U.S. side rejects emphatically the DRV contention that responsibility for implementation of Article 7 of the Paris Agreement

[regarding infiltration] rests only with the two South Vietnamese parties. All four parties to the Agreement are responsible for its strict implementation. The U.S. side holds the DRV side fully responsible for the continued violation of Article 7 and insists that the DRV side accept its responsibility and cease the infiltration of men and materiel into South Vietnam in violation of that article and Article 20. The U.S. side further insists that the DRV side withdraw its forces from Laos and Cambodia unconditionally as required by Article 20. . . . The U.S. side wishes to point out that continuation of these violations will have most serious consequences.

The end of our message coupled another warning with a proposal for a meeting with Le Duc Tho:

In order to arrest any further deterioration, Dr. Kissinger proposes a meeting in Paris with special adviser Le Duc Tho at a mutually agreeable time during the first week of May.

Our strategy was to use April to bomb the Ho Chi Minh Trail and other infiltration routes and then confront Le Duc Tho after having shown our determination to enforce the agreement.

But Hanoi had strong nerves. By the end of April, the Ho Chi Minh Trail would be shut down as the rainy season turned it into a quagmire. So Hanoi played for time while continuing its illegal infiltration. It took ten days to reply, then on April 15 accepted the meeting for any day after May 15. Le Duc Tho wanted as long an interval as possible, calculating that we would not attack until after negotiations had taken place. His calculations were wrong; he prevailed for reasons connected with Watergate, not diplomacy. But for Watergate, we would surely have acted in April.

By mid-April, some 35,000 North Vietnamese troops had entered South Vietnam or nearby sanctuaries; the total increase in combat personnel and supplies was greater than before the 1972 Easter offensive—all this in total violation of the Paris Agreement. The normal Nixon would have surely acted, but the Watergate Nixon continued to dither. To gain time he had, on April 8, sent Al Haig, now Vice Chief of Staff of the Army, on a five-day fact-finding trip to Indochina. In the past, this would have been the precursor to strong decisions. Not now. When Haig reported on April 15, Nixon procrastinated again, which would soon make the projected attack pointless as the rainy season rendered the Ho Chi Minh Trail unusable. We were instructed to call yet one more WSAG meeting to consider the options.

Nixon was simply unable to concentrate his energies and mind on Vietnam. The record shows that he was engaged in incessant meetings and telephone calls on Watergate.

Largely oblivious of these developments, I was convinced, as I told Defense Secretary Elliot Richardson, that hesitation was the most dangerous course. "The only chance we have got is not to let the other guys calibrate the price that they have to pay at each stage." We reviewed the options the next day in the WSAG. In addition to the resupply down the Ho Chi Minh Trail threatening South Vietnam's safety, we were now faced with a new North Vietnamese offensive in northern Laos. The WSAG recommended that we should respond by bombing in Laos, and that we should suspend mine clearing. These recommendations were accepted almost immediately. But they fudged the fundamental issue, which was the transgressions in the main theater—South Vietnam itself. American B-52 bombers and fighter planes struck targets in Laos on April 16 in retaliation for the North Vietnamese seizure of Tha Vieng, south of the Plain of Jars. On April 17, the raids continued for a second day, and Secretary Richardson at a news conference described them as a response to "a flagrant violation" of the Laotian cease-fire. But no action was taken against the North Vietnamese infiltration down the Ho Chi Minh Trail or against the illegal infiltration across the DMZ, and that was, after all, the heart of the matter.

By then I was undeceived. On April 14, Leonard Garment (who later became Nixon's beleaguered White House counsel) informed me that Watergate (and the suspected cover-up) might touch the President himself. I was appalled, seeing, for the first time clearly, how Watergate could destroy all authority. In these circumstances, it would be reckless to urge Nixon to put his diminishing prestige behind a bombing campaign of several weeks' duration that the situation required and that he was clearly reluctant to undertake. I therefore suggested at the next WSAG meeting that we wait for an unambiguous direct challenge while continuing with our planning. The members of the WSAG, who were finely tuned to bureaucratic and political intangibles, understood immediately that this represented a sea change. Up to then our strategy had been to prevent a major challenge rather than wait for it to occur. The decision meant that we were postponing a preemptive strike indefinitely. Thus, sooner or later, South Vietnam would have to cope with the full fury of the unimpeded North Vietnamese buildup.

By April 23, it was clear that the President was in no position to order any kind of meaningful retaliation. I told Haig:

> My problem is I don't see how we can get anything done in this climate. I mean supposing we start bombing. This will crystalize all the Congressional opposition. . . . I have no doubt that if it weren't for the mess, we'd back them off [that is, the North Vietnamese].

By the end of April 1973, therefore, both carrots and sticks for enforcing the Vietnam agreement were in tatters. In the light of flagrant North Vietnamese violations and the stories of abuse told by returning prisoners of war, the carrot of economic aid to Hanoi was understandably all but eliminated by Congress. First the Byrd amendment, which barred direct or indirect assistance (to any of the parties) unless specifically authorized by Congress, went through by 88 votes to 3. Then the stick of bombing was lost by our domestic turmoil. Congress in June prohibited a military response by law, but the window we had in those few months in early 1973 had already been closed by Watergate's enfeeblements.

Within six months of the Paris accords, the traditional opponents of American involvement in Indochina succeeded in legislating their preferred outcome by means of binding congressional acts—something they had never managed to accomplish while the war was raging. When, in June 1973, Congress prohibited the use of military force "in or over Indochina," the United States was effectively forbidden to enforce an agreement for which over 55,000 Americans and hundreds of thousands of Vietnamese had given their lives. At the same time, military assistance to Vietnam was slashed from $2.1 billion for fiscal year 1973 to $1.4 billion in FY 1974 and $700 million in FY 1975, despite the fact that oil prices were quadrupling and draining Saigon's scant reserves of hard currency.

In these circumstances, Hanoi infiltrated over 130,000 soldiers with tanks and heavy artillery into South Vietnam over the year and a half after the agreement and constructed a network of roads to shift its troops rapidly from sector to sector. The United States was throttling South Vietnam and paralyzing its own capacity to act. Not surprisingly, the tragedy ended with the entire North Vietnamese army invading South Vietnam while the United States stood by paralyzed and cultivating its own divisions.

The Search for Peace in Cambodia

It is one thing to have opposed, at the time, the measures the Nixon administration considered necessary to support Cambodia, thereby to preserve South Vietnam. The fear that America might get "bogged down" in Cambodia as it had in Vietnam represents an honorable difference of judgment. But the debate shades into hypocrisy when the tragedy of Cambodia inspires not sober second thoughts, but a campaign to shift the indictment for all *Communist* misdeeds to those who tried to save Cambodia and spare it the horrors that befell it.

It was North Vietnam that occupied portions of Cambodia in 1965 to implant military bases from which it killed Americans and South Vietnamese for four years before there was any American response—and that response was limited to the narrow belt a few miles wide where the North Vietnamese sanctuaries were located. It was Hanoi that had spurned American proposal to restore Cambodia's neutrality, which I made to Le Duc Tho in a secret meeting on April 4, 1970. It was Hanoi that refused to talk of peace except with the prior condition that any non-Communist structure in Cambodia should be destroyed. It was Hanoi that rejected offers of cease-fire in October 1970, May 1971, October 1971, January 1972, and from October 1972 to January 1973. It was the Communist Khmer Rouge, organized, armed, and sponsored by Hanoi, that blocked Cambodia's inclusion in the Paris Agreement, something the United States had repeatedly sought. Determined to fight on to total victory, the Khmer Rouge rejected Lon Nol's proclamation of a unilateral cease-fire and America's unilateral cessation of hostilities on January 27, 1973.

It was Hanoi, therefore, if it was anyone, that brought the war to Cambodia and made possible the genocide by the Khmer Rouge. No doubt we overestimated Hanoi's influence on the Khmer Rouge; the Cambodian Communists were intractably different from the submissive Pathet Lao. But there can be no doubt that the decision on a fight to the finish was Hanoi's. Hanoi promoted the unconditional victory of the Communists, calculating—correctly, as it turned out—that the collapse of Cambodia would speed the demoralization of South Vietnam and that it would be able to deal with a fractious Communist Cambodia at leisure afterward.

Cambodia was misrepresented in America as a separate "war" that must be avoided. But it was not any such thing. The enemy was the same as in Vietnam. North Vietnamese troops shifted back and forth across the border as if the concept of sovereignty did not exist. America contributed to the disaster in Cambodia not because it did too much but because it did too little. In 1970, after American and South Vietnamese troops withdrew from their brief incursion into the sanctuaries—designed to destroy North Vietnamese base areas from which Americans and South Vietnamese had been killed for years—antiwar critics sought to achieve by legislation what had eluded them in the street demonstrations of May 1970. Between 1970 and the end of the war, the following restrictions on American assistance to Cambodia were passed into law, always over Nixon's veto or vigorous objection:

• The Fulbright amendment to the Armed Forces Appropriation Authorization for Fiscal Year 1971, enacted on October 7, 1970, specified that South Vietnamese and other free world forces (such as Thailand's) could not use funds provided by the act to furnish military support and assistance to Cambodia. It also prohibited South Vietnamese or other free world forces from transferring to Cambodia any military supplies furnished under the act. Thus the ceiling placed on our aid was imposed as well on our allies in Southeast Asia, as if our primary national problem was to close every loophole by which Cambodia might be saved. It was passed three months after our incursion was over and on the same day that Nixon offered a cease-fire throughout Indochina—which the Communists quickly rejected.

• The Cooper-Church amendment to the Supplementary Foreign Assistance Act of 1970, enacted on January 5, 1971, prohibited the use of funds for "the introduction of United States ground combat troops into Cambodia, or to provide United States advisors." Thus the United States was barred by law from giving the Cambodians the kind of advice and training that they needed to become an effective fighting force.

• The Symington-Case amendment to the Substitute Foreign Assistance Act and Related Assistance Act, enacted on February 7, 1972, limited the total number of "civilian officers and employees of executive agencies of the United States Government who are United States citizens" in Cambodia to 200 at any one time. It also limited the number of third-country nationals employed by the United States in Cambodia to eighty-five. This made any effective military *or civilian* advice to the Cambodians impossible.

• The Second Supplemental Appropriations Act for Fiscal Year 1973 (signed into law reluctantly by Nixon on July 1, 1973) prohibited the use of funds appropriated in the act to "support directly or indirectly combat activities in or over Cambodia, Laos, North Vietnam and South Vietnam or off the shores of Cambodia, Laos, North Vietnam and South Vietnam." Also, it prohibited any funds appropriated under *any* act to be used after August 15 for the above purposes. Thus any American military action anywhere in or around Indochina became illegal. With it vanished any Communist fear of a penalty for violating the Agreement.

• The Continuing Appropriations Act for Fiscal Year 1974 likewise prohibited the use of any funds to finance directly or indirectly combat activities by U.S. forces "in or over or from off the shores of North Vietnam, South Vietnam, Laos or Cambodia." This continued the prohibition of the previous year.

• The Foreign Assistance Act of 1973, which became law on December 17, 1973, provided that no funds authorized or appropriated under any provision of law would be available to finance military or paramilitary combat operations by foreign forces in Laos, Cambodia, North Vietnam, South Vietnam, or Thailand unless such operations were conducted by the forces of the recipient government within its borders. This meant that allies like Thailand, threatened from Indochina, could not use American equipment—and therefore not their forces—to assist the countries whose survival they judged important to their security.

In addition, Congress limited the total amount of aid for Cambodia to $250–$300 million a year, about 2 percent of what was being spent to help Vietnam.

These cumulative constraints not only prevented effective American assistance; they also precluded our allies in Southeast Asia from helping their Cambodian neighbors. Military advisers were prohibited, which the American embassy in Phnom Penh interpreted to bar even field trips by military attachés. Thus the Cambodian army grew in size but not in competence. Congressional restrictions forced it to rely on firepower rather than mobility (and the rigidity our critics imposed was then invoked as an indictment of the Cambodians' military effort). Only airpower was available to stave off disaster—until that too was prohibited by those who had blocked the more discriminating methods of resistance.

Sadly, Cambodia became a symbol and a surrogate for the whole controversy over Vietnam. To Nixon, it was "the Nixon doctrine in its purest form,"* meaning that our policy was to help it defend itself without Ameri-

---

* Nixon used the phrase in his news conference of November 12, 1971.

can troops. To his opponents, it was an opportunity retrospectively and symbolically to defeat by legislation both our incursion into the sanctuaries and Nixon's very effort to achieve a defense against aggression by building up local forces. They sought, and succeeded, in imposing on Cambodia the restrictions they had failed to inflict on South Vietnam. Their failure over South Vietnam prevented collapse; but their success over Cambodia doomed that country and, in time, South Vietnam as well. The restrictions made inevitable the diplomatic impasse that served Hanoi's purposes. Once Hanoi was committed to conquest and the Khmer Rouge to total victory, the only way to extricate America honorably was to demonstrate that these goals were unfulfillable. Our domestic divisions produced the opposite result. The restrictions on American aid saved the Khmer Rouge from defeat in 1970–1972 when it was still an embryonic force; and thereafter they prevented the leverage over the Khmer Rouge and Hanoi that was essential to induce a political negotiation.

Beginning in early 1973, we strove to bring about a cease-fire in Cambodia, to follow the cease-fires in Laos and Vietnam. On the day the Paris Agreement was signed, January 27, the Cambodian government, on our advice, made a bid for peace by halting all offensive military operations and declaring a unilateral cease-fire. Simultaneously, we stopped American air operations.

Whatever hopes Sihanouk may have had to emerge as the indispensable balance wheel disappeared when he turned himself into a prisoner of the Khmer Rouge and of his own 1970 declaration of total war against the Cambodian government. The official position of the Khmer Rouge remained the outraged appeal of Sihanouk of March 23, 1970, less than a week after he was deposed. He had called then for dissolution of the Lon Nol government and legislature and for formation of a Government of National Union, a National Liberation Army, and a National United Front, whose essential task was to fight "American imperialism" at the side of the Vietnamese and Laotian Communists.

In the period leading up to the Paris accords, Sihanouk reiterated this position. And the signs of flexibility afterward evaporated in the light of closer inspection. In an interview with Agence France Presse on January 29, 1973, Sihanouk noted that "our friends" (probably Hanoi and China) had urged his government in exile not to maintain its intransigent stance. He was willing to talk to the United States, he said, but he would never negotiate with

Lon Nol and would never accept a solution like that reached for South Vietnam. In any case, he said significantly, the ultimate position would be determined not by him but by the "Cambodian resistance, which is operating in the interior"—that is to say, the Khmer Rouge. An official four-point statement of January 26, 1973, issued in the name of Sihanouk, his Prime Minister Penn Nouth, and Khmer Rouge leader Khieu Samphan, reiterated that the solution to the Cambodian problem could be found *only* on the basis of Sihanouk's declaration of March 23, 1970—in other words, a complete Communist takeover.

On February 2, the Khmer Rouge radio broadcast an official statement by its insurgent leadership. Rejecting both the American and Lon Nol unilateral cease-fire, it proclaimed that "the Cambodian nation and people are obliged to continue their struggle against the U.S. aggressors and the traitors Lon Nol and Sirik Matak in order to liberate the people." The statement contemptuously ruled out all negotiation with the "U.S. imperialists," declaring that "it is necessary to obstruct and oppose their diplomatic maneuvers." The Khmer Rouge bitterly denounced Hanoi for signing the Paris Agreement; they saw the Vietnam settlement as a betrayal, and not only because they thought it allowed us to shift the brunt of American military operations to Cambodia. In a document published after they came into power, they admitted that they resisted all pressures for a cease-fire because "if the Kampuchean [Cambodian] revolution had accepted a cease-fire it would have collapsed."[7] Later they blocked a settlement because they were bent on total victory.

The same day, the Khmer Rouge command issued orders that the fighting continue, that any political negotiation or compromise with the Cambodian government was ruled out, and that Sihanouk was not to engage in negotiations with the Americans or anyone else. In short, by the time I left for a trip to Asia in February 1973, the Cambodian Communists had decided on at least one more attempt at total victory.

When I visited Beijing after the trip to Hanoi, the Chinese leaders were beginning to understand that the domination of Indochina by Hanoi might be an ideological victory but a geopolitical defeat for China, as it would place at China's southern border a powerful state drawn to Moscow and with a record of historical enmity toward China. Perhaps China had always understood it but—like many other nations—could not believe that the United States would accept military defeat, much less engineer it. Both of us, in any event, wanted an independent and neutral Cambodia, and both of us were moving toward the return of Sihanouk—the United States hesitantly because it saw no other unifying force, the Chinese with conviction because they considered him their most reliable friend in Cambodia and the best counterweight to the Khmer Rouge. Both Beijing and the Nixon administration were convinced that the best solution for Cambodia was some sort of coalition headed by Sihanouk, whose influence would depend on the continued existence of some of the non-Communist forces represented by the Lon Nol government.

In June 1972, even while the war was still going on, Zhou Enlai had told me that, in Laos and Cambodia, China preferred an outcome in which "bourgeois elements" would participate in the government and the traditional rulers would become heads of state:

> In solving the Indochina question it is not Vietnam alone—it is still a question of Cambodia and Laos, but they are comparatively easier. Because no matter what happens we can say for certain that elements of the national bourgeoisie will take part in such a government; and we can be sure in Cambodia Prince Sihanouk will be the head of state, and in Laos the King will be the head of state. So if it can be solved through negotiations such an outcome would be a matter of certainty.

In February 1973, upon conclusion of the Vietnam agreement, Zhou elaborated on this thought when he told me that a completely "red" Cambodia would result in greater problems, meaning that it would doom Sihanouk and assure Hanoi's hegemony over Indochina. I responded by proposing an immediate meeting between Sihanouk's Prime Minister Penn Nouth and a representative of Lon Nol. We would not insist on the participation of Lon Nol in a government that might emerge from such a negotiation so long as the forces he represented were included. Zhou offered to take this proposition to the Cambodians "in our wording," meaning that he would identify himself to some extent with our position.

The situation was complex. The Chinese saw their best guarantee of Cambodian independence in Sihanouk. But the Soviet Union continued to recognize Lon Nol—thus transferring the Sino-Soviet rivalry to Cambodia. The irony was that the major Communist rivals each backed the wrong horse because both overestimated the American determination to support the existing structure in Phnom Penh, for without this both the Lon Nol government as well as Sihanouk were doomed.

Our analysis was that the Khmer Rouge would agree to a negotiated settlement only if deprived of hope of a military victory. That the Khmer Rouge had made exactly the same analysis became evident in July. We learned that in the spring of 1973, the executive committee of the Khmer Communist leadership had made a crucial policy decision. It decided to keep open two basic options: total victory or a compromise. The choice between them was to be determined by the military situation in Cambodia later in the year. In the event that military victory was out of reach and a stalemate emerged, the Khmer Rouge would negotiate for the best conditions obtainable. If, on the other hand, the military situation was favorable, negotiations would be avoided and total victory sought. It was thus a contest between the American quest for equilibrium and the Khmer Rouge determination to prevail.

On my return from Asia at the end of February, I called a series of WSAG meetings. My attitude was summed up by what I told the group on March 28:

> We've been meeting here for four years and we've been through it all. I'm not looking for alibis from you for losing this whole thing. There are a hundred ways we could make it look good while turning it over to the Communists, but that's not what we're here to do.

If there were officials favoring an elegant collapse of the free Cambodians, they did not speak up at the meeting. Nevertheless, we were caught in a vicious circle. We could not achieve a cease-fire without a stronger government in Phnom Penh, and the government could not be strengthened without a more active American policy, which in turn was prevented by legislative restrictions.

Not unnaturally, the strain began to show in Cambodia. The guerrilla war conducted with unparalleled cruelty by the Khmer Rouge, assisted by the North Vietnamese, drove refugees from the countryside into the cities, especially into Phnom Penh, destroying the social equilibrium of the country. It imposed a war on a Cambodian army that had first been deliberately kept small and ineffective by Sihanouk to discourage any temptation for a coup and then had been deprived of effective training and adequate supplies by American legislation. Assaulted by ferocious indigenous Communists, the free Cambodians fought with extraordinary bravery that was both made possible and shackled by an American aid program legislated to prevent any decisive success.

The Lon Nol government was in reality Sihanouk's without the Prince; its institutions and personalities were the leadership cadre that had governed Cambodia since independence. As in many authoritarian societies, there had always been corruption. This is partly because in traditional societies the distinction between the private and public sectors tends to be less sharply defined and partly because the insufficient power to tax invites corruption as a means of financing the costs of government. It was perhaps inevitable that Lon Nol should lean increasingly on the few people he trusted, who tended to be his family, especially his younger brother, Lon Non; the latter unfortunately carried corruption and favoritism to heights beyond what could be explained by sociological analysis. Lon Non came to be described in the world's press as the "evil genius." The brothers' *pas de deux* resembled a similar drama in 1963, a decade earlier, in Saigon when the Ngo Dinh Diem government began to disintegrate under the impact of Communist guerrilla war, American pressure to reform, and its own inherent rigidities, and Diem and his brother Ngo Dinh Nhu were assassinated in an American-sponsored coup.

In Washington, participants at the WSAG meeting proposed that, to lay the groundwork for a return of Sihanouk, Lon Nol should be persuaded to "broaden the base of his government" and indeed to resign. A scheme emerged to invite Lon Non to military school in the United States and Lon Nol abroad for medical treatment. Prince Sisowath Sirik Matak, perhaps the ablest Cambodian leader (who had been Sihanouk's Deputy Prime Minister until the 1970 coup), was to become Vice President and acting President during Lon Nol's absence. In early April, Al Haig visited Phnom Penh to present the scheme. Lon Nol agreed to send his brother into exile and to bring Sirik Matak into the government. We decided to recommend delaying Lon Nol's departure as a bargaining chip for an eventual negotiation.

Sihanouk was of no help. In light of later developments, it is hard to believe that the Chinese did not indicate to him that in the right circumstances he could go back as head of state with American support. But to make himself more acceptable to the implacable and dreaded Khmer Rouge, Sihanouk kept on parroting their insistence on a fight to the finish. Despite his obvious self-interest in Beijing's and Washington's preferred solution, Sihanouk understood that the Khmer Rouge and Hanoi were determined to block such an outcome. He was too weak to abandon the only base he had, which was the Communists—whatever his convictions. Sihanouk repeatedly let it be known that the "interior resistance," that is to say, the Khmer Rouge, opposed all compromise.

That Sihanouk's assessment of Khmer Rouge dominance was accurate soon became evident. Sihanouk made a brief visit to the "liberated zone" of Cambodia in March 1973, widely publicized afterward. But the Communists were trying to undermine Sihanouk's standing in the country even while exploiting his prestige internationally. The Khmer Rouge, for example, refused to disseminate Sihanouk's statements within Cambodia. Other reports revealed that the Khmer Rouge were systematically purging pro-Sihanouk elements from the internal structure in Cambodia and launching a propaganda campaign to discredit him and eliminate all vestiges of his popularity in the countryside.[8]

The sole remaining card to produce a negotiation was to work for a military stalemate. And to achieve this, the sole asset was American airpower—advice and training to improve Cambodian military performance and increases in American aid having been precluded by legislation. Part of the new Cambodia guilt-shifting myth is that American bombing was indiscriminate, that it produced monstrous civilian casualties, and that the "punishment" inflicted on the Khmer Rouge turned them from ordinary guerrillas into genocidal maniacs driven by "Manichean fear."[9] The reality is otherwise.

Ambassador to Cambodia Emory C. Swank, often critical of our policy, and his deputy Thomas O. Enders set out the facts about the bombing in a document written for the Historical Division of the Department of State years after I had left office. (The document is in the Appendix. The analysis here follows their account.) On January 27, 1973, when the Cambodian government unilaterally halted all offensive military actions in the hope of achieving a cease-fire, American tactical air and B-52 operations also stood down. The bombing was to be resumed only if the Khmer Rouge insisted on continued hostilities, and only at the request of the Cambodian government.

These conditions were fulfilled in February 1973. The Khmer Rouge answered the cease-fire appeal by launching an offensive; the North Vietnamese, in violation of Article 20 of the agreement, refused to withdraw their forces and continued to give logistical and occasional rocket and artillery support to their Cambodian allies. The United States had to respond or face the collapse of free Cambodia—and probably South Vietnam as well. American air operations were resumed, as Swank and Enders demonstrate, through regular channels by instructions from the Department of State to the ambassador.

The targeting was controlled by the Seventh Air Force, which relied on up-to-date photography, precision radar, and infrared sensors and conducted reconnaissance both before and after every strike. Air operations were subject to rules of engagement that prohibited the use of B-52s against targets closer than one kilometer to friendly forces, villages, hamlets, houses, monuments, temples, pagodas, or holy places. There were tragic accidents—only two serious ones, Swank and Enders note—but they hardly amounted to systematic slaughter of civilians. On a number of occasions, Cambodian requests for air strikes were turned down because reconnaissance showed risks to the civilian population that those controlling air operations were unwilling to take.

The myth that Khmer Rouge brutality was the result of American bombing may fulfill some masochistic imperatives, but it makes even less sense than to blame the Holocaust on the bombing of Cologne, for the target of the bombing of Cambodia was largely unpopulated areas. What evidence there is regarding Khmer Rouge conduct suggests something completely different. As early as 1971, the Khmer Rouge were carrying out deliberately, in all areas of Cambodia they controlled, the same totalitarian practices that horrified the world when applied to Phnom Penh after their victory in 1975. The forced uprooting and dispersal of village populations; destruction of traditional local social organization, religious practices, and family structures; forced collectivization of agriculture; deliberate liquidation of the middle class as an obstacle to a "new society"; and the systematic terror of the Communist police state—all these features of the post-1975 holocaust in Cambodia were in evidence in Khmer Rouge–controlled areas for several years before 1975. They represented *deliberate policy*, founded on ideological fanaticism.

In the summer of 1973, we strove through all available means to end the Cambodian war. Both the broadening of the Phnom Penh government and the intensification of the bombing were designed to prompt resumption of negotiation. Sihanouk's public remarks, unfortunately, continued virulently negative about the prospects. On April 13, after returning from his visit to the "liberated zone" in Cambodia, undoubtedly reflecting what he had been told by the Khmer Rouge inside Cambodia, Sihanouk told a press conference in Beijing that he would "never accept a cease-fire nor compromise."

The Aborted Chinese Mediation

Despite all the obstacles, there was a brief moment when a prospect for a negotiated solution with Chinese assistance emerged, though it has been resolutely ignored by writers on the subject.

The news of Khmer Rouge intransigence could not have been welcome to Sihanouk's Chinese hosts. They knew that a total Khmer Rouge victory would ruin the viability of their carefully nurtured Sihanouk card and guarantee Hanoi's domination of Indochina. China doubtless also calculated that the United States would resist a total defeat of the forces with which it had been associated. A continuation of the war would therefore increase Beijing's foreign policy problems. At a minimum, it would delay the rapprochement with the United States that was a principal objective of Chinese policy.

Zhou Enlai tried to cut through these perplexities—at first a bit too obliquely. He used the occasion of Sihanouk's return to Beijing from his trip to Cambodia to articulate Chinese preferences. At a state banquet for Sihanouk on April 11, Zhou condemned the United States for continuing its "wanton bombing" in Cambodia and its support of the "traitorous Lon Nol clique." Zhou's unusual public statement critical of the United States temporarily obscured the thrust of his remarks: China's emphatic backing for Sihanouk as Cambodian head of government. According to Zhou, Sihanouk's visit to Cambodia had proved what the Khmer Rouge had emphatically denied: that Sihanouk was "beloved and supported by the Cambodian people."

We noticed mainly the explicit criticism of the United States rather than the subtle dissociation from Hanoi and the Khmer Rouge. On April 13, therefore, was sent a sharp note to Beijing expressing our "extreme disappointment" at Zhou's remarks. It called attention to Hanoi's flagrant violations of the Paris Agreement, especially of Article 20, which required withdrawal from Laos and Cambodia. But even this note ended with an affirmation that we were willing to proceed with negotiations on the basis of what I had outlined to Zhou.

That Beijing was stung was apparent in the rapidity of its reply. Huang Hua, then Chinese ambassador to the United Nations, asked to see me on

April 16 in a "personal" capacity—an inconceivable procedure for a Chinese diplomat unless he wished to say something that could be officially disavowed. He could not understand, he said, our expression of extreme disappointment; China had done no more than restate its previous positions. He urged that the United States end its support of Lon Nol. The formulation, aimed at an individual and not a structure, stressed the ambassador, left open the prospect discussed in Beijing in February of including other elements of the Phnom Penh government in a coalition without their present chief.

I picked up the theme in my response:

> With respect to Cambodia, we are prepared to work with you to bring about some coalition structure along the lines that the Prime Minister and I discussed in Peking [Beijing]. We are not committed to any particular personality. And we would encourage negotiations between representatives of Prince Sihanouk and the other forces.
>
> Our objective in Southeast Asia seems to us not totally dissimilar from yours. We want to prevent a security system extending in South and Southeast Asia controlled by one unit and one outside power. We believe this is best achieved if each country in the region can develop its own national identity.

The Chinese did not respond immediately. However, on May 18, 1973, in his first meeting with David Bruce, recently appointed the head of America's new liaison office in Beijing, Zhou turned the conversation to Cambodia: He told Bruce that "the only way to find a solution was for the parties concerned to implement fully all the subsidiary clauses of Article 20." China thus agreed with the American interpretation that North Vietnamese forces had to vacate Cambodian territory. Zhou added that Huang Zhen, the newly designated head of China's liaison office in Washington, would leave on May 25 for the United States and would be authorized to pursue the subject. Clearly, Zhou hoped for an answer by the time Huang Zhen reached Washington.

Meanwhile, Le Duc Tho's interpretation of the Paris Agreement increasingly equated Cambodian neutrality and independence with North Vietnamese hegemony. Implementing Article 20—regarding North Vietnamese withdrawals—required a prior political settlement, according to Le Duc Tho, and he would not discuss a political solution out of respect for the "sovereignty" of his Cambodian allies. So tender was Hanoi's regard for the independence of a country it had first invaded in 1965 and was to invade again in 1978 that Le Duc Tho would not even agree to my proposal for a joint recommendation of a cease-fire to both parties in Cambodia.

To follow up the exchanges with Zhou Enlai, I approached the Chinese with a formal proposal. On May 27, I told Huang Hua in New York that, in my view, American and Chinese interests were compatible. We both sought to prevent "a bloc which could support the hegemonical objectives of outside powers." In other words, we did not want Indochina under Hanoi's tutelage aligned with the Soviet Union. To achieve this purpose, I made the following proposal:

> We are prepared to stop our bombing in Cambodia, and we are prepared to withdraw the very small advisory group we have there. And we are prepared to arrange for Lon Nol to leave for medical treatment in the United States. In return we would like a cease-fire—if necessary, say for ninety days—a negotiation between the Sihanouk group and the remainder of the Lon Nol group; and while this negotiation is going on in Cambodia, we would authorize some discussions between the staff of Ambassador Bruce and Prince Sihanouk in Peking [Beijing]. And when this process is completed, in some months, we would not oppose the return of Prince Sihanouk to Cambodia. But it is a process that has to extend over some time, and it must not be conducted in a way that does not take into account our own necessities.

Huang Hua was a thoroughgoing professional. He asked a few clarifying questions. Huang Hua knew that Hanoi would not favor such a scheme but might not be able to block it. He reminded me that Premier Zhou Enlai had told David Bruce that both Sihanouk and the Khmer Rouge were in principle willing to talk to the United States. This might not mean much if the precondition was the destruction of the non-Communist forces, but the Chinese had to have something more in mind. For, after all, Zhou himself had said in February that a completely "red" government would compound everybody's problems.

Huang Hua did not reject my proposition, as he surely would have done had it been Beijing's policy to keep aloof from events in Indochina. He said he would report to Beijing.

On May 29, I reiterated the same proposal to Huang Zhen on his first call on me at the White House. He, too, said he would report back; he, too, pointedly reminded me of Zhou's conversation with Bruce and its emphasis on the strict implementation of Article 20. The next day, Nixon used the occasion of an Oval Office courtesy call by Huang Zhen to stress the importance he attached to a peaceful solution for Cambodia.

The Chinese followed up swiftly. On June 4, eight days after my original proposal, Huang Hua in New York requested a meeting with me to hand over a message. It noted our "tentative thinking on the settlement of the question of Cambodia." It stressed that all parties concerned—and therefore by implication Hanoi as well—needed to respect the sovereignty of Cambodia. China could not conduct talks with the United States on behalf of Cambodia; direct talks with Sihanouk would therefore be necessary at some point. Nevertheless, China was now prepared to:

> communicate the U.S. tentative thinking to the Cambodian side, but as Samdech [Prince] Sihanouk is still visiting Africa and Europe, it is inconvenient for us to contact him through diplomatic channels. For the sake of accuracy, the Chinese side would like to repeat the U.S. tentative thinking.

The Chinese note then repeated verbatim the proposal that I had read to Huang Hua, and concluded: "If there are any inaccuracies in the above, it is expected that the U.S. side will provide corrections."

Anyone familiar with Zhou Enlai could be certain that he would not check so meticulously except to signal that he was engaging himself, and he would not act as intermediary unless he expected to succeed. The careful Chinese would never risk demonstrating their impotence to affect events in Southeast Asia; they would never offer to pass on a message that they thought would be turned down. And it was significant, too, that when Beijing designated Sihanouk as our interlocutor, no reference whatever was made to the "internal resistance," that is to say, the Khmer Rouge. Still, it was inconceivable that the Chinese would expose themselves in this manner without having checked with the Khmer Rouge. And if the Cambodian Communists were ready to deal, the military stalemate that the Khmer Rouge had decided in March would cause them to negotiate by July must be imminent.

Zhou had clearly committed China to a compromise that preserved key elements of the Lon Nol structure—that was the thrust of everything we both had been insisting on for nearly a year. The proposal, reflecting the military balance, would stop short of the total victory the Khmer Rouge had heretofore demanded. The cease-fire would preserve the structure of free Cambodia; Sihanouk would return with the support of the United States and China, not simply as a temporary figurehead, as the Cambodian Communists preferred, but with the power inherent in the necessity of acting as the balance wheel between different factions.

Zhou Enlai could have sold any such proposition to the Politburo in Beijing—and especially to Chairman Mao—only with the argument that total Khmer Rouge victory was impossible because Washington would never tolerate it and that any other course would aid the hegemonic aims of Hanoi. Nor could he possibly have made it palatable to the Khmer Rouge without the argument that only this scheme would bring about the end of American bombing. And the Khmer Rouge would not have acquiesced unless convinced that they could not prevail militarily in the face of continued bombing. Hence, even though he would not admit it, Zhou needed America's military actions in Cambodia for the effectiveness of his policy almost as much as America did. The bombing was a bargaining chip for two parties, even though one formally condemned it.

But the American domestic situation, it soon appeared, would not sustain American policy as it was approaching its culmination. By early June, the President had been brought to bay. In Los Angeles on June 5, a grand jury began hearings on a Watergate-related break-in at the office of the psychiatrist of Daniel Ellsberg who had leaked the Pentagon Papers to the press. On June 6, Nixon agreed, under pressure from the Senate Watergate committee, to reverse a refusal of two days earlier to release the logs of his conversations with John Dean, his White House counsel, who had turned state's evidence. And on June 8, one of the Watergate burglars, James McCord, asked Judge John Sirica for a new trial on grounds that the government had withheld evidence and perjury had been committed at his trial.

Neither Zhou Enlai nor, for that matter, I appreciated the extent to which presidential authority had been eroded, so we proceeded on the agreed path. On June 13, in a meeting in Paris with Chinese Acting Foreign Minister Ji Pengfei, I confirmed the accuracy of what Zhou intended to convey to Sihanouk. I emphasized the importance of a transition period of several months before Sihanouk could return to Cambodia. There was no disagreement between us about the Prince's ultimate role as head of state.

That was the sense, too, of a conversation I had with Huang Zhen the next day, June 14, in Washington. We both expressed our impatience for Sihanouk's early return to Beijing and our frustration at the unpredictability of his movements. Huang Zhen and I began to discuss a trip by me to Beijing. Ostensibly it was to brief Zhou on the results of Brezhnev's imminent visit to the United States. It would also be the occasion for beginning contact with Sihanouk.

On June 19, I told Huang Zhen that if a cease-fire existed in Cambodia by the time of my visit to China—expected around August 6—I would be prepared to meet Sihanouk for political discussions. We had gone to the limit of what was possible. Meantime, Sihanouk continued his travels, apparently oblivious to my talks with the Chinese. He seemed, above all, concerned that Le Duc Tho and I might settle Cambodia over his head. Sometime in June, while visiting Yugoslavia, he gave an interview to the Italian journalist, Oriana Fallaci. Sihanouk emphasized that Hanoi had no right to speak for the Khmer insurgents. Then he repeated the Communist hard-line position, again in the subtle form of reporting the views of his allies—not his own: "The Khmer Rouge will never accept a cease-fire. They will never bow to an agreement. Never." (The only explanation I have for the Chinese failure to inform Sihanouk on his travels was that they did not trust their codes to convey the complexity of their scheme, and they distrusted above all Sihanouk's discretion while so far away from Beijing.)

Sihanouk paid tribute to the American bombing: it was "the only thing that prevents us from entering Phnom Penh right now." But he also showed his awareness of Watergate and Congress's efforts to terminate American military activities: "Nixon is in a very difficult situation. The Watergate scandal has done him a great disservice and in the end the Senate and Congress will oppose his expenditures." As for his relationship with the Khmer Rouge, Sihanouk had few illusions and many premonitions: "The Khmer Rouge do not love me at all. I know it! . . . I am useful to them. . . . I understand very well that when I shall no longer be useful to them, they'll spit me out like a cherry pit." Cambodia would one day be Communist, he said ruefully. He disdained any ambition, saying he had no desire to be a figurehead like Queen Elizabeth or Hirohito.[10]

We did not learn of the interview until August 12, when the die had already been cast. In all likelihood, we would have interpreted it as showing that Sihanouk was almost surely out of touch during his travels; that Zhou

knew what he was doing; that he would not have committed himself to a
course unless confident that he would succeed in it.

In mid-June, we believed that we were on the homestretch to a cease-fire
and Sihanouk's return, followed by Sihanouk's achieving the room to maneuver between the existing political forces and the Communists with all that it
would have meant for Cambodia's future. But the inability to maintain domestic support was to doom Cambodia—and probably to shake Mao's confidence in his Prime Minister (who disappeared from his office six months
later).

For in late June, Congress legislated a final halt to the bombing to take
effect in mid-August.

Many factors contributed to the final series of events that led to the abandonment of Cambodia. Simple war weariness in the United States played a
major role. Some legislators sincerely thought they were conferring a great
boon on the peoples of Indochina by prohibiting American military action.
Congressman Thomas O'Neill, then Democratic Majority Leader, remarked
in the House that Cambodia was not worth the life of one American flier.[11]
Conservatives, already disheartened by the ambiguities of ten years of war,
were demoralized by the travails of their old standard-bearer, Nixon. The collapse of Nixon's public standing as a result of Watergate was without doubt
the single most important factor. So it happened that Congress marked the
final breakdown of domestic consensus by prohibiting United States military
operations in Indochina.

Congressional agitation against the bombing started in April and May.
America's air operations were denounced as "illegal," though their constitutional basis was substantial (as elaborated in the notes).[12] Le Duc Tho had
gloated in May of the congressional pressures on us. We were heading for a
dilemma described by me in a press conference on May 12:

> No one can expect that an agreement for a cease-fire will be ob-
> served simply because it is written down, and the Congress and oth-
> ers have to ask themselves whether it is possible to maintain an
> agreement without either sanctions or incentives.

It turned into a race between our efforts to achieve a cease-fire in Cambodia
and the congressional timetable. By early June, the legislative scene turned
bleak. On June 4, the Senate approved the Case-Church amendment to cut

off all funds for military operations in Indochina. I knew only too well that a bombing cutoff would destroy our only bargaining chip—and the sole incentive for Chinese involvement. Zhou Enlai needed to be able to argue that, in exchange for a political solution involving Sihanouk and preservation of the existing structure, he had brought the Khmer Rouge an end of American bombing. The negotiations now in tenuous train were our last throw of the dice. If they failed, Cambodia, and soon thereafter South Vietnam and Laos, would be doomed. On June 18, I appealed to Mel Laird, after Watergate temporarily brought him back to government as Counselor to the President for Domestic Affairs. I told Laird that the Chinese had promised to intercede: "I can't imagine that they would commit themselves to saying that they would do something unless they felt they had a chance of bringing it off." I offered to make a gentleman's agreement with the Speaker of the House, Carl Albert, and the venerable Chairman of the House Appropriations Committee, George Mahon, that, succeed or fail in the negotiations, we would stop bombing on September 1. But they had to give us their word not to reveal the deadline; once it was known, our capacity to use the end of bombing diplomatically was gone; the Khmer Rouge would simply wait until the deadline passed. Laird agreed to put forward my proposal, but he was not optimistic. That master manipulator of congressional committees was convinced we had reached the end of the line: "Mahon says it's never been as tough as it is right now."

Every day counted. We learned that Sihanouk would return to Beijing from his travels on July 5 and that our plan could then unfold. But Congress would brook no further delay. On June 25—the day John Dean started testifying before the Senate—came a crucial vote in the House on the Eagleton amendment, a Senate-passed rider to cut off funds for Cambodian bombing. Attached to a supplemental appropriations bill to fund the activities of the U.S. government after the end of the current fiscal year (June 30), it could be vetoed by the President only at the risk of shutting down the government. For if the bill did not pass, all government agencies would be out of funds. From San Clemente, I appealed by telephone to a number of congressmen: We would end the bombing by September 1 come what may, but this pledge had to be kept secret if prospects for a cease-fire in Cambodia were not to be derailed. I could not be explicit about the Chinese initiative, but I gave enough hints about negotiations.

But the secrecy of the September 1 deadline could not be preserved. Only by a public "compromise" in which September 1 was named as a cutoff date could administration supporters hope to stave off the pressure for an immediate end to bombing. Yet once the deadline was public, our strategy was dead; the Khmer Rouge would simply wait it out. Then on June 25, the administration failed on a tie vote, 204 to 204, to obtain even this brief extension. The House by voice vote approved the Eagleton amendment, which cut off funds immediately.

The next day, June 26, similar amendments were attached to a continuing resolution, the means by which existing budgets are extended pending congressional consideration of new appropriations. The same amendments were tied to the bill raising the national debt ceiling. Our opponents, in short, were prepared to stop the operation of the entire government in order to emasculate military operations in Indochina.

American diplomacy had for six months painstakingly put the pieces into place for a neutral Cambodia ruled by Sihanouk. But military pressure was one such piece, and the legislated end of military activity destroyed all possibility of a neutral, free Cambodia. With a total Communist victory now guaranteed, Sihanouk became nearly as irrelevant as Lon Nol—barely tolerated by the Khmer Rouge for international consumption, rapidly discarded when total power was achieved. Congressional action had doomed America to become a passenger in a vehicle hurtling out of control down a steep mountainside.

The Negotiations Unravel

For a few weeks, the existing plan kept going by momentum, perhaps in part because the Chinese leaders needed time to adjust to the spectacle of a superpower voluntarily abandoning its options. On July 6, coinciding with Sihanouk's return to Beijing, the Phnom Penh government officially offered to negotiate with the "other side." This step had been planned to provide a diplomatic framework for the Chinese initiative, which presumably would now unfold even though its premises had been shattered.

But Sihanouk, the great survivor, understood the new situation faster than either Lon Nol or Zhou Enlai. For months he had been denouncing America for failure to negotiate, while at the same time explaining his intransigence not as his preference but as imposed by the Khmer Rouge. Returned to Beijing, he must have been aware that we had offered a bombing halt, negotiations, and a meeting between him and me early in August. Clearly, too, Zhou Enlai favored such a course. Yet after the congressional action, Sihanouk understood that the negotiating route was dead. Obviously the Khmer Rouge had studied the military situation, as we knew they had planned to do in the early summer, and had concluded that, with the bombing ended, there was no need for compromise after all. On July 5, Sihanouk's public line eschewed all hints of a willingness to negotiate: It was now "useless" to talk, he said. It was now "too late." The Khmer insurgency, he admitted, had decided "to struggle to the end."

During the first week of July, the Soviet Union also shifted its position. Throughout, it had recognized Lon Nol and maintained an embassy in Phnom Penh. Now *Pravda* and *Izvestia* both began to refer to Sihanouk as chief of state, for the first time since his ouster on March 18, 1970. Communist diplomats briefed newsmen in Moscow that Moscow was shifting its bets—an augury that these practitioners of power politics, who prided themselves on their assessment of objective factors, had grasped the significance of the congressional action.[13] Two weeks later, Soviet Ambassador Dobrynin informed me that the Soviets, Chinese, and North Vietnamese had all come to the conclusion after July 1 that negotiations were dead and the Khmer Rouge were going to win.

We nonetheless tried to pursue the negotiation through the Chinese; we had, in fact, no other option. On July 6, 1973, Ambassador Huang Zhen was my guest at the summer White House in San Clemente. He brought with him a message hinting that Zhou Enlai was getting nervous and looking for an exit. The Chinese complained about "rumors" and "speculation" in the American press about a negotiation between the Lon Nol "clique" and Sihanouk. The message tactfully attributed the leaks in part to the Lon Nol government although "U.S. officials" had recently "made some disclosures" on this question. Interestingly, the Chinese did not claim the speculation was wrong; on the contrary, they expressed concern that such speculation "is extremely disadvantageous to seeking a settlement of the Cambodian question and will even cause trouble." (The "disclosures" of a negotiation, of course, had been provoked by the administration's desperate attempt to head off the congressional bombing halt.)

I replied by reiterating our plan. Huang Zhen confirmed that Beijing would, as promised, inform Sihanouk of our "tentative thinking" now that Sihanouk had returned from abroad. If Zhou was still willing to transmit an offer whose central element—the cease-fire—had been made irrelevant by legislation, the Chinese must have been eager indeed for a political settlement. Huang Zhen confirmed that a visit by me in Beijing in early August would be welcome. Zhou Enlai clearly would not give up the joint plan easily.

The tension in Beijing caused by the new and unexpected turn of events in Washington was revealed in an encounter that same day between the Chinese Premier and a visiting congressional delegation headed by Senator Warren Magnuson. Zhou Enlai made the standard boilerplate criticism of America's Cambodian policy, including the bombing. The agreed plan, indeed, depended on his ability to claim later that he had induced Washington to end the bombing as his contribution to the peace process. Suddenly Zhou Enlai found handed to him in front of many witnesses what his design required to appear to be extracted from us. Senator Magnuson informed Zhou grandiloquently that he need not worry about the bombing; Zhou should be patient; it would soon be over—specifically, on August 15; Zhou had Congress to thank for it. Zhou grew visibly irritated. Desperately seeking to preserve his bargaining chip, he said that it was hard to be patient while bombs were falling. Not to worry, intoned Magnuson, Congress would take care of everything. "Zhou was visibly angered," to the growing bafflement of the congressional delegation, David Bruce reported. And Zhou's annoyance seemed to mount uncontainably when Magnuson continued to mutter: "We stopped the bombing."

I understood. Zhou saw emerging before him his geopolitical nightmare: an Indochina dominated from Hanoi and allied with the Soviet Union, brought into being by an obtuse superpower that did not deign to give its own diplomacy a chance to succeed.

And the prospect raised premonitions of a yet deeper sort for him. Watergate had heretofore appeared as an incomprehensible domestic squabble in America. But now it seemed possible, even likely, that China would have to deal with a President whose authority was so weakened that his commitments, and perhaps even his communications, had become unreliable; that—to use a favorite Chinese phrase—his word no longer counted. If America proved so incapable as a superpower, it had profound implications for China's security; indeed, it undercut the premise on which the Chinese rapprochement with the United States had been based.

After the Zhou-Magnuson exchange, signs of hesitation from Beijing multiplied. On July 11, David Bruce back-channeled an assessment of the Cambodia diplomacy in light of my projected visit to China. The Chinese seemed to be backing away from involvement in a Cambodia negotiation.

On the same day, there was another straw in the ill wind. The Chinese had already agreed to receive me in Beijing in the first week of August; they had invited us to pick the date. When at the end of June we proposed August 6, they had even allowed that date to leak to the press in Beijing. We had then suggested an announcement for July 16. On July 11, we received the bland reply that Huang Zhen had been recalled to Beijing—in itself an unexpected development—and that the announcement would have to await his consultations. This was a clear hint that there were second thoughts.

The guillotine finally fell on the evening of July 18. Han Xu delivered a note to General Scowcroft declaring that for a variety of rather contrived reasons, China was no longer willing even to communicate the American proposal to Sihanouk. The Chinese note simply repeated the most extreme demands of the Khmer Rouge, all of which had been known in the months in which the Chinese had engaged themselves in the search for a compromise.

And since the Chinese could never be sure that the Western mind fathomed the intricacies of any situation, Zhou Enlai sent us another unmistakable signal: The very next day—July 19—we were informed that my visit on August 6 was no longer "convenient." The most appropriate date would be August 16, the day *after* the bombing halt America had imposed on itself. If Cambodia were to be discussed in these circumstances, we would be suppliants. The implication was clear. America had become largely irrelevant to Chinese policy in Indochina—and so had Sihanouk. They might continue to pay lip service to Sihanouk, but henceforth they had to place all their bets on the Khmer Rouge. Chinese mediation was over.

I summed up the situation to my staff on July 19:

> The bombing cut-off had fundamentally changed the situation in Cambodia. Formerly, Sihanouk's utility to the Khmer Rouge had been that he gave them legitimacy they had not had. Now they didn't need legitimacy; they saw they could win. Sihanouk's utility to the Chinese had been that he gave them influence over the Khmer Rouge and could resist other outside influences. The utility of the Chinese to us was that they had some control over Sihanouk.

Sihanouk's utility to us was that, once he returned to Cambodia, he might be able to keep things balanced. Ironically the Chinese needed the Lon Nol group—this was a restraint on Sihanouk and on the Khmer Rouge. The congressmen had totally misjudged the situation. Now this was all lost. Sihanouk couldn't deliver the Khmer Rouge and the Chinese couldn't deliver Sihanouk.

There is no guarantee that this negotiating effort would have succeeded. The Khmer Rouge might well have violated any agreement they did not block. The fact remains that even if the plan we were negotiating ultimately failed, it would have brought a transitional period to ease the fate of the Cambodian people and perhaps spare them the genocidal suffering that the abdication of their friends and the ferocity of their conquerors eventually inflicted on them. This was the most promising negotiating opportunity, if not the only one—with the Chinese and us working actively in parallel—and it was torpedoed by our domestic turmoil.

After the summer of 1973, Cambodia was doomed, and only a miracle could save South Vietnam. North Vietnamese communications to us grew progressively more insolent. There was no longer even the pretense of preserving the Paris Agreement. America's legislated impotence added humiliation to irrelevance. We struggled to furnish what economic and military aid for Cambodia was obtainable from Congress. But by the fall of 1973, collapse was just a question of time.

12

FORD AND VIETNAM

After the events of the summer of 1973, Vietnam disappeared as a policy issue. There was nothing the administration could do to alter the course of events, and the opponents were content with the strategy of attrition they had adopted. In August, I was appointed Secretary of State. In September, I was awarded, together with Le Duc Tho, the Nobel Peace Prize for the negotiation of the Vietnam agreement. It was a complete surprise, for I had not even been aware that I was under consideration. The happiness at this greatest distinction a statesman can achieve was balanced, if not overcome, by the foreboding regarding the ultimate outcome. I turned the prize money over to a scholarship fund for the education of children of American servicemen killed in Vietnam. I did not attend the award ceremony in Oslo because the authorities feared demonstrations. Le Duc Tho answered my note of congratulations with an insolent message regarding American violations. The Middle East war soon demanded much of our attention. As for Indochina, I observed it with the melancholy shown toward a terminally ill relative, hoping for a long respite and a miracle cure I was unable to describe.

Gerald Ford succeeded Richard Nixon as President on August 9, 1974, and asked me to stay on as Secretary of State. As it happened, the President's first decision was how to react to a desperately inadequate military assistance budget for Vietnam wending its way through Congress. Support for military or economic assistance to Indochina was disintegrating. Appropriations for Vietnam had been reduced by 50 percent each year since the signing of the Paris Agreement, from $2.1 billion in 1973, to $1.4 billion in 1974, and to $700 million for fiscal year 1975. The Nixon administration had requested

$1.4 billion for military assistance for FY 1975. The Senate Armed Services Committee, headed by the venerable and conservative John Stennis from Mississippi, had reduced this to $1 billion. Now the Senate Appropriations Committee, headed by the equally conservative John McClellan from Arkansas, was slashing another $300 million from the military assistance program. At the same time, economic aid was being reduced from $650 million to $250 million. The impact of these cuts was compounded because the increase in oil prices and inflation reduced the effective value of the aid package to about one quarter of the 1973 amount.

The budgetary battles were surrogates for a fundamental challenge being pressed on the new President first by the Congress he had inherited from Nixon and even more insistently by the predominantly McGovernite Congress elected in 1974. What had started out as a campaign to reduce American forces had by 1973 turned into a campaign to liquidate American support for Indochina altogether. At the same time, some of Ford's associates from his congressional days, having seen career after career blighted by Vietnam, were urging him to avoid being drawn into the Indochina vortex, especially in what would clearly be a losing battle. In their more innocent moments, some of them even entertained the illusion that their old friend might wind up garnering public credit for ending America's involvement in Indochina.

Ford had no such misconceptions. He understood instinctively that the oath of office drew him into the fray, and it is to his credit that he recognized the fashionable slogan for ending American economic and military assistance for what it was: a euphemism for abandoning Indochina. Nevertheless, the opponents were gaining ground because no one was left to contest the field. The conservatives had lost heart with the bombing halt ordered by Johnson in 1968; the Nixon supporters were demoralized by Watergate; and the new White House staff had no stomach for the brutal fight they had heretofore watched from the sidelines.

To symbolize his commitment to maintaining a free South Vietnam, Ford had made it a point to receive the South Vietnamese ambassador, Tran Kim Phuong, for a private meeting the evening of his first day in office. The President assured Phuong that he was committed to Saigon's survival and would do his best to increase aid levels. On the same day, Ford reiterated this assurance in a letter to Thieu, adding to the NSC draft a paragraph of his own:

Our legislative process is a complicated one and it is not yet completed. Although it may take a little time I do want to reassure you of my confidence that in the end our support will be adequate on both counts.

Neither Ford nor I had yet grasped the depth and scope of the congressional opposition about to be elected in the aftermath of Watergate, or the letter would surely have been modified. Congressional support for aid to Vietnam had evaporated on both ends of the political spectrum. In June, while Nixon was still in office, Senator James Allen of Alabama, a conservative and master at legislative maneuvering, stated that he had supported the administration until the troops and the prisoners had come home but, once that task had been accomplished, "now, we should get out." [1] Senator Hubert Humphrey, the floor manager of the foreign aid bill, testified to the same exhaustion in liberal rhetoric: "We ignore the most important lesson, that political battles cannot be resolved by force of arms." [2] This is not a conclusion which most historians have reached. And the neoconservatives—recent converts to the conservative camp from the liberal side and busy excoriating the Ford administration for alleged softness toward Communist pressures—were nowhere to be found in the domestic debate over how to resist the only Communist military aggression actually taking place.

It was not until September 5 that Ford was able to turn to the issue of aid for Indochina in a systematic way. During one of my daily meetings, I warned:

Without massive effort on your part, we are in trouble on Vietnam. If we don't do enough, it doesn't matter how much too little you do. North Vietnam seems undecided. You might want to consider meeting with the congressional leaders next week. We are in trouble both with the restrictions and the dollar amounts. . . .

For symmetry's sake, I presented the option of abandoning Vietnam:

You do have an option as a new President. You could let it go—and not be blamed, at least through '76. I must say I think it is wrong. The liberals who would applaud it would fail you when the going was tough.

Ford never considered that option. He had been the ranking Republican member of the Defense Subcommittee of the House Appropriations Committee throughout the Vietnam war and had considerable knowledge of the significance of the aid levels. He needed no briefing to understand that the constantly declining levels of aid posed an ominous psychological and military danger. On September 12, I sent Ford a memorandum that described the impact of a $700 million level for military aid:

> —insufficient funds to replace damaged or lost equipment;
> —a 50 percent reduction in aircraft utilization on top of the 11 squadrons of aircraft already grounded;
> —reductions in operations by sea-going vessels by 30 percent and by riverine vessels by 82 percent;
> —medical supplies would be completely expended by the end of May 1975;
> —fuel for ground forces would be exhausted by late April 1975;
> —by the end of FY 75, the Army would have only one-quarter of the minimum ammunition reserve necessary to meet a major offensive;
> —unutilized aircraft and ground equipment will deteriorate rapidly.

By September 1974, South Vietnamese casualties were mounting in direct proportion to the aid shortfalls, which forced them to ration ammunition. They had reached 26,000 combat deaths since the signing of the Paris Agreement twenty months earlier. Though the congressional leaders were impressed by these figures, the most Ford could extract from them was a promise by Senator Stennis to consider favorably a request for $300 million for a supplemental budget in January 1975. That did not help matters much because, as far as Saigon was concerned, funds would be disbursed at the rate implied by the $700 million budget until the supplemental budget could be passed, which would not be until well into 1975.

The supplemental request turned into a forum for another assault on funding for Indochina, the abandonment of which was being advocated more and more openly and with increasingly insistent alibis: Did we have a legal commitment to extend aid to Vietnam? Should we gear our assistance to the levels of Soviet and Chinese aid to Hanoi? Should we not seek a political rather than a military solution? Every argument produced weeks of procrastination as new hearings were conducted by skeptical congressional committees. Finally the opponents of aid, now in a majority, abandoned their rear-guard action and began to rally around the proposition that South Vietnam had to learn to stand on its own and could expect at best a final lump sum grant as a sort of severance payment.

Within the administration, I was the chief advocate for meaningful aid levels. Having had the principal role in negotiating the Paris accords, I felt a special responsibility. I would never have concluded the negotiation had I not been convinced that Congress would supply adequate assistance after our withdrawal. It never occurred to me that America might end up simply jettisoning an allied people. As Vietnam was collapsing, my appeal was to such unfashionable concepts as "honor" and "moral obligation," not to *Realpolitik*—as critics had it. On March 22, 1974, I told a staff meeting:

> I do feel very strongly that having lost fifty thousand men, torn our country apart, staggered to a conclusion which was at least not dishonorable, to throw it all away now for $100 million one way or the other is a disgrace. And I would much rather tell Congress what we think we need and let them take the responsibility for cutting it.

At a minimum, America owed Vietnam a reasonable opportunity to defend itself by supplying the wherewithal to do it. What would have happened in Europe, Korea, or the Gulf had the United States, after a cease-fire, withdrawn its troops, cut off aid, and then legislated a prohibition against responding to aggression with American forces?

In 1971–1973, when we were extricating America from Vietnam, there had been many expressions of congressional support for the idea of giving substantial aid after an American troop withdrawal, as can be seen in the backnotes.[3] Once the Paris Agreement was concluded, however, collective amnesia suddenly set in. Congress displayed an extraordinary penchant for disavowing what it had heretofore been proclaiming as articles of faith. One such argument was that American aid to Saigon should be no greater than Soviet and Chinese deliveries to Hanoi. But this compared the incommensurable. Saigon was obliged to defend a jungle frontier of nearly 700 miles; the North Vietnamese could concentrate on any one point and, in flagrant violation of the Paris Agreement, were expanding and upgrading their logistics system to enable them to concentrate their forces rapidly and at decisive points. Until the summer of 1974, the South Vietnamese armed forces had been able to compensate with superior artillery and airpower; now congressional budget cuts were forcing dramatic reductions in these activities. The best description of the impact of these budgetary cuts could be found in an analysis in the authoritative theoretical journal of the North Vietnamese Communist Party, *Hoc Tap,* of January 1975:

> The intensity of firepower and the amount of mobile equipment of the puppet troops [Saigon] have markedly decreased. In the third quarter of 1974, the monthly number of artillery rounds fired by the puppet troops decreased approximately by three-fourths, compared with the monthly number in 1973. The number of daily tactical sorties of the puppet air force only equaled approximately one-fifth of those conducted in 1972. The present number of aircraft in the South, compared with the greatest number of aircraft on hand in the period of the limited war, has decreased by 70 percent, with the number of helicopters decreasing by 80 percent. . . . The bomb and ammunition reserves of the puppet troops have decreased and they are encountering great difficulties in fuel and in the maintenance, repair and use of various types of aircraft, tanks, combat vessels and heavy weapons.

All the evidence at the time and even more since in the various accounts of the North Vietnamese commanders leaves no doubt that Hanoi was preparing for a military showdown from the day the peace accords were signed—in complete disregard of their pledged undertakings. Starting immediately, the North Vietnamese undertook a monumental effort to reequip and reorganize their forces in the South. They constructed a network of strategic roads totaling 12,000 miles north and south, east and west, including an eight-meter wide, all-weather road suitable for trucks; they built 3,000 miles of oil pipelines to fuel the tens of thousands of vehicles moving down the roads—all in flagrant violation of the Paris Agreement. As early as October 1973, the Twenty-first Plenum of the Central Committee of the North Vietnamese Communist Party decided to resume its program of "revolutionary violence." By March 1974, a Central Military Committee meeting was drawing up operational plans for resuming the "strategic offensive." The memoirs of North Vietnamese General Van Tien Dung, who commanded the final assault, relate that, between April and October 1974, North Vietnamese units attacked the enemy "with no let-up, winning greater victories each day, at a greater pace," from which the general staff drew the conclusion that "the fighting capability of our mobile main-force units was superior to that of the enemy's."[4]

The reason, according to the same North Vietnamese general, was that great quantities of "tanks, armored cars, rockets, long-range artillery, and anti-aircraft guns" (all, of course, prohibited by the Paris Agreement) had been sent south. This was made possible by the network of roads, which, in the vivid words of Dung, were like "strong ropes inching gradually day by day, around the neck, arms and legs of a demon, awaiting the order to jerk tight and bring the creature's life to an end."[5]

While South Vietnam was being gradually strangled, Washington had grown tired of Vietnam.

The Strangulation of South Vietnam

Lawrence Durrell has written that every individual possesses a finite reservoir of courage or commitment which, however deep, is neither inexhaustible nor replenishable. This is what happened to the United States with respect to Indochina in 1975, two years after the Paris Agreement to end the war. Idealism had propelled America into Indochina, and exhaustion caused it to leave.

The passage of time has mercifully eased some of the pain of those somber months. Nevertheless, the way Indochina was brought to collapse in 1975 still evokes a sinking feeling in me, composed in equal parts of sadness for the victims that were abandoned and melancholy for what America did to itself. What makes the ultimate collapse so heartbreaking is that, by 1975, the debates of the Kennedy, Johnson, and Nixon years should have become irrelevant. Once the agreement to end the war was signed in January 1973, whatever the views regarding the wisdom of undertaking the war or of how it had been conducted, the peoples of South Vietnam and Cambodia who had stood with America deserved the economic and military aid without which they had no chance of defending themselves.

Instead the United States, as if suddenly seized by a collective obsession to extrude a past which was, in fact, inescapable, seemed bent on extinguishing its witnesses. Whether South Vietnam, Laos, and Cambodia could have survived by their own efforts indefinitely had they received the assistance promised to them will never be known. There is no doubt in my mind that, with anything close to an adequate level of American aid, they would not have collapsed in 1975. And with anything like the support extended to allies in Korea, the Gulf, and the Balkans, they might have survived until the erosion of Communism set in.

The end came to Indochina as it does in a Greek tragedy where the principals are driven by their very natures to fulfill their destiny sometimes in full foreknowledge of the anguish that awaits them. In Indochina, the manner in which the chief actors had conducted themselves in the previous decade ultimately shaped their actions in 1975. The choices they made in the end were permutations of choices they had made years earlier. What had started as an almost philosophical controversy over what constitutes a nation's honor ended up as a technical debate about modalities of extrication. Even the new American President, really the only free agent among the principals, was forced to the realization that there was no heretofore undiscovered way out of this morass; given what had gone before, the tragedy had become inevitable.

The overwhelming Democratic victory in the 1974 congressional elections brought a group of congressional freshmen to Washington who, in the words of *The Almanac of American Politics, 1978,* represented a political realm "in which opposition to the Vietnam War was the most compelling source of motivation."[6] Only two years earlier, in the presidential election of 1972, George McGovern had been defeated in the second largest landslide in American history importantly over the issue of Vietnam. In the congressional elections of 1974, in the aftermath of Nixon's forced resignation, his erstwhile supporters prevailed on the issue of Watergate and emerged in a position to reverse the voters' earlier verdict on Vietnam.

Hanoi's determination to step up pressures received a boost from an apparent change in Soviet attitudes. In late December 1974, a high-ranking Soviet official visited Hanoi for the first time since the signing of the Paris Agreement. It turned out to be anything but a courtesy call. The Chief of the Soviet General Staff, Viktor Kulikov, participated in the Politburo strategic discussions then under way (the last similar visit had been in 1971 prior to the Tet offensive of 1972).

Memoirs have yet to recount the gist of the Soviet advice, but it seems clear that some previous restraints were lifted; Soviet shipments of military matériel increased fourfold in the months that followed. Until Soviet archives are opened, we cannot know the Soviet motives—whether it was a reaction to the congressional attacks on the trade bill in the Jackson amendment and on the Vladivostok Agreement just concluded between President Ford and Brezhnev, or whether it had been part of Soviet strategy all along. Whatever the answer, there is little doubt that Moscow was now encouraging Hanoi's bellicosity.

The only remaining element of uncertainty for Hanoi was the attitude of the United States. According to General Dung's account, Le Duan, the party's general secretary, concluded in October 1974 that "the internal contradictions within the United States administration and between the American political parties, too, were growing sharper. The Watergate affair had agitated the whole country. . . . American aid to the Saigon quisling administration was on the decline" to the point that the United States "cannot rescue the Saigon administration from its disastrous collapse." The 1975 offensives would test this judgment. While there are disagreements among the North Vietnamese military leaders who have written memoirs (largely over who gets credit for the winning strategy), they all agree on this central point: The offensives planned for 1975 were expected to be only a prelude to final victory in 1976 or even 1977. The American reaction to these offensives—or lack of it—would be a crucial test of how they would then proceed.[7]

The tone of communications from Le Duc Tho was always a good indicator of the level of the confidence of Hanoi's Politburo. Nixon's resignation, coupled with congressional budget cuts for Vietnam, produced an arrogance which suggested that Hanoi was feeling the wind at its back. On August 9, 1974, we used the occasion of Ford's swearing-in to send a message warning against treating the transition as a military opportunity and expressing our desire for improved relations with Hanoi:

> President Ford, as you must be aware, has been a firm supporter
> of President Nixon's policy in Indochina for five and one-half years.
> In the spirit of mutual respect and candor which has always characterized our exchanges, Mr. Special Advisor, I must convey to you that
> President Ford is a man with a keen sense of American honor. He also

shares the view, as we all do on the American side, that the DRV has a positive path open to it—of peaceful settlement, reconstruction, constructive ties with the United States and the western world, and a truly independent role in world affairs. The President is ready to engage with you on this path.

In a brutal reply on August 25, Le Duc Tho not only took credit for bringing about Nixon's resignation but threatened Ford with a similar fate:

> Mr. Nixon met with failure in the enterprise and had to leave the White House. Should Mr. Ford continue doing so, he would certainly and inevitably fail too.

After accusing me of betraying my "signature and my commitment"—a charge one makes in diplomacy only if one expects to prevail with no need for further negotiations—Le Duc Tho concluded on this ominous note:

> In case the US continues the implementation of the Nixon Doctrine without Nixon and the use of the Nguyen Van Thieu group to pursue the war and to undermine the Paris Agreement on Vietnam, then the Vietnamese people will resolutely carry on their struggle to defend peace and the Paris Agreement until complete victory.

While Hanoi opted for military victory, Washington was waffling over whether even the aid package of $700 million—which, as noted, in real terms amounted to a reduction by two thirds of the first peacetime year— might be too high. When Ford appealed to Senator Stennis for a restoration of the $300 million that had been cut from the military assistance budget, this staunch friend of the Pentagon and anything but a dove replied:

> I said if 700 million [for Vietnam] wasn't enough I would work for more. But I was getting information from some military people that we could cut down, and I wanted you to send someone out there to appraise it.

A few, albeit at a relatively low level, managed to rise above the Beltway preoccupations. On December 20, 1974, James R. Bullington, the State De-

partment's Vietnam desk officer, wrote a moving and extraordinarily prescient report after a visit to Saigon. He pointed out that even a supplemental
of $300 million would only barely cover expenditures for consumables and
would leave no funds for replacements. A minimum of $1.3 billion would be
needed for the same purpose in 1976. By then, the replacement of damaged
and destroyed equipment could no longer be delayed, implying the need
for an additional—and substantial—financial request. Interspersing his report with human interest vignettes of the growing despair among South
Vietnamese, Bullington concluded that, without the supplemental, South
Vietnam's position was hopeless. The point had been reached where, if the
supplemental failed to materialize, only one option would be left to mitigate
our country's dishonor—to save as many Vietnamese as possible:

> If the supplemental fails, we should also consider ways and means of
> saving as many anti-Communist South Vietnamese as possible. For
> example, do we not have a certain obligation to those many thou-
> sands of Vietnamese and their families who are present or former em-
> ployees of the USG? To fail to help such people escape would, I
> believe, add considerable dishonor to our defeat in South Vietnam.

On December 30, 1974, in Vail, Colorado, Ford reluctantly signed the
Foreign Assistance Act and coupled it with a strong objection to the deep
cuts in aid for Vietnam it contained (made even more onerous by many legislative limitations on the use of the aid). The survival of Vietnam now depended on our ability to obtain the supplemental appropriation promised by
the congressional leadership.

Hanoi Resumes the Offensive

One of the nightmarish aspects of the Vietnam tragedy was that debates
about it had a liturgical quality: They were their own end; they required no relationship to observable reality. Thus, in Washington, the fateful
year began as if nothing extraordinary were happening in Indochina even
though Hanoi had just run through a dress rehearsal of its options by launching the first of the limited offensives ordered by the Politburo. In mid-

December, it initiated a series of sharp attacks throughout the southern provinces of South Vietnam. On January 7, 1975, Communist forces over-ran Phuoc Binh, capital of Phuoc Long province, the first provincial capital in the entire war to have been lost and never retaken by Saigon. While the of-fensive was under way, the Hanoi Politburo met to assess its results and chart its strategy. Phuoc Binh was the test case.[8] If the United States reacted, there was still a chance for Hanoi to withdraw from the brink.

But Washington was determined to withhold funds from an ally when the knife was at its throat. Congress was not ready to act quickly, to say the least. Thus the issue came down to whether other measures might be avail-able to resist the Phuoc Long move. The previous pattern repeated itself. There had been little enough enthusiasm for a supplemental; there was now even less for other forms of assistance. Fortunately, there was at least one per-son in the executive branch who held the view that America was honor-bound to extend aid, and he happened to be the President of the United States. Under pressure from the media, urged by his immediate staff to disso-ciate from Vietnam, disavowed by many of his former congressional col-leagues, Ford remained steadfast and calm. Before every interdepartmental meeting, I would check with him to make sure I was reflecting his views, as I did on January 7 before the WSAG meeting to deal with the Phuoc Long offensive. The President's response was brief and decisive:

> KISSINGER: We are having a WSAG on Vietnam. I plan to take a tough line. I assume you are prepared to ask for a supple-mental.
>
> FORD: By all means.

And again, on January 8, when I reported to Ford about the military mea-sures discussed at the WSAG meeting, he replied: "I think we should do it."

Unfortunately, the cupboard was bare when the discussion turned to measures to show Hanoi that we viewed its actions with increasing gravity. The checklist of available diplomatic measures was far more likely to demon-strate American impotence than it was to give Hanoi pause. It included such frightening measures as appeals to Moscow, Beijing, and to the U.N. Secu-rity Council (in which both Beijing and Moscow had vetoes), and protesting to the eleven other parties and countries that had signed on as guarantors of the Paris Peace Agreement at the March 2, 1973, International Conference on Vietnam.*

None of these measures offered the slightest prospect of averting the looming North Vietnamese offensive and South Vietnamese debacle. We did send a circular dispatch to the guarantors as well as to the four members of the International Commission of Control and Supervision (Canada, Hungary, Poland, and Indonesia). This elicited a few evasive replies but mostly silence—which I would feel better about if I could describe it as embarrassed.

I had learned from experience that Hanoi would pay attention only to measures which might affect the situation on the ground. We now know from memoirs how carefully its leaders were studying every American military and political move. The administration had no intention of violating the congressional prohibitions against direct American military involvement, but given Hanoi's near paranoid suspiciousness, there was a slight chance that moving some American forces closer to Indochina might cause Hanoi to take a second look. The Defense Department provided a list of permitted possibilities:

- Increasing reconnaissance activity over North Vietnam;
- Detouring the aircraft carrier *Enterprise,* which was scheduled to move to the Indian Ocean from Subic Bay in the Philippines, via the Gulf of Tonkin;
- Redeploying F-4 fighter planes to the Philippines and Thailand and B-52s from the United States to Guam.

I favored all these proposals, arguing: "It has been my experience that when we move timidly, we lose. When we are bold, we are successful."

Ford approved the entire list. But before any deployments could be implemented, the Defense Department recoiled in the face of the probable congressional and media assaults. The annual congressional budget battle was coming up—this time with the new McGovernite Congress—and the Pentagon was in no mood to expend any more capital on Vietnam. It either

---

* There were twelve participants: United States, France, China, United Kingdom, Canada, Soviet Union, Hungary, Poland, Indonesia, Democratic Republic of Vietnam (DRV, i.e., North Vietnam), Republic of Vietnam (GVN, i.e., South Vietnam), and Provisional Revolutionary Government of the Republic of South Vietnam (PRG, i.e., the South Vietnamese Communists).

dragged its feet on implementing the WSAG recommendations or shifted the onus for them to the State Department. As expected, Hanoi protested the increase in reconnaissance flights as a violation of the Paris Agreement, most provisions of which it had been flagrantly violating for months. The media and Congress instantly clamored for clarification, whereupon the Pentagon announced that the State Department would do the briefing—thus passing the buck and implying that the Pentagon was washing its hands of the entire project. In the end, Secretary of Defense James Schlesinger stepped up and, on January 14, 1975, undertook a strong defense of the reconnaissance flights. By then, Hanoi had learned what it needed to know: that this was the maximum we were capable of doing and not the opening maneuver of determined resistance.

The deployment of a carrier group into the Gulf of Tonkin never took place. The *Enterprise* had barely left Subic Bay on the way to the Indian Ocean—and before the orders for diversion to the Gulf of Tonkin had even been received—when Hanoi started to beat the propaganda drums, claiming American provocation. By now we were quite familiar with the characteristic North Vietnamese tactic: Hanoi would appeal to Congress and the media for reassurances regarding measures they actually feared, then use the reassurance to demonstrate American impotence to the South Vietnamese. The Pentagon was so concerned about avoiding congressional wrath—and so reluctant to testify about its measures—that it ordered the *Enterprise* to proceed on its original course. Not until the *Enterprise* had traversed the Strait of Malacca did the White House learn that there had been a change of signals. By then, of course, turning the carrier around would have magnified the firestorm.

The Defense Department offered to substitute another carrier—the *Coral Sea*—for the Gulf of Tonkin mission. But it was clear that we had lost the ability to move military forces in Southeast Asia without debilitating controversy.

Even the White House staff was infected by the prevailing mood of abdication. Several of the new President's friends were urging two fantasies, already noted: that they could somehow get credit for Ford for ending the Vietnam war; at a minimum, they sought to "protect" their President from too close an association with the looming disaster. Neither option really existed. "Credit" for ending the Vietnam war was not to be gained by consigning those who had relied on America to a tragic end. Nor was there any way for Ford to avoid playing the hand which fate had dealt him, however unfairly. To the President's credit—in the way history, and not contemporaries, measures credit—he remained firm in the refusal to dishonor his office by colluding with Hanoi in the destruction of an ally.

The attitude of the newly arrived White House staff was epitomized by Ron Nessen, who had been brought in as press secretary after Ford's initial choice resigned over the pardon of Nixon. In his memoirs, Nessen describes a wonderful "fantasy" of his, according to which he would one day announce the end of the Vietnam war. He then proudly recounts his determination to *prevent* the White House from sending any message to the North Vietnamese by means of his daily briefings:

> He [the NSC staffer responsible for press guidance] wanted to scare the North Vietnamese a little, or at least leave them guessing about American intentions. I replied that I didn't think Hanoi devised its strategy according to my answers.[9]

Despite Nessen's belief to the contrary, the North Vietnamese *were* watching. According to two North Vietnamese military sources, Premier Pham Van Dong wisecracked to a Politburo meeting at the end of 1974 that Washington was so paralyzed that "even if we offered the Americans a bribe to intervene again, they would not accept it." Thus he concluded that the campaign in the South should resume.[10] Another North Vietnamese source reports the similar conclusion of Hanoi Communist leader Le Duan, who persuaded the Politburo that, in view of the "weakening position of the enemy," Hanoi's original plan for a two-year campaign for 1975–1976 should be modified to include another option: to seize "the opportune moment" to "win" and "immediately liberate the South in 1975."[11]

The End of the Road

Our sole remaining card to prevent Saigon's collapse was the supplemental appropriation. Without it, everybody agreed, South Vietnam was doomed. But if the supplemental was delayed very much longer, it would be too late to reverse the slide toward disaster.

Of course, no one had any idea whether the figure of $300 million would be adequate.

A money bill has to pass through two stages in each house of Congress: authorization, followed by the actual appropriations. These decisions are handled by separate committees, require separate testimony, and are subject to separate votes. The Appropriations Committee cannot exceed the authorized amount, but it is free to reduce it. It might later restore its cuts up to the authorized limit; that additional sum is called a supplemental appropriation. If the administration wanted a larger increase, it had to ask the Armed Services Committee for a new authorization.

The bureaucracy fastened on the $300 million figure primarily because it would avoid the authorization process. In fact, there was no reasonable basis for it. The administration had requested $1.4 billion; the Armed Services Committee had authorized $1 billion; and the Appropriations Committee had reduced the amount by another $300 million. It was this last cut we were now seeking to restore. Reluctant to start the entire authorization process over again, the Pentagon declared the $300 million to be precisely what was needed. I told a State Department staff meeting on January 20, 1975:

> I simply call attention to the amazing coincidence that a figure that corresponds to nothing that anyone ever asked for, and that emerged by accident out of the authorization process at a quiet time should be exactly the figure you need at a period [of increased warfare].

Thieu, by now desperate, appealed to Ford in two letters dated January 24 and 25, 1975. He protested the capture of Phuoc Binh as "certainly the most massive and the most blatant violation of the Paris Agreement." He described the intensity of the North Vietnamese attacks, backed by the "massive application of fire power and armor." By contrast, the South Vietnamese troops "had to count every single shell they fired in order to make the ammunition last." Thieu pointedly reminded Ford of the assurances of continued American aid which had induced him to sign the Paris Agreement.

The letters triggered Ford's decision to overrule the White House staff, which had opposed the supplemental. He launched his effort in a televised interview with John Chancellor and Tom Brokaw on January 23, continued it at a meeting with congressional leaders on January 28, and culminated it with firm instructions to the Cabinet on January 29. The request to Congress provided grim details of the North Vietnamese buildup and the South Vietnamese shortfalls. Ford reminded Congress:

> We told the South Vietnamese, in effect, that we would not defend them with our military forces, but that we would provide them the means to defend themselves, as permitted by the Agreement. The South Vietnamese have performed effectively in accepting this challenge.

And he appealed to his Cabinet to close ranks:

> Yesterday I sent up an Indochina supplemental. I want it clearly understood that this Administration is clearly, firmly, unequivocally behind that. We want it, we are going to fight for it, and I want everyone behind it. I think it is vital and right, and I want no misunderstanding about that.

I weighed in with an appeal to the congressional leadership on June 28:

> . . . The overwhelming objective of the national debate was to disengage our military forces and return our prisoners. There was no objection to the principle of supporting a government that was prepared to defend itself by its own efforts. They are now defending themselves. The South Vietnamese agreed to go it alone on the basis that we could give them the wherewithal to do it. They have a chance to defend themselves. That chance exists. That chance depends on American assistance.

It was to no avail; Congress was beyond being moved by such appeals. Senate Majority Leader Mike Mansfield explained that he would vote against the supplemental because "our friends are in this country, not in Southeast Asia or the Middle East." Speaker Carl Albert, usually a strong supporter of administration policy, did not even pretend that his decision had any substantive basis: "I won't say what I will do, but when all your fellows are against you, what can you do?" Senate Minority Leader Hugh Scott made a valiant effort to support the President, but the bulk of commentary ranged from hostile to fence-sitting.

The favorite theme of those who opposed the supplemental was that the administration should seek political rather than military solutions. But the aging revolutionaries in Hanoi had nothing but contempt for the proposition that diplomacy was somehow separable from strategy. They were not to be deprived of their ultimate victory by diplomatic sleights of hand or academic theories of conflict resolution. If America could not influence the situation on the ground, it stood no chance of making any impact on Hanoi via diplomacy.

Most of the domestic attacks came from by now familiar quarters. But to our immense surprise and huge disappointment, the cause of Vietnam was abandoned also by Senator Henry Jackson, scourge of détente and Ford administration critic for its alleged softness on Communism. With his own presidential candidacy looming and primaries in New York and California on the horizon, Jackson decided to throw in the towel. Announcing his opposition to the supplemental, he stated:

> I voted to cut that $300 million last year and I am not going to
> vote to hand it back this year. There has to be a limit. There has to be
> a ceiling. There has to be an end. The problems of Southeast Asia are
> not going to be solved by $300 million more in ammunition.[12]

When even the traditional anti-Communist sentinels abandoned the ramparts, the chasm between the views of the administration and Congress became unbridgeable. For the supplemental to have any impact on the ground in Vietnam, it needed to be passed by March so that the money for consumables could be made available immediately. The longer the delay, the more the South Vietnamese army, demoralized by shortages in fuel and ammunition and the mounting casualties, ran the risk of disintegration.

The issue before Thieu was no longer how to defend his country but what he could afford to give up. Yet every redeployment into presumably more defensible areas only increased Hanoi's incentive to step up its attacks and to try for a knockout. In February, still waiting for the supplemental, Thieu decided to move his crack airborne units from the Central Highlands to Danang along the coast. That move settled the issue for Hanoi and triggered an all-out attack. The Army Chief of Staff, General Van Tien Dung, took over as its field commander in the South. According to Dung's memoirs, the plan was to fight in the Central Highlands through the dry season of 1975 and then move to the area near Saigon for the following year.[13]

Hanoi's burgeoning confidence produced a new political offer. It was hailed immediately as "moderate" by the peace movement but sounded all too familiar to veterans of the negotiations. It was the old standby of an end to United States involvement, the overthrow of Thieu, and the formation in Saigon of a new administration that would implement the Paris Agreement, which Hanoi had totally violated from the beginning.

In the meantime, since Congress exhibited no urgency about responding to Ford's request for a supplemental, Hanoi became convinced that it did not need even the pretense of a political solution. Indeed, South Vietnam's reverses, far from spurring Congress to action, set up another vicious cycle: The more Congress dissociated itself from Vietnam, the more a demoralized Saigon retreated; the weaker Saigon appeared, the more the congressional opposition insisted on the need to "end the war"—its euphemism for strangling America's allies.

Sir Robert Thompson, the British expert on counterinsurgency, visited South Vietnam in February and reported to President Ford that, if Hanoi became sufficiently emboldened to commit its reserve divisions just north of the demarcation line (DMZ) dividing South from North Vietnam:

> ARVN [the South Vietnamese army] would lose at least the airborne, marine, 1 and 3 divisions and would collapse. The war would be over. . . . The whole issue hinges on the restraints and sanctions still operating on Hanoi. . . . The decision rests in part with the Congress and the American people. . . . It [Saigon] is ready to continue fighting and, given the minimum of support sufficient to encourage its people and to deter Hanoi, to hold out successfully so that the long American involvement can be ended. But, if the support is not forthcoming, South Vietnam will go down fighting to the eternal disgrace of the United States.

The trouble was that the most vocal groups within Congress and the media—the ones setting the terms of the debate and fiercely denouncing an opposing view—thought the opposite: They saw disgrace in having any association, even financial ties, with the government in Saigon. The protest movement reached its ultimate position: No longer content with American withdrawal, it sought to deprive non-Communist Vietnam (and Laos and Cambodia) of the means of resistance. That point of view was epitomized in an editorial in the *Los Angeles Times* of March 6, 1975, urging not only the rejection of the proposed supplemental but drastic *cuts* in military assistance to well below the $700 million level already approved:

> The key element must be to set the level of military aid to South Vietnam so that it serves as an incentive for political movement, compromise and concession by Nguyen Van Thieu, and not as encouragement for him to consolidate his personal rule.

Congress retreated into procrastination. Hearings consumed the better part of February, during which the North Vietnamese offensive rolled on. At that point, Senator Humphrey came up with the idea of a bipartisan congressional fact-finding mission to Vietnam on the theory that it would learn enough to support a responsible assistance program (and, in the process, waste some more time). Ford accepted Humphrey's proposal only reluctantly. He feared that none of the senior senators Humphrey had proposed would be willing to identify themselves with so controversial a mission, while junior members would neither carry the necessary weight nor be prepared to risk the certain media assault.

Ford's misgivings were borne out by events. The Senate leadership refused to endorse the project, and senior senators refused to go when the White House tried to organize the trip on its own. After weeks of discussion, only one senator—Dewey Bartlett from Oklahoma, with a reputation as a maverick—and seven representatives embarked on the trip, none from the leadership of either house. The representatives included Bella Abzug, a protest movement activist; Paul McCloskey, long an opponent of an American role in Indochina; and Donald M. Fraser, former head of the liberal advocacy group Americans for Democratic Action. Not surprisingly, the congressional delegation accomplished nothing except to waste a few weeks during which Vietnam descended into catastrophe.

Senator Frank Church from Idaho, who had a long history of opposition to America's Indochina policy, took Ford up on a compromise suggestion the President had made in an interview with the *Chicago Tribune:* a terminal grant of two to three years, after which South Vietnam would be on its own.

I did not like the idea of a terminal grant because it made it seem as if American assistance to Vietnam was an act of charity rather than of policy. I did not see how we could in good conscience ask of South Vietnam, under all-out attack, what we had never asked of far less threatened allies. And I feared the inevitable haggling over an appropriate amount and the reality that one Congress cannot bind its successor. But our ambassador in Saigon, Graham Martin, favored a terminal grant to gain time, and Ford had embraced the idea. In the end, I reluctantly supported a terminal grant in a press conference as a "second-best choice."

As soon as we had accepted the principle, the terminal grant was turned into another device for cutting off Saigon from all aid. We were thinking in terms of several billion dollars; Church offered a one-time grant of at most $750 million—less than half of what we thought was needed for one year. And to obtain even that would require that the entire budgetary process start all over, which would take months. By then, it was the end of March, and events proceeded toward tragedy on their own momentum.

13

THE COLLAPSE OF
CAMBODIA

The limitations on aid to Vietnam were applied even more ferociously to Cambodia. Congress, which had been voting yearly appropriations for Vietnam, acted as if successive American Presidents had sneaked into the war by subterfuge. And to prevent this imaginary sequence from being repeated in Cambodia, congressional restrictions imposed an almost vindictive constraint both on the scale of American assistance to impoverished, mortally menaced Cambodia and on the flexibility with which Cambodia could use it, even to the extent of banning training and matériel aid from neighboring friendly countries.

By 1974, an overall ceiling of $377 million in aid to Cambodia had been established, and every individual expenditure was being counted against this total. The number of American civilians (including embassy personnel) was limited to 200 and third country nationals employed by the United States to eighty-five. Assistance from America's Southeast Asian allies was similarly restricted.[1] As a result, food or economic aid could not be provided without reducing military expenditures and vice versa. Restrictions such as these had enabled the Khmer Rouge to survive when they were still embryonic and gradually turned the tide in their favor once they gained strength. Brigadier General William W. Palmer, chief of the Military Equipment Delivery Team in Cambodia, described in his final report how congressional restrictions led to the cumulative strangulation of the Cambodian military effort: Limitations on American training produced excessive reliance on American airpower; when this was banned by Congress, Cambodian artillery and tactical airpower became crucial. But American instructors had not been permitted to train Cambodians in the field on how to use these weapons. In the end, even purely Cambodian defense efforts were choked off by escalating munitions costs due to inflation and reduced funding.

In the face of these restrictions, the Cambodian army did manage to resist the Khmer Rouge dry-season offensive in 1973 (with the help of American airpower). It did so again in 1974, this time entirely with its own forces, in part due to Hanoi's ambivalent attitude toward the Khmer Rouge. Hanoi was willing to use the Khmer Rouge to expel the last vestige of American influence from Indochina. But it distrusted the movement's passionate nationalism, suspecting that it would be turned against Vietnam in the wake of a complete victory.

Hanoi therefore kept the Khmer Rouge on a short leash for the first eighteen months after the cease-fire. In the fall of 1974, however, it changed course and poured in weapons and ammunition—perhaps as part of its own general offensive, perhaps because it had decided that congressional shortfalls had doomed the Lon Nol government and there was no point in antagonizing the Khmer Rouge further.

In a countrywide offensive beginning on January 1, 1975, the Khmer Rouge cut the Mekong River supply line to Phnom Penh. The combined result of increased combat activity and congressional ceilings was that the Cambodian army began to run out of ammunition. At the existing rate of expenditures, its stockpiles would not last beyond March. On January 28, Ford therefore asked Congress to lift the ceiling of $200 million for military assistance to Cambodia and to approve an additional $222 million. (I cannot determine at this remove how a figure of such precision was arrived at; perhaps some budget officer had a warped sense of humor.)

In addition to his formal request, Ford wrote a letter to House Speaker Carl Albert in which he eloquently stated the moral issue:

> Are we to deliberately abandon a small country in the midst of its life and death struggle? Is the United States, which so far has consistently stood by its friends through the most difficult of times, now to condemn, in effect a small Asian nation totally dependent upon us?[2]

I echoed this theme in many press briefings. The voluminous records of State Department and White House staff meetings show that our private concerns for America's honor, self-respect, and credibility were identical with what we stated publicly; there was no hidden "geopolitical" agenda for the sake of which we pursued assistance to the countries of Indochina. "Countries around the world," Ford wrote to Albert, "who depend on us for support— as well as their foes—will judge our performance." Cambodia was especially on our minds because, coinciding with its final agony, I was conducting shuttles meant to convince another small, friendly country—this time Israel— that it ought to put some of its security at risk by giving up territory at least partly on the basis of assurances of increased American support.

All appeals by Ford met with the same reception as they had regarding Vietnam—in even more absolute terms. The other departments preferred to avoid Congressional buffeting or media assaults for what they considered a losing cause, unless directly ordered to do so by the White House. Media and congressional commentary paralleled the arguments against aid to Vietnam with the added twist that Cambodia's mounting agony was invoked as one more reason to terminate its suffering. Experts, questioning whether Cambodia really needed additional aid, were quoted approvingly.[3] Conversely, it was said to be too late for extending aid since Cambodia was beyond saving.[4] Still others discerned no reason for aid because no binding commitment to Cambodia existed. Indeed, antiwar legislation from the early 1970s onward had specified that no "commitment" was implied. On February 13, 1975, the *Baltimore Sun* took the highly unusual step of exonerating the Nixon administration of complicity in the overthrow of Sihanouk but only to conclude that, since America had not connived in his ouster, it had no obligation to his successors.[5] Aid would just prolong the killing and prevent the Cambodians from solving their own problems peacefully.[6] Since America really had nothing at stake, it was a mistake for the administration to create the impression that American credibility would be harmed if Cambodia fell.[7]

The theme that nothing could be worse for the Cambodian people than a continuation of American military aid was pervasive. That a cutoff of arms aid would end the suffering was treated as self-evident; the administration's warnings of a possible bloodbath were derided as baseless and insincere, outweighed by the presumed horror of the continuing battles, or rejected as a McCarthyesque ploy to blame Congress for the imminent loss of Indochina.

An article in the *New York Times* datelined March 13, headed "The Enigmatic Cambodian Insurgents," disparaged the warnings of a bloodbath on a variety of grounds: The stories of deliberate Khmer Rouge atrocities in areas conquered by them were predictable examples of military indiscipline after hotly contested battles, or else they were the self-serving accounts of POWs and, as such, were probably "less than totally reliable." Once the Khmer Rouge had won, "some diplomats and other long-time observers" were quoted as saying that there would be "no need for random acts of terror." "Most Cambodians do not talk about a possible massacre and do not expect one," concluded the same reporter reassuringly. "Since all are Cambodians, an accommodation will be found." In any event, the Communist leadership was "more nationalist than Communist." The insurgent movement included some non-Communists and "possibly anti-Communists"; Communist leader Khieu Samphan was described as a "French-educated intellectual" who had joined the Communists in the 1960s "to fight against feudal privileges and social inequities." He was said to be highly regarded for his "integrity" and might be expected to "move somewhat to the right" once he came into power. The outcome would probably be "a more flexible nationalist socialism or Communism for Cambodia."[8]

Congress needed little encouragement to throttle Cambodia. It did so less by any explicit decision to which blame might later be attached than by simply failing to act on the various administration requests. On March 12, the House Democratic caucus, by a vote of 189–49, rejected any further military aid to Cambodia. The administration was urged to accept a "compromise" put forward by a subcommittee of the House Foreign Affairs Committee chaired by Representative Lee Hamilton which would have given a terminal grant with a cutoff date of June 30. The administration was saved from the embarrassment of either vetoing or signing this stay of execution of three months because, on March 13, the full House Foreign Affairs Committee rejected the Hamilton compromise by an 18–15 vote—and, while it was at it, refused to consider any other compromise. Representative Donald Fraser was explicit about his objectives. He favored surrender, he said, "under controlled circumstances to minimize the loss of life."[9] That same day, the Senate Democratic caucus joined its House counterpart by voting 38–5 to oppose military aid to Cambodia and to reject the military aid supplemental for Vietnam by a vote of 34–6.

At this point, there occurred one of those "credibility gaps" by which Washington periodically flagellated itself and which, in the atmosphere of the time, was both nearly inevitable and a convenient excuse for avoiding decisions. It suddenly transpired that we had not run out of funds for Cambodia after all. On March 14, Secretary Schlesinger reported that the Defense Department had discovered that $21.5 million of funds from fiscal year 1974 had been set aside as a contingency for inflation and not been used. In other words, we had funds for two to three more weeks of ammunition deliveries than we had told Congress.

This unexpected windfall amounting to a brief stay of execution for Phnom Penh was greeted not with relief but with dismay as a potential public relations catastrophe. Had we created another "credibility gap"? Ford's reaction was to order that Congress be notified immediately—as if he were conveying some terrible discovery: "It never hurts to be honest, even in a tough spot like this." Mercifully, Congress adjourned for the Easter recess at this point, sparing the country for at least a few weeks the humiliation of a public debate on the best way to abandon a helpless ally totally dependent on America. By the time Congress returned in early April, Cambodia was beyond help, and Vietnam was unraveling.

The Myth of the Failure to Negotiate on Cambodia

The standard alibi for the steps which made the catastrophe irreversible was to press the administration to bring about a negotiated end to the war in Cambodia. Indeed, cutting assistance off was increasingly put forward as the best means to facilitate a political solution by the device of eliminating Cambodia's ability to defend itself. Not all who used this argument were cynical—though hypocrisy was not in short supply. But for some, the quest for pure diplomacy based solely on negotiating legerdemain, unsupported by any leverage, reflected a very American nostalgia. It is difficult to conceive a more sweeping misapprehension than that the ruthless Hanoi Politburo and the murderous Khmer Rouge could let themselves be persuaded to forgo total military victory by the verbal facility of American diplomacy.

Hanoi's aim was total victory. It would only compromise on the basis of a balance of forces that it could not hope to alter; any other premise amounted to either an alibi or an abdication. The Khmer Rouge wanted the same thing with the additional purpose of revolutionizing Cambodian society by murdering its educated segment. In Cambodia, this balance of forces on the ground could only be achieved with the help of American airpower and American military assistance. In its absence, there were no diplomatic means available to alter the impending disaster.

In the immediate aftermath of the Paris Agreement, a certain military balance seemed within reach. The Khmer Rouge were much weaker than the North Vietnamese and had very few outside sources of supply other than Hanoi, already stretched to the limit in South Vietnam. A relatively small military effort, combined with a serious attempt to train the Cambodian army, might well have achieved a military balance and possibly even military superiority. Had the administration been allowed to establish a military balance and—heaven forbid—perhaps even gain the upper hand, a negotiation might have ensued and been enthusiastically welcomed by the administration. The one serious exploration to this end collapsed when Congress legislated a bombing halt—as described earlier.

What we lacked after the bombing halt was not commitment to the desirability of a diplomatic solution but the objective conditions to achieve one. The more Congress reduced aid, the more certain became the victory of the Khmer Rouge; the more confident the Khmer Rouge were of success, the less open they were to a diplomatic outcome. No amount of negotiating skill could get around this dilemma. America was being urged to abandon a military solution for a political one at the precise moment when the elements on which a political compromise might have been based were being systematically dismantled. In their absence, the demand for a political solution amounted to a discussion of the modalities of surrender.

As the end in Indochina came more and more clearly into view, a debate on how to manage the debacle broke out within the administration. The American ambassadors in Saigon and Phnom Penh, manning increasingly besieged battlements, were driven to contemplate their responsibilities. Both found themselves in a heartbreaking situation. They were obliged to preside over the liquidation of their embassies and charged with rescuing their employees and as many Cambodians and Vietnamese as possible—especially those who had cast their lot with the United States. Each ambassador faced an extremely fast-moving collapse, testing his initiative and his capacity to improvise because Washington was geographically too remote and too unfamiliar with the local intangibles to give meaningful day-to-day operational guidance. As a result, each ambassador developed proconsular attitudes and often felt free to disregard explicit instructions from Washington. Yet in their interpretation of the scope and purpose of their proconsular roles, the two men diverged dramatically.

In Saigon, Graham Martin, tough and self-assured, was a classic cold warrior. Prepared to take great risks with his own career, he insisted on strict discipline within his embassy without applying the same strictures to his own conduct vis-à-vis Washington. In pursuit of his perception of his mission, Martin would take upon himself initiatives that more circumspect and less driven ambassadors would not have launched without first checking with Washington. And his style was sufficiently convoluted so that Washington could not always determine how he was interpreting its decisions. In this manner, Martin upheld to the bitter end the American commitment to a free South Vietnam for which so many thousands, including—as it happened— his adopted son, had given their lives. To induce Washington to go along with his recommendations, Martin was not above shading his analysis to accord with his preconceptions. Philip Habib, recently appointed Assistant Secretary of State for East Asia who had served many years in Vietnam and leaned toward a more pessimistic view, supplied the corrective.

Faced with imminent disaster, Martin decided to go down with his ship and battled for his convictions until the last second of the last day. Believing that the United States Congress had erred grievously in abandoning South Vietnam, he resisted conventional media and congressional wisdom and made no concessions to the illusory "compromises" with which they salved their consciences. I understood very well that Martin's many hortatory messages were designed in part to create a record which might later be published—perhaps even to my disadvantage. For Martin tended to consider anything less than 100 percent support as betrayal. But whatever the public relations impact, it would show Martin struggling to maintain America's moral commitments. In the meantime, my heart went out to Martin as I watched him mask his anguish with bravado.

The ambassador in Phnom Penh, John Gunther Dean, represented a different generation. Just as confident as Martin of the correctness of his views, Dean took great care to stay within the parameters of conventional wisdom. He always made sure that the media were aware of his commitment to the "politically correct" solution—labeled "political compromise"—even as whatever objective conditions might once have existed for it were evaporating.

Highly intelligent and well informed, Dean understood clearly that congressional restrictions on American funding and advisory activities were certain to doom the country to which he was accredited. And he made clear from the start that he would not go down with the sinking ship. Like the congressional doves, Dean advocated a "political" way out of the disaster he had been asked to administer. He therefore bent every effort to get a negotiation started, usually under his own auspices. A deluge of cables descended on Washington with a persistence that led to the perhaps unworthy suspicion that, like Martin, Dean was building a record. But where Martin exhibited an excessive zeal in pursuing what was, after all, the approved strategy, Dean took it upon himself to alter national strategy from the improbable venue of Phnom Penh.

Dean's strategy was to urge negotiations now with the Khmer Rouge, now with Sihanouk, at one moment through Indonesian President Suharto, at another via Prime Minister Lee Kuan Yew of Singapore. A stream of tactical suggestions, coupled with increasingly shrill demands for more rapid action, poured forth from the Phnom Penh embassy. Dean's basic strategy was to replace the government to which he was accredited with a coalition structure of some kind as a prelude for negotiations with the Khmer Rouge.

Being obliged to deal with Congress on a daily basis, the precariousness of Cambodia's situation was clear enough to those who held the fort in Washington, and they shared with Dean the strong desire to ease Cambodia's fate. But whatever chances existed for a negotiated outcome—and, in light of the military situation and aid cutoff, we judged them to be minimal—the ambassador in Phnom Penh was not the appropriate focal point for exploring them. America had precious few bargaining chips, the two principal ones being the military establishment and the government structure headed by Lon Nol. Congress was dismantling the military, and the thrust of Dean's recommendations was to dismantle the Phnom Penh government at the beginning of some undefined diplomatic process.

We judged the key to whatever negotiation might develop to be Sihanouk, who was in Beijing. We were willing to explore that and other channels, including those suggested by Dean, such as using Suharto or Lee as intermediaries. Dean, however, was not well positioned with respect to any of these venues. Assuming a negotiation was even possible, his role in American strategy was to hold Phnom Penh together until an interlocutor willing to negotiate emerged.

On February 18, 1975, while on a shuttle in the Middle East, I instructed the State Department:

Dean has now gone so far as to invite key Khmer military and civilian leaders to his home to discuss openly and with considerable enthusiasm the removal of the chief of state of [Cambodia].

As far as I am concerned, if we are to leave Cambodia, we will leave with dignity. I am willing to listen to any recommendation that is consistent with that objective. But the frenzied approach which Dean seems to have adopted will solve nothing. I want him to adhere to a sober, deliberate policy that neither precludes positive action on our part nor rushes us into it headlong.

The subsequent careers of the two ambassadors are proof that it is far more dangerous to challenge conventional congressional and media wisdom than to harass the Secretary of State. Martin never received another ambassadorial post because he was henceforth considered impossible to confirm; Dean went on to serve—ably—as ambassador in Denmark and India before retiring.

Our strategy was to seek contacts preferably with Sihanouk either directly or through such trusted ambassadors as David Bruce and later George H. W. Bush in Beijing, or through capitals that had some influence on the Cambodian parties, such as those of Algeria or Indonesia. We far preferred Sihanouk as our interlocutor, for we judged the Khmer Rouge adamant against compromise and determined to disintegrate the Phnom Penh structure and make Sihanouk irrelevant. What we sought to avoid was the destruction of the Phnom Penh government as an entrance price into negotiations—as Dean was urging.

After the collapse of Zhou's tentative mediation in 1973, we had on several occasions throughout 1974 raised the basic formula of cease-fire, coalition government, and Lon Nol's departure with Chinese leaders (including Deng Xiaoping) and with then Algerian Foreign Minister Abdelaziz Bouteflika (at this writing President of Algeria), who represented the Nonaligned Movement that year. In addition, in the fall of 1974, we tried to organize an international conference on Cambodia but were unable to generate any interest. In February and March of 1975—partly at the urging of Dean—we approached Prime Minister Lee Kuan Yew and President Suharto to explore negotiating possibilities. They saw no chance so long as the government in Phnom Penh was facing imminent collapse.

Another attempt at negotiation occurred in December 1974. It was initiated when French President Valéry Giscard d'Estaing told Ford at their summit in Martinique of the conviction of his ambassador in Beijing, Etienne Manac'h, that a negotiated agreement with Sihanouk was attainable and would be supported by China. We had our doubts that, after Zhou's debacle, China would engage itself again or that, if it did, it would do so through French intermediaries. Despite our reservations, we authorized the French Foreign Ministry to proceed with an exploration. We would go along with Sihanouk as head of government; to be able to govern independently, we argued, he would have to include strong non-Communist elements in his administration. In practice, this meant members of the Lon Nol structure, though not Lon Nol. Any other terms would have meant surrender and, to arrange this, we did not require a French intermediary. Our requirements were contained in a formal paper on December 24, 1974:

> We are prepared to accept Sihanouk as the leader of Cambodia,
>
> —If Sihanouk returns to Phnom Penh as a genuine national leader and not figurehead.
>
> —For Sihanouk to be a genuine national leader, he must have supporting him in his Government strong elements representing all important tendencies, including those of the present structure. How does he plan to bring this about? What is the structure and nature of the government envisaged by Sihanouk?
>
> Discussions cannot be used to demoralize the existing government in Phnom Penh. If there is agreement in principle it should be implemented rapidly.
>
> We favor that the new government would follow the principle of neutrality in foreign relations.
>
> There must be assurance of durability in the compromise solution. We are not interested in a subterfuge for settlement which will be followed shortly thereafter by another upheaval.

Still smarting from its experience of the previous year, Beijing refused even to discuss the subject on the ground that foreign countries should not interfere in Cambodian affairs. Lest the point be missed and to shut off further discussions, Beijing denied a visa to the French emissary who was supposed to deliver the above message to Sihanouk.[10]

Far too late Sihanouk understood his dilemma. On March 25—after having rebuffed our overtures for nearly two years—he suddenly established contact in a manner that lent considerable credit to his subtlety, if not to his timing. In a letter to Ford via the French ambassador in Beijing, the exiled Prince requested American assistance in returning to him his collection of Cambodian music and instruments which he had left behind on being deposed in 1970. On March 26, 1975, we instructed George H. W. Bush, then chief of mission in Beijing, to seek a meeting with Sihanouk to inform him that we would do our utmost to respond to his request and to sketch for him one more time a solution to the Cambodian tragedy we had been proposing for two years:

> As guidelines for this part of your meeting, you should open by advising him that we remain vitally interested in receiving his ideas for settling the war in Cambodia. We therefore invite him to use this opportunity to convey to us through you his latest thinking on how the war in Cambodia can be brought to a close in a manner which will preserve the integrity of his nation and enable him to exercise a personal leadership in unifying the Khmer people.
>
> You should also indicate that we continue to believe that it will be necessary to preserve a balance of forces between the opposing Khmer elements if a true peace settlement is to be achieved. Such a balance would serve as the indispensable basis not only for achieving a settlement, but also for assuring that Sihanouk will be able to realize the decisive leadership role we envisage.

On March 28, John Holdridge, the deputy chief of mission in Beijing, met with Phung Peng Chen, Sihanouk's Chief of Staff, at the French embassy and delivered an invitation from Bush to Sihanouk for a discussion at a mutually agreed venue. Sihanouk rejected the proposal on March 29 via the same aide, who used the excuse that the Prince did not wish to confuse "international opinion" by giving rise to rumors about the imminence of a political negotiation. Bush was thereupon instructed to inform Sihanouk that we had succeeded in safeguarding his cultural possessions and to use the occasion to deliver the political part of our message.

On April 1, Holdridge met with Phung Peng Chen and reported his response as follows:

It would be very bad for Cambodia if the Red Khmer took over the entire government in Cambodia, since they were "very doctrinaire." It would be far better "for the free world" if Prince Sihanouk, who had the support of the peasants and the people of Phnom Penh, could be brought back to Cambodia and with the backing of the superpowers exercise some balance over the other forces. Phung indicated that he hoped that the US could assist in bringing Sihanouk back.

We agreed with this analysis and had for several years. A "political" solution could have been built on it had Sihanouk acted earlier and had Congress understood that a military balance was the precondition. But by now, given the events on the ground, it was much too late.

The Final Collapse

The Khmer Rouge offensive that began on January 1, 1975, closed in on Phnom Penh at the beginning of April when Neak Luong, the government's last foothold on the lower Mekong, was captured. This freed at least 6,000 more Communist troops for the final assault on Phnom Penh, now cut off from American supplies.

The remaining government troops fought until their ammunition ran out. That there was no dearth of inefficiency and even corruption on the Cambodian side cannot be denied. But it was also the case that, despite stifling congressional restrictions, an essentially ceremonial force under Sihanouk had been transformed into an army that, with American help, fought the ferocious Khmer Rouge to a standstill for two years.

By early April, reflections about what might have been had become irrelevant. For, as the end approached, the American superpower had already turned itself into an impotent spectator absorbed in a narcissistic pursuit of its own domestic controversy. There was nothing left to do other than to watch first in anguish, and then with a growing sense of horror as the Khmer Rouge turned the victory that American actions had facilitated into genocide against their own people.

Ambassador Dean, now confined to his basic mission, conducted the

American withdrawal and attendant political transformations with great skill and professionalism. Lon Nol left Phnom Penh on April 1, ostensibly to go "on vacation." A number of changes in personnel at the top were initiated to ease the transition and perhaps to retain a foothold for the old order. Touchingly (and shamingly), the Cambodians still had so much confidence in the United States that they consulted us at every step. Even at this late stage, the new acting President, Saukham Khoy, made a pathetic last-minute appeal to Ford on April 6:

> For [a] number of years now the Cambodian people have placed their trust in America. I cannot believe that this confidence was misplaced and that suddenly America will deny us the means which might give us a chance to find an acceptable solution to our conflict.

As everything was about to disintegrate, Sihanouk was suddenly heard from again. He had been punctuating the death throes of the Lon Nol government with intransigent statements in which he rejected any talk of a last-minute compromise as a "political plot." Labeling all the newly appointed ministers in Phnom Penh as traitors, Sihanouk asserted that:

> Under no circumstances, neither in the near future nor in the more remote future, will the Cambodian resistance agree to be reconciled with the traitors in the clique of Saukham Khoy, [Vice Prime Minister] Pan Sothi and company.[11]

These bloodthirsty words were the now unavoidable tribute Sihanouk paid to his ostensible allies, the Khmer Rouge. What he thought privately was quite different and was conveyed to us in Beijing in an elliptical manner. Another meeting between Holdridge and Phung took place, this time on the pretext that Sihanouk wanted to send some Cambodian recordings to Ford in appreciation of his intercession in Phnom Penh on behalf of his cultural treasures. Holdridge had been instructed to convey the President's good wishes and to invite "any further messages Sihanouk might have for us." The meeting took place on April 10, forty-eight hours before the American evacuation. Phung, according to Holdridge, passed on the following observations:

It is important that [a] solution be reached in Cambodia prior to the fall of Saigon; otherwise North Vietnamese and Red Khmer will take over all of Cambodia in same way Soviets took over Czechoslovakia. Phung stated that on this point he was expressing Sihanouk's personal views.

Sihanouk is "helpless" in Peking [Beijing] to do anything about situation in Cambodia. However, he does not want Red Khmer to take over the country completely.

It is a good thing to keep "the army" intact in Cambodia, since Sihanouk has the support of the soldiers and also of the Cambodian peasants. Phung made it very clear when questioned that by "the army" he meant the forces now defending Phnom Penh and not the Red Khmer forces.

Once again Sihanouk—if Phung was, in fact, speaking for him—had outlined the same strategy we had been attempting to implement. Sihanouk either had hoped that a military stalemate would occur in which he would be called back as the indispensable balancing factor, or else he had concluded that the Khmer Rouge were certain to prevail, so that any diplomatic initiative on his part could only weaken his long-term influence. Probably he had pursued both convictions simultaneously. Now, at the last second when the counterweights to the Khmer Rouge were disintegrating, Sihanouk realized that his position was scarcely better than that of the remnants of the Lon Nol administration, and he finally engaged himself to achieve what might well have been possible earlier had he been more forthright and America more united.

We undertook one last convulsive attempt to respond to Phung's message. Dean was instructed to suggest to Cambodia's acting President that he make an appeal to Sihanouk to return as the head of a government of national union. At the same time, Holdridge was instructed to contact Sihanouk to inform him of this overture and, if he agreed, to suggest that the Chinese fly him to Phnom Penh in a Chinese airplane.

The end of an era provides a kind of laboratory for studying how difficult it is to break established patterns of thought. By then, America had been dominant in Phnom Penh for so long that, though literally within hours of leaving, we were not emotionally prepared to accept the implications. This pathetic overture was put forward as the Cambodian army was collapsing and the American embassy in Phnom Penh was packing. By then, in a grim coincidence, the Cambodians had totally run out of ammunition, and the situation had turned so perilous that Dean was instructed to proceed with evacuation whatever Sihanouk's reply. Had the scheme worked, Sihanouk, upon his return, would have found no Americans to assist him, only Cambodian military forces without ammunition.

Sihanouk spared us this embarrassment by replying with a message proving that he was either very subtle or totally out of touch. When, on April 11, Holdridge told Phung of our overture to Cambodia's acting President, Phung professed to be highly pleased but added that Sihanouk could not return on the basis of an appeal made by a leader he had only recently called a traitor. Phung therefore urged that Saukham Khoy buttress his request by appeals from "two chief Bonzes, other members of the priesthood, students, army men, Phnom Penh residents in general, and the peasants." We knew, even if Phung—seduced by a belief in America's invincibility—did not, that there was no longer any time left for such fancy maneuvers, since the American embassy would be leaving April 12, the next day.

Incongruously, as the curtain fell on Cambodia, Washington returned to bureaucratic business as usual. Evacuation is heartrending for the victims; to those implementing it, it is above all a technical problem. In no time, Washington was consumed by perennial discord. Stories were soon being leaked, rendering Cambodia's death throes as yet another installment of a running turf battle between the Pentagon and the State Department and of the media's quest for credibility gaps.

These internal debates turned out to be a dress rehearsal for the much more complex evacuation of Saigon two weeks later. The dispute did not concern the necessity of evacuation, only its timing and modalities. The Defense Department, which would be responsible for the actual movement, wanted to start immediately, using fixed-wing aircraft. The State Department, on the advice of Dean, preferred to evacuate in a way that would reduce panic and enable as many Khmer who had worked with us as possible to flee. On April 3, there was a decision to evacuate with the actual timing left to the ambassador. Dean decided to delay a few days to avoid a panic and to better organize the departure. The ensuing tensions are illustrated by the following exchange at an 8:00 A.M. State Department staff meeting on April 11:

HABIB: Defense—the Pentagon—is trying to tell us that if we don't do certain things fast enough, God help us. If they have an accident, they're going to blame us.

KISSINGER: No doubt. The Pentagon has said, "It's your fault." I've heard it three times. . . .

Why was it delayed, as a matter of fact?

HABIB: It was delayed because Dean came in with a message saying, "I can't do it at this time," and all his military advisers agreed. . . .

KISSINGER: I know all these guys around town and I know their position—that if one guy breaks a leg in the evacuation it will be our fault. We'll just have to take that.

Yet we knew that all the quibbling was a dispute over arranging the deck chairs on the *Titanic*. Dean told us on April 10 that both the airport and the road leading to it were no longer safe and that evacuation by helicopter should start immediately. For technical reasons, the airlift could not start until 8:00 A.M. local time on April 12. Eighty-two Americans, 159 Cambodians, and thirty-five other nationals were evacuated in a little more than two hours.

Messages were sent to top-level Cambodians offering to evacuate them as well. To our astonishment and shame, the vast majority refused, including Lon Nol's brother, Lon Non, and Premier Long Boret, both of whom were on the Khmer Rouge's published death list. Ron Nessen reacted perceptively: "In other words, the Cambodians are telling us, 'Okay, you chickenshits, go ahead and bug out, but we are going to stay and fight.' " [12]

Sirik Matak, former Prime Minister and the only leader of the 1970 coup still in Phnom Penh, expressed the attitude of the Khmer leaders in more elevated language. Responding to Dean's offer to be evacuated, he sent a note, handwritten in elegant French, on April 12 while the evacuation was in progress:

Dear Excellency and Friend:

I thank you very sincerely for your letter and for your offer to transport me towards freedom. I cannot, alas, leave in such a cowardly fashion. As for you, and in particular for your great country, I never

believed for a moment that you would have this sentiment of abandoning a people which has chosen liberty. You have refused us your
protection, and we can do nothing about it.

You leave, and my wish is that you and your country will find
happiness under this sky. But, mark it well, that if I shall die here on
the spot and in my country that I love, it is no matter, because we all
are born and must die. I have only committed this mistake of believing in you [the Americans].

Please accept, Excellency and dear friend, my faithful and
friendly sentiments.

S/Sirik Matak.

On April 13, the *New York Times* correspondent reported the American departure under the headline, "Indochina Without Americans: For Most, a
Better Life." [13]

The Khmer Rouge took Phnom Penh on April 17. Long Boret was executed immediately as was every member of the previous government who
had remained behind. All former government employees and their families
were killed in the weeks that followed. The two million citizens of Phnom
Penh were ordered to evacuate the city for the countryside ravaged by war
and incapable of supporting urban dwellers unused to fending for themselves. Between one and two million Khmer were murdered by the Khmer
Rouge until Hanoi occupied the country at the end of 1978, after which a
civil war raged for another decade.

Sirik Matak was shot in the stomach and left without medical help. It
took him three days to die.

Final Note

The participants on both sides of the American domestic debate shared
one vast gap of understanding: They could not imagine the incarnate
evil represented by the Khmer Rouge. Those who sought to end the war by
throttling Lon Nol—even the radical fringe—cannot be blamed for the
holocaust they helped bring about. Incapable of imagining that a govern-

ment would murder millions of its own people, and convinced that nothing could be worse than a continuation of the war, they were prepared to ensure its end by cutting off supplies to America's allies. But they have since devalued this honorable motive by an implacable vendetta and rewriting of history. Seeking to obscure their fallibility in a cocoon of righteousness, they refuse to face their own tragedy that, like all actors in the Indochina tragedy, they contributed to results immeasurably different from what they intended.

14

THE END OF VIETNAM

Those who thought that the agony of Cambodia might inure them to the pain of South Vietnam's collapse soon learned better. The tragic end of two decades of American sacrifice, dedication, and national division proved beyond getting used to.

On March 10, the North Vietnamese, no longer even pretending to be bound by the Paris Agreement, launched a major offensive in the Central Highlands using divisions recently introduced from the North. They overran the strategic junction of Ban Me Thuot in two days, cutting all the roads from Saigon to the Central Highlands except for one very poor road constantly being harassed by Vietcong guerrillas.

While the Central Highlands were tottering, Foreign Minister Tran Van Lam was sent by President Thieu to Washington to plead for the supplemental aid package. He reported to Saigon that there was no hope of obtaining any additional aid from the sitting Congress. Fear turned into certainty when the House and Senate Democratic caucuses (then the majority in Congress) voted overwhelmingly on March 12 and 13 against any further aid to South Vietnam.

Thieu understood that, with his shrinking resources, he would no longer be able to defend the entire territory of his besieged country and ordered a strategic withdrawal from the Central Highlands. At the same time, he redeployed the 1st Airborne Division from the northern border to the area around Danang—both moves to start a few days hence, on March 16. Thieu's intent was to create a defensible redoubt which might be held until a perhaps more sympathetic Congress was elected in 1976.

As a war college exercise, Thieu's move made good sense. In terms of Vietnamese realities, it ushered in catastrophe. Launched without preparation or detailed guidance from the Joint General Staff in Saigon, the "strategic withdrawal" had to be carried out over a single road—Route 7B—in bad repair and heavily mined. A major engineering job would have been required to make it usable, including the rebuilding of several collapsed bridges—tasks for which the South Vietnamese divisions were inadequately equipped. In addition to the combat units, Route 7B would have to accommodate a horde of fleeing civilians, for the dependents of the Army of the Republic of Vietnam divisions were always billeted close to the fighting units—in this case, in Pleiku, the capital of the Central Highlands. As soon as word of the withdrawal order filtered down, panic set in, and a mass exodus followed. To compound the chaos, the regional militias, composed mostly of local tribes called Montagnards, rioted upon hearing that they were to be left behind.

The lone escape route was soon clogged by an estimated 60,000 troops and 400,000 civilians. The system of food distribution broke down, and hungry soldiers started to pillage the villages along the way. South Vietnamese air force planes mistakenly bombed an ARVN armored unit, killing many troops and dependents. The North Vietnamese attacked this traveling conflagration. Only a small fraction of the fleeing soldiers and civilians made it to the coast; the Vietnamese divisions that had defended the Central Highlands evaporated.

Originally the North Vietnamese had intended to devote the 1975 campaigning season to the capture of the Central Highlands and to fight the decisive battles for Saigon in 1976. Within a matter of days, however, the North Vietnamese achieved their initial goal and without suffering any significant casualties or loss of equipment. The divisions aimed at the Central Highlands were now free to attack Danang and Hue along the coast, which they soon besieged. The flood of refugees from the Central Highlands engulfed the elite airborne division just transferred from the northern border, preventing any sustained defense of these major strategic bases.

The news from Vietnam recorded an endless stream of disasters. The old imperial city of Hue fell on March 25, Danang on March 30. With a million refugees in Danang and food supplies running out, the key issue in the northern part of the country was humanitarian, not defense.

Nevertheless, WSAG meetings addressing these problems soon turned into a bizarre legalistic wrangle over the use of American LSTs (Landing

Ship/Tank) to help evacuate refugees. Congressional experts were fretting whether this would violate Article 7 of the Paris Agreement prohibiting the introduction of military equipment except to replace losses—an article never observed for one day by the North Vietnamese. Another dispute was over whether the frantic refugees could be evacuated by military vehicles before notification of Congress under the War Powers Act, passed the year before to limit executive discretion in the use of military equipment. The matter was judged sufficiently important to require a presidential decision. Ford ruled: "I think we ought to do it, notify them, and make a public announcement." I interpreted the ruling to mean that we were to do so in that order.

The collapse of the Vietnamese civil and military structure was tragic and poignant. For those of us making the decisions, the challenge took the form of how to manage the by now nearly inevitable evacuation of the remaining 6,000 Americans as well as those Vietnamese who were in jeopardy by virtue of their association with the United States. "I want the list of categories of people," I said at a State Department staff meeting of April 8, "how they're going to be moved to a place from which they can be evacuated, in what order, and with what prior consultation with the government."

Surrealistically, evacuation planning was taking place side by side with an internal debate about whether to request military aid for South Vietnam at this late stage and how much. Ford and I were the principal advocates of continuing with the request to Congress for additional aid until the last moment. How to reconcile that seeming inconsistency between my insistence on evacuation planning with continued advocacy of aid appropriations for South Vietnam?

The overwhelming majority of the media (I can think of no significant exception) clamored for the dismantling of Saigon, for the replacement of Thieu, and for an immediate complete withdrawal from Vietnam. Congress was not far behind. Within the administration, CIA Director William Colby favored offering a deal whereby we would jettison Thieu for unimpeded evacuation of Americans. Ford's White House staff was eager to liquidate Vietnam to avoid tarnishing his presidency with further Vietnam controversies.

But those of us who were meeting daily in the White House Situation Room faced real, not theoretical, choices. We would need to withdraw the 6,000 Americans still remaining in Vietnam and try to help evacuate the tens of thousands of Vietnamese who had jeopardized their lives by working with

America. But we would not be able to evacuate any South Vietnamese friends unless we prolonged the withdrawal of Americans, for Congress would surely cut off all funds with the departure of the last American.

Whatever course we adopted required maintaining the request for assistance to Vietnam. The moment the request was abandoned, panic would be compounded and what was left of a civil structure would disintegrate. At that point, the battered South Vietnamese army might turn on the American remnants in despair and rage over what it was bound to consider America's betrayal. And they might do so also if we started the final withdrawal too precipitately. In early April, I told Colby that, though Thieu would probably fall soon, if we offered him up in any bargain, Hanoi would immediately demand the head of his successor as well until it had destroyed the entire South Vietnamese political structure (which is essentially what happened). On April 3, a document of a provincial committee of the South Vietnamese Communist Provisional Revolutionary Government confirmed this prediction. It described the various offers of tripartite government—Hanoi's perennial scheme for a decade—as "merely stratagems to isolate the GVN."

We needed time to synchronize the evacuations of both Americans and Vietnamese to whom we had incurred a moral obligation. Maintaining the request for aid was the only way to preserve the morale of those Vietnamese still prepared to fight for a decent outcome—now unhappily to be defined in terms of people rescued.

But what level of assistance should be requested? My recommendation was to propose a figure relevant to South Vietnam's actual needs. On January 28, Ford had requested the supplemental of $300 million which Senator John Stennis had promised. Even then the figure bore no relationship to the need, but at least Vietnam had been relatively calm. That sum was no longer even remotely adequate for the catastrophe all around us. Therefore, Ford sent General Fred C. Weyand, the Army Chief of Staff who had commanded the 1st Cavalry Division in Vietnam, to Saigon to come up with a realistic recommendation.

Throughout this controversy, Ford stood tall; he quite simply could not imagine abandoning those who had risked their lives for decades by cooperating with what five Presidents of both American parties had declared essential for the security of the free world. I did my best to ensure that this courageous and decent man would have the widest range of choices available and took great care to give Ford a way out. On March 27, as the extent of the military debacle was becoming apparent, I concluded an Oval Office briefing on Saigon's military requests as follows:

> I say this with a bleeding heart—but maybe you must put Vietnam
> behind you and not tear the country apart again. The Vietnam agree
> ments were based on two things: our threat of military support and
> the continuation of aid. In July '73 we stopped our support, and we
> also cut the aid below the minimum they needed. Now we are faced
> with a desperate situation.

Ford would not hear of it because, he said, it would go "against my grain." His reply was much the same on April 3 when I reminded him that he had the option of doing nothing. On April 9, the day before Ford formally requested additional funds for Vietnam, I called to his attention Ron Nessen's view that the President should lead America out of Vietnam, not into it. Ford replied: "That is not the way I am. . . . I couldn't do it."

At a press conference on April 3, Ford stood by his request for both economic and military aid for South Vietnam. He accused the North Vietnamese of blatant violations of the Paris Agreement, criticized Congress for reducing our requests for assistance to South Vietnam, and ordered an emergency airlift for 2,000 Vietnamese orphans. Ford refused the journalists' needling that he jettison Thieu because "I don't believe that it is my prerogative to tell the head of state elected by the people to leave office." He added:

> We will stand by our allies, and I specifically warn any adversaries
> they should not, under any circumstances, feel that the tragedy of
> Vietnam is an indication that the American people have lost their
> will or their desire to stand up for freedom anyplace in the world.

Media reaction was predictable. Ford was accused by the *New York Times* of being confused[1] and by the *Washington Post* of engaging in a shell game.[2] Somewhat more charitably, the *Los Angeles Times* demanded a "new direction," which it defined as a cutoff of military aid for Indochina.[3] When I repeated Ford's arguments at a press conference on April 5, I encountered the same reception, reflected in questions such as these: How could we expect congressional cooperation while we were blaming Congress for what was happening? What made us think that any more money would do any good?

Wasn't it all Thieu's fault? How could we have signed the Paris Agreement expecting any other outcome? And, most insistently, just what was the nature of our commitment in South Vietnam?

I reiterated what I had been saying for months. Our request was based on a moral, not a legal, obligation:

> It is a very important moral question for the United States whether when people who, with its encouragement, have fought for many years should in their hour of extremity be told by the United States that while they want to continue fighting that the United States would no longer help them.

I ended with this appeal:

> Many of you have heard me brief on this subject now for six years, and I think none of you have ever heard me question the travail and concern of those who have opposed the war. All we can ask is that those of you who have been critical ought to keep in mind that there is a great human tragedy that those in the administration are viewing and they are trying to deal with it in the best interest of the United States and in the best interests of world peace.

Neither Ford nor I ever based our appeal on the existence of formal commitments. All we claimed with Vietnam under assault was an underlying moral obligation. Not the least irony of the death throes of Vietnam was that those who were usually being attacked for *Realpolitik* insisted on honor and moral obligations, while their critics, usually so free with moral claims, were acting like lawyers looking for escape clauses in a contract. Nor was the issue incompatible with a properly understood *Realpolitik*. For, in the end, a nation's reliability affects the steadiness of its allies and the calculations of its adversaries.

General Weyand reported to President Ford in Palm Springs on April 5. The military situation, he said, was deteriorating, and he described the choices as follows: The $300 million supplemental would replace consumables only partially. It would not make up for the vast amount of equipment lost in the disasters of the past few weeks. The South Vietnamese army had, in fact, received no replacement equipment for two years. Therefore,

Weyand argued, the original supplemental was no longer adequate. Instead he submitted a list of what would be needed to reconstitute some of the units destroyed in recent battles. The minimum amount that made sense was $722 million.

On one level, it was preposterous. Vietnam was likely to collapse before any equipment at all could arrive. At the same time, if we were going to submit any figure, we might as well pick one associated with a program that had some intellectual basis. It was the minimum amount with which something might still be salvaged, the one most likely to give the South Vietnamese the shot in the arm with which to gain time for evacuation. And if Vietnam collapsed before any aid could reach it, America would at least have partially discharged its moral obligations. Ford accepted Weyand's number.

Ford announced his decision to the NSC on April 9 with a longer and more eloquent explanation than was his custom:

> I will ask for $722 million because we can justify it. At least the record will be clear. I will ask that it be done by a date certain, perhaps May 1, though we still have to decide that.
>
> I will ask for humanitarian aid but not through the United Nations. Third, I will ask for authority, which I think is needed, to evacuate the Americans and others to whom we have an obligation.
>
> I gather, Jim [Schlesinger], that you have reservations. But this is the decision. This will be the only group that knows it. I have spent a lot of time on this, now and even earlier, going back to 1952. I think our policy, going back to Presidents Truman and Eisenhower, was the right policy. We did not always implement it well, and we may have made many mistakes. But it was the right policy.

On April 10, the President addressed a joint session of Congress. In a firm and unapologetic speech, he endorsed the purposes which had caused his predecessors to involve the United States in Indochina; traced the evolution of the Paris Agreement; and stressed that the United States had neither supplied adequate aid to its ally nor enforced the agreement. Ford concluded by warning:

> That the national interests of the United States and the cause of world stability require that we continue to give both military and hu-

manitarian assistance to the South Vietnamese. . . . We cannot in the meantime abandon our friends while our adversaries support and encourage theirs. We cannot dismantle our defenses, our diplomacy, or our intelligence capability while others increase and strengthen theirs.

The next day, I summed up my view of what was at stake in a pep talk to the senior staff of the State Department:

If the President last night had said what so many congressmen say he should have said—namely, "We've done enough; we can no longer give military aid," I think Phil Habib [Assistant Secretary for East Asia] will agree there will be total uncontrollable, chaotic collapse in Saigon starting this morning. Once the President decided he was not going to do nothing, he might just as well ask for what is right on this because the opposition on the Hill is not hinged on a figure; it's hinged on the principle. . . .

This thing is now going to go its course; its course is reasonably predictable. And what we are trying to do is to manage it with dignity and to preserve a basis for which we can conduct the foreign policy in which people can have some confidence in us. . . .

We're not going to accuse anybody of having been wrong. I have no intention, when this thing is over, of turning it into a vendetta and going around the country. I think people are going to feel badly when it's over. I don't think there are going to be many heroes left in this. But this department . . . is going to stand for what's right. We have no other choice in the world.

The Debate over Evacuation

Within the administration, the President's speech shifted the controversies from whether to request aid to how to deal with the increasingly likely collapse of South Vietnam. In practice, this reduced itself to the question of how quickly to evacuate and with what concern for the Vietnamese who had worked with America.

The Pentagon wanted to evacuate as rapidly as possible. As in Cambodia, it made daily representations to speed up the process. It did not want to run risks of casualties, congressional inquiries, or accidents by prolonging evacuation. Daily warning memos or phone calls to that effect arrived at my office. C-141 transports were leaving Saigon each day with well-documented empty seats to prove that, if there were any American casualties, it would be someone else's fault—Ambassador Martin's or mine.

Graham Martin stood at the other extreme. The management of evacuations is the responsibility of the State Department, with the ambassador acting as field commander. Martin was a born generalissimo—the Foreign Service's equivalent of Douglas MacArthur. He had his own very definite views on the optimum rate of evacuation and not exactly excessive regard for directives from faraway Washington. Passionately committed to the people he would soon be obliged to abandon, Martin considered it his duty to space the American withdrawal over the longest period of time in order to leave enough of an American presence to justify rescuing Vietnamese. Believing that, in the short term, panic in Saigon was a greater worry than Hanoi's military moves, Martin strove for a much slower pace of evacuation than even Ford, Scowcroft, or I—the administration "hawks"—thought appropriate. With the State Department being harassed by the Pentagon because we were evacuating too slowly and by Martin because we were leaving too fast, the mean emerged as far more precarious than golden.

Where I parted company with the ambassador was in our respective assessments of South Vietnam's prospects for survival—hence of the time available for evacuation. Even after the collapse of the Central Highlands, Martin was arguing that a viable redoubt could be constructed around Nha Trang, Saigon, and the Delta—a proposition vehemently disputed by the irrepressible Phil Habib, who was no shrinking violet either. When Saigon's collapse became too obvious to be explained away, Martin argued that we could manage the transfer of power in Saigon by means of a coalition government gradually enough to maintain a refugee airlift for many more weeks than I considered feasible. Having sat across from Le Duc Tho for all these years, I was certain that he would never acquiesce in a gradual transfer of authority or any autonomous political structure in Saigon, however temporary—not even an autonomous Communist one. Hanoi would take no chances on the emergence of Titoism in South Vietnam.

Much as I sympathized with Martin's objectives, U.S. policy had to take account of the increasingly ominous intelligence assessments that South Vietnam would be able to hold out for only a matter of weeks.

Based on these considerations, the President approved the following plan. First we determined the helicopter lift capacity for one day, which turned out to be around 1,250. On that basis, on April 18 (a week after the President's address), Martin was ordered to reduce the American personnel to that level by April 22. This last group of Americans, together with as many remaining Vietnamese employees as possible, would be evacuated from the embassy grounds at the point when the Saigon airport (Tan Son Nhut) was threatened. During the intervening period, a maximum effort would be made to evacuate Vietnamese, with preference given to those who had exposed themselves on America's behalf.

Senatorial pressures for a speedy retreat from Vietnam were mounting daily. On April 14, the entire Senate Foreign Relations Committee called on the President in the Cabinet Room, the first time this had happened since Woodrow Wilson. Schlesinger and I delivered grim, nearly identical briefings about the military situation and Saigon's prospects. The senators replied that they had not come to discuss Vietnam strategy but to speed the evacuation of Americans and to make sure we were not delaying it in order to rescue Vietnamese. Giving priority to saving South Vietnamese, they held, would get us involved militarily all over again. Ford tells the story in his memoirs:

> The message was clear: get out, *fast.* "I will give you large sums for evacuation," New York's Jacob Javits said, "but not one nickel for military aid." Idaho's Frank Church saw grave problems which "could involve us in a very large war" if we attempted to evacuate all the South Vietnamese who had been loyal to us. Delaware's Joseph Biden echoed a similar refrain. "I will vote for any amount for getting the Americans out," he said; "I don't want it mixed with getting the Vietnamese out."[4]

The President's reply was polite but unyielding on the principle of evacuation:

> Believe me, we need to buy time, even a few days. Thank you for coming down. We've had a good discussion but the decision is my responsibility and I'll accept the consequences.[5]

The Search for a Political Solution

Commentators and Congress kept pushing for their cherished "political solution." But the side facing total defeat has nothing to offer to the adversary and little more than risk to possible intermediaries. France showed a keen interest in playing a diplomatic role. But even while we politely discussed various French schemes for partitioning South Vietnam, we judged their démarches—as on Cambodia—to be more a reflection of nostalgia for lost colonial influence than a realistic assessment of how to conclude the Vietnam tragedy.

The only "political" move we could think of was to approach Moscow, which, despite a series of stalemated U.S.-Soviet negotiations, continued to have a stake in the American relationship. Brezhnev still pined after the summit conference on European security he had been pursuing for three years and which was now tentatively planned to be held in late July. I told my daily State Department senior staff meeting on April 18 that we would approach the Soviet Union even though I rated the chances of its doing something constructive on the order of one in a thousand. We were in the humiliating position summed up by British historian Edward Gibbon: that persuasion is the recourse of the feeble and the feeble are seldom able to persuade.

On April 19, I delivered an "oral note" from Ford to Brezhnev via Dobrynin. (An oral note is a written document having the same status as an oral conversation but put in writing for precision and emphasis.) The note stated that a cease-fire in Vietnam was needed to accomplish the "evacuation of American citizens and those South Vietnamese to whom we have a direct and special obligation." We were approaching Moscow, we said, because "it is in our long-term mutual interest that the situation be brought to its conclusion in a manner that does not jeopardize Soviet-American relations, or affect the attitude of the American people toward other international problems."

To give a more realistic cast to this essentially threadbare appeal, we stressed our willingness "to discuss the special political circumstances that could make this [a cease-fire] possible"—in other words, a change in the political situation in Saigon. In the meantime, Saigon's position had become desperate. We bluffed about the dangerous consequences of an attack on airfields and passenger planes—though so expert an observer of American congressional debates as Dobrynin was unlikely to take that threat very seriously.

While awaiting the Soviet reply, Martin, on April 20, hinted to Thieu that the South Vietnamese President might consider resigning. Martin purported to speak in his personal capacity, though in fact the démarche had been specifically approved by Ford and me. I had no illusions about what the North Vietnamese response would be to such a step, but I acquiesced on the slim hope that our approach might lead to a negotiation, giving us a few extra days for evacuating Vietnamese associated with America. Rather icily, Thieu replied that he would do what was best for his country. Martin ended his report to Washington on this poignant note: "I went home, read the daily news digests from Washington, took a shower, scrubbed very hard with the strongest soap I could find. It didn't help very much." Ford, Scowcroft, and I felt the same way. In retrospect, I think what we lost in self-respect outweighed whatever extra evacuation time we gained, if any.

The White House sense of urgency about evacuating the maximum number of Vietnamese had not yet engaged the Justice Department, which refused to waive visa requirements. It may seem strange to those unfamiliar with Washington that a President can be in a position to be obliged to fight bitter battles with a Cabinet agency about its willingness to "extend parole"—the technical term for waiving visa requirements—which was within the executive branch's authority. At last, on April 22, the Justice Department—with the approval of the Senate Judiciary Committee—agreed to waive restrictions for up to 130,000 refugees from Indochina, including 50,000 in the high-risk category. The last such exception had been made in 1960 on behalf of Cuban refugees.

While many of their seniors in Washington were engaged in passing the buck, junior Foreign Service officers who had served earlier in Vietnam exerted themselves on their own to ease the suffering. Among these were Lionel Rosenblatt and Craig Johnstone. On April 20, they left their posts at the State Department without permission. Traveling at their own expense and with regular (not diplomatic) passports, they arrived in Saigon and helped some of the Vietnamese who had worked with them escape. It was an egregious breach of Foreign Service discipline and who knows how many State Department regulations. The State Department bureaucracy was outraged and recommended penalties ranging from dismissal to a severe reprimand, which would have blighted Rosenblatt's and Johnstone's careers. When they returned to Washington two weeks later, I told Larry Eagleburger, then Deputy Undersecretary of State for Administration, to read them the riot act and then bring them to my office. After making some formal noises of disapproval, I said: "There has been little of which we can be proud these last months. But you have brought credit to your country and to the Foreign Service." No disciplinary action was taken. A year later, I saw to it that each received the State Department Superior Honor Award. Johnstone remained in the Foreign Service, later becoming ambassador to Algeria; Rosenblatt has devoted his life and career to nongovernmental organizations for helping refugees.

On the evening of April 21, Nguyen Van Thieu resigned with a bitter speech castigating the United States for failing either to enforce the Paris Agreement or to extend the promised material assistance to South Vietnam. The media hailed his departure. A "negotiated agreement" in accordance with the Paris Agreement was now possible at last, argued the *Washington Post* and *New York Times,* as if Thieu had been the obstacle to a negotiated outcome. Thieu's complaints against the United States were dismissed as the rantings of a "discredited and embittered Vietnamese politician"; for once, the liberal media were happy to defend the administration.[6]

Thieu had every reason to resent America's conduct. He had never been the obstacle to peace that antiwar critics alleged. Both Thieu and his country deserved a better fate. Had I thought it possible that Congress would, in effect, cut off aid to a beleaguered ally, I would not have pressed for an agreement as I did in the final negotiations in 1972.

Hopes for a "political solution" proved to be every bit as fragile as all experience had indicated they would be. Radio Hanoi attacked Thieu's successor, Tran Van Huong, as viciously as it had the departed President. No sooner had Thieu resigned than Hanoi escalated its demands, insisting on the immediate departure of all American personnel, both civilian and military.

Twenty years of hope, frustration, and discord over Vietnam had now been reduced to a single objective: to save the maximum number of potential Vietnamese victims from the consequences of America's abandonment. The White House clung to every refugee flight as if it could somehow redeem the accumulated anguish of America's war with itself. Starting on April 21, a round-the-clock airlift from Saigon was begun with C-141s flying in the daytime and C-130s at night. Over the next ten days, this helped to save close to 50,000 Vietnamese (another 80,000 escaped by other means, often with American assistance). The almost exclusive preoccupation of America's Indochina diplomacy had become to keep the airlift going.

The Communist incentive to grant us that crucial time diminished when White House staffers masterminded a typical inside-the-Beltway bureaucratic victory. They inserted into a presidential speech at Tulane University in New Orleans on April 23 a phrase to the effect that, as far as Ford was concerned, the war was over. The relevant passage read as follows:

> Today, America can regain the sense of pride that existed before Vietnam. But it cannot be achieved by refighting a war that is finished as far as America is concerned. As I see it, the time has come to look forward to an agenda for the future, to unify, to bind up the Nation's wounds, and to restore its health and its optimistic self-confidence.

Background briefings by White House staffers stressed that neither Scowcroft nor I had been consulted about the wording and described the speech as a presidential "declaration of independence" from his Secretary of State.

What the gloaters failed to understand was that the war *was* over, with or without the paragraph; the only remaining issue was how many Vietnamese could be saved and how much longer we would be permitted to carry on this essentially humanitarian activity. Some ambiguity about how far we were willing to go to achieve that objective was the sole bargaining card left.

In practice, the Tulane speech did not alter Ford's conduct of affairs. Later that day, he instructed Ron Nessen to inform the media that he stood by his request for $722 million in aid to Vietnam. In the midst of the heartbreaking turmoil all around us, I saw no point in debating speechwriting prerogatives with the President. I never raised the issue, and Ford never volunteered an explanation. Apparently he did not consider the Tulane speech as significant as some of his entourage did, for he made no mention of it in his memoirs.

The Evacuation

For a few days after the Tulane speech, all was quiet, though the Communists had advanced to within artillery range of Tan Son Nhut airport. Were they regrouping for a final assault, or had they opened up a window for evacuation?

Actually they were doing both. On April 24, Dobrynin telephoned at

4:00 P.M. and read me the Soviet reply to our note of April 19. It sounded like an explicit green light to evacuate Americans, and it claimed that Hanoi would seek a political outcome guided by the Paris Agreement. The North Vietnamese allegedly told Moscow that they "do not intend to damage the prestige of the United States." This emboldened Brezhnev to try to restrain nonexisting American adventurousness by expressing his hope that we would take no action "fraught with a new exacerbation of the situation in Indochina."

If the Soviet note meant what it seemed to say, there might be some breathing room for evacuation. Though the note confined itself to the evacuation of Americans, its practical effect was to help extricate Vietnamese as well, since we were evacuating both groups simultaneously. And if Hanoi really intended to bring about the political change by the procedures according to its interpretation of the Paris Agreement, some more time might be gained.

The outcome, of course, would be the same: the total Communist takeover four American administrations had resisted so strenuously for two decades. Yet, for the sake of saving more Vietnamese lives, we were prepared to grit our teeth and play along. Grasping for every last possible extension, we replied to the Soviets at 8:25 P.M. on April 24. We posed a number of questions in the hope that the refugee airlift might continue while the Soviets concerted answers with Hanoi. The message noted that in view of the "constructive [Soviet] reply . . . the U.S. side is proceeding with the evacuation of Americans under the assumption that conditions will remain favorable." It invited Hanoi's views on how to implement the provisions of the Paris Agreement "relative to the achievement of a political settlement." The President reassured Brezhnev that we would desist from what Congress was, in any event, prohibiting. So long as there was no interference with the evacuation, our note continued, the United States would "take no steps which might exacerbate the situation."

Four days later, on the evening of April 28 Washington time (April 29 in Vietnam), the final collapse of Saigon began with a rocket attack on Tan Son Nhut airport. Eight thousand particularly endangered Vietnamese and 400 Americans had been assembled there in order to enable the evacuation planes to be filled and turned around without delay.

Though the firing soon ceased, the refugees' fear became their undoing. Panicked, they swarmed over the runways, and in effect stopped the airlift.

At 10:45 P.M. (Washington time) on April 28, Ford very reluctantly ordered the final evacuation. Shortly before, we had talked though not in the apocalyptic terms in which the occasion may appear in history books. Rather it was dominated by pain for the unfortunate victims we were about to leave behind:

> KISSINGER: They have the authority to call for the emergency airlift anytime tonight—our night—and they must call for it before the end of the day out there.
>
> FORD: By the end of the day out there or by tomorrow morning here?
>
> KISSINGER: By tomorrow morning here if the C-130s haven't taken them off, then the helicopters will.
>
> FORD: That's a real shame! Twenty-four more hours—or twelve more hours?
>
> KISSINGER: Twelve more hours and we would have saved eight thousand lives.
>
> FORD: Henry, we did the best we could.
>
> KISSINGER: Mr. President, you carried it single-handedly against all the advice and we played it out as far as it would play.
>
> FORD: Well, I just hope [General Homer] Smith [Jr., U.S. Defense Attaché in Saigon] and [Graham] Martin now understand where we are and will not hesitate to act.
>
> KISSINGER: Well, we checked with Martin. I talked with him fifteen minutes ago. I can't say that he's doing it willingly but he's going to do it. He wants to stay behind with two people to take care of Americans that might come out of the woodwork. But I just don't think we can justify it.
>
> FORD: I don't think so either, Henry.

At 11:00 P.M., I called Graham Martin and told him to pull the plug: All Americans must come out together with as many Vietnamese as could be loaded on the helicopters in what would irrevocably be the final day of the airlift. Martin agreed to the evacuation but proposed staying behind with two volunteers to supervise an orderly transfer of power, confirming my suspicion that he planned to go down like General George "Chinese" Gordon—the famed British commander who was killed in Khartoum by the Mahdi in 1885 after refusing to leave. We needed few things less than to have our ambassador in Saigon taken hostage by the North Vietnamese on the day our effort there collapsed. So I ordered Martin to leave: "We need our heroes back in Washington; there aren't too many of them here."

At the time, I believed that Ford's Tulane speech had advanced Hanoi's timetable because, in effect, it removed the last danger of American reinter-vention—though actually it would have required a truly extraordinary level of North Vietnamese paranoia to take such a threat seriously. The memoirs of General Van Tien Dung, the commander, do not refer to Ford's speech, as they do to almost every other milestone in the American domestic debate.[7] According to Dung, what seems to have hastened Hanoi's decision-making, however, were the "cunning diplomatic plans" of the "United States and its puppets":

> The Americans' and puppets' cunning diplomatic plans coming one
> on top of the other, coupled with threatening hints to us, were aimed
> at blocking our troops' general offensive on Saigon, and showed all
> the more that we must fight more urgently, attack more quickly, and
> make the best use of each hour, each minute for total victory.[8]

Hanoi's idea of "cunning diplomatic plans" was that Saigon tried to im-plement the steps which the American protest movement had been demand-ing for a decade: Thieu's removal and broadening of the government.

On April 24, Thieu's successor, President Tran Van Huong, broadened the government by inviting General Duong Van Minh to take over as Prime Minister. "Big Minh," as he was nicknamed, had been the great hope of the anti-Vietnam protesters since 1967, when he had lost out in a power struggle with Thieu. Alleged to be a neutralist, Minh was deemed to be acceptable to the Communists, though Le Duc Tho had given me the opposite im-pression.

In the final struggle over who would be captain of the sinking ship, Minh refused to serve as Prime Minister because he said the offer came from the old power structure, now overthrown. Instead, he asked that the National As-sembly appoint him President with the charge to end the war and to create a transitional administration. Two days were spent accomplishing this maneu-ver, and Big Minh was finally installed as President on April 27. Big Minh remained in office less than seventy-two hours, only long enough to undertake two significant acts: He asked Hanoi for a cease-fire and political negotiations—which were rejected—and, on April 29, he demanded that all Americans leave within twenty-four hours. Since this coincided precisely with our withdrawal schedule, it in fact helped our extrication by avoiding the charge that America was abandoning its friends. Simultaneously, the French Foreign Office attempted to establish diplomatic contact between the PRG representative in Paris and American diplomats—for which the PRG envoys were allegedly eager.

But Hanoi's leaders had not fought for three decades to tolerate a transitional government in Saigon, much less an independent—even if Communist—state. Paradoxically, the installation of Minh may well have speeded up Hanoi's timetable. It might have been more prepared to grant Thieu a period of grace than to his increasingly abject successors. Thieu's regime was collapsing, and a few extra days would not resuscitate it. But if an internationally recognized government emerged in Saigon capable of negotiating a cease-fire and dealing with the United States, it might lead to a kind of independence for South Vietnam—albeit a Communist one. This Hanoi would not countenance. Ironically, Hanoi's last battle in Saigon may well have been aimed at the South Vietnamese Communists whose guerrilla movement had started the entire tragedy all those years earlier.

Not surprisingly, the contact with the PRG in Paris never materialized.

The Last Day

As Americans were being lifted from the roof of the American embassy during the morning of April 29 (Washington time), Ford, Schlesinger, and I briefed the congressional leadership. Continuing to fight yesterday's battles, the legislators kept harping on a "political" solution, oblivious to the fact that the evacuation we were describing ended America's ability to influence the political outcome.

After that, all was silence. I sat alone in the National Security Adviser's corner office in the West Wing of the White House, enveloped by the eerie solitude that sometimes attends momentous events. The White House NSC office was the Washington command center for the evacuation of Vietnam even though the actual airlift was being conducted by the Pentagon. The careful record established by the Pentagon of its repeated requests for a speedy evacuation guaranteed that Ford and I would be held accountable should anything go wrong at this last moment. On the other hand, neither Ford nor I could influence the outcome any longer; we had become spectators. So we each sat in our offices, freed of other duties yet unable to affect the ongoing tragedy, suspended between a pain we could not still and a future we were not in a position to shape.

In that almost mystical stillness, I felt too drained to analyze the various decisions that had led to this moment of dashed hopes. But I reviewed them as if in slow motion. What was the turning point? The overthrow of Diem in the Kennedy administration? The decision of the Johnson administration to pursue a strategy of attrition incompatible with what the American public would sustain? Or the Nixon choice of Vietnamization, which required a subtle combination of withdrawal, warfare, and negotiation amidst a domestic maelstrom? Had I thought systematically, I would probably have concluded that the tragedy was that, by the time the Nixon administration came into office, no other options than those it pursued were left. The possibility of victory had been given up by our predecessors—simple abandonment was precluded by our concept of honor. Unilateral rapid withdrawal—proposed by so many critics but not before 1970—would have produced a nightmare far more searing than what we were now facing. The complexities that a withdrawal of 6,000 had imposed on us in recent weeks showed the nightmare that would have faced America had it tried to withdraw hundreds of thousands surrounded by millions of armed Vietnamese.

But what did torment me in these hours was a more tactical issue—my own role in the next-to-last act: the acceleration of negotiations after Le Duc Tho's breakthrough offer of October 8, 1972. What has torn at me ever since is whether the demoralizations of the Saigon structure which led to its collapse in 1975 started with the pace of negotiations we imposed in 1972, however favorable we considered the terms. Was there a basis for the elation of my negotiating team and me on October 8, 1972, when Le Duc Tho, in effect, accepted our proposals, and we thought ourselves on the verge of both an honorable end of the war and national reconciliation?

My colleagues and I believed that it was our duty to seize the opportunity for an outcome other than abdication. No doubt had I stalled, the North Vietnamese would have gone public even earlier than they did. Thieu would have dug in his heels anyway; the diplomatic outcome (if any) would have been less favorable. Congress would have forced a conclusion by cutting off funds.

None of us could imagine that a collapse of presidential authority would follow the expected sweeping electoral victory. We were convinced that we were working on an agreement that could be sustained by our South Vietnamese allies with American help against an all-out invasion. Protesters could speak of Vietnam in terms of the excesses of an aberrant society, but when my colleagues and I thought of Vietnam, it was in terms of dedicated men and women—soldiers and Foreign Service officers—who had struggled and suffered there and of our Vietnamese associates now condemned to face an uncertain but surely painful fate. These Americans had honestly believed that they were defending the cause of freedom against a brutal enemy in treacherous jungles and distant rice paddies. Vilified by the media, assailed in Congress, and ridiculed by the protest movement, they had sustained America's idealistic tradition, risking their lives and expending their youth on a struggle that American leadership groups had initiated, then abandoned, and finally disdained. It was they and not the few bad apples, their goals and not their ultimate failures, American responsibility for the safety of the free world and not the frustrations associated with it that were on my mind as I sat at my desk and Vietnam wound down.

My reflections were interrupted by the one telephone call I received that day not related to the helicopter lift. It was from Lew Wasserman, then head of MCA, the Hollywood communications giant, and a recent friend: "The purpose of the call is to tell you that with all the problems you're having there are a lot of your friends out here who are thinking about you." He hung up before I could reply. Lew Wasserman was a devout Democrat, a constant critic of our Vietnam policies, and I could not be of any conceivable use to his business. It was a genuine act of grace, and I have never forgotten it.

Then, in its very death throes, Vietnam swept me back into its frustrations and tragedy. By now it was early afternoon in Washington, well after midnight in Saigon. Despite his original decision to end the airlift at dusk in Vietnam, Ford had ordered it to continue all night so that the largest number of Vietnamese might be rescued—especially those still inside the embassy compound. Around 2:00 P.M., I learned that there were still 760 people there and that, for whatever reason, only one helicopter had landed in the previous two hours. I called Schlesinger to discuss how we could evacuate this group and at the same time establish a deadline by which the evacuation would be completed. For it was clear that the North Vietnamese would occupy Saigon at daybreak. Schlesinger and I were in complete harmony. We computed that thirteen helicopters would do the trick. But to throw in a safety factor, we agreed on a total of nineteen. Martin was to be on the last helicopter.

The conversation between Schlesinger and me during which this decision was reached conveys the atmosphere of those hours better than any narrative could:

> KISSINGER: Jim.
>
> SCHLESINGER: Yeah, Henry. We are sending a message to them because of the 46s as well as the 53s [types of helicopters]—that the 19 choppers, which should handle 760 people—[are] all that he gets, and we expect them—him—out on the 19th chopper at the latest at the pace to terminate around 3:30.
>
> KISSINGER: All right. Now, you tell him, Jim; if you don't add that this is a presidential order, he won't come out.
>
> SCHLESINGER: Right. We shall do that.
>
> KISSINGER: That's what I wanted to make sure that you add.
>
> SCHLESINGER: Shall do. He is a man with a mission.
>
> KISSINGER: Well, he lost a son there.
>
> SCHLESINGER: Yes. You have got to admire that man.
>
> KISSINGER: Look, his thoughts are in the right direction.
>
> SCHLESINGER: That's right. Dedication and energy.
>
> KISSINGER: And I think . . .
>
> SCHLESINGER: You weep.
>
> KISSINGER: I think you and I will be glad we went this way.

I mention this episode because, some twenty years later, I was watching a cable television program in which a very impressive colonel expressed his outrage that 400 Vietnamese friends of the United States had been left behind inside the embassy compound where he had helped supervise the evacuation. I was stunned and tracked down the colonel at the Army War College and confirmed his statements on the program. No one had told me any such thing, nor is there any record of such abandonment in the many staff meetings surrounding the event. I still do not understand what happened. I know that nineteen helicopters left—because I was receiving a report on each departure—and that Martin was on the last one. I have no explanation as to why anyone was left behind unless the gates of the embassy had been reopened to let in another group beyond the original 760. I sought out the colonel at the Army War College where he taught and apologized to him.

Shortly after 4:00 P.M., I was able to reassure George Meany, president of the AFL-CIO, that Vietnamese labor leaders had just been rescued. His was one of many requests we had received to rescue some Vietnamese with special ties to the United States. At 3:58 P.M. Washington time (4:58 the next morning in Saigon), Martin left on the nineteenth or last helicopter—or what we thought was the last. He had done an extraordinary job. Imperious, occasionally insubordinate, he was as dedicated and courageous as he had been contentious. Over a two-week period, Martin had orchestrated the evacuation of over 50,000 South Vietnamese and 6,000 Americans with only four casualties. The accolade I sent him on the rescue ship came from the heart:

> I am sure you know how deeply I feel about your performance under
> the most trying circumstances. My heartfelt thanks. Warm regards.

Brent Scowcroft, who had had to bear the brunt of the nearly daily exchanges with Martin, added his own postscript: "Graham: You were superb. Brent." For the taciturn Brent, this was the equivalent of decorating Martin with the Scowcroft Medal of Honor.

As soon as I thought the last helicopter had left, I crossed the passageway between the White House and the Executive Office Building to brief the press. Summarizing the day's events, I responded to questions, the overwhelming thrust of which was to get me to confirm the journalists' established view that everything that had ever happened had been an unforgivable mistake. Awed by the tragedy taking place halfway around the globe, I refused to take the bait:

> I think this is not the occasion, when the last American has barely left
> Saigon, to make an assessment of a decade and a half of American
> foreign policy, because it could equally well be argued that if five ad-
> ministrations that were staffed, after all, by serious people dedicated
> to the welfare of their country came to certain conclusions, that

maybe there was something in their assessment, even if for a variety
of reasons the effort did not succeed.

As I have already pointed out, special factors have operated in recent years. But I would think that what we need now in this country,
for some weeks at least, and hopefully for some months, is to heal the
wounds and to put Vietnam behind us and to concentrate on the
problems of the future.[9]

Returning to my office, I found that Vietnam still would not let go.
While Graham Martin and the remnants of the embassy staff had indeed departed at 4:58 A.M. Saigon time, elements of the 9th Marine Amphibious
Brigade protecting the evacuation—comprising 129 marines—had been left
behind for some inexplicable reason. Huge credibility gaps had been manufactured from far less than this, but those of us in the White House Situation
Room had no time to worry about public relations. The helicopter airlift was
resumed. It was 7:53 P.M. Washington time (and broad daylight in Saigon)
when the helicopter carrying the last marines left the embassy roof.

Two hours later, North Vietnamese tanks rolled into Saigon. One of the
first smashed through the gates of the Presidential Palace. There was no
turnover of authority because that would have implied the existence of an independent, or at least autonomous, South Vietnam. Instead, Big Minh and
his entire Cabinet were arrested and disappeared from public view.

The Provisional Revolutionary Government, the reincarnation of the
National Liberation Front—advertised in the West for a decade as the puta-
tive centerpiece of a South Vietnamese democratic coalition government—
disappeared with Big Minh. Within a year, the two Vietnams were unified.
Not a shred of autonomy remained for the South. Hundreds of thousands of
South Vietnamese, including all those who had been in the government or
armed forces, were herded into so-called reeducation camps—a euphemism
for concentration camps—where they stayed for the better part of a decade.
Tens of thousands fled as boat people. The Buddhist monks, whose quest for
autonomy from the Saigon authorities had contributed to inducing the Kennedy administration to overthrow South Vietnamese President Ngo Dinh
Diem and his government, were imprisoned under the most brutal conditions.

In Washington, not much changed as a result of the tragedy of Vietnam.
On May 1, 1975, the day after Saigon fell, the House of Representatives re-

fused to approve a request by Ford for $327 million for the care and transportation of Indochinese refugees. Congressional leaders for weeks had argued against efforts to save Vietnamese, and now the House turned down refugee relief for those who had already been saved. Second thoughts have been few and far between.[10]

For the sake of our long-term peace of mind, we must some day undertake an assessment of why good men on all sides found no way to avoid this disaster and why our domestic drama first paralyzed and then overwhelmed us. But, on the day the last helicopter left the roof of the embassy, only a feeling of emptiness remained. Those of us who had fought the battles to avoid the final disaster were too close to the tragedy to review the history of twenty years of American involvement.

And now it was too late to alter the course of events.

EPILOGUE

During the last days of Vietnam, I set down, in response to a request by President Ford, some observations about the events through which we were living. It was a melancholy memorandum, resigned to circumstances and seeking to place the divisions within our society into some kind of perspective. It read in full:

> At your request, I have prepared some thoughts on the "lessons of Vietnam" for your consideration and for your background information in dealing with further press questions on the subject.
>
> It is remarkable, considering how long the war lasted and how intensely it was reported and commented, that there are really not very many lessons from our experience in Vietnam that can be usefully applied elsewhere despite the obvious temptation to try. Vietnam represented a unique situation, geographically, ethnically, politically, militarily and diplomatically. We should probably be grateful for that and should recognize it for what it is, instead of trying to apply the "lessons of Vietnam" as universally as we once tried to apply the "lessons of Munich."
>
> The real frustration of Vietnam, in terms of commentary and evaluation, may be that the war had almost universal effects but did not provide a universal catechism.
>
> A frequent temptation of many commentators has been to draw conclusions regarding the tenacity of the American people and the ultimate failure of our will. But I question whether we can accept

that conclusion. It was the longest war in American history, the most distant, the least obviously relevant to our nation's immediate concerns, and yet the American people supported our involvement and its general objectives until the very end. The people made enormous sacrifices. I am convinced that, even at the end, they would have been prepared to support a policy that would have saved South Vietnam if such an option had been available to use.

It must not be forgotten that the decisions of American administrations that involved this nation in the war were generally supported at the time they were taken, and that they were supported not only among the people at large but among the political elements and among the journalists who later came to oppose the war. The American people generally supported and applauded President Eisenhower for the decision to partition Vietnam and to support an anti-Communist government in the South. The American people, and particularly the American media, supported President Kennedy's decision to go beyond the restrictions on American involvement that President Eisenhower had set and they also supported his decision to permit American involvement in the removal of President Diem although the extent of that involvement was not clear at the time. Many who were later to be labeled as "doves" on Vietnam then insisted that South Vietnam had to be saved and that President Diem's removal was essential to save it. You yourself will remember the strong support that the Tonkin Gulf resolution won on the Hill and the general support for President Johnson's decision to send troops. President Nixon won an outpouring of support for the decision to withdraw American forces at a gradual pace, as well as for the Paris Peace Agreement.

If one could offer any guidelines for the future about the lessons to be drawn regarding domestic support for foreign policy, it would be that American political groups will not long remain comfortable in positions that go against their traditional attitudes. The liberal Democrats could not long support a war against a revolutionary movement, no matter how reactionary the domestic tactics of that movement. They had accepted the heavy commitment to Vietnam because of President Kennedy, whom they regarded as their leader, but they withdrew from it under President Johnson.

One clear lesson that can be drawn, however, is the importance of absolute honesty and objectivity in all reporting, within and from the Government as well as from the press. U.S. official reports tended for a long time to be excessively optimistic, with the result that official statements did not make clear to the American people how long and how tough the conflict might turn out to be. After a while the pessimistic reports from journalists began to gain greater credence because such positive trends as did emerge came too slowly to justify optimistic Washington assessments. In Vietnam, the situation was generally worse than some reported and better than others reported. But the pessimistic reports, even if they were inaccurate, began to look closer to the mark until almost any government statement could be rejected as biased, not only by the opposition but by an increasingly skeptical public.

Another lesson would be the absolute importance of focusing our own remarks and the public debate on essentials—even if those essentials are not clearly visible every night on the television screen. The Vietnam debate often turned into a fascination with issues that were, at best, peripheral. The "tiger cages" were seen as a symbol of South Vietnamese Government oppression, although that Government was facing an enemy who had assassinated, tortured and jailed an infinitely greater number; the "Phoenix" program became a subject of attack although North Vietnamese and Vietcong tactics were infinitely more brutal. The Mylai incident tarnished the image of an American Army that had generally—though not always—been compassionate in dealing with the civilian population. Even at the end, much of the public discussion focused on President Thieu's alleged failure to gain political support, but it was the Communists who rejected free elections and who brought in their reserve divisions because they did not have popular support. And at home, it was argued that your aid request meant American reinvolvement when nothing was further from your mind.

Of equal importance may be a dedication to consistency. When the United States entered the war during the 1960s, it did so with excesses that not only ended the career and the life of an allied leader but that may have done serious damage to the American economy and that poured over half a million soldiers into a country where we never had more than 100,000 who were actually fighting. At the end, the excesses in the other direction made it impossible to get from the Congress only 2 or 3 percent as much money as it had earlier appropriated every year. When we entered, many did so in the name of morality. Before the war was over, many opposed it in the name of morality. But nobody spoke of the morality of consistency, or of the virtue of seeing something through once its cost had been reduced to manageable proportions.

In terms of military tactics, we cannot help draw the conclusion that our armed forces are not suited to this kind of war. Even the Special Forces who had been designed for it could not prevail. This was partly because of the nature of the conflict. It was both a revolutionary war fought at knifepoint during the night within the villages. It was also a main force war in which technology could make a genuine difference. Both sides had trouble devising tactics that would be suitable for each type of warfare. But we and the South Vietnamese had more difficulty with this than the other side. We also had trouble with excesses here: when we made it "our war" we would not let the South Vietnamese fight it; when it again became "their war," we would not help them fight it. Ironically, we prepared the South Vietnamese for main force warfare after 1954 (anticipating another Korean-type attack), and they faced a political war; they had prepared themselves for political warfare after 1973 only to be faced with a main force invasion 20 years after it had been expected.

Our diplomacy also suffered in the process, and it may take us some time to bring things back to balance. We often found that the United States could not sustain a diplomatic position for more than a few weeks or months before it came under attack from the same political elements that had often advocated that very position. We ended up negotiating with ourselves, constantly offering concession after concession while the North Vietnamese changed nothing in their diplomatic objectives and very little in their diplomatic positions. It was only in secret diplomacy that we could hold anything approaching a genuine dialogue, and even then the North Vietnamese could keep us under constant public pressure. Our diplomacy often degenerated into frantic efforts to find formulas that would evoke momentary support and would gloss over obvious differences between ourselves and the North Vietnamese. The legacy of this remains to haunt us, making it difficult for us to sustain a diplomatic position for any length of time, no matter how obdurate the enemy, without becoming subject to domestic attack.

In the end, we must ask ourselves whether it was all worth it, or at least what benefits we did gain. I believe the benefits were many, though they have long been ignored, and I fear that we will only now begin to realize how much we need to shore up our positions elsewhere once our position in Vietnam is lost. We may be compelled to support other situations much more strongly in order to repair the damage and to take tougher stands in order to make others believe in us again.

I have always believed, as have many observers, that our decision to save South Vietnam in 1965 prevented Indonesia from falling to Communism and probably preserved the American presence in Asia.

This not only means that we kept our troops. It also means that we kept our economic presence as well as our political influence, and that our friends—including Japan—did not feel that they had to provide for their own defense. When we consider the impact of what is now happening, it is worth remembering how much greater the impact would have been ten years ago when the Communist movement was still widely regarded as a monolith destined to engulf us all. Therefore, in our public statements, I believe we can honorably avoid self-flagellation and that we should not characterize our role in the conflict as a disgraceful disaster. I believe our efforts, militarily, diplomatically and politically, were not in vain. We paid a high price but we gained ten years of time and we changed what then appeared to be an overwhelming momentum. I do not believe our soldiers or our people need to be ashamed.

Ten years later, I wrote an article for the *Washington Post,* drawing some additional conclusions:

Guerrilla wars are best avoided by preemption, by generous programs of assistance and reform in countries the United States considers vital. But once a war is in progress, victory cannot be achieved by reform alone.

Before America commits combat troops, it should have a clear understanding of the nature of the threat and of realistic objectives.

When America commits itself to military action, there is no alternative to achieving the stated objective.

A democracy cannot conduct a serious foreign policy if the contending factions do not exercise some restraint in their debate. The United States owed the peoples of Indochina a decent opportunity for survival; its domestic divisions made it impossible for the United States to pay this debt.

Since then, another fifteen years have passed and provided the perspective of a quarter-century. I would not change my conclusions but supplement them with a few observations.

The dominoes did not fall in Southeast Asia after the collapse of Indochina, as the originators of America's involvement had feared in the 1950s—in all likelihood because America's effort in Indochina permitted shaky new states to consolidate themselves. Other dominoes fell instead, in regions where it had not been anticipated or imagined. The causes for their fall were not confined to the Vietnam tragedy, but the debacle in Indochina provided a psychological impetus for them. A Cuban expeditionary force appeared in Africa within six months of Saigon's fall and decided a civil war. Other Cuban and Soviet military adventures in Africa and Afghanistan followed. Would such daring moves have been attempted had not a technologically backward country already demonstrated the vincibility of the United States and had not America's internal divisions suggested a creeping paralysis?

Three years later, the Shah of Iran was overthrown and, with that major shift of power, the entire geopolitical equilibrium of the Gulf and parts of the Indian Ocean was shaken—and has not been fully restored to this writing. A year later, American diplomats were held as hostages in Tehran for over a year. The policies of the Shah and of the United States no doubt contributed to the outcome, but the question remains: To what extent were these developments influenced by the Shah's loss of confidence in American protection, by his opponents' growing conviction that the wave of history was on their side, and by America's seeming reluctance, in the wake of Vietnam, to deal with crises in geopolitical terms?

But it is even more the case that the "domino effect" had a more unpredictable and devastating impact on our Cold War adversary, the Soviet Union. Perceived American weakness tempted it into adventures in Africa and Afghanistan. It overextended itself, accelerating the Soviet Union's eventual collapse fifteen years later.

For the United States, the domino effect was, above all, psychological. For over a quarter-century after the war ended, the Vietnam era divisions persisted in the conflicting ways Americans interpreted the world. The liberal wing of the generation whose formative experience had been during the war recoiled from the use of American power. It focused its efforts on the so-called "soft issues," such as the environment, that did not imply reliance on military force. Some of them derided what they called "Cold War attitudes" as if the Cold War had been some sort of misunderstanding, if not an American invention. On the whole, this group distrusted the concept of national interest unless it could be presented as in the service of some "unselfish" cause—hence the devotion to multilateralism. The ambivalence about the use of power came to expression in a fear of casualties so that even when American power was committed, it appeared as a symbol of American inhibitions.

As a result, strategy became largely the provenance of American conservatives and neoconservatives. Uncomfortable with commitments on distant battlefields, the American right concentrated on rigorous anti-Communist diplomacy and vigilance in maintaining the strategic nuclear balance; they were ambivalent about preserving the geopolitical equilibrium of the various continents. Nevertheless, against an adversary himself paying the price for overextension and inherent weakness, the conservative administrations of the 1980s achieved great successes in dismantling the Soviet empire. The challenge of building a new world order was left largely in abeyance.

As the generation whose seminal experience was the Vietnam war passed from the scene, so did the two-power world of the Cold War period. The post-Vietnam generation is not shaped by the debates over the war in Indochina, with which it is largely unfamiliar. Nor does it have feelings of guilt about a doctrine of self-interest, which it has pursued strenuously in its economic activities, especially in the salad days of the 1990s. For a time, it was tempted by the concept of riskless gratification and the belief that the hardheaded pursuit of economic self-interest would ultimately produce global reconciliation via globalization—thereby moving much of the debate from strategy to self-indulgence.

At that point, in September 2001, the post-Vietnam generation had a wake-up call: the first direct attack on American soil. For the first time since the Civil War, Americans have experienced the impact of war on the American continent and for the first time ever at the hands of foreign enemies. The debates that grew out of the Vietnam war have been superseded by this challenge. The first reaction was a defiant unity, a recognition that this is a country worth defending not only for its own sake but for the peace and progress of the rest of the world. But the struggle is likely to be long and complex. Disagreements are inevitable. History never repeats itself precisely. Many of the lessons of the Vietnam war are no longer applicable. But one should surely be engraved in the consciousness of those who endured the period and of the majority that has learned of it only secondhand: Democracies achieve dynamism by confronting their differences, but they achieve meaning only if they remember that societies thrive not through the victories of factions over each other but through their reconciliations and their common purposes.

ACKNOWLEDGMENTS

Turning material written over a period of twenty years into a narrative, together with assessments from a more recent period, presented a special challenge. I am indebted to Michael Korda, who, as editor, friend, and amateur psychologist, participated in all these efforts and contributed his penetrating judgment. John Cox was his indispensable assistant during every phase of this effort. Gypsy da Silva supervised the copyediting and proofreading with her characteristic efficiency, reinforced by unfailing good cheer.

Winston Lord, my closest associate during the events recounted here, read the entire manuscript and contributed important insights.

The dedication and extraordinary ability of Theresa Cimino Amantea and Jody Williams of my staff contributed to every stage of this process. They typed, collated, edited, and advised efficiently and indefatigably. Jessee Incao calmly and effectively took over those administrative duties her colleagues had to abandon during this period. Peter Mandaville reviewed the manuscript, assisting ably with fact-checking and research.

Fred Chase copyedited the entire first draft of the manuscript. Sydney Wolfe Cohen produced the index.

I am grateful as well for the cooperation and assistance of Mark Gompertz, Touchstone publisher; Caroline Sutton, Touchstone editor, and her assistant, Nicole Diamond; Jennifer Love, managing editor; George Turianski, production manager; and Francine Kass, cover designer.

My wife, Nancy, made many perceptive editorial comments and provided her indispensable moral support.

I have dedicated this book to the memory of two remarkable public servants. Ambassador Ellsworth Bunker and General Creighton ("Abe") Abrams vindicated, in a time of turbulence and controversy, the permanent honor and values of this country.

APPENDIX

The 1973 Bombing Campaign in Cambodia

Memorandum for the Historian of the State Department from Emory C. Swank, U.S. Ambassador to the Khmer Republic, 1970–73, and Thomas O. Enders, Deputy Chief of Mission, Phnom Penh, 1970–74, and dated October 10, 1979.

    (Following this memorandum are Tab A: State Department Instruction 015050, January 26, 1973; Tab B: Letter from William N. Harben, Chief of the Political Section, Phnom Penh, 1972–1973; and Tab C: Letter from John W. Vogt, General USAF, Ret., Commander of the US Seventh Air Force and of the United States Support Activities Group, 1973.)

In a book published earlier this year (*Sideshow: Kissinger, Nixon and the Destruction of Cambodia,* Simon and Schuster, New York, 1979) William Shawcross makes assertions and inferences which misrepresent the conduct and consequences of the 1973 bombing campaign in Cambodia and the roles each of us played in it. Although they are by no means the only errors of fact and interpretation contained in Mr. Shawcross's book, these are of particular importance historically, because they appear to be the main basis for his conclusions concerning the "destruction of Cambodia."

    According to Mr. Shawcross,

- Embassy Phnom Penh "approved and controlled" the bombing;
- It was instructed to do so by Assistant to the President for National Security Affairs Kissinger without the knowledge of the Secretary of State;
- Bombing was "indiscriminate" because out-of-date maps were used rather than photography;
- Control of bombing was shifted to the Cambodian armed forces after a Congressional sub-committee investigation in April 1973;
- The bombing resulted in massive civilian casualties.

None of these statements is correct.

    1. *Assertion:* That from early February 1973 on, Embassy Phnom Penh was no longer to be merely "a conduit, passing Cambodian requests for bombing strikes on to the Seventh Air Force,"

but "was to be actively involved in the entire bombing process, selecting, examining, approving and controlling the bombing." [1] Mr. Shawcross cites no source for this statement.

Clarification: The Embassy did not approve or control air strikes; only Military Assistance Command Vietnam (MACV) and its successor command—the United States Support Activities Group (USSAG)—had that authority. The role of the Embassy was to receive FANK requests for air support, validate them "consistent with means and time available" and forward them to MACV for decision. The operative part of the Embassy's instructions, as sent to Swank in State Department cable 15050, dated January 26, 1973 and classified Secret/NODIS, reads:

> "At the time when the FANK [Forces Armées Nationales Khmeres] suspend offensive military operation all U.S. TACAIR and B-52 strikes in Cambodia will cease. RECCE, airlift, medevac and other U.S. air operations that are not ordnance delivery associated are permitted.
>
> "U.S. TACAIR and B-52 forces will be prepared to strike designated targets in Cambodia in order to assist FANK forces when the situation so dictates. To this end a simple, rapid request-validation-execute procedure will be set up between US Ambassador Cambodia and MACV. In essence, US Ambassador will be responsible for receiving requests for air support from GKR [Government of the Khmer Republic] and validating requests consistent with his means and time available. The Ambassador will pass the requests to MACV who has the authority to validate and direct air strikes by US TACAIR or B-52's as the situation dictates. All air strikes executed under this guidance are to counter specific hostile acts against GKR/FANK. Escort of Mekong convoys is authorized." [2]

As explained to Swank on February 8, 1973, by then Assistant to the President for National Security Affairs Kissinger, the purpose of these arrangements was to back up the unilateral U.S. statement on Cambodia made at the last session of the Paris Peace Talks on January 23, 1973. The U.S. had been unsuccessful in engaging the Khmer Rouge in the talks either directly or indirectly. In the absence of any agreement, the U.S. offered to suspend hostilities in Cambodia, if reciprocated. If the Khmer Rouge attacked, government forces and the Seventh Air Force would respond. The role of the Embassy, Dr. Kissinger told Swank, was to make sure the response to any such attacks was no more than required to back up the unilateral statement.

In implementing this instruction, the Embassy, according to the report prepared for Senator Stuart Symington of the Senate Foreign Relations Committee by Staff Members James G. Lowenstein and Richard M. Moose, performed three functions, none of which included the approval or control of air strikes:[3]

> "A. *As a communications relay point*
> We were shown the radio-telephone relay system, known as 'Area Control' located in the Air Attache's Office in the Embassy which is manned by an augmented staff of U.S. military personnel temporarily assigned to the Defense Attache's Office. It provides a communications link between the Cambodian General Staff, Seventh Air Force, the Airborne Battlefield Command and Control Center plane and the U.S. Forward Air Control planes.
> "B. *As an on-the-spot coordinator of forward air control planes and strike aircraft*
> U.S. Forward Air Control planes which are assigned daily to the control of the Air Attache and which regularly refuel at Phnom Penh airport are shifted by

Area Control from place to place in response to requests from the Cambodian General Staff or in response to tactical emergencies; and

"C. *As a screener of Cambodian or Seventh Air Force requests for strikes except in eastern Cambodia*

A panel of Embassy officers, both civilian and military, validates each request for B-52 and F-111 strikes, and the Defense Attache screens tactical air requests.

The degree and nature of the Embassy's involvement varies depending on the location of air activity and on whether strategic or tactical air is involved. The Embassy has relatively little to do with air activity in the eastern third of Cambodia where there is no Cambodian Government presence. (This area is designated for air operations purposes as 'Freedom Deal.') Its role in both strategic and tactical air operations is much greater in the remainder of Cambodia where Cambodian Government forces are engaged with an enemy which is now composed almost entirely of Khmer Communist insurgents and North Vietnamese."

The first two functions—communications with and coordination of the U.S. Forward Air Controllers operating in light planes over Cambodia, who validated and authorized TACAIR strikes—were performed by the Embassy only pending construction of a Direct Air Support Center (DASC) in FANK headquarters. When the DASC was completed in late April, they were transferred from the Embassy to it.

The third function—screening of B-52 and F-111 bombing requests—was exercised by the Embassy throughout the bombing campaign. These steps were involved:[4]

"The Embassy validates all B-52 and F-111 strikes outside the 'Freedom Deal' area. When the Cambodian General Staff submits a request, it does so on a form which contains information regarding the nature of the target, its justification, and a certification that friendly forces, villages, hamlets, houses, monuments, temples, pagodas or holy places are not within certain specified distances of the target area.

"The Embassy Air Attache's Office then plots the target and the bombing 'box,' the area in which the bombs will fall, on a one-to-fifty thousand map which is supposed to show the exact location of all permanent houses and buildings. The Air Attache told us that the maps being used by the Embassy were several years old and that the Embassy did not have current photography on proposed target areas which would permit the identification of new or relocated villages.

"The original Cambodian request and the map are then considered by an Embassy bombing panel which meets daily. The panel is chaired by the Deputy Chief of Mission. Its other members are the Defense Attache who is an Army Colonel, the Chief of the Military Equipment Delivery team who is an Army Brigadier General, the Counselor for Political-Military Affairs and the Embassy intelligence chief.

"The panel discusses the target in terms of consistency with the Rules of Engagement, the probable utility of the target, air safety and political factors. The final decision rests, according to the rules of the panel, with the Deputy Chief of Mission. According to him, decisions are, as a practical matter, made unanimously and approximately 40 percent of the requests are turned down. The Ambassador does not sit on the panel but is informed of decisions as they are made, and, according to the rules of the panel, before any particularly sensitive decision. [Note: Swank joined the panel in May 1973; Enders remained a member.] The panel then sends its recommendation to Seventh Air Force through Embassy communications facilities in the form of a message from the Ambassador to the Seventh Air Force Commander. Targets are again reviewed at Seventh Air Force for consistency with the Rules of Engagement. The Embassy is then informed by message from Seventh Air Force of targets scheduled for attack, and, subsequently, of the results. The Embassy then relays this information to Cambodian General Staff Headquarters."

2. *Assertion:* That instructions for making the Embassy into "the command post for the new aerial war in Cambodia" were given in Bangkok to Swank directly by Dr. Kissinger on February 8, 1973. "Although the general instructions were laid out in a cable from the State Department," Secretary of State Rogers "was not told how fully his subordinates in Phnom Penh were now involved in the bombing."[5] No source is cited by Mr. Shawcross.

Clarification: We cannot say for certain that Secretary Rogers knew of the instruction to the Embassy cited above, which laid out succinctly what the Embassy was to do. According to the file copy, two of his senior associates were involved in its preparation (Assistant Secretary of State for East Asian and Pacific Affairs Marshall Green as drafter, and Undersecretary of State for Political Affairs U. Alexis Johnson as authorizer), and two copies were distributed to the Secretary. The cable is dated January 23, 1973, two weeks before Dr. Kissinger met with Swank in Bangkok.

3. *Assertion:* That the bombing was not done "carefully"[6] by the Embassy and was "indiscriminate,"[7] because recent photography was not available and targets were plotted on large-scale, out-of-date maps that did not "show the location of new settlements in the massive forced migrations that the Khmer Rouge were now imposing on the areas they controlled."[8] Mr. Shawcross cites as the source for his comment on maps and photography the Lowenstein and Moose report.[9]

Clarification: All B-52 strikes were subject to detailed Rules of Engagement and executed on the basis of pre-strike photography. As noted above the Embassy never had a substantive role in tactical air operations.

Rules of Engagement prohibited use of B-52 ordnance closer than one kilometer to friendly forces, villages, hamlets, houses, monuments, temples, pagodas or holy places.[10]

General John W. Vogt, who as commander of the United States Support Activities Group and the Seventh Air Force had responsibility for the bombing, states:[11]

> "The choice of targets was made by my headquarters, the United States Support Activities Group in Thailand. The personnel in the headquarters were skilled professionals from all of the Services (Army, Navy, Marines and Air Force). Many of them had been with me in Vietnam when I conducted the Linebacker operation of 1972. By 1973 we had developed targeting techniques based heavily on reconnaissance and employing sophisticated sensors such as infra-red (IR) and precision radar (SLAR). We had up-to-the-minute photography on all areas of Cambodia in which the bombing was conducted. LORAN coordinates were obtained on all B-52 targets and were completely independent of map accuracy. We bombed in all cases with B-52s by reference to this sensor or photographic information. In all cases the targets were covered by reconnaissances

both pre-strike and post-strike. On a number of occasions we turned down FANK requests for targets because our recon showed risks to civilian population we were unwilling to take."

Mr. Shawcross appears to have been misled by the fact that the *Embassy* did not have available to it such photography. But it did not have to, since any FANK target the Embassy validated was re-validated or rejected by *USSAG* on the basis of photography. Messrs. Lowenstein and Moose did visit USSAG headquarters in April 1973. It is not known whether they were told of use of photography in USSAG target validation. In any case, they do not mention it in their report, and that omission appears to be the basis for Mr. Shawcross's charges. General Vogt is categorical on the question: "The B-52s bombed without the need for maps at all."[12]

4. *Assertion:* That "after the Moose and Lowenstein investigation in April [1973], control of the bombing was shifted to FANK."[13] Mr. Shawcross gives no source.

Clarification: At no point did FANK control B-52, F-111 or U.S. TACAIR strikes; only USSAG did.[14]

The only change in the arrangements made after April 1973 was the establishment of a direct communications link with FANK headquarters (DASC), by-passing the Embassy on TACAIR (see Point 1 above). Processing of B-52 and F-111 strikes was not involved. Throughout the war, control of U.S. TACAIR was in the hands of U.S. Forward Air Controllers, not the FANK.

5. *Inference:* That the bombing resulted in massive civilian casualties. Mr. Shawcross does not make an explicit statement to this effect, but he implies it in the map/photography misinterpretation cited above and in the three (and three only) pieces of evidence he cites on civilian casualties. First he quotes Embassy political officer William Harben as saying "I began to get reports of wholesale carnage. One night a mass of peasants from a village near Sa[']ang went out on a funeral procession. They walked straight into a 'box.' Hundreds were slaughtered.' "[15] Second, he cites the bombing of Neak Luong on August 7, 1973 (the town was held at that time by Khmer Republic forces) due to bombardier error, and writes: "The accident inevitably raised the question of how often such errors occurred in parts of the country where reporters could never penetrate."[16] Finally Cambodian generals "took a casual view of the risks to civilians." "As one air attache, Mark Berent, recalls, 'They never plotted anything. We could have given the coordinates of the palace and they would have said yes.' "[17]

Clarification: There is no evidence of massive civilian casualties. Two major B-52 accidents are known, one at Sa'ang and the other at Neak Luong; both were reported by the Embassy as well as cited by Mr. Shawcross. The former could not have been prevented (the target, in conformance to the Rules of Engagement, was well away from an inhabited area); the latter was Seventh Air Force responsibility. No doubt there were other civilian casualties, although on a smaller scale.

Mr. Harben, who is often portrayed in *Sideshow* as a bitter critic of U.S. (and Embassy) policy, makes these comments on casualties:[18]

> "In retrospect I think it likely that accidents involving TACAIR, particularly Khmer Air Force, may have been confused with B-52's in the retelling during the heightened public awareness of the latter. . . . In the case of the Sa'ang tragedy . . . it is clear that the rules of engagement were respected . . . (as regards my statement that) 'I began to get reports of wholesale carnage . . . ' [Mr. Shawcross] garbled it slightly: In referring to the Sa'ang raid, I used the expression used by my informant on that raid: 'c'etait un veritable carnage.' Shawcross seems to have written this down in such a way as to give the impression that such

a description applied to all the raids about which I had heard. The context was simply a narration of events."

Mr. Harben concludes:

"So civilian casualties were unavoidable, but far fewer, I am sure, than Shawcross and others claim. Had they been so great, the reports I received would not have been so vague. It is curious also that, although thousands of Khmers who were living in enemy-held areas at that time have fled to Thailand, and some have even gone to Europe, Shawcross seems to have made no effort to question them, although he made the effect of bombing upon them a major theme of his book. He did not even speak to So Satto, ex-chief of the Khmer Air Force, as I suggested. Nor did he contact In Tam, who was speaking to dozens of peasants every day recently arrived from the other side—and to enemy emissaries discussing defection."

General Vogt makes this comment about the possibility of other offset bombing errors like that at Neak Luong:[19]

"Every accident my headquarters was aware of was made known immediately, the worst being the off-set bombing error by B-52s against Neak Luong. To set the record straight, B-52s employed this off-set technique on only a handful of missions. The beacons were there primarily for F-111 use. The latter used them successfully throughout 1973 without a single incident. Their equipment, of course, was much better as they were much later generation airplanes. After Neak Luong the B-52s stopped using this practice . . . Virtually all of the B-52 bombing was precisely controlled by Seventh Air Force control systems. They were led in by F-4 LORAN-equipped pathfinders. These lead planes had a demonstrated accuracy by photo-recon confirmation of less than 400 feet miss distance."

Finally, since at no time did FANK control B-52 strikes (or for that matter F-111 or TACAIR strikes), Mr. Shawcross's third and last piece of evidence—an air attache's comment on FANK's own concern for civilians—does not apply.

It is worth noting that all B-52 strikes were photographed afterwards, as well as before. Not only was there available to General Vogt immediate evidence of any accident, but such evidence is preserved in Air Force archives. Seventh Air Force post-strike photography on Cambodia could be examined by a photo-reconnaissance specialist to confirm the conclusions on casualties reported here.

> [*signed*] Emory C. Swank 10/10/79
> U.S. Ambassador to the
> Khmer Republic, 1970–73

> [*signed*] Thomas O. Enders 10/10/79
> Deputy Chief of Mission
> Phnom Penh, 1970–74

Tab A

IMMEDIATE   PHNOM PENH

PRIORITY   SAIGON, BANGKOK PRIORITY, VIENTIANE PRIORITY,
FRANCE PRIORITY

STATE 015050

260022Z JAN 73

FOR AMBASSADOR SWANK

SUBJECT: USAF ACTIVITIES IN CAMBODIA FOLLOWING A CEASEFIRE IN
VIETNAM

REF: PHNOM PENH 634

1. USAF activities in Cambodia will be related to Lon Nol's proposed announcement of unilateral suspension by FANK of offensive military actions while reserving the right of self-defense. Thus, we propose from the time Lon Nol takes this action that USAF will stand down TACAIR and B-52 strikes. If a FANK unit is in trouble due to enemy action, we can react locally to provide appropriate air support clearly commensurate with the defensive requirements of the units under attack. You may inform Lon Nol that USAF activities in Cambodia will be related to his proposed declaration but that US air support will be provided, as necessary, in accordance with the JCS instructions below:

2. Chief JCS has just sent CINCPAC, info COMUSMACV, following guidance:

3. Quote: At the time when the FANK suspend offensive military operation all US TACAIR and B-52 strikes in Cambodia will cease. RECCE, airlift, MEDEVAC and other U.S. air operations that are not ordinance delivery associated are permitted.

4. Quote: U.S. TACAIR and B-52 forces will be prepared to strike designated targets in Cambodia in order to assist FANK forces when the situation so dictates. To this end a simple, rapid request-validation-execute procedure will be set up between U.S. Ambassador Cambodia and MACV. In essence, US Ambassador will be responsible for receiving requests for air support from GKR and validating requests consistent with his means and time available. The Ambassador will pass the requests to MACV who has the authority to validate and direct air strikes by US TACAIR or B-52's as the situation dictates. All air strikes executed under this guidance are to counter specific hostile acts against GKR/FANK. Escort of Mekong convoys is authorized. Unquote.

5. MACV requested to set up procedures as outlined above as soon as possible and to inform Chief JCS of details agreed upon.

ROGERS

Tab B

Ambassador Thomas O. Enders   June 22, 1979
American Embassy
Ottawa, Canada

Dear Tom:

Recently I had an opportunity to read the Shawcross book. Your questions assume that I knew much more than I did. I knew hardly more than any literate Cambodian about the bombing—nothing, for example, of the rules of engagement, or the fact that there was an Embassy targeting committee which you chaired.

(i) Is the account of the bombing campaign given in Mr. Shawcross' book on pages 270–272 accurate?

Answer: I know too little, even now, to assess his accuracy. The assertion that only maps of 1:50,000 were used is absurd on the face of it, but beyond that I cannot comment.

(ii) What accidents causing civilian casualties did you learn of?

Answer: As the B-52 raids began to hit near Phnom Penh foreign journalists told me they had heard of many civilian casualties. One quoted a woman refugee who said her husband had been killed "with blood coming from his eyes and ears" in what sounded from her description like a B-52 attack. Another was said to have been near Kompong Speu, and still another mentioned by a Khmer Red Cross official to a journalist. Then In Tam summoned me and said that many civilians had been killed by "B-52's" near Skoun. You checked and said it must have been Tacair. In retrospect I think it likely that accidents involving Tacair, particularly Khmer Air Force, may have been confused with B-52's in the retelling during the heightened public awareness of the latter. Perhaps some of the reports mentioned above applied to the same raid. About this time an airgram from one of our border posts in Vietnam quoted Cambodian refugees as saying that hundreds of peasants conscripted for work in enemy camps had been killed by B-52's. I had this in mind when I told Shawcross that most civilian casualties were certainly due to the Communists drafting peasants for use as porters and laborers in legitimate target areas. He chose to omit this comment. Another incident was reported to me by a Democratic Party official who was a mathematics professor at the university. He said his uncle, mayor of Sa'ang, near Phnom Penh, had sent word that some hundreds of peasants had walked into a B-52 box while on a nocturnal procession some kilometers from that village to bury or burn a deceased favorite bonze. They did not go by day fearing that such a column would invite Tacair attack, he said. I reported it to you, and a few days later it was mentioned in the Khmer press.

About this time also the only remaining Khmer newspaper which had not been banned—the Army organ—published an editorial condemning the B-52 bombing and saying that it would be more appropriate for us to bomb North Vietnam, and not our Cambodian ally. I believe this editorial mentioned some civilian casualties or implied that there had been some.

About this time I met Liz Trotta, a rather bold NBC television reporter, with whom one day I watched Tacair bombing a retreating enemy unit on the east bank of the Mekong from the Chrui Changwar peninsula. Refugees with sampans loaded with bedding, furniture, bicycles, and even farm animals were streaming toward us from the far bank, fleeing either the bombing or the enemy or both.

Liz insisted on going to the other side when a Khmer soldier told us it was safe for about a kilometer back of the riverbank, and I accompanied her and her TV crew. We followed Khmer troops of the rearguard in their leisurely pursuit southward, and stopped to question some peasants through a French-speaking schoolteacher. Miss Trotta, having heard the uproar about civilian casualties, asked them if they could cite specific instances of civilian deaths. After some palaver they cited three in that area from all bombings: a farmer who had gone too close in order to rescue his strayed cattle, a bonze, and another villager. Miss Trotta thought this rather a small and unavoidable toll, and did not bother to report it. When she asked the peasants if they opposed the bombing, they said they did not mind as long as it was not on *their* village. Liz was so surprised that she thought the teacher was giving us a bit of government propaganda, but when I questioned him he quite freely said he had no use for Lon Nol or any of the other politicians either.

(iii) Were they caused by B-52 or Tacair strikes?

Answer: I have no other information other than that given above.

(iv) If B-52, were the rules of engagement respected (i.e., no strikes closer than one kilometer to inhabited areas)?

Answer: It was not until I received this question that I knew what the rules of engagement were. In any case I did not seek or obtain enough detail on the raids to determine this. In the case of the Sa'ang tragedy, however, it is clear that the rules of engagement *were* respected.

(v) Were these accidents caused or made more likely by use of maps several years old, or by lack of care by the Embassy or the Seventh Air Force?

Answer: I do not think the accidents were due to old maps or lack of care. I believe they were due to factors I will explain in answer to your question (vii) below. You refer only to B-52 attacks, but I feel that in order to be complete I should say what I knew of the rules of engagement in Tacair strikes, about which I knew more, since they were more easily observed.

Conversations in the staff meetings convinced me that we were exercising great care to avoid civilian casualties in Tacair bombing, and I assumed that the same care was exercised with respect to B-52 raids. On one occasion Gen. Cleland complained that the enemy were so confident that we would not bomb villages that they had set up their guns in villages on the banks of the Mekong to shoot at our convoys. I recall that I suggested that smoke bombs be dropped upwind of these positions to blind them. He replied that that had been considered by the "High Command" and rejected as impractical since it would obstruct navigation. Although that might be true only for certain azimuths I did not pursue it, but on the way down the stairs I met the Naval Attache coming up. I told him that "someone" had suggested smoke bombs. He said it was a good idea—it ought to be tried. I then said that "someone" had objected that it would blind the navigators. He scoffed at that and pointed out that they had brought a convoy up in the middle of a moonless night a few nights earlier. I mentioned to Shawcross that the enemy put guns in villages confident that they would not be attacked, but he chose to omit this also.

Rules of engagement were mentioned on one other occasion in my presence. A Jesuit priest, a speechwriter in the White House, arrived and was shunted to me. He was quite interested in the bombing, and I asked one of the Assistant Air Attaches over for a drink, since I could not enlighten him. The priest questioned him quite closely as to whether the rules of engagement were being observed, and even pretended to be a "firebreather"—claiming that there are no neutrals in total war—in order to provoke the Ass't Air Attache into admitting some departure from the rules. The latter insisted, however, that deliberate violations were rare and minor. He would go no further than to say that a pilot receiving fire from a cluster of huts slightly over the maximum attackable size might stretch a point. The priest asked what the size of the cluster was, and the Ass't Air Attache declined to give it to him, saying that it was information which could be of great use to the enemy.

(vi) Is the quotation attributed to you accurate? If so, to whom did you make it, when, and in what context?

Answer: There are several, but I assume you mean that in which I said "I began to get reports of wholesale carnage . . ." etc. This was said to Shawcross in my house in 1977, I believe. I think he garbled it slightly. In referring to the Sa'ang raid, I used the expression used by my informant on that raid: "c'etait un veritable carnage". Shawcross seems to have written this down in such a way as to give the impression that such a description applied to all the raids about which I had heard. The context was simply a narration of events. Shawcross is inaccurate in a number of other quotations: When I said that Lon Nol, when Washington was distracted elsewhere, resumed his dictatorship with the usual army backing, Shawcross inserted in brackets "United States" in front of "army", although I meant *Khmer* Army. If I had meant United States Army I would have used the word "acquiescence", although some might think that Gen. Cleland's threats of terminating U.S. aid made to officers who were discussing a coup against Lon Nol might amount to more than that. Shawcross also says that my proposals were rejected "contemptuously." I did not use such a word and did not feel that you or Coby were ever contemptuous toward me. The General was another matter. Shawcross also states that officers in the Political Section "like Bill Harben" were unhappy over your allegedly more vigorous prosecution of the "Nixon Doctrine". I am not sure what he means by that. I do not recall such sentiments in my section. If anything, I found your more vigorous approach a refreshing change.

(vii) Did you cut out a B-52 box, apply it to Central Cambodia, and conclude that nowhere could bombing be carried out without civilian casualties? Is that your view now?

Answer: I did. I did not attend the Air Attache's briefings, but journalists told me that the Embassy claimed that there were *no* civilian casualties, and jeered at the idea. Convinced, for reasons given below, that it was impossible to conduct such bombing without inflicting *some* civilian casualties, I felt the Embassy might once again be creating a "credibility gap". On the spur of the moment I decided to demonstrate to myself how easily hostile outsiders might make us appear to be cruel and foolish. I tried to orient the B-52 "box", cut to scale, on my office map and covered a village in Central Cambodia in all positions.

I felt I should apprise someone of this, but had clashed with Gen. Cleland whenever I reported Khmer Army corruption. He had even insisted I burn a memo of Carney's on front-line bribes for delivery of US munitions, though I felt it might even be a violation of federal law for the Political Section to conceal such information which had come to its attention. So I shunned the military and wrote a memorandum to Paul Gardner, since the title of his "Political Military" Section seemed to indicate some responsibility.

But it was not just this exercise with the map which convinced me that some civilian casualties were unavoidable. Most of my career had been spent on international Communist matters, and I thought that if a public scandal about civilian casualties would hurt our war effort, they would see to it that we did kill civilians, despite our caution. Furthermore I had knocked about rural Java a good deal in the early 60's, and had encountered mysterious religious processions at night far out in the countryside. While climbing mountains I had come upon small villages hidden under palms not shown on my maps. They were so remote from the national life that they did not know what money was, and dropped it on the ground when I paid them for coconuts. Such villages would have been wiped out in any "carpet bombing" of "uninhabited" areas. In war the problem is worse. People whose draft animals have been commandeered or whose rice has been confiscated go foraging in the jungle for food. They hide in unusual places at night to avoid enemy conscription. Often they are fleeing by night to the safety of the government lines. Some of our reports from the other side spoke of the Communists marching villagers to bases at night to harangue them with political speeches. No air force can know where such people are at any given moment.

So civilian casualties were unavoidable, but far fewer, I am sure, than Shawcross and the others claim. Had they been so great, the reports I received would not have been so vague. It is curious also that, although thousands of Khmers who were living in enemy-held areas at that time have now fled to Thailand, and some have even gone to Europe, Shawcross seems to have made no effort to question them, although he made the effect of bombing upon them a major theme of this book. He did not even speak to So Satto, ex-chief of the Khmer Air Force, as I suggested. Nor did he contact In Tam, who was speaking to dozens of peasants every day recently arrived from the other side—and to enemy emissaries discussing defection. (Actually I suspect that Shawcross' French is too poor to have done a complete job).

Shawcross quotes me as "appalled" at the time. I was not appalled by the casualties to civilians, which I think were minor and unavoidable, but by the fact that they were in vain in the absence of vigorous measures to stamp out Khmer Army corruption, build an efficient fighting force, ensure the coming to power of the honest and much more capable In Tam, whose popularity as demonstrated in his election victory and his contacts with disaffected enemy held out a prospect of victory. When he described to me his plan of buying off the Khmer Rumdoh piecemeal with FANK ranks and wages, gradually thus reducing the Communists to a minority and isolating them back in the Cardamoms, I thought it workable, but asked him where he would get the money. He replied: "Your own figures, announced in Washington, say that Lon Nol and his officers are stealing the wages of enough men to buy off the whole insurgent army—that is where I intend to get the money." That would have required strong support from us—and I did not think Congress could raise protests on behalf of embezzlers of US funds and equipment.

The B-52 bombing even made corruption worse. When Cheng Heng pleaded with Lon Nol to act against corrupt officers, Nol told him to calm down, since "the American B-52's are killing a thousand enemy every day and the war will soon be over."

With regard to the morality of killing any civilians at all, I feel it was justified in the attempt to save them from a much greater slaughter at the hands of the Communists, who in every country have liquidated far more people than may have been accidentally killed in Cambodia. The bombing of German extermination camps is now debated in retrospect. We are criticized for failing to do so. Would Shawcross object to such bombing on the grounds that "hundreds" of noncombatants would have been killed? In the invasion of Normandy we killed many French civilians. In Sicily we even bombed our own troops. In World War II Mr Shawcross' country devised a policy of deliberately aiming at civilians, and made the author of that policy a peer of the realm, whereas our country is probably the only one in recent decades in which strict rules of engagement were imposed to avoid or reduce civilian deaths.

There will be a next time, and when that time comes I think we should be more attentive to the problem of public relations and history. We might, for example, shower enemy-occupied areas with leaflets announcing our intention in a general way and urging civilians to avoid enemy military concentrations at night, etc. Still there will be civilian casualties, but we will have visible evidence of concern for their safety.

In retrospect I do not envy you the role you were asked to play, which I am sure you exercised as humanely as possible. Our commissions read that we serve "at the pleasure of the president". If the press or the public regards some of the results of our obedience as unfortunate, then they should devote their attention to the faults of the system which "program" such occurrences, instead of to the pursuit of villains. Any embassy, under the circumstances, would have come up with about the same cast of characters, doing, or not doing, the same things.

Sincerely

[*signed*] *Bill*

W. N. Harben

Tab C

The Honorable Thomas Ostrom Enders   July 8, 1979
Ambassador of the USA
100 Wellington Street
Ottawa, Ontario K1P 5T1

Dear Tom,

I delayed this response until I finished reading Shawcross' book which you kindly sent me. My comments on his charges and answers to your questions follow.

First let me say that his description of the 1973 bombing as "indiscriminate" is completely contrary to fact. As one who led his squadron over the beaches of Normandy in World War II and later operated against targets in support of Allied troops on the Western front, I can assure you I have some basis for judging the nature of bombing activities. I state flatly that the precision, degree of control, validity of targets attacked and professionalism of the crews involved in the 1973 Cambodian campaign were as high or perhaps even higher than all of World War II bombing, the 1965–68 Rolling Thunder campaign, or the Linebacker campaigns in 1972 in North and South Vietnam.

There were some accidents, but surprisingly few considering the weight of effort involved (which as the author points out was far higher than World War II).

Every accident my headquarters was aware of was made known immediately, the worst being the off-set bombing error by B-52s against Neak Luong. To set the record straight, B-52s employed this off-set technique on only a handful of missions. The beacons were there primarily for F-111 use. The latter used them successfully throughout 1973 without a single incident. Their equipment, of course, was much better as they were much later generation airplanes. After Neak Luong the B-52s stopped using this practice so the author's statement "The accident inevitably raised the question of how often such errors occurred in parts of the country where reporters could never penetrate", is groundless speculation like so much of his description of the 1973 bombing campaign.

Virtually all of the B-52 bombing was precisely controlled by 7th Air Force control systems. They were led in by F-4 LORAN-equipped pathfinders. These lead planes had a demonstrated accuracy by photo-recon confirmation of less than 400 feet miss distance.

The choice of targets was made by my headquarters, The United States Support Activities Group in Thailand. The personnel in the headquarters were skilled professionals from all of the Services (Army, Navy, Marines and Air Force). Many of them had been with me in Vietnam when I conducted the Linebacker operations of 1972. By 1973 we had developed targeting techniques based heavily on reconnaissance and employing sophisticated sensors such as infra-red (IR) and precision radar (SLAR). We had up-to-the-minute photography on all areas of Cambodia in which the bombing was conducted. LORAN coordinates were obtained on all B-52 targets and were completely independent of map accuracy. We bombed in all cases with B-52s by reference to this sensor or photographic information. In all cases the targets were covered by reconnaissances both pre-strike and post-strike. On a number of occasions we turned down FANK requests for targets because our recon showed risks to civilian population we were unwilling to take.

As you will recall, charges were constantly being made in 1973 that we were hitting Cambodian villages. Except for the very few accidents, in not one single case were we able to substantiate such charges. A prime example occurred in June or July '73 when the Assistant Secretary of Defense for Public Affairs, Jerry Friedheim, sent me a message including the full text of an East Coast newspaper article which stated B-52s had destroyed or heavily damaged 10 Cambodian villages causing the villagers to flee. The reporter stated he had personally interviewed many of these villagers. He named each village supposedly involved. Friedheim wanted an immediate answer to the charges. I dispatched recon aircraft to each village and took low altitude photography of excellent quality. *In no case* could we find any evidence of B-52 bomb drops (the pattern of craters is unmistakable). The majority of the villages were relatively untouched by war damage of any kind. A few near the Vietnam border showed some damage from artillery fire or 250 lb. bombs (dropped only by the South Vietnamese Air Force; we did not use them at all). Even in these cases the amount of damage was relatively small and usually was found at the edges of the towns. This hard photographic evidence was immediately dispatched to Washington with a full explanatory text. It was never used by OSD to refute the story because (I was told later) "the whole incident had died down in the Press and they didn't want to rekindle it". I am afraid the author's charges are based largely on such unsubstantiated evidence.

Now to your specific questions:—In what cases was photography used prior to target adoption? Ans. In the case of B-52 operations it was used in *all* cases. Tac Air which was under FAC control (forward air controllers) did not require such pre-strike recon but the combat areas were photographed each day for precise location of enemy and friendly positions and was available to the FACs.

—How often was it used? Ans. Answered in the first question.

—Is there evidence that in those where photography was not used accidents occurred or the risk of accidents was significantly greater? Ans. As I indicated above photography on the precise target was not required in the case of Tactical aircraft only. The precise nature of FAC control virtually precluded accidents. I can recall no accidents occurring with TAC air all during 1973.

—Were your photo surveillance assets adequate to your needs or were you constrained? Ans. Fully adequate. I retained within 7th Air Force following the Vietnam settlement RF-4 assets which gave me proportionately far better coverage than I had when we were operating throughout all of S.E. Asia.

—What is your view of the adequacy of available mapping? Could up-to-date maps have been prepared? How long would it have taken? Ans. As I indicated above, we were relying far more on up-to-the-minute photography, LORAN precision coordinates gained from that photography or, in the case of F-111 op-

erations, highly precise off-set radar beacon techniques than on the maps themselves. The B-52s bombed without the need for maps at all. In the case of TAC
air good maps are an asset to help the FAC find the target quickly, but from that
point on, the pilot's eyeballs plus the photography available to him fixed the actual target. All FACs had strict orders to avoid villages and did so with remarkable professionalism. So while up-to-date maps would have helped the FACs
find the target more quickly they were not a factor in the actual bomb delivery.
The Defense Mapping Agency was fully responsive to my mapping needs and
sent us the latest available to them. They were constantly updating from our
photography. Nevertheless there was a lag in some areas like Cambodia, but I
doubt very much the involved process of map making could have been speeded
up much more than it was.

A few general comments: I suspect Shawcross had determined his theme before he gathered
the evidence and wrote the book. For example, much of what I have said above I told to Shawcross
when I discussed the bombing campaign with him in February of 1977. He chose to use none of
this information. Even if he didn't believe what I said an objective presentation would have required that he include it. After all I was the commander running the bombing operations and had
access to far more hard data than his hear-say reporters.

There is ample documentary evidence of the 1972 Cambodian air operations. My own oral
report to the Air Force Historical Research Center at Air University at Maxwell AFB, Alabama, for
example, contains a full statement of the 10 village incident I mentioned above. Unfortunately the
report is classified secret but parts of it I am sure could be declassified if the effort were made.

Shawcross does quote my statement to him that the 1973 bombing "saved Phnom Penh by
killing 16,000 enemy". There is an interesting sidelight to this. After the Washington announcement to stop all bombing by August 15, 1973 the enemy launched a series of all-out attacks to capture the city even though they knew the job would be much easier after 15 August. Why? We
found out later. Captured intelligence revealed the Khmer Rouge had issued direct orders to their
forward commanders to take the city before August 1973 so they could prove to the world that
they could humble the U.S. In callous disregard for human life they threw in their troops in repeated attacks and since they were no longer able to use jungle cover, they suffered huge losses to
air attack. This should have given us some clue as to how this regime would treat its own people
after they seized control. They so decimated their elite forces that after the bombing stopped they
took until April 1975 to finally take the city. Had we remained steadfast in support of the Cambodian government and provided air support as needed the country would be in non-communist
hands today instead of North Vietnam's. I am not proud of my country's bug-out in either Vietnam or Cambodia. After losing more than 50,000 American lives we quit even though we had
turned back the Easter offensive in Vietnam. Air power had applied great pressure on Hanoi itself
causing them to accept terms which would have kept South Vietnam free if enforced by a meaningful threat of the resumption of that bombing. We turned our backs on our friends when they
called on us to back up our promises made in January 1973. Likewise in Cambodia we had broken
the back of the Khmer Rouge forces in 1973 and then let them regain their strength to reattack a
year and a half later while denying our friends ammunition. The pervasive effects of Watergate had
set in.

One final comment: Shawcross has gone to great lengths to disparage the leadership in Cambodia. I knew all the key Cambodian generals through close personal contact. Having worked

with the military in South Vietnam and Laos, I think I had a valid basis for comparison. Considering their limited means and experience (because of Sihanouk's policy of making them no more than a palace guard) they displayed remarkable qualities. They had to go from the role of company commanders to that of division and larger in just a few months. They had the ability to defeat the enemy and would have done so if we had not pulled the rug out from under them.

In Lon Nol, whom I met and talked to on a number of occasions, I found a man truly dedicated to preventing his country from falling to the communists. I hope future historians will present the case of Cambodian leaders' ability and patriotism in a better light than Shawcross has done.

Please feel free to use any or all of the above as you find necessary to set the record straight. The distortion of the true state of events in Cambodia which has occurred in the liberal press, of which Shawcross is obviously a part, needs to be set straight.

> With all best wishes
> [*signed*] *John*
> John W. Vogt, General USAF (Ret.)

NOTES

CHAPTER 1: AMERICA'S ENTRY INTO THE MORASS (1950–1969)

1. Inaugural Address, January 20, 1949, in *Public Papers of the Presidents of the United States: Harry S. Truman,* 1949 vol. (Washington, D.C.: U.S. Government Printing Office, 1964), pp. 112–14.

2. Inaugural Address, January 20, 1953, in *Public Papers of the Presidents of the United States: Dwight D. Eisenhower,* 1953 vol. (Washington, D.C.: U.S. Government Printing Office, 1960), p. 6 (hereinafter cited as *Eisenhower Papers*).

3. Inaugural Address, January 20, 1961, in *Public Papers of the Presidents of the United States: John F. Kennedy,* 1961 vol. (Washington, D.C.: U.S. Government Printing Office, 1962), p. 1 (hereinafter cited as *Kennedy Papers*).

4. Inaugural Address, January 20, 1965, in *Public Papers of the Presidents of the United States: Lyndon B. Johnson,* 1965 vol. (Washington, D.C.: U.S. Government Printing Office, 1966), p. 72 (hereinafter cited as *Johnson Papers*).

5. Jeffrey P. Kimball, ed., *To Reason Why: The Debate About the Causes of U.S. Involvement in the Vietnam War* (New York: McGraw-Hill, 1990), p. 54.

6. Quoted in Kimball, *To Reason Why,* p. 73.

7. Ibid.

8. Quoted in Thomas J. Schoenbaum, *Waging Peace and War: Dean Rusk in the Truman, Kennedy and Johnson Years* (New York: Simon and Schuster, 1988), p. 234.

9. NSC 68, "United States Objectives and Programs for National Security," April 7, 1950, in U.S. Department of State, *Foreign Relations of the United States,* 1950, vol. I (Washington, D.C.: U.S. Government Printing Office, 1977), pp. 237–38.

10. George C. Herring, *America's Longest War, The United States and Vietnam 1950–1975* (New York: Alfred A. Knopf, 2nd ed., 1986), p. 18.

11. Ibid.

12. Schoenbaum, *Waging Peace and War,* p. 230.

13. "United States Objectives and Courses of Action with Respect to Southeast Asia," Statement of Policy by the National Security Council, 1952, in Neil Sheehan, Hedrick Smith, W. W. Kenworthy, Fox Butterfield, *The Pentagon Papers, as Published by the New York Times* (New York: Quadrangle Books, 1971), p. 29.

14. Ibid., p. 28.

15. Ibid., p. 29.

16. Quoted in Herring, *America's Longest War,* p. 26.

17. Eisenhower to Churchill, April 4, 1954, in Peter G. Boyle, ed., *The Churchill-Eisenhower*

Correspondence, 1953–1955 (Chapel Hill and London: University of North Carolina Press, 1990), pp. 137–40.

18. Anthony Eden, *Full Circle: The Memoirs of the Rt. Hon. Anthony Eden* (Boston: Houghton Mifflin, 1960), p. 124.

19. Quoted in Martin Gilbert, *Winston S. Churchill,* vol. VIII, *"Never Despair," 1945–1965* (Boston: Houghton Mifflin, 1988), pp. 973–74.

20. Quoted in ibid., p. 973.

21. Townsend Hoopes, *The Devil and John Foster Dulles* (Boston: Little, Brown, 1973), p. 239.

22. Richard M. Nixon, *No More Vietnams* (New York: Arbor House, 1985), p. 41.

23. U.S. Declaration on Indochina, July 21, 1954, in *State Bulletin,* vol. XXXI, no. 788 (August 2, 1954), p. 162.

24. Herring, *America's Longest War,* p. 45.

25. Eisenhower letter to Diem, October 23, 1954, in Marvin E. Gettleman, ed., *Viet Nam: History, Documents, and Opinions on a Major World Crisis* (Greenwich, Conn.: Fawcett Publications, 1965), pp. 204–5.

26. Herring, *America's Longest War,* p. 56.

27. Ibid., p. 68.

28. Dwight D. Eisenhower, *Waging Peace: The White House Years, 1956–1961* (Garden City, N.Y.: Doubleday, 1965), p. 610.

29. *Kennedy Papers,* 1961 vol. (1962), p. 23.

30. Lin Piao, "Long Live the Victory of People's War!," *Peking Review,* vol. VIII, no. 36 (September 3, 1965), pp. 9–30.

31. Quoted in David Halberstam, *The Best and the Brightest* (New York: Random House, 1972), p. 76.

32. From Kennedy's opening statement at a news conference of March 23, 1961, in *Kennedy Papers,* 1961 vol. (1962), p. 214.

33. *"Let the Word Go Forth": The Speeches, Statements, and Writings of John F. Kennedy, 1947–1963,* selected and with an introduction by Theodore C. Sorensen (New York: Dell Publishing, 1988), pp. 370ff.

34. Senator John F. Kennedy, "America's Stake in Vietnam, the Cornerstone of the Free World in Southeast Asia," address delivered before the American Friends of Vietnam, Washington, D.C., June 1, 1956, in *Vital Speeches of the Day,* August 1, 1956, pp. 617–19.

35. Acting Assistant Secretary of Defense William Bundy, quoted in Sheehan, Smith, Kenworthy, Butterfield, *Pentagon Papers,* p. 103.

36. Quoted in Herring, *America's Longest War,* p. 83.

37. Quoted in ibid., p. 86.

38. Kennedy's Special Message to Congress on Defense Policies and Principles, March 28, 1961, in *Kennedy Papers,* 1961 vol. (1962), pp. 229ff.

39. Quoted in Guenter Lewy, *America in Vietnam* (New York: Oxford University Press, 1978), p. 26.

40. State Department telegram to Lodge in Saigon, August 24, 1963, in *Pentagon Papers,* p. 200.

41. Ibid.

42. Quoted in Lewy, *America in Vietnam,* p. 28.

43. Quoted in ibid., p. 29.

44. Harrison Salisbury, *Behind the Lines—Hanoi* (New York: Harper & Row, 1967), pp. 194–97.

45. Johnson Address to the American Alumni Council, July 12, 1966, in *Johnson Papers,* 1966 vol. II (1967), p. 720.

46. James Reston, "Washington: The Flies That Captured the Flypaper," *New York Times,* February 7, 1968, p. 46.

47. For a brilliant analysis of this group, see Norman Podhoretz, *Why We Were in Vietnam* (New York: Simon and Schuster, 1982), pp. 85ff.

48. Quoted in ibid., p. 105.

49. Lewy, *America in Vietnam*, p. 76; Don Oberdorfer, *Tet!* (Garden City, N.Y.: Doubleday, 1971), pp. 329ff.
50. Arthur M. Schlesinger, Jr., *Robert Kennedy and His Times* (Boston: Houghton Mifflin, 1978), p. 843.
51. "Report from Vietnam by Walter Cronkite," CBS News special, February 27, 1968, quoted in Oberdorfer, *Tet!*, p. 251.
52. "The Logic of the Battlefield," *Wall Street Journal*, February 23, 1968, p. 14.
53. "Frank Magee Sunday Report," NBC, March 10, 1968, quoted in Oberdorfer, *Tet!*, p. 273.
54. "The War," *Time*, vol. 91, no. 11 (March 15, 1968), p. 14.
55. Johnson television broadcast to the American people, March 31, 1968, in *Johnson Papers, 1968–69* vol. I (1970), pp. 469–96.

CHAPTER 2: EVOLUTION OF A STRATEGY

1. Addicts of secret documents may read this NSC staff summary of the agencies' responses to NSSM I in the *Washington Post* of April 25, 1972.
2. Christopher Hitchens, *The Trial of Henry Kissinger* (London: Verso, 2001). I allegedly bore part of the responsibility because I had told Nixon of my view that an agreement was imminent. The facts supported by the documentary record are as follows: I had no contact with any of the Vietnamese parties. I did not meet Nixon during the campaign (and, indeed, had met him only once for a handshake). John Mitchell, then one of Nixon's top aides, invited me to two meetings to inquire about the basic concern of any candidate: whether there would be a surprise agreement before the election. Based on my experience in 1967 described in the previous chapter, I told him that I thought it probable Hanoi would seek to conclude negotiations regarding a bombing halt before the election. As William Bundy, the Assistant Secretary of State in charge of the negotiations, has written, I had no access to information on the negotiations. [See William Bundy, *A Tangled Web: The Making of Foreign Policy in the Nixon Presidency* (New York: Hill and Wang, 1998), pp. 39–40.] I had no knowledge of what, if anything, Nixon did with my prediction.
3. Anatoly Dobrynin, *In Confidence: Moscow's Ambassador to America's Six Cold War Presidents (1962–1986)* (New York: Times Books, 1995), pp. 178–81, 190–91.
4. This is the thesis of William Shawcross, *Sideshow: Kissinger, Nixon and the Destruction of Cambodia* (New York: Simon & Schuster, 1979). For an analysis of the book's errors and misleading documentation, see Peter W. Rodman, "Sideswipe: Kissinger, Shawcross and the Responsibility for Cambodia," *The American Spectator* 14, no. 3 (March 1981), and the exchange between Rodman and Shawcross in *The American Spectator* 14, no. 7 (July 1981).
5. See Elizabeth Becker, "Cambodia: A Look at Border War with Vietnam," *Washington Post*, December 27, 1978; Henry Kamm, "Pol Pot Confirmed Assertion by Nixon," *New York Times*, March 18, 1979, p. 7.
6. See the address by State Department legal adviser John Stevenson to the Bar Association of the City of New York on May 28, 1970, explaining our legal position with respect to operations in Cambodia by U.S. and South Vietnamese forces from April 30 to June 30, 1970 (in *Department of State Bulletin*, vol. 62, June 22, 1970, pp. 765–70).
7. The following is an excerpt of a memo prepared by the Historical Office of the Secretary of Defense on civilian casualties in Cambodia:

> Cambodia and North Vietnam were comparable in size, but the population of North Vietnam was more than twice that of Cambodia even before Pol Pot's genocidal regime—18 million in North Vietnam versus 7 million in Cambodia. While North Vietnam was sending its troops to South Vietnam, a civil war like the one in Cambodia was not raging within the borders of North Vietnam. On the other hand, B-52 area bombers accounted for a much higher proportion of bomb tonnage in Cambodia than in North Vietnam—two-thirds in Cambodia versus a quarter in North Vietnam.
>
> During 1969–73 in Cambodia, it was difficult for reporters in Phnom

Penh to estimate the proportion of civilian casualties caused by air operations. There is no doubt that most of those casualties occurred in 1973. Pol Pot's forces laid siege to Phnom Penh while cease-fire agreements in Vietnam and Cambodia permitted American air power to focus on Cambodia. Reporters in Phnom Penh could see that many nearby villages had been destroyed by bombing. According to the American air commander, General Vogt, those villages had already been vacated by civilians fleeing into the city. His forces were using a range of intelligence sources (including infrared sensors) to determine which villages were occupied. The worst error occurred at Neak Luong, where more than a hundred civilians were killed when a B-52 crew failed to calculate an offset and dropped on a beacon in the town.

8. An even fuller account can be found in Bernard C. Nalty, *Air War over South Vietnam, 1968–1975* (Washington, D.C.: Air Force History and Museums Program, United States Air Force, 2000), especially pp. 129–33.

9. Clark M. Clifford, September 29, 1968.

10. Clark M. Clifford, press conference, December 10, 1968.

11. The text of Nixon's July 15 letter to Ho Chi Minh and of Ho's reply was released by the White House at the time of Nixon's November 3, 1969 speech on Vietnam.

12. MEMORANDUM FOR THE PRESIDENT September 10, 1969
FROM: Henry A. Kissinger
SUBJECT: Our Present Course in Vietnam
I have become deeply concerned about our present course in Vietnam. This memorandum is to inform you of the reasons for my concern. It does not discuss alternative courses of action, but is provided for your background consideration. You know my recommendations.

While time acts against both us and our enemy, it runs more quickly against our strategy than against theirs. This pessimistic view is based on my view of Hanoi's strategy and the probable success of the various elements of our own.

I. *U.S. Strategy*

In effect, we are attempting to solve the problem of Vietnam on three highly interrelated fronts: (1) within the U.S., (2) in Vietnam, and (3) through diplomacy. To achieve our basic goals through diplomacy, we must be reasonably successful on *both* of the other two fronts.

a. *U.S.*

The pressure of public opinion on you to resolve the war quickly will increase—and I believe increase greatly—during the coming months. While polls may show that large numbers of Americans now are satisfied with the Administration's handling of the war, the elements of an evaporation of this support are clearly present. The plans for student demonstrations in October are well known, and while many Americans will oppose the students' activities, they will also be reminded of their own opposition to the continuation of the war. As mentioned below, I do not believe that "Vietnamization" can significantly reduce the pressures for an end to the war, and may, in fact, increase them after a certain point. Particularly significant is the clear opposition of many "moderate" leaders of opinion, particularly in the press and in the East (e.g., *Life* Magazine). The result of the recrudescence of intense public concern must be to polarize public opinion. You will then be somewhat in the same position as was President Johnson, although the substance of your position will be different. You will be caught between the Hawks and the Doves.

The effect of the public pressures on the U.S. Government will be to accentuate the internal divisiveness that has already become apparent to the public and Hanoi. Statements by government officials which attempt to assuage the Hawks or Doves will serve to confuse Hanoi but also to confirm it in its course of waiting us out.

b. *Vietnam*

Three elements on the Vietnam front must be considered—(1) our efforts to "win the war" through military operations and pacification, (2) "Vietnamization," and (3) the political position of the GVN [Government of Vietnam, i.e., South Vietnam].

(1) I do not believe that with our current plans we can win the war within two years, although our success or failure in hurting the enemy remains very important.

(2) "Vietnamization" must be considered both with regard to its prospects for allowing us to turn the war over to the Vietnamese, and with regard to its effect on Hanoi and U.S. public opinion. I am not optimistic about the ability of the South Vietnamese armed forces to assume a larger part of the burden than current MACV [Military Assistance Command, Vietnam] plans allow. These plans, however, call for a thirty-month period in which to turn the burden of the war over to the GVN. I do not believe we have this much time.

In addition, "Vietnamization" will run into increasingly serious problems as we proceed down its path.

—Withdrawal of U.S. troops will become like salted peanuts to the American public: the more U.S. troops come home, the more will be demanded. This could eventually result, in effect, in demands for unilateral withdrawal—perhaps within a year.

—The more troops are withdrawn, the more Hanoi will be encouraged—they are the last people we will be able to fool about the ability of the South Vietnamese to take over from us. They have the option of attacking GVN forces to embarrass us throughout the process or of waiting until we have largely withdrawn before doing so (probably after a period of higher infiltration).

—Each U.S. soldier that is withdrawn will be relatively more important to the effort in the South, as he will represent a higher percentage of U.S. forces than did his predecessor. (We need not, of course, continue to withdraw combat troops, but can emphasize support troops in the next increments withdrawn. Sooner or later, however, we must be getting at the guts of our operations there.)

—It will become harder and harder to maintain the morale of those who remain, not to speak of their mothers.

—"Vietnamization" may not lead to reduction in U.S. casualties until its final stages, as our casualty rate may be unrelated to the total number of American troops in South Vietnam. To kill about 150 U.S. soldiers a week, the enemy needs to attack only a small portion of our forces.

—"Vietnamization" depends on broadening the GVN, and Thieu's new government is not significantly broader than the old (see below). The best way to broaden the GVN would be to create the impression that the Saigon government is winning or at least permanent. The more uncertainty there is about the outcome of the war, the less the prospect for "Vietnamization."

(3) We face a dilemma with the GVN: The present GVN cannot go much farther towards a political settlement without seriously endangering its own existence; but at the same time, it has not gone far enough to make such a settlement likely.

Thieu's failure to "broaden" his government is disturbing, but not because he failed to include a greater variety of Saigon's Tea House politicians. It is disturbing because these politicians clearly do not believe that Thieu and his government represent much hope for future power, and because the new government does not offer much of a bridge to neutralist figures who could play a role in a future settlement. This is not to mention his general failure to build up political strength in non-Catholic villages. In addition, as U.S. troops are withdrawn, Thieu becomes more dependent on the political support of the South Vietnamese military.

c. *Diplomatic Front*

There is not therefore enough of a prospect of progress in Vietnam to persuade Hanoi to make real concessions in Paris. Their intransigence is also based on their estimate of growing U.S. domestic opposition to our Vietnam policies. It looks as though they are prepared to try to wait us out.

II. *Hanoi's Strategy*

There is no doubt that the enemy has been hurt by allied military actions in the South, and is not capable of maintaining the initiative on a sustained basis there. Statistics on enemy-initiated activities, as well as some of [Chief Military Strategist for Hanoi, General Vo Nguyen] Giap's recent statements, indicate a conscious decision by Hanoi to settle down to a strategy of "protracted warfare." This apparently consists of small unit actions with "high point" flurries of activity, and emphasis on inflicting U.S. casualties (particularly through rocket and mortar attacks). This pattern of actions seems clearly to indicate a low-cost strategy aimed at producing a psychological, rather than military, defeat for the U.S.

This view of their strategy is supported by our estimates of enemy infiltration. They *could* infiltrate more men, according to intelligence estimates, despite growing domestic difficulties. The only logical reason for their not having done so is that more men were not needed in the pipeline—at least for a few months—to support a lower-cost strategy of protracted warfare. It seems most unlikely that they are attempting to "signal" to us a desire for a *de facto* mutual withdrawal, although this cannot be discounted. There is no diplomatic sign of this—except in Xuan Thuy's linkage of points two and three of the PRG program—and I do not believe they trust us enough to "withdraw" a larger percentage of their men than we have of ours, as they would be doing.

Hanoi's adoption of a strategy designed to wait us out fits both with its doctrine of how to fight a revolutionary war and with its expectations about increasingly significant problems for the U.S.
III. *Conclusion*

In brief, I do not believe we can make enough evident progress in Vietnam to hold the line within the U.S. (and the U.S. Government), and Hanoi has adopted a strategy which it should be able to maintain for some time—barring some break like Sino-Soviet hostilities. Hence my growing concern.

CHAPTER 3: SECRET NEGOTIATIONS AND A WIDENING WAR

1.   On earlier Vietnamese dominance of Laos and Cambodia, see Bernard Fall, *The Two Vietnams,* rev. ed. (London: Pall Mall Press, 1965), pp. 12–19, 33.
2.   Ibid., p. 386.
3.   See, e.g., *New York Times,* February 25, 1970.
4.   Sihanouk interview in *New York Times,* March 12, 1970.
5.   See his memoirs, *My War with the CIA: The Memoirs of Prince Norodom Sihanouk as Related to Wilfred Burchett* (New York: Random House, Pantheon Books, 1973), p. 24. See also pp. 21–22, 24–26, 42–43, 50, 54, 201–2.
6.   John Mitchell took notes of the meeting and wrote a concise two-page memorandum:
     MEMORANDUM OF MEETING April 28, 1970
     PRESENT: The President, Secretary of State, Secretary of Defense, Attorney General
     SUBJECT: Cambodia/South Vietnam
     The subject meeting was held in the Oval Office of The President on Tuesday, April 28, 1970, commencing at 10:20 A.M. and lasting for approximately twenty minutes.
     The President stated that the purpose of the meeting was to advise those present of the decisions he had reached with respect to the developing situation in South Vietnam and Cambodia. The President further stated that he had had the subject under constant consideration for the past ten days and had taken into consideration all of the information provided by the Director of Central Intelligence, the Joint Chiefs of Staff and Admiral McCain and his staff at the briefing in Hawaii. The President further stated that, in arriving at his decision, he had taken into consideration the positions taken by the Secretary of State and Secretary of Defense in opposition to the use of U.S. Forces in Cambodia and the fact that Dr. Kissinger was leaning against the recommendation of such use.
     The President further stated that the previous day he had made certain inquiries of Ambassador Bunker and General Abrams. The President read his communication to Ambassador Bunker and the Ambassador's reply received late Monday evening.
     The President further stated that, based upon his review of the general Cambodian situation, he had decided not to change the current U.S. position with respect to military assistance to Cambodia or his authorization for the ARVN [Army of the Republic of Vietnam] operation in the Parrot's Beak. The President further stated that he had decided to confirm the authorization for a combined U.S./GVN operation against COSVN headquarters in Fish Hook in order to protect

U.S. Forces in South Vietnam. The President expressed the opinion that the COSVN operation was necessary in order to sustain the continuation of the Vietnamization Program and would possibly help in, but not detract from, U.S. efforts to negotiate peace.

The President further stated that he had taken into consideration, in arriving at his decisions, the probable adverse reaction in some Congressional circles and some segments of the public. The President further stated that, in order to establish the record of the events leading to his decisions and the advice he had received concerning the subject matter thereof, the previous evening he had dictated a tape which included the contrary recommendations of the Secretary of State and the Secretary of Defense.

At the close of the President's statements he left the Oval Office to attend another meeting in the Cabinet Room. There was no discussion of the subject matter of the meeting by others in attendance during the presence of the President.

[Signed:] J. N. Mitchell

7. See Elizabeth Becker, "Cambodia: A Look at Border War with Vietnam," *Washington Post,* December 27, 1978; Henry Kamm, "Pol Pot Confirmed Assertion by Nixon," *New York Times,* March 18, 1979, p. 7.

8. *New York Times,* May 18, 1970.

9. E.g., Shawcross, *Sideshow,* pp. 372–73, 389. Shawcross, who thus excused the Khmer Rouge atrocities, was amazingly upbraided in turn by another writer who alleged that there was insufficient evidence the atrocities ever took place. Richard Dudman, *New York Times Book Review,* April 22, 1979. Some of our critics seemed to be ready to give Khmer Rouge leader Pol Pot the benefit of the doubt before their own government.

10. *Congressional Record* (daily ed.), December 16, 1970, pp. S20283, 20289ff.

CHAPTER 4: DIPLOMACY AND STRATEGY: FROM A CEASE-FIRE PROPOSAL TO THE INTERDICTION OF THE HO CHI MINH TRAIL

1. *Washington Post* editorials, August 28 and September 1, 1970.

2. See the *New York Times,* June 16, 1969; The *New York Times Magazine,* September 21, 1969.

3. See, e.g., *New York Times* editorials, August 5, August 21, August 24, and October 15, 1969.

4. They included Henry Jackson, who drafted the letter, Hugh Scott, Mike Mansfield, Barry Goldwater, Jacob Javits, Warren Magnuson, Bob Dole, Alan Bible, Thomas J. McIntyre, Winston Prouty, Birch Bayh, Charles Percy, Milton Young, and Ted Stevens.

5. Proposed, for example, by Morton Halperin and Leslie Gelb in the *Washington Post,* October 11, 1970, and by Halperin again in the *New York Times,* November 7, 1970.

6. Nixon Address to the Nation, April 7, 1971; see also news conferences of February 17 and March 4, 1971.

7. Muskie and Humphrey quoted in *Newsweek,* February 7, 1972.

CHAPTER 5: HANOI THROWS THE DICE: THE VIETNAMESE SPRING OFFENSIVE

1. See Lewis Sorley, *A Better War: The Unexamined Victories and Final Tragedy of America's Last Years in Vietnam* (New York: Harcourt Brace & Company, 1999), pp. 343–44.

2. Safire's account, from the speech-writing perspective, is in *Before the Fall* (Garden City, N.Y.: Doubleday, 1975), pp. 417–20.

3. See, e.g., Richard Nixon, *RN: The Memoirs of Richard Nixon* (New York: Grosset & Dunlap, 1978), p. 591.

4. Ibid., pp. 590–91.

CHAPTER 6: THE SHOWDOWN

1. Excerpts from Nixon's April 30 memorandum to me are printed in Nixon, *RN*, pp. 593–94.
2. See ibid., p. 594.
3. I was not present at the May 8 leadership meeting. An account of it is in Safire, *Before the Fall*, pp. 422–27.
4. The senators are quoted in *Congressional Quarterly*, May 13, 1972.
5. *New York Times* editorial, May 9, 1972.
6. *New York Times, Washington Post*, and *Christian Science Monitor* editorials of May 10, 1972.
7. Marvin Kalb and Bernard Kalb, *Kissinger* (Boston: Little, Brown, 1974), p. 310.
8. This memorandum is quoted in Nixon, *RN*, pp. 606–7.

CHAPTER 7: FROM STALEMATE TO BREAKTHROUGH

1. See Larry Berman, *No Peace, No Honor* (New York: The Free Press, 2001).
2. The result can best be judged by comparing Hanoi's original draft with the version that emerged on October 11. Le Duc Tho's draft of October 8 read:

> Immediately after the cease-fire, the two South Vietnamese parties shall hold consultations in a spirit of national concord, equality, mutual respect, and mutual non-elimination to set up the three-segment administration of national concord and to settle all other internal matters of South Viet Nam in keeping with the South Viet Nam people's aspirations for peace, independence, democracy, and neutrality. The two South Vietnamese parties shall as soon as possible sign an agreement on the internal matters of South Viet Nam, and not later than three months after the enforcement of cease-fire.

The version on October 11 read:

> Immediately after the cease-fire, the two South Vietnamese parties shall hold consultations in a spirit of national reconciliation and concord, mutual respect, and mutual non-elimination to set up an administrative structure called the National Council of National Reconciliation and Concord of three equal segments. The Council shall operate on the principle of unanimity. After the National Council of National Reconciliation and Concord has assumed its functions, the two South Vietnamese parties will consult about the formation of councils at lower levels. The two South Vietnamese parties shall sign an agreement on the internal matters of South Vietnam as soon as possible and do their utmost to accomplish this within three months after the cease-fire comes into effect, in keeping with the South Vietnamese people's aspirations for peace, independence and democracy.

This was weakened further in later negotiations by dropping the phrase "administrative structure," the Vietnamese translation of which was controversial.

CHAPTER 8: THE TROUBLED ROAD TO PEACE

1. Nixon, *RN*, p. 693.
2. See, e.g., Nixon's news conference of March 15, 1973; his address of March 29, 1973; the joint statement of Presidents Nixon and Thieu, April 3, 1973; Secretary of Defense Richardson on *Meet the Press*, April 1, 1973; Richardson testimony to the Senate Armed Services Committee, April 2, 1973; Richardson remarks to newsmen prior to appearing before the House Appropriations Committee, April 3, 1973; my interview with Marvin Kalb, CBS-TV, February 1, 1973; remarks of Ambassador William Sullivan on *Meet the Press*, January 28, 1973; and other sources collected in U.S. Congress, Senate, Committee on Appropriations, *Emergency Military Assistance*

and Economic and Humanitarian Aid to South Vietnam, 1975; Hearings before the Committee on Appropriations, 94th Cong., 1st Sess., 1975, pp. 19–24.

3. The relevant assurances I had recited back to Hanoi in a message on October 20 read:
    With respect to Cambodia, the U.S. side operates on the basis of the following statements made by Special Advisor Le Duc Tho at private meetings with Dr. Kissinger on September 26 and 27 and October 8 and 11, 1972:
    —"The questions of the war in Vietnam and Cambodia are closely linked: when the war is settled in Vietnam, there is no reason for the war to continue in Cambodia" (September 27);
    —"Once the Vietnam problem is settled, the question of Cambodia certainly will be settled; and the end of the Vietnamese war will create a very great impact that will end the war in Cambodia perhaps immediately" (October 8);
    —"It is an understanding between us that the DRV will abide by the principle that all foreign forces, including its own, must put an end to their military activities in Cambodia and be withdrawn from Cambodia and not be reintroduced" (September 26);
    —"The DRV will follow the same principles in Cambodia that it will follow in South Vietnam and Laos, that is, it will refrain from introducing troops, armament, and war material into Cambodia" (October 11); and
    —"As Article 18 [later 23] states, the obligations of this agreement come into force on the day of its signing" (October 11).
    The United States reiterates its view as expounded by Dr. Kissinger on October 11, 1972, that if, pending a settlement in Cambodia, offensive activities are taken there which would jeopardize the existing situation, such operations would be contrary to the spirit of Article 15(b) [later 20(b)] and to the assumptions on which this Agreement is based.
    Hanoi confirmed these statements in a written message on October 21 and added a written assurance that it would "actively contribute to restoring peace in Cambodia."

CHAPTER 9: "PEACE IS AT HAND"

1. Henry A. Kissinger, press conference, October 26, 1972.
    Dr. Kissinger Discusses Status of Negotiations Toward Vietnam Peace: *Following is the transcript of a news conference by Henry A. Kissinger, Assistant to the President for National Security Affairs, held at the White House on October 26, 1972.*
    Dr. Kissinger: Ladies and gentlemen: We have now heard from both Vietnams, and it is obvious that a war that has been raging for 10 years is drawing to a conclusion, and that this is a traumatic experience for all of the participants. The President thought that it might be helpful if I came out here and spoke to you about what we have been doing, where we stand, and to put the various allegations and charges into perspective.
    First, let me talk about the situation in three parts: Where do we stand procedurally; what is the substance of the negotiations; and where do we go from here?
    We believe that peace is at hand. We believe that an agreement is within sight, based on the May 8th proposal of the President and some adaptation of our January 25th proposal which is just to all parties. It is inevitable that in a war of such complexity that there should be occasional difficulties in reaching a final solution, but we believe that by far the longest part of the road has been traversed and what stands in the way of an agreement now are issues that are relatively less important than those that have already been settled.
    Let me first go through the procedural points, the arguments with respect to particular dates for signing the agreement. As you know, we have been negotiating in these private sessions with the North Vietnamese for nearly four years. We resumed the discussions on July 19th of this year. Up to now, the negotiations had always foundered on the North Vietnamese insistence that a political settlement be arrived at before a military solution be discussed, and on the companion

demand of the North Vietnamese that the political settlement make arrangements which, in our view, would have predetermined the political outcome.

We have taken the view, from the earliest private meetings on, that rapid progress could be made only if the political and military issues were separated; that is to say, if the North Vietnamese and we would negotiate about methods to end the war and if the political solution of the war were left to the Vietnamese parties to discuss among themselves. During the summer, through many long, private meetings, these positions remained essentially unchanged.

As Radio Hanoi correctly stated today, on October 8th the North Vietnamese for the first time made a proposal which enabled us to accelerate the negotiations. Indeed, for the first time they made a proposal which made it possible to negotiate concretely at all. This proposal has been correctly summarized in the statements from Hanoi; that is to say, it proposed that the United States and Hanoi, in the first instance, concentrate on bringing an end to the military aspects of the war; that they agree on some very general principles within which the South Vietnamese parties could then determine the political evolution of South Vietnam, which was exactly the position which we had always taken.

They dropped their demand for a coalition government which would absorb all existing authority. They dropped their demand for a veto over the personalities and the structure of the existing government.

They agreed for the first time to a formula which permitted a simultaneous discussion of Laos and Cambodia. In short, we had for the first time a framework where, rather than exchange general propositions and measure our progress by whether dependent clauses of particular sentences had been minutely altered, we could examine concretely and precisely where we stood and what each side was prepared to give.

I want to take this opportunity to point out that from that time on, the North Vietnamese negotiators behaved with good will and with great seriousness. And so did we. We have no complaint with the general description of events as it was given by Radio Hanoi.

However, there grew up the seeds of one particular misunderstanding. The North Vietnamese negotiators made their proposal conditional on the solution of the problem by October 31st, and they constantly insisted that we give some commitment that we would settle the war and complete the negotiations by October 31st.

I want to stress that these dates were not dates that we invented or proposed. I would like to stress that my instructions from the President were exactly those that were stated by him at a press conference; that is to say, that we should make a settlement that was right, independent of any arbitrary deadlines that were established by our own domestic processes.

In order to avoid an abstract debate on deadlines, which at that time still seemed highly theoretical, we did agree that we would make a major effort to conclude the negotiations by October 31st, and it is true that we did, from time to time, give schedules by which this might be accomplished. It was, however, always clear, at least to us, and we thought we made it clear in the records of the meetings, that obviously we could not sign an agreement in which details remained to be worked out simply because in good faith we had said we would make an effort to conclude it by a certain date.

It was always clear that we would have to discuss anything that was negotiated first in Washington and then in Saigon. There has been a great deal of discussion whether Saigon has a veto over our negotiations, and I would like to explain our position with respect to that.

Clearly, the people of South Vietnam, who have suffered so much, and the Government of South Vietnam, with which we have been allied, who will be remaining in that country after we have departed, have every right to participate in the making of their own peace. They have every right to have their views heard and taken extremely seriously.

We, of course, preserve our own freedom of judgment and we will make our own decisions as to how long we believe a war should be continued. But one source of misunderstanding has been that Hanoi seemed to be of the view that we could simply impose any solution on Saigon and that their participation was not required. But I also want to make clear that the issues that remain to be settled have a number of sources, and I will get into them in some detail.

Saigon, as is obvious from the public record, has expressed its views with its customary forcefulness both publicly and privately. We agreed with some of their views. We didn't agree with all of them and we made clear which we accepted and which we could not join.

In addition, while my colleagues and I were in Saigon, we visited other countries of Southeast Asia and we had extensive conversations with American officials, and it appeared there that there were certain concerns and certain ambiguities in the draft agreement that we believe required modification and improvement. But I want to stress that what remains to be done is the smallest part of what has already been accomplished, and as charges and counter-charges fill the air, we must remember that, having come this far, we cannot fail and we will not fail over what still remains to be accomplished.

Now, let me first go briefly over the main provisions of the agreement as we understand them, and then let me say what, in our view, still remains to be done. We believe, incidentally, what remains to be done can be settled in one more negotiating session with the North Vietnamese negotiators lasting, I would think, no more than three or four days, so we are not talking of a delay of a very long period of time.

Let me, however, before I go into the issues that still remain, cover those that are contained in the draft agreement, of which, on the whole, a very fair account has been given in the radio broadcast from Hanoi. I don't refer to the last two pages of rhetoric; I am referring to the description of the agreement.

The principal provisions were and are that a cease-fire would be observed in South Vietnam at a time to be mutually agreed upon—it would be a cease-fire in place; that U.S. forces would be withdrawn within 60 days of the signing of the agreement; that there would be a total prohibition on the reinforcement of troops; that is to say, that infiltration into South Vietnam from whatever area, and from whatever country, would be prohibited. Existing military equipment within South Vietnam could be replaced on a one-to-one basis by weapons of the same characteristics and of similar characteristics and properties, under international supervision.

The agreement provides that all captured military personnel and foreign civilians be repatriated within the same time period as the withdrawal; that is to say, there will be a return of all American prisoners, military or civilian, within 60 days after the agreement comes into force.

North Vietnam has made itself responsible for an accounting of our prisoners and missing in action throughout Indochina and for the repatriation of American prisoners throughout Indochina.

There is a separate provision that South Vietnamese civilians detained in South Vietnam, that their future should be determined through negotiations among the South Vietnamese parties, so that the return of our prisoners is not conditional on the disposition of Vietnamese prisoners in Vietnamese jails on both sides of the conflict. With respect to the political provisions, there is an affirmation of general principles guaranteeing the right of self-determination of the South Vietnamese people and that the South Vietnamese people should decide their political future through free and democratic elections under international supervision.

As was pointed out by Radio Hanoi, the existing authorities with respect to both internal and external policies would remain in office; the two parties in Vietnam would negotiate about the timing of elections, the nature of the elections, and the offices for which these elections were to be held.

There would be created an institution called the National Council of National Reconciliation and Concord whose general task would be to help promote the maintenance of the cease-fire and to supervise the elections on which the parties might agree.

That council would be formed by appointment, and it would operate on the basis of unanimity. We view it as an institutionalization of the election commission that we proposed on January 25th in our plan.

There are provisions that the disposition of Vietnamese armed forces in the South should also be settled through negotiations among the South Vietnamese parties.

There are provisions that the unification of Vietnam also be achieved by negotiations among the parties without military pressure and without foreign interference, without coercion and without annexation.

There is a very long and complex section on international supervision which will no doubt occupy graduate students for many years to come and which, as far as I can tell, only my colleague Ambassador Sullivan [William H. Sullivan, Deputy Assistant Secretary of State for East Asian and Pacific Affairs] understands completely.

But briefly, it provides for joint commissions of the participants, either two-party or four-party, for those parts of the agreement that are applicable either to two-parties or to four-parties; it provides for an international supervisory commission to which disagreements of the commissions composed of the parties would be referred, but which also has a right to make independent investigations, and an international conference to meet within 30 days of the signing of the agreement to develop the guarantees and to establish the relationship of the various parties to each other in greater detail.

There is finally a section on Cambodia and Laos in which parties to the agreement agree to respect and recognize the independence and sovereignty of Cambodia and Laos, in which they agree to refrain from using the territory of Cambodia and the territory of Laos to encroach on the sovereignty and security of other countries.

There is an agreement that foreign countries will withdraw their forces from Laos and Cambodia and there is a general section about the future relationship between the United States and the Democratic Republic of Vietnam in which both sides express their conviction that this agreement will usher in a new period of reconciliation between the two countries, and in which the United States expresses its view that it will in the postwar period contribute to the reconstruction of Indochina and that both countries will develop their relationships on a basis of mutual respect and noninterference in each other's affairs, and that they will move from hostility to normalcy.

Now, ladies and gentlemen, in the light of where we are, it is obvious that most of the most difficult problems have been dealt with. If you consider what many of you might have thought possible some months ago compared to where we are, we have to say that both sides have approached this problem with a long-term point of view, with the attitude that we want to have not an armistice, but peace, and it is this attitude which will govern our actions despite occasional ups and downs which are inevitable in a problem of this complexity.

Now, what is it, then, that prevents the completion of the agreement? Why is it that we have asked for one more meeting with the North Vietnamese to work out a final text? The principal reason is that in a negotiation that was stalemated for five years, and which did not really make a breakthrough until October 8th, many of the general principles were clearly understood before the breakthrough, but as one elaborated the text, many of the nuances on which the implementation will ultimately depend became more and more apparent.

It was obvious, it was natural, that when we were talking about the abstract desirability of a cease-fire that neither side was perhaps as precise as it had to become later about the timing and staging of a cease-fire in a country in which there are no clear front lines. And also the acceptance on our part of the North Vietnamese insistence on an accelerated schedule meant that the text could never be conformed, that English and Vietnamese texts tended to lag behind each other.

And that ambiguities in formulation arose that require one more meeting to straighten out. Let me give you a few examples, and I think you will understand that we are talking here of a different problem than what occupied us in the many sessions I have had with you ladies and gentlemen about the problem of peace in Vietnam, sessions which concerned abstract theories of which approach might succeed.

We are talking here about six or seven very concrete issues that with anything like the good will that has already been shown, can easily be settled. For example, it has become apparent to us that there will be a great temptation for a cease-fire to be paralleled by a last effort to seize as much territory as possible, and perhaps to extend operations for long enough to establish political control over a given area.

We would like to avoid the dangers of the loss of life, perhaps in some areas even of the massacre that may be inherent in this, and we, therefore, want to discuss methods by which the international supervisory body can be put in place at the same time that the cease-fire is promulgated.

The Secretary of State has already had preliminary conversations with some of the countries that are being asked to join this body in order to speed up this process.

Secondly, because of the different political circumstances in each of the Indochinese countries, the relationship of military operations there to the end of the war in Vietnam, or cease-fire there in relation to the end of the war in Vietnam, is somewhat complex, and we would like to discuss more concretely how to compress this time as much as possible.

There were certain ambiguities that were raised by the interview that the North Vietnamese Prime Minister, Pham Van Dong, gave to one of the weekly journals, in which he seemed to be, with respect to one or two points, under a misapprehension as to what the agreement contained and, at any rate, we would like to have that clarified.

There are linguistic problems. For example, we call the National Council of Reconciliation an administrative structure in order to make clear that we do not see it as anything comparable to a coalition government. We want to make sure that the Vietnamese text conveys the same meaning.

I must add that the words "administrative structure" were given to us in English by the Vietnamese, so this is not a maneuver on our part.

There are some technical problems as to what clauses of the Geneva Accords to refer to in certain sections of the document, and there is a problem which was never settled in which the North Vietnamese, as they have pointed out in their broadcast, have proposed that the agreement be signed by the United States and North Vietnam; we on behalf of Saigon, they on behalf of their allies in South Vietnam.

We have always held the view that we would leave it up to our allies whether they wanted a two-power document or whether they wanted to sign themselves a document that establishes peace in their country. Now, they prefer to participate in the signing of the peace, and it seems to us not an unreasonable proposal that a country on whose territory a war has been fought and whose population has been uprooted and has suffered so greatly, that it should have the right to sign its own peace treaty.

This again strikes us as a not insuperable difficulty, but its acceptance will require the redrafting of certain sections of the document, and that, again, is a job that will require several hours of work.

We have asked the North Vietnamese to meet with us on any date of their choice. We have, as has been reported, restricted our bombing, in effect, to the battle area in order to show our good will and to indicate that we are working within the framework of the existing agreement.

We remain convinced that the issues that I have mentioned are soluble in a very brief period of time. We have undertaken, and I repeat it here publicly, to settle them at one more meeting and to remain at that meeting for as long as is necessary to complete the agreement.

So this is the situation in which we find ourselves. With respect to Hanoi, we understand its disappointment that a schedule toward the realization of which it had made serious efforts could not be met for reasons beyond the control of any party, but they know, or they should know, and they certainly must know now, that peace is within reach in a matter of weeks, or less, depending on when the meeting takes place, and that once peace is achieved, we will move from hostility to normalcy, and from normalcy to cooperation with the same seriousness with which we have conducted our previous less fortunate relationships with them.

As far as Saigon is concerned, it is, of course, entitled to participate in the settlement of a war fought on its territory. Its people have suffered much, and they will remain there after we leave. Their views deserve great respect. In order to accelerate negotiations, we had presented them with conclusions which obviously could not be fully settled in a matter of four days that I spent in Saigon. But we are confident that our consultations with Saigon will produce agreement within the same time frame that I have indicated is required to complete the agreement with Hanoi, and that the negotiations can continue on the schedule that I have outlined.

With respect to the American people, we have talked to you ladies and gentlemen here very often about the negotiations with respect to the peace, and we have been very conscious of the division and the anguish that the war has caused in this country. One reason why the President has been so concerned with ending the war by negotiation, and ending it in a manner that is consistent with our principles, is because of the hope that the act of making peace could restore the unity that had sometimes been lost at certain periods during the war, and so that the agreement could be an act of healing rather than a source of new division. This remains our policy.

We will not be stampeded into an agreement until its provisions are right. We will not be deflected from an agreement when its provisions are right. And with this attitude, and with some cooperation from the other side, we believe that we can restore both peace and unity to America very soon.

Thank you. I will be glad to answer your questions.

Q. Do you feel that this program could not have been achieved four years ago?

Dr. Kissinger: There was no possibility of achieving this agreement four years ago because the other side consistently refused to discuss the separation of the political and military issues, because it always insisted that it had to settle the political issues with us, and that we had to predetermine the future of South Vietnam in a negotiation with North Vietnam.

As the statement from Hanoi said on October 8th, Hanoi, for the first time, made what it called a very significant proposal in which it accepted the principles that the military issues should be settled first, and that the political issues should be left essentially to a negotiation among the South Vietnamese parties, with just the most general principles to be settled in the private negotiations.

As they say, "With a view to making the negotiations progress"—this is reading from the Hanoi statement—"at the private meeting on October 8th, the DRV side took a new, extremely important initiative. It put forward a draft agreement and proposed that the government" and so on, "immediately agree upon and sign this agreement to rapidly restore peace in Vietnam."

In that draft agreement, the DRV side proposed the cessation of the war throughout Vietnam, a cease-fire in South Vietnam, and a total withdrawal of U.S. forces, and then it said, "The two South Vietnamese parties shall settle together the internal matters of South Vietnam within three months after the cease-fire comes into effect."

This is not an exact description of what the agreement says. The agreement does not say it must be done within three months. The agreement says that the two parties will do their utmost to get it done within three months. The exact text to which I referred is as follows:

"Therefore, as the U.S. side has many times proposed, the Vietnam problem would be solved in two steps. The first step is to end the war in Vietnam, to have a cease-fire in South Vietnam, to end military involvement in South Vietnam. In the second step, the South Vietnamese sides will jointly solve South Vietnamese internal problems."

This has been our position since the beginning of these negotiations. It was never accepted four years ago, three years ago, or two months ago. The first time it was accepted was on October 8th. As soon as it was accepted, we completed within four days a rough draft of an agreement from which we have since been operating.

Q. What is the recourse if the negotiations for the elections break down? That has been a point at which the North Vietnamese have balked in the past.

Dr. Kissinger: The agreement provides that the cease-fire is without time limit.

Q. Does President Thieu go along with this whole deal?

Dr. Kissinger: As I have pointed out, the South Vietnamese agree with many parts of it and disagree with some aspects of it. We agree with some of their disagreements and not with all.

Q. Have the South Vietnamese been informed of the negotiations?

Dr. Kissinger: The South Vietnamese were informed of the negotiations as they went along. However, the negotiations really were composed of two phases. There were the negotiations between July 19th and October 8th. In that negotiation, the other side constantly proposed various formulas for the institution of a coalition government which would replace the existing government in Saigon and which would assume governmental power, and Saigon was informed.

I took a trip to Saigon in the middle of August to have a long discussion with the South Vietnamese Government. My deputy, General [Alexander M.] Haig, took another trip to present to them the various formulations that had been developed.

On October 8th, for the first time, Hanoi presented the different approach which they have correctly described in their statement. They then insisted that we, on the basis of this approach, begin to draft the outline of an agreement in order to meet their deadline for October 31st.

Now, if we had wanted to protract negotiations, we could easily have said that we have to return to Washington first, or return to Saigon for further consultation. We believed that this was such an important step on the part of the North Vietnamese that took into account so many of the proposals that we had made, and such a significant movement in the direction of the position consistently held by this administration, that we had an obligation, despite the risks that were involved, of working with them to complete at least an outline of an agreement, and we spent four days, sometimes working 16 hours a day, in order to complete this draft agreement, or at least the outline of this draft agreement.

I mention this only because, if we had wanted to delay, we had much better opportunities than to raise a few objections of the kind that I have described, at the very end. But we did insist and we constantly emphasized that we could not conclude this agreement without a full discussion with our allies in Vietnam.

I want to make clear another thing: that many of the concerns I have expressed here, while they are also shared by Saigon, are ours as well, and the particular issues that I raise would require a solution if the agreement is to bring a real peace, and if it is not to lead immediately to endless disputes as to what its provisions mean.

Q. Why are you waiting for Hanoi to propose the date of the next meeting? Why don't you suggest that you start tomorrow?

Dr. Kissinger: Because we are not eager to score debating points. Obviously, the North Vietnamese negotiators have to get wherever we are going to meet from where they are. We have told them that any day they are ready to meet, we will be there. We have suggested Paris, but we have also told them that we would meet in other locations that might be more convenient for them.

Q. Would you go to Hanoi, Dr. Kissinger?

Dr. Kissinger: I think we should complete the agreement elsewhere.

Q. Dr. Kissinger, you have, in effect, encouraged the American people that you are on the brink of peace. By coincidence—this happens to come by coincidence, you say at any rate—this happens to come at a time when the American people are about to vote for a President. What assurance can you give the American people that this will not somehow fall down; that is, that it will not come off after the election?

Dr. Kissinger: We can only give the assurance of our record. We have conducted these negotiations for four years, and we have brought them to this point with considerable difficulty and with considerable anguish. We cannot control if people believe or if people choose to assert that this is simply some trick.

We have negotiated seriously and in good faith. We stand by what we have agreed to, and we give the assurance that we will stick by what we have negotiated and what we have achieved so laboriously.

As for the point that this is by a so-called coincidence, I can only repeat that the deadline was established by Hanoi and not by us, and that we were prepared to keep this whole agreement secret until it was consummated, and we would not have revealed it if it had not been consummated before the election.

Q. Dr. Kissinger, what are the main differences between Saigon and Washington now, and what will happen if agreement is not reached?

Dr. Kissinger: We are confident that agreement will be reached. No useful purpose would be served by going into the details of consultations that are still in process, but we are confident that we will reach agreement within the time frame that I have described to you.

Q. Is the United States prepared to sign a separate agreement with North Vietnam if President Thieu refuses to sign the agreement?

Dr. Kissinger: I see no point in addressing a hypothetical question which, as I have said, we are confident will not arise; and as I have indicated, the particular objectives which we seek for ourselves in the remainder of the negotiations are all views which we strongly hold as the United States Government.

Q. Dr. Kissinger, you haven't said whether President Thieu accepts a cease-fire.

Dr. Kissinger: I think I have expressed my conviction that President Thieu will accept a cease-fire.

Q. Dr. Kissinger, President Thieu said in his speech that the Communists were demanding a coalition government, and you did not mention one. Could this National Council be turned into a coalition?

Dr. Kissinger: This settlement is a compromise settlement in which neither side achieves everything, and in which both parties have the necessity of posturing themselves for their constituency.

We do not consider this a coalition government, and we believe that President Thieu was speaking about previous versions of a Communist plan and not about this version of the Communist plan. I think we all recognize the fact that political leaders speak to many audiences at the same time.

Q. Are you going to make the text available that you had?

Dr. Kissinger: No.

Q. Do you believe the North Vietnamese will leave on the negotiating table the proposals they have accepted thus far, if you don't make the October 31 deadline?

Dr. Kissinger: I cannot believe that when this major progress has been made, that an arbitrary deadline should be the obstacle to peace, and we believe that the negotiations will continue.

Q. On the same point, with respect to the 8th of November deadline, what is to assure them that our side will not harden our negotiating stance once the pressure of the election is off?

Dr. Kissinger: Our negotiation has not been framed by the election. We have not revealed any of our positions throughout the election, and had not Hanoi revealed the text or the substance of the agreement, we would have had no intention of disclosing it until or unless an agreement had been reached.

We have given a commitment that a text that will be agreed to at the next session will be the final text and that no new changes will be proposed. We will maintain this commitment. We are not engaged in Vietnam for the purpose of conducting a war.

I would like to suggest to you ladies and gentlemen that while it is possible to disagree with provisions of an agreement, the implication that this is all a gigantic maneuver which we will revoke as soon as this period is over is unworthy of what we have gone through.

Q. Dr. Kissinger, can you say whether President Thieu himself would insist on signing an agreement or whether somebody else might, for his government?

Dr. Kissinger: The level at which the agreement will be signed has not been finally determined, but it is almost certainly not at the Presidential level.

Q. Dr. Kissinger, does the resupplying and re-equipment of the Communist forces apply only to those in South Vietnam and if so, are the North Vietnamese at liberty to take as much from the Soviet Union as they can get?

Dr. Kissinger: The formal provisions apply only to South Vietnam, but there is no question, and there can be no question, that the general conditions in Indochina will govern the actions of many of the countries, but I don't want to go into greater detail.

Q. Does your formal explanation there cover U.S. support, the status of continuing U.S. support?

Dr. Kissinger: There is no limitation of any kind on economic aid. Military aid is governed by the replacement provisions that I have described. There is no limitation of any kind on economic advisors, and the military presence is governed by the withdrawal provisions.

Q. Is bombing covered within the concept of a withdrawal of U.S. forces?

Dr. Kissinger: It covers an end to all military activities over the territory of North Vietnam from whatever direction.

Q. What effect does it have on Thailand and the Seventh Fleet?

Dr. Kissinger: There are no limitations on American forces in Thailand nor on the Fleet.

Q. Dr. Kissinger, do you think that the mining of the harbor and the bombing of North Vietnam contributed to the acceleration by the North Vietnamese of negotiations?

Dr. Kissinger: I don't want to speculate on North Vietnamese motivation.

Q. Would you tell us, please, what concessions did the United States make to get this agreement, in your judgment?

Dr. Kissinger: The United States made the concessions that are described in the agreement. There are no secret side agreements of any kind.

Q. Did you discuss with Le Duc Tho at any time the deadline of October 31st to sign the agreement, and if he raised this question, what did you reply?

Dr. Kissinger: We believe that it is quite possible that an honest misunderstanding arose. We always said that we would make a major effort to meet the deadline and we developed various hypothetical ways by which this deadline could be met. We also said, and that is equally in the record, that all of this depended on a satisfactory completion of various parts of the agreement. But they may have misunderstood, honestly, the conditional or hypothetical nature of some of the schedules.

But the most significant aspect cannot be whether one signs on one date or another. The significant aspect is that when one is so close to an agreement, whether one perfects it and then signs it regardless of the deadline. There is no magic about any one date.

Q. Why did Hanoi want that deadline?

Dr. Kissinger: You will have to ask Hanoi.

Q. Is it still possible to achieve that deadline of October 31? What countries would participate in the cease-fire and in the conference?

Dr. Kissinger: We are committed to achieving an agreement in another session of several days duration, and it is up to the other side to determine when they want to meet.

As to the second question, until all countries are approached, I don't think it would be proper for me—

Q. Is the United States one of them?

Dr. Kissinger: The United States is a party. It cannot be part of the supervisory mechanism, but the United States is a party to the four-power Joint Military Commission. That is one of the bodies that supervises those provisions that apply to the four parties. It is not part of the international body, but it is part of the international conference.

Q. How broad would the conference be, sir?

Dr. Kissinger: Again, it would be inappropriate to list the countries until they have been approached.

Q. Would you amplify somewhat on the Cambodian-Laos agreements. Both sides must withdraw forces and cease major supplying, is that what you implied before?

Dr. Kissinger: Well, I have given the general outline of the agreement, but it is envisaged that foreign forces are withdrawn from these countries.

Q. When was Hanoi advised one more meeting would be necessary?

Dr. Kissinger: I believe on Sunday morning our time here, and we also informed them that we would stop military activities north of the 20th Parallel.

THE PRESS: Thank you, Dr. Kissinger.
2. The full text of the President's message to me of December 6 is in Nixon, *RN,* pp. 729–30.
3. Nixon, *RN,* p. 733.
4. Guenter Lewy, *America in Vietnam* (New York: Oxford University Press, 1978), pp. 413–14.

CHAPTER 10: A VISIT TO HANOI

1. See the sources collected in Martin F. Herz, *The Prestige Press and the Christmas Bombing, 1972: Images and Reality in Vietnam* (Washington: Ethics and Public Policy Center, 1980), pp. 54–60; and in Lewy, *America in Vietnam,* pp. 413–14. See also Henry Kissinger, *White House Years* (Boston: Little, Brown and Co., 1979), pp. 1454–55.
2. Harrison E. Salisbury, "Hanoi Premier Tells View; Some in U.S. Detect a Shift," *New York Times,* January 4, 1967. See also Harrison E. Salisbury, *Behind the Lines: Hanoi* (New York: Harper & Row, 1967), Chapter XVIII.
3. See Kissinger, *White House Years,* p. 1109.
4. The relevant portion of Article 20 of the Paris Agreement reads as follows:

(*a*) The parties participating in the Paris Conference on Vietnam shall strictly respect the 1954 Geneva Agreements on Cambodia and the 1962 Geneva Agreements on Laos, which recognized the Cambodian and the Lao peoples' fundamental national rights, i.e., the independence, sovereignty, unity, and territorial integrity of these countries. The parties shall respect the neutrality of Cambodia and Laos. The parties participating in the Paris Conference on Vietnam undertake to refrain from using the territory of Cambodia and the territory of Laos to encroach on the sovereignty and security of one another and of other countries.

(*b*) Foreign countries shall put an end to all military activities in Cambodia and Laos, totally withdraw from and refrain from reintroducing into these two countries troops, military advisers and military personnel, armaments, munitions and war material.

5. Sihanouk, *War and Hope,* pp. 21–23, 64–65. It is confirmed also by a Khmer Rouge document of 1978, Democratic Kampuchea, *The Black Book: Facts and Proofs of Vietnam's Acts of Agression and Annexation against Kampuchea* (Phnom Penh: September 1978), Chapter V, section 2 (b).

CHAPTER 11: ENFORCEMENT AND AID

1. See, e.g., the illuminating memoir by David Horowitz, *Radical Son: A Generational Odyssey* (New York: Free Press, 1997), Parts 3 and 4, and James Webb, "Peace? Or Defeat? What Did the Vietnam War Protesters Want?," *The American Enterprise,* Vol. 8, No. 3 (May/June 1997), pp. 46–49.
2. Larry Berman, *No Peace No Honor: Nixon, Kissinger, and Betrayal in Vietnam* (New York: Free Press, 2001).
3. E.g., Horowitz, *Radical Son,* p. 202.
4. See, e.g., President John F. Kennedy's contribution to the genre in Kissinger, *White House Years,* p. 895 and note 7 on p. 1488, and in Henry Kissinger, *Years of Upheaval* (Boston: Little, Brown and Co., 1982), note 5 on p. 1236.

5. Statements on United States enforcement of the Paris Agreement included the following:

President Nixon's address to the nation, January 23, 1973:

[T]he terms of the agreement must be scrupulously adhered to. We shall do everything the agreement requires of us, and we shall expect the other parties to do everything it requires of them. We shall also expect other interested nations to help insure that the agreement is carried out and peace is maintained.

Kissinger, press conference, January 24, 1973:

QUESTION: If a peace treaty is violated and if the ICC proves ineffective, will the United States ever again send troops into Vietnam?

KISSINGER: I don't want to speculate on hypothetical situations that we don't expect to arise.

Deputy Assistant Secretary William Sullivan on NBC-TV's Meet the Press, January 28, 1973:

QUESTION: There's also reports from Saigon today, Mr. Ambassador, that the United States has given official but private assurances to Saigon that we would intervene militarily again if Hanoi commits serious violations. Just what is our commitment? What would we do if a cease-fire breaks down?

SULLIVAN: I am not going to speculate on that, Mr. Rosenfeld. I think you have seen Dr. Kissinger's statement concerning the method in which the agreement has stipulated the requirements for carrying out this accord. There are no inhibitions upon us, but we are not going to discuss any hypothetical questions at this time about what the future prospects may bring.

Kissinger, interview on CBS News with Marvin Kalb, February 1, 1973:

KALB: Dr. Kissinger, I think what I was trying to get at is what happens—and I suppose this question must be asked. In the best of all possible worlds the cease-fire is going to hold. In the world that we live in it may not. President Thieu said in an interview tonight on CBS that he would never call upon American airpower to go back. And Ambassador Sullivan said only last Sunday that there are no inhibitions—I believe were his words—in the use of this airpower. Is that correct?

KISSINGER: That is legally correct.

KALB: Politically and diplomatically?

KISSINGER: We have the right to do this. The question is very difficult to answer in the abstract. It depends on the extent of the challenge, on the nature of the threat, on the circumstances in which it arises; and it would be extremely unwise for a responsible American official at this stage, when the peace is in the process of being established, to give a checklist about what the United States will or will not do in every circumstance that is likely to arise.

For the future that we can foresee, the North Vietnamese are not in a position to launch an overwhelming attack on the South, even if they violate the agreement. What happens after a year or two has to be seen in the circumstances which then exist.

Most of the violations that one can now foresee should be handled by the South Vietnamese.

KALB: So that for the next year or two, if I understand you right, there would be no need for a reinvolvement of American military power?

KISSINGER: Marvin, we did not end this war in order to look for an excuse to reenter it, but it would be irresponsible for us at this moment to give a precise checklist to potential aggressors as to what they can or cannot safely do.

President Nixon's news conference, March 15, 1973:

I will only suggest this: that we have informed the North Vietnamese of our concern about this infiltration and of what we believe it to be, a violation of the cease-fire, the cease-fire and the peace agreement. Our concern has also been expressed to other interested parties. And I would only suggest that based on my actions over the past four years, that the North Vietnamese should not lightly disregard such expressions of concern when they are made with regard to a violation. That is all I will say about it.

Undersecretary for Political Affairs William Porter, speech in Grand Rapids, MI, March 21, 1973:

President Nixon has made clear our concern at North Vietnamese infiltration of large amounts of equipment into South Vietnam. If it continued, this infiltration could lead to serious consequences. The North Vietnamese should not lightly disregard our expressions of concern.

President Nixon's address to the nation, March 29, 1973:

There are still some problem areas. The provisions of the agreement requiring an accounting for all missing in action in Indochina, the provisions with regard to Laos and Cambodia, the provisions prohibiting infiltration from North Vietnam into South Vietnam have not been complied with. We have and will continue to comply with the agreement. We shall insist that North Vietnam comply with the agreement. And the leaders of North Vietnam should have no doubt as to the consequences if they fail to comply with the agreement.

Defense Secretary Elliot Richardson on NBC-TV's Meet the Press, *April 1, 1973:*

RON NESSEN: Mr. Secretary, can you say that the United States will never under any circumstances send military forces back to Indochina?

RICHARDSON: No. I cannot give any categorical assurance, Mr. Nessen. Obviously the future holds possible developments that are unforeseeable now. But certainly we very much hope that this will not be necessary.

NESSEN: And if I ask you the same question about, can you say whether the United States will never bomb again in North or South Vietnam, your answer would be the same?

RICHARDSON: Yes, but of course our hope and expectation is that the cease-fire agreements will be observed.

NESSEN: President Nixon has warned several times North Vietnam that it should have no doubt about the consequences if it violates the cease-fire. What does he mean, what are the consequences?

RICHARDSON: This is obviously something that cannot be spelled out in advance, Mr. Nessen. . . .

They have, I think, had some reason, looking back over the past, to know that the President has been willing to do what has been necessary in order to bring about a negotiated solution and to bring an end to the war.

Defense Secretary Elliot Richardson to the Senate Armed Services Committee, April 2, 1973:

QUESTION: There are reports out of South Vietnam today that President Thieu of South Vietnam says that the United States and the South Vietnamese government have an agreement that if there is an offensive, that if the North Vietnamese do come in, that the United States will come back with its airplanes and with its air support. Do we have such a commitment?

RICHARDSON: This is a question simply of very possible contingencies. I wouldn't want to try to amplify on anything he said or to subtract from it. . . .

We, of course, continue to adhere to the proposition that the cease-fire agreements not only have been signed but are in the interest of all the parties and our objective is to assure so far as is possible that they are carried out. . . .

Our job is to reinforce the considerations that will, we trust, lead them to carry out the agreement. . . .

If he [the President] had the constitutional power to carry on the war while winding it down, we think it's a natural extension of this to say that he has the constitutional power to take whatever incidental steps that are now required in order to assure that the cease-fire agreements are carried out.

U.S.-GVN Communiqué (San Clemente), April 3, 1973:
Both Presidents, while acknowledging that progress was being made toward military and political settlements in South Vietnam, nevertheless viewed with great concern infiltrations of men and weapons in sizeable numbers from North Vietnam into South Vietnam in violation of the Agreement on Ending the War, and considered that actions which would threaten the basis of the agreement would call for appropriately vigorous reactions. They expressed their conviction that all the provisions of the Agreement, including in particular those concerning military forces and military supplies, must be faithfully implemented if the cease-fire is to be preserved and the prospects for a peaceful settlement are to be assured. President Nixon stated in this connection that the United States views violations of any provision of the Agreement with great and continuing concern.

Defense Secretary Elliot Richardson, interviewed by newsmen prior to his appearance before the House Appropriations Subcommittee on Defense, April 3, 1973:
QUESTION: Mr. Secretary, under what conditions might we have to begin bombing in support of the South Vietnamese?
RICHARDSON: It would be one of those questions that it's impossible to answer in general terms. We can only see what develops, and hopefully, what will develop is the full and complete implementation of the cease-fire agreements.
QUESTION: But is it possible that we will have to bomb either North Vietnam or in support of the South Vietnamese army again?
RICHARDSON: It's certainly something we cannot rule out at this time.

Kissinger, press conference, May 2, 1973:
QUESTION: You say if North Vietnam does not obey the call for an honorable cease-fire, it would risk revived confrontation with us. Could you spell out a little bit more clearly what you mean there [in the foreign policy report]?
KISSINGER: . . . Now, on the confrontation, we have made clear that we mean to have the agreement observed. We are now engaged in an effort to discuss with the North Vietnamese what is required to bring about the strict implementation of the agreement. We have every intention and every incentive to make certain that our side of the agreement is maintained, and to use our influence wherever we can to bring about the strict implementation of the agreement.
But the United States cannot sign a solemn agreement and within weeks have major provisions violated without our making an attempt to indicate it. Now, the particular measures: some of them are, of course, obvious and we would prefer, as we state in the report and as we have stated publicly many times, to move our relationship with the North Vietnamese toward normalization, and to start a process which would accelerate, such as other processes normally have.
So the general thrust of this paragraph is that the tension existing between us certainly cannot ease as rapidly as we want if the agreement is not observed.

President Nixon's foreign policy report, May 3, 1973:
We hope that the contending factions will now prefer to pursue their objectives through peaceful means and political competition rather than through the brutal and costly methods of the past. This choice is up to them. We shall be vigilant concerning violations of the Agreement. . . .
Hanoi has two basic choices. The first is to exploit the Vietnam Agreement and press its objectives in Indochina. In this case it would continue to infiltrate men and materiel into South Vietnam, keep its forces in Laos and Cambodia, and through pressures or outright attack renew its aggression against our friends.

Such a course would endanger the hard won gains for peace in Indochina. It would risk revived confrontation with us. . . . The second course is for North Vietnam to pursue its objectives peacefully, allowing the historical trends of the region to assert themselves. . . .

The Republic of Vietnam will find us a steady friend. We will continue to deal with its government as the legitimate representative of the South Vietnamese people, while supporting efforts by the South Vietnamese parties to achieve reconciliation and shape their political future. We will provide replacement military assistance within the terms of the Agreement. We expect our friends to observe the Agreement just as we will not tolerate violations by the North Vietnamese or its allies. . . .

We have told Hanoi, privately and publicly, that we will not tolerate violations of the Agreement.

Kissinger, press conference, June 13, 1973:
QUESTION: Do you feel now that with the signing of the document you have more or less ended your work in the Indochina area or that you will still have a lot of difficulties, especially concerning Cambodia?
KISSINGER: The remaining issues in Indochina will still require significant diplomatic efforts, and we expect to continue them. Of course, we remain committed to the strict implementation of the Agreement, and we will maintain our interest in it.

President Nixon's message to the House of Representatives, June 27, 1973, opposing the Indochina bombing halt:
A total halt would virtually remove Communist incentive to negotiate and would thus seriously undercut ongoing diplomatic efforts to achieve a cease-fire in Cambodia. It would effectively reverse the momentum toward lasting peace in Indochina set in motion last January and renewed in the four-party communiqué signed in Paris on June 13. . . .

A Communist victory in Cambodia, in turn, would threaten the fragile balance of negotiated agreements, political alignments and military capabilities upon which the overall peace in Southeast Asia depends and on which my assessment of the acceptability of the Vietnam agreements was based.

Finally, and with even more serious global implications, the legislatively imposed acceptance of the United States to Communist violations of the Paris agreements and the conquest of Cambodia by Communist forces would call into question our national commitment not only to the Vietnam settlement but to many other settlements or agreements we have reached or seek to reach with other nations. A serious blow to America's international credibility would have been struck—a blow that would be felt far beyond Indochina.

Kissinger, letter to Senator Edward Kennedy, March 25, 1974:
As a signator of the Paris Agreement, the United States committed itself to strengthening the conditions which made the cease-fire possible and to the goal of the South Vietnamese people's right to self-determination. With these commitments in mind, we continue to provide to the Republic of Vietnam the means necessary for its self-defense and for its economic viability. . . .

We have . . . committed ourselves very substantially, both politically and morally.

Interview with Tran Van Lam, former South Vietnamese Foreign Minister, April 14, 1975, Saigon (press report):
Foreign Minister Lam stated that President Nixon promised to "react immediately and vigorously" to any large-scale North Vietnamese offensive. But, he added, "no secret agreement was signed."

6. See note 5.

7. Democratic Kampuchea, *The Black Book: Facts and Proofs of Vietnam's Acts of Aggression and Annexation against Kampuchea* (Phnom Penh: September 1978), Chapter V, Section 2 (c).

8. See Kenneth M. Quinn, "Political Change in Wartime: The Khmer Krahom Revolution in Southern Cambodia, 1970–1974," *Naval War College Review* (Spring 1976), pp. 8–9.

9. See, e.g., Shawcross, *Sideshow,* p. 389 and *passim.*

10. "Sihanouk: The Man We May Have to Settle for in Cambodia," *New York Times,* August 12, 1973.

11. Versions of this remark by Congressman O'Neill appear in several sources: e.g., remarks by Congressman Robert Giaimo on *The CBS-TV Evening News,* June 25, 1973; Shawcross, *Sideshow,* p. 285. Members of Congress have the privilege of amending or rewriting their statements before publication in the *Congressional Record,* and this remark does not appear there.

12. The President's legal authority to continue air operations in Cambodia after the Paris Agreement was spelled out in detail in a memorandum that Secretary Rogers submitted to the Senate Foreign Relations Committee on April 30, 1973 (footnotes omitted):

PRESIDENTIAL AUTHORITY TO CONTINUE U.S. AIR COMBAT OPERATIONS IN CAMBODIA

The purpose of this memorandum is to discuss the President's legal authority to continue United States air combat operations in Cambodia since the conclusion of the Agreement on Ending the War and Restoring Peace in Vietnam on January 27, 1973 and the completion on March 28, 1973 of the withdrawal of United States armed forces from Vietnam and the return of American citizens held prisoner in Indochina. The memorandum also discusses the background of the Agreement of January 27 and the purposes of various United States actions in order to clarify the legal issues.

For many years the United States has pursued a combination of diplomatic and military efforts to bring about a just peace in Vietnam. These efforts were successful in strengthening the self-defense capabilities of the armed forces of the Republic of Vietnam and in bringing about serious negotiations which culminated in the Agreement on Ending the War and Restoring Peace in Vietnam, signed at Paris on January 27, 1973. This Agreement provided for a cease-fire in Vietnam, the return of prisoners, and the withdrawal of United States and allied armed forces from South Vietnam within sixty days. The Agreement (in Article 20) also required the withdrawal of all foreign armed forces from Laos and Cambodia and obligated the parties to refrain from using the territory of Cambodia and Laos to encroach on the sovereignty and security of other countries, to respect the neutrality of Cambodia and Laos, and to avoid any interference in the internal affairs of those two countries. This Article is of central importance as it has long been apparent that the conflicts in Laos and Cambodia are closely related to the conflict in Vietnam and, in fact, are so inter-related as to be considered parts of a single conflict.

At the time the Vietnam Agreement was concluded, the United States made clear to the North Vietnamese that the armed forces of the Khmer Government would suspend all offensive operations and that the United States aircraft supporting them would do likewise. We stated that, if the other side reciprocated, a *de facto* cease-fire would thereby be brought into force in Cambodia. However, we also stated that, if the Communist forces carried out attacks, government forces and United States air forces would have to take necessary counter measures and that, in the event, we would continue to carry out air strikes in Cambodia as necessary until such time as a cease-fire could be brought into effect. These statements were based on our conviction that it was essential for Hanoi to understand that continuance of the hostilities in Cambodia and

Laos would not be in its interest or in our interest and that compliance with Article 20 of the Agreement would have to be reciprocal.

It has recently been suggested that the withdrawal of all U.S. armed forces from South Vietnam and the return of all U.S. prisoners has created a fundamentally new situation in which new authority must be sought by the President from the Congress to carry out air strikes in Cambodia. The issue more accurately stated is whether the constitutional authority of the President to continue doing in Cambodia what the United States has lawfully been doing there expires with the withdrawal of U.S. armed forces from Vietnam and the return of American prisoners despite the fact that a cease-fire has not been achieved in Cambodia and North Vietnamese troops remain in Cambodia contrary to clear provisions of the Agreement. In other words, the issue is not whether the President may do something new, but rather whether what he has been doing must automatically stop, without regard to the consequences even though the Agreement is not being implemented by the other side.

The purposes of the United States in Southeast Asia have always included seeking a settlement to the Vietnamese war that would permit the people of South Vietnam to exercise their right to self-determination. The President has made this clear on many occasions. For example, on May 8, 1972, when he made the proposals that formed the basis for the ultimately successful negotiations with North Vietnam, he said there were three purposes to our military actions against Vietnam: first, to prevent the forceful imposition of a Communist government in South Vietnam; second, to protect our remaining forces in South Vietnam; and third, to obtain the release of our prisoners. The joint communiqué issued by the President and Mr. Brezhnev in Moscow on May 29, 1972 in which the view of the United States was expressed said that negotiations on the basis of the President's May 8 proposals would be the quickest and most effective way to obtain the objectives of bringing the military conflict to an end as soon as possible and ensuring that the political future of South Vietnam should be left for the South Vietnamese people to decide for themselves, free from outside interference. The recent opinion of the United States Court of Appeals for the District of Columbia Circuit in *Mitchell* v. *Laird* makes it clear that the President has the constitutional power to pursue all of these purposes. In the words of Judge Wyzanski the President properly acted "with a profound concern for the durable interests of the nation—its defense, its honor, its morality."

The Agreement signed on January 27, 1973 represented a settlement consistent with these objectives. An important element in that Agreement is Article 20 which recognizes the underlying connections among the hostilities in all the countries of Indochina and required the cessation of foreign armed intervention in Laos and Cambodia. The importance of this article cannot be overestimated, because the continuation of hostilities in Laos and Cambodia and the presence there of North Vietnamese troops threatens the right of self-determination of the South Vietnamese people, which is guaranteed by the Agreement.

The United States is gratified that a cease-fire agreement has been reached in Laos. It must be respected by all the parties and result in the prompt withdrawal of foreign forces. In Cambodia it has not yet been possible to bring about a cease-fire, and North Vietnamese forces have not withdrawn from that country. Under present circumstances, United States air support and material assistance are needed to support the armed forces of the Khmer Republic and thereby to render more likely the early conclusion of a cease-fire and implementation of Article 20 of the Agreement. Thus, U.S. air strikes in Cambodia do not represent a commitment by the United States to the defense of Cambodia as such but instead represent a meaningful interim action to bring about compliance with this critical provision in the Vietnam Agreement.

To stop these air strikes automatically at a fixed date would be as self-defeating as it would have been for the United States to withdraw its armed forces prematurely from South Vietnam while it was still trying to negotiate an agreement with North Vietnam. Had that been done in Vietnam, the Agreement of January 27 would never have been achieved; if it were done in Cambodia, there is no reason to believe that a cease-fire could be brought about in Cambodia or that the withdrawal of North Vietnamese forces from Cambodia could be obtained. It can be seen from this analysis that unilateral cessation of our United States air combat activity in Cambodia without the removal of North Vietnamese forces from the country would undermine the central achievement of the January Agreement as surely as would have a failure by the United States to insist on the inclusion in the Agreement of Article 20 requiring North Vietnamese withdrawal from Laos and Cambodia. The President's powers under Article II of the Constitution are adequate to prevent such a self-defeating result. It is worth noting that in reaching a similar conclusion, the report entitled "Congress and the Termination of the Vietnam War" recently prepared for your Committee by the Foreign Affairs Division of the Congressional Research Service, arrived at the same general conclusion as to the President's Constitutional power.

One must recognize that the scope and application of the President's powers under Article II of the Constitution are rarely free from dispute. Under the Constitution, the war powers are shared between the Executive and Legislative branches of the Government. The Congress is granted the powers "to provide for the common defense", "to declare war, grant letters of marque and reprisal, and make rules concerning captures on land and water", "to raise and support armies", "to provide and maintain a navy", "to make rules for the government and regulation of the land and naval forces", and "to make all laws which shall be necessary and proper for carrying into execution the foregoing powers. . . ." On the other hand, the Constitution provides that "the executive power shall be vested in a President," that he "shall be Commander-in-Chief of the army and navy of the United States," and that "he shall take care that the laws be faithfully executed." The President is also given the authority to make treaties with the advice and consent of two thirds of the Senate, to appoint ambassadors with the advice and consent of the Senate, and to receive ambassadors and other public ministers.

The proceedings of the Federal Constitutional Convention in 1787 suggest that the ambiguities of this division of power between the President and the Congress were deliberately left unresolved with the understanding that they were to be defined by practice. There may be those who wish the framers of the Constitution would have been more precise, but it is submitted that there was great wisdom in realizing the impossibility of foreseeing all contingencies and in leaving considerable flexibility for the future play of political forces. The Constitution is a framework for democratic decision and action, not a source of ready-made answers to all questions, and that is one of its great strengths.

There is no question but that Congress should play an important role in decisions involving the use of armed forces abroad. With respect to the continuation of U.S. air combat activity in Cambodia, what is that role? The Congress has cooperated with the President in establishing the policy of firmness coupled with an openness to negotiation which has succeeded in bringing about the Agreement of January 27 and which can succeed in securing its implementation. This cooperation has been shown through consultations and through the authorization and appropriation process. The Congress has consistently rejected proposals by some members to withdraw this congressional participation and authority by cutting off appropriations for necessary military expenditures and foreign assistance. The Congress has also enacted several provisions with specific

reference to Cambodia. The President's policy in Cambodia has been and continues to be fully consistent with these provisions.

It was, of course, hoped that the Agreement signed at Paris on January 27
would be strictly implemented according to its terms, including the prompt conclusion of cease-fires in Laos and Cambodia and the withdrawal of foreign troops
from those two countries. What has happened instead is that, in Laos, the cease-
fire has been followed by continuing Communist stalling in forming the new
government and, in Cambodia, the Communists responded to the efforts of the
Khmer Government to bring about a *de facto* cease-fire with a fierce, general offensive. North Vietnamese forces remain in Laos and Cambodia and continue to
infiltrate men and war material through these countries to the Republic of Vietnam. North Vietnamese forces in Cambodia continue to participate in and to
support Communist offensive operations.

United States air strikes in Laos were an important element in the decision
by North Vietnam and its Laotian allies to negotiate a cease-fire in Laos. If
United States air strikes were stopped in Cambodia despite the Communist of-
fensive, there would be little, if any, incentive for the Communists to seek a
cease-fire in that country, and the temptation would doubtless be great for North
Vietnam to leave its troops and supply lines indefinitely in Laos and Cambodia.
Such a situation would be the opposite of that prescribed by Article 20 of the
Vietnam Agreement and would so threaten the viability of the settlement in
Vietnam and the right to self-determination of the South Vietnamese people as
to be totally unacceptable to the Republic of Vietnam and to the United States.
In light of these facts, it seems clear that the argument that the Constitution re-
quires immediate cessation of U.S. air strikes in Cambodia because of the Paris
Agreement is, in reality, an argument that the Constitution which has permitted
the United States to negotiate a peace agreement—a peace that guarantees the
right of self-determination to the South Vietnamese people as well as the return
of United States prisoners and withdrawal of United States armed forces from
Vietnam—is a Constitution that contains an automatic self-destruct mechanism
designed to destroy what has been so painfully achieved. We are now in the
process of having further discussions with the North Vietnamese with regard to
the implementation of the Paris Agreement. We hope these discussions will be
successful and will lead to a cease-fire in Cambodia.

See also the excellent constitutional analysis and testimony submitted by Senator Barry M.
Goldwater on May 10, 1973, to the House Foreign Affairs Committee. U.S. Congress, House
Committee on Foreign Affairs, *U.S. Policy and Programs in Cambodia,* Hearings before the Subcommittee on Asian and Pacific Affairs, 93d Cong., Ist sess., 1973, pp. 41–52 and 82.
13. See, e.g., Michael Parks, "Soviet Trying to End Feud with Sihanouk," *Baltimore Sun,* July 8,
1973.

CHAPTER 12: FORD AND VIETNAM

1. Remarks by Senator Allen to a State Department official, June 25, 1974.
2. As quoted in Allan E. Goodman, *The Lost Peace, America's Search for a Negotiated Settlement
of the Vietnam War* (Stanford: Hoover Institution Press, 1978), p. 177.
3. Following are additional examples of expressions of congressional support for aid to South
Vietnam after an American troop withdrawal:
Senator Hubert Humphrey had declared in favor of continued aid on February 10, 1972.
The *New York Times* of February 12, 1972 (Robert B. Semple, Jr., "Democrats to Get Briefings on
War"), described his position as follows:
Mr. Humphrey . . . said he would provide American military and economic

aid—in the form of equipment but not men—after the United States with-
draws, but only if South Vietnam comes under renewed attacks and such aid is
judged to be in the United States interests.

Senator Mike Mansfield, in early 1973, had supported "backup help of an economic nature" and
also "logistical support" for our allies, in accordance with the Nixon Doctrine. He viewed the Paris
Agreement as achieving what he wanted—U.S. withdrawal—and acknowledged explicitly that a
price had to be paid for it in terms of other commitments:

> And may I say that I would anticipate that the Nixon Doctrine, which was
> promulgated almost three years ago . . . would now go into effect. That means,
> as I interpret it, that we would gradually withdraw militarily from various coun-
> tries throughout Asia and the world, that those countries would henceforth have
> to depend upon themselves primarily. As far as our allies are concerned, we
> would be willing to extend backup help of an economic nature, but would not
> intervene or interfere in any way in the affairs of any nation. (*Congressional
> Record,* January 26, 1973, p. 2202)

> The Nixon Doctrine as I understand it calls for the gradual withdrawal of our
> forces all over the world and a greater dependence on the nations with whom we
> have ties, with the United States furnishing in specific instances only logistical
> support. . . .
> So as I look at this picture, the things I have been arguing for have, in effect,
> been achieved. I realized that there is a price attached to such an agreement and
> after I see the details, after proposals are made to the Congress, it is my intention,
> insofar as I possibly can, to support proposals of that nature because I wanted the
> war to end. I wanted our men withdrawn. I wanted our POWs and recoverable
> MIAs returned home. Those are the factors in which I was most interested.
> Therefore, I will be most interested and, insofar as I am able, most supportive in
> any negotiations which led to commitments of various kinds which have not yet
> been finally consummated, because I think you have to balance that one against
> the other. (Briefing, Senate Foreign Relations Committee hearing, February 21,
> 1973, pp. 16–17)

Other congressional leaders, not all of them liberals, had spoken in the same vein. Senator
Robert Byrd, Democrat of West Virginia, said on the Senate floor on January 26, 1973:

> It is to America's credit . . . that, even in the face of criticism at home and abroad,
> she did not abandon an ally. . . . We got into this war little-by-little, unable to
> see where day-to-day and week-to-week events would ultimately lead us. But we
> became involved in behalf of an ally, and our country kept the promise of its
> leaders—Presidents Eisenhower, Kennedy, Johnson and Nixon—that we would
> not desert South Vietnam. I hope I do not live to see the day when this nation,
> forged in the crucible of courage, will ever forsake the pursuit of national honor.
> For the honor of a nation is the sum of the honor of its sons and daughters. If
> honor ever ceases to be a part of the American character there can be no future
> for our country. (*Congressional Record,* January 26, 1973, p. 2309)

Chairman George Mahon of the House Appropriations Committee was quoted as follows in
the *Washington Post* on January 28, 1973:

> Following the President's briefing on the Paris Agreement, Chairman Mahon
> . . . said "it is inherent in the cease-fire that we will continue to provide assistance
> to South Vietnam and rehabilitation assistance to North Vietnam." He said this
> must be accepted as a fact of life, and "is a better alternative than continuation of
> the war."

In Senate hearings in February 1973, Senator Hugh Scott, at testimony by Secretary of State
William Rogers, said:

> On the question of aid to Vietnam, I agree with you [Rogers] it would be bet-
> ter not to be frozen into any position because we have no way of knowing

what suggestion will come up in regard to possible bilateral aid or U.S. aid. (Briefing, Senate Foreign Relations Committee hearing, February 21, 1973, p. 27)

Representative Samuel Stratton of New York made the point in general terms: We cannot simply abandon Asia just because we got a cease-fire. Stability in Asia will depend on our continuing participation in that area to maintain that new triangle of Russia, China, and America. If we go isolationist, then Asia polarizes again and peace goes out the window. (*Congressional Record,* January 29, 1973, p. 2519)

Senator Jesse Helms of North Carolina declared: We must do what we can to make the truce work. We must share our material strength with the South Vietnamese, our allies, so they can defend themselves if the truce does not work. (*Congressional Record,* January 31, 1973, p. 2732)

4. General Van Tien Dung, *Our Great Spring Victory: An Account of the Liberation of South Vietnam,* translated by John Spragens, Jr. (New York: Monthly Review Press, 1977), pp. 10–12. See also Col.-Gen. Tran Van Tra, *Vietnam: History of the Bulwark B2 Theatre,* Vol. 5: *Concluding the 30-Years War* (Ho Chi Minh City: Van Nghe Publishing House, 1982), translated in FBIS/JPRS 82783, Southeast Asia Report No. 1247, February 1983, pp. 45, 103.

5. Dung, *Our Great Spring Victory,* p. 15.

6. Michael Barone, Grant Ujifusa, and Douglas Matthews, *The Almanac of American Politics, 1978* (New York: E. P. Dutton, 1978), p. viii.

7. Dung, *Our Great Spring Victory,* pp. 19–20; Tra, *Vietnam,* p. 125.

8. Dung, *Our Great Spring Victory,* pp. 22–23. See also "How North Vietnam Won the War," interview with North Vietnamese Col. Bui Tin by Stephen Young, *Wall Street Journal,* August 3, 1995, and Bui Tin, *Following Ho Chi Minh: Memoirs of a North Vietnamese Colonel* (Honolulu: University of Hawaii Press, 1995), pp. 81–82.

9. Ron Nessen, *It Sure Looks Different from the Inside* (Chicago: Playboy Press, 1978), p. 92.

10. Bui Tin, *Following Ho Chi Minh,* p. 79; Tra, *Vietnam,* p. 125.

11. Dung, *Our Great Spring Victory,* pp. 24–25.

12. Kenneth Reich, "Jackson Opposes Increase in Aid to South Vietnam," *Los Angeles Times,* January 27, 1975.

13. Dung, *Our Great Spring Victory,* p. 24.

CHAPTER 13: THE COLLAPSE OF CAMBODIA

1. The various restrictions were as follows:

• The Fulbright amendment to the armed forces appropriations authorization for fiscal year 1971, passed on October 7, 1970, specified that South Vietnam and other allied countries could not use their funds for military support or assistance to Cambodia. It also prohibited South Vietnam and other allied countries such as Thailand from transferring military supplies furnished under the act to Cambodia. In other words, Cambodia's neighbors were prohibited from improving their own security by assisting Cambodia with American equipment, the only equipment they had.

• The Cooper-Church amendment to the Supplementary Foreign Assistance Act of 1970, passed on January 5, 1971, prohibited the use of American funds for financing "the introduction of United States ground combat troops into Cambodia, or to provide United States advisers." Not only were American combat troops prohibited, but American advisers were barred from training or instructing Cambodian units on the use of the American equipment the United States was supplying.

• The Symington-Case amendment to the Substitute Foreign Assistance Act and Related Assistance Act, passed on February 7, 1972, placed severe restrictions on civilians serving in Cambodia. It limited the total number of "civilian officers and employees of executive agencies of the United States Government who are United States citizens" to

200 and the number of third country nationals to eighty-five. This made effective military *or civilian* advice to the Cambodians impossible.
• The Second Supplemental Appropriations Act for fiscal year 1973 (signed reluctantly into law by President Nixon on July 1, 1973) prohibited the use of funds appropriated in the act to "support directly or indirectly combat activities in or over Cambodia, Laos, North Vietnam, and South Vietnam or off the shores of Cambodia, Laos, North Vietnam, and South Vietnam."
• The Continuing Appropriations Act for fiscal year 1974, likewise signed into law on July 1, 1973, prohibited the use of any funds to finance directly or indirectly combat activities by U.S. forces "in or over or from off the shores of North Vietnam, South Vietnam, Laos or Cambodia."
• The Foreign Assistance Act of 1973, which became law on December 17, 1973, provided that no funds authorized or appropriated under any of its provisions would be available to finance military or paramilitary combat operations by foreign forces in Laos, Cambodia, North Vietnam, South Vietnam, or Thailand.
2. President Ford's letter to Speaker of the House of Representatives Carl Albert, February 25, 1975, in Ford, *Public Papers,* 1975, pp. 279–80.
3. E.g., Sydney H. Schanberg, "Aid Request for Cambodia Said to Exceed Needs Now," *New York Times,* February 7, 1975.
4. E.g., commentary by Eric Sevareid, *CBS-TV Evening News,* February 26, 1975.
5. "Congress and the Mekong," *Baltimore Sun* editorial, February 13, 1975.
6. E.g., Jim Adams, "House Leaders See Aid Losing," *Washington Star-News,* February 26, 1975; "Cambodian Climax," *New York Times* editorial, February 28, 1975.
7. E.g., "Aid for Cambodia," *Washington Post* editorial, February 5, 1975; "U.S. 'Word' Isn't at Stake in the Cambodian Civil War," *Philadelphia Inquirer* editorial, February 27, 1975.
8. Sydney H. Schanberg, "The Enigmatic Cambodian Insurgents: Reds Appear to Dominate Diverse Bloc," *New York Times,* March 13, 1975.
9. Staff reporter, "Ford Bid for More Arms Aid to Cambodia Is Dealt Two Severe Setbacks in Congress," *Wall Street Journal,* March 14, 1975.
10. An unrecognizable version of some of these events may be found in Shawcross, *Sideshow,* Chapter 22.
11. Statement by Sihanouk issued in Beijing on April 2, as reported in "Compromise Is Ruled Out by Sihanouk," *Baltimore Sun,* April 3, 1975.
12. Nessen, *It Sure Looks Different from the Inside,* p. 103.
13. Sydney H. Schanberg, "Indochina Without Americans: For Most, a Better Life," *New York Times,* April 13, 1975.

CHAPTER 14: THE END OF VIETNAM

1. "Mr. Ford's Confusion," *New York Times* editorial, April 4, 1975.
2. "Vietnam: The Shell Game Goes On, and On," *Washington Post* editorial, April 4, 1975.
3. "A New Direction in Vietnam," *Los Angeles Times* editorial, April 4, 1975.
4. Gerald Ford, *A Time to Heal: The Autobiography of Gerald R. Ford* (New York: Harper & Row and The Readers Digest Association, Inc., 1979), p. 255.
5. Ibid.
6. "Next Steps in Vietnam After President Thieu," *New York Times* editorial, April 22, 1975; "The Departure of Nguyen Van Thieu," *Washington Post* editorial, April 22, 1975; "Mr. Thieu Steps Down," *Baltimore Sun* editorial, April 22, 1975; "After the Fall," *New York Daily News* editorial, April 22, 1975; "After Vietnam," *Christian Science Monitor* editorial, April 22, 1975; "Exit President Thieu," *Chicago Tribune* editorial, April 22, 1975; "It Was Thieu Who Betrayed the People of Vietnam," *Philadelphia Inquirer* editorial, April 22, 1975; "Saigon's Denouement and Washington's Role," *New York Times* editorial, April 23, 1975.
7. Dung, *Our Great Spring Victory,* pp. 201–2.

8. Ibid., p. 234.
9. Press conference, April 29, 1975, in *Department of State Bulletin,* Vol. 72, No. 1873, May 19, 1975, p. 631.
10. William Shawcross, my gadfly in many treatises, seems to have had second thoughts. He had this to say in 1994: "Those of us who opposed the American war in Indochina should be extremely humble in the face of the appalling aftermath: a form of genocide in Cambodia and horrific tyranny in both Vietnam and Laos. Looking back on my own coverage for *The Sunday Times* of the South Vietnamese war effort of 1970–75, I think I concentrated too easily on the corruption and incompetence of the South Vietnamese and their American allies, was too ignorant of the inhuman Hanoi regime, and far too willing to believe that a victory by the Communists would provide a better future. But after the Communist victory came the refugees to Thailand and the floods of boat people desperately seeking to escape the Cambodian killing fields and the Vietnamese gulags. Their eloquent testimony should have put paid to all illusions." (William Shawcross, "Shrugging Off Genocide," *The Times* [London], December 16, 1994.) See also Horowitz, *Radical Son,* for an even more thoroughgoing recantation.

APPENDIX: THE 1973 BOMBING CAMPAIGN IN CAMBODIA

1. Shawcross, *Sideshow,* p. 265.
2. Text at Tab A.
3. *U.S. Air Operations in Cambodia: April 1973,* a staff report prepared for the use of the Subcommittee on U.S. Security Agreements and Commitments Abroad of the Committee on Foreign Relations, p. 5.
4. *U.S. Air Operations in Cambodia: April 1973,* pp. 5–6.
5. Shawcross, *Sideshow,* p. 265.
6. Ibid., p. 271.
7. Ibid., p. 396.
8. Ibid., p. 271.
9. *U.S. Air Operations in Cambodia: April 1973,* p. 6.
10. Seventh Air Force OPORD 71–17.
11. Vogt to Enders letter, July 8, 1979, p. 2, Tab C [pp. 578–79].
12. Vogt to Enders letter, p. 3 [p. 580].
13. P. 295n.
14. *U.S. Air Operations in Cambodia: April 1973,* report on visit to Seventh Air Force Headquarters, p. 1.
15. Ibid., p. 272.
16. Ibid., p. 294.
17. Ibid., p. 271.
18. Harben to Enders letter, June 22, 1979. Tab B.
19. Vogt to Enders letter, p. 1, Tab C [p. 578].

INDEX